Index
to
Loudoun County, Virginia
Land Deed Books 2A-2M
1800-1810

By
Patricia B. Duncan

WILLOW BEND BOOKS

WILLOW BEND BOOKS

AN IMPRINT OF HERITAGE BOOKS, INC.

Books, CDs, and more – Worldwide

For our listing of thousands of titles see our website
at
www.HeritageBooks.com

Published 2003 by
HERITAGE BOOKS, INC.
Publishing Division
1540 Pointer Ridge Place #E
Bowie, Maryland 20716

International Standard Book Number: **1-58549-868-8**

Introduction

The following is an extended index to Loudoun County, Virginia Land Deed Books 2A-2M. In addition to providing the basic information of book:page number, parties involved, and type of document, I have also included the date of the document, the date recorded in court, a brief description of the item, including adjourning neighbors, and witnesses. Please note that neighbors were listed if there were complete names, and those with only initials were usually omitted. Witness designation may include providers of certificates of execution.

Microfilms of these records are currently available from the Library of Virginia Interlibrary Loan Service. Copies of the documents may be obtained from the Office of Clerk of Circuit Court County of Loudoun, Box 550, Leesburg, VA 20178-0550.

Abbreviations used in this text:
Admr - Administrator
A/L – Assignment of Lease
AlexVa – Alexandria, Virginia
B/S – Bargain and Sale
BaltMd – Baltimore, Maryland
BerkVa – Berkeley County, Virginia
Bk:Pg – Book:Page
BoS - Bill of Sale
br/o – brother of
CamP – Cameron Parish in Loudoun
ChstrPa – Chester County, Pennsylvania
CoE - Certificate of Examination [of wife]
CoI – Certificate of Importation [slaves]
dau – daughter
d/o - daughter of
DiffRn – Difficult Run
DittP – Dittingen Parish in Prince William County, Virginia
DoE – Deed of Emancipation [slaves]
Exor – Executor
Ffx – Fairfax County, Virginia
Fqr – Fauquier County, Virginia
FrdkMd – Frederick County, Maryland
FrdkVa – Frederick County, Virginia
Gent. – gentleman
GrB – Great Britain
Hllb - Hillsborough
h/o - husband of
HdnNJ – Hunterdon County, New Jersey
JeffVa – Jefferson County, Virginia
KingG – King George County, Virginia
L/L – Lease for Life

L/R – Lease/Release
Ldn – Loudoun County, Virginia
Lsbg - Leesburg
Mdbg – Middleburg
MontMd – Montgomery County, Maryland
[number]ac = number of acres
NwCslDel – New Castle County, Delaware
OverP – Overwharton Parish in Stafford County, Virginia
PhilPa – Philadelphia County, Pa
PoA – Power of Attorney
PrG – Prince George County, Maryland
PrWm – Prince William County, Virginia
RcCt - Received in Court
RichVa – Richmond County, Virginia
S/L – Surrender of Lease
s/o - son of
ShelP – Shelburne Parish in Loudoun
SpotVa – Spotsylvania County, Virginia
StafVa – Stafford County, Virginia
TruP – Truro Parish in Fairfax County, Virginia
w/o - wife of
WashMd – Washington County, Maryland
wd/o – widow of
Wstm – Westmoreland County [no state given]
WstmVa – Westmoreland County, Virginia
Wtfd - Waterford

LAND DEED BOOKS 2A-2M

Bk:Pg: 2A:001   Date: 4/14/1800   RcCt: 14 Apr 1800
James McILHANEY, Thomas Ludwell LEE, George LEE, Samuel
CLAPHAM, James HEATON. Bond on McILHANEY as Sheriff. Wit: C.
BINNS.

Bk:Pg: 2A:002   Date: 4/14/1800   RcCt: 14 Apr 1800
James McILHANEY, Thomas Ludwell LEE, George LEE, Samuel
CLAPHAM, James HEATON. Bond on McILHANEY as Sheriff. Wit: C.
BINNS.

Bk:Pg: 2A:003   Date: 4/14/1800   RcCt: 14 Apr 1800
James McILHANEY, Thomas Ludwell LEE, George LEE, Samuel
CLAPHAM, James HEATON. Bond on McILHANEY as Sheriff to collect
taxes. Wit: C. BINNS.

Bk:Pg: 2A:004   Date: 4/7/1800   RcCt: 14 Apr 1800
Andrew BROWN & wife Jane of Adams Co. PA to Fleming PATTERSON
of Ldn. B/S of lot in Wtfd BROWN bought from estate of John JANNEY.
Wit: James GILLIS, Patrick McKAIG.

Bk:Pg: 2A:006   Date: 10/17/1799   RcCt: 14 Apr 1800
Ferdinando FAIRFAX & wife Eliza Blair FAIRFAX of Shannon Hill
Berkeley Co. VA to farmer James NIXON of Ldn. B/S of 302ac of
Piedmont tract of Short Hill, adj Beaverdam branch, Thompson Mill,
George SHAFFER, John MORRIS, Rachel WHITE, Michael ROUSE,
Nicholas FRANTZ. Wit: Isaiah MORRIS, David MORRIS, William NIXON,
Jacob JACOBS, George NIXON Sr, Jesse JANNEY.

Bk:Pg: 2A:009   Date: 12/18/1799   RcCt: ___ [14 Apr 1800?]
John LYONS & wife Anne late of Hanover Co, now of Fairfax to William
HORSEMAN of Ldn. B/S of 306¾ac (part of suit between Charles
CARTER and Robert CARTER, land in Frying Pan area); lots occupied by
William & Isaias HORSEMAN, adj. John PAGE of Rosewell, John PAGE
of North River, Robert PAGE of Broad neck, Hardage LANE, Amos
DAVIS. Wit: Johnston CLEVELAND, William WHALEY, William
HORSMAN, Saml. LOVE.

Bk:Pg: 2A:013   Date: 11/16/1799   RcCt: 14 Apr 1800
Adam RHORBACH of Ldn to John MILLER & Michael BALLMER of Ldn.
BoS of farm and household items. Wit: Frederick SMITH, Jacob
WALTMAN, Jonathan ROCKAFIELD.

Bk:Pg: 2A:014   Date: 10/6/1799   RcCt: 14 Apr 1800
Frederick SMITH of Ldn to George SUNEFRANK of Ldn. BoS for mare.
Wit: Tunis TITUS, Jacob WALTMAN, John BAYER.

Bk:Pg: 2A:015   Date: 4/1/1800   RcCt: 14 Apr 1800
Jonathan MATTHEW of Ldn attorney for Chas. CHALFINT (Admr for
Robert CHALFINT dec'd, and assignee of Michael WHITMIRE son & heir
at law to John WHITMIRE) to Samuel EVANS of Ldn. Assignment of

100*ac* between short hill and blue ridge, adj Simon ADAMS, Thomas JACKSON.

Bk:Pg: 2A:018   Date: 4/14/1800   RcCt: 14 Apr 1800
Bartholomew HOLDREN & wife Horpy of Ldn to William COLTON Jr. of Ldn. B/S of 217*ac* on branch of Goose Creek, adj Thomas CARR, John ALEXANDER, George CARTER, Thomas MOSS. Wit: Joseph MOXLEY, Benjamin MAHUGH, Enoch SLACK.

Bk:Pg: 2A:020   Date: 4/14/1800   RcCt: 14 Apr 1800
William CARR. DoE for Negro man Lewis, abt 35y old, freed 8y 8m from this date.

Bk:Pg: 2A:020   Date: 2/20/1800   RcCt: 14 Apr 1800
Patrick CAVAN of Lsbg & wife Sarah to John Henry SHELGESS of Ldn. B/S of 1*ac* lot in Lsbg formerly owned by Alexander McINTYRE dec'd. Wit: John MATHIAS, Robt ADAMS, John CAVAN.

Bk:Pg: 2A:022   Date: 2/22/1800   RcCt: 14 Apr 1800
John Henry SHELGESS to Patrick CAVAN. Agreement to pay additional money within a year. Wit: John MATHIAS, Robt ADAMS, John CAVAN.

Bk:Pg: 2A:023   Date: 1/11/1794   RcCt: 14 Apr 1800
William WILKINSON. Col for unnamed slaves from Md.

Bk:Pg: 2A:024   Date: 4/15/1800   RcCt: 15 Apr 1800
Patrick MURRAY to William ROBERTS. BoS for bay horse. Wit: Jacob STUMP, Simon BINNS.

Bk:Pg: 2A:024   Date: 9/8/1795   9 Feb 1796
John WRENN & wife Hannah of Fqr to Frances HARRIMAN of Ldn. B/S for lot on NE side of main road from Lsbg to AlexVa, part Samuel Dorsey HARRIMAN purchased from WRENN and sold back. Wit: John LITTLEJOHN, Benjamin EDWARDS, John FRY.

Bk:Pg: 2A:026   Date: 2/11/1796   RcCt: 12 Apr 1796
John WRENN & wife Hannah of Fqr to Thomas Ludwell LEE of Ldn. B/S of 100*ac;* originally Samuel Dorsey HARRIMAN agreed to give LEE use of water of Goose Creek for a mill in exchange for land but HARRIMAN died. Wit: C. BINNS Jr, Thomas SWAIN, Wm. H. HARDING.

Bk:Pg: 2A:029   Date: 5/22/1798   RcCt: 15 Apr 1800
Patrick CAVAN & wife Sarah of Ldn to George RINE of Ldn. B/S of lot in Lsbg on Loudoun St adj George HEAD. Wit: George McCABE, Alex COUPER Jr, James CAVAN Jr, John LITTLEJOHN, Saml. MURREY.

Bk:Pg: 2A:031   Date: 4/15/1800   RcCt: 15 Apr 1800
Abraham DAVIS & wife Hannah of Ldn to Reuben HIXON of Ldn. B/S of 193*ac* purchased of John GISS, except that sold to William MUIRHEAD adj Means VANDEVENTER, William ROBERTS. Wit: Isaac LARROWE, Timothy HIXON, Godfrey KIPHART.

Bk:Pg: 2A:033   Date: 12/3/1799   RcCt: 15 Apr 1800
Abram/Abraham DAVIS & wife Hannah of Ldn to Joseph DANIEL of Ldn.
B/S of 48½ac on Kittoctan Mt adj Isaac VANDEVENTER, William
ROBERTS. Wit: Timothy HIXON, Isaac LARROWE, M. SULLIVAN.

Bk:Pg: 2A:036   Date: 9/30/1799   RcCt: 15 Apr 1800
James HAMILTON of Lsbg to Thomas LEWIS of Lsbg. Mortgage on Lsbg
Lot #34; also 400ac in KY on big Carrin River which HAMILTON (as heir
to father) obtained by military warrant located by Capt Samuel GILL of
Lincoln Co. KY.

Bk:Pg: 2A:037   Date: 2/25/1800   RcCt: 15 Apr 1800
Thomas PURSEL & wife Lydia of Ldn to Thomas Darnal STEVENS of
Ldn. B/S of ½ & ½ of ¼ac adj James ROACH on turnpike from AlexVa to
Keyes Ferry. Wit: Stacy TAYLOR, Abner OSBURN, John McILHANEY.

Bk:Pg: 2A:039   Date: 3/1/1800   RcCt: 15 Apr 1800
Samuel CONNER (s/o Charles CONNER dec'd) of Ldn to Thomas MOSS
of Ldn. B/S of 64ac.

Bk:Pg: 2A:040   Date: 4/1/1800   RcCt: 15 Apr 1800
Thomas MOSS & wife Milla to Samuel CONNER (s/o Charles CONNER
dec'd). B/S of 32ac where MOSS now lives.

Bk:Pg: 2A:042   Date: 4/14/1800   RcCt: 15 Apr 1800
Samuel CONNER of Ldn (s/o Charles CONNER dec'd) of Ldn to Samuel
TILLETT of Ldn. B/S of 310ac TILLETT now lives plus adj tract, adj Jonas
POTTS, James RICE.

Bk:Pg: 2A:044   Date: 4/16/1800   RcCt: 15 Apr 1800
Thomas SWANN of AlexVa. DoE for Negro James who now lives in Lsbg.

Bk:Pg: 2A:045   Date: 4/15/1800   RcCt: 15 Apr 1800
John CROSS of Bernards, Somerset Co. NJ, attorney for William CROSS
& John CROSS of same place to Cornelius SKINNER of Ldn. PoA to
receive their legacy from estate of Joseph CROSS dec'd of Ldn. Wit: Wm.
CHILTON.

Bk:Pg: 2A:045   Date: 4/16/1800   RcCt: 15 Apr 1800
Samuel MURREY of Lsbg. DoE for Negro Phillis 30y old & Negro Sarah
34y old.

**Bk:Pg: 2A:046   Date: 11/23/1799   RcCt: Ffx 20 Jan 1800, Ldn 14 Apr
1800**
Hardage LANE of MontMd and Mary GREENFIELD. Marriage contract -
LANE gives her 100ac called Fortune in Montgomery, slave Eliza and
other items; also lands in TN; she paid LANE 5 shillings. Wit: Wm.
SMITH, J. LACKLAND, John SMITH, James SMITH, J'h MOORE, Josh
AXLIN, Benjn THOMAS, Charles ROGERS, Weathers SMITH.

Bk:Pg: 2A:049   Date: 5/13/1800   RcCt: 13 May 1800
John WRENN & Hannah his wife. DoE. Wit: John ALEXANDER and John
LITTLEJOHN.

Bk:Pg: 2A:050   Date: 5/10/1800   RcCt: 13 May 1800
Jeremiah FAIRHURST of Ldn to George FAIRHURST of Ldn. B/S of 162ac adj Blackstone JANNEY, James HATCHER, William HATCHER, Benjamin MEAD. Wit: Benjamin MEAD, Blackston JANNEY, Eli JANNEY.

Bk:Pg: 2A:052   Date: 5/10/1800   RcCt: 13 May 1800
Samuel IDEN & wife Catharine of Ldn to William PIGGOTT of Ldn. B/S of 99ac adj William NICKOLS, John PIGGOTT, Mahlon TAYLOR, James HEATON. Wit: William NICKOLS, Ebenezer PIGGOTT, Bernard TAYLOR.

Bk:Pg: 2A:055   Date: 5/10/1800   RcCt: 13 May 1800
Isaac MILLER of Ldn to Samuel POTTERFIELD of Ldn. A/L of 100ac. Wit: Frederick SMITH, Mathias SMITLEY, Jacob EMREY.

Bk:Pg: 2A:057   Date: 5/12/1800   RcCt: 13 May 1800
James BRADFIELD & wife Ruth of Ldn to Thomas PRICE of Ldn. B/S of 60ac adj NW fork of Goose Creek, James McILHANEY. Wit: Thomas WHITACRE, Benjamin PHILIPS.

Bk:Pg: 2A:059   Date: 2/13/1800   RcCt: 13 May 1800
John THRELKELD of MontMd to Conrod LICKEY of Ldn. B/S of 226ac on Catoctin Mt near Canby's Mill. Wit: Daniel REINTZELL, George FENWICK, Francis FENWICK.

Bk:Pg: 2A:061   Date: 4/25/1800   RcCt: 13 Apr 1800
William THORNTON of Spottsylvania VA to Edmund DENNY of Ldn. B/S of ½ac Lot #26 on Market Street adj courthouse in Lsbg. Wit: Pat'k CAVAN, John MATHIAS, John CAVAN, Philip TRIPLETT.

Bk:Pg: 2A:062   Date: 4/25/1800   RcCt: 13 May 1800
Edmond DENNY of Lsbg to William THORNTON of Ldn. Mortgage of above ½ac lot #26. Wit: Patrick CAVAN, John MATHIAS, John CAVAN, Philip TRIPLETT.

Bk:Pg: 2A:064   Date: 5/12/1800   RcCt: 13 May 1800
Patrick CAVAN & wife Sarah of Lsbg to Benjamin STEER of Ldn. B/S of 95½ac in Catoctan adj Mahlon JANNEY, nr mouth of Clymores Lane (Joseph JANNEY dec'd granted to CAVAN). Wit: Jno. MATHIAS, John CAVAN, Abner WILLIAMS.

Bk:Pg: 2A:065   Date: 5/12/1800   RcCt: 13 May 1800
Patrick CAVAN & wife Sarah of Lsbg to Joshua CHILTON. B/S of Lot #49 in Lsbg, reserving graveyard adj meeting house. Wit: John MATHIAS, John CAVAN, Benjamin STEER.

Bk:Pg: 2A:068   Date: 11/27/1799   RcCt: 13 May 1800
William THORNTON of Fredericksburg to Robert WELFORD of Fredericksburg. Trust on 54ac adj Lsbg & 1/3 of lot #52 in Lsbg. Wit: W. CARTER, David C. KEN, John ENGLISH, John ALRICK, John C. CARTER, John LITTLEJOHN, Wylless SILMAN, John CAVAN, Pat'k CAVAN.

Bk:Pg: 2A:069 Date: 2/15/1800 RcCt: 13 May 1800
Sampson TURLEY of Ffx to John TURLEY. B/S of 176*ac,* part of 416*ac* where Giles TURLEY now resides adj Joseph LACEY, George LEWIS. Wit: Wm. DENEALE, Thomas POLLARD Jr, Sandford PAYNE, Johnston CLEVELAND, Matthew HARRISON, Fleet SMITH, Tho. SWANN.

Bk:Pg: 2A:072 Date: 10/14/1799 RcCt: 13 May 1800
Daniel LOSH & wife Elizabeth of Lsbg to George NIXON of Ldn. B/S of lot on E side of King Street from Lsbg to Noland's Ferry adj Benjamin WHITMORE. Wit: Wm. MAINS, Amos LACEY, Jno. MATHIAS.

Bk:Pg: 2A:073 Date: 4/25/1799 RcCt: 13 May 1800
Jonas POTTS & wife Phebe of Ldn to Joshua DANIEL of Ldn. Mortgage for 300*ac* Grist Mill plantation on Pine Hill branch of Goose Creek, adj James RICE, Amos THOMPSON. Wit: Wm. H. HARDING, Samuel CARR, Wm. ROBERTS.

Bk:Pg: 2A:076 Date: 5/1/1800 RcCt: 13 May 1800
Samuel SPENCER (Admr of Edmond PHILIPS dec'd) of Ldn to George TAVENOR Jr. of Ldn. B/S of 66*ac* on W side of Kitoctan Mt, adj Joshua GORE.

Bk:Pg: 2A:078 Date: 3/10/1800 RcCt: 13 Jun 1800
William Byrd PAGE & wife Anne of AlexVa to William WILSON of AlexVa and John Thomas RICKETTS & William NEWTON of AlexVa. B/S of 1600*ac* on Goose Creek and Tuscarora branch; WILSON sold to RICKETTS & NEWTON part of that land but lost original indenture. Wit: Wm. HARTSHORNE, Jonah THOMPSON, Thomas WILLIAMS, James H. HOOE.

Bk:Pg: 2A:083 Date: 2/20/1800 RcCt: 13 Jun 1800
William WILSON of AlexVa to Colin AULD of AlexVa. B/S of 425*ac.* Wit: Thomas LAMYON, Edmd J. LEE, G. DENEALE, John HOOF.

Bk:Pg: 2A:086 Date: 12/31/1799 RcCt: 13 Jan 1800
John Carlyle HERBERT, Carlyle Fairfax WHITING & wife Sarah Manley of Ffx to William HALL of Ldn. B/S of 100*ac* adj HALL's other land. Wit: Edmd. J. LEE, Chs. LITTLE Jr, Wm. P. ROPER, John EVANS, Christo. ROPER.

Bk:Pg: 2A:088 Date: 12/21/1799 RcCt: 14 Jan 1800
John C. HERBERT & Carlisle F. WHITING & wife Sarah Manley of Ffx to William CARR of Ldn. B/S of 294*ac.* Wit: Charles LITTLE, Wm. Byrd PAGE, Wm. P. ROPER, John EVANS, Christo. ROPER.

Bk:Pg: 2A:091 Date: 6/9/1800 RcCt: 9 Jun 1800
Hugh DOUGLAS of Ldn. DoE for Negro Molly. Wit: Chs. BINNS Jr.

Bk:Pg: 2A:092 Date: 5/15/1800 RcCt: 14 Jul 1800
Frances HARRIMAN of Ldn to John BOGUE of AlexVa. B/S of 87*ac* on S side of Goose Creek adj G. KIPHEART; plus adj 19*ac.* Wit: Elias COCKRILLE, Godfrey KIPHEART, John HAMILTON.

Bk:Pg: 2A:094   Date: 1/15/1800   RcCt: 15 Jan 1800
John Carlyle HERBERT, Carlyle Fairfax WHITING & wife Sarah Manley of Ffx to James LEITH Jr. of Ldn. B/S of 116ac on Goose Creek. Wit: Edmd. J. LEE, Charles LITTLE, Christo. ROPER, John EVANS, Wm. P. ROPER.

Bk:Pg: 2A:096   Date: 9/9/1795   RcCt: 9 Feb 1896
Frances HARRIMAN of Ldn to John WRENN of Ldn. Mortgage for land WRENN sold due to decree and repurchased by WRENN who sold to HARRIMAN. Wit: John LITTLEJOHN, Benjamin EDWARDS, Jno. FRY.

Bk:Pg: 2A:098   Date: 7/8/1800   RcCt: 15 Jul 1800
Jacob TAWNER/TOWNER Jr. & wife Elizabeth R. of Lsbg to John TAWNER of Lsbg. B/S of Lot #62 in Lsbg. Wit: John MATHIAS, Jacob TAWNER Jr.

Bk:Pg: 2A:100   Date: 12/21/1799   RcCt: 15 Jul 1800
John Henry SHELGESS of Lsbg to John DULIN of Ldn. Mortgage for lot and house in Lsbg where SHELGESS now lives, SHELGESS gets to remain for 18m, then DULIN can do what he wants with the property. Wit: Thos. JONES, Jas. CAVAN Jr, Jesse ELGIN.

Bk:Pg: 2A:101   Date: 12/21/1799   RcCt: 15 Jul 1800
Patrick CAVAN to John Henry SHELGESS. Release of mortgage. Wit: Tho. JONES, James CAVAN Jr.

Bk:Pg: 2A:101   Date: 3/28/1800   RcCt: 15 Jul 1800
David DAVIS & wife Parnella of Ldn to George LEE of Ldn. B/S of 200ac. Wit: Albert RUSSELL, William ELLZEY, Absalom HAWLEY, Alexander MILTON.

Bk:Pg: 2A:105   Date: 6/2/1800   RcCt: 14 Jul 1800
John MINOR of AlexVa to John BOGUE of Ldn. Mortgage - MINOR wants to go to school in Europe, sells slaves James, Mary, Susannah, Judah & boy Adam abt 9y old for $100/yr while in Europe. Wit: John RITCHTER, Adam LONGDEN.

Bk:Pg: 2A:108   Date: 7/1/1800   RcCt: 14 Aug 1800
William HALLING of Ldn. Col for Slave Sall received by wife's right of dower and removed from PA to VA on June last.

Bk:Pg: 2A:109   Date: 8/14/1800   RcCt: 14 Aug 1800
John HAMILTON of Ldn to Edward SPENCER of Ldn. BoS for Negro woman Nan abt 70 or 80y old, black complexion; also Negro slave Man. Wit: Alex SUTHERLAND, Alex WAUGH.

Bk:Pg: 2A:110   Date: 8/16/1800   RcCt: 16 Aug 1800
Francis TRIPLETT and William TAYLOR & wife Ann (Executrix of William ANSLEY dec'd). Contract between TRIPLETT and ANSLEY for lot, suits by both parties, agree to arbitration.

Bk:Pg: 2A:110   Date: 11/10/1798   RcCt: 8 Sep 1800
John Beale HOWARD & wife Margarett and Thomas HOLLAND & wife Sybil of Md (formerly Margarett & Sybil WEST) to Josias CLAPHAM of Ldn. B/S of land on Kittoctan Mt. wives acquired at death of brother

George William WEST as well as "Hollands Land" in Ldn from death of uncle George WEST. Wit: Wm. Young LEWIS, Sam Weston LEWIS.

Bk:Pg: 2A:113   Date: 3/22/1800   RcCt: 8 Sep 1800
Dorothy SCHOOLEY (wd/o Samuel SCHOOLEY) of Ldn to James CAMPBELL of Ldn. Assignment of 100ac in Catoctan Manor. Wit: Farling BALL, John JACKSON, Adam HOUSEHOLDER Jr, John HANKS.

Bk:Pg: 2A:115   Date: 9/8/1800   RcCt: 8 Sep 1800
Joseph JANNEY & wife Mary of Ldn to William LODGE of Ldn. B/S of 10ac, adj Phinehas THOMAS, Harmon COX, William FOWLER. Wit: Jonas JANNEY, Israel JANNEY, Samuel MEAD, George TAVENOR Jr.

Bk:Pg: 2A:117   Date: ___ 1800   RcCt: 8 Sep 1800
Nathan BALL & wife Mary of Ldn to John FAWLEY Jr. of Ldn. B/S of 100½ac, adj John COLVILLE, Timothy HIXON, Roach Mill Road. Wit: Frederick SMITH, foreign name, George FAWLEY.

Bk:Pg: 2A:119   Date: 9/8/1800   RcCt: 8 Sep 1800
George LEE of Ldn to Joseph WATSON of Ldn. BoS for Negroes Dolly & Joe. Wit: Job RACE, Thomas Eskridge MINOR, William VEALE.

Bk:Pg: 2A:119   Date: 9/8/1800   RcCt: 8 Sep 1800
James BALL & wife Ruth of Ldn to James PAXON of Ldn. B/S of 17ac adj Jonathan MYERS heirs. Wit: Asa MOORE.

Bk:Pg: 2A:121   Date: 4/17/1800   RcCt: 8 Sep 1800
Scarlett BERKELEY of Ldn to Vincent DAVIS. PoA. Wit: John LINTON, James LEWIS, John L. BERKELEY.

Bk:Pg: 2A:122   Date: 9/17/1798   RtCt 8 Sep 1800
Josiah HALL & wife Mary of Ldn to George HIXON of Ldn. Mortgage on 140ac adj Samuel MEAD, Richard WHITE, Samuel WILK, Francis WILK plus 1ac adj lot. Wit: Wm. H. HARDING, Thomas LESLIE, Henry SETTLE.

Bk:Pg: 2A:124   Date: 4/16/1800   RcCt: 8 Sep 1800
Amos DAVIS of Ldn to John L. BERKELEY of Ldn. PoA. Wit: Jos. LEWIS, Richd KEEN, Chas. LEWIS, Vincent DAVIS.

Bk:Pg: 2A:124   Date: 4/16/1800   RcCt: 8 Sep 1800
James DAVIS of Ldn to John L. BERKELEY of Ldn. PoA. Wit: Jos. LEWIS, Richd' KEEN, Chas. LEWIS, Vincent DAVIS.

Bk:Pg: 2A:124   Date: 2/20/1800   RcCt: 8 Sep 1800
James COLEMAN & wife Jane of Ffx to son William COLEMAN of Ldn. B/S of 315ac of Valley Land, adj John WILLIAMS, Peter CARR, William ROBERTS, Israel VANDEVENDER, Abraham DAVIS, also slaves yellow woman Milley, yellow boy Will & Ellick. Wit: Ferdno. FAIRFAX, Wm. H. HARDING, James COLEMAN Jr, Richard COLEMAN.

Bk:Pg: 2A:126   Date: 1/11/1800   RcCt: 8 Sep 1800
Joseph ALLEN (s/o William ALLEN dec'd) & wife Frances of Ldn to Joshua LEE of Ldn. B/S of 100ac adj Abraham WARFORD, David

SMALLEY, David LEE. Wit: Israel LACEY, Thomas KEEN, George LEWIS.

Bk:Pg: 2A:128   Date: 7/21/1800   RcCt: 8 Sep 1800
William LANE Sr. & wife Sarah of Ffx to Hardage LANE of MontMd. B/S of 851ac adj Thomas BLINCOE, Elizabeth & Frances BARNS' patent, heirs of Elizabeth KING, Frances KING. Wit: Richard Bland LEE, Harrison FITZHUGH, William FOX, Thomas GUNNELL, Amos FOX, A. FOX.

Bk:Pg: 2A:131   Date: 8/15/1800   RcCt: 8 Sep 1800
Patrick CAVAN & wife Sarah to Joshua CHILTON. CoE for sale of 2 lots. Wit: Samuel MURREY, Joseph SMITH, Wilson C. SELDON.

Bk:Pg: 2A:132   Date: 9/6/1800   RcCt: 8 Sep 1800
George FAIRHURST of Ldn to Hamilton ROGERS of Ldn. B/S of 2ac adj Thomas GREGG. Wit: Jesse JANNEY, Samuel GREGG.

Bk:Pg: 2A:134   Date: 3/10/1800   RcCt: 8 Sep 1800
Pierce BAYLEY & wife Mary of Ldn to John SPENCER of Ldn. B/S of 200ac adj Richard McGRAW, Philip PALMER, Andrew REDMOND, Benjamin JAMES, James LEWIS, Daniel & Hugh THOMAS, Steven ROZEL. Wit: Joseph LANE.

Bk:Pg: 2A:138   Date: 9/8/1800   RcCt: 8 Sep 1800
Joseph SANDS of Ldn to John ROBERTSON of Ldn. Title bond - Joseph is entitled to 1/7 of 170ac of Isaac SANDS dec'd. Wit: Wm. H. HARDING, George ROWAN, Jonah SANDS.

Bk:Pg: 2A:140   Date: 9/4/1800   RcCt: 8 Sep 1800
William GROVES of Ldn to John SPENCER of Ldn. B/S of 100ac devised to GROVES by George RALLS. Wit: Andrew REDMOND, Benjamin JAMES, Stephen GROVE.

Bk:Pg: 2A:142   Date: 4/14/1800   RcCt: 8 Sep 1800
George CLEVELAND of Clarke Co. KY to Johnston CLEVELAND of Ldn. B/S of 400ac inherited from Frances CLEVELAND on Cub Run. Wit: John MITCHELL, John L. BERKELEY, Benja. THOMAS, J. H. LEWIS.

Bk:Pg: 2A:143   Date: 9/1/1800   RcCt: 8 Sep 1800
Jeremiah FAIRHURST of Ldn to John IREY of Ldn. B/S of 106ac adj Hamilton ROGERS, Bleackston JANNEY, George FAIRHURST, James HATCHER, George HATCHER. Wit: Jesse JANNEY, Hamilton ROGERS, John UPDIKE.

Bk:Pg: 2A:145   Date: 8/28/1799   RcCt: 14 Apr 1800
John SPENCER & wife Pheby of Ldn to Andrew REDMON of Ldn. B/S of 3071ac adj on road from Clarksburg to Muskingdom River. Wit: Israel LACEY, Joseph DAVIS, William HOSKINS.

Bk:Pg: 2A:147   Date: 4/4/1800   RcCt: 14 Apr 1800
John SPENCER & wife Phoebe of Ldn to William GROVE of Ldn. B/S of 1000ac adj Andrew REDMON. Wit: Andrew REDMOND, Benjamin JAMES, Stephen GROVE.

Bk:Pg: 2A:149   Date: 11/2/1799   RcCt: 14 Apr 1800
John SPENCER & wife Phoebe of Ldn to Richard SKINNER of Ldn. B/S of 100*ac* nr Broad Run where SPENCER now lives adj Barnebas CURTIS, the lot which Stout BENNETT leased. Wit: Cornelius SKINNER Jr, Joseph LEWIS Sr, John SKILLMAN.

Bk:Pg: 2A:151   Date: 9/10/1791   RcCt: 10 Apr 1792
Charles WEST & wife Sally of Fqr to Thomas WILLIAMS of Ffx. LS of 102*ac* S side of Goose Creek, adj Major McCARTY, Capt. William AYLET. Wit: Wm. HALE, James LEITH, Whitman LEITH, Jno. P. HARRISON.

Bk:Pg: 2A:153   Date: 9/10/1791   RcCt: 10 Apr 1792
Charles WEST & wife Sally of Ldn to Thomas WILLIAMS of Ffx. LS 102*ac* on S side of Goose Creek. Wit: Wm. HALE, James LEITH, Whitman LEITH, Jno. P. HARRISON.

Bk:Pg: 2A:156   Date: 6/7/1800   RcCt: 8 Sep 1800
Patrick CAVAN & wife Sarah to Benjamin STEER. CoE for sale of 95½*ac*. Wit: John LITTLEJOHN, Saml. MURREY, Joseph SMITH.

Bk:Pg: 2A:157   Date: 3/5/1800   RcCt: 9 Sep 1800
Matthew RUST & wife Martha [signed Patty] of Ldn to William TOMLINSON of Ldn. B/S of 20*ac* adj Bernard TAYLOR. Wit: Bernard TAYLOR, John MUDD, Temple SMITH.

Bk:Pg: 2A:159   Date: 3/25/1800   RcCt: 9 Sep 1800
Mary COMBS, John COMBS & wife Ann [signed Nancey], Mahlon COMBS & wife Sarah, Israel COMBS & wife Jane of Ldn to William TOMLINSON of Ldn. B/S of 70*ac*, half of tract of Andrew COMBS dec'd. Wit: Matthew RUST, John MUDD, Temple SMITH.

Bk:Pg: 2A:162   Date: 1/20/1795   RcCt: 9 Feb 1795
Rev. Mr. Bryan FAIRFAX of Ffx to John STANHOPE (wife Ann, son Lewis) of Ldn. LS of 153*ac* adj Allen DAVIS. Wit: Thomas GUNNELL Sr, Henry GUNNELL Sr, Henry GUNNELL Jr.

Bk:Pg: 2A:163   Date: 1/20/1795   RcCt: 9 Feb 1795
Bryan FAIRFAX of Ffx to Thomas GUNNELL Sr. of Ffx. LS of 150*ac* adj Robert CARTER. Wit: John STANHOPE, Henry GUNNELL Sr. and Jr.

Bk:Pg: 2A:165   Date: 9/9/1800   RcCt: 9 Sep 1800
Robert COOPER and Sarah HALBERT. Marriage contract - child Margrett to receive all that Sarah now possesses (if Margrett dead given to Samuel BEAVERS son of Robert) gives up slaves and property from father Michael HALBERT's estate. Wit: Sampson BLINCOE, W. DAWSON, Daniel DILLON, Edin B. MOORE.

Bk:Pg: 2A:166   Date: 7/23/1798   9 Sep 1800
John CAMPBELL & wife Sarah of Ldn to Thomas PEAKE of Ldn. B/S of 60*ac* on Turnpike road from Lsbg to AlexVa, adj Mary GORDEN, William Bird PAGE. Wit: Charles BINNS Jr., Robert ADAMS, Step. C. ROZELL, Alex. WAUGH.

Bk:Pg: 2A:167   Date: 5/17/1800   RcCt: 9 Sep 1800
Stacy HANES & wife Mary and Charles DRISH & wife Susanna of Lsbg to William CHILTON. B/S of lot on King St adj reps of David CLINE dec'd. Wit: Thomas L. SIM, John DREAN, Simeon HAINS.

Bk:Pg: 2A:170   Date: 7/20/1800   RcCt: 10 Sep 1800
Thomas FRANCIS & wife Mary of Ldn to Isaac HARRIS of Lsbg. B/S of part of Lot #1 on Loudoun St in Lsbg where Jane HAMILTON now lives, adj Matthew WETHERBY. Wit: Stephen G. ROZELL, James HAMILTON, John DREAN.

Bk:Pg: 2A:173   Date: 5/13/1790   RcCt: 13 Oct 1800
Thomas John CHILTON of Lincoln Co. KY (heir at law to George CHILTON dec'd, wife Anne later m. John WILLIAMS) to Jacob REED (son Joseph) of Ldn. B/S of 321ac. Wit: Hugh JOHNSTON, George JOHNSTON, Henry TAYLOR, George JOHNSTON Jr.

Bk:Pg: 2A:175   Date: 5/28/1800   RcCt: 13 Oct 1800
Devault NIECE & wife Gertrude of Ldn to Jacob FAWLEY of Ldn. B/S of 59ac adj Peter HOLLER & Francis COST. Wit: Frederick SMITH, John SLATER, John FAWLEY Sr.

Bk:Pg: 2A:177   Date: 10/29/1799   RcCt: 13 Oct 1800
Thomas PURSELL & wife Lydia of Ldn to Thomas HEBURN of Ldn. B/S of ½ac lot in gap of Short Hill on N side of turnpike road, adj William COPELAND, David SMITH. Wit: Newton BRADLEE, Bernard TAYLOR, Ann WILLIAMS.

Bk:Pg: 2A:180   Date: __ 1800   RcCt: 13 Oct 1800
Richard OSBURN of Ldn to Thomas LESLIE of Ldn. LS of 76ac. Sons Joseph FISHER, John FISHER and Saml FISHER named.

Bk:Pg: 2A:181   Date: 10/1/1800   RcCt: 13 Oct 1800
Absalom HAWLEY of Ldn to Barton D. HAWLEY of Ldn. Memo of payment for farm and household items for present years of schooling as teacher. Wit: James FOX, Charles McBRIDE, John McBRIDE.

Bk:Pg: 2A:182   Date: 9/8/1800   RcCt: 13 Oct 1800
Benjamin EDWARDS & wife Elizabeth to Thomas Ludwell LEE. B/S of 232ac on Goose Creek. Wit: Samuel MURREY, Joseph SMITH, William MINOR.

Bk:Pg: 2A:186   Date: 11/20/1793   RcCt: 13 Feb 1797
Sandford CONNELLY & wife Mary and John CONNELLY & wife Frances to David DAVIS of Ffx. B/S of I500ac devised to CONNELLY by will of Sandford REAMY, adj Col. Henry ASHTON, Col. Thomas LEE, John PILE, John DAVIS. Wit: Wm. REDWOOD, John GROVES, Wm. HUMMER.

Bk:Pg: 2A:190   Date: 8/18/1800   RcCt: 13 Oct 1800
Sampson TURLEY Sr. & wife Martha of Ffx to Sampson TURLEY Jr. of Ffx. B/S of 200ac on Broad Run where John TURLEY now lives. Wit: Fleet SMITH, M. HARRISON, Thomas JONES, Thos. SWANN.

Bk:Pg: 2A:192   Date: 5/12/1800   RcCt: 14 Oct 1800
Thomas OSBURN and Joel OSBURN of Ldn to Morris OSBURN of Ldn.
B/S of 60*ac* at foot of Blue Ridge, adj Abel MARKS, Thomas SADEN. Wit:
Abraham VICKERS, And'w COPELAND, Chas. CHAMBLIN.

Bk:Pg: 2A:194   Date: 12/18/1897   RcCt: 13 Aug 1798
Isaac MILLER & wife Catharine of Ldn to merchant Terence FIGH of Ldn.
B/S of 100*ac* in Catoctan. Wit: John DAVIS, Jacob FRY?, Isaac RICHIE,
Farling BALL, James McILHANEY.

Bk:Pg: 2A:197   Date: 10/13/1800   RcCt: 14 Oct 1800
Patrick CAVAN of Lsbg to Samuel PROBASCOE of Lsbg. LS of 1*ac* Lot
#10 in Lsbg. Wit: John MATHIAS, John CAVAN.

Bk:Pg: 2A:198   Date: 4/11/1800   RcCt: 14 Oct 1800
James LEGG & wife Elizabeth of PrWm to Thomas COCKRILL of Ldn.
B/S of 115*ac* in CamP adj John Turley's Spring branch, road from Baptist
meeting house to Gum Spring, John SPENCER. Wit: Rich'd B.
ALEXANDER, John H. GIBBS, George LEWIS, John BROWN, Edmd.
BROOKE.

Bk:Pg: 2A:201   Date: 8/12/1800   RcCt: 14 Oct 1800
Charles DRISH & wife Susanna of Lsbg to Thomas Nielson BINNS of
Ldn. B/S of ½*ac* lot on King St in Lsbg adj Stacy HAINS. Wit: William
CLINE, William TAYLOR, Barton LUCAS, Leven POWELL, Abner
OSBORNE, Thomas Ludwell LEE.

Bk:Pg: 2A:203   Date: 3/10/1800   RcCt: 14 Oct 1800
John GARNER & wife Rebekah of Ldn to Joshua GREGG of Ldn. B/S of
48¾*ac* adj Samuel ARNETT, Joseph GREGG, Joseph REED. Wit: Wm.
BRONAUGH, A. RUSSELL, Abijah JANNEY, Stacey TAYLOR.

Bk:Pg: 2A:205   Date: 10/14/1800   RcCt: 14 Oct 1800
Thomas N. BINNS & wife Amelia of Ldn to Benjamin H. CANBY of Lsbg.
B/S of ½*ac* lot on King St in Lsbg adj Stacy HAINS. Wit: Leven POWELL,
Abner OSBURN, Thomas Ludwell LEE.

Bk:Pg: 2A:206   Date: 9/12/1800   RcCt: 11 [Nov?] 1800
Philip PALMER to Thomas REASE. B/S of 10*ac* in CamP adj Benjamin
JAMES. Wit: M. HARRISON, Wm. CHILTON, Wm. B. HARRISON, Wm.
R. TAYLOR.

Bk:Pg: 2A:208   Date: 10/20/1800   RcCt: 11 Nov 1800
Henry ACTON. Col from Md on 4 Oct 1800 for Negro boy John abt 8y old
left to wife Lucy as legacy by Susannah SMALLWOOD of Md.

Bk:Pg: 2A:209   Date: 11/8/1800   RcCt: 8 Dec 1800
Nathan BALL & wife Mary of Ldn to John FALLEY Jr. CoE for sale of
100½*ac*. Wit: Farling BALL, Charles BENNETT, John HAMILTON.

Bk:Pg: 2A:210   Date: 11/8/1800   RcCt: 8 Dec 1800
Devault NIECE & wife Gertrude to Jacob FALLEY. CoE for sale of 59*ac*.
Wit: Farling BALL, Charles BENNETT, John HAMILTON.

Bk:Pg: 2A:211   Date: 12/2/1800   RcCt: 8 Dec 1800
Ann GORDEN of Hancock Co. GA late Ann HARDY (niece of Thomas DENT of Piscattaway PrG, dau of George & Lucy HARDY his sister) to Rufus UPDIKE. B/S of 223ac adj Gidney CLARK, Isaac NICKOLS on NW fork of Goose Creek. Wit: C. BINNS Jr., Stacy TAYLOR, James DILLON, Sampson BLINCOE.

Bk:Pg: 2A:213   Date: 11/20/1800   8 Dec 1800
Peter ROMINE of Ldn to James GRADY of Ldn. Mortgage for 140¾ac now in tenure of John BALDWIN Sr adj Thomas HEREFORD, Saml. TALBOTT, James DILLON, Spencer PUE. Wit: Joseph READ, Edw'd B. GRADY, Jonathan WARTERS.

Bk:Pg: 2A:214   Date: 12/4/1800   8 Dec 1800
Samuel RITCHIE of Ldn to John GEORGE of Ldn. Deed of 2¼ac (part where RITCHIE now lives) for GEORGE to use for his mill dam. Wit: Adam SHOWER, Wm. THOMAS, Henry POTTERFELT.

Bk:Pg: 2A:215   Date: 12/6/1800   RcCt: 8 Dec 1800
James MASH & wife Ruth of Ldn to John VERNON of Ldn. B/S of 102ac on Beaver Dam adj Annanias RANDLE, Matthew RUSS, Joseph TAYLOR. Wit: David JAMES, Andrew CAMPBELL, Samuel PROBASCO.

Bk:Pg: 2A:217   Date: 10/9/1800   RcCt: 8 Dec 1800
Ann GORDON (late Ann HARDY) of Hancock Co. GA to son-in-law William McGAUGHEY. PoA for land transactions in Md and Va. Wit: James McGAUGHEY, John COUTTER.

Bk:Pg: 2A:218   Date: 11/4/1800   RcCt: 8 Dec 1800
James MASH & wife Ruth of Ldn to Andrew CAMPBELL of Ldn. B/S of 110ac on Beaverdam adj Matthew RUST, Andrew McMULLIN. Wit: August LOVE, John VERNON, David JAMES.

Bk:Pg: 2A:221   Date: 11/4/1800   RcCt: 8 Dec 1800
Andrew CAMPBELL & wife Jane of Ldn to Annanias RANDLE of Ldn. Mortgage of 100ac at Beaver Dam. Wit: Augs't LOVE, John VERNON, David JAMES.

Bk:Pg: 2A:223   Date: 12/8/1800   RcCt: 8 Dec 1800
Jacob SCOTT & wife Elizabeth (both dec'd, he died intestate). Agreement - children Rebecca ROBERTS, Martha WILSON, Stephen SCOTT, Elizabeth had difficulty settling Jacob's estate, children Hannah SCOTT, Merab SCOTT, John ROBERTS & Stephen WILSON make no claims against father's estate. Wit: James MOORE, Asa MOORE.

Bk:Pg: 2A:224   Date: 6/9/1800   RcCt: 8 Dec 1800
Thomas GIST to Charles LEWIS. BoS for Negro girls Beck & Chloe. Wit: Daniel C. LANE.

Bk:Pg: 2A:224   Date: 10/28/1800   RcCt: 8 Dec 1800
James HIXON & wife Ezebel of Ldn to Thomas Brook BEALL of MontMd. B/S of 284ac on Catoctan Mt adj John OXLEY, Hannah STEPHENS, Isaac LARROWE. Wit: Pat'k CAVAN, John ROSE, Joseph SMITH.

Bk:Pg: 2A:227   Date: 12/12/1791   RcCt: 12 Dec 1791
Joshua DANIEL & wife Jean of Ldn to John HAMILTON. LS of 100*ac* adj
John CAVINS, Jonathan MYERS. Wit: James HAMILTON, Wm.
COPELAND, Benjamin BIRD.

Bk:Pg: 2A:229   Date: 12/13/1791   RcCt: 12 Dec 1791
Joshua DANIEL & wife Jane/Jean of Ldn to John HAMILTON of Ldn. B/S
of 100*ac* adj John CAVANS, Jonathan MYERS. Wit: James HAMILTON,
Wm. COPELAND, Benj. BIRD.

Bk:Pg: 2A:231   Date: 11/13/1800   RcCt: 8 Dec 1800
John THRELKELD of MontMd to Isaac HUGHS & wife Elizabeth of Ldn.
B/S of 250*ac* adj Daniel WHITE, George NIXON, William JONES. Wit:
Danl. REINTZEL, Thomas WATSON.

Bk:Pg: 2A:232   Date: 3/8/1793   RcCt: 9 Sep 1793
John HOUGH of Ldn to Anthony CONARD of Ldn. LS of 100*ac* on S side
of N fork of Kittoctan Creek. Wit: William PAXON, John MARTIN, Thomas
GILLINGHAM.

Bk:Pg: 2A:235   Date: 3/9/1793   RcCt: 9 Sep 1793
John HOUGH of Ldn to Anthony CONNARD of Ldn. B/S of 100*ac* on S
side of N fork of Kittoctan Creek. Wit: William PAXSON, John MARTIN,
Thomas GILLINGHAM.

Bk:Pg: 2A:237   Date: 12/8/1800   RcCt: 8 Dec 1800
Benjamin GARRETT & wife Mary of Hampshire Co. VA to William
WILKISON of Ldn. B/S of 113*ac* adj Thomas GARRETT Jr, Abel
GARRETT, Silas GARRETT. Wit: Thos. HUMPHREY, Augu't LOVE,
Reuben TRIPLETT.

Bk:Pg: 2A:240   Date: 11/1/1799   RcCt: 8 Dec 1800
Richard Weaver JOHNS. Col for Negroes Priscilla, Hannah & Phil brought
in Va as natives of America.

Bk:Pg: 2A:241   Date: 12/8/1800   RcCt: 8 Dec 1800
Ste's Tho'n MASON. DoE for slave Richard Williams. Wit: Wm. CHILTON,
Chas. BINNS Jr, Patrick H. DOUGLASS.

Bk:Pg: 2A:242   Date: 12/9/1800   RcCt: 9 Dec 1800
William H. HARDING & wife Nancy. CoE for sale of land. Wit: Thos. Lud
LEE, Samuel MURREY.

Bk:Pg: 2A:243   Date: 12/10/1800   RcCt: 9 Dec 1800
Thomas Ludwell LEE & wife Fanny to Ludwell LEE. B/S of 1456*ac* adj
Thomas Ludwell LEE, Ludwell LEE, George LEE, Houghs Mill road. Wit:
Fleet SMITH, Wm. CHILTON, Chas. BINNS Jr.

Bk:Pg: 2A:245   Date: 11/10/1800   RcCt: 9 Dec 1800
Francis TYTUS & wife Jane of Ldn to Jonas POTTS & Jacob BAUGH of
Ldn. B/S of 1¾*ac* adj John HOUGH. Wit: George NIXON Sr, John
HENRY, Saml. CARR.

Bk:Pg: 2A:247   Date: 12/9/1800   RcCt: 9 Dec 1800
John BOARD & wife Nancy of Ldn to John HENRY of Ldn. B/S of lot in
Lsbg adj Stacy HAINS on Loudoun St. Wit: Wm. H. HARDING, Wm.
MAINS, Reuben HIXON, Nathan BALL

Bk:Pg: 2A:248   Date: 10/26/1800   RcCt: 9 Dec 1800
Thomas PEAKE of Ldn to William MEANS of Ldn. B/S of 60ac on turnpike
road from Lsbg to AlexVa adj Mary GORDEN, William B. PAGE. Wit:
Wm. H. HARDING, John PEAKE, Benja' SHREVE, Jno. ALEXANDER.

Bk:Pg: 2A:250   Date: 11/6/1794   RcCt: 9 Dec 1800
Ann HAIT (wd/o Benjamin HAIT of Elizabeth borough, Essex Co. NJ) &
surviving children Elizabeth HAIT, Mary HAIT, Benjamin HAIT and James
HAIT to William MAINS of Ldn. B/S of 807ac nr Lsbg adj James
RADICAN, Joseph COX. Wit: David BONNEL, D. CAMPBELL, William
BRANTOP.

Bk:Pg: 2A:253   Date: 12/8/1800   RcCt: 9 Dec 1800
Daniel LOSH & wife Elizabeth of Lsbg to George NIXON Jr. of Ldn. B/S of
3ac nr Lsbg on W side of eastern most street. Wit: Wm. MAINS, George
FAIRHURST.

Bk:Pg: 2A:254   Date: 11/15/1800   Jan 1801
Charles BINNS Jr, Matthew HARRISON, Thomas SWANN & Stes. Tho'n.
MASON of Ldn. Bond on BINNS as clerk of Ldn. Wit: Thos. Tho'n
JONES, Wm. R. TAYLOR, Wm. CHILTON.

Bk:Pg: 2A:255   Date: 11/20/1800   RcCt: 12 Jan 1801
Robert ARMISTEAD of Ldn. DoE for slave boy Stephen abt 14y old.

Bk:Pg: 2A:256   Date: 12/8/1800   RcCt: 12 Jan 1801
William DULIN of Ldn. DoE for Negro man Sam abt 45y old, woman Lucy
abt 37y old, man Harry 29y old, woman Nell 28y old. Wit: Samuel
MURREY, Samuel DONOHOE, Amos DONOHOE.

Bk:Pg: 2A:257   Date: 1/9/1801   RcCt: 12 Jan 1801
Charles HUNGERFORD. Col: 23 Dec 1800 moved from Md to Ldn and
brought Negroes Joseph, Elijah, Fillis, Gabriel, Henna & Jane. On last day
of Dec brought in Negroes Sarah, Hannah & Brice.

Bk:Pg: 2A:257   Date: 7/4/1800   RcCt: 13 Jan 1801
John LITTLEJOHN of Ldn. DoE for Negro man Charles GIBSON.

Bk:Pg: 2A:258   Date: 4/9/1800   RcCt: 13 Jan 1801
John REIGOR & wife Margarett of Ldn to John LITTLEJOHN of Ldn. L/L
of land belonging to heirs of John THORNTON dec'd. Wit: Joseph
BENTLEY, James JOHNSTON.

Bk:Pg: 2A:259   Date: 1/12/1801   RcCt: 13 Jan 1801
John LITTLEJOHN of Ldn. DoE for Negro woman Rachel freed from 1
Jan 1804.

Bk:Pg: 2A:259   Date: 10/25/1800   RcCt: 13 Jan 1801
Benjamin WOODLEY & wife Elizabeth of Ldn to James DAWSON of Ldn.
B/S of ¼ac lot in Lsbg. Wit: B. HOUGH, Jas. HAMILTON, Samuel
HOUGH.

Bk:Pg: 2A:261   Date: 1/13/1801   RcCt: 13 Jan 1801
Joseph SMITH of Ldn. DoE for Negro girl/woman Lukey freed on 1 Jan
1810.

Bk:Pg: 2A:261   Date: 1/13/1801   RcCt: 13 Jan 1801
Patrick CAVAN of Lsbg to John McCORMICK of Lsbg. LS of lots #23 &
#24, part leased from James HEREFORD dated 10 Aug 1798.

Bk:Pg: 2A:263   Date: 1/13/1801   RcCt: 13 Jan 1801
Samuel MURREY of Ldn. DoE for Negro man Sige from 1 Jun 1803, man
Bob from 1 Jun 1806, girl Hannah from 1 Jun 1808, boy Charles from 1
Jun 1812, girl Betty after she becomes 18y old.

Bk:Pg: 2A:263   Date: 11/29/1800   RtCt 8 Dec 1800
John REIGOR & wife Margaret of Ldn to Charles BINNS Jr. of Ldn. B/S of
¼ac Lot #25 in Lsbg. Wit: Josiah MOFFETT, William TAYLOR, Benjamin
SHREIVE, Samuel MURREY, Joseph SMITH.

Bk:Pg: 2A:266   Date: 1/13/1801   RcCt: 13 Jan 1801
Frederick WILDBAHN & wife Catharine of Ldn to Thomas JANNEY of
AlexVa. B/S of 26ac conveyed in 1799 in trust, adj John CAMPBELL. Wit:
Chas. BENNETT, Joseph SMITH.

Bk:Pg: 2A:269   Date: 1/13/1801   RcCt: 13 Jan 1801
John Hough CANBY of Ldn to Thomas JANNEY of AlexVa. B/S of 26ac
that Frederick WILDBAHN conveyed in 1799 to JANNEY in trust adj John
CAMPBELL.

Bk:Pg: 2A:270   Date: 2/2/1801   RcCt: 9 Feb 1801
John LEWIS of Ldn to daughter Ann MATCHIN of Washington Co. Md.
Gift of mulatto Negro girl Jane. Wit: James LEWIS, Danl. LEWIS, David
LEWIS.

Bk:Pg: 2A:271   Date: 11/20/1800   RcCt: 9 Feb 1801
Jenkin PHILIPS of Jefferson Co. KY by PoA to his son Thomas PHILIPS
to Peter HANN of Ldn. B/S of 208ac on drains of Goose Creek, sold to
PHILIPS by waggoner Thomas PHILIPS, adj Joseph BURSON, Jesse
HUMPHREY, James DILLION, Benjamin BURSON, Elisha MARKS,
Samuel ARRETT. Wit: Jesse HUMPHREY, Aaron ASHFORD, Isaac
KENT, Matthew HANN.

Bk:Pg: 2A:273   Date: 11/29/1800   RcCt: 9 Feb 1801
Burr POWELL of Mdbg to Peter HAND of Ldn. Trust for debt to Thomas
PHILIPS using of 208ac adj Joseph BURSON, Jesse HUMPHREY,
James DILLON, Elisha MARKS, Samuel ARRETT. Wit: Jesse
HUMPHREY, Matthias HANN, Isaac KENT.

Bk:Pg: 2A:274   Date: 9/20/1800   RcCt: 9 Feb 1801
Jenkin PHILIPS of Jefferson Co. KY to son Thomas PHILIPS. PoA for
sale of 208ac to Thomas PHILIPS and 170ac (from Samuel BUTCHER,
f/o wife Hannah).

Bk:Pg: 2A:276   Date: 2/9/1801   RcCt: 9 Feb 1801
Joseph CARR Jr. of Ldn to Francis ELGIN of Ldn. B/S of 81ac on road
from Lsbg to Laswell's ford, adj John ALEXANDER, Christopher
GREENUP, Thomas CARR. Wit: Wm. H. HARDING

Bk:Pg: 2A:278   Date: 1/13/1801   RcCt: 9 Feb 1801
Benjamin CUMMINGS & wife Ann of Ldn to Joshua OSBORNE of Ldn.
A/L of 111ac. Wit: Joseph GORE, Daniel EACHES, Jonathan CARTER.

Bk:Pg: 2A:280   Date: 1/13/1801   9 Feb 1801
Benjamin CUMMINGS & wife Ann of Ldn to Joshua OSBORN of Ldn. B/S
of 43ac. Wit: Daniel EACHES, Joseph GORE, Jonathan CARTER.

Bk:Pg: 2A:282   Date: 3/20/1794   RcCt: 13 Apr 1794
Charles DULIN & wife Anne (formerly Anne GRAYSON) of Fqr to Leven
POWELL Jr. of Ldn. B/S of 139¾ac, part of tract left by Lewis ELLZEY
dec'd to Anne, her brother Benjamin & sisters Susanna & Sarah. Wit:
Thomas LEWIS, Josiah DILLON, Robert DAGG, John MCFARLAND,
Leven POWELL.

Bk:Pg: 2A:285   Date: 2/9/1801   RcCt: 9 Feb 1801
William GRUBB Sr of Ldn to son William GRUBB of Ldn. A/L of 100ac
and plantation. Wit: Wm. H. HARDIN.

Bk:Pg: 2A:287   Date: 2/10/1801   RcCt: 10 Feb 1801
Simon TRIPLETT of Ldn. DoE for Negro man David abt 44y old.

Bk:Pg: 2A:287   Date: 2/10/1798   RcCt: 12 Feb 1802 [1801?]
Sarah FAIRFAX (of Ferdinando FAIRFAX) by attorney Battaile MUSE to
farmer John MORRIS of Ldn. LS of 100ac in Piedmont, part L/L to Jenkin
MORRIS, then to son John MORRIS (for life of sons Isaiah & David
MORRIS). Wit: Thomas DAVIS, Ebenezer GRUBB, John CAMPBELL.

Bk:Pg: 2A:292   Date: 9/15/1796   RcCt: 12 Dec 1796
Jonah THOMPSON and William HOUGH (Exors of Israel THOMPSON
dec'd) of Ldn to Garlock STICKLER. A/L of 81ac. Wit: Thomas
THOMPSON, John LOVE, Craven P. THOMPSON, John SCHOOLEY Jr,
Joseph THOMPSON, Isaac BALL.

Bk:Pg: 2A:294   Date: 3/12/1799   RcCt: 10 Feb 1801
Charles BINNS Jr. of Ldn. DoE - on 12 Feb 1796 advanced $200 to John
ROBISON otherwise John HULLS of Ldn for purchase of his wife a yellow
woman Cate (late the property of Francis ELGIN dec'd) from William
ELGIN, now set free.

Bk:Pg: 2A:295   Date: 8/26/1800   RcCt: 12 Feb 1801
William STABLER & wife Deborah of MontMd to Thomas MATTHEWS of
AlexVa. B/S of ¼ac lot #60 in Lsbg. Wit: Ben. H. CANBY, Jas.
HAMILTON, Thos. EDWARDS.

Bk:Pg: 2A:297   Date: 9/23/1771   RcCt: 12 Feb 1801
John GLASFORD and Archibald HENDERSON by PoA to Alexander
HENDERSON Jr. to Thomas BLINCOE of Ldn. Mortgage deed for two
Negro slaves James and Winny to secure bond in suit. Wit: Ths. BOTTS.

Bk:Pg: 2A:298   Date: 3/9/1801   RcCt: [10 Mar 1801?]
Jesse JANNEY assignee of John MATTHIAS. 25ac of waste and
unpropriate land on warrant No. 2994 for 50ac dated 23 Oct 1800, adj
George LEWIS, John WEST, Thomas DENT, John HISKETT; no surveyor
available at this time.

Bk:Pg: 2A:299   Date: 3/9/1801   RcCt: [10 Mar 1801?]
Jesse JANNEY assignee of John MATHIAS. 16ac of waste and
unpropriated land from warrant No. 2994 for 50ac dated 23 Oct 1800; no
surveyor available at this time.

Bk:Pg: 2A:299   Date: 3/9/1801   RcCt: 10 Mar 1801
Samuel SINGLETON. DoE for Negro man Muler. Wit: Sn. BLINCOE, ?
HARRISON.

Bk:Pg: 2A:300   Date: 1/22/1801   RcCt: 10 Mar 1801
William HALLING. Col for Negro girl Mint abt 12y old whom he brought to
VA from PA on 28 Dec 1800, obtained by right of marriage with his wife.

Bk:Pg: 2A:300   Date: 7/18/1800   RcCt: 10 Mar 1801
James ROACH to Stephen PHINNALL of Ldn. BoS for farm and
household items from partnership with John NICKLIN Jr., also Thomas
PURSELL. Wit: Mahlon ROACH.

Bk:Pg: 2A:301   Date: 3/9/1801   RcCt: 12 Mar 1801
Randolph RHODES of Ldn to brother Samuel RHODES. PoA for sale on
Morris's Creek in Wilks Co. GA.

Bk:Pg: 2A:302   Date: 3/12/1801   RcCt: 12 Mar 1801
Jonas STRUTS. Col for Negro girl Bett abt 14y old brought from MD to
VA on 11 Mar 1801, right of inheritance with his wife.

Bk:Pg: 2A:302   Date: 8/11/1800   RcCt: 13 Mar 1801
George DEA of Ldn to John HOLME of Ldn. BoS for mare. Wit: Wm.
SHEPHERD.

Bk:Pg: 2A:303   Date: 2/14/1801   RcCt: 13 Apr 1801
John A. BINNS & wife Dewannah of Ldn to Michael BOGAR of Ldn. B/S
of 134¾ac. Wit: Frederick SMITH, John SHAFFER, Samuel WARD,
foreign name.

Bk:Pg: 2A:304   Date: 2/14/1801   RcCt: 13 Apr 1801
John Alexander BINNS & wife Dewanner of Ldn to Michael BOGAR of
Ldn. B/S of 50ac on Broad Run. Wit: Frederick SMITH, John SHAFFER,
Samuel WARD, foreign name.

Bk:Pg: 2A:307   Date: 3/6/1801   RcCt: 13 Apr 1801
Dewanner BINNS. CoE for sale to Michael BOGER. Wit: Farling BALL,
Chas. BENNETT.

Bk:Pg: 2A:308   Date: 9/15/1800   RcCt: 13 Apr 1801
William McNAB. Deposition - oath that Gideon CUMMINGS, when abt 7 or 8y old, had his ear bit off by a horse.

Bk:Pg: 2A:308   Date: 2/9/1801   RcCt: 13 Apr 1801
George GRIMES/GRYMES of Ffx to Jno. BLAKER of Ldn. A/L of 69ac. Wit: Ariss BUCKNER, John GILL, Elizabeth GILL.

Bk:Pg: 2A:310   Date: 4/13/1801   RcCt: 13 Apr 1801
Nathan SPENCER Sr. & wife Hannah of Ldn to John SPENCER. B/S of 194ac on NW fork of Goose Creek.

Bk:Pg: 2A:312   Date: 4/13/1801   RcCt: 13 Apr 1801
Griffith PIERCE & wife Alice, Samuel PIERCE & wife Delilah, John HIXON & wife Susannah and Thomas PIERCE of Ldn to William WOODFORD of Ldn. B/S of 342ac (legacy to Alice PIERCE from father Samuel BUTCHER) on Round Hill adj John DIXON, John MARKS, William LODGE, Samuel PALMER. Wit: Jos. CARR Jr, George BROWN, foreign name.

Bk:Pg: 2A:314   Date: ___ 1801   RcCt: 13 Apr 1801
Richard KEEN to Lendorus LUCAS. A/L of lot. Wit: Chas. BINNS Jr, Simon BINNS, Sn. BLINCOE.

Bk:Pg: 2A:315   Date: 9/15/1800   RcCt: 13 Apr 1801
Wilson Cary SELDON & wife Eleanor of Ldn to Thomas SWANN of Ldn. B/S of 260ac in big spring adj John Thompson MASON, Col. Burgess BALL.

Bk:Pg: 2A:317   Date: 1/16/1801   RcCt: 13 Apr 1801
Thomas DAVIS & wife Leah of Ldn to John Alexander BINNS of Ldn. B/S of land on broad run. Wit: John HAMILTON, Benjamin SHRIEVES, Mortho SULLIVAN, Chas. BENNETT, Henry HUFF.

Bk:Pg: 2A:320   Date: 10/29/1800   RcCt: 13 Apr 1801
John BOGUE of Ldn to Benjamin EDWARDS of Ldn as agent for John MINOR late of AlexVa. Assignment of mortgage using slaves James, Mary, Susannah, Judah and Adam as security.

Bk:Pg: 2A:323   Date: 7/21/1794   RcCt: 13 Apr 1801
Daniel KING of Ldn. DoE for slave James a bright mulatto abt 36y old, purchased his freedom. Wit: William CHICK Jr., Michael ROONEY, Mountjoy KING.

Bk:Pg: 2A:324   Date: 2/14/1801   RcCt: 13 Apr 1801
Merchant Jeremiah RINKER of BaltMd to William HALLING of Ldn. Release of mortgage. Wit: Jonas POTTS, Barnett HOUGH, W. H. HARDING, Jonathan FOUCH, Thos. WILKISON/WILKERSON.

Bk:Pg: 2A:326   Date: 4/13/1801   RcCt: 13 Apr 1801
William JENKINS of Ldn to Adam SHOVER. BoS for Negro man Isaac, 20-25y old. Wit: John STOUTSENBARGER, Reuben HIXON, James TUCKER.

Bk:Pg: 2A:327   Date: 10/25/1800   RcCt: 14 Apr 1801
House joiner Mathew WEATHERBY of Ldn to Benjamin WOODLEY of
Ldn. B/S of land nr Lsbg on Caroline Road. Wit: B. HOUGH, James
HAMILTON, Samuel HOUGH.

Bk:Pg: 2A:329   Date: 4/18/1801   RcCt: 14 Apr 1801
William TAYLOR & wife Ann of Lsbg to Benjamin WOODLEY of Ldn. B/S
of land on Carolina road WOODLEY, John TRIBBEE. Wit: Joseph KNOX,
John DRISH, John RIEGER.

Bk:Pg: 2A:332   Date: 1/31/1801   RcCt: 14 Apr 1801
Benjamin WOODLEY of Ldn to Charles BINNS Jr. of Ldn Mortgage of
½ac on Carolina Road where Hugh SURGHNOR now lives. Wit: W.
CHILTON, Thos. T. JONES, Patrick H. DOUGLASS.

Bk:Pg: 2A:334   Date: 8/20/1800   RcCt: 14 Apr 1801
John LITTLEJOHN & wife Monica of Ldn to Marcy TOMKINS of Ldn. B/S
of 1ac nr Lsbg on road to Mains Mill next to where TOMKINS now lives.
Wit: Alexander SUTHERLAND, George ROWAN, Charles ROWAN,
Patrick CAVAN, Samuel MURREY.

Bk:Pg: 2A:337   Date: 11/11/1800   RcCt: 14 Apr 1801
Thomas TAYLOR and Benjamin CANBY (Exors of Thomas TAYLOR
dec'd) to Joseph TAYLOR. B/S of 107ac on Katocton Creek (land
purchased of Mercer BROWN less 200ac left to son Henry TAYLOR). Wit:
John DREAN, Jacob FADELEY, Saml. HAMILTON.

Bk:Pg: 2A:338   Date: 8/26/1800   RcCt: 12 Jan 1801
William STABLER & wife Deborah of MontMd to Benjamin H. CANBY of
Lsbg. B/S of ½ac nr Lsbg adj land CANBY recently bought of Francis
HAGUE & Isaac THOMPSON. Wit: Jas. HAMILTON, Isaac MYERS,
Thos. EDWARDS, Samuel MURREY, Joseph SMITH.

Bk:Pg: 2A:341   Date: 4/11/1801   RcCt: 14 Apr 1801
Stacey TAYLOR of Ldn to James HEATON of Ldn. B/S of 13ac adj
Samuel IDEN, Mahlon TAYLOR.

Bk:Pg: 2A:343   Date: 3/31/1801   RcCt: 11 May 1801
James MOORE & Joshua GORE as Exors of John UPDIKE dec'd of Ldn
to Abel DAVIS of Ldn. B/S of 117ac adj Blackstone JANNEY, Joseph
HOLMES, Hamilton ROGERS, George HATCHER, Ish IREY. Wit: Gideon
DAVIS, John IREY, Hamilton ROGERS.

Bk:Pg: 2A:345   Date: 1/12/1801   RcCt: 11 May 1801
Isaac RICHARD and Cage TRIPLETT of Ldn to Benjamin GRAYSON. S/L
of 100ac. Wit: Ezer DILLON, Aaron ARDEN, Wm. FOWKE, Abner
HUMPHREY, Benjn. BARTON.

Bk:Pg: 2A:346   Date: 2/9/1801   RcCt: 11 May 1801
Joseph HOLMES & wife Elizabeth of Ldn to Abel DAVIS of Ldn. B/S of
1ac on NW fork of Goose Creek. Wit: Isaac LARROWE, George
TAVENOR Jr, Samuel GREGG, John LITTLEJOHN, Benjamin
EDWARDS.

Bk:Pg: 2A:349   Date: 4/14/1801   RcCt: 11 May 1801
John A. BINNS & wife Duanna of Ldn to William MOXLEY of Ldn. B/S of
17½ac nr Carolina Road adj Samuel MURREY. Wit: Samuel HOUGH,
James HAMILTON, Benja. SHREIVE, Murtho SULLIVAN, Samuel
MURREY, Joseph SMITH.

Bk:Pg: 2A:352   Date: 11/26/1778   RcCt: ___ [May 1801?]
Craven PEYTON of Ldn to James KIRK of Ldn. B/S of 11¼ac. Wit: James
COLEMAN, Jeremiah MOORE, Jonah THOMPSON.

Bk:Pg: 2A:353   Date: 9/4/1778   RcCt: 15 Apr 1794 and 14 May 1801
Craven PEYTON & wife Ann of Ldn to James KIRK of Ldn. L/R of 11¼ac.
Wit: James COLEMAN, Jeremiah MOORE, Jonah THOMPSON.

**Bk:Pg: 2A:355   Date: 11/22/1779   RcCt: 15 Apr 1794 and 11 May
1801**
Craven PEYTON & wife Ann of Ldn to James KIRK OF Ldn. B/S of ½ac
Lot #5 in Lsbg. Wit: James COLEMAN, Jeremiah MOORE, Jonah
THOMPSON.

Bk:Pg: 2A:357   Date: 4/1/1801   RcCt: 11 May 1801
Abel DAVIS & wife Catharine of Ldn to John IREY of Ldn. B/S of 10ac adj
IREY, Hamilton ROGERS. Wit: Blackstone JANNEY, Joseph HOLMES,
Hamilton RODGERS, Joseph TAVINOR.

Bk:Pg: 2A:360   Date: 4/1/1801   RcCt: 11 May 1801
Abel DAVIS & wife Catharine of Ldn to Hamilton ROGERS of Ldn. B/S of
48ac adj Hamilton ROGERS, George HATCHER, John IREY, Joseph
HOLMES. Wit: Blackstone JANNEY, Joseph HOLMES, John IREY,
Joseph TAVENOR.

Bk:Pg: 2A:362   Date: 4/1/1801   RcCt: 11 May 1801
Abel DAVIS & wife Catharine of Ldn to Eli JANNEY of Ldn. B/S of 29ac
adj Hamilton ROGERS, John IREY, Blackstone JANNEY. Wit: Blackstone
JANNEY, Joseph HOLMES, John IREY, Hamilton ROGERS.

Bk:Pg: 2A:365   Date: 11/11/1800   RcCt: 11 May 1801
Thomas PURSELL & wife Lydia of Ldn to Josiah WHITE of Ldn. B/S of
½ac in short hill, adj William ADAM. Wit: Mahlon ROACH, James
UNDERWOOD, Mahlon MORRIS. Stacy TAYLOR, Abner OSBORNE.

Bk:Pg: 2A:368   Date: 3/9/1801   RcCt: 11 May 1801
Robert WELFORD of Frederick as attorney and trustee for Wm.
THORNTON to Edmond DENNY of Ldn. Release of mortgage for
purchase of horse and ½ac lot in Lsbg adj the courthouse. Wit: Wm.
CHILTON, Patrick H. DOUGLASS, Charles DRISH.

Bk:Pg: 2A:369   Date: 6/14/1800   RcCt: 11 May 1801
John DAVIES dec'd of Ldn to Baptist Church in South Wales, Pembroke
Co, Parish of Manerdivy - ministers Benjamin DAVIES & David EVANS,
deacons Jonathan DAVIES and John HUGHES to Thomas W. JONES &
Simon JAMES of Cambria, Somersett Co PA. PoA - will of 29 Nov 1791
gives £100 to Church; rest of estate to brother's children Jenkin and

Thomas DAVIES and sister's children Mary and Margaret (nee DAVIES). Wit: Richard JONES, Evan GEORGE, Lewis MILES, Owen DANIEL.

Bk:Pg: 2A:371   Date: 11/10/1800   RcCt: 11 May 1801
Christopher ROPER of Lsbg to Joshua CHILTON. BoS for Negro boy Nall 8-10y old. Wit: Jno. MATHIAS, John BINNS.

Bk:Pg: 2A:371   Date: 11/10/1800   RcCt: 11 May 1801
Joshua CHILTON. Assignment of BoS for Negro boy Nall. Wit: John MATHIAS, foreign name.

Bk:Pg: 2A:372   Date: 1/26/1801   RcCt: 11 May 1801
Samuel NICKOLS to George TAVENOR. Assignment of rights of deed of trust. Wit: Mary McCULLAH, Nicholas OSBURN.

Bk:Pg: 2A:372   Date: 4/4/1801   RcCt: 11 May 1801
Nehemiah SMITH & Aaron SMITH of Blumstead Township, Bucks Co., PA to Benjamin BRADFIELD of Ldn. PoA for mortgage. Wit: Moses KELLY, John HANNA.

Bk:Pg: 2A:373   Date: 5/11/1801   RcCt: 11 May 1801
Benjamin BRADFIELD & wife Rachel of Ldn to Abner HUMPHREY of Ldn. B/S of 26¾ac adj Thomas BLACKBURN & Benjamin BARTON. Wit: Benjn. GRAYSON, John OSBURN, Wm. FOWKE.

Bk:Pg: 2A:376   Date: 5/11/1800   RcCt: 11 May 1801
Benjamin BRADFIELD of Ldn to Abel PALMER of Ldn. B/S of 100ac adj Spencer PUGH. Wit: Benj'n GRAYSON, William FOWKE, Abner HUMPHREY.

Bk:Pg: 2A:378   Date: 5/11/1801   RcCt: 11 May 1801
William TREYHORN of Ldn to Stephen McPHERSON of Ldn. B/S of 12ac on N fork of Beaver Dam nr Quaker Road, adj Samuel NICKOLS, Samuel PUGH. Wit: William DEBELL, Stephen G. ROZELL, Stephen C. ROZELL.

Bk:Pg: 2A:380   Date: 5/11/1801   RcCt: 11 May 1801
George FAIRHURST of Ldn to Hiland CROW of Ldn. B/S of 4½ac on branch of Crooked Run. Wit: Jesse JANNEY, Jesse HIRST, Hamilton ROGERS.

Bk:Pg: 2A:381   Date: 2/20/1794   RcCt: 15 Apr 1794, 11 May 1801
Thomas WILLIAMS of AlexVa to Thomas MOORE Jr. of Ldn. B/S of 102ac on Goose Creek adj Capt. William AYLETT, reserving 5ac adj Mill Dam of Rawleigh COLSTON. Wit: John JANNEY, Benniah WILLETT, Caleb BENTLY, Tho. SWANN, Asa MOORE.

Bk:Pg: 2A:384   Date: 5/17/1801   RcCt: 11 May 1801
Thomas MOORE & wife Mary of Md to Burr POWELL and William BRONAUGH Jr. of Ldn. B/S of 10ac. Wit: Abner WILLIAMS, John WILLIAMS, Richard GRIFFITH, Asa MOORE, Tho. PHILLIPS.

Bk:Pg: 2A:385   Date: 7/10/1800   RcCt: 12 Jan 1801
Francis HAGUE & wife Mary of Ldn to Benjamin Hough CANBY of Lsbg. B/S of 1¾ac lot nearly adj Lsbg, adj Adam GOUGH on W side of Carolina

Wit: Ths. SIM, Thomas EDWARDS, James HAMILTON, Pat'k
CAVAN, Samuel MURREY.

Bk:Pg: 2A:388 Date: 12/9/1800 RcCt: 11 May 1801
John SCATTERDAY & wife Rebecca of Ldn to John JANNEY of AlexVa.
B/S – 62ac of Peter ROMINE adj John ROMINE & John SOUTHWARD,
devised to daughter Sarah now dec'd, leaving to 5 children - son Daniel
sold his 1/5th to SCATTERDAY. Wit: Eden B. MOORE, John MATHIAS,
Geo. McCABE.

Bk:Pg: 2A:390 Date: 4/14/1798 RcCt: 14 May 1798
George JEWELL & wife Mary (d/o David EVANS dec'd) of Ldn to James
COLEMAN of Ldn. B/S of 153ac devised in will of John EVANS dated 4
Oct 1766 to son David, gave son Griffith EVANS Abraham Lay's lot,
Griffith's will of 12 Dec 1767 in PA gave brother David his lot, David's will
of 4 Jun 1771 in Philadelphia gave 1/3 to dau Mary, wife of Jewell (rest to
daus. Hannah & Sarah EVANS). Right of dower to Elizabeth EVANS. Wit:
Joseph COLDWELL, Griffin TAYLOR, Charles BRENT, Joshua GORE,
Js. H. DAVIDSON, Arch'd MAGILL, Jonathan LOVETT.

Bk:Pg: 2A:393 Date: 4/20/1801 RcCt: 11 May 1801
John RIEGOR & wife Margaret of Lsbg to Charles BINNS Jr. of Ldn. B/S
of ¼ac lot #26 on Market St. Wit: Samuel MURREY, Joseph SMITH,
Patrick H. DOUGLAS.

Bk:Pg: 2A:396 Date: 5/5/1801 RcCt: 12 May 1801
William WILSON of AlexVa to Barnett HOUGH of Ldn. B/S of ¼ac lot #14
in Lsbg. Wit: Jonathan FOUCH, Stephen DONOHOE, Obadiah
CLIFFORD, Jno. SCHOOLEY Jr.

Bk:Pg: 2A:397 Date: 5/19/1801 RcCt: 12 May 1801
John MATTHEWS, Wm. H. HARDING and Matthew HARRISON of Ldn.
Bond on MATTHEWS as Surveyor of Ldn.

Bk:Pg: 2A:397 Date: 3/10/1801 RcCt: 12 May 1801
Robert WELFORD of Fredericksburg as trustee for William THORNTON
to John LITTLEJOHN of Ldn. Mortgage on 54ac. Wit: Thos. SIM, Wm.
CHILTON, Daniel GANTT.

Bk:Pg: 2A:398 Date: 2/3/1801 RcCt: 12 May 1801
Peter DOWE of Ldn to Robert CALDWELL, heir of William CALDWELL
dec'd of MontMd. B/S of 100ac known as Tavener's Field, part of tract of
348ac granted to Hugh CALDWELL dec'd by patent of 5 Jun 1844; 248ac
were sold to John CARGYLL by widow Sarah CALDWELL and eldest son
William CALDWELL.

Bk:Pg: 2A:400 Date: 2/24/1801 RcCt: 14 Apr 1801
Catesby GRAHAM and Jane GRAHAM to William CHILTON of Ldn. B/S
of 152ac nr Lsbg on Tuscarora, adj Samuel MURREY. Wit: Matthew
HARRISON, Edward TURNER, Arch'd MAINS, Jas. BATSON, Patrick H.
DOUGLAS.

Bk:Pg: 2A:401   Date: 1/10/1801   RcCt: 14 Apr 1801
Edward CONRAD & wife Judith of Ldn to Nathan PIGGOTT of Ldn. B/S of
100ac adj Thomas JOHN, John HOUGH, Thomas JANNEY, Samuel
WILSON. Wit: Stacy TAYLOR, Abner OSBURN, Josiah WHITE Jr.

Bk:Pg: 2A:404   Date: 1/10/1801   RcCt: 14 Apr 1801
Edward CONRAD & wife Judith of Ldn to Enos POTTS of Ldn. B/S of
39ac adj James BEANS, Lewis MASSEY, Isaac NICKOLS. Wit: Stacy
TAYLOR, Abner OSBURN, Josiah WHITE Jr.

Bk:Pg: 2A:406   Date: 4/14/1801   RcCt: 11 May 1801
Stacey JANNEY of Ldn to Benjamin WHITACRE of Ldn. A/L of 164ac
(from Gidney CLART [CLARK] late of Barbadoes 17 Apr 1772). Wit: Stacy
TAYLOR, Henry L. WILSON, Nathan PIGGOTT, Enos POTTS.

Bk:Pg: 2A:407   Date: 8/22/1799   RcCt: 8 Jun 1801
Thomazin ELLZEY of Ffx to William ELLZEY of Ldn. PoA to collect rents
from Robert TODD and David LACY on Kittoctan tract of land. Wit:
Thomas WRENN, Peter JETT Jr, Geo. NEWMAN, Wm. CHILTON, Jno
MATHIAS.

Bk:Pg: 2A:408   Date: 3/12/1800   RcCt: __ Mar 1801 MontMd
Benjamin RAY Jr. & wife Eleanor of MontMd to Walter & Elizabeth
LANHAM of MontMd (Exors of Aaron LANHAM dec'd). Eleanor RAY a d/o
Aaron LANHAM inherits one Negro woman; will also devises to Eleanor,
widow Elizabeth LANHAM, Sethe LANHAM and Mary Ann LANHAM 25ac
called Littleworth in FredMd; and 150 acre called Chestnut Level in Ldn to
daus. Wit: John L. SUMMERS, J. H. McPHERSON.

Bk:Pg: 2B:001   Date: 7/13/1801   RcCt: 13 Jul 1801
Thomas N. BINNS. Col for Negro Thomas "Tom" obtained on division of
estate of John DURHAM dec'd (father of wife Amelia) of Heartford Co.
MD brought to VA on 1 Nov 1778.

Bk:Pg: 2B:001   Date: 2/21/1801   RcCt: 13 Jul 1801
David LEE of PrWm to son Joshua LEE of Ldn. B/S of 150ac adj
Abraham WARFORD nr N fork of Broad run. Wit: Aligah FRYAR, Ret
BRETT, Margarett BRETT, John LEE.

Bk:Pg: 2B:003   Date: 5/7/1800   RcCt: 13 Jul 1801
Joseph SMITH, C. BINNS, S. C. ROZELL. Bond on SMITH as coroner of
Ldn.

Bk:Pg: 2B:003   Date: 5/7/1801   RcCt: 13 Jul 1801
Thomas PURSELL & wife Lydia of Ldn to Edward CUNARD of Ldn. B/S
of 2 lots (1ac & 17 perches) nr gap of short hill on turnpike road, adj
Richard COPELAND, John JANNEY. Wit: Thos. HOUGH, John B.
STEPHENS, Edward CUNARD Sr.

Bk:Pg: 2B:006   Date: 5/7/1801   RcCt: 13 Jul 1801
Thomas PURSELL & wife Lydia of Ldn to Edward CUNARD of Ldn. B/S
of 3¼ac nr Gap of Short Hill nr turnpike road adj Edward CUNARD, David
SMITH. Wit: Thos. HOUGH, John B. STEPHENS, Edward CUNARD Jr.

Bk:Pg: 2B:009   Date: 7/13/1801   RcCt: 13 Jul 1801
Thomas PURSELL & wife Lydia of Ldn to Thomas HOUGH of Ldn. B/S of 4¼ac on turnpike road from Keys Ferry to AlexVa, adj John STEPHENS, Edward CUNARD. Wit: Mahlon HOUGH, Edward CUNARD, Thomas BEST.

Bk:Pg: 2B:010   Date: 6/8/1801   RcCt: 13 Jul 1801
Thomas HARRISON Jr. of Dumphries to Mahlon HOUGH. B/S of 240ac of Scotland Mills tract, now rented by James LARROWE. Wit: Char. BENNETT, Edward CUNARD, Thomas HOUGH, Abner WILLIAMS.

Bk:Pg: 2B:012   Date: 4/17/1801   RcCt: 13 Jul 1801
Jacob SHOMAKER & wife Elizabeth of Ldn to Simon SHOMAKER of Ldn. B/S of 153¾ac. Wit: Frederick SMITH, 2 in foreign language.

Bk:Pg: 2B:013   Date: 12/17/1800   RcCt: 13 Jul 1801
Sarah MAJOR of CamP to daughter Sarah HUTCHISON of CamP. Gift of all possessions she now owns. Wit: Benjamin HUTCHISON, George HUTCHISON, Major HUTCHISON, John HUTCHISON.

Bk:Pg: 2B:014   Date: 4/17/1772   RcCt: 14 Apr 1801
Gidney CLARK of Barbadoes Island to Stacy JANNEY (brothers Mahlon & William JANNEY) of Ldn. L/L of 164ac. Wit: Henry VARNOVER, Henry CARNSWORTH, Hezekiah HOWELL, Stephen JONES, Stephen DONALDSON, Charles WEST, Har. LANE.

Bk:Pg: 2B:017   Date: 1/6/1801   RcCt: 13 Jul 1801
Elisha POWELL & wife Ann of Ldn to John KEIL of Ldn. B/S of 8¾ac on Goose Creek [gives plat], adj Samuel GUY, William MARTIN & John KILE. Wit: Joseph LANE, Nicholas KILE, Thomas LEWIS, Eleanor LEITH.

Bk:Pg: 2B:020   Date: 7/13/1801   RcCt: 13 Jul 1801
Orsburne KING. Several bills of sale, deemed they should be included in his liabelities. Wit: W. W. WILLIAMS, Thomas L. LEE, Wm. GUNNELL.

Bk:Pg: 2B:020   Date: 3/2/1801   RcCt: 13 Jul 1801
Orsburne KING of Ldn to William WHALEY. BoS for Negro woman Cate. Wit: Barton JOHNSTON, John CARTER.

Bk:Pg: 2B:021   Date: 12/20/1800   RcCt: 13 Jul 1801
Thomas PURCELL & wife Lydia of Ldn. CoE for sale of ½ac to James ROACH. Wit: Stacy TAYLOR & Abner OSBURN.

Bk:Pg: 2B:022   Date: 6/13/1801   RcCt: 13 Jul 1801
William George FAIRFAX of Lee Co. to Archibald MORRISON of Ldn. B/S of 125ac leased to Thos. WYATT & adj 45ac lot, both now in possession of Jones RANDALL & Enoch SCHRIDLEY. Wit: Josias CLAPHAM, Joseph STEERE.

Bk:Pg: 2B:023   Date: 11/13/1800   RcCt: 14 Jul 1801
John SCATTERDAY to James McILHANEY. Deed of trust for farm and household items. Wit: Tho. Tho'n. JONES, Francis TRIPLETT, Edward TALBOTT.

Bk:Pg: 2B:025   Date: 8/14/1801   RcCt: 15 Aug 1801
Pat'k CAVAN & wife Sarah. CoE for sale of 1*ac* to John Henry
SHELGESS. Wit: Leven POWELL, Samuel MURREY.

Bk:Pg: 2B:026   Date: 7/24/1801   RcCt: 14 Sep 1801
Elias LOVETT of Ldn to James LOVE of Ldn. B/S of 115*ac* on Kittocton
Creek adj Jesper POULSON, Edward LOVETT; 1/2 of tract Daniel
LOVETT bequeathed to sons Elias & Edward LOVETT. Wit: Jesse
JANNEY, Stacy JANNEY, Mahlon JANNEY.

Bk:Pg: 2B:028   Date: 5/13/1801   RcCt: 14 Sep 1801
Michael BALLMER & wife Barbara of Ldn to Laurrence MINK of Ldn. B/S
of 79*ac* in Catoctin adj William ALT, Peter HICKMAN, John SHEAVER.
Wit: Frederick SMITH.

Bk:Pg: 2B:029   Date: 5/18/1801   RcCt: 14 Sep 1801
Jonathan McVEIGH of Ldn to William VICKERS of Ldn. LS of 50*ac* on
Goose Creek adj French DUNHAM, nr the schoolhouse. Wit: Jesse
McVIGH, Jacob REEDER, Joseph BURSON.

Bk:Pg: 2B:031   Date: 9/13/1801   RcCt: 14 Sep 1801
John TODHUNTER (grandson of John TODHUNTER) of Ldn to Jacob
DEHAVEN of Ldn. B/S of 100*ac* adj Josias CLAPHAM, John ELLIOTT,
George RAZOR. Wit: George MAUL, John DODD Jr, Jacob AXLINE.

Bk:Pg: 2B:032   Date: 9/10/1801   RcCt: 14 Sep 1801
John Daniel LOSCH & wife Elizabeth of Lsbg to Alexander
SUTHERLAND of Lsbg. B/S of part of 98½ perches adj George NIXON,
heirs of Henry McCABE, easternmost street of Lsbg, Peter BELL, Presley
CORDELL. Wit: James CAVAN Jr, William P. ROPER, Presley
SANDERS Jr.

Bk:Pg: 2B:034   Date: 8/15/1801   RcCt: 14 Sep 1801
John ROAN & wife Mary of Ldn to daughter Catharine ROAN of Ldn. Gift
of farm and household items. Wit: John LINTON, Joseph LEWIS Sr.

Bk:Pg: 2B:035   Date: 5/1/1801   RcCt: 14 Sep 1801
James McILHANEY & wife Margaret to Nathan SPENCER Jr. B/S of
170¾*ac* on Goose Creek. Wit: Stacy TAYLOR, Abner OSBERN.

Bk:Pg: 2B:037   Date: 9/14/1801   RcCt: 14 Sep 1801
John HESKETT & wife Amelia of Ldn to John HATCHER Jr. of Ldn. B/S
of 63*ac* adj Richard CLARK, Abel PALMER, Benjamin BARTON.

Bk:Pg: 2B:038   Date: 9/17/1798   RcCt: 14 Sep 1801
James McILHANEY & wife Peggy of Ldn to James BRADFIELD of Ldn.
B/S of 158*ac* on NW fork of Goose Creek. Wit: Nancy McILHANEY,
Rosannah McILHANEY, Benjamine BRADFIELD, Stacy TAYLOR, Abner
OSBURN.

Bk:Pg: 2B:041   Date: 4/16/1801   RcCt: 14 Sep 1801
John HERBERT of AlexVa and Carlisle F. WHITING & wife Sarah Manly
of Ffx to William MEANS and William CARR of Ldn. B/S of 381½*ac* on
Kittocton Mt adj Tuskorara, William CARR, Daniel LOVETT, William

RHODES. Wit: Francis TRIPLETT, Geo. ROWAN, Jas. HAMILTON, Wm. H. HARDING, James WREN, Charles LITTLE.

Bk:Pg: 2B:044   Date: 12/19/1800   RcCt: 14 Sep 1801
William WILKERSON of Ldn to Benjamine GARRETT of Ldn. B/S of 113ac adj Thomas GARRETT, Thomas GARRETT Jr, Able GARRETT. Wit: Stephen G. ROSZEL, Joseph GARRETT, Levi TATE, Thos. VANANDER, Edward GARRETT.

Bk:Pg: 2B:045   Date: 3/21/1801   RcCt: 14 Sep 1801
Michael VERTS of Ldn to John SLACK. B/S of land purchased from estate of Andrew THOMPSON dec'd. Wit: William LaMAR, John MARTIN, Jeremiah PURDUM.

Bk:Pg: 2B:048   Date: 4/11/1801   RcCt: 14 Sep 1801
John DUNLAP of Ldn to Richard KEEN of Ldn. B/S of 353ac adj Capt. Lewis ELLZEY & John DISKINS, bequeathed to widow Sarah KEEN (sons Richard & James Keen), Sarah has since married John DUNLAP. Wit: James BRASHEARS, John STUMP, Peter STUMP.

Bk:Pg: 2B:049   Date: 9/14/1801   RcCt: 14 Sep 1801
Cornelious WYNKOOP & wife Catharine [signed as Cornela] of Ldn to William WILKERSON of Ldn. B/S of 10ac on Long Branch, adj Thomas GARRETT, Thomas VANNANDER. Wit: Thomas GHEEN, Joseph FOX, John MUDD.

Bk:Pg: 2B:051   Date: 4/10/1801   RcCt: 14 Sep 1801
Thomas LESLIE of Ldn to Philip DERRY of Ldn. A/L from lease of 1 Apr 1786 from Geo. Wm. FAIRFAX to Cunard NEAR. Wit: John AXLINE, foreign name.

Bk:Pg: 2B:053   Date: 10/12/1796   RcCt: 14 Sep 1801
Thomas TAYLOR and wife Caleb of Ldn to Joseph TAYLOR of Ldn. B/S of ¼ac on Milford Lot #18 adj Henry TAYLOR. Wit: Isaac LAROWE, A. SUTHERLAND, Jacob DEHAVEN

Bk:Pg: 2B:054   Date: __Sep 1801   RcCt: 14 Sep 1801
John ADAMS & wife Margarett of Ldn to William CRAIG of Ldn. B/S of 42ac on NW fork of Goose Creek adj Jacob BROWN. Wit: John McGEATH, Griffith G. PEARS, Samuel NICHOLS.

Bk:Pg: 2B:056   Date: 8/11/1801   RcCt: 14 Sep 1801
Stephen WILSON & wife Martha of FredMd to Jonathan BRADFIELD of Ldn. B/S of 170ac adj Nathanial SPENCER & Gidney CLARKE. Wit: Stacy TAYLOR, Bernard TAYLOR, Benjamine BRADFIELD, Abner OSBURN.

Bk:Pg: 2B:060   Date: 9/14/1801   RcCt: 14 Sep 1801
James STEVENS and Ann STEVENS (Exors of Hezekiah STEVENS dec'd) to James BALL. B/S of 61ac, part of 153ac adj Thompson MASON. Wit: William HAMMILTON, Abner WILLIAMS, Elizabeth TALBOTT.

Bk:Pg: 2B:062   Date: 9/3/1801   RcCt: 14 Sep 1801
Samuel PROBASCO & wife Elizabeth of Ldn to William CARR of Ldn. B/S
of 50ac on Beaverdam adj George NIXON. Wit: John LITTLEJOHN,
George HEAD, John MARTS.

Bk:Pg: 2B:063   Date: 4/1/1800   RcCt: 13 May 1800
Ferdinando FAIRFAX & wife Eliza Blain FAIRFAX of Shannonhill, Berkley
Co. VA to William Byrd PAGE of Alexander VA. Mortgage for land called
Shannondale located partly in Ldn and partly in Berkley Co., lying
between the Blue Ridge and Short Hill Mts. bordered on W & N sides by
Shannondoah and Potomac Rivers, original patent dated 17 May 1739.
Wit: Thomas Thornton JONES, G. Wythe BAYLER, Derick CRUESON.

Bk:Pg: 2B:066   Date: 9/15/1801   RcCt: 14 Sep 1801
Archibald McVICKER. DoE for slave Thomas LEGAL paid £40 for his
freedom.

Bk:Pg: 2B:066   Date: 2/23/1801   RcCt: 15 Sep 1801
John DRISH & wife Elioner of Lsbg to Barton LUCAS of Lsbg. B/S of ¼ac
Lot #44 in Lsbg. Wit: Presley CORDELL, Samuel MORAN, William
HAWKE.

Bk:Pg: 2B:069   Date: 7/2/1800   RcCt: 15 Sep 1801
John WOLF and wife Abigal to Adam HOUSHOLDER. CoE for sale
103ac. Wit: Farling BALL, Chas. BENNETT.

Bk:Pg: 2B:070   Date: 3/3/1800   RcCt: 15 Sep 1801
Elizabeth HICKMAN of Alleganey Co. MD to Peter HICKMAN of Ldn. PoA
to sell 103ac to Adam HOUSEHOLDER. Wit: John RICE, Roger
PERREY.

Bk:Pg: 2B:072   Date: 3/3/1800   RcCt: 15 Sep [1801]
Peter SMOUSE & wife Catharine of Allegany Co. Md to Peter HICKMAN.
PoA for sale of 103ac to Adam HOUSEHOLDER. Wit: Roger PERRY,
John RICE.

Bk:Pg: 2B:074   Date: 1/18/1800   RcCt: 15 Sep 1801
John ENGLEBUCHT & wife Mary and Jacob HICKMAN of Colerain,
Bedford Co. PA to Peter HICKMAN. PoA for sale of 103ac to Adam
HOUSEHOLDER. Wit: Martin REILEY, David REILEY.

Bk:Pg: 2B:077   Date: 10/27/1800   RcCt: 15 Sep 1801
Sarah HICKMAN (w/o Jacob HICKMAN) of Bedford Co. PA to Peter
HICKMAN. PoA for sale of 103ac to Adam HOUSEHOLDER. Wit: Martin
REILEY, David REILEY.

Bk:Pg: 2B:079   Date: 9/16/1800   RcCt: 13 Jan 1801
David DAVIS & wife Parnella of Ffx to George LEE of Ldn. B/S of 80ac.
Wit: Jno. MATHIAS, Absalom HAWLEY, Joseph WATSON, Thomas L.
LEE, Benjamine EDWARDS.

Bk:Pg: 2B:081   Date: 6/25/1801   RcCt: 15 Sep 1801
William HAWK of Lsbg to Martin KITZMILLER of Ldn. BoS for household
items. Wit: Fleet SMITH.

**Bk:Pg: 2B:084	Date: 8/11/1800	RcCt: 15 Sep 1801**
Henry WHITMORE & wife Esther of FredMd to Alexander SUTHERLAND of Ldn. B/S of ¼ac lot in Lsbg on road to Nolands Ferry, adj lot SUTHERLAND bought from Daniel LOSH. Wit: Thomas SIM, Wm. H. HARDING, John EVANS, Henry WILLIAMS.

**Bk:Pg: 2B:087	Date: 9/16/1801	RcCt: 16 Sep 1801**
Isaac CRAVEN of Cumberland Co. PA to Abner CRAVEN of Ldn. B/S for Isaac's share of his father Thomas CRAVEN dec'd land. Wit: Isaac LARROWE, S'n. BLINCOE, Samuel HOUGH.

**Bk:Pg: 2B:088	Date: 5/12/1801	RcCt: 14 Sep 1801**
John LITTLEJOHN & Jonas POTTS of Ldn as trustees to John JANNEY Sr and Adam HOUSEHOLDER Jr. B/S of 60ac Isaac BALL conveyed to trustees. Wit: Geo. ROWAN, Abner CRAVEN, William HAWLING.

**Bk:Pg: 2B:090	Date: 8/3/1801	RcCt: 16 Sep 1801**
John DREAN & wife Nancy of Lsbg to William Rust TAYLOR of Lsbg. B/S of ¼ac Lot #56 in Lsbg at N side of Back St adj William BAKER. Wit: John LITTLEJOHN, Francis TRIPLETT, Simon TRIPLETT Jr, Samuel MURREY.

**Bk:Pg: 2B:093	Date: 9/26/1801	RcCt: 17 Oct 1801**
Cooper William DIXON & wife Catharine of Mill Creek Hundred, New Castle Co., Delaware to farmer Boston WOFTER of Ldn. B/S of 191ac in Ffx (then, but now Loudoun) adj James YOUNG & James PHILLIPS. PoA to George BROWN & Thomas GREGG of Ldn. Wit: Robert McCULLAH, John JACKSON.

**Bk:Pg: 2B:096	Date: 11/16/1786	RcCt: 12 Oct 1801**
Archibald JOHNSTON of Ffx to Richard CRUPPER of Ldn. Reacknowledgement of deed for 156ac adj Bryan FAIRFAX, Col. Francis PEYTON, John WALKER. Wit: Benj. B. DOWNES, Burr POWELL, Jno. P. HARRISON, Wm. BRONAUGH Jr.

**Bk:Pg: 2B:099	Date: 9/14/1801	RcCt: 12 Oct 1801**
Solomon HOGE of Ldn as attorney for Harman COX of Randolph Co. NC to Phineas THOMAS of Ldn. B/S of 274½ac adj Joseph JANNEY, William LODGE, Samuel PALMER, Leven POWELL. Wit: Isaac NICHOLS, Israel JANNEY, Amos GIBSON, David JANNEY.

**Bk:Pg: 2B:102	Date: 9/15/1801	RcCt: 12 Oct 1801**
Phineas THOMAS of Ldn to Solomon HOGE of Ldn as attorney of Harmon COX of Randolph Co. NC. Mortgage for two debts. Wit: Isaac NICHOLAS, Israel JANNEY, Amos GIBSON, David JANNEY.

**Bk:Pg: 2B:106	Date: 7/13/1801	RcCt: 12 Oct 1801**
Mary OSBURN of Ldn to Morris OSBURN of Ldn. B/S of 44ac at foot of Blue Ridge at head branch of NW fork of Goose Creek adj Abel MARKS, James NICHOLS, Nathan NICHOLS. Wit: James NICHOLS, Ignatious BYRNES, Thomas OSBURN.

Bk:Pg: 2B:108   Date: 3/23/1801   RcCt: 12 Oct 1801
David ELLIOT of Ldn to brother John ELLIOT Jr. of Ldn. B/S of 160*ac*
where John now lives (to discharge bond given to father John ELLIOT in
1794) adj David BEATTY, Samuel CLAPHAM, Josias CLAPHAM. Wit:
Charles BINNS Jr, Joseph SMITH, Hugh DOUGLAS, Francis STONE.

Bk:Pg: 2B:110   Date: 7/14/1801   RcCt: 12 Oct 1801
Ferdinando FAIRFAX of Shannon Hill, Berkely Co. VA to William
HORSEMAN of Ldn. B/S of 93¼*ac* on Broad run part called page lot (part
in Ldn and part in Fairfax) awarded to John PAGE of Rosewell, John
PAGE of north river and Robert PAGE of Broadneck. Wit: Richard
COLEMAN, Isaac MYERS, Patrick McINTYRE, Wm. H. HARDING,
Samuel HOUGH.

Bk:Pg: 2B:112   Date: 10/12/1801   RcCt: 12 Oct 1801
David TAYLOR & wife Catharine of Ldn to Eliazor EVANS & wife Mary of
Ldn. B/S of 30*ac* adj Isaac NICHOLS (devised to TAYLOR by will of
Mahlon KIRKBRIDE in 1774, part conveyed from Timothy TAYLOR & wife
Achea and Jonathan TAYLOR & Ann in 1796). Wit: James BRADFIELD,
Benj'a BRADFIELD.

Bk:Pg: 2B:114   Date: 2/22/1799   RcCt: 13 May 1799, 14 Oct 1801
James MONTEITH of StafVA to Jesse McVEIGH of Ldn. LS and
assignment. Wit: James CHANNEL, Thomas CHINN Jr, Swanson
LUNSFORD, Amos DENHAM, John LYONS, Amos DENHAM Jr.

Bk:Pg: 2B:116   Date: 10/12/1801   RcCt: 12 Oct 1801
Josiah HALL & wife Mary of Ldn to William HALL of Ldn. B/S of 245½*ac*
purchased by Josiah & William from Charles HOLE & wife Mary on 14
Feb 1792 adj Geo. NIXON. Wit: James HAMILTON, Stephen HENRY,
Samuel HALL.

Bk:Pg: 2B:118   Date: 5/9/1800   RcCt: 12 Oct 1801
Ferdinando FAIRFAX of Berkley Co VA to Adam RHORBACK of Ldn.
Reacknowledgement of deed of 48*ac* in Piedmont, adj William VERTS,
John ROLERS, Isaac RICHEYES. Wit: James MILTON, Theodorick LEE,
Wm. H. HARDING, Richard COLEMAN, Sampson BLINCOE, Fleet
SMITH.

Bk:Pg: 2B:120   Date: 5/9/1800   RcCt: 12 Oct 1801
Ferdinando FAIRFAX of Berkley Co VA to Frederick SLATES of Ldn.
Reacknowledgment of deed of 169*ac* in Piedmont adj William H.
HARDING, old mill lot on Dutchman Run adj Frederick BELTZ, John
GEORGE, Daniel SHOEMAKER Jr. Wit: James MILTON, Theodorick
LEE, Wm. H. HARDING, Richard COLEMAN, Sampson BLINCOE, Fleet
SMITH.

Bk:Pg: 2B:122   Date: 10/11/1801   RcCt: 12 Oct 1801
William Smith BELT & wife Nancy [signed Anne] of Ldn to John
WILDMAN of Ldn. B/S of Lot #7 in Lsbg adj Patrick CAVAN, William
MOXLEY.

Bk:Pg: 2B:124   Date: 10/12/1801   RcCt: 12 Oct 1801
Thomas STONESTREET of Ldn to son Richard William STONESTREET.
Gift of Negro land Sam and horse.

Bk:Pg: 2B:125   Date: 1/14/1801   RcCt: 13 Jul 1801
Asa MOORE & wife Sarah of Ldn and Henry BURKETT & wife Elizabeth
of MD to Patrick McGAVICK of Ldn. B/S of 5985 sq ft lot in Wtfd adj
Mahlon JANNEY. Wit: Daniel STONE, Richard GRIFFITH, Thos.
PHILLIPS, John McGAVACK.

Bk:Pg: 2B:128   Date: __ May 1801   RcCt: 12 Oct 1801
Moses COLWELL of Ldn to Abner CRAVEN of Ldn. Mortgage for 113ac
adj James BALL, Patrick HOLLAND, Stevens Thompson MASON.

Bk:Pg: 2B:131   Date: 10/12/1801   RcCt: 11 Oct 1801
Samuel PROBASCO & wife Elizabeth of Ldn to John BROWN of Ldn. LS
of 1ac Lot #10. Wit: Isaac LAROWE, Jacob SANDS, Sn. BLINCOE.

Bk:Pg: 2B:133   Date: 10/13/1801   RcCt: 13 Oct 1801
Jacob STONEBURNER & wife Barbara of Ldn to John HAMILTON of
Ldn. B/S of land for mill on Kittocton Creek adj John COMPHER. Wit:
John BINNS, Levi HOLE, Joseph SPOOND.

Bk:Pg: 2B:135   Date: 11/9/1801   RcCt: 9 Nov 1801
Mary VALENTINE of MD (Exor & w/o George VALENTINE dec'd) to
Leonard CROWE. PoA. Wit: Sam LUCKETT, Isaac LAROWE.

Bk:Pg: 2B:136   Date: 3/31/1801   RcCt: 2 Mar 1801
George Fairfax LEE of WstmVa to Peter STUMP of Ldn. B/S or 640ac on
Goose Creek adj George CARTER. Wit: Jno. Tas. MAUND, Thomas
CHANDLER, Wm. CHANDLER.

Bk:Pg: 2B:138   Date: 4/1/1778   RcCt: 11 Dec 1801
Patrick MOLEN. Col of slaves Precella and Ann Minte.

Bk:Pg: 2B:139   Date: 10/12/1801   RcCt: 14 Dec 1801
Alexander SUTHERLAND & wife Nancy of Lsbg to John HAMILTON of
Ldn. B/S of 107ac on Kittocton Creek willed by Joseph TAYLOR dec'd
(left son Henry TAYLOR 200 acres). Wit: John EVANS, Robert
HAMILTON, George MILNER, Samuel MURREY, Joseph SMITH.

Bk:Pg: 2B:142   Date: 4/14/1801   RcCt: 14 Dec 1801
Henry LEE & wife Anna of Stretford, WstmVa to Thomas LANG Jr. of NY
City. B/S of 600ac nr Mdbg. Wit: J. MAUND, W. P. TEBBS, Orrick
CHILTON, Thomas HUFF, Anthony PAYTON.

Bk:Pg: 2B:144   Date: 7/14/1801   RcCt: 14 Dec 1801
Sheriff John LITTLEJOHN & wife Monica of Ldn to Overseer of the Poor.
B/S of 20ac for poor house on Market St in Lsbg. Wit: James HAMILTON,
Isaac HARRISON, Samuel MURREY, Samuel CARR, Joseph SMITH.

Bk:Pg: 2B:147   Date: 11/5/1801   RcCt: 14 Dec 1801
David TAYLOR & wife Catharine of Ldn to George TAVENER of Ldn. B/S
of 158ac on NW fork of Goose Creek adj James JANNEY, John WEST,

Timothy TAYLOR, Eleazor EVANS, Jonas JANNEY. Wit: Stacy TAYLOR, Jno. WEST, John HAMILTON.

Bk:Pg: 2B:150   Date: 11/5/1801   RcCt: 14 Dec 1801
Timothy TAYLOR of Ldn to George TAVENER. Bond for purchase of 158 acres; David TAYLOR abt to move out of Va, Mary HARDING wd/o Edward HARDING dec'd pretends to have right of dower to land so TAVENER will have to pay any damages if TAYLOR is sued. Wit: John HAMILTON, Jno. WEST.

Bk:Pg: 2B:150   Date: 12/14/1801   RcCt: 14 Dec 1801
Peter VERTS of Ldn to Joseph SMITH of Ldn then to Adam MILLER. B/S of lease [lease is signed by SMITH]. Wit: Josh'a BAKER, John EVANS, Samuel SMITH.

Bk:Pg: 2B:152   Date: 5/7/1801   RcCt: 14 Dec 1801
John HATCHER & wife Sarah of Ldn to Noah HATCHER of Ldn. B/S of 150ac adj Mercer BROWN, Mahlon KIRKBRIDE. Wit: Stacy TAYLOR, William BEANS, Ruth BEANS, Abner OSBURN.

Bk:Pg: 2B:155   Date: 11/26/1801   RcCt: 14 Dec 1801
Benjamin OVERFIELD. Revocation of PoA - had appointed son-in-law Isaac LEWIS as attorney, states LEWIS used the profits of sale for his own use. Wit: Jos. LANE, Wm. CASTLEMAN.

Bk:Pg: 2B:156   Date: 1/3/1800   RcCt: 14 Dec 1801
George BROWN & wife Mary. CoE for B/S of 10 Jan 1799 to Notley C. WILLIAMS. Wit: Stacy TAYLOR, Abner OSBURNE.

Bk:Pg: 2B:157   Date: 2/17/1800   RcCt: 8 Sep 1800 & 14 Dec 1801
Thomas GARRETT Jr. & wife Anna of Pensylvania Co. VA to Thomas GEEN of Ldn. B/S of 112ac adj John GARRETT. Wit: Joseph GARRETT, John GARRETT, Abel GARRETT, Silas GARRETT, Henry GARRETT, John GARRETT Jr., Joseph MORTON.

Bk:Pg: 2B:160   Date: 12/8/1801   RcCt: 14 Dec 1801
Abraham MOORE and Margarett MOORE (formerly HARTMAN) of Ldn to Alexander McLELAND of Spring Hill township, Fayett Co. PA. BoS for 3 Negro slaves - woman Easter aged 22y in Feb next and her children mulatto boy Charles aged 3y on 9 Nov last, Negro girl Harriett aged 1y on 3 Oct last. Wit: John STEER, Isaac STEER.

Bk:Pg: 2B:161   Date: 4/14/1801   RcCt: 14 Dec 1801 ✓
John GREEN of Ffx to William HUMMER of Ldn. BoS for slaves Negro man Sam (abt 22y old, 5' 10") and Charles (yellow complexion, abt 20y, same size). Wit: Wm. H. HARDING, Wm. GUNNELL Jr.

Bk:Pg: 2B:162   Date: 11/24/1801   RcCt: 14 Dec 1801
James SINCLAIR & wife Mary of Ldn to James HIXON of Ldn. B/S of 330ac on the little river, part of tract patented to Thomas OWSLEY adj John SINCLAIR, James SINCLAIR & James MERCER. Wit: John SINCLAIR, William SINCLAIR, Traverse GEORGE, William GEORGE, Francis PEYTON, Israel LACEY.

Bk:Pg: 2B:166   Date: 10/18/1801   RcCt: 14 Dec 1801
Widow Ann STEVENS (Admr of Hezekiah STEVENS dec'd) and James
STEVENS to James BALL. B/S of 87ac; on 14 Sep 1801 sold to BALL
part Capt. John ROSE claimed, arbitration by Charles BINNS awarded
land to BALL. Wit: Thomas FOUCH, Josh BAKER, James McLEAN, John
MATHIAS.

Bk:Pg: 2B:168   Date: 12/6/1798   RcCt: 12 Dec 1801
Thomas FRANCIS & wife Mary of Ldn to Edward LLOYD of Ldn.
Mortgage on 62ac on Beverdam. Wit: Wm. BRONAUGH, Jos. HALE, Jos.
LANE.

Bk:Pg: 2B:171   Date: 12/10/1801   RcCt: 15 Dec 1801
Commissioners Samuel MURREY, Jonas POTTS, Aaron SAUNDERS,
James HAMILTON. Report - having difficulty completing the building of
poor house on time due to lack of materials and workmen, 8 rooms have
been completed.

Bk:Pg: 2B:172   Date: 4/25/1799   RcCt: 15 Dec 1801
Joseph LANE as attorney for Henry GULICK to Silas REESE. Release of
mortgage. Wit: C. BINNS Jr., Step. C. ROZEL, Thos. PEAKE.

Bk:Pg: 2B:172   Date: 8/28/1801   RcCt: 15 Dec 1801
Patrick CAVAN of Lsbg to George FEISTER of Ldn. LS for Lots #19 and
#16 totaling 4ac. Wit: Thos. EDWARDS, Alx. LANGLEY, John SHAW Jr.

Bk:Pg: 2B:174   Date: 12/15/1801   RcCt: 15 Dec 1801
James McILHANEY, Wm. R. TAYLOR and Benjamin SHRIEVE to John
ALEXANDER, Wilson C. SELDEN, Ludwell LEE & Thos. SIM as Justices
of County Ct. Bond on McILHANEY to collector levy. Wit: Sn. BLINCOE.

Bk:Pg: 2B:175   Date: 7/24/1801   RcCt: 11 Jan 1802
John CRUMBAKER (s/o John dec'd) of Ldn to John SEAGER of Ldn [also
given as SERGER]. BoS of leased land. Wit: Adam SHOVER, Jacob
FILLER, ? FILLER.

Bk:Pg: 2B:177   Date: 1/7/1802   RcCt: 11 Jan 1802
Joshua LEE & wife Theodocia of Ldn to William WARFORD of Ldn. B/S of
50ac, adj Abraham WARFORD. Wit: Wm. STEPHENSON, James
HIXON, Obadiah CLIFFORD.

Bk:Pg: 2B:179   Date: 1/10/1802   RcCt: 11 Jan 1802
John MARSHALL of Ldn to William MARSHALL of Ldn. Will of Thomas
MARSHALL dec'd gave son John 100ac, he will keep 86ac and gives to
William 201ac [gives plat]. Wit: Thos. T. JONES, Thos. LESLIE, John
TRIPLETT.

Bk:Pg: 2B:181   Date: 10/30/1801   RcCt: 11 Jan 1802
Thomas LESLIE of Ldn to John GEORGE Sr. BoS for Negro woman
Ellender. Wit: Adam SHOVER, J. SNYDER, John GEORGE Jr.

Bk:Pg: 2B:182   Date: 10/2/1801   RcCt: 11 Jan 1802
Patrick CAVAN of Lsbg to John BROWN of Ldn. LS for 1ac Lot #7 leased
by CAVAN of James HEREFORD. Wit: John CAVAN, Fleet SMITH,
James CAVAN Jr.

Bk:Pg: 2B:184   Date: 4/20/1801   RcCt: 9 Nov 1801
Leven POWELL of Mdbg to Elias LACEY of Mdbg. LS of ½ac Lot #27 in
Mdbg. Wit: Burr POWELL, John CRAIN, A. GIBSON, James BATTSON.

Bk:Pg: 2B:186   Date: 1/2/1802   RcCt: 11 Jan 1802
Leven POWELL & wife Sarah of Ldn to John HESKETT of Ldn. B/S of
109ac adj John HANBY; also 51ac adj John ROMINE dec'd. Wit: Simon
TRIPLETT, Burr POWELL.

Bk:Pg: 2B:189   Date: 1/11/1802   RcCt: 11 Jan 1802
John HESKETT of Ldn to William BRONAUGH of Ldn. Trust for debt to
Leven POWELL using 161ac adj John HANBY, and 51ac adj John
ROMINE dec'd.

Bk:Pg: 2B:191   Date: 12/21/1801   RcCt: 11 Jan 1802
Stacy HAINS & wife Mary of Ldn to Charles GULLATT of Lsbg. B/S of Lot
#57 in Lsbg. Wit: John LITTLEJOHN, Charles BINNS, Sn. BLINCOE,
Wm. HAINS, Samuel MURREY, Joseph SMITH.

Bk:Pg: 2B:194   Date: 12/21/1801   RcCt: 11 Jan 1802
Mahlon MEANS & wife Mary of Ldn to Stacy HAINS of Ldn. B/S of 60ac
on turnpike road from Lsbg to Goose Creek adj Mary GORDEN. Wit: C.
BINNS, Patrick H. DOUGLAS, John LITTLEJOHN, Sn. BLINCOE, Samuel
MURREY, Joseph SMITH.

Bk:Pg: 2B:197   Date: 1/2/1802   RcCt: 11 Jan 1802
Leven POWELL & wife Sarah of Ldn to Joseph READ of Ldn. B/S of
280ac adj James GRADY, Leven POWELL & Thomas GREGG. Wit:
Simon TRIPLETT, Burr POWELL.

Bk:Pg: 2B:200   Date: 1/1/1802   RcCt: 11 Jan 1802
Mrs. Sarah FAIRFAX of GrB to farmer Philip EVERHART of Ldn & son
Daniel. B/S of 100ac (1765 L/L to Daniel MATTHENY, wife Judith, son
Thomas) adj John PAGET, Samuel SMITH; MATTHENY & son are dead.

Bk:Pg: 2B:202   Date: 9/10/1801   RcCt: 11 Jan 1802
Daniel LOSH & wife Elizabeth of Lsbg to Peter BELTZ of Ldn. B/S of lot
on King St Lsbg adj Alexander SUTHERLAND. Wit: Wm. R. TAYLOR,
Thos. WILKERSON, Simon TRIPLETT Jr.

Bk:Pg: 2B:203   Date: 12/10/1801   RcCt: 11 Jan 1802
Benjamin Rhode HACKNEY late of Ldn now of MD to Peter BELTS. A/L
from George Wm. FAIRFAX dated 10 Sep 1787. Wit: James RUSSEL,
Job MORGEN, Abraham SUNFRANK.

Bk:Pg: 2B:204   Date: 12/14/1801   RcCt: 11 Dec 1801
Sarah CAVAN and Joshua BAKER of Lsbg to Ann DONAHOE of Ldn. B/S
of part of Lot #56 adj Barnett HOUGH & Lot #57 in Lsbg. Wit: James
HAMILTON, William DRISH, Robt. HAMILTON.

Bk:Pg: 2B:206   Date: 1/11/1802   RcCt: 8 Feb 1802
James HEATON & wife Lydia of Ldn to Notley C. WILLIAMS. CoE for sale of 3½ac. Wit: Stacy TAYLOR, Abner OSBURN.

Bk:Pg: 2B:208   Date: 12/13/1801   RcCt: 8 Feb 1802
David BAKER of Somerset Co PA to Samuel BAKER of Ldn. B/S of 150ac on S side of Broad Run of Kittocton (Philip BAKER bequeathed to his children). Wit: Sn. BLINCOE, Jas. OFFUTT.

Bk:Pg: 2B:210   Date: 2/8/1802   RcCt: 12 Feb 1802
John DRISH & wife Eleanor of Ldn to Charles BINNS of Ldn. B/S of Lot #45 on King St in Lsbg. Wit: William ELLZEY, Benj'a EDWARDS, Henry JENKINS.

Bk:Pg: 2B:213   Date: 2/6/1802   RcCt: 12 Feb 1802
Jonah HAGUE & wife Martha of Fqr to William HALE Jr. of Mdbg. B/S of ½ac Lot #17 in Mdbg, adj Jonah HAGUE, Thomas C. WELLS. Also ½ac lot where Enock WHITACRE now lives. Wit: Burr POWELL, Jesse McVEIGH, John BEVERIDGE, Enoch WHITACRE, Thomas RUSSELL, Leven POWELL.

Bk:Pg: 2B:216   Date: 1/11/1802   RcCt: 8 Feb 1802
John TUCKER late of Ldn, now of Culpeper Co. DoE for Negro man Samuel, abt 31-32y old. Wit: Stacy TAYLOR, Abner OSSBURN, Price JACOBS.

Bk:Pg: 2B:217   Date: 4/13/1801   RcCt: 14 Dec 1801
William SUDDITH of Ldn to David ALEXANDER of Ldn. B/S of 5ac on NW fork of Goose Creek. Wit: John HANDEY, John MUDD, James TERRY.

Bk:Pg: 2B:219   Date: 12/28/1801   RcCt: 8 Feb 1802
James HAMILTON & wife Elizabeth of Ldn to widow Martha WILLIAMS, Owen, John, Ellias, Mary, Martha, Daniel and William WILLIAMS surviving children of John. B/S of 30ac adj Peter CARR where John WILLIAMS lived. Wit: Fielden BROWN, John CARR, John CARLILE.

Bk:Pg: 2B:221   Date: __ Dec 1801   RcCt: 8 Feb 1802
Benjamin H. CANBY & wife Sarah of Lsbg to William CHILTON of Lsbg. B/S of ½ lot on King St. Wit: Wm. MOXLEY, George HAMMAT, Jno. MATHIAS, John LITTLEJOHN, Samuel MURREY.

Bk:Pg: 2B:224   Date: 8/18/1801   RcCt: 8 Feb 1802
Joseph TALBOTT of Ldn to James McILHANEY of Ldn. B/S of house & ¼ ac lot on Water St. in Wtfd adj Janney's Mill race, Fleming PATTERSON. Wit: Lewis ELLZEY, James MOORE, Jacob WINE.

Bk:Pg: 2B:227   Date: 1/13/1798   RcCt: [8 Feb 1802]
Sanford RAMEY to James GRIFFITH. BoS for Negro man Butler abt 30y old. Wit: Robert YATES, James McILHANEY.

Bk:Pg: 2B:227   Date: 2/8/1802   RcCt: [8 Feb 1802]
Jas. GRIFFITH to James McILHANEY. Transfer of rights to Negro man Butler (see above). Wit: Uriah WILLIAMS, Jos. TRIBBEY.

Bk:Pg: 2B:227   Date: 2/8/1802   RcCt: 8 Feb 1802
James McILHANEY of Ldn. DoE for Negro Butler. Wit: Isaac LAREW, Thomas WHITE.

Bk:Pg: 2B:228   Date: 1/16/1802   RcCt: 9 Feb 1802
William CHILTON of Lsbg to Peter BOSS. BoS for Negro girl Esther (born on 15 Sep 1788) to be free when she reaches 31y old, her children to serve until they are 21y old. Wit: B. HOUGH, Thos. WILKINSON.

Bk:Pg: 2B:228   Date: 2/9/1802   RcCt: 9 Feb 1802
John Daniel LOSH & wife Elizabeth of Ldn to Charles BINNS of Ldn. B/S of ¼ac, part of Lot #45 in Lsbg where BINNS now lives. Wit: Burr POWELL, Stacy TAYLOR, John H. CANBY.

Bk:Pg: 2B:231   Date: __ 1802   RcCt: 9 Feb 1802
Benjamin WOODLEY & wife Elizabeth of Ldn to Benjamin SHREVE of Ldn. B/S of land on main road from Lsbg to the red house, adj Matthew WEATHERBY, ½ of lot conveyed by WEATHERBY to WOODLEY.

Bk:Pg: 2B:234   Date: 8/15/1801   RcCt: [9 Feb 1802?]
Christopher ROPER of Lsbg to John STOUSABERGER of Ldn. BoS for horse & Negro female Caty age 37y old and Mahlon age 9m.

Bk:Pg: 2B:235   Date: 8/15/1801   RcCt: 9 Feb 1802
Christopher ROPER & Thomas WILKINSON of Lsbg to John STOUSABERGER of Ldn. BoS for Negro Caty age 37y and Mahlon age 9m. Wit: Simon TRIPLETT.

Bk:Pg: 2B:236   Date: 12/15/1801   RcCt: 9 Feb 1802
Benjamin WOODLEY & wife Elizabeth of Ldn to Benjamin HOUGH of Lsbg. B/S of land on Carolina Road between lot where WOODLEY lives and John TRIBBY, adj John LITTLEJOHN, James McNELLAGE. Wit: Eden B. MOORE, Wm. MOXLEY, Joseph COMBS, Samuel MURREY, John LITTLEJOHN.

Bk:Pg: 2B:239   Date: 2/16/1795   RcCt: 14 Apr 1795 and 9 Feb 1802
Farling BALL of Ldn to Simon SHUMAKER of Ldn. A/L for land on Broad Run adj Thomas SHEPERD. Wit: Jeremiah PURDUM, Isaac BALL, George SHOEMAKER.

Bk:Pg: 2B:240   Date: 10/14/1799   RcCt: 12 Jan 1800
Chambers HALL of New Castle Co. Del to John GARRET of Ldn. B/S of 112ac adj Thomas GHEEN. Wit: Stacy TAYLOR, Levi TATE, Joseph GARRETT, Jesse R. PURNELL.

Bk:Pg: 2B:243   Date: 1/14/1802   RcCt: 9 Feb 1802
William TAYLOR & wife Ann of Lsbg to Presley CORDELL of Lsbg. B/S of part of Lot #13 on King St in Lsbg adj John DRISH, Samuel MURREY, Jacob FAIDLEY. Wit: John LITTLEJOHN, Joseph SMITH, Geo. ROWAN.

Bk:Pg: 2B:246   Date: 8/15/1801   RcCt: 8 Mar 1802
Thomas TRIPLETT & wife Elizabeth (d/o John SANDERS dec'd of Ldn) of Amherst Co. VA to Presley SANDERS of Ldn. B/S – per will of John leased 140ac where he lived should be sold 10y after date of will, money

to go to daughters. Wit: Thomas FOUCH, Aaron SANDERS, Thos.
Thornton JONES, Joseph SPOOND, Samuel MEREDITH, Jos. BURRUS.

Bk:Pg: 2B:250   Date: 2/13/1802   RcCt: 9 Mar 1802
Mary WEST of Ldn. DoE for Negro man James HOGINS abt 7y old. Wit:
Thos. N. BINNS, William WILKINSON.

Bk:Pg: 2B:251   Date: 2/13/1802   RcCt: 9 Mar 1802
Mary WEST of Ldn. DoE for Negro man Nathaniel GRYMES abt 50y old.
Wit: Thos. N. BINNS, William WILKINSON.

Bk:Pg: 2B:252   Date: 12/21/1801   RcCt: 12 Apr 1802
James BEANS & wife Ruth of Ldn to Israel JANNEY of Ldn. B/S of 4ac
adj Israel JANNEY. Wit: Benjamin MEAD, Blackstone JANNEY, Abijah
JANNEY, Jonathan JANNEY.

Bk:Pg: 2B:255   Date: 3/10/1802   RcCt: 12 Apr 1802
Israel JANNEY of Ldn to Abijah JANNEY of Ldn. B/S of 115ac on NW fork
of Goose Creek where Abijah JANNEY now lives, adj Isaac NICHOLS,
Enos POTTS, James BEANS, James CRAIG, John YOUNG. Wit: David
JANNEY, Rus JUREY, Jonathan JANNEY.

Bk:Pg: 2B:257   Date: 12/1/1801   RcCt: 12 Apr 1802
John QUEEN & wife Mary of Ldn to Israel JANNEY of Ldn. B/S of 200ac
adj James BEANS, Abijah JANNEY, Sollomon HOGE. Wit: Benjamin
MEAD, Blackstone JANNEY, James BEANS, Ruth BEANS, Abijah
JANNEY.

Bk:Pg: 2B:261   Date: 2/17/1802   RcCt: 12 Apr 1802
Thomas RUSSELL Sr. & wife Margarett of Ldn to William REEDER of
Ldn. B/S of 80ac, part adj Thomas MOORE. Wit: Leven POWELL, Burr
POWELL, Thomas CHINN.

Bk:Pg: 2B:265   Date: 3/15/1800   RcCt: 12 Apr 1802
Ferdinando FAIRFAX of Shannon Hill, JeffVa to Archibald MORRISON of
Ldn. B/S of 263ac in Piedmont, adj Thomas WYATT, William GEORGE,
Thomas DAVIS, James McILHANEY, John STATLER, Charles CHRIMM,
Margaret SANDERS. Wit: Geo. McCABE, John H. CANBY, Wm. H.
HARDING, Ezekiel POTTS, Theodorick LEE.

Bk:Pg: 2B:267   Date: 3/25/1799   RcCt: 14 Oct 1799
John SHOEMAKER & wife Mary, Henry AXLINE & wife Catharine (nee
BAKER), Jacob EVERLY & wife Molly, William BAKER, George MAN &
wife Hannah, George BRENOR & wife Barbara, Jacob BAKER,
Christener BAKER and David BAKER (heirs of Philip BAKER dec'd of
Ldn) to Samuel BAKER of Ldn. B/S of 150ac on Broad Run. Wit: Isaac
LAROWE, James McILHANEY, John JACKSON, Jeremiah PURDUM,
Peter STONE, John McILHEANY, Martin REILEY, David REILY, Ch.
TRIBBEY, Robt. DICKEY (some in Colrain, Bedford Co. & Westmoreland
Co PA).

Bk:Pg: 2B:274   Date: 4/1/1802   RcCt: 12 Apr 1802
John SKILLMAN & wife Catharine, Christopher SKILLMAN & wife
Heneriette of Ldn to Jesse McVEIGH of Mdbg. B/S of 105ac adj Henry

PETERSON, Col. Albert RUSSELL. Wit: Chas. DUNKIN, Lewis GARNER, Zephaniah LEGG.

Bk:Pg: 2B:277   Date: 11/24/1801   RcCt: 12 Apr 1802
James HIXON of Ldn to James SINCLAIR of Ldn. B/S of 330*ac* as collateral on little River, adj John SINCLAIR, James HIXON, James MERCER dec'd. Wit: John SINCLAIR, Wm. SINCLAIR, Traverse GEORGE, William GEORGE.

Bk:Pg: 2B:280   Date: 12/16/1800   RcCt: 12 Aug 1801
Archibald JOHNSTON & wife Jemima of Ldn to Leven LUCKETT of Ldn. B/S of 119*ac* adj John Peyton HARRISON, Richard CRUPPER, Townshead D. PEYTON & Thaddius McCARTY. Wit: John SINCLAIR, Townshend D. PEYTON, Stephen W. LEWIS, Thomas FIELDS, Fra. H. PEYTON.

Bk:Pg: 2B:282   Date: 4/6/1802   RcCt: 12 Apr 1802
Robert BRADEN of Ldn to John EBLEN of Ldn. B/S of 10½*ac*.

Bk:Pg: 2B:285   Date: 4/11/1800   RcCt: 14 Oct 1800
Thomas COCKRILL & wife Million of Ldn to William SMALLEY of Ldn. B/S of 115*ac* in CamP, adj John TURLEY, road from Baptist Meeting House to Gum Spring. Wit: Richd. B. ALEXANDER, John H. GIBBS, George LEWIS.

Bk:Pg: 2B:286   Date: 4/6/1802   RcCt: 12 Apr 1802
John ADAMS & wife Margarett of Ldn to Isaac NICHOLAS/NICKOLS of Ldn. B/S of 125*ac* on NW fork of Goose Creek, adj John HANDY. Wit: James CRAIG, William CRAIG, Isaac CRAIG, Garret CRAVEN.

Bk:Pg: 2B:288   Date: 3/18/1802   RcCt: 12 Apr 1802
Christian NIGHSWANGER & wife Ruth of Ldn to Henry PLEASHER of Ldn. B/S of 100½*ac* on Catocton. Wit: Adam SHOVER, Jacob SNYDER, Jacob DOFFMAN?, John GEORGE Sr.

Bk:Pg: 2B:290   Date: 2/20/1802   RcCt: 12 Apr 1802
Robert SEARES of Ldn to John LUKE of Ldn. BoS for horse and farm items. Wit: Jas. McNABB, Samuel CAREY.

Bk:Pg: 2B:291   Date: 3/15/1802   RcCt: 12 Apr 1802
Ferdinando FAIRFAX of Shannon Hill, JeffVa to Henry Joseph FRY of Ldn. B/S of 108*ac* in Piedmont, adj George SHOEMAKER, Jeremiah PURDUM, William GEE. Wit: Geo. McCABE, John H. CANBY, Wm. H. HARDING, Ezekiel POTTS, Theodorick LEE.

Bk:Pg: 2B:293   Date: 7/14/1801   RcCt: 12 Apr 1802
William HORSEMAN & wife Helen of Ldn to Ferdinando FAIRFAX of Shannon Hill, Berkley Co. VA. B/S of 20¼*ac*. Wit: Wm. H. HARDING, Richard COLEMAN, Patrick McINTYRE, Isaac MYERS.

Bk:Pg: 2B:295   Date: 12/7/1801   RcCt: 12 Apr 1802
Ferdinando FAIRFAX of JeffVa to John AXLINE of Ldn. B/S of 235*ac* in Piedmont, adj Peter WHIP, Daniel HOUSEHOLDER, John JACKSON,

Adam AXLINE, Frederick BELTZ, Conrod ROALER & Philip EVERHART. Wit: Wm. H. HARDING, Henry MOSCOP, Elijah CHAMBERLIN.

Bk:Pg: 2B:297   Date: 3/8/1802   RcCt: 13 Apr 1802
Elizabeth HOMAN of Ldn to Hugh DOUGLAS of Ldn. B/S of 14ac. Wit: C. BINNS, Patrick H. DOUGLAS, John E. COOKE, John H. CANBY.

Bk:Pg: 2B:299   Date: 4/12/1802   RcCt: 13 Apr 1802
Adam HOUSEHOLDER Jr. of Ldn to John HALE of JeffVa. A/L of 60ac. Wit: Isaac LAROWE.

Bk:Pg: 2B:301   Date: 4/12/1802   RcCt: 13 Apr 1802
Adam HOUSEHOLDER Jr. of Ldn to John HALL of JeffVa. Mortgage for 91ac on Catocton Creek adj George MAN. Wit: Isaac LAROWE.

Bk:Pg: 2B:303   Date: 4/12/1802   RcCt: 13 Apr 1802
John HALL of JeffVa to Adam HOUSEHOLDER Jr. of Ldn. Mortgage on 60ac. Wit: Isaac LAROWE.

Bk:Pg: 2B:305   Date: 4/13/1802   RcCt: 13 Apr 1802
William CHILTON & wife Sarah of Lsbg to James Jr. & John CAVAN of Lsbg. B/S of ½ac lot on Market St next to Lot #9, Lot #23 on which was lately a distillery but now owned by William TAYLOR.

Bk:Pg: 2B:308   Date: 4/13/1802   RcCt: 13 Apr 1802
Matthew RUST & wife Patty/Patsy of Ldn (distributee of William RUST dec'd) to Samuel BOGGESS of Ldn. B/S of Lot #4 on survey by Joseph LANE. Wit: Jos. LANE, Stacy TAYLOR, Wm. R. TAYLOR.

Bk:Pg: 2B:311   Date: 4/24/1802   RcCt: 10 May 1802
John ADAMS & wife Margarett to Isaac NICKOLS. CoE for sale of 125ac. Wit: John LITTLEJOHN, Thos. SIM.

Bk:Pg: 2B:313   Date: 5/8/1802   RcCt: 10 May 1802
Conrad VIRTS of Ldn to Joseph SMITH of Ldn. A/L of 105ac. Wit: Francis WHITELY, Jesse TAYLOR, Adam CARNAHAM.

Bk:Pg: 2B:315   Date: 5/10/1802   RcCt: 10 May 1802
William BEANS & wife Hannah of Ldn to David GOODWIN of Ldn. B/S of 49ac on Kittocton Creek adj Jesper POULTON, Thos. HUGHESE, Jesse SILCOTT. Wit: Stacey TAYLOR.

Bk:Pg: 2B:318   Date: 12/1/1801   RcCt: 12 Apr 1802
John B. ARMISTEAD of Fqr to Leven POWELL Jr. BoS - ARMISTEAD owes Abner GIBSON, sells Negro girl Sally abt 14y old he got from Mrs. Lucey ARMISTEAD; ARMISTEAD must pay debt within 12 months or POWELL can sell girl. Wit: Thomas GIBSON, Leven D. POWELL, Joshua RUBY, Leven POWELL, Noble BEVERIDGE, Mesheck LACEY.

Bk:Pg: 2B:319   Date: 10/6/1801   RcCt: 10 May 1802
John SPENCER of Ldn to son David SPENCER of Ldn. B/S of 80ac where John now lives, adj William SMALLEY, road leading from mountain meeting house to gum spring.

Bk:Pg: 2B:320   Date: 5/10/1802   RcCt: 10 May 1802
William BURK of PhilPa to Andrew HESSER of Ldn. B/S of 156*ac* on S of
main road from Israel Janney's mill to Snickers gap, adj William WEST.
Wit: Stacy TAYLOR, Timothy TAYLOR, Wm. BRONAUGH.

Bk:Pg: 2B:323   Date: 4/19/1802   RcCt: 10 May 1802
Jonas POTTS of Lsbg to Thomas HOUGH of Ldn. Release of mortgage
on 262*ac* adj Amos JANNEY, Francis WILSON. Wit: Sn. BLINCOE, Jesse
ELGIN, Saml. CARR, Levi HOLE.

Bk:Pg: 2B:325   Date: 5/10/1802   RcCt: 10 May 1802
Joseph TALBOTT to Robert BRADEN. B/S of plantation where father
Joseph TALBOTT dec'd formerly lived, adj Mahlon JANNEY, now in
possession of widow, devised to Jos. by will.

Bk:Pg: 2B:327   Date: 10/23/1801   RcCt: 11 May 1802
John SPENCER & wife Phebey of Ldn to John ASHFORD. B/S of 22*ac*
on old mountain road, adj Stephen ROZELL, Richard McGRAW. Wit:
Henry SETTLE, Ruben SETTLE, Daniel SETTLE, Newman SETTLE,
William ELLZEY, Chas. LEWIS.

Bk:Pg: 2B:330   Date: 5/10/1802   RcCt: 10 May 1802
Ferdinando FAIRFAX & wife Elizabeth Blair of Shannon Hill, JeffVa to
Charles CRIMM of Ldn. B/S of 98½*ac* on SE side of short hill where Isaac
MILLER now lives. Wit: John STOUSENBERGER, Wm. H. HARDING.

Bk:Pg: 2B:332   Date: 10/19/1801   RcCt: 12 May 1802
John SPENCER & wife Phebe of Ldn to Jonah THOMPSON & Richard
VEITCH (copartners in trade in the firm of THOMPSON & VEITCH of
AlexVa). B/S of 400*ac* nr Gum Spring, part of 2 patents (to Mrs. Ann
FAIRFAX & John SPENCER). Wit: Wm. R. TAYLOR, John L. BURKLEY,
Wm. B. HARRISON, Charles LEWIS.

Bk:Pg: 2B:336   Date: 10/19/1801   RcCt: 12 May 1802
John SPENCER & wife Phebe of Ldn to Jonah THOMPSON and Richard
VEITCH (copartners in trade under the firm of THOMPSON and VEITCH
of AlexVa). B/S of 372*ac* called Broad run old Church tract (part of
Sturman's Patent). Wit: John L. BERKLEY, Wm. R. TAYLOR, Wm. B.
HARRISON, Charles LEWIS.

Bk:Pg: 2B:340   Date: 10/19/1801   RcCt: 12 May 1802
John SPENCER Jr. & wife Selah of Ldn to John SPENCER of Ldn. B/S of
82*ac* nr Gum Spring. Wit: Wm. R. TAYLOR, John L. BERKLEY, Wm. B.
HARRISON, Chas. LEWIS.

Bk:Pg: 2B:344   Date: 5/11/1802   RcCt: 12 May 1802
Ferdinando FAIRFAX of Shannon Hill, JeffVa to William ELLZEY of Ldn.
B/S of 848¾*ac* in Piedmont nr Dutchmans Run adj Samuel RITCHIE,
George's mill, Conroad ROLER, Jacob VIRTZ, Isaac RITCHIE. Wit:
William LITTLEJOHN, Thomas WILKINSON, James HAMILTON, Wm. H.
HARDING.

Bk:Pg: 2B:346   Date: 3/4/1802   RcCt: 12 May 1802
Yowman John HINES Ldn to John HENRY of Ldn. BoS for cow and household items. Wit: William GARROT, Stephen HENRY.

Bk:Pg: 2B:347   Date: 4/23/1802   RcCt: 14 Jun 1802
Deborah RAMEY (wd/o Jacob RAMEY). Allotment of dower - Negroes Jack & Darkes, horse, household items. Subscribers - Chas. BENNETT, John HAMILTON, Robert BRADEN.

Bk:Pg: 2B:347   Date: 6/17/1802   RcCt: 16 Jun 1802
James SWARTS. Col - has imported no slaves since 1 Nov 1778.

Bk:Pg: 2B:348   Date: 12/13/1801   RcCt: 12 Jul 1802
Charles McMANNAMY & wife Jane of Ldn to Benjamin WHITE of Ldn. B/S of 23ac on Kittocton Mt. adj Levi HOLE. Wit: Levi HOLE, James McMANAMAN, Thomas KERRICK.

Bk:Pg: 2B:350   Date: 5/21/1802   RcCt: 12 Jul 1802
James THOMAS to Lucinda DARBY. BoS for farm animals. Wit: J. LINTON, Samuel HOUGH, John KIPHART.

Bk:Pg: 2B:351   Date: 10/12/1801   RcCt: 12 Jul 1802
Daniel LOSH & wife Elizabeth of Lsbg to William WRIGHT of Ldn. B/S of Lot #22 adj Fleet SMITH. Wit: John MATTHIAS, Joseph GARDNER, Fred'k WILDBAHN.

Bk:Pg: 2B:352   Date: 5/10/1802   RcCt: 12 Jul 1802
John HOLLINGSWORTH to James ROACH, George TAVENER & wife Tabitha, Owen ROGERS & wife Mary, Hannah DONALDSON & Edmund ROACH (reps of Richard ROACH dec'd). B/S of 123ac. Wit: Stacy TAYLOR, George TAVENER, Chas. BENNETT, John HAMILTON.

Bk:Pg: 2B:355   Date: __ 1802   RcCt: 12 Jul 1802
Jonas POTTS, Robert BRADEN, James HEATON as commissioners to John HOLLINGSWORTH. Suit of 15 Dec 1801 with defts James ROACH and Robert WHITE decrees public sale of land; sold to HOLLINGWORTH.

Bk:Pg: 2B:355   Date: 1/13/1802   RcCt: 8 Feb 1802
Hezikiah ODEN & wife Elizabeth of Ldn to Ariss BUCKNER of Ldn. B/S of 35½ac decreed ODEN by his father, part of lot divided amongst several heirs. Wit: And. REDMOND, John BLAKER, Israel LACEY, Chas. LEWIS.

Bk:Pg: 2B:359   Date: 7/12/1802   RcCt: 12 Jul 1802
Leven POWELL, Simon TRIPLETT, Burr POWELL, Francis ADAMS, Charles ESKRIDGE, Israel LACEY, John CRAIN, John LITTLEJOHN & Joseph SMITH. Bond on LANE as Sheriff of Ldn to collect all taxes.

Bk:Pg: 2B:360   Date: 7/12/1802   RcCt: 12 Jul 1802
Leven POWELL, Simon TRIPLETT, Burr POWELL, Francis ADAMS, Charles ESKRIDGE, Israel LACEY, John CRAIN, John LITTLEJOHN & Joseph SMITH. Bond on LANE as Sheriff of Ldn to collect all levies.

Bk:Pg: 2B:360   Date: 7/12/1802   RcCt: 12 Jul 1802
Joseph LANE, Leven POWELL, Simon TRIPLETT, Burr POWELL, Francis ADAMS, Charles ESKRIDGE, Israel LACEY, John CRAIN, John

LITTLEJOHN & Joseph SMITH. Bond on LANE as Sheriff of Ldn to collect & receive all officers fees & distribute fees.

Bk:Pg: 2B:361   Date: 10/5/1801   RcCt: 10 Aug 1802
Jane CUNARD of Ldn to friend Edward CUNNARD of Ldn. PoA to receive from John JOHNSTON of Gurmantown PA money due from estate of late husband Henry CUNARD dec'd of Upper Dublin. Wit: Jos. LANE.

Bk:Pg: 2B:362   Date: 12/14/1801   RcCt: 10 Aug 1802
Jacob MILLER (an heir of Christian MILLER dec'd late of Ldn) now of Augusta Co. VA to Edward CUNNARD. PoA to convey unto Valentine MILLER, Christian MILLER & George MILLER 3 of the sons of Christian MILLER dec'd claims to 2 tracts of land. Wit: Vincent SAPP, William ANDERSON.

Bk:Pg: 2B:363   Date: 2/15/1802   RcCt: 10 Aug 1802
Adam HOUSEHOLDER Jr. & wife Sarah to George MANN. B/S of 103*ac,* conveyed to Conrod HICKMAN now dec'd on 14 Mar 1796, sold to HOUSEHOLDER by his children (Peter HICKMAN & wife Regina, Jacob HICKMAN, Elizabeth HICKMAN, Peter SMOUSE & wife Catharine, John WOLF & wife Abigail, John INGLEBREAK & wife Charity). Wit: Jeremiah PURDUM, John MARTIN, foreign name.

Bk:Pg: 2B:365   Date: 2/15/1802   RcCt: 10 Aug 1802
George MANN & wife Barbara of Ldn to Adam HOUSEHOLDER Jr. of Ldn. B/S of 91*ac* nr Cotoctan creek. Wit: Frederick SMITH, John MARTIN, foreign name.

Bk:Pg: 2B:367   Date: 4/10/1788   RcCt: [Aug 1802?]
Josiah LUSBY, practitioner of physick in Philadelphia PA, & wife Elizabeth to sadler John LITTLEJOHN of ShelP. B/S of 100*ac* in ShelP on Goose Creek and 240*ac,* being part of 348*ac* patent to Hugh COLWELL dec'd of 5 Jun 1745, seized by eldest son William COLWELL (widow Sarah), conveyed to James CARGILE, then to Amos THOMPSON then to Elizabeth BUCKHILL now wife of Josiah LUSBY. Wit: Jonas POTTS, Mordicai MILLER, Sarah HOUGH.

Bk:Pg: 2B:369   Date: 4/12/1788   RtCt 11 Jan 1789 and 11 Aug 1802
Sarah HOUGH (now Sarah MASON) and Josiah LUSBY & wife Elizabeth of Philadelphia PA (practitioner of phisick) to sadler John LITTLEJOHN of ShelP. L/R of previous mentioned two tracts of land. Wit: Jonas POTTS, Mordecai MILLER, Sarah HOUGH, Thos. MATTHEWS.

Bk:Pg: 2B:375   Date: 10/21/1801   RcCt: 13 Sep 1802
Mahlon JANNEY of Ldn to James MOORE of Ldn. B/S of Lots #11 & #12 in new addition to Wtfd on SW side of the street. Wit: Abner WILLIAMS, Joseph TALBOTT, Thos. PHILLIPS.

Bk:Pg: 2B:376   Date: 3/16/1802   RcCt: 13 Sep 1802
John CARTER & Morriss CARTER of Ldn to Jeremiah CULLERSON. BoS for Negro man Jo age 33y old. Wit: Joseph HAVENNER, William COLLETT.

Bk:Pg: 2B:376   Date: 3/27/1800   RcCt: 13 Sep 1802
George TAVENER & wife Martha of Ldn [signed Patty] to Constantine
HUGHESE of Ldn. B/S of 35ac on W side of Kittoctin Mt, adj Joshua
GORE, main road from Israel JANNEY's to Lsbg. Wit: Jesse JANNEY,
John DODD, Thomas CLOWES, Stacey JANNEY.

Bk:Pg: 2B:378   Date: 3/27/1802   RcCt: 13 Sep 1802
George TAVENER & wife Martha of Ldn [signed Patty] to Thomas
CLEWS and Joseph CLEWS of Ldn. B/S of 24½ac on road from Israel
JANNEY to Lsbg, adj Constantine HUES. Wit: Jesse JANNEY, Stacy
JANNEY, Constantine HUGHES, John DODD.

Bk:Pg: 2B:380   Date: 2/9/1802   RcCt: 13 Sep 1802
William H. HARDING (devisee and Exor of John HANBY dec'd) and Job
HARDING and Elihue HARDING (devisees of John HANBY) to William
HUGH of Ldn. B/S of 154½ac, adj Joseph JANNEY dec'd, William
GREGG, William HICKSON dec'd. Wit: Thomas HAGUE, Thos.
PHILLIPS, Mahlon JANNEY Jr, James RUSSELL.

Bk:Pg: 2B:382   Date: 2/24/1802   RcCt: 13 Sep 1802
John JANNEY (Exor of Jos. JANNEY dec'd) to Benjamin STEER. Receipt
for A/L. Wit: Abner WILLIAMS, Isaac STEER, Asa MOORE.

Bk:Pg: 2B:382   Date: 3/4/1802   RcCt: 13 Sep 1802
Joshua SINGLETON & wife Hannah of KY to Elizabeth BAKER of Ldn.
B/S of Lot #5, part of tract William RUST died seized and was distributed
to SINGLETON. Wit: Benja' GRAYSON, Elia SWEAREGEN, Thos. A.
HEREFORD, Wm. H. POWELL.

Bk:Pg: 2B:385   Date: 9/13/1802   RcCt: 13 Sep 1802
Andrew HEATH, David SMALLEY & Joshua SMALLY heirs at law of
Ezekiel SMALLEY dec'd to William SMALLEY of Ldn: PoA for any
property Ezekiel SMALLEY would have been entitled to from John
SPENCER per agreement dated 21 Jan 1797 - SPENCER refused to give
over lands. Wit: John MILLON, Thos. COCKERILL, Chas. LEWIS,
Benjamine JAMES.

Bk:Pg: 2B:386   Date: 1/15/1802   RcCt: 13 Sep 1802
Jonathan PALMER to daughter Martha ORANDURFF. Gift of use in Ldn
for her lifetime. Wit: Henry B. MORGAN, Thomas COOPER, John
COOPER.

Bk:Pg: 2B:386   Date: 5/13/1802   RcCt: 13 Sep 1802
Jonas JANNEY & wife Ruth of Ldn to George TAVENER of Ldn B/S of
142ac adj Joseph CLOWES, Blackstone JANNEY, Israel JANNEY &
Joshua GORE. Wit: Israel JANNEY, David JANNEY, Jonathan JANNEY,
Daniel JANNEY.

Bk:Pg: 2B:390   Date: 9/15/1801   RcCt: 14 Sep 1801
Archibald McVICKER. DoE for slave man Thomas SEAGAL paid £40 to
be free. Wit: William CHILTON, Isaac LARROWE.

Bk:Pg: 2C:001 Date: 5/14/1802 RcCt: 13 Sep 1802
George TAVENER of Ldn to Jonas JANNEY of Ldn. Trust using 142*ac* nr Israel Janney's Mill. Wit: Israel JANNEY, David JANNEY, Jonathan JANNEY.

Bk:Pg: 2C:005 Date: 9/11/1802 RcCt: 13 Sep 1802
Cyrus (free black man) of Ldn. DoE frees wife Lucy whom he purchased from James MAHONY.

Bk:Pg: 2C:005 Date: 5/10/1802 RcCt: 13 Sep 1802
Ferdinando FAIRFAX of JeffVa to Christian VIRTZ and Michael VIRTZ (Exor of Peter VIRTZ dec'd) of Ldn. B/S of 138*ac* in Piedmont adj John ROLER. Wit: Josh DANNIEL, Levi HOLE, James HAMILTON, Wm. H. HARDING, Jas. CAVAN Jr, Pat'k McINTYRE, Charles T. JONES.

Bk:Pg: 2C:007 Date: 4/13/1802 RcCt: 13 Sep 1802
Ferdinando FAIRFAX of Shannon Hill, JeffVa to Samuel Wade JANNEY of Ffx. B/S of 480*ac*, part of the division of the Broad run and Sugarland run tract adj William HORSEMAN. Wit: Richard COLEMAN, James COLEMAN, Alexander YOUNG, Wm. H. HARDING, Abiel JENNERS.

Bk:Pg: 2C:009 Date: 4/28/1802 RcCt: 13 Sep 1802
John McGEATH & wife Elizabeth of Ldn to Murtho SULLIVAN of Ldn. B/S of 3*ac* nr Fairfax Quaker Meeting House. Wit: Wm. R. TAYLOR, Benja. SHREVE.

Bk:Pg: 2C:011 Date: 8/2/1802 RcCt: 13 Sep 1802
William TAYLOR & wife Ann to Jacob FADELY. B/S of Lot #___ in Lsbg adj Matthew WEATHERBY & Samuel MURREY. Wit: John LITTLEJOHN, Joseph SMITH, George HAMMAT.

Bk:Pg: 2C:014 Date: 9/13/1802 RcCt: 13 Sep 1802
George FOUCH & wife Susanna and Daniel FOUCH & wife Sarah of Ldn to Gustavus ELLGIN of Ldn. B/S - Isaac FOUCH dec'd (father of George, Daniel, Thomas & Jonathan) left land to widow Mary for use, now sons are selling their 149*ac* share; ¼*ac* reserved for family graveyard. Wit: Stacy TAYLOR, Steph. C. ROSZEL, Jeremiah RIDDLE

Bk:Pg: 2C:018 Date: 9/6/1802 RcCt: 13 Sep 1802
Elizabeth GREEN. Col - owns 7 slaves in MD, bringing 3 to Va - girl Amy abt 14y old, boy Jim abt 12y old & boy Greenberry abt 11y old.

Bk:Pg: 2C:018 Date: 1/19/1802 RcCt: 13 Sep 1802
Adam HOUSEHOLDER Jr. of Ldn to Jacob SKINNER of Ldn. LS for use of house, orchard and fields where Abner TITUS now lives. Wit: Frederick SMITH.

Bk:Pg: 2C:019 Date: 6/14/1802 RcCt: 13 Sep 1802
John DAVIS of Ldn. Release - will dated 29 Nov 1791 - bequeathed to Baptist church meeting at the white house named Kilfower in Pembroke Co., Maenardife Parish money to nephew Evan DAVIS in SC, named David THOMAS & William OSBURN as Exors. Wit: Mahlon TAYLOR, Stacy TAYLOR.

Bk:Pg: 2C:021   Date: 4/14/1794   RcCt: 8 Dec 1794, 13 Sep 1802
John JANNEY and John JANNEY Jr. (Exors of Joseph JANNEY dec'd) of
Ldn to John WILLIAMS of Ldn. B/S of lot in Wtfd on road leading from
Mahlon Janney's Mill to Lsbg, adj Ann MYARS, William HOUGH. Wit:
Benjamin MEAD, Wm. HOUGH, R. BRADEN, Stephen WILSON.

Bk:Pg: 2C:023   Date: 7/20/1798   RcCt: 13 Sep 1802
Burr POWELL & wife Catherine of Ldn to Ezekiel MOUNT of Ldn. B/S of
14ac. Wit: Jos. LANE, Thos. LEWIS, Richard CHINN.

Bk:Pg: 2C:026   Date: 5/13/1802   RcCt: 13 Sep 1802
Asa MOORE & wife Sarah of Wtfd to Conrod VERTS/VIRTS of Ldn. B/S
of 16 ¼ac adj John HOUGH dec'd & Conrod VIRTS. Wit: Wm.
HAMILTON, Thos. PHILIPS, James RUSSELL.

Bk:Pg: 2C:028   Date: 5/1/1802   RcCt: 13 Sep 1802
William HOUGH, Samuel HOUGH & Mahlon HOUGH of Ldn (Exors of
John HOUGH dec'd) to Asa MOORE of Ldn. B/S of 104¾ac on Kittocton
Creek, adj Jacob SHEBELEY, Ebenezer GRUBB & Conrod VERTS. Wit:
James MOORE, Daniel STONE, Thos. PHILLIPS, Jonah HOUGH.

Bk:Pg: 2C:030   Date: 8/6/1802   RcCt: 13 Sep 1802
Solomon HOGE & Joshua GORE of Ldn (Exor of William HOGE dec'd) to
James CARRUTHERS of Ldn. B/S of 187ac, tract conveyed 2 Jul 1770 by
Soloman HOGE & wife Anne to William HOGE, adj William HOLMES,
Daniel WHITE, Asher CLAYTON, William MORELAND. Wit: George
TAVENOR Sr, Israel JANNEY, Daniel EACHER, Abijah JANNEY.

Bk:Pg: 2C:033   Date: 8/7/1802   RcCt: 13 Sep 1802
James CARRUTHERS of Ldn to Joshua GORE of Ldn. B/S of 93ac. Wit:
George TAVENOR Sr, Israel JANNEY, Daniel EACHES, Abijah JANNEY.

Bk:Pg: 2C:036   Date: 4/16/1802   RcCt: 13 Sep 1802
Ferdinando FAIRFAX of Shannon Hill, JeffVa to Jacob VIRTZ of Ldn. B/S
of 80½ac in Piedmont on Dutchmans run, adj Michael WELMAN, Matthias
SMITLEY, Conrod ROLER & John George's mill. Wit: Wm. H. HARDING,
James HAMILTON, Elizabeth HAMILTON

Bk:Pg: 2C:038   Date: 3/31/1796   RcCt: 12 Sep 1796
Dr. Charles DOUGLAS & wife Susanna of Lsbg to William MOXLEY of
Ldn. B/S of lot in Lsbg. Wit: Alex. DOW, Asa BACON, Jonas POTTS,
Pat'k CAVAN, Samuel MURREY.

Bk:Pg: 2C:040   Date: 6/15/1802   RcCt: 13 Sep 1802
Ferdinando FAIRFAX of Shannon Hill, JeffVa to Richard BROWN of Ldn.
B/S of 182ac of Piedmont on Kittoctan Creek, adj William WILDMAN,
Edward McDANIEL, William WILDMAN Jr. Wit: Wm. GUNNELL Jr.,
James COLEMAN Jr., Wm. H. HARDING, Jesse MOORE.

Bk:Pg: 2C:042   Date: 1/21/1802   RcCt: 10 May 1802
Thomas ODEN & wife Lydia of Ldn to Ariss BUCKNER of Ldn. B/S of
63¾ac, part of tract ODEN & others inherited from his father. Wit: Wm. B.
HARRISON, Charles LEWIS, Thos. GIST.

Bk:Pg: 2C:046   Date: 1/8/1802   RcCt: 13 Sep 1802
Leonard CROWE of Ldn to William WILLIAMS & Peter STUCK of Ldn.
BoS for farm and household items. Wit: Isaac LAROWE, Jacob
DEHAVEN.

Bk:Pg: 2C:046   Date: 6/4/1802   RcCt: 13 Sep 1802
John Dalrymple ORR & wife Lucinda of Ldn to Isaac GOUCHNAUER of
PrWm. B/S of 11½ac on Goose Creek, part of 200ac taken up by Charles
SEMPLE and granted Capt. William AYLETT on 19 Oct 1741. Wit: Thos.
STONESTREET, Ludwell LEE, Thomas Lud. LEE.

Bk:Pg: 2C:048   Date: 6/4/1801   RcCt: 13 Sep 1802
John Dalrymple ORR & wife Lucinda of PrWm to Burr POWELL of Ldn.
B/S of 205ac on Goose Creek and Wonkopin tract on road leading from
Mdbg to Colston's Mill. Wit: Thos. STONESTREET, Ludwell LEE, Thos.
Lud LEE.

Bk:Pg: 2C:051   Date: 6/15/1802   RcCt: 14 Sep 1802
Edmund DENNEY & wife Elizabeth of DC to Lee DURHAM of Lsbg. B/S
of Lot #10 with 2 houses on Loudoun St. Wit: Geo. ROWAN, Wm.
CHILTON, Patk. McINTYRE, John DRISH, Wm. H. HARDING, Daniel
DOWLING, Job HARDING, A. FAW, Cuthbert POWELL.

Bk:Pg: 2C:055   Date: 3/1/1796   RcCt: 10 Oct 1796
Jonah HAGUE (s/o John HAGUE dec'd) & wife Martha of Ldn to William
H. HARDING of Ldn. B/S of 170ac adj William MEADE, Robert CARTER.
Wit: Leven POWELL, Cuthbert POWELL, Thos. N. BINNS.

Bk:Pg: 2C:057   Date: 7/5/1802   RcCt: 14 Sep 1802
Ferdinando FAIRFAX of Shannon Hill, JeffVa to Samuel UNDERWOOD
of Ldn. B/S of 19¾ac in Piedmont adj Archibald MORRISON, James
WHITE, Daniel SHOEMAKER. Wit: Wm. H. HARDING.

Bk:Pg: 2C:058   Date: 9/11/1802   RcCt: ___ [14 Sep 1802?]
Heirs of Jas. WHITE, Peter STONE, Samuel UNDERWOOD, George
MULL, Thomas DAVIS, Richd BROWN, Sanford RAMEY, Thomas
LESLIE, James HAMILTON, John SHAFFER, Michl. VIRTZ, William
ELLZEY - purchasers parts of Piedmont, Stes. Thom. MASON, John D.
ORR, Wm. H. HARDING to Thomas FAIRFAX of JeffVa. Reconfirms to
William HORSEMAN, Thomas MARSHALL, John GUNNELL, John
COLEMAN, James COLEMAN Sr, Richard COLEMAN, David HOLMES,
Baldwin DADE, James & Samuel SCOTT, Abiel JENNERS, Samuel
Wade YOUNG & Alexander YOUNG purchases of parts of Page Lot. Wit:
George SHOEMAKER Sr., Jacob SHOEMAKER Sr, John GEORG, Jacob
VIRTS, Jacob WALTMAN, Jacob EVERHART, Jacob EMERY, John
AXLINE, Henry Jos. FRY, Fredk. SHLATZ, Adam RHORBACK, Charles
CRIM, John STADLER, Daniel HOUSEHOLDER, Archd. MORRISON,
James NIXON.

Bk:Pg: 2C:061   Date: 7/18/1801   RcCt: 14 Sep 1802
Joshua CHILTON & wife Nancy to John DREAN of Lsbg. B/S of 2 parts of lot at Market and Back St in Lsbg, Rosanna HOUGH relinquishes right to claim on lots. Wit :Wm. R. TAYLOR, Joseph SMITH, Simon TRIPLETT Jr.

Bk:Pg: 2C:064   Date: 9/14/1802   RcCt: 14 Sep 1802
Stephens Thomson MASON of Ldn to Thomas Thornton JONES of Ldn. B/S of 67ac, adj John CLAREY & Moses COLWELL.

Bk:Pg: 2C:065   Date: 2/4/1802   RcCt: 14 Sep 1802
Jared MASTER of Ldn to Charles ROBERTS of Ldn. BoS for horses and cows. Wit: Israel LACEY, Wm. COOKE.

Bk:Pg: 2C:065   Date: 2/12/1802   RcCt: 14 Sep 1802
Thomas Darnall STEVENS & wife Mary Eleanor of Ldn to John Brewis STEVENS of Ldn. B/S of ¼ac part of lot. Wit: Stacy TAYLOR, Abner OSBURN.

Bk:Pg: 2C:068   Date: 2/12/1802   RcCt: 14 Sep 1802
Thomas PURSELL & wife Lydia of Ldn to John Brewis STEVENS of Ldn. B/S of Market #2 adj Thomas D. STEVENS on turnpike road. Wit: Stacy TAYLOR, Abner OSBURN.

Bk:Pg: 2C:071   Date: __ Sep 1800   RcCt: 14 Sep 1802
Patrick CAVAN of Lsbg to John BUCKY of Ldn. LS of 1ac, part of James HEREFORD's lease to CAVAN land nr Lsbg. Wit: Joseph NEWTON, John MATHIAS, Stacy TAYLOR.

Bk:Pg: 2C:072   Date: 9/10/1802   RcCt: 13 Sep 1802
Matthew WEATHERBY of Ldn to John LITTLEJOHN of Ldn. B/S of 12ac purchased from William ANSLEY & 10ac from John DREAN. Wit: George HAMMAT, John MILNER, George HEAD.

Bk:Pg: 2C:074   Date: ___   RcCt: 14 Sep 1802
Benjamin HUFTY of Ldn to David LACEY of Ldn. B/S of Lot #43 on Cornwell St in Lsbg, also remainder of Lot #42 (Edward RINKER owns rest). Wit: John LITTLEJOHN, Jno. SCHOOLEY Jr, Thomas WILKINSON, Joseph BURSON.

Bk:Pg: 2C:076   Date: 8/16/1802   RcCt: 11 Sep 1802
George EMREY & wife Margaret of Ross Co., Territory of the US North, West of Ohio River to Joseph SMITH of Lsbg. B/S of Lot in Lsbg adj Lot #12, John RIGOR, Henry McCABE dec'd, Thomas WILLKINSON. Wit: William W. HALL, George NELSON.

Bk:Pg: 2C:079   Date: 4/14/1794   RcCt: 11 Oct 1802
Anthony THORNTON & wife Jinny to John LITTLEJOHN. CoE for sale of 66ac. Wit: W. Wm. LANE Jr, & H. PEAKE in Ffx.

Bk:Pg: 2C:080   Date: 7/19/1797   RcCt: 12 Feb 1798 and 11 Oct 1802
Thomas ROOKARD & wife Sarah of Ldn to Israel LACEY of Ldn. B/S of 170ac adj David REEDER, Nathaniel PEGG. Wit: Thomas COCKERILL, Moses DOWDLE, Francis PEYTON, Peirce BAYLY.

Bk:Pg: 2C:083   Date: 10/11/1802   RcCt: 11 Oct 1802
William POWELL of Ldn to Isaias HORSEMAN of Ldn. BoS for Negro girl
Sary and her son John. Wit: Charles TURLEY.

Bk:Pg: 2C:084   Date: 10/4/1802   RcCt: 11 Oct 1802
Nathan GREGG of Ldn (s/o Stephen GREGG dec'd) to Richard
OSBURNE of Ldn. B/S of 106½ac at foot of Short Hill adj Edward POTTS,
Ezekiel POTTS. Wit: Isall WILLIAMS, Samuel GREGG, Thomas GREGG.

Bk:Pg: 2C:086   Date: 10/11/1802   RcCt: 11 Oct 1802
Thomas GHEEN & wife Margaret of Ldn to David HIRST of Ldn. B/S of
112ac on long branch, adj Abel GARRETT, John GARRETT.

Bk:Pg: 2C:088   Date: __ 1802   RcCt: 13 Sep 1802
George LEE & wife Evelyn Byrd to Peter OATYAR. B/S of 153ac. Wit:
Cornelius MEHER, David POOLE, Mathias SHRY, Thos. Lud LEE,
Ludwell LEE.

Bk:Pg: 2C:091   Date: 7/30/1802   RcCt: 11 Oct 1802
Ferdinando FAIRFAX of Shannon Hill, JeffVa to James ROACH of Ldn.
B/S of 118ac on SE side of Short hill adj Silas PRYOR, James BROWN.
Wit: Mahlon MORRIS, George CASTLE, Mahlon ROACH, Wm. H.
HARDING, Thos. LESLIE, Thos. HOUGH.

Bk:Pg: 2C:093   Date: 9/13/1802   RcCt: 11 Oct 1802
Ferdinando FAIRFAX of Shannon Hill, JeffVa to Mahlon ROACH of Ldn.
B/S of 107ac, 2 lots numbered 495 on survey of SE side of short hill in
Shannondale, adj James McILHANEY, John McILHANEY, James
ROACH. Wit: Thos. HOUGH, James ROACH, Thos. LESLIE, Wm.
HOUGH, Benjamin LESLIE.

Bk:Pg: 2C:095   Date: 10/9/1802   RcCt: 11 Oct 1802
Thomas PURSELL & wife Lydia of Ldn to Mahlon MORRIS of Ldn. B/S of
2ac by mill race. Wit: James McILHANEY, John HAMILTON, Mahlon
ROACH, Thos. HOUGH.

Bk:Pg: 2C:099   Date: 9/13/1802   RcCt: 11 Oct 1802
Ferdinando FAIRFAX of Shannon hill, JeffVa to Thomas HOUGH of Ldn.
B/S of 47¼ac on SE side of short hill in Shannondale. Wit: James
ROACH, Thos. LESLIE, Mahlon ROACH, Wm. H. HARDING.

Bk:Pg: 2C:101   Date: 10/9/1802   RcCt: 11 Oct 1802
Thomas PURSEL & wife Lydia of Ldn to Thomas HOUGH. CoE for sale of
¼ac. Wit: James McILHANEY, John HAMILTON.

Bk:Pg: 2C:102   Date: 2/11/1786   RcCt: 12 Oct 1801
David SIMMONS & wife Catherine of Fredericksburg, Spotsilvania Co. VA
to Patrick CAVAN of Lsbg. B/S of Lot #45 in Lsbg adj Henry McCABE.
Wit: Andrew SPECHT, Sebestion LOSH, Catherine SPECK.

Bk:Pg: 2C:103   Date: 10/6/1802   RcCt: 11 Oct 1802
Thomas BRAND & wife Phebe of Ldn to John C. STRAHAN and Samuel
BOGGESS of Ldn. BoS for Negro man Ben abt 29y old, Negro girl Kitty
abt 11y old & household items. Wit: Uriel GLASCOCK, George RUST.

Bk:Pg: 2C:104   Date: 6/12/1802   RcCt: 13 Sep 1802
Mrs. Sarah FAIRFAX of GrB (wd/o George Wm. FAIRFAX dec'd) to Adam
RORBAUGH of Ldn. LS on 43*ac* from FAIRFAX transferred to John
STOUTSENBARGER, then to John LOUSCH, then to Christian
REEPOLD (died intestate and brother George transferred to
RHORBAUGH w/o consent) reverted back to FAIRFAX. Wit: Michael
VERTS, Charles CHINN, Jacob WALTMAN.

Bk:Pg: 2C:107   Date: 4/13/1802   RcCt: 12 Oct 1802
William P. ROPER (died intestate - heirs Christopher ROPER & Ann
ROPER now MORRISON, William P. ROPER, Thomas ROPER and
Catharine ROPER's (since dec'd) children) of Lsbg to Thomas
WILKINSON of Lsbg. B/S of part of Lot #12 on King St adj John REIGOR.
Wit: John H. CANBY, Geo. ROWEN, Samuel MORAN.

Bk:Pg: 2C:109   Date: 4/23/1802   RcCt: 9 Nov 1802
George Fairfax LEE and John Tasker CARTER of WstmVa to Thomas
Ludwell LEE of Ldn, Spencer BALL of PrWm and John KEENE of Ffx.
PoA for sale of Goose Creek tract. Wit: J. J. MAUND, Jas. A.
THOMPSON, Thos. ROWAN, John CAMHELLE, Meredith M. HACKNEY,
Benja. HACKNEY, M. WRIGHT.

Bk:Pg: 2C:111   Date: 3/30/1802   RcCt: 9 Nov 1802
George Fairfax LEE and John Tasker CARTER of WstmVa to Thomas
Ludwell LEE of Ldn, Spencer BALL of PrWm and John KEENE of Ffx.
PoA for land on Goose Creek. Wit: Jno. Jas. MAUND, Jas. N.
THOMPSON, William BRICKEY, Thomas OMEHUNDRO.

Bk:Pg: 2C:113   Date: 3/22/1802   RcCt: 13 Dec 1802
Jacob DEHAVEN & wife Nancy of Ldn to John ELLIOT of Ldn. B/S of
80*ac* where DEHAVEN has lived many years, adj George RAZOR,
Charles BELL, Josiah CLAPHAM, John ELLIOT. Wit: Hugh DOUGLAS,
Samuel CLAPHAM, David BEATY, Wm. WILLIAMS, Charles BELL.

Bk:Pg: 2C:114   Date: 10/11/1802   RcCt: 13 Dec 1802
Joseph FREDD & wife Sarah of Ldn to Joshua FREDD of Ldn. B/S of
111¼*ac* at foot of Blue Ridge adj Francis FRED, Thomas FRED. Wit:
William POWELL, Isaac RICHARDS, Thomas FRED.

Bk:Pg: 2C:116   Date: 11/9/1802   RcCt: 13 Dec 1802
Thomas GARRET (by attorney Chambers HALL of Newcastle Co. DE) to
Joseph GARRETT of Ldn. B/S of 23*ac* on Long Branch adj Thomas
GHEEN. Wit: Samuel TODD, Thomas GHEEN, Aaron RAWLINGS.

Bk:Pg: 2C:118   Date: ___   RcCt: 13 Dec 1802
Benjamin HIXON & wife Elizabeth of Ldn to William PAXSON of Ldn.
Bond on sale of 220*ac* plantation less 28*ac*. Wit: William AHLINE, Reuben
HIXSON, Mahlon JANNEY Jr.

Bk:Pg: 2C:119   Date: 12/11/1802   RcCt: 13 Dec 1802
David HIRST & wife Ann of Ldn to Stephen WILSON of Ldn. B/S of 20*ac*
nr Goose Creek Meeting House. Wit: Stacy TAYLOR, Bernard TAYLOR.

Bk:Pg: 2C:121   Date: 4/21/1802   RcCt: 13 Dec 1802
Thomas BRENT of Ldn to Burr POWELL. Negro man Anthony, Negro boy
Nelson, and horse held in trust on $150 BRENT owes to Abner GIBSON.
Wit: Robert DAGG, Saml. HENDERSON, Thomas CHINN.

Bk:Pg: 2C:122   Date: 6/3/1802   RcCt: 13 Dec 1802
Joseph REED & wife Agness (d/o William RUST dec'd intestate) of Ldn to
Samuel BOGGESS of Ldn. B/S of 70ac assigned to REED from division
of RUST's estate. Wit: Michael EBLEN, Samuel PEW, John MARKS, Jno.
ROSE, Joseph SMITH.

Bk:Pg: 2C:125   Date: 5/1/1802   RcCt: 13 Dec 1802
William HOUGH, Samuel HOUGH & Mahlon HOUGH of Ldn (Exors of
John HOUGH dec'd) to Isaac STEER of Ldn. B/S of 325ac, where John
HOUGH lived, adj Ebenezer GRUBB, road leading to German Settlement,
Jacob WINE, Anthony CUNARD, William PAXSON, William HOUGH,
Jesse TAYLOR. Wit: James MOORE, Asa MOORE, Jonah HOUGH,
Thos. PHILLIPS.

Bk:Pg: 2C:128   Date: 4/9/1802   RcCt: 13 Sep 1802
John A. BINNS & wife Dewanner of Ldn to Jonathan CUNNARD of Ldn.
B/S of 58ac, on Broad Run on road from Roaches Mill to German
Settlement, adj Michael BOGER. Wit: John LITTLEJOHN, Tho. SIM, Wm.
PAXSON.

Bk:Pg: 2C:132   Date: 4/9/1802   RcCt: 13 Sep 1802
John Alexander BINNS & wife Dewanner of Ldn to William PAXSON of
Ldn. B/S of 57¾ac, adj Anthony SOWDER, George MANN, Daniel LONG.
Wit: John LITTLEJOHN, Tho. SIM.

Bk:Pg: 2C:135   Date: 5/29/1802   RcCt: 13 Sep 1802
David SMITH of FrdkVa to Thomas LESLIE of Ldn. B/S of 2 rods on gap
of short hill on NE side of turnpike, adj John JENNEY. Wit: Israel
THOMPSON, Bernard TAYLOR, Patterson INGLEDUE, Edward
CUNARD, Wm. H. HARDING, Jas. HAMILTON, Jonah WHITE.

Bk:Pg: 2C:137   Date: 10/12/1802   RcCt: 13 Dec 1802
Ferdinando FAIRFAX of Shannon hill, JeffVa to Edward McDANIEL of
Ldn. B/S of 175ac where McDANIEL now lives in Piedmont, adj Thomas
D. STEVENS, Joseph THOMPSON. Wit: William HAMILTON, Jesse
HIRST, Thomas HIRST.

Bk:Pg: 2C:139   Date: 9/10/1802   RcCt: 13 Dec 1802
Ferdinando FAIRFAX & wife Eliza Blair of Shannon Hill, JeffVa to brother
Thomas FAIRFAX of JeffVa. B/S of land on Blue Ridge and Short Hill
(mostly in Ldn) called Shannondale, originally granted 17 May 1739 to
John COLVILLE, then to William FAIRFAX (grandfather of above) on 23
Jan 1740, gifted to eldest son George Wm. FAIRFAX, bequeathed to
widow Sarah FAIRFAX, on East side of Blue Ridge nr Shenandoa Falls.
Wit: George NORTH, Abram DAVENPORT, Edwd. GANTE.

Bk:Pg: 2C:142   Date: 6/14/1802   RcCt: 13 Dec 1802
Jacob VIRTS to John GEORG. Mortgage of $1000 for land VERTS
purchased from Ferdinando FAIRFAX. Wit: Wm. H. HARDING, Jacob
WALTMAN, Samuel UNDERWOOD.

Bk:Pg: 2C:143   Date: 5/7/1802   RcCt: 14 Dec 1802
John SPENCER of Ldn to Hiland CROWE of Ldn. B/S of 100ac where
William GROVES lately lived, and 206ac where SPENCER lives adj
Benjamin JAMES. Wit: Wm. R. TAYLOR, John L. BERKLEY, Joseph
BLINCOE.

Bk:Pg: 2C:146   Date: 12/11/1802   RcCt: 14 Dec 1802
James JOHNSON & wife Jane of Ldn to John JOHNSON of Ldn. B/S of
128¼ac on Goose Creek, Lot #2. Wit: John WILSON, Henry ROBERTS,
Joseph PULLER.

Bk:Pg: 2C:147   Date: 12/4/1802   RcCt: 14 Dec 1802
Peter BELTS of Ldn to Peter JACOBS of Ldn. Mortgage for Lot in Lsbg on
the continuation of King St. Wit: Job MORGIN

Bk:Pg: 2C:148   Date: 6/19/1802   RcCt: 11 Oct 1802
John PAGE dec'd late of Buckroe in Elizabeth City Co. to Wilson C.
SELDEN. Agreement - land in Matthews Co., will devised estate to
children after wife's death, Thomas SWANN and Wm. Byrd PAGE (br/o
John PAGE) bound to collect. Wit: Ferdno. FAIRFAX, Richard H. LOVE,
Joseph BEARD.

Bk:Pg: 2C:150   Date: 1/10/1802   RcCt: 14 Dec 1802
William RUST dec'd (died intestate). Dower & division of estate: dower
waved in lieu of annual sum, Negros to Mrs. Elizabeth BAKER (Lizza,
Winny & Carter), Matthew RUST & Patty (Jacob, Daniel & Emily), Joseph
REID & Agnes (Letty & Leana), Vincent BOGGESS & Anne (Jude &
Lemon), Joshua SINGLETON & Hannah (Peter & Mary Ann), Sarah
Taylor (Peg & Jimm) George RUST & wife Elizabeth (Daphne & Simon),
plat showing land division. Subscribers: Wm. H. POWELL, Benjamin
GRAYSON, Thomas A. HEREFORD.

Bk:Pg: 2C:155   Date: 1/8/1803   RcCt: 10 Jan 1803
Terrence FIGH of Ldn to Jacob BAKER of Ldn. B/S of 100ac. Wit: Henry
HUFF, Adam HOUSEHOLDER Jr, Joseph SPOOND.

Bk:Pg: 2C:156   Date: 3/31/1796   RcCt: 10 Oct 1796 and 11 Jan 1803
Robert SCOTT, William SCOTT, Martha SCOTT (now ROGERS), James
FOX & wife Hannah of Ldn to Nicholas HARPER of Ldn. B/S of 200ac, adj
Richard COLEMAN, Nathan DAVIS, Col. James COLEMAN. Tract sold by
Joseph MARSHALL & wife Rachel to Joseph SCOTT on 8 Feb 1769 and
bequethed to wife Hannah until son Robert reached 23y old, then divided.
Wit: Francis MOORE, James MARSHALL, Samuel MARSHALL, William
EHICK, John GREEN.

Bk:Pg: 2C:159   Date: 1/10/1803   RcCt: 10 Jan 1803
Thomas BINNS of Ldn. DoE for Negro man Simon SWEENER, abt 38y
old.

Bk:Pg: 2C:160   Date: 11/15/1802   RcCt: 10 Jan 1803
Jonathan FOUCH (s/o Isaac FOUCH dec'd) of Ldn to Thomas FOUCH of
Ldn. B/S of 50*ac* on Seconnel Branch adj Thomas FOUCH.

Bk:Pg: 2C:163   Date: 12/6/1802   RcCt: 11 Jan 1802
Nathaniel CRAWFORD & wife Sarah of PrG to Samuel BOYD of Ldn. B/S
of 54*ac,* part of lease by Thomas BLACKBURNE to Isaac NOTAU in
1771, adj Thomas GREGG, Beaverdam Creek, and part of 113*ac*
BLACKBURNE conveyed to CRAWFORD and Bushrod WASHINGTON &
wife Ann.

Bk:Pg: 2C:166   Date: 12/6/1802   RcCt: 11 Jan 1803
Nathaniel CRAWFORD & wife Sarah of PrG to Amos HIBBS of Ldn. B/S
of 125*ac* on Beaverdam leased by Thomas BLACKBURNE to John
LEMING in 1771, adj Henry SMITH, Malon CUMMINGS, Joseph HOGE,
Isaac COWGIL.

Bk:Pg: 2C:170   Date: 12/6/1802   RcCt: 11 Jan 1803
Nathaniel CRAWFORD & wife Sarah of PrG to William REEDER of Ldn.
B/S of 85*ac* leased by Thomas BLACKBURNE to William HUFF in 1771,
adj Beaverdam, Isaac NOTAU, George CHILTON.

Bk:Pg: 2C:174   Date: 12/1/1802   RcCt: 11 Jan 1803
Nathaniel CRAWFORD & wife Sarah of PrG to Jacob SILCOTT of Ldn.
B/S of 60*ac* at branch called Buckhorn, adj Beaverdam, Richard
RICHARDS, Michael EBLIN, William WYNN, part of tract SILCOTT rented
from Thomas BLACKBURNE.

Bk:Pg: 2C:177   Date: 12/6/1802   RcCt: 11 Jan 1803
Nathaniel CRAWFORD & wife Sarah of PrG to Samuel SMITH of Ldn.
B/S of 102½*ac,* leased by Thomas BLACKBURNE to Joseph BROWN in
1771, adj Hezekiah GUY, Beaverdam.

Bk:Pg: 2C:181   Date: 12/6/1802   RcCt: 11 Jan 1803
Nathaniel CRAWFORD & wife Sarah of PrG to Isaac COGILL of Ldn. B/S
of 75*ac,* tract leased by Thomas BLACKBURN to COGILL in 1771, adj
Henry SMITH, Joseph HOGUE, Joseph SMITH.

Bk:Pg: 2C:185   Date: 12/6/1802   RcCt: 11 Jan 1803
Nathaniel CRAWFORD & wife Sarah of PrG to Richard RICHARDS of
Ldn. B/S of 63*ac* adjoining Amos HIBS.

**Bk:Pg: 2C:188 [misnumbered as 187]   Date: 12/6/1802   RcCt: 11 Jan
1803**
Nathaniel CRAWFORD & wife Sarah of PrG to William GALLIHER. B/S of
115*ac,* part of tract leased by Thomas BLACKBURNE to Frederick
CLYNE in 1772, adj Dawson BROWN, Thomas GREGG.

Bk:Pg: 2C:190   Date: 12/6/1802   RcCt: 11 Jan 1803
Nathaniel CRAWFORD & wife Sarah of PrG to John WILKINSON of Ldn.
B/S of 75*ac,* tract the Thomas BLACKBURNE leased to Joseph SMITH in
1771, adj Henry SMITH, Isaac BROWN.

Bk:Pg: 2C:194   Date: 1/11/1803   RcCt: 11 Jan 1803
Walter TAYLOR & Mary TAYLOR (Exors of John TAYLOR dec'd). DoE
for black man Anthony abt 42y old, freed in will if $100 paid by 25 Dec
1802, which he does. Wit: C. BINNS.

Bk:Pg: 2C:195   Date: __ 1802   RcCt: 11 Jan 1803
James HAMILTON & wife Cassandra, Alexander COOPER & wife
Margaret, John MATTHIAS & wife Anne, James McCABE and Robert
HAMMILTON, all of Lsbg to Obadiah CLIFFORD of Lsbg. B/S of Lot #3
on Loudoun St in Lsbg, adj George ROWEN, Daniel DOWLING. Wit: B.
HOUGH, George HAMMET, Samuel HOUGH, Thomas SIM, John
LITTLEJOHN.

Bk:Pg: 2C:198   Date: 1/11/1803   RcCt: 12 Jan 1803
Ferdinando FAIRFAX of Shannon hill, JeffVa to James HAMILTON of
Ldn. B/S of 4 lots totaling 428ac, adj Nicholas FRANCIS, John HOUGH,
Michael ROOCE, George SHAVER, John MARTIN, James NIXON,
James McCAMY, Daniel SHOEMAKER. Wit: Thomas WILKINSON,
Archibald MAINS, Wm. H. HARDING.

Bk:Pg: 2C:201   Date: 1/10/1803   RcCt: 12 Jan 1803
Ferdinando FAIRFAX of Shannon Hill, JeffVa to John McILHANY of Ldn.
B/S of l97¼ac lot #3 on plat of Short Hill, SE side, in Shannondale, adj
James McILHANEY, Mahlon ROACH. Wit: James HAMILTON, Armstead
LONG, Thos. T. JONES, John H. CANBY.

Bk:Pg: 2C:203   Date: __ 1802   RcCt: 12 Jan 1803
James HAMILTON & wife Cassandra, Alexander COOPER & wife
Margaret, John MATTHIAS & wife Ann, Jane McCABE & Robert
HAMILTON, all of Lsbg to Daniel DOWLING of Lsbg. B/S of Lot #3 on
Loudoun St in Lsbg adj Obadiah CLIFFORD. Wit: B. HOUGH, George
HAMMET, Samuel HOUGH, Thomas SIM, Jno LITTLEJOHN.

Bk:Pg: 2C:206   Date: 1/1/1802   RcCt: 12 Jul 1802
Abraham B. T. MASON & wife Sarah of Ldn to Jonas POTTS & Jacob
BAUGH of Ldn. B/S of 40ac on Potomac, devised from will of Thomson
MASON dec'd. Wit: Thomas Thornton JONES, Ariana SIM, Patrick SIM,
John LITTLEJOHN, Samuel CARR, Thomas SIM, Samuel MURREY.

Bk:Pg: 2C:209   Date: 9/13/1802   RcCt: 14 Feb 1803
Jonah SANDS of Ldn to John ROBERTSON of Ldn. Bond as colateral for
completion of sale of 150ac (his 1/7 share of father Isaac SANDS dec'd
land). Wit: William WRIGHT, John OXLEY, Isaac LARROWE.

Bk:Pg: 2C:210   Date: 3/10/1798   RcCt: 15 Feb 1803
Sarah LANE (Admr for James LANE Jr. dec'd) to Elisha GREEN &
Hannah GREEN. Receipt for their share of said father's estate. Wit: Will
LANE, Susanna LANE, Sally LANE.

Bk:Pg: 2C:211   Date: 1/17/1803   RcCt: 15 Feb 1803
James CAVAN Jr. and John CAVAN (heirs of Patrick CAVAN dec'd) both
of Lsbg to Thomas BEATTY of Creigors Town MD. Mortgage for ½ac Lot
#10 in Lsbg now occupied by free negro Wm. COSSEY and Griffith

ROBERTS, adj Robert KIRK, heirs of Alexr. McINTYRE dec'd, John H.
SCHELLGY, Dr. James McLEAN, graveyard. Wit: Alexr. SUTHERLAND,
John EVANS, Benja. MYERS.

Bk:Pg: 2C:213   Date: 9/17/1802   RcCt: 15 Feb 1803
John LITTLEJOHN & wife Monica of Ldn to William LITTLEJOHN of Ldn.
B/S of 100*ac,* adj Joseph SMITH, head of Rock Spring, George HAMMIT,
Giles TILLETT. Wit: Geo. ROWAN, Obadiah CLIFFORD, George HEAD,
Samuel MURREY, Joseph SMITH.

Bk:Pg: 2C:216   Date: 2/15/1803   RcCt: 15 Feb 1803
James CAVAN Jr. and John CAVAN (heirs of Patrick CAVAN dec'd) both
of Lsbg to Robert J. TAYLOR (Admr of Jesse TAYLOR dec'd of AlexVa)
and Charles DRISH of Lsbg. Mortgage to TAYLOR for 2*ac* nr Lsbg
purchased from Townshend DADE, to DRISH went lot on S side of
Market St. Wit: Alexr. SUTHERLAND, John MATHIAS, Jno. EVANS.

Bk:Pg: 2C:218   Date: 9/13/1802   RcCt: 11 Oct 1802
Ferdinando FAIRFAX of Shannon Hill, JeffVa to Thomas LESLIE of Ldn.
B/S of 46¼*ac,* at Short Hill adj James McILHANEY. Wit: Wm. H.
HARDING, James ROACH, Thomas HOUGH, David LOVETT, Mahlon
ROACH.

Bk:Pg: 2C:220   Date: 8/25/1786   RcCt: 10 Apr 1787 and 15 Feb 1803
Wilfred JOHNSON of Ffx to John Peyton HARRISON of Fqr. B/S of 268*ac*
bequeathed to JOHNSON by George JOHNSTON. Wit: Val. HARRISON,
Joseph JACKSON, John DYER, Hugh NEILSON.

Bk:Pg: 2C:223   Date: 12/13/1802   RcCt: 16 Feb 1803
Richard Bland LEE & wife Elizabeth of Ffx to John Thomas RICKETTS
and William NEWTON of AlexVa. B/S for parts of tract Lee purchased
from Ferdinando FAIRFAX, including 150*ac* leased to Samuel SCHOOLY
and 150*ac* leased to John SCHOOLY, both now in possession of Richard
CONNOR, also 105*ac* leased to John NICKLIN and 102*ac* leased to John
MARTIN. Wit: Elisha C. DECK, George TAYLOR, John BOUSALL, John
MILL Jr., Benja. RICKETTS.

Bk:Pg: 2C:227   Date: 2/17/1803   RcCt: 16 Feb 1803
Ferdinando FAIRFAX of Shannon Hill, JeffVa to John SHAVOR of Ldn.
B/S of 5½*ac* in Piedmont, adj Michael BOGER, late Frederick BOGERS,
Peter HICKMAN.

Bk:Pg: 2C:228   Date: 2/16/1803   RcCt: 16 Feb 1803
Ferdinando FAIRFAX of Shannon Hill, JeffVa to John SWANK of Ldn. B/S
of 120*ac* in Piedmont.

Bk:Pg: 2C:230   Date: ___   RcCt: 13 Mar 1801
Mary LEE of StafVa to John D. ORR. B/S with affection of 858*ac* abt 2
miles from Mdbg on Goose Creek. Wit: Richd. B. ALEXANDER, Bartlett
LEACH, Ferdno. FAIRFAX.

Bk:Pg: 2C:232   Date: 11/1/1778   RcCt: 16 Feb 1803
Jonathan EDWARDS Jr. Col for boy Dennis abt 9y old from MD.

Bk:Pg: 2C:233   Date: 8/27/1802   RcCt: 14 Feb 1803
William STABLER & wife Deborah to Thomas MATTHEWS. CoE for lot in
Lsbg. Wit: George SLACUM, Jacob HOFFMAN.

Bk:Pg: 2C:234   Date: 4/17/1802   RcCt: 16 Feb 1803
Jonathan EDWARDS Jr. Col on 21 Mar last brought in Negro girl Tilda
from Md, a gift to his wife by her father.

Bk:Pg: 2C:234   Date: 6/15/1802   RcCt: 15 Feb 1803
William H. HARDING of JeffVa at request of Ferdinando FAIRFAX to
George CARTER of Oatland. Mortgage for 170ac, adj William MEADE,
Catesby COCKS, patent of Robert CARTER, widow HOLLING. Wit: R. J.
TAYLOR, Jas. CAVAN Jr., Armisted LONG, Tho. SWAN, James
COLEMAN.

Bk:Pg: 2C:237   Date: 4/11/1803   RcCt: 11 Apr 1803
John LITTLEJOHN, Matthew HARRISON, Charles BENNETT, Thomas
SIM, Abraham B. T. MASON, Hugh DOUGLAS. Bond on LITTLEJOHN as
Sheriff of Ldn to collect taxes.

Bk:Pg: 2C:238   Date: 4/11/1803   RcCt: 11 Apr 1803
John LITTLEJOHN, Matthew HARRISON, Charles BENNETT, Thomas
SIM, Abraham B. T. MASON, Hugh DOUGLASS. Bond on LITTLEJOHN
as Sheriff of Ldn to collect levies.

Bk:Pg: 2C:239   Date: 4/11/1803   RcCt: 11 Apr 1803
John LITTLEJOHN, Matthew HARRISON, Charles BENNETT, Thomas
SIM, Abraham B. T. MASON, Hugh DOUGLASS. Bond on LITTLEJOHN
as Sheriff of Ldn to collect Officers fees and dues.

Bk:Pg: 2C:240   Date: 3/2/1803   RcCt: 11 Apr 1803
John LITTLEJOHN & wife Monica of Ldn to Joseph SMITH of Ldn. B/S of
2ac lot at NE end of Lsbg, adj William LITTLEJOHN. Wit: Samuel
MURREY, Thomas SIM, John DREAN.

Bk:Pg: 2C:242   Date: 4/9/1803   RcCt: 11 Apr 1803
Leven POWELL of Mdbg to Mesheck LACY of Ldn. LS of ½ac Lot #33 in
Mdbg on Madison St. Wit: Noble BEVERIDGE, Burr POWELL, Andrew
COCKRAN.

Bk:Pg: 2C:242   Date: 12/23/1802   RcCt: 14 Feb 1803
William WILSON of AlexVa. DoE for Negro man Wm. CAUSEY, under
45y old. Wit: R. J. TAYLOR, Edm. J. LEE, Edmund DENNY.

Bk:Pg: 2C:244   Date: 4/2/1803   RcCt: 12 Apr 1803
Francis TITUS & wife Jane of Ldn to Jonas POTTS and Jacob BAUGH of
Ldn. B/S of 119ac. Wit: Sampson BLINCOE, G. W. BLINCOE, Thomas
SIM, John LITTLEJOHN, Walker REID.

Bk:Pg: 2C:247   Date: 4/4/1803   RcCt: 12 Apr 1803
Abraham SKILMAN & wife Violinda to Francis TYTUS. Bond for 2 lots
conveyed to SKILMAN by Francis TYTUS & wife Jane. Wit: Sn.
BLINCOE, Jonas POTTS, Walker REID.

Bk:Pg: 2C:249   Date: 1/11/1800   RcCt: 12 Jan 1802
Edmund J. LEE of AlexVa to Stephen COOK of AlexVa. LS of 500*ac*
between Goose Creek and Lsbg. Wit: Charles SIMMS, M. HARRISON, R.
J. TAYLOR.

Bk:Pg: 2C:250   Date: 8/12/1802   RcCt: 12 Apr 1803
Robert MARTIN of Ldn to John KLEINHOFF. BoS for farm and household
items. Wit: James MOTE.

Bk:Pg: 2C:251   Date: 2/25/1803   RcCt: 12 Apr 1803
Samuel CLAPHAM of Ldn to George ELLIOT Sr. of Ldn. LS of 35*ac* in
ShelP. Wit: Vincent WHALY, Geo. ELLIOTT.

Bk:Pg: 2C:253   Date: 3/1/1803   RcCt: 12 Apr 1803
Joseph SMITH & wife Mary to John LITTLEJOHN. B/S of 2*ac* at NE end
of Lsbg. Wit: Thomas SIM, Samuel MURRY, John DREAN.

Bk:Pg: 2C:256   Date: 4/5/1796   RcCt: 11 Jul 1797 and 12 Apr 1803
Henry McCABE & wife Jane of Lsbg to Joseph SMITH of Lsbg. B/S of
43*ac* adj Lsbg. Wit: Patk. CAVAN, John LITTLEJOHN, George
HAMMETT, Thomas MILBURNE.

Bk:Pg: 2C:259   Date: 12/14/1802   RcCt: 12 Apr 1803
Thomas BRENT of Ldn to Martin BRENT. BoS for Negro man Anthony
and boy Nelson. Wit: Jesse McVEIGH, Thomas CHINN, A. GIBSON.

Bk:Pg: 2C:259   Date: 4/11/1803   RcCt: 12 Apr 1803
John HENRY of Ldn to Samuel MURRY of Ldn. B/S of lot on Loudoun St
in Lsbg, purchased by HENRY from John BOARD.

Bk:Pg: 2C:261   Date: 4/5/1803   RcCt: 12 Apr 1803
George TAVENNER & wife Tabitha of Ldn to Joseph TAVENNER of Ldn.
B/S of 18*ac* on road leading to Wtfd, adj Stacy JENNY, Samuel GREGG.
Wit: Jesse JANNY, Jonah SANDS, William CARTER.

Bk:Pg: 2C:263   Date: 12/25/1802   RcCt: 12 Apr 1803
George TAVENNER & wife Tabitha of Ldn to Jesse JANNY of Ldn. B/S of
1*ac* adj Stacy JANNEY on S side of main road to Lsbg, road leading to
Wtfd. Wit: Jonah SANDS, Joseph TAVENNER, Stacy JANNY, Joshua
HIKMAN?

Bk:Pg: 2C:265   Date: 9/28/1795   RcCt: 11 Apr 1796
John ALEXANDER & wife Elizabeth of Ldn to William WILSON of Ffx. B/S
of 314*ac* on west side of mountain. Wit: Thos. SWANN, Jacob MYERS,
Saml. TILLETT Jr, Sn. BLINCOE, Saml. BOGGESS, Leven POWELL,
Burr POWELL.

Bk:Pg: 2C:270   Date: 5/7/1803   RcCt: 9 May 1803
Thomas SIM of Ldn to Jacob WALTMAN. BoS for Negro boy Tom. Wit:
Benjamin DEWELL.

Bk:Pg: 2C:271   Date: 10/14/1802   RcCt: 9 May 1803
James LEITH & wife Sarah to William VICKERS. B/S of 50*ac* on Goose
Creek. Wit: Burr POWELL, Leven POWELL, Martin BRENT, John
MORRIS, Jacob REEDER.

Bk:Pg: 2C:274   Date: 4/13/1801   RcCt: 13 Apr 1801
Thomas SCHOLEFIELD & wife Rebeckah of Ldn to John SCHOLEFIELD
of Ldn. B/S of 100*ac* on Bull run on Carolina Road, adj Jacob ISH. Wit:
William SKINNER, Jacob ISH, Israel LACY, William SHOLFIELD.

Bk:Pg: 2C:276   Date: 10/1/1802   RcCt: 11 Apr 1803
Anne BINNS of Ldn (wd/o Charles BINNS) to son William Alexander
BINNS of Ldn. Gift of all rights received from husband's will and 50*ac,* adj
George NIXON, Thomas N. BINNS. Wit: C. BINNS, Simon A. BINNS,
Joseph ROSS.

Bk:Pg: 2C:277   Date: 3/25/1803   RcCt: 9 May 1803
Mahlon JANNEY of Ldn to Thomas HIRST of Wtfd. B/S of Lots #3 & #4 in
new addition of Wtfd, adj Mahlon JANNY, William HOUGH. Wit: Wm.
HAMILTON, Francis WHITELY, Richard GRIFFITH.

Bk:Pg: 2C:279   Date: 10/20/1801   RcCt: 13 Sep 1802
Mahlon JANNEY & wife Sarah of Ldn to Isaac HOUGH of Ldn. B/S of Lots
#14 & #15 in addition to Wtfd. Wit: Abner WILLIAMS, J. W. L. L. H. S.,
Amasa HAGUE.

Bk:Pg: 2C:281   Date: 3/14/1803   RcCt: 9 May 1803
Eleazer EVANS & wife Mary of Ldn to Charles JOHNSON of Ldn. B/S of
30*ac* on NW fork of Goose Creek, adj Isaac NICKOLS. Wit: Stacy
TAYLOR, Timothy TAYLOR, John HEAD, Wm. JONES, Leven POWELL.

Bk:Pg: 2C:284   Date: 5/2/1803   RcCt: 9 May 1803
Asa MOORE of Wtfd to Mahlon JANNEY of Ldn. B/S of Lot #1 & #2 in
Wtfd, adj Mahlon JANNEY, Richard GRIFFITH. Wit: Jonah HOUGH,
James MOORE, James RUSSELL.

Bk:Pg: 2C:286   Date: 4/6/1803   RcCt: 9 May 1803
Frederick BELTS of Ldn to Jacob AXLINE of Ldn. A/L. Wit: John AXLINE,
Jeremiah PURDUM, David AXLINE.

Bk:Pg: 2C:288   Date: 11/28/1792   RcCt: 11 Feb 1793 and 9 May 1803
John MOORE of Ldn to Jacob ISH of Ldn. LS of 2*ac* in CamP. Wit: Israel
LACEY, Cornelius SKINNER, James PENDERGRASS.

Bk:Pg: 2C:289   Date: 12/29/1792   RcCt: 11 Feb 1793 and 9 May 1803
John MOORE & wife Sarah of Ldn to Jacob ISH of Ldn. Mortgage on
above 2*ac*. Wit: Z. BAYLY, Israel LACEY, Cornelious SKINNER, James
PENDERGAS.

Bk:Pg: 2C:293   Date: 4/15/1803   RcCt: 9 May 1803
Sarah OSBURN of Ldn to Morris OSBURN of Ldn. B/S of 44*ac* at foot of
Blue Ridge. Wit: John OSBURN, John REED, Joel OSBURN.

Bk:Pg: 2C:295   Date: 3/14/1803   RcCt: 9 May 1803
James CRAVAN Jr (Admr of Patrick CAVAN dec'd - died intestate) of
Lsbg to Casper ECKART of Ldn. A/L of 1*ac* adj John LITTLEJOHN. Wit:
George HAMMAT, J. HARDING, John EVANS.

Bk:Pg: 2C:297   Date: 11/22/1802   RcCt: 9 May 1803
Sarah OSBURN and Mary OSBURN of Ldn to Joel OSBURN. Bond for their share of 150*ac* now in possession of Hannah OSBURN wd/o Richard OSBURN, her dower until she pays $100 to Joel OSBURN and other heirs. Wit: John OSBURN, Ignatious BYRNS, Thomas OSBURN.

Bk:Pg: 2C:299   Date: 3/1/1803   RcCt: 9 May 1803
Timothy HIXSON of Ldn to Reuben HIXSON of Ldn. B/S of 63*ac,* adj heirs of William HIXON dec'd; also ½*ac* on Kittocton for to use as abutment for a dam. Wit: Henry HUFF, Jno. MARTIN Jr, John KLEINHOFF, Geo. MULL.

Bk:Pg: 2C:302   Date: 4/7/1803   RcCt: 9 May 1803
Ferdinando FAIRFAX of JeffVa to Pateson WRIGHT of Ldn. B/S of 84¾*ac* in Piedmont, on Kittocton Creek. Wit: Wm. HARDING, Sanford RAMEY, Jonathan CUNNARD, Patrick McGAVOCK.

Bk:Pg: 2C:303   Date: 4/7/1803   RcCt: 9 May 1803
Ferdinando FAIRFAX of Shannon Hill, JeffVa to Patrick McGAVACK of Ldn. B/S of 64½*ac* in Piedmont on Kittocton Creek adj Patterson WRIGHT. Wit: Wm. H. HARDING, Sanford RAMEY, Jonathan CUNARD, Patson WRIGHT.

Bk:Pg: 2C:304   Date: 4/7/1803   RcCt: 9 May 1803
Ferdinando FAIRFAX of Shannon Hill, JeffVa to Sandford RAMEY of Ldn. B/S of 300*ac* in Piedmont on Kittocton Creek on road from Wtfd to Thompson's Mill, adj Anthony WRIGHT, Edward CONNER. Wit: Wm. H. HARDING, Peteson WRIGHT, Jonathan CUNARD, Patrick McGAVACK.

Bk:Pg: 2C:306   Date: 4/7/1803   RcCt: 9 May 1803
Ferdinando FAIRFAX of Shannon Hill, JeffVa and William B. PAGE of Walsingham Co. VA (holds the mortgage) to Henry NEUSCHWANGER of Ldn. B/S of 122½*ac* on Piney Run in Shannondale, adj James RUSSELL & Beltz's Mill. Wit: Wm. H. HARDING, Levi HOLE, Thomas LESLIE, Sanford RAMEY, Jonathan CUNARD.

Bk:Pg: 2C:309   Date: 7/6/1802   RcCt: 9 May 1803
Theophilus HAINS of AlexVa to Peter MILLER of Ldn. B/S of 148*ac* at foot of Short Hill, adj Abel JANNEY. Wit: John WILD, Matthew SMITH, Hugh SMITH.

Bk:Pg: 2C:313   Date: 5/9/1803   RcCt: 9 May 1803
Stephen REED (Exor of Jonathan REED dec'd) of Ldn to Thomas MARKS of Ldn. B/S of 2*ac*. Wit: John McGEATH, Timothy TAYLOR, Price JACOBS.

Bk:Pg: 2C:315   Date: __ 1803   RcCt: 9 May 1803
James GRADY of Ldn to Peter ROMINE of Ldn. Release of mortgage on 140*ac* adj Thomas A. HEREFORD, Samuel TORBERT, James DILLON, Spencer PEW. Wit: Philip THOMAS, Benja. JENKINS, Wm. JENKINS.

Bk:Pg: 2C:317   Date: 3/14/1803   RcCt: 9 May 1803
Anthony CUNARD & wife Mary of Ldn to Asa MOORE of Wtfd. B/S of
9*ac,* adj William PAXSON, Patterson WRIGHT. Wit: James MOORE, Jos.
TALBOTT, Thomas PHILLIPS.

Bk:Pg: 2C:319   Date: 4/8/1803   RcCt: 9 May 1803
Richard Bland LEE & wife Elizabeth of Ffx to Benjamin STEER of Ldn.
B/S of 153½*ac,* adj John HOUGH. Wit: John NICKLIN, Samuel EVANS,
John HOLLINGSWORTH, Francis ADAMS, John KEENE.

Bk:Pg: 2C:322   Date: 6/14/1802   RcCt: 9 May 1803
Peter ROMINE to Benjamin JENKINS and William JENKINS. B/S of
140*ac* adj Spencer PEW, James DILLON. Wit: Stacy TAYLOR, Timothy
TAYLOR, Robt. HAMILTON.

Bk:Pg: 2C:324   Date: 2/12/1803   RcCt: 9 May 1903
Mahlon HOUGH & wife Mary of Ldn to Thomas HOUGH of Ldn. B/S of lot
nr Gap of the Short Hill. Wit: Edward CUNARD Sr., Edward CUNARD Jr,
John B. STEPHENS, John WOLFCALE.

Bk:Pg: 2C:326   Date: 2/12/1803   RcCt: 9 May 1803
Richard MATHEWS & wife Elizabeth of FredVa to Thomas HOUGH of
Ldn. B/S of 2¾*ac* nr Gap of Short Hill on S side of great road, adj Edward
CUNARD, Thomas PURSSELL. Wit: James McILHANEY, Edward
CUNARD Jr, Edward CUNARD Sr, John B. STEPHENS, John
WOLFCALE, Stacy TAYLOR.

Bk:Pg: 2C:329   Date: 5/4/1803   RcCt: 4 May 1803
Mahlon HOUGH & wife Mary to Thomas HOUSE. CoE for sale of 45
perches. Wit: James McILHANEY, Stacy TAYLOR.

Bk:Pg: 2C:330   Date: 2/12/1803   RcCt: 9 May 1803
Mahlon HOUGH & wife Polly of Ldn [signed as Mary] to John B.
STEPHENS of Ldn. B/S of 45 perches nr Gap of Short Hill on S side of
turnpike road, adj Richard COPELAND. Wit: Edward CUNARD Sr.,
Edward CUNARD Jr, Thos. HOUGH, John WOLFCALE, James
McILHANEY, Stacy TAYLOR.

Bk:Pg: 2C:333   Date: 6/12/1798   RcCt: 9 May 1903
Leven POWELL & wife Sarah of Ldn to James M. GARNETT & John T.
BROOKE of Honbl. James MERCER dec'd. Release for land lying part in
Fqr & Ldn commonly called Allen Reed's farm. Wit: Thos. JONES,
Charles BINNS Jr, Asa BACON, Tho. SWANN, A. HARRISON.

Bk:Pg: 2C:335   Date: 2/12/1803   RcCt: 9 May 1803
Richard MATHEWS & wife Elizabeth of FrdkVa to John WOLFCALE of
Ldn. B/S of 1¼*ac* contegious with Gap of the Short Hill, adj Thomas
HOUGH, Richard MATHEWS. Wit: James McILHANEY, Thos. HOUGH,
Edward CUNARD Jr, Edward CUNARD Sr, John B. STEPHENS, Stacy
TAYLOR.

Bk:Pg: 2C:339   Date: 5/9/1803   RcCt: 9 May 1803
Benjamin MEADE & wife Ann of Ldn to Henry BROWN of Ldn. B/S of
24*ac* on NW fork of Goose Creek, adj William SUDDITH.

Bk:Pg: 2C:341   Date: 5/9/1803   RcCt: 9 May 1803
Mahlon JANNEY of Ldn to Edward DORSEY of Wtfd. B/S of Lot #13 in new addition of Wtfd, adj Isaac HOUGH, James MOOR.

Bk:Pg: 2C:342   Date: 5/9/1803   RcCt: 9 May 1803
Mahlon JANNEY of Ldn to William PAXSON of Ldn. B/S of Lots #16 & #17 in new addition to Wtfd, adj Isaac HOUGH.

Bk:Pg: 2C:344   Date: 4/2/1803   RcCt: 9 May 1803
Reuben SETTLE & wife Susanna to son Reuben SETTLE Jr. A/L of 50*ac* (part of L/L on Reuben SETTLE Jr, James LYNE Jr, Thadius DULING). Wit: Israel JANNEY, Ariss BUCKNER, Thomas ODEN.

Bk:Pg: 2C:345   Date: 4/2/1803   RcCt: 9 May 1803
Reuben SETTLE & wife Susanna to son Henry SETTLE. B/S of 50*ac*. Wit: Israel LACEY, Arris BUCKNER, Thomas ODEN.

Bk:Pg: 2C:347   Date: 5/9/1803   RcCt: 9 May 1803
Jacob GREGG & wife Mary of Ldn to Robert McHULLAH of Ldn. B/S of 104*ac*. Wit: Bernard TAYLOR, John SINCLAIR, Isaac NICHOLS.

Bk:Pg: 2C:349   Date: 3/12/1803   RcCt: 9 May 1803
John HEAD & wife Elizabeth of Ldn to Benjamin MEREDITH of Ldn. B/S of 6*ac* adj Thomas GREGG, Timothy HOWELL. Wit: Mahlon HOWELL, Richard ENERS, Henry HOWELL, Leven POWELL, Stacy TAYLOR.

Bk:Pg: 2C:353   Date: 7/29/1796   RcCt: 8 Jul 1799 and 9 May 1803
Jonah THOMPSON, Samuel THOMPSON and William HOUGH (Exors of Israel THOMPSON dec'd) of Ldn to Theopilus HARRIS of AlexVa, Ffx. B/S of 148*ac*, part of Thompson's Cool Spring Plantation at the foot of Short Hill. Wit: Leven POWELL, W. ELLZEY, Thos. Lud LEE.

Bk:Pg: 2C:357   Date: 4/18/1796   RcCt: 9 May 1796 and 9 May 1803
Isaac THOMPSON of Ldn to Andrew THOMPSON of Ldn. LS of 75*ac*. Wit: John TUCKER, Isaac SHUNK, John TUCKER.

Bk:Pg: 2C:358   Date: 11/11/1802   RcCt: 9 May 1803
Ferdinando FAIRFAX of Shannon Hill, JeffVa to Richard Bland LEE of Sully, Ffx. B/S of 2325*ac* in Piedmont, on S fork of Kittocton creek, adj Israel THOMPSON, main road to Lsbg, Patrick McGORLICK, Charles LAWSON, John HOUGH, Isaac SEDDLE, John MARTIN, John HAMILTON, George SHAFFER, Samuel EVANS. Wit: Theodorick LEE, Wm. H. HARDING, Pateson WRIGHT, Presley CORDELL, David EVELANE, Wm. B. HARRISON, Levi HOLE.

Bk:Pg: 2C:362   Date: 4/7/1803   RcCt: 9 May 1803
Ferdinando FAIRFAX of Shannon Hill, JeffVa to John CUMMINGS of Ldn. B/S of 65*ac* in Shannondale. Wit: Wm. H. HARDING, Sanford RAMEY, Thos. LESLIE, Levi HOLE.

Bk:Pg: 2C:364   Date: 4/7/1803   RcCt: 9 May 1803
Ferdinando FAIRFAX of Shannon Hill, JeffVa and William B. PAGE of Washington Co. VA to John CONROD of Ldn. B/S of 224*ac* on W side of Short Hill in Shannondale adj Peter DOUPERMAN. Wit: Wm. H.

HARDING, Levi HOLE, Thos. LESLIE, Sanford RAMEY, Jonathan CUNARD.

Bk:Pg: 2C:366   Date: 12/31/1802   RcCt: 9 May 1803
Ferdinando FAIRFAX & wife Elizabeth Blair of Shannon Hill, JeffVa to Philip LIGHTFOOT of Culpeper Co. VA. Secure debt due of FAIRFAX to John JAMESON assignee of John PAGE of Rosewell for 400ac purchased from James HAMILTON. Wit: Geo. HITE, Cyrus SANDERS, John D. ORR, Wm. Byrd PAGE.

Bk:Pg: 2C:368   Date: 3/31/1803   RcCt: 9 May 1803
Philip LIGHTFOOT of Culpeper Co. VA to Richard Y. WIGGENTON of Culpeper Co. VA. B/S of 400ac nr Lsbg.

Bk:Pg: 2C:371   Date: 4/19/1803   RcCt: 9 May 1803
Richard Y. WIGGINTON & wife Mary of Culpeper Co. VA to John JAMESON of Culpeper Co. VA. B/S of 400ac.

Bk:Pg: 2C:374   Date: 5/9/1803   RcCt: 9 May 1803
Charles DRISH & wife Susanna of Ldn to Thomas SANDERS (s/o Henry) of Ldn. B/S of ¼ac - eastern most half of Lot #42 on N side of Cornwall St in Lsbg, adj William TAYLOR, Frederick DRISH.

Bk:Pg: 2C:375   Date: 5/9/1803   RcCt: 9 May 1803
Simon SHOEMAKER of Ldn to Peter COMPHER of Ldn. LS of land on Broad Run.

Bk:Pg: 2C:378   Date: 1/16/1803   RcCt: 9 May 1803
Ferdinando FAIRFAX of Shannon Hill, JeffVa to George MULL of Ldn. B/S of 157ac in Piedmont adj Michael COOPER, Reuben HIXON, George MULL, Jacob SHUMAKER. Wit: Wm. H. HARDING, Laurence MINK, Fredk. BOGER.

Bk:Pg: 2C:380   Date: 4/7/1803   RcCt: 9 May 1803
Ferdinando FAIRFAX of Shannon Hill, JeffVa to Lawrence MINK of Ldn. B/S of 50ac in Shannondale on SE side of Short Hill (#24 on plat). Wit: Wm. H. HARDING, Thos. LESLEY, John CONARD, Levi HOLE.

Bk:Pg: 2C:381   Date: 3/15/1803   RcCt: 9 May 1803
Ferdinando FAIRFAX of Berkley Co. VA to John STATLER of Ldn. B/S of 179ac in Piedmont adj James McILHANEY, Charles CRUMMER, Arch'd MORRISON. Wit: James MILSON, Theodorick LEE, Wm. H. HARDING, Richard COLEMAN, Sn. BLINCOE, Fleet SMITH, Jos. LEWIS Jr, Sanford RAMEY, James NIXON.

Bk:Pg: 2C:383   Date: 3/15/1802   RcCt: 9 May 1803
Ferdinando FAIRFAX of Shannon Hill, JeffVa to John STATLER of Ldn. B/S of 75ac, #16 on plat of Short Hill, SE side, in Shannondale. Wit: Jos. LEWIS Jr, Wm. H. HARDING, James NIXON, Sanford RAMEY.

Bk:Pg: 2C:384   Date: 3/15/1803   RcCt: 9 May 1803
Ferdinando FAIRFAX of Shannon Hill, JeffVa to James NIXON of Ldn. B/S of 58ac, Lot #10 on Short Hill plat, SE side, in Shannondale. Wit: Jos. LEWIS Jr, Sanford RAMEY, Wm. H. HARDING, ?

Bk:Pg: 2C:386   Date: 4/7/1803   RcCt: 9 May 1803
Ferdinando FAIRFAX of Shannon Hill, JeffVa to Peter RIDENBAUGH of Ldn. B/S of 88*ac* in Piedmont adj David MULL, Geo. SHULTZ, Michael EVERHARD. Wit: Wm. H. HARDING, Thos. LESLIE, Levi HOLE.

Bk:Pg: 2C:388   Date: 4/7/1803   RcCt: 9 May 1803
Ferdinando FAIRFAX of Shannon Hill, JeffVa to Jacob KEYLOR of Ldn. B/S of 4*ac* on SE side of Short Hill in Piedmont adj Michael EVERHARD. Wit: Wm. H. HARDING, Thos. LESLIE, John CONARD, Levi HOLE.

Bk:Pg: 2C:389   Date: 4/7/1803   RcCt: 9 May 1803
Ferdinando FAIRFAX of Shannon Hill, JeffVa to Michael EVERHARD of Ldn. B/S of 21*ac* on SE side of Short Hill in Piedmont adj Jacob KEYLOR, Peter RIDENBAUGH. Wit: Wm. H. HARDING, Thos. LESLIE, John CONARD, Levi HOLE.

Bk:Pg: 2C:391   Date: 1/13/1803   RcCt: 9 May 1803
Ferdinando FAIRFAX of JeffVa to Abiel JENNERS of Ldn. B/S of 637*ac*, Lot #2 & #3 on plat made by Wm. H. HARDING, part of Page's Lot, adj Thomas MARSHALL, William HORSEMAN. Wit: Fleet SMITH, Joseph BLINCOE, Wm. H. HARDING.

Bk:Pg: 2C:392   Date: 1/22/1802   RcCt: 9 May 1803
George EMREY & wife Margaret of Ross Co., Territory of the US, NW of River Ohio to Joseph SMITH of Ldn. PoA for sale of Lot #12 in Lsbg.

Bk:Pg: 2C:394   Date: 5/10/1803   RcCt: 9 May 1803
George EMREY & wife Margaret of Ross Co., OH by attorney Joseph SMITH of Lsbg to Peter BOSS of Lsbg. B/S of Lot #12 in Lsbg. Wit: John LITTLEJOHN, Ths. EDWARDS, Isaac HARRIS.

Bk:Pg: 2C:396   Date: 5/10/1803   RcCt: 9 May 1803
Peter BOSS of Lsbg to Samuel MURREY, Isaac HARRISON and John LITTLEJOHN of Ldn. Bond using mortgage on above land.

Bk:Pg: 2C:397   Date: 5/14/1803   RcCt: 13 Jun 1803
Benjamin SHREVE to heirs of Alexander McINTYRE dec'd. Writ and inquisition - SHREVE to erect a mill on Tuscarora, damages to heirs by overflow of water on them, awarded $30 by committee - John LITTLEJOHN, Geo. ROWAN, Charles DRISH, John DREAN, Peter CARR, Thomas CIMMINGS, John WILDMAN, William HAWLING, Jonas POTTS, Presley CORDELL, John DRISH, Wm. ROBERTS, Benja. SANDERS.

Bk:Pg: 2C:399   Date: 5/10/1803   RcCt: 10 May 1803
John ELLIOTT and Rebeckah ELLIOTT (Admr of John ELLIOTT dec'd) to John ELLIOTT & wife Esther. Aaron SANDER, William DULIN and/or Isaac STEERS shall determine allowance as payment for bond entered into by John ELLIOTT dec'd and David ELLIOTT.

Bk:Pg: 2C:400   Date: 5/13/1803   RcCt: 13 Jun 1803
Dr. Wilson Cary SELDON. Inquisiton - for damages caused by SELDON building Grist Mill dam on Tuscarora, panel - Jno. LITTLEJOHN, William MEANS, Joseph BENTLEY, Barton LUCAS, Robert WARD, Thomas N.

BINNS, David WHITE, Giles TILLETT, James GARNER, Mat
WETHERBY, Thomas MOSS, John DRISH.

Bk:Pg: 2C:402   Date: 10/13/1802   RcCt: 13 Jun 1803
Abel GARRETT & wife Nancy of Pittsyvania Co. VA to John EAR of Ldn.
B/S of 105ac. Wit: Cornelius WINKOOP, William WILKINSON, David
HIRST, Thomas GREGG, Wm. HARRISON, Philip JENKINS.

Bk:Pg: 2C:404   Date: 11/19/1792   RcCt: 13 Jun 1803
Thomas BISSETT in Anne Arundle Co. DoE for Negro man Dublin. Wit:
Chas. A. WARFIELD.

Bk:Pg: 2C:405   Date: 3/14/1803   RcCt: 11 Jul 1803
William WILSON of Alexandria in DC. to John RAMSAY of Alexandria in
DC: B/S of 440ac & 31⁴ac. Wit: Colin AULD.

Bk:Pg: 2C:407   Date: 5/10/1802   RcCt: 10 May 1802
John SPENCER & wife Phebe of Ldn to Benjamin JAMES of Ldn. B/S of
105ac, adj Benjamin JAMES, Stephen ROZELL, Richard McGRAW.

Bk:Pg: 2C:410   Date: 5/10/1803   RcCt: 11 Jul 1803
Jacob VANREED & wife Elizabeth of Berks Co. PA to William DULIN of
Ldn. B/S of 202½ac on Clerks Run adj Thomas NOLAND, Charles BELL,
Jacob WARREN. Wit: John SNELL, Henry BETZ.

Bk:Pg: 2C:413   Date: 3/1/1803   RcCt: 11 Jul 1803
Zepheniah LEGG of Ldn to Israel LACEY of Ldn. BoS for Negro woman
(slave for life) Henney, abt 17y old and child at her breast abt 4m named
James, and farm and household items. Wit: Gust'a. A. MORAN, Thos.
BEVERIDGE.

Bk:Pg: 2C:414   Date: 4/14/1803   RcCt: 11 Jul 1803
Mary WEST of Ldn. DoE for mulatto woman Suckey GOINGS on 23 Mar
1809 and her son Leonard GOINGS on 6 Oct 1816. Wit: William
HARNED, Philip HOUSER.

Bk:Pg: 2C:414   Date: 4/9/1803   RcCt: 11 Jul 1803
John BOGUE of Ldn (for benefit of Judith, Robert, Maria, John Jr &
Francis BOGUE Jr and other children he might have by wife Frances) to
Joseph CARR living nr Asley's Gap in the Blue Ridge and John
LITTLEJOHN. B/S of 19ac Bogues Farm below Goose Creek now
occupied by BOGUE purchased from Francis HEREMAN now Mrs.
Francis LITTLETON; and Negro Dick abt 19y old and farm items. Wit:
Lewis GRIGSBY, John ROLLISON.

Bk:Pg: 2C:418   Date: 6/18/1803   RcCt: 11 Jul 1803
James CAVAN Jr. (Admr of Patrick CAVAN dec'd) of Lsbg to Thomas N.
BINNS of Ldn. LS of 5ac adj John LITTLEJOHN. Wit: Joseph SMITH,
Jno. MATHIAS, Samuel HOUGH, John H. CANBY.

Bk:Pg: 2C:421   Date: 6/2/1802   RcCt: 11 Jul 1803
Joseph LEWIS Jr. of Ldn to Joseph TIDBALL of Winchester. Mortgage on
203ac called Clifford Mills conveyed to LEWIS by Benjamin MYERS. Wit:

Adam DOUGLASS, Wm. CHRISTIE, S. McNEIL, Richard CHURCHILL, Lewis BECKWITH.

Bk:Pg: 2C:424   Date: 4/11/1803   RcCt: 11 Jul 1803
Francis TITUS & wife Jane to Abraham SKILLMAN. Mortgage on 229*ac* (includes plat). Wit: John LITTLEJOHN, Thos. SIM, G. W. BLINCOE, Wm. REID, Isaac HOOK, Ambrose D. CRETES, Henson SIMPSON.

Bk:Pg: 2C:429   Date: 12/10/1800   RcCt: 13 Jul 1801 and 11 Jul 1803
Reuben SETTLE & wife Susannah of Ldn to John ASHFORD of Ldn. B/S of ½*ac* on turnpike road leading through Mdbg and Centreville to AlexVa. Wit: Henry SETTLE, Reuben SETTLE Jr, Daniel SETTLE.

Bk:Pg: 2C:430   Date: 5/13/1803   RcCt: 11 Jul 1803
Daniel LOSH & wife Elizabeth of Lsbg to Francis TRIPLETT of Lsbg. B/S of ½ of Lot #13 in Lsbg. Wit: Sn. BLINCOE, Wm. WOODY, George HAMMAT.

Bk:Pg: 2C:433   Date: 12/24/1802   RcCt: 11 Jul 1803
Rhoda EVANS of Ldn (Admr & wd/o John BOYD dec'd, died intestate) and George ROSE & wife Jane (d/o John BOYD) to Ludwell LEE of Ldn. B/S of 300*ac*. Wit: John LYONS, Wm. COLEMAN, Wm. W. WILLIAMS, Jno. ROSE, Presley SANDERS, James ROSE.

Bk:Pg: 2C:434   Date: 5/16/1803   RcCt: 11 Jul 1803
John HAMILTON. Inquisition - writ of 15 Oct 1803 on lands of John HAMILTON for proposed Water Grist Mill, possible overflow on John COMPHER. Jury - Timothy HIXON, David GOODEN, William GOODEN, Jacob BAKER, Asa HARRIS, Enas WILLIAMS, Thomas HIRST, Jacob SANDS, Eligah MYERS, Thomas PHILIPS, John SCHOOLEY, William GREGG.

Bk:Pg: 2C:436   Date: 7/11/1803   RcCt: 11 Jul 1803
James McNAB, William FIELDS, Archibald McVICKER & John VERNON. Bond on McNAB as Constable of Ldn.

Bk:Pg: 2C:436   Date: 7/11/1803   RcCt: 11 Jul 1803
David GOODEN, Benjamin SHREVE and Murtho SULLIVAN. Bond on GOODEN as Constable of Ldn.

Bk:Pg: 2C:437   Date: 7/11/1803   RcCt: 11 Jul 1803
Richard CLARK, John HANDY, Benjamin GRASON, Thomas A. HEREFORD and William BRONAUGH. Bond on CLARK as Constable of Ldn.

Bk:Pg: 2C:437   Date: 7/11/1803   RcCt: 11 Jul 1803
James TUCKER, John CUMMINGS and Nicholas TUCKER. Bond on TUCKER as Constable of Ldn.

Bk:Pg: 2C:437 [should be 438]   Date: 7/11/1803   RcCt: 11 Jul 1803
Thomas KEEN, Charles LEWIS and Israel LACEY. Bond on KEEN as Constable of Ldn.

Bk:Pg: 2C:437 [should be 438]   Date: 7/11/1803   RcCt: 11 Jul 1803
George HAMMAT and Thomas SIM. Bond on HAMMAT as Constable of Ldn.

Bk:Pg: 2C:438   Date: 2/20/1802   RcCt: 13 Sep 1802 and 11 Jul 1803
Abraham HAWLEY and wife Mary (d/o Thomas ODEN) of Fluvannah Co. VA to Aris BUCKNER of Ldn. B/S of 41ac in CamP. Wit: Geo. HUTCHISON, Jeremiah HUTCHISON, John DAVIS, Thomas ODEN, Sn. BLINCOE, J. PAYNE, A. BARNERD.

Bk:Pg: 2C:441   Date: 6/13/1803   RcCt: 11 Jul 1803
James FRAZIER, John CRAIN and Geo. BERKLEY. Bond on FRAZIER as Constable of Ldn. Wit: W. REID.

Bk:Pg: 2C:441   Date: 6/13/1803   RcCt: 11 Jul 1803
John DAVIS, Thomas SWANN and Fleet SMITH. Bond on DAVIS as Constable of Ldn.

Bk:Pg: 2C:442   Date: 6/13/1803   RcCt: 11 Jul 1803
Andrew SMARR, Thomas C. WELLS, Joseph MOORE and John WHITE. Bond on SMARR as Constable of Ldn. Wit: Sn. BLINCOE.

Bk:Pg: 2C:442   Date: 6/13/1803   RcCt: 11 Jul 1803
Thomas E. MINOR, Charles JENNINGS and William WHALEY. Bond on MINOR as Constable of Ldn. Wit: W. REID.

Bk:Pg: 2C:443   Date: 6/1/1803   RcCt: 13 Jun 1803
David GOODEN, Asa HARRIS and Benjamin SHREVE. Bond on GOODEN as Constable of Ldn.

Bk:Pg: 2C:443   Date: 8/12/1803   RcCt: 12 Jun 1803
Peter FERNANDIS, Abraham SKILLMAN and Jacob GOOLEY. Bond on FERNANDIS as Constable of Ldn. Wit: W. Reid.

Bk:Pg: 2C:444   Date: 8/12/1803   RcCt: 12 Aug 1803
Elisha TIMMS, George SHIVELY and John WHITE. Bond on TIMMS as Constable of Ldn. Wit: Walker REID.

Bk:Pg: 2C:445   Date: 12/12/1802   RcCt: 12 Aug 1803
Burr POWELL to Martin BRENT. Receipt - deed of trust paid of Thomas BRENT to Burr POWELL. Wit: Henry BRAWNER.

Bk:Pg: 2C:445   Date: 1/10/1803   RcCt: 9 Aug 1803
Nathaniel CRAWFORD & wife Sarah of PrG and Bushrod WASHINGTON & wife Anne to Robert McCORMACK of Ldn. B/S of 100ac adj Thomas GREGG, John LEMING, Isaac COGILL. Wit: Samuel HOUGH, Samuel DUNKIN, A. HARRISON, W. ELLZEY, Samuel HEPBURN, William W. BERRY.

Bk:Pg: 2C:448   Date: 1/10/1803   RcCt: 9 Aug 1803
Nathaniel CRAWFORD & wife Sarah of PrG to Isaac BROWN of Ldn. B/S of 150ac adj Robert SMITH, Samuel SMITH, Dawson BROWN, Ben OVERFIELD. Wit: W. ELLZEY, William VICKERS, Samuel DUNKIN, Jacob SILCOTT, Saml. HEPBURN, William W. BERRY.

Bk:Pg: 2C:452   Date: 9/10/1801   RcCt: 14 Sep 1801 and 9 Aug 1803
Mary WEST of Ldn to Jason GOINGS. DoE - £28 from GOINGS to free woman slave Ann and her children James, Harriet, Sophia, Joel, Wily, George & Fanny as well as Negroes Hannah and Fanny from the time WEST dies. Wit: Amos THOMPSON, Wm. HARNED, ?

Bk:Pg: 2C:453   Date: 8/12/1803   RcCt: 12 Sep 1803
Abner HUMPHREY & wife Mary of Ldn to Jane HUMPHREY of Ldn. B/S of 60*ac* adj Richard THATCHER, John GREGG. Wit: Hugh DOUGLAS, Wm. BRONAUGH, Jere. W. BRONAUGH, Ben. GRAYSON.

Bk:Pg: 2C:456   Date: __ May 1790   RcCt: 8 Jun 1795, 12 Sep 1803
Townshend DADE of King George Co. VA to Patrick CAVAN of Ldn. B/S of 2½*ac* adj Lsbg on Market St. Wit: John RAMSAY, Henry McCABE, John LITTLEJOHN.

Bk:Pg: 2C:457   Date: 4/18/1803   RcCt: 12 Sep 1803
William CHILTON & wife Sarah of Lsbg to William HOLMES of Lsbg. B/S of 135¾*ac* nr Lsbg on Carolina Rd. Wit: Sn. BLINCOE, G. W. BLINCOE, Charles BINNS, Samuel MURRY, Thomas SIMM.

Bk:Pg: 2C:460   Date: 3/21/1803   RcCt: 12 Sep 1803
Isaac VANDEVENTER Sr. & wife Elizabeth of Ldn to son Isaac VANDEVENTER of Ldn. B/S of 100*ac* on branch of Catoctin adj John DODD. Wit: John HAMILTON, Joseph DANIEL, William DODD, Andrew HOSPITAL.

Bk:Pg: 2C:462   Date: 4/9/1803   RcCt: 12 Sep 1803
Spencer PUGH of Ldn to Mary HOPEWELL of Ldn. If pending marriage takes place and Mary outlives Spencer, she to release all claim to dower for £50 child's portion of estate. Wit: William POWELL, Jesse BATES, Christian HOPE.

Bk:Pg: 2C:463   Date: 2/12/1803   RcCt: 12 Sep 1803
Francis HAGUE & wife Mary of Lsbg to Benjamin H. CANBY of Ldn. B/S of land nr Lsbg on W side of Carolina Road being 1/2 of HAGUE's lot where Joseph COOMS now lives. Wit: John LITTLEJOHN, Joseph SMITH, John MATTHIAS.

Bk:Pg: 2C:465   Date: 5/2/1803   RcCt: 12 Sep 1803
Jesse JANNEY of Ldn to Rufus UPDIKE of Ldn. B/S of 23¼*ac,* adj George LEWIS, John HOUGH, Thomas DENT. Wit: John WEST, Jonathan JAMES, James TUCKER, John PEAKOCK, Giles CRAVAN.

Bk:Pg: 2C:467   Date: 9/9/1803   RcCt: 12 Sep 1803
Mahlon JANNEY of Ldn to Asa MOORE of Ldn. B/S of 7*ac* on 2 lots in Wtfd, adj Mahlon JANNY, William HOUGH, Asa MOORE, James MOORE, Francis HAGUE. Wit: John WILLIAMS, Richard GRIFFETH, Abijah TAYLOR, Hiram HAGUE.

Bk:Pg: 2C:469   Date: 5/9/1803   RcCt: 12 Sep 1803
Thomas LANG Jr. of New York City to Theodoerick LEE of Winchester: PoA for sale of 640*ac* nr Mdbg currently occupied by George IDEN and

others. Wit: John SHACKELFORD, Daniel F. STROTHER, Benj. SHACKELFORD.

Bk:Pg: 2C:470   Date: 4/8/1803   RcCt: 12 Sep 1803
James KINCHELOW & wife Elizabeth to Richard VANPELT of Ldn. B/S of 119ac, adj John NORTON. Wit: Burr POWELL, Washington COCKE, Martin BRENT, Leven POWELL.

Bk:Pg: 2D:001   Date: 9/10/1803   RcCt: 12 Sep 1803
Joseph LEWIS Jr. of Ldn to Jacob VERTZ of Ldn. B/S of 103½ac in Piedmont now under L/L to VERTS, adj David AXLINE, Conrad ROLLER. Wit: Samuel PAIRPOINT.

Bk:Pg: 2D:002   Date: 9/10/1803   RcCt: 12 Sep 1803
Joseph LEWIS Jr. of Ldn to Joseph SMITH of Ldn. B/S of 123¾ac in Piedmont which SMITH L/L adj John SLACK, Philip EVERHART, Jacob AXLINE, John WITTERMAN, Peter VERTZ, Henry FRYE. Wit: Samuel PAIRPOINT.

Bk:Pg: 2D:004   Date: 9/10/1803   RcCt: 12 Sep 1803
Joseph LEWIS Jr. of Ldn to Joseph SMITH of Ldn. Mortgage for 153¾ac. Wit: Samuel PAIRPOINT.

Bk:Pg: 2D:005   Date: 9/12/1803   RcCt: 12 Sep 1803
Joseph LEWIS Jr. of Ldn to Jacob WALTMAN of Ldn. B/S of 3½ac in Piedmont.

Bk:Pg: 2D:007   Date: 9/10/1803   RcCt: 12 Sep 1803
Joseph LEWIS Jr of Ldn to John WITTERMAN of Ldn. B/S of 100ac in Piedmont which WITTERMAN L/L adj Peter VERTS, Joseph SMITH, Cristian RUSE. Wit: Samuel PAIRPOINT.

Bk:Pg: 2D:008   Date: 9/10/1803   RcCt: 12 Sep 1803
Joseph LEWIS Jr. to John WITTERMAN. Mortgage for above land. Wit: Samuel PAIRPOINT.

Bk:Pg: 2D:010   Date: 9/12/1803   RcCt: 12 Sep 1803
Joseph LEWIS Jr. of Ldn to Michael BOGER of Ldn. B/S of 165¾ac in Piedmont, adj Christian RUSE, George WINSELL, Church lot.

Bk:Pg: 2D:011   Date: 9/12/1803   RcCt: 12 Sep 1803
Joseph LEWIS Jr. of Ldn to Peter HICKMAN of Ldn. B/S of 90ac in Piedmont adj Lawrence MINK, Farling BALL. Wit: Simon SHOEMAKER.

Bk:Pg: 2D:013   Date: 9/10/1803   RcCt: 12 Sep 1803
Joseph LEWIS Jr. of Ldn to George COOPER of Ldn. B/S of 128¾ac in Piedmont where COOPER has L/L adj John SLACK, Daniel HOUSHOLDER, William BAKER, John JACKSON, Jacob EMRY. Wit: Samuel PAIRPOINT.

Bk:Pg: 2D:014   Date: 9/10/1803   RcCt: 12 Sep 1803
Joseph LEWIS Jr to George COOPER. Mortgage for above land. Wit: Samuel PAIRPOINT.

Bk:Pg: 2D:016   Date: 9/10/1803   RcCt: 12 Sep 1803
Joseph LEWIS Jr. of Ldn to George SHOEMAKER Jr. of Ldn. B/S of
154½ac in Piedmont adj George MULL, Jeremiah PURDUM, William
GEE, Broad run. Wit: Samuel PAIRPOINT.

Bk:Pg: 2D:017   Date: 9/10/1803   RcCt: 12 Sep 1803
Joseph LEWIS Jr. to George SHOEMAKER. Mortgage for above land.
Wit: Samuel PAIRPOINT.

Bk:Pg: 2D:019   Date: 9/9/1803   RcCt: [12 Sep 1803?]
Joseph LEWIS Jr. of Ldn to David AXLINE of Ldn. B/S of 129¼ac in
Piedmont where AXLINE has L/L adj Jacob VERTZ, John AXLINE, John
JACKSON, Michael MILLER. Wit: Samuel PAIRPOINT.

Bk:Pg: 2D:021   Date: 9/9/1803   RcCt: 12 Sep 1803
Joseph LEWIS Jr. to David AXLINE. Mortgage on above land. Wit:
Samuel PAIRPOINT.

Bk:Pg: 2D:022   Date: 9/10/1803   RcCt: 12 Sep 1803
Joseph LEWIS Jr. of Ldn to Laurence MINK of Ldn. B/S of 125ac in
Piedmont where MINK has L/L. Wit: Samuel PAIRPOINT.

Bk:Pg: 2D:024   Date: 9/10/1803   RcCt: 12 Sep 1803
Joseph LEWIS Jr. to Laurence MINK. Mortgage on above land. Wit:
Samuel PAIRPOINT.

Bk:Pg: 2D:025   Date: 9/2/1803   RcCt: 12 Sep 1803
Hugh HOLMES & wife Elizabeth of Winchester to Michael COOPER of
Piedmont manner in Ldn. B/S of 194 where COOPER has L/L adj Lydia
HOUGH, Jo. WILKINSON, Reuben HIXON, Geo. MULL. Wit: Simon
SHOEMAKER, Joseph LEWIS Jr., James McILHANY.

Bk:Pg: 2D:027   Date: 9/1/1803   RcCt: 12 Sep 1803
Hugh HOLMES of Winchester to Michael COOPER. Mortgage on above
land. Wit: Jos. LEWIS Jr., James McILHANY, Simon SHUMAKER.

Bk:Pg: 2D:029   Date: 6/28/1803   RcCt: 12 Sep 1803
William TAYLOR & wife Ann of Ldn to John EVANS of Ldn. B/S of 300ac
part of Mary's Grove (Mary FOSTER), the rest of this land to go to John
EVANS. Wit: Alexander COUPER, Joseph GARDNER, Robert
HAMILTON.

Bk:Pg: 2D:030   Date: 6/30/1803   RcCt: 12 Sep 1803
Ann TAYLOR. CoE for sale of above land. Wit: Wilson C. SELDON,
Francis H. PEYTON.

Bk:Pg: 2D:031   Date: 6/11/1803   RcCt: 12 Sep 1803
John EVANS of Ldn to William TAYLOR of Ldn. B/S of 300ac previously
mentioned. Wit: Ben H. CANBY, David EVANS, John CAVAN.

Bk:Pg: 2D:033   Date: 3/5/1803   RcCt: 12 Sep 1803
Jacob LODGE of Ldn to Robert MORRIS of Ldn. A/L of 67ac. Wit: Mahlon
ROACH, Josiah WHITE Jr., Mahlon MORRIS, Thomas STEPHENS.

Bk:Pg: 2D:035   Date: 6/30/1803   RcCt: 12 Sep 1803
Rachel SANDS of Ldn to John ROBERTSON of Ldn. Bond - SANDS sold her share of lands (of her father Isaac SANDS) nr Catocton Creek (1/7th of two tracts containing 150ac). Wit: John OXLEY, Mary WOLLARD, Aaron WOLLARD.

Bk:Pg: 2D:036   Date: 8/20/1803   RcCt: 12 Sep 1803
Jonathan BURSON & wife Rebekah of Ldn to John BURSON of Ldn. B/S of 50ac on N branch of Beaverdam adj Jonathan BURSON, Benjamin BURSON, James BURSON. Wit: Joseph BURSON, Ruth DYER, Aaron BURSON.

Bk:Pg: 2D:038   Date: 7/1/1803   RcCt: 12 Sep 1803
Ferdinando FAIRFAX of Shannon Hill, JeffVa to Jacob VIRTS of Ldn. B/S of 53¼ac lot #23 on survey and plat of SE side of mountain on Shannondale. Wit: Wm. H. HARDING, Simon SHOVER, foreign name, George SWANK.

Bk:Pg: 2D:039   Date: 8/10/1803   RcCt: 12 Sep 1803
Samuel CLAPHAM. DoE for Esther a mulatto woman aged 38y. Wit: Isaac STEER.

Bk:Pg: 2D:040   Date: 9/12/1803   RcCt: 12 Sep 1803
Samuel CLAPHAM. Manumission - frees Negro George alias George DRADEN.

Bk:Pg: 2D:040   Date: 3/21/1803   RcCt: 12 Sep 1803
Isaac VANDEVENTER Sr. of Ldn to son Isaac VANDEVENTER Jr. of Ldn. Bond for 100ac bought of George DYKE. Wit: John HAMILTON, Joseph DANIEL, William DODD.

Bk:Pg: 2D:041   Date: 12/14/1802   RcCt: 12 Sep 1803
Thomas MATTHEWS & wife Sak of Alexandria, D. C., heirs of Joseph JANNY (Charles HARPER who married Sarah JANNY one of the heirs now dec'd as natural Guardian to his children, Joseph & Sarah HARPER, Thomas IRWIN & wife Elizabeth, Samuel HOPKINS & wife Hannah, John LOYD & wife Rebekah, Susannah JANNY and Mary JANNY) to Presley SANDERS of Ldn. B/S of 55¾ac on Kittocton Mt. MATTHEWS and JANNY bought jointly in 1791, adj Clare AXLEY. Wit: Isaac LARROWE, Aaron SANDERS, Henry M. DAVIS.

Bk:Pg: 2D:045   Date: 10/6/1802   RcCt: 9 May 1803
Burr POWELL & wife Catharine of Ldn to Mahlon BALDWIN of Ldn. B/S of 90ac of Aylett's 609 acre tract, adj road from Mdbg to Colston's Mill. Wit: Jesse McVEIGH, A. GIBSON, Martin BRENT, Peter MYERS.

Bk:Pg: 2D:048   Date: 9/12/1803   RcCt: 12 Sep 1803
Joseph LEWIS Jr. of Ldn to Christian RUSE of Ldn. B/S of 185ac in Piedmont which RUSE now L/L, adj John WITTERMAN, Michael BOGER, Isaac RITCHIE.

Bk:Pg: 2D:050   Date: 9/12/1803   RcCt: 12 Sep 1803
Joseph LEWIS Jr. to Christian RUSE. Mortgage on above land.

Bk:Pg: 2D:052   Date: 9/12/1803   RcCt: 12 Sep 1803
Joseph LEWIS Jr. of Ldn to Michael EVERHEART of Ldn. B/S of 29¼ac in Piedmont now L/L by EVERHEART, adj Peter DERRY, Christian EVERHEART.

Bk:Pg: 2D:054   Date: 9/12/1803   RcCt: 12 Sep 1803
Joseph LEWIS Jr. to Michael EVERHEART. Mortgage for above land.

Bk:Pg: 2D:056   Date: 7/1/1803   RcCt: 12 Sep 1803
Ferdinando FAIRFAX of Shannon Hill, JeffVa to Conrod ROLER of Ldn. B/S of 54ac on Short Hill, #17 on survey & plat of SE side of Mountain in Shannondale, adj John STATLER. Wit: Simon SHOVER, Jacob VIRTS, George SWANK.

Bk:Pg: 2D:058   Date: 3/10/1803   RcCt: 12 Sep 1803
Ferdinando FAIRFAX of Shannon Hill, JeffVa to Hugh HOLMES of Winchester. B/S of 1015ac in Piedmont, adj John HOUGH, James HAMILTON, Michael RUSE, James NIXON, Samuel UNDERWOOD, Daniel SHOEMAKER, Margareta SANDERS, Geo MULL, Michael COOPER.

Bk:Pg: 2D:061   Date: 3/5/1803   RcCt: 12 Sep 1803
James BRADFIELD & wife Ruth of Ldn to Cornelius SHAWEN of Ldn. B/S of 227ac adj John STEER. Wit: James FITCH, Joseph BEARD, Joseph SMITH, Saml MURRAY.

Bk:Pg: 2D:064   Date: 9/12/1803   RcCt: 12 Sep 1803
George NIXON & wife Ann of Ldn to Thomas JACOBS of Ldn. B/S of part of lot on road from King St in Lsbg to Noland's Ferry, adj Daniel LOSH, Joseph GORE. Wit: Joseph BURSON, John EVANS, Philip VANSICKLER.

Bk:Pg: 2D:066   Date: 4/23/1803   RcCt: 12 Sep 1803
Conrad TRITIPAUGH & wife Mary to Cornelius SHAWEN of Ldn. B/S of 41ac on Beaverdam branch, adj land formerly Nathan BALL. Wit: Isaac LARROWE, John McNEALE, John WOLLARD, Farling BALL, Chas BENNETT.

Bk:Pg: 2D:069   Date: 4/29/1803   RcCt: 12 Sep 1803
Levy PRINCE of Ldn to Isaac GRIFFITH of Ldn. B/S of 108ac on Catocton Creek. Wit: Isaac LARROWE, Philip SOWDER, Matthias PRINCE.

Bk:Pg: 2D:071   Date: 9/6/1803   RcCt: 12 Sep 1803
Thomas COCKERILL of Ldn to Christopher SKILLMAN. BoS for Negro boy Ben about 6y old. Wit: Abraham SKILLMAN, Hezekiah ATHEY.

Bk:Pg: 2D:071   Date: 9/6/1803   RcCt: 12 Sep 1803
Samuel COCKERILL of Ffx to Christopher SKILLMAN of Ldn. BoS for Negro boy Ben about 6y old. Wit: Hezekiah ATHEY, Abraham SKILLMAN.

Bk:Pg: 2D:072   Date: 1/13/1803   RcCt: 12 Sep 1803
Ferdinando FAIRFAX of Shannon Hill, JeffVa to Nicholas HARPER of Ffx. B/S of 293ac in Ldn & Ffx, part of the Page lots, adj James COLEMAN, Alexander YOUNG, John COLEMAN. Wit: Fleet SMITH, Wm. H. HARDING, Joseph BLINCOE, Abiel JENNERS.

Bk:Pg: 2D:074   Date: 8/13/1803   RcCt: 12 Sep 1803
Ferdinando FAIRFAX of Shannon Hill, JeffVa to Thomas LESLIE of Ldn. B/S of 115ac in Piedmont, adj David GEE, Peter HICKMAN, Lawrence MINK, German Church lot. Wit: Wm. H. HARDING, Adam WOLF, George FOLAY.

Bk:Pg: 2D:076   Date: 6/14/1803   RcCt: 12 Sep 1803
William TAYLOR & wife Ann of Ldn to Thomas A. HEREFORD of Ldn. B/S of part of Lot #14 in Lsbg between Samuel MURRY and Barnet HOUGH. Wit: Wm. BRONAUGH, Robert HEREFORD, George NIXON.

Bk:Pg: 2D:077   Date: 3/22/1803   RcCt: 12 Apr 1803
Arthur ROGERS to Jesse McVEIGH. A/L - no further details. Wit: James BATTSON, James STEPHENSON, James CHAMIL, Martin BRENT, Andrew SMARR, Silas BEATY, Thos. BISCO, Wm. T. TAYLOR, Jonathan McVEIGH.

Bk:Pg: 2D:078   Date: 9/12/1803   RcCt: 12 Sep 1803
Henry Joseph FRY & wife Christian of Ldn to John SLACK of Ldn. B/S of 4ac adj Joseph SMITH.

Bk:Pg: 2D:079   Date: 8/19/1803   RcCt: 12 Sep 1803
John Alexander BINNS & wife Dewanna of Ldn to Enoch FRANCIS of Ldn. B/S of 19ac at fork of Catocton and Beaverdam Creeks. Wit: Isaac LARROWE, Cornelius SHAWEN, Samuel WARD.

Bk:Pg: 2D:082   Date: 8/19/1803   RcCt: 12 Sep 1803
Enoch FRANCIS & wife Nancy of Ldn to Cornelius SHAWEN of Ldn. B/S of 19ac at fork of Catocton and Beaverdam Creeks. Wit: Isaac LARROWE, John A. BINNS, Samuel WARD.

Bk:Pg: 2D:084   Date: 8/19/1803   RcCt: 12 Sep 1803
Enoch FRANCIS to Cornelius SHAWEN. Mortgage for above land. Wit: Isaac LARROWE, John A. BINNS, Samuel WARD.

Bk:Pg: 2D:086   Date: 8/19/1803   RcCt: 12 Sep 1803
John Alexander BINNS of Ldn to Enoch FRANCIS of Ldn. Mortgage for 127ac on Clarks Run adj John STEER, 143ac on Goose Creek adj Samuel D. HARRIMAN, also land purchased of Peter HARBOURT near Goose Creek toll bridge. Wit: Isaac LARROWE, Cornelius SHAWEN, Samuel WARD.

Bk:Pg: 2D:089   Date: 7/9/1803   RcCt: 11 Jul 1803
John DRISH & wife Nelly of Ldn to Martin CORDELL of Ldn. B/S part of 3ac nr Lsbg DRISH purchased of Henry McCABE, adj John DEALEHUNT, John MANSFIELD. Wit: John MYERS, Samuel MORAN, Thomas WILKINSON, Joseph SMITH, Francis H. PEYTON.

Bk:Pg: 2D:092   Date: 8/19/1803   RcCt: 12 Sep 1803
Cornelius SHAWEN & wife Mary of Ldn to Enoch FRANCIS of Ldn. B/S of 127*ac*, adj James STEER and James BRADFIELD. Wit: Isaac LARROWE, John A. BINNS, Samuel WARD.

Bk:Pg: 2D:094   Date: 6/4/1802   RcCt: 11 Oct 1803
John EBLIN & wife Anne of Ldn to Thomas HOUGH of Ldn. B/S of 186*ac*, land devised by father John EBLIN dec'd except 14*ac* of the E corner of the tract now the property of Robert BRADEN and the life estate of widow Eliza PARKER in 8*ac* on N corner of plantation, adj William BROWN. Wit: Stacy TAYLOR, John HAMILTON, George TAVENDER, Henry ROBERTS.

Bk:Pg: 2D:096   Date: 9/8/1803   RcCt: 12 Sep 1803
William HOUGH of Ldn. DoE for Negro woman Phebe and her 5 children Charlotty (when she arrives at 18y old), Neroe, Abraham, Amasa and George (the last four when they arrives at 21y old). Wit: James MOORE, Asa MOORE, Thomas PHILIPS, Israel H. THOMPSON.

Bk:Pg: 2D:097   Date: 7/5/1803   RcCt: 13 Sep 1803
William LITTLEJOHN of Ldn to George ROWAN of Ldn. B/S of lots #15 & #16 nr Lsbg beginning at corner of Market and Air Sts.

Bk:Pg: 2D:099   Date: 9/13/1803   RcCt: 13 Sep 1803
William LITTLEJOHN of Ldn to Thomas Neilson BINNS of Ldn. B/S of 3*ac*, lots #35, #36 & #37, beginning at corner of lot #26 on Market St to corner of Air St.

Bk:Pg: 2D:101   Date: 9/13/1803   RcCt: 13 Sep 1803
Mahlon JANNEY of Ldn to Anna BALL of Ldn. B/S of lot in Wtfd, on road from Fairfax Meeting House, adj Mahlon JANNEY.

Bk:Pg: 2D:102   Date: 6/13/1803   RcCt: 11 Jul 1803
Henry Ashly BENNETT of GrB to Stephen BALL & John BALL of Ldn. Mortgage on 109*ac* on branches of Catocton, adj Ball's Mill; this land sold by BENNETT to Farling BALL, Farling to his son Isaac, Isaac to Stephen & John. Wit: Nathan BALL, Francis TRIPLETT, Daniel TRIPLETT, R. T. HOOE.

Bk:Pg: 2D:105   Date: 9/13/1803   RcCt: 13 Sep 1803
William LITTLEJOHN of Ldn to Anthony LAMBAG of Ldn. B/S of two ½*ac* lots #30 & #39, on Market St continued from Lsbg to the Poor House lot.

Bk:Pg: 2D:107   Date: 7/11/1803   RcCt: 13 Sep 1803
Mahlon JANNEY. Writ of adquoddamnum - assess damages caused by erecting a water Grist Mill on the waters of a stream of Katocton upon his own land below William Hough's Mill; panel includes George TAVENNER, Abner WILLIAMS, Thomas PHILIPS, Reuben SCHOOLEY, Anthony WRIGHT, Paterson WRIGHT, John NICHLIN, James BALL, Asa HARRIS, John SCHOOLEY, Patrick McGAVACK & Ozzy CLEMANS.

Bk:Pg: 2D:109   Date: 9/12/1803   RcCt: 13 Sep 1803
Yowman John HENRY of Ldn to Stephen HENRY of ShelP. BoS for girl
slave named Barbary aged 17y old. Wit: Corn. SKINNER Jr., Edward
DAVIS, David CLINE.

Bk:Pg: 2D:110   Date: 1/10/1803   RcCt: [13 Sep 1803?]
Adam HOUSHOLDER Jr. Writ of adquoddamnum - to condemn as much
of the land of William BROWN in ShelP as necessary for erecting an
abutment or dam across the Katocton Creek for a water grist mill; panel
includes Peter RICHIE, Frederick STONEBURNER, Andrew SPRING,
William CHAMBERS, Simon SHOMAKER, Frederick SLATES, Michael
BOGER, William AULT, Lawrence MINK, Philip SOWDER, Jacob
TUSTIMER, George VINCEL.

Bk:Pg: 2D:113   Date: 5/14/1803   RcCt: 13 Sep 1803
Widow Esther BROWN (relict of Henry BROWN dec'd) & John BROWN
and William BROWN (Exors of Henry) to Adam HOUSHOLDER Jr.
Selling the land for abutment of dam. Wit: Isaac LARROW, Mahlon
STRUP?, ?

Bk:Pg: 2D:115   Date: __   RcCt: 13 Sep 1803
Jesse TAYLOE to William ELLIOTT of Ldn. B/S of for 2ac; in 1794 Patrick
CAVAN was indebted to Jesse TAYLOE for mortgage on lot in Lsbg but
didn't pay, TAYLOE sued, but then TAYLOE and CAVAN both died
intestate; appt commissioners sold the land to Francis TRIPLETT who
gave title to ELLIOTT. Wit: Alexander COOPER Jr., Barton LUCAS,
Daniel DOWLING, John E. COOK, Patrick H. DOUGLAS, Jas.
STEPHENSON, John HAMMERLY.

Bk:Pg: 2D:118   Date: 6/1/1802   RcCt: 14 Dec 1802
Samuel MURREY & wife Betsy of Ldn to Martin KITSMILLER of Ldn. B/S
of 2½ac lot adj Lsbg on Alexandria Road, adj James KIRK. Wit: Danl
DOWLING, John LITTLEJOHN, Joseph SMITH.

Bk:Pg: 2D:121   Date: 5/29/1793   RcCt: 13 Jan 1794
James McLEAN & wife Martha of Lsbg to George Emrey GOFF of Ldn.
B/S of ½ of lot #60 in Lsbg. Wit: Patk CAVAN, James HAMILTON, Wm.
H. HARDING.

Bk:Pg: 2D:124   Date: 5/1/1803   RcCt: 13 Sep 1803
James McLEAN of Lsbg to Charles BINNS of Lsbg. B/S of Lot #60 where
McLEAN now lives, adj John MATHIAS which belongs to Thomas
FRANCIS. Wit: Sn. BLINCOE, Benedict M. LANE, Levi ?, Martin
KITZMILLER, William CLINE.

Bk:Pg: 2D:125   Date: 4/10/1803   RcCt: 13 Sep 1803
William CAMEL of Ldn to Joseph CARR of Ldn. BoS for Negro man Cato
and Negro Anne and her children now in the possession of Mary
PORTER. Wit: Spencer GIBSON, Minor FURR?

Bk:Pg: 2D:126   Date: 4/11/1803   RcCt: 12 Sep 1803
Ferdinando FAIRFAX of Shannon Hill, JeffVa to Thomas LESLIE of Ldn.
B/S of 87*ac* in Piedmont, adj James McILHANY, Andrew THOMPSON,
William WILDMAN. Wit: John A. BINNS, C. BINNS, Wm. H. HARDING.

Bk:Pg: 2D:128   Date: 4/11/1803   RcCt: 12 Sep 1803
Ferdinando FAIRFAX of JeffVa to Thomas LESLIE of Ldn. B/S of 47*ac* lot
#22 on SE side of Short Hill in Shannondale, adj John STAGER. Wit: C.
BINNS, John A. BINNS, Wm. H. HARDING.

Bk:Pg: 2D:130   Date: 3/1/1803   RcCt: 12 Sep 1803
Nicholas GARRET of FrdkMd to Christopher HOWSER of Ldn. LS of
cleared land GARRET holds by A/L from Jonas STREET in 1801. Wit: G.
W. BLINCOE, Walker REED.

Bk:Pg: 2D:133   Date: 9/17/1803   RcCt: 10 Oct 1803
Peter WARRICK. DoE - frees his wife Nancy, daughter Betsey, daughter
Marquis, and grandchild Courtney. Wit: S. BLINCOE, Walker REID, G. W.
BLINCOE.

Bk:Pg: 2D:133   Date: ___   RcCt: 10 Oct 1803
Thomas PURSEL & wife Lidia to Edward CUNNARD Sr. CoE for sale of 2
lots. Wit: James McILHANEY, Stacy TAYLOE.

Bk:Pg: 2D:135   Date: 9/29/1803   RcCt: 10 Oct 1803
Thompson MASON (late of StafVa) dec'd Exor Abraham Barnes
Thompson MASON to John Thompson MASON of Georgetown, DC. B/S
of 302*ac* in ShelP. Wit: Chas TUTT, Armisted T. MASON, John T.
MASON Jr.

Bk:Pg: 2D:137   Date: 12/13/1802   RcCt: 10 Oct 1803
Barnett HOUGH & wife Louisa of Ldn to Daniel BROWN of FrdkVa. B/S of
80*ac* with water grist and saw mill on Goose Creek. Wit: Samuel
DONOHOE, William HOUGH, James CAVAN Jr., Jos. SMITH, Fra. H.
PEYTON.

Bk:Pg: 2D:140   Date: 12/13/1802   RcCt: 10 Oct 1803
Barnet HOUGH of Lsbg to Daniel BROWN of FrdkVa. Mortgage- for
above 80*ac*. Wit: Samuel DONOHOE, William HOUGH, James CAVAN
Jr.

Bk:Pg: 2D:142   Date: 8/1/1803   RcCt: 10 Oct 1803
Martha ORENDURF of Ldn to Jonathan BONHAM of Ldn. LS of ½*ac* at
foot of Blue Ridge. Wit: Wm. POWELL, Ezekiel YOUNG.

Bk:Pg: 2D:143   Date: 8/8/1803   RcCt: 10 Oct 1803
Merchant Joseph USHER of Baltimore by attorney Thomas SWANN to
Sampson HUTCHISON of Ldn. B/S of 62*ac*. Wit: Moses DOWDLE, Jacob
ISH, Joseph BEARD.

Bk:Pg: 2D:146   Date: 10/10/1803   RcCt: 10 Oct 1803
Jonathan LOVETT & wife Ann of FrdkVa to Daniel EACHES and Joseph
GORE of Ldn. B/S of 196*ac,* adj David LOVETT, Joseph LOVETT,

Beaverdam Creek, meeting house lot. Wit: Joshua GORE, Solomon GORE, Thomas GORE.

Bk:Pg: 2D:148   Date: 10/10/1803   RcCt: 10 Oct 1803
Joseph LEWIS Jr of Ldn to Peter DERRY of Ldn. B/S of 76½ac in Piedmont where DERRY now L/L, adj Michael EVERHART, John GEORGE, Adom MILLER.

Bk:Pg: 2D:150   Date: 10/10/1803   RcCt: 10 Oct 1803
Joseph LEWIS Jr. of Ldn to Peter COMPHER of Ldn. B/S of 147½ac in Piedmont where COMPHER now L/L adj George SHOEMAKER Jr., John MARTIN, Farling BALL, Reuben HIXON, George MULL.

Bk:Pg: 2D:152   Date: 10/10/1803   RcCt: 10 Oct 1803
Joseph LEWIS Jr. of Ldn to Christian EVERHART of Ldn. B/S of 96¾ac in Piedmont where EVERHART L/L, adj Peter DERRY, Michael EVERHART, Jacob SMITH, John GEORGE.

Bk:Pg: 2D:154   Date: 10/10/1803   RcCt: 10 Oct 1803
Joseph LEWIS Jr. of Ldn to William JAY of Ldn. B/S of 88ac in Piedmont where JAY L/L, adj George SHOEMAKER Jr., Peter VERTS, Henry Joseph FRY, Jeremiah PURDUM.

Bk:Pg: 2D:156   Date: 10/10/1803   RcCt: 10 Oct 1803
Joseph LEWIS Jr. to Peter COMPHER. Mortgage for land in Piedmont he leases.

Bk:Pg: 2D:157   Date: 10/10/1803   RcCt: 10 Oct 1803
Joseph LEWIS Jr. to William JAY of Ldn. Mortgage for land in Piedmont he L/L.

Bk:Pg: 2D:159   Date: 10/10/1803   RcCt: 10 Oct 1803
Joseph LEWIS Jr. to Christian EVERHART. Mortgage for land in Piedmont he L/L.

Bk:Pg: 2D:161   Date: 7/17/1779   RcCt: 10 Oct 1803
William HATCHER of Ldn. DoE for my mulatto child Susa when she arrives at 18y old on 8 Jan 1795. Wit: John HIRST, William HATCHER Jr., Mary HATCHER.

Bk:Pg: 2D:162   Date: 5/15/1803   RcCt: 10 Oct 1803
John STOUSEBERGER & wife Margeret of Ldn to John STONE of Ldn. B/S of 53¾ac, recorded in Liber L, folio 460. Wit: William JENKINS, George HUFF, Adam CORTEL.

Bk:Pg: 2D:164   Date: 11/1/1801   RcCt: 12 Dec 1803
Merchant Joseph USHER of BaltMd (Exor of Thomas USHER dec'd) to Thomas SWANN of Alexander VA. PoA to sell land in Ldn. Wit: Geo Washington LIGGETT.

Bk:Pg: 2D:165   Date: 10/5/1803   RcCt: 10 Oct 1803
Christopher GREENUP of KY to Josiah MOFFETT of VA. On 12 Sep 1789 in DC court GREENUP gave PoA to Charles BINNS the younger to sell 38ac in Ldn to MOFFETT, land adj Jacob BINKS now Peter

HARBOURT, Landon CARTER dec'd. Wit: John LITTLEJOHN, Christo. ROPER, Wm. WOODY.

Bk:Pg: 2D:167   Date: 7/12/1803   RcCt: 10 Oct 1803
George LEWIS & wife Violett of CamP to Ariss BUCKNER of Paris Co. VA. B/S of 142*ac* in CamP. Wit: Israel LACY, Charles LEWIS, William LEWIS.

Bk:Pg: 2D:171   Date: 4/7/1803   RcCt: 11 Oct 1803
Thomas Ludwell LEE of Ldn and Landon CARTER of RichVa (Exors for George CARTER dec'd late of StafVa) to Benjamin SHREVE of Ldn. B/S of 131¼*ac* on S side of Tuscarora in Ldn. Wit: Ignatius ELLGIN, Samuel DONOHOE, Henry JENKINS, Benjamin DOWELL, Jno. MATHIAS.

Bk:Pg: 2D:173   Date: 4/7/1803   RcCt: 11 Oct 1803
Thomas Ludwell LEE & Landon CARTER (Exors for George CARTER dec'd) to Benjamin SHREVE. Mortgage for above land. Wit: Jno. MATHIAS, Henry JENKENS, Samuel DONOHOE.

Bk:Pg: 2D:176   Date: 4/7/1803   RcCt: 11 Oct 1803
Thomas Ludwell LEE & Landon CARTER (Exors of George CARTER dec'd) to Benjamin H. CANBY. Mortgage for 174*ac* on Secolon Branch. Wit: Samuel MURREY, Ignatius ELGIN, Samuel DONOHOE, Thomas WILKINSON.

Bk:Pg: 2D:180   Date: 9/12/1789   RcCt: 10 Oct 1803
Christopher GREENUP of Danville KY to Charles BINNS the younger. PoA for sale of 38*ac* to Josiah MOFFETT.

Bk:Pg: 2D:181   Date: 4/17/1803   RcCt: 11 Oct 1803
Thomas Ludwell LEE of Ldn & Landon CARTER of RichVa (Exors of George CARTER dec'd late of StafVa) to Benjamin SHREEVE of Ldn. B/S of 63*ac* on N side of Tuskorora, adj William CHILTON, junction of Foxes Mill Road with the Turnpike Road, William WRIGHT. Wit: Ignatius ELGIN, Samuel DONOHOE, Henry JENKENS, Benjamin DOWELL, Jno. MATHIAS.

Bk:Pg: 2D:185   Date: 4/17/1803   RcCt: 11 Oct 1803
Thomas Ludwell LEE of Ldn & Landon CARTER of RichVa (Exors of George CARTER late of StafVa) to Ignatius ELGIN of Ldn. B/S of 82*ac,* adj Benjamin H. CANBY, Samuel DONOHOE. Wit: Benj'n SHREEVE, John CAVAN, Samuel DONOHOE, Henry JENKENS, Jno MATHIAS.

Bk:Pg: 2D:188   Date: 10/31/1797   RcCt: 11 Oct 1803
John CAMPBELL & wife Sarah of Ldn to William MAINS of Ldn. B/S of 122*ac* adj Middleton SHAW. Wit: C. BINNS Jr., Alexr WAUGH, Tho. FOUCH.

Bk:Pg: 2D:191   Date: 9/1/1803   RcCt: 11 Oct 1803
William MAINS & wife Mary of Ldn to Thomas CIMMINGS of Ldn. B/S of 98*ac,* adj Cobler's Gap road and CIMMINS. Wit: S. BLINCOE, Walker REID, G. W. BLINCOE.

Bk:Pg: 2D:193   Date: 8/4/1803   RcCt: 11 Oct 1803
Ferdinando FAIRFAX of Shannon Hill, JeffVa to Joseph LEWIS Jr of Ldn.
B/S of 4000ac in Piedmont, adj Potomack River, Dutchman Run, near
German Calvenist Church, Ph. HOFF, Peter RICKEY, Peter HICKMAN,
Reuben HIXON, Geo. SHOEMAKER, Peter COMPHER, Jacob
SHOEMAKER, Geo. MULL, Archey MORRISON, Chas CRIMM, Jno.
STADLER, Polser DERRY. Wit: Wm. H. HARDING, Cyrus SAUNDERS,
Nancy A. HARDING.

Bk:Pg: 2D:199   Date: 10/9/1803   RcCt: 12 Oct 1803
Ferdinando FAIRFAX of Shannon Hill, JeffVa to Edward McDANIEL of
Ldn. B/S of 176ac where McDANIEL now lives near Kittockton Creek, adj
Thomas D. STEVENS, Jos. THOMPSON. Wit: Cyrus SAUNDERS.

Bk:Pg: 2D:202   Date: 9/11/1803   RcCt: 11 Oct 1803
William MAINS & wife Mary of Ldn to Isaac CURREY of Ldn. B/S of 18ac.
Wit: S. BLINCOE, ? REID, G. W. BLINCOE.

Bk:Pg: 2D:205   Date: 10/7/1803   RcCt: 12 Oct 1803
James CAVAN Jr. and John CAVAN of Lsbg to Joseph SMITH of Lsbg.
B/S of lot on west end of Lsbg between Loudoun & Market Sts, adj
William ELLIOTT, Presbyterian Meeting house, Benjamin H. CANBY,
Joseph SMITH, William SMITH. Wit: Geo. ROWAN, James HAMILTON,
Saml. SMITH.

Bk:Pg: 2D:207   Date: 4/13/1803   9 May 1803
Andrew BROWN of Adams Co. PA to Jesse TAYLOR of Ldn. B/S of
190ac, adj S fork of Kittocton, John HOUGH, Mary McGEATH, John
BINNS, road to Isaac Sture's mill. Wit: Josh'a DANIEL, Timothy HIXON,
William WRIGHT.

Bk:Pg: 2D:211   Date: 9/29/1803   RcCt: 12 Oct 1803
Samuel MURREY & wife Elizabeth of Lsbg to James CAVAN Jr. & John
CAVAN of Lsbg. B/S of lot at W end of Lsbg between Loudoun & Market
Sts, adj William SMITH dec'd. Wit: George HAMMAT, C. BINNS, Robert
WAID, Joseph SMITH, W. C. SELDEN.

Bk:Pg: 2D:215   Date: 6/28/1800   RcCt: 15 Dec 1801
Patrick CAVAN & wife Sarah of Lsbg to William HARDING of Ldn and
Samuel MURREY of Ldn. Trust - in 1796 HARDING was the security for
bonds of Cavan now due, selling to MURREY 90ac on Broad Run of
Kittocton adj Samuel SCHOOLEY and 97ac on Broad Run. Wit: Jno
MATHIAS, James CAVAN Jr., John CAVAN, Joseph SMITH, John
LITTLEJOHN.

Bk:Pg: 2D:220   Date: 10/10/1803   RcCt: 12 Oct 1803
James BALL & wife Ruth of Ldn to Hugh DOUGLAS of Ldn. B/S of 87ac.

Bk:Pg: 2D:222   Date: 7/8/1800   RcCt: 12 Feb 1801
Isaac WREN to John BYOTT. A/L - on 13 Oct 1777 William MORLAN
annexed a lease to BYOTT. Wit: John WREN, Isaac HARRIS, Turner
WREN.

Bk:Pg: 2D:223   Date: 2/1/1803   RcCt: 12 Oct 1803
Samuel MURREY of Lsbg to William H. HARDING of JeffVa. B/S of
187*ac*, selling to cover the security bonds on Patrick CAVAN.

Bk:Pg: 2D:226   Date: 6/13/1803   RcCt: 11 Oct 1803
James TUCKER. Bond as constable of Ldn. Wit: William YOE, James
BRADFIELD, Jos. THOMPSON.

Bk:Pg: 2D:227   Date: 8/22/1803   RcCt: 14 Nov 1803
Samuel S. HARWOOD to William S. BELT. BoS for Negro boy named
Otha. Wit: Richard HARWOOD, Thos. N. HARWOOD, Sn. BLINCOE,
Walker REID.

Bk:Pg: 2D:227   Date: ___   RcCt: 15 Nov 1803
List of residents of Lsbg who agree to a fire company - Samuel MURREY,
Charles GULLATT, Geo. ROWAN, Obadiah CLIFFORD, Thomas SIM,
William WOODY, B. HOUGH, John SHAW, James HAMILTON, D.
DOWLING, Presly CORDELL, R. HAMILTON, Geo. FORTNEY, John
MYERS, Thos. WILKINSON, Saml. HOUGH, James CAVAN, John
EVINS, John CAVAN, Thos. EDWARDS, Henry COOK, John COOK,
Patrick DOUGLAS, John NEWTON, Alexr COUPER Jr., Martin
CORDELL, Martin KITZMILLER, Barton LUCAS, Wm. CLINE, Joseph
BEARD, Isaac HARRIS, James GARNER, Hen. GLASSGOW, Geo.
HEAD Sr., A. SUTHERLAND, Jacob TOWNER, Jacob FADELY, Thos.
JACOBS, George HEAD Jr., John MINDETT, Fleet SMITH, A. LAMBAG,
James SANDERS, Lee DERAM, Fr. H. PEYTON, John WILDMAN,
Christ'o. ROPER & Sn. BLINCOE.

Bk:Pg: 2D:228   Date: 4/29/1803   RcCt: 11 Nov 1803
William BROWN of Wstm to William Jett BROWN of Wstm: PoA to sell
estate in Ldn. Wit: S. JETT, Wm. THOMPSON, Jno. M. SMITH, Wm.
BROWN, Danl. CARMICHAEL.

Bk:Pg: 2D:229   Date: 11/15/1803   RcCt: 12 Dec 1803
James HAMILTON & wife Elizabeth of Ldn to David LACEY of Ldn. B/S of
405½*ac* on Kittoctan Mt, adj Peter CARR, William MAINS, Isaac CURRY.
Wit: Wm. H. HARDING, Joseph WILKINSON, Wm. MAINS, Thomas
WILKINSON.

Bk:Pg: 2D:231   Date: 11/2/1803   RcCt: 12 Dec 1803
Hugh HOLMES & wife Elizabeth to Michael COOPER. CoE for sale of
194*ac*. Wit: Robt MACKY, Chas. SMITH of Frederick Co.

Bk:Pg: 2D:232   Date: 11/3/1803   RcCt: 12 Dec 1803
Samuel CLAPHAM of Ldn and father Josias CLAPHAM dec'd of Ldn to
Thomas NOLAND of FrdkMd. B/S of 19*ac* below mouth of Clarks Run nr
Potomac and another 16½*ac*. Wit: Saml LUCKETT, Fr. H. PEYTON,
Benj'a PRICE, W. NOLAND.

Bk:Pg: 2D:236   Date: 11/3/1803   RcCt: 12 Dec 1803
Thomas NOLAND of FrdkMd to Samuel CLAPHAM of Ldn. B/S of
151½*ac* on Potomac adj Albin THACKER and 16½*ac* adj Enoch FLOYD.
Wit: Samuel LUCKETT, Fr. H. PEYTON, W. NOLAND, Benja PRICE.

Bk:Pg: 2D:240   Date: 12/9/1803   RcCt: 12 Dec 1803
William COTTON & wife Janey of Ldn to Joseph MOXLEY of Ldn. B/S of 217ac on branch of Goose Creek, adj Cornelius HOLDRIN, Thomas CARR, John ALEXANDER, George CARTER. Wit: Francis ELGIN, Saml TILLETT, John COTTON, Cornelius ATCHER.

Bk:Pg: 2D:242   Date: 12/2/1803   RcCt: 12 Dec 1803
Joseph MOXLEY of Ldn to William COTTON of Ldn. BoS for Negro man Harry, man Adam, girl Rebecca, Negro woman Hannah and her 5 children Eve, Francis, Benjamin, William & Samuel, and horses. Wit: Cornelius ATCHER, Christopher ATCHER, Thos. MOSS.

Bk:Pg: 2D:244   Date: 12/12/1803   RcCt: 12 Dec 1803
Mahlon JANNEY Sr. & wife Sarah of Ldn to Richard GRIFFITH of Wtfd. B/S of lots #1 & #2 in Wtfd, adj Janney's Mill lot. Wit: James MOORE, Joseph TALBOTT, Paterson WRIGHT, Samuel GOVER.

Bk:Pg: 2D:246   Date: 10/13/1803   RcCt: 12 Dec 1803
Joseph PEIRPOINT & wife Catrenah of FrdkVa to Richard GRIFFITH of Ldn. B/S of part of lot in Wtfd, adj Francis PEIRPOINT, Main St, Evan GRIFFITH. Wit: Fleet SMITH, Francis TRIPLETT, John NEWTON, Samuel MURREY, Joseph SMITH.

Bk:Pg: 2D:249   Date: 12/12/1803   RcCt: 12 Dec 1803
Thomas HIRST of Ldn to Jacob WALTMAN. BoS for Negro boy Tolbert. Wit: Wm. HAMILTON, Wm. PAXSON.

Bk:Pg: 2D:249   Date: 12/10/1803   RcCt: 12 Dec 1803
Thomas A. HEREFORD & wife Margarett to William WOODEY. B/S of part of Lot #14 in Lsbg between houses of Samuel MURREY and Barnet HOUGH. Wit: Sampson BLINCOE.

Bk:Pg: 2D:251   Date: 12/12/1803   RcCt: 12 Dec 1803
George SINCLAIR & wife Margarett of Ldn to Abner CRAVEN of Ldn. B/S of undivided share from her father Thomas CRAVEN dec'd. Wit: Isaac LARROWE.

Bk:Pg: 2D:253   Date: 12/12/1803   RcCt: 12 Dec 1803
Samuel SINCLAIR & wife Edith of Ldn to Abner CRAVEN of Ldn. B/S of Edith's undivided share from her father Thomas CRAVEN dec'd. Wit: Isaac LARROWE.

Bk:Pg: 2D:254   Date: 12/1/1803   RcCt: 12 Dec 1803
Abner CRAVEN & wife Sarah of Ldn to George SINCLAIR of Ldn. B/S of 35¼ac, Sarah's share of father John SINCLAIR dec'd. Wit: Isaac LARROWE.

Bk:Pg: 2D:256   Date: 11/5/1803   RcCt: 12 Dec 1803
Mary ARMSTEAD to granddaughter Elizabeth ARMSTEAD d/o son Robert ARMSTEAD. Gift of Negro girl Kity abt 10y old. Wit: Armistead LONG, David ENGLISH.

Bk:Pg: 2D:257   Date: 10/25/1803   RcCt: 12 Dec 1803
Stephen DONALDSON & wife Susanna of Lsbg to Jessy DAILEY of Ldn.
B/S of lot on Loudoun St in Lsbg where Joseph BEARD now lives, adj
James GARNER. Wit: Samuel MURREY, Turner WRENN, Joseph
SMITH.

Bk:Pg: 2D:260   Date: 11/18/1803   RcCt: 12 Dec 1803
Writ of adquoddamnum - awarded to Benjamin DUEL, inquiry into
possible damages by his erecting a water grist mill on the Secolon - found
there would be no damage. Panel - Samuel BOGGESS, John
McCORMICK, Geo. ROWAN, Thomas WILKINSON, John DODD, William
CARR, John COTTON, John DREAN, Ignatius ELGIN, Matth
WEATHERBY, Samuel DONOHOE, John DRISH.

Bk:Pg: 2D:262   Date: 4/13/1803   RcCt: 12 Dec 1803
John DRISH & wife Nelly of Lsbg to Joseph GORE of Ldn. B/S of land adj
Daniel LOSCH, road from Lsbg to Nolands Ferry, Henry McCABE dec'd,
part of 3ac bought from Henry McCABE dec'd. Wit: James SANDERS Jr.,
John EVANS, George HAMMATT.

Bk:Pg: 2D:263   Date: 5/16/1803   RcCt: 12 Dec 1803
Amos DONOHOE to Samuel DONOHOE. BoS for Negro boy Harry abt
13y old. Wit: Isaac HARRIS, George HAMMAT.

Bk:Pg: 2D:264   Date: 8/14/1796   RcCt: 11 Sep 1797
Thomas SMITH & wife Martha of Culpeper Co, formerly of Ldn to
Ebenezer GRUBB of Ldn. B/S of 235ac between Short hill and blue ridge,
conveyed to Thomas and brother George by father Henry dec'd, adj
Christian MILLER, David POTTS. Wit: Isaac LAROWE, Uriah WILLIAMS,
James McILHANEY, Phil SLAUGHTER, William GRAY.

Bk:Pg: 2D:268   Date: 12/12/1803   RcCt: 12 Dec 1803
Thomas N. BINNS & wife Amelia of Ldn to George RODES of Ldn. B/S of
8ac on Tuscarora branch.

Bk:Pg: 2D:270   Date: 12/10/1803   RcCt: 12 Dec 1803
John ROSE & wife Anna of Ldn to Thomas Brook BEALL of DC. B/S of
20ac, adj Henry OXLEY, John OXLEY. Wit: Chs. BENNETT & Thos. SIM.

Bk:Pg: 2D:274   Date: 3/16/1803   RcCt: 12 Dec 1803
Patrick CAVAN dec'd by Joseph SMITH, John LITTLEJOHN & Stephen
COOK commissioners appointed by court to Peter DOWE. B/S of lot #8
on W end of Lsbg, conveyed by deed of mortgage from CAVAN now
dec'd to Jesse TAYLOR, adj George RINE. Wit: Fleet SMITH, James
CAVAN Jr., G. W. BLINCOE.

Bk:Pg: 2D:276   Date: 12/7/1803   RcCt: 12 Dec 1803
James GRADY & wife Susannah of Ldn to Elisha MARKS of Ldn. B/S of
29ac. Wit: Edward GRADY, Ury GRADY, Jane GRADY.

Bk:Pg: 2D:279   Date: 10/17/1803   RcCt: 13 Dec 1803
James CAVAN Jr. (Admr of Patrick CAVAN dec'd) of Lsbg to Thomas N.
BINNS of Ldn. B/S of 3ac leased by James HEREFORD to Patrick

CAVAN (now dec'd) adj John LITTLEJOHN. Wit: Jno. MATHIAS, Alexr SUTHERLAND, Wm. WILLIAMS.

Bk:Pg: 2D:282   Date: 11/15/1803   RcCt: 12 Dec 1803
Bazil STONESTREET of Ldn to Henry JONES of Ldn. A/L. Wit: Sn. BLINCOE.

Bk:Pg: 2D:283   Date: 5/25/1803   RcCt: 12 Dec 1803
Thomas GIST to Thomas ODEN. BoS for Negro woman Dealey and child Matilda. Wit: Jos. LEWIS, Joseph EVERITT.

Bk:Pg: 2D:284   Date: 12/12/1803   RcCt: 13 Dec 1803
John CRAVEN & wife Elizabeth of Albemarle Co VA to Abner CRAVEN of Ldn. B/S of CRAVEN's undivided share from father Thomas CRAVEN dec'd. Wit: William CLINE, Josiah MOFFETT, Thos. WILKINSON, Samuel MURREY, Fra. H. PEYTON.

Bk:Pg: 2D:286   Date: 10/13/1803   RcCt: 13 Dec 1803
James CAVAN Jr (Admr of Patrick CAVAN dec'd) of Lsbg to George FEICHTER of Ldn. A/L of land lease from James HEREFORD. Wit: John MATHIAS, John SHAW, John DRISH.

Bk:Pg: 2D:290   Date: 12/13/1803   RcCt: 13 Dec 1803
William PARROTT to James HAMILTON for Joshua DANIEL. BoS for Negro fellow Jess abt 28y old. Wit: Josiah MOFFETT, John A. BINNS, Thos. N. BINNS.

Bk:Pg: 2D:291   Date: 12/1/1803   RcCt: 13 Dec 1803
Jacob JACOBS dec'd of Lsbg. William HAWKE and John JACOBS. Commissioners Jno. SCHOOLEY Jr, Geo. ROWAN & Obadiah CLIFFORD by Court order dated 15 Feb 1803 to sell house & lot, sold part to HAWKE and remaining part & house to JACOBS.

Bk:Pg: 2D:292   Date: 9/20/1803   RcCt: 13 Dec 1803
Writ of adquoddamnum - awarded to Benjamin H. CANBY of ShelP to assess possible damages to Benjamin THORNTON if he erects a water grist mill on Secolon; panel states no damage will occur. Panel - Samuel BOGGESS, Francis TRIPLET, William HALLING, Constantine HUGHES, Joseph WHITE, James CARR, John PYOT, John BROWN, James CRAIGE, John IREY, William SUDDITH, John HANDEY & John COTTON.

Bk:Pg: 2D:294   Date: ___   RcCt: 14 Dec 1803
John THRELKELD of Georgetown, MontMd to William JONES of Ffx. A/L of 150ac indenture of 11 May 1761 between Bryant FAIRFAX of Ffx and Solomon HOGE (wife Ann, son Solomon) of Ldn lease on Kittocton Mt, transferred to William JONES of Ldn; boundaries in dispute so new lease is drawn.

Bk:Pg: 2D:300   Date: 1/9/1804   9 Jan 1804
George TAVENNER & wife Martha [signed as Patty] of Ldn to Jonah SANDS of Ldn. B/S of 6ac, adj Constantine HUGHES.

Bk:Pg: 2D:302   Date: 1/9/1804   9 Jan 1804
Barton EWERS dec'd. Plots and descriptions by Josiah PALLY, of 67*ac*
plot, 133*ac* plot, 25*ac* plot, 112*ac* plot; Thomas EWERS, Jonathan
EWERS and Barton EWERS make bond on these divisions. Wit: Sn.
BLINCOE, G. W. BLINCOE, Eli OFFUTT.

Bk:Pg: 2D:306   Date: ___   RcCt: 10 Jan 1804
Writ of adquoddamnum - to Reuben HIXON to assess possible damages
to heirs of William HIXON dec'd if he erects water grist mill on Catocton,
panel awards $13.50 to heirs. Panel - John WILLIAMS, Abner WILLIAMS,
Jacob SANDS, John MARTIN, Patrick MILHOLLEN, Peter HICKMAN,
William AULT, Henry WOLF, John FAWLEY, John ERSKINS, John
SLACK & Philip SOWDER.

Bk:Pg: 2D:309   Date: 9/13/1803   9 Jan 1804
George TAVENNER Jr. & wife Martha [signed as Patty] of Ldn to Joshua
GORE of Ldn. B/S of 20*ac,* adj Joseph CLEWES, Blackstone & Israel
JANNY. Wit: Israel JANNY, Jonathan JANNY, David LUPTON Jr, Daniel
JANNY.

Bk:Pg: 2D:314   Date: 12/30/1803   9 Jan 1804
Joseph GREGG & wife Mary of Ldn to Barton EWERS of Ldn. B/S of
30*ac* on Beaverdam branch. Wit: Thomas EWERS, Jonathan EWERS.

Bk:Pg: 2D:316   Date: 1/5/1804   9 Jan 1804
Samuel CLAPHAM & wife Elizabeth of Ldn to Isaac STEERE of Ldn. B/S
of 62½*ac,* adj John STEERE, Isaac STEERE, Capt Thomas CHILTON,
William DULIN, Samuel LUCKETT. Wit: W. NOLAND, Thos. NOLAND,
Joseph STEERE, Johnston CLEVELAND.

Bk:Pg: 2D:320   Date: 2/1/1804   RcCt: 13 Feb 1804
Isaac RICHEY Sr. to Michael SHAVER. A/L for remainder of lease. Wit:
G. W. BLINCOE, Eli OFFUTT, Sn. BLINCOE.

Bk:Pg: 2D:321   Date: 12/20/1803   RcCt: 13 Feb 1804
Ferdinando FAIRFAX of JeffVa to William ELLZEY of Ldn. B/S of 123¾*ac*
on Dutchman Run in Piedmont. Wit: Wm. H. HARDING, Abiel JENNERS,
Alexander YOUNG, Saml W. YOUNG.

Bk:Pg: 2D:323   Date: 1/6/1804   RcCt: 13 Feb 1804
James MOORE of Ldn to Edward DORSEY of Wtfd. B/S of ½ lot in Wtfd,
adj James MOORE.

Bk:Pg: 2D:324   Date: 1/11/1804   RcCt: 13 Feb 1804
John H. HARWOOD of Ldn to Nathaniel SKINNER of Ldn. Trust - to
secure payment on two $250 bonds to Moses DOWDLE of PrWm, sells
trust to SKINNER. Wit: William LEWIS, Cornelius SKINNER, Peter
SKINNER, John SCHOLFIELD.

Bk:Pg: 2D:327   Date: 9/22/1803   RcCt: 13 Feb 1804
Mahlon JANNEY of Ldn to Edward DORSEY of Wtfd. B/S of 2¾*ac* lot in
Wtfd, adj James MOORE, John WILLIAMS. Wit: Thomas HIRST, James
MOORE, Abner MOORE.

Bk:Pg: 2D:329   Date: 1/6/1804   RcCt: 13 Feb 1804
Abiel JENNERS & wife Deborah of Ldn to Ferdinando FAIRFAX of JeffVa.
B/S of 637*ac* on Broad Run in Pages lot, adj Thomas MARSHALL,
William HORSEMAN. Wit: Wm. H. HARDING, John McKENDREE, Nichs.
ROPER.

Bk:Pg: 2D:331   Date: 1/3/1804   RcCt: 13 Feb 1804
Peter DEMERY of Ldn [signed as DEMERY but document states
TEMERY] to William B. PAGE of JeffVa and Ferdinando FAIRFAX of
JeffVa. Trust for debt to FAIRFAX using 122¼*ac* in Shannondale. Wit:
Abiel JENNERS.

Bk:Pg: 2D:334   Date: 2/13/1803   RcCt: 13 Feb 1804
Esther GREGG (wd/o Samuel GREGG). Renunciation of claim to property
secured to her by will of her late husband. Wit: Lewis ELLZEY, Uriah
WILLIAMS.

Bk:Pg: 2D:335   Date: 2/13/1804   RcCt: 13 Feb 1804
Thomas FRANCIS & wife Mary of Ldn to Price JACOBS of Ldn. B/S of
62*ac* on S side of Beaverdam Run, adj John ONEALE, Reuben
TRIPLETT, Lovet JACKSON, Joshua DUNKIN.

Bk:Pg: 2D:337   Date: 2/13/1804   RcCt: 13 Feb 1804
Thomas FRANCIS of Ldn to Price JACOBS of Ldn. Mortgage for above
land.

Bk:Pg: 2D:338   Date: 12/12/1803   RcCt: 13 Feb 1804
Leven POWELL for President and directors of Little River turnpike
company. Writ of adquoddamnum - for potential damage to heirs of
Robert LYLE, heirs of Hardage LANE, Isaac WYCOFF, John SPENCER
and Benjamin JAMES from turnpike running through their land - each
awarded by panel for some damages. Panel - Jos. BLINCOE, James
COLEMAN Jr., George SHIVELY, Peter OAYER, Nicholas GRIMES,
Thomas STONESTREET, Richard FREEMAN, William WOLHARD,
William MARSHALL, John TURLEY, Reuben MORGAN, Thomas
WILLIAMSON & Elisha TIMMS.

Bk:Pg: 2D:341   Date: 10/25/1803   RcCt: 13 Feb 1804
Henry AWBREY of Ldn to Thomas AWBREY and Samuel AWBREY of
Ldn Partition - Henry and Thomas hold land as tenants in common,
Samuel sold his part without making partition, 207*ac* at foot of Blue Ridge
adj Thomas Alexander BROOKE, Benjamin GRAYSON, Enoch FURR.
Wit: William FOWKE, Samuel DILLON, Benj GRAYSON, Aaron ARDEN.

Bk:Pg: 2D:344   Date: 2/13/1804   RcCt: 13 Feb 1804
George FAIRHURST of Ldn to Hamilton ROGERS of Ldn. B/S of 1*ac*, adj
William DIGGS, Thomas GREGG. Wit: Jesse JANNY, John IREY, Daniel
LOVET.

Bk:Pg: 2D:346   Date: 2/13/1804   RcCt: 13 Feb 1804
Jacob BRAUFF & wife Rebeckah to Joel NIXON. B/S - Jonathan NIXON
purchased land from John THRELKELD but died intestate leaving

children Rebeckah, Joel, Sarah, Jonathan and John to share in equal portions. Wit: John SCATTERDAY, Jesse HARRIS, Josias HALL.

Bk:Pg: 2D:340   Date: 6/15/1803   RcCt: 13 Feb 1804
Isaac BALL of Ldn to Stephen BALL and John BALL of Ldn. B/S of 109*ac* in Catocton tract purchased by his father Farling BALL, near Ball's Mill. Wit: Wm. WOODDY, William TAYLOR, Francis TRIPLET.

Bk:Pg: 2D:350   Date: 10/10/1803   RcCt: 13 Feb 1804
Jonas POTTS & wife Phebe of Ldn and Jacob BAUGH & wife Mary of Ldn to Aaron SANDERS of Ldn. B/S of 42*ac* that POTTS & BAUGH purchased from Francis TITUS. Wit: Samuel CARR, Samuel HOUGH, Jas. CAVAN Jr., John MATHIAS, W. ELLZEY, John HAMILTON.

Bk:Pg: 2D:353   Date: 11/15/1803   RcCt: 12 Dec 1803
Joseph WHITE and George TAVENNER Jr (Exors of George NIXON dec'd) of Ldn to Josiah HALL of Ldn. Remortgage on land. Wit: Wm. ROBERTS, Ths. PEAKE, I. BALL, Walker REID, Benj. SHREVE.

Bk:Pg: 2D:354   Date: 2/13/1804   RcCt: 13 Feb 1804
Joshua WHITACRE & wife Ann of Ldn to Samuel LACY of Ldn. B/S of 150*ac* in Harrison Co. VA. Wit: Benjamin STEER, Reuben SCHOOLEY.

Bk:Pg: 2D:356   Date: 2/10/1804   RcCt: 13 Feb 1804
Henry AWBREY (s/o Thomas AWBREY dec'd & br/o Samuel) & wife Charity of Ldn to Benjamin GRAYSON of Ldn. B/S of 103½*ac*, adj Jonathan McCARTER. Wit: Burr POWELL, Wm. BRONAUGH, Saml BOGGESS.

Bk:Pg: 2D:360   Date: 12/13/1803   RcCt: 14 Feb 1803
Burr POWELL & wife Catharine of Ldn to Harmon BITZER of Ldn. B/S of 107¼*ac*. Wit: Raw'h CHINN, A. GIBSON, E. DOWELL, Leven POWELL, Wm. BRONAUGH.

Bk:Pg: 2D:364   Date: 12/17/1803   RcCt: 14 Feb 1804
Burr POWELL & wife Catharine of Ldn to William BRONAUGH of Ldn. B/S of ½ of 10*ac* tract. Wit: Thomas CHINN, Martin BRENT, A. GIBSON, Leven POWELL, Ben GRAYSON.

Bk:Pg: 2D:367   Date: 2/13/1804   RcCt: 13 Feb 1804
Samuel HOUGH & wife Ann of Ldn to George RHODES of Ldn. B/S of 2 pieces (2*ac*) where RHODES now lives, adj Will'm MAINS, Thomas CIMMING. Wit: Thos. LOWE, Robt HAMILTON, John CAMPBELL.

Bk:Pg: 2D:370   Date: 3/21/1803   RcCt: 13 Feb 1804
Archibald JOHNSON & wife Jemimah to Leven LUCKETT. CoE for sale of 119*ac*. Wit: Francis PEYTON, Burr PEYTON.

Bk:Pg: 2D:371   Date: 6/20/1803   RcCt: 13 Feb 1804
Michael BOGAR & wife Elizabeth of Ldn [signed as BOGAR but BOGART in rest of document] to George FULTON of Ldn. B/S of 4*ac* on Broadrun just above Fulling Mill. Wit: Frederick SMITH, George FAWLEY, Samuel AMICK.

Bk:Pg: 2D:374   Date: 10/18/1803   RcCt: 14 Feb 1804
John DRISH & wife Nelly of Lsbg to John MANSFIELD of Lsbg. B/S of lot adj Martin CORDELL on main road from Lsbg to Nolands Ferry. Wit: John WIRT, Henry M. DAVIS, Samuel MORAN.

Bk:Pg: 2D:376   Date: 9/10/1803   RcCt: 10 Jan 1804
James CAVAN Jr. and John CAVAN of Lsbg to Samuel MURREY of Lsbg. B/S of 130 square perches lot adj Lsbg, at side of main road leading through Loudoun St on NW side, adj lot #57 of Charles GULLATT. Wit: Francis TRIPLETT, John WILDMAN, Isaac HARRIS, Thomas CUMMINGS.

Bk:Pg: 2D:378   Date: ___   RcCt: ___ [Jan or Feb 1804?]
Robert J. TAYLOR (Admr of Jesse TAYLOR dec'd). Acknowledgement - Ct decreed that TAYLOR can foreclose on mortgage of Patrick CAVAN and sell mortgaged premises.

Bk:Pg: 2D:378   Date: 8/25/1803   RcCt: 14 Feb 1804
Richard Bland LEE & wife Elizabeth of Ffx to Thomas SWANN of Alexandria, DC. Deed of assignment- Ferdinando FAIRFAX conveyed to Lee tract called Hill and Dale in Frederick Co which on same date Lee conveyed to SWANN, land is now subject to mortgage to Raleigh CHINN, so FAIRFAX conveyed to LEE tract called Shannon Dale in Ldn and Jefferson Co except part that was previously sold and subject to mortgage.

Bk:Pg: 2D:383   Date: 1/5/1804   RcCt: 14 Feb 1804
John DRISH & wife Eleanor of Lsbg to Smallwood MIDDLETON of Lsbg. B/S of ¼ac lot near Lsbg at North and King St. Wit: Richard PURDY, Henry M. DAVIS, John WIRT.

Bk:Pg: 2D:385   Date: 3/12/1804   RcCt: 12 Mar 1804
Casper JOHNSON. DoE for Negro Priss paid $200 for her freedom. Wit: Sn. BLINCOE, G. W. BLINCOE.

Bk:Pg: 2D:386   Date: ___   RcCt: 12 Mar 1804
David LACEY. Writ and inquisition- LACEY intends to build a water grist mill on Kittockton Creek adj land of Mortho SULLIVAN, panel accessed possible damages and awarded $500 to Anthony WRIGHT. Panel - Benj SHREVE, Richard GRIFFITH, Moses COLDWELL, Sandford RAMEY, John MILHOLLAND, Patrick MILHOLLAND, John McGEATH, Patrick McGAVOCK, Lambert MYERS, Elijah MYERS, James BALL, John NICKLIN & Abner WILLIAMS.

Bk:Pg: 2D:389   Date: ___   RcCt: 9 Apr 1804
George VINCEL & wife Catharine of Ldn to William AULT of Ldn. B/S of 34¾ac. Wit: Sn BLINCOE.

Bk:Pg: 2D:391   Date: 2/22/1804   RcCt: 9 Apr 1804
Robert CHINN & wife Sarah to Thomas CHINN Sr & wife Sarah and Noble BEVERIDGE & Mesheck LACEY. Mortgage on 200ac. Wit: Burr POWELL, Francis PEYTON, Thos. CHINN Jr., Thos. A. HEREFORD, Wm. HALE.

Bk:Pg: 2D:397   Date: 5/16/1803   RcCt: 10 Jan 1804
William CHILTON & wife Sarah Harrison CHILTON of Lsbg to Samuel
MURRAY of Lsbg. B/S of 1*ac* lot on King St. Wit: John LITTLEJOHN,
George ROWAN, James HAMILTON, Jno. ROSE, Thos. SIM.

Bk:Pg: 2D:402   Date: 3/30/1804   RcCt: 9 Apr 1804
Burr POWELL & wife Catharine of Ldn to Peter TOWERMAN of Ldn. B/S
of 199*ac* nr road from Mdbg to Handy Mill. Wit: Leven POWELL, Thomas
SIM.

Bk:Pg: 2D:406   Date: 11/1/1803   RcCt: 9 Apr 1804
Joseph WEST of Ldn to James CHANNEL of Ldn. LS of 137*ac*. Wit:
Leven POWELL Jr, Martin BRENT, Thomas C. WELLS, Rawleigh CHINN,
James BATSON, Robert DAGG, Leven D. POWELL, Wm. MARTIN, Wm.
THOMAS.

Bk:Pg: 2D:407   Date: 8/26/1803   RcCt: 9 Apr 1804
George Emrey GOFF (s/o Rachel GOFF) & wife Mary of Washington Co.
to Richard PURDY of Lsbg. B/S of part of lot #12 on King St. Wit: Jacob
FADELY, Joseph KNOX.

Bk:Pg: 2D:409   Date: 3/29/1802   RcCt: 12 Apr 1802
Leven POWELL Sr. of Ldn to William HALE Sr. of Fqr. B/S of 2*ac* nr
Mdbg, adj Robert DAGG, Abner GIBSON. Wit: Jesse McVEIGH, Thomas
CHINN, Wm. T. TAYLOR, Samuel HENDERSON, A. GIBSON.

Bk:Pg: 2D:411   Date: 2/10/1804   RcCt: 9 Apr 1804
Nathaniel CRAWFORD & wife Sarah of PrG to Michael EBLIN of Ldn. B/S
of 63*ac*, leased by Thomas BLACKBURNE to Hezekiah GUY, adj
Thomas GREGG, Jos. HAGUE, John LEMINGS. Wit: W. ELLZEY, Tho.
SWANN, Jos. LEWIS Jr., Saml HEPBURNE, David CRAWFORD.

Bk:Pg: 2D:415   Date: 3/5/1804   RcCt: 9 Apr 1804
Thomas NOLAND & wife Elenor of FrdkMd to William NOLAND of Ldn.
B/S of 140*ac*, 60*ac*, 13*ac*, 30*ac*, 2*ac*, also part of 116*ac*. Wit: Abm.
SHRIVER, Saml CLAPHAM, Jane NOLAND.

Bk:Pg: 2D:420   Date: 5/28/1803   RcCt: 12 Dec 1803
William BROWN by Attorney Wm. Jett BROWN of WstmVa to Robert M.
POWELL of Ldn. B/S of 50*ac*. Wit: Burr POWELL, G. LOVE, Wm. P.
HALE, Thomas VIOLETT, Thomas TRIPLETT.

Bk:Pg: 2D:423   Date: 10/15/1803   RcCt: 12 Dec 1803
John WILLIAMS (s/o John WILLIAMS d. intestate) & wife Agnes of KY to
Ellis WILLIAMS of Ldn. B/S of 1/7th of undivided tract father John
purchased from James HAMILTON. Wit: John LITTLEJOHN, Archd
MAINS, James MILES.

Bk:Pg: 2D:425   Date: ___   RcCt: 9 Apr 1804
Thomas FOUCH and Charles BINNS. Bond on FOUCH as Coroner of
Ldn.

Bk:Pg: 2D:426   Date: 4/7/1804   RcCt: 9 Apr 1804
John DRISH & wife Nelly of Lsbg to Charles BINNS of Lsbg. B/S of part of
lot #45 in Lsbg adj Robert HAMILTON dec'd. Wit: Sn. BLINCOE, A.
ALDRIGE, John H. HOFFMAN, William NOLAND, Johnston
CLEVELAND.

Bk:Pg: 2D:430   Date: 3/10/1804   RcCt: 9 Apr 1804
John DRISH & wife Nelly of Ldn to Martin CORDELL of Ldn. B/S of part of
3ac nr Lsbg, adj Richard PURDY. Wit: Presly CORDELL, John WIRTS,
William GEORGE, W. C. SELDON, Samuel MURREY.

Bk:Pg: 2D:434   Date: 2/18/1804   RcCt: 9 Apr 1804
Joseph SMITH & wife Mary of Alexandria, DC late of Lsbg to Charles
BINNS of Lsbg. B/S of 43ac nr Lsbg. Wit: Samuel MURREY, Jno.
SCHOOLEY Jr., Isaac HARRIS, Thomas SIM.

Bk:Pg: 2D:438   Date: 3/13/1804   RcCt: 9 Apr 1804
Joseph SMITH of Alexandria, DC to Charles BINNS & wife Hannah of
Ldn. Mortgage on above land. Wit: Samuel MURREY, Jno. SCHOOLEY
Jr., Isaac HARRIS, Tho. SIM.

Bk:Pg: 2D:442   Date: 3/30/1804   RcCt: 9 Apr 1804
Samuel Wade YOUNG & wife Ruth of Ldn to Ferdinando FAIRFAX of
JeffVa. B/S of 80ac, part of division of the Broad and Sugarland run tract.
Wit: Elizabeth CANON, Wm. H. HARDING, W. ELLZEY, Chas. LEWIS,
Johnston CLEVELAND.

Bk:Pg: 2D:446   Date: 10/4/1803   RcCt: 9 Apr 1804
Archibald MORRISON & wife Ann of Cumberland Co. VA formerly of Lsbg
to Thomas WILKINSON of Lsbg. B/S of Ann's share of lot #12 (from
Thomas ROPER dec'd who died intestate, land went to Christopher
ROPER, Ann ROPER (now MORRISON), William P. ROPER, Thomas
ROPER and Catherine ROPER (who died interstate), and children of
Thomas ROPER dec'd). Wit: Jas. CAVAN Jr., Joseph SMITH, Sebastian
LOSH, Joseph BENTLY, Samuel MURREY, Joseph SMITH.

Bk:Pg: 2D:451   Date: 11/21/1803   RcCt: 9 Apr 1804
Samuel CLAPHAM of Ldn to Samuel LUCKETT of Ldn. B/S of 26ac, adj
William DULIN, Sarah LUCKETT, John STEER. Wit: Isaac STEER, John
MONTGOMERY.

Bk:Pg: 2D:453   Date: 11/3/1803   RcCt: 10 Apr 1804
Samuel CLAPHAM of Ldn to Samuel LUCKETT & wife Sarah of Ldn. B/S
of 31½ac. Wit: Thos. NOLAND, William NOLAND, Benja PRICE, Fra. H.
PEYTON.

Bk:Pg: 2D:456   Date: 8/22/1803   RcCt: 10 Apr 1804
Samuel CLAPHAM of Ldn to Benjamin PRICE of Ldn. Gift (consideration
of natural love) of 18ac purchased by Col. Josias CLAPHAM, adj Capt.
Benjamin PRICE, Capt. Thomas CHILTON. Wit: William NOLAND,
Thomas CHILTON, Fleet SMITH.

Bk:Pg: 2D:457   Date: 4/1/1804   RcCt: 10 Apr 1804
Thomas FRANCIS & wife Mary of Ldn to Thomas Neilson BINNS of Ldn.
B/S of ½ac Lot #59 in Lsbg between West and Loudoun Sts adj Charles
BINNS Jr.

Bk:Pg: 2D:459   Date: 2/27/1804   RcCt: 10 Apr 1804
Asa HARRIS & wife Elizabeth of Ldn to William FOX of Ldn. B/S of 80ac
where HARRIS lives (willed by Samuel HARRIS dec'd to sons William
and Asa HARRIS), adj John HAMILTON, Abner WILLIAMS, Jonathan
MOYERS dec'd. Wit: Abner WILLIAMS, Josh'a DANIEL, Rob. BRADEN,
Charles BENNETT Jr., John HAMILTON, Chs. BENNETT.

Bk:Pg: 2D:463   Date: 3/19/1804   RcCt: 10 Apr 1804
Samuel CLAPHAM of Ldn to William NOLAND of Ldn. B/S of 28ac
conveyed by Richard AWBREY to Josiah CLAPHAM and another 8ac.
Wit: Jno. MATHIAS, Jas. JOHNSON Jr., Thos. NOLAND.

Bk:Pg: 2D:466   Date: 4/10/1804   RcCt: 10 Apr 1804
Sarah FAIRFAX of GrBr by agent William H. HARDING to James
McKIMMEY of Ldn. LS of 97ac in ShelP, adj Michael RUSE, James
NIXON, Daniel SHOEMAKER. Wit: Wm. MAINS, Thos. N. BINNS, Corn.
SKINNER.

Bk:Pg: 2D:473   Date: 4/9/1804   RcCt: 10 Apr 1804
James PAXSON & wife Sarah of Ldn to Melcher STRUPE of Ldn. B/S of
81½ac nr Roach's Mill road. Wit: John HENRY, Jonathan CUNNARD.

Bk:Pg: 2D:475   Date: 4/10/1804   RcCt: 10 Apr 1804
Melcher STRUPE & wife Mary Ann of Ldn to William PAXSON of Ldn. B/S
of 94ac, adj John A. BINNS, Geo. MANN; also 81½ac. Wit: Josh'a
DANNIEL, Isaac BALL, John DAYLY.

Bk:Pg: 2D:479   Date: 4/10/1804   RcCt: 10 Apr 1804
Nathan PIGGOTT & wife Lydia of Ldn to William PIGGOTT of Ldn. B/S of
122ac on NW fork of Goose Creek, adj Nathon SPENCER.

Bk:Pg: 2D:482   Date: 11/16/1803   RcCt: 10 Apr 1804
Wilson C. SELDON & wife Nelly of Ldn to Edmund I. LEE of Alexandria,
DC. B/S of 183ac; corrects an error made in earlier recording about true
course. Wit: Jno. LOVE, Lewis ELLZEY, Thos. SWANN, Benj'a SHREVE,
Burr POWELL, Fra. H. PEYTON.

Bk:Pg: 2E:001   Date: 8/9/1803   RcCt: 10 Apr 1804
William WILSON of Alexandria, DC to Edmund I. LEE of Alexandria, DC.
B/S - further correction on the 183ac mentioned above. Wit: James
PATTON, Wm. RAMSEY, P. RAMSAY.

Bk:Pg: 2E:005   Date: ___   RcCt: 10 Apr 1804
Joseph CRAVEN of Ldn to Abner CRAVEN of Ldn. B/S of share left to
Joseph by father Thomas CRAVEN.

Bk:Pg: 2E:006   Date: 11/7/1803   RcCt: 10 Jan 1804
Robert William KIRK & wife Sarah of Alexandria, DC to John SHAW of
Lsbg. B/S of part of Lot #5 in Lsbg. Wit: R. J. TAYLOR, Tho. SWANN, R.

T. HOOE, Jno. Thos. RICKETTS, Archd McCLEAN. Alexr SMITH, George TAYLOR.

Bk:Pg: 2E:011 Date: ___ RcCt: 10 Apr 1804
James BOYD, John KEMP & wife Nancy late Nancy BOYD, John BOYD, William BOYD and John BOYD as Guardian of Elizabeth BOYD which John William and Elizabeth are ch/o William BOYD dec'd, William WATSON & wife Polly late Polly BOYD a d/o Elizabeth BOYD and George ROSE & wife Jane late Jane BOYD d/o John BOYD dec'd, and said person on behalf of Will BELL a s/o Jane BOYD dec'd who are the legal distributees of the estate of Thomas BOYD dec'd to Charles BINNS of Ldn. PoA for sale of property. Wit: Jas. HAMILTON, Josiah MOFFETT Jr., George HAMMAT.

Bk:Pg: 2E:012 Date: 4/10/1804 RcCt: 10 Apr 1804
James BOYD & wife Sinah, John KEMP & wife Nancy, John BOYD, William BOYD, William WATSON & wife Polly, George ROSE & wife Jane of Ldn to Presley CORDELL of Ldn. B/S of 100*ac,* land conveyed by Wilson C. SELDON & wife Nelley to Thomas BOYD now dec'd, adj Wilson Cary SELDON, Burges BALL.

Bk:Pg: 2E:016 Date: ___ RcCt: 10 Apr 1804
James BOYD to Presley CORDELL. Bond - Thomas BOYD died intestate leaving 131*ac* in Ldn and brother James BOYD, sister Nancy who married John KEMP, John BOYD, William BOYD and Elizabeth BOYD which John Williams and Elizabeth are children of William BOYD dec'd another brother, William WATSON who married Polly a daughter of sister Elizabeth BOYD, George ROSE who married Jane a daughter of brother John BOYD dec'd and William BELL alias BOYD a son of sister Jane BOYD dec'd; Elizabeth BOYD was a minor when they sold the land to CORDELL and William BELL has been missing for 7 years; once Elizabeth is of age and William BELL is found the land goes to CORDELL.

Bk:Pg: 2E:018 Date: 3/30/1804 RcCt: 10 Apr 1804
James BOYD, John KEMP, John BOYD, William BOYD, William WATSON, George ROSE and John BOYD as Guardian of Elizabeth BOYD and on behalf of William BELL as representatives of Thomas BOYD dec'd. Agreement - Negro woman Anne late the property of Thomas BOYD dec'd is an incumberance and is sold to James BOYD who will care for her at the lowest price.

Bk:Pg: 2E:019 Date: 4/10/1804 RcCt: 10 Apr 1804
James BOYD, John KEMP, John BOYD, William BOYD, William WATSON, and George ROSE of Ldn to James BOYD. BoS for Negro James alias Jim.

Bk:Pg: 2E:020 Date: 1/25/1804 RcCt: 10 Apr 1804
William ASHFORD of Monnongahala Co to Michael ASHFORD of Ldn. BoS for 3 horses and wagon. Wit: Thomas HITE, George DARR, Jane ASHFORD.

Bk:Pg: 2E:021   Date: 10/3/1803   RcCt: 10 Oct 1803
Ferdinando FAIRFAX and William Byrd PAGE of JeffVa to James
McILHANEY of Ithaia Farm in Ldn. B/S of 756¾ac, the South division of
Short Hill Mt. in Shannondale, adj Mahlon HOUGH, Josiah WHITE. Wit:
Edward CUNNARD, Wm. H. HARDING, John McILHANEY, Lewis
ELLZEY.

Bk:Pg: 2E:024   Date: 10/3/1803   RcCt: 10 Oct 1803
Ferdinando FAIRFAX of Shannon Hill, JeffVa to James McILHANEY of
Ithaia Farm in Ldn. B/S of for 3 lots in Piedmont - 142 3/4ac lately held by
John MORRIS adj Jonah THOMPSON, James NIXON and Thomas
DAVIS; 182ac lot of Isaac SIDDLE adj William WILLIAMS, Benjamin
PURDUM, Benjamin STEER, John HOUGH and John MARTIN; and 55ac
adj Archy MORRISON, Thomas DAVIS, James NIXON, Jonah
THOMPSON, Samuel CLENDENING and Andrew THOMPSON. Wit:
Edward CUNNARD, Wm. H. HARDING, John McILHANEY, Lewis
ELLZEY.

Bk:Pg: 2E:027   Date: 11/6/1803   RcCt: 14 Feb 1804
Abraham Barnes Thompson MASON, Westwood Thompson MASON and
William Temple Thompson MASON of Ldn to Hugh DOUGLAS of Ldn.
B/S of 24ac. Wit: Robt ARMISTEAD, Jno. MATHIAS, Thomas FLOWERS.

Bk:Pg: 2E:030   Date: 4/9/1804   RcCt: 11 Apr 1804
Martin KITSMILLER of Ldn to George KITSMILLER of Adams Co. PA.
Mortgage for lot where MARTIN now lives on Alexandria road S of Lsbg,
adj James KIRK.

Bk:Pg: 2E:032   Date: 4/3/1804   RcCt: 11 Apr 1804
Robert William KIRK & wife Sarah of Alexandria, DC to Martin
KITSMILLER of Ldn. B/S of lot on western end of Lsbg on S side of the
main road through town. Wit: Thos. SWANN, R. J. TAYLOR, Arch.
McCLEAN, George TAYLOR, Alexr SMITH.

Bk:Pg: 2E:036   Date: 3/30/1804   RcCt: 11 Apr 1804
Robert William KIRK & wife Sarah of Alexandria, DC to James DAWSON
(a free man of color) of Lsbg. B/S of part of Lot #5 (inherited from James
KIRK) in Lsbg, adj John SHAW, Patrick CAVAN dec'd. Wit: Thos.
SWANN, R. J. TAYLOR, Arch McCLEAN, George TAYLOR, Alexr
SMITH.

Bk:Pg: 2E:041   Date: 4/11/1804   RcCt: 11 Apr 1804
Reuben HIXON & wife Mary of Ldn to Timothy HIXON of Ldn. B/S of
193ac that except what Reuben sold to William MUREHEAD, adj Ellzey
MAINS, Vandevanter ROBERTS.

Bk:Pg: 2E:044   Date: 4/11/1804   RcCt: 11 Apr 1804
Timothy HIXON (s/o Mathew HIXON) & wife Margaret of Ldn to Reuben
HIXON of Ldn. B/S of 184ac.

Bk:Pg: 2E:047   Date: 10/11/1803   RcCt: 12 Apr 1804
Samuel MURREY & wife Betsey of Lsbg to Wilson Cary SELDON of Ldn.
B/ S of 141ac on Tuscarora. Wit: Joseph SMITH, Fra. H. PEYTON, Jno.
MATHIAS.

Bk:Pg: 2E:051   Date: 3/29/1804   RcCt: 10 Apr 1804
Wilson Cary SELDON & wife Nelly of Ldn to James BOYD, John KEMP &
wife Nancy, John BOYD, William BOYD, Elizabeth BOYD, William
WATSON & wife Polly, Geo. ROSE & wife Jane and William BELL as
legal representatives of Thomas BOYD dec'd. B/S of 31ac. Wit: C.
BINNS, Alexr COOPER Jr., Wm. COTTON, Samuel MURREY, Thos.
FOUCH.

Bk:Pg: 2E:056   Date: 5/12/1804   RcCt: 14 May 1804
Amos THOMPSON & wife Jane of Ldn to Daniel GHANT of Ldn. B/S of
41ac. Wit: David MOFFETT, Samuel STONE, Alexr DOW.

Bk:Pg: 2E:059   Date: 5/12/1804   RcCt: 14 May 1804
Amos THOMPSON to Daniel GHANT & wife Lucy of Ldn. Mortgage on
above 41ac known as Thompson's Mill. Wit: Alexr DOWE, David
MOFFET, Samuel STONE.

Bk:Pg: 2E:062   Date: 5/4/1804   RcCt: 14 May 1804
Jonathan CUNNARD & wife Elizabeth of Ldn to George MULL of Ldn. B/S
of 8ac. Wit: Josh'a DANNIEL, Nathan CUNNARD, Samuel CUNNARD.

Bk:Pg: 2E:063   Date: ___   RcCt: 14 May 1804
Susannah SETTLE of Ldn to daughter Eliza HUGHES of Ldn. Gift of
Negro boy William. Wit: Daniel SETTLE, Newman SETTLE.

Bk:Pg: 2E:064   Date: ___   RcCt: 14 May 1804
Susannah SETTLE of Ldn to daughter Mary SETTLE. Gift of Negro girl
Milly. Wit: Daniel SETTLE, Newman SETTLE.

Bk:Pg: 2E:065   Date: ___   RcCt: 14 May 1804
Susannah SETTLE of Ldn to son-in-law Henry HARMON of Ffx. Gift of
Negro boy Alfred. Wit: Daniel SETTLE, Newman SETTLE.

Bk:Pg: 2E:066   Date: 11/10/1803   RcCt: 14 May 1804
Richard RICHARDS & wife Mary of Ldn to Samuel RICHARDS of Ldn.
B/S of 100ac. Wit: William CARTER, David POPKINS, Jesse CARTER.

Bk:Pg: 2E:068   Date: 4/9/1804   RcCt: 14 May 1804
Thomas HOUGH & wife Mary of Ldn to William SMITH of Ldn. B/S of
262ac adj Amos JANNEY, Francis WILSON. Wit: Stacy TAYLOR, James
HAMILTON, Louisa HOUGH.

Bk:Pg: 2E:071   Date: 3/10/1804   RcCt: 14 May 1805
William H. HARDING & wife Anne Alexander of JeffVa to James
CAMPBELL of Ldn. B/S of 96ac, adj Michael BOGER. Wit: Timothy
TAYLOR, James HAMILTON, John CAMPBELL, John H. CANBY, Wm.
PAXON, Jacob WALTMAN, Ferdn. FAIRFAX, David HUMPHREY.

Bk:Pg: 2E:075   Date: 5/14/1804   RcCt: 14 May 1804
Enos GARRETT. Col for woman Sally, boy Charles, boy Quill, girl Sally and girl Harriott brought from MD.

Bk:Pg: 2E:075   Date: 4/3/1804   RcCt: 14 May 1804
Joshua BAKER and Sarah CAVAN of Lsbg to Catherine McCaleb RICE. B/S of lot in Lsbg on Loudoun St, adj Jacob SHOPE. Wit: Jno. SCHOOLEY Jr., Jacob SWOPE, Thomas EDWARDS, C. BINNS.

Bk:Pg: 2E:077   Date: 3/17/1804   RcCt: 10 Apr 1804
Ferdinando FAIRFAX of JeffVa to John NICKLIN of Ldn. B/S of 114½ac where NICKLIN now lives in Piedmont, adj Thomas PHILLIPS, William WILLIAMS dec'd, John CUMMINGS, Richard WILLET, Patk McGAVUCK, Luke SMALLWOOD. Wit: James McILHANEY, John WILLIAMS, Wm. H. HARDING, Thomas PHILIPS.

Bk:Pg: 2E:080   Date: 5/14/1804   RcCt: 14 May 1804
William LITTLEJOHN of Ldn to Mungo DYKES of Ldn. B/S of ½ac Lot #17 in Lsbg.

Bk:Pg: 2E:081   Date: 5/14/1804   RcCt: 14 May 1804
John BROWN of Ldn to Edward RINKER of Ldn. LS lots #7 and #10 [Lsbg].

Bk:Pg: 2E:083   Date: 5/14/1804   RcCt: 14 May 1804
John BROWN of Ldn to Edward RINKER & wife Sally of Ldn. Mortgage.

Bk:Pg: 2E:085   Date: 5/14/1804   RcCt: 14 May 1804
Jonathan McCARTER & wife Mary of Ldn to Benjamin GRAYSON of Ldn. B/S of 48¼ac, adj Henry AWBREY, Enoch FURR, Joseph FRED. Wit: Thos. HUMPHREY, Wm. BLEAKLY, Wm. FRANCIS.

Bk:Pg: 2E:089   Date: 5/14/1804   RcCt: 14 May 1804
Jonathan McCARTER & wife Mary of Ldn to Abner HUMPHREY of Ldn. B/S of 21ac. Wit: Thos. HUMPHREY, Wm. BLEAKLY, Wm. FRANCIS.

Bk:Pg: 2E:092   Date: 5/14/1804   RcCt: 14 May 1804
John HESKET & wife Milley of Ldn to Phineas THOMAS of Ldn. B/S of 52ac, adj John ROMINE dec'd.

Bk:Pg: 2E:094   Date: 5/14/1804   RcCt: 14 May 1804
Joseph LEWIS Jr. of Ldn to Henry Joseph FRYE of Ldn. B/S of 94ac in Piedmont Manor now L/L by David JAY and son William JAY, adj John MARTIN, Peter VERTS, George SHOEMAKER.

Bk:Pg: 2E:096   Date: 5/14/1804   RcCt: 14 May 1804
Joseph LEWIS Jr. of Ldn to Henry Joseph FRYE of Ldn. Mortgage on 94ac.

Bk:Pg: 2E:097   Date: 5/14/1804   RcCt: 14 May 1804
John HESKET & wife Milley of Ldn to Amos JANNEY of Ldn. B/S of 2ac, adj road from Martin OVERFIELD to Israel JANNEY, Joseph JANNEY.

Bk:Pg: 2E:100   Date: 10/11/1803   RcCt: 14 May 1804
Joseph LEWIS Jr. of Ldn to Robert BRADEN of Ldn. B/S of 103ac in Piedmont L/L by Adam MILLER, adj Jacob VERTS, Mathias SMIDLEY,

Peter DERRY, John GEORGE. Wit: Timothy TAYLOR, Levi HOLE, Francis TRIPLETT, Philip TRIPLETT, Thomas A. HEREFORD.

Bk:Pg: 2E:102   Date: 5/4/1804   RcCt: 14 May 1804
Joseph LEWIS Jr. of Ldn to Philip FITZHUGH, lately of Marmion, King George Co. VA. B/S of 173ac "Clifton" on Panther Skin, adj Edward GARRETT, John GIBSON, Isaac GIBSON. Wit: George W. HUMPHREYS, I SANDERS, Wm. STEPHENSON, Wm. H. HARDING.

Bk:Pg: 2E:104   Date: 5/14/1804   RcCt: 14 May 1804
John THOMAS (s/o Joseph) & wife Leach of Ldn to William BLAKELY. B/S of 62ac at fork of Beaverdam of Goose Creek, adj John ROMINE. Wit: Thos. HUMPHREY, Wm. POWELL, Wm. ROBERTS.

Bk:Pg: 2E:107   Date: 1/23/1796   RcCt: 19 May 1796
William W. HARDING & wife Ann of Ldn to William WILSON. B/S of 440ac, adj Mary BOLAN. Wit: Thomas LEWIS, Philip WEAVER. Wilson C. SELDON, Samuel MURREY.

Bk:Pg: 2E:110   Date: 2/14/1804   RcCt: 14 May 1804
Peter LEE of Mason Co KY to Robert BRADEN of Ldn. PoA (because of moving) to adjust accts LEE authorized by Debby RAMEY Admr of Jacob RAMEY dec'd late of Ldn and as his attorney for him as Guardian to the heirs of RAMEY. Wit: John HAMILTON, Susanah LINDSAY.

Bk:Pg: 2E:110   Date: 1/12/1804   RcCt: 14 May 1804
Debby RAMEY of Mason Co KY to brother Peter LEE of Mason Co KY. PoA (because of moving) for her accts of Jacob RAMEY dec'd. Wit: Joseph DONIPHAN, Benj BAYLES.

Bk:Pg: 2E:112   Date: 4/5/1804   RcCt: 13 Oct 1794 and 14 May 1804
Joshua DANIEL & wife Jane of Ldn to James HAMILTON Jr. of Ldn. B/S of 430ac, adj Peter CARR, John WILLIAMS, William MAINS. Wit: Daniel McILROY, Cornelius ATCHER, Martha TEMPLER.

Bk:Pg: 2E:114   Date: 4/5/1794   RcCt: 13 Oct 1794 and 14 May 1804
Joshua DANIEL & wife Jane of Ldn to James HAMILTON of Ldn. B/S of 430ac on E side of Catocton Mt, adj Peter CARR, William MAINS. Wit: Daniel McILROY, Cornelius ATCHER, Martha TEMPLER.

Bk:Pg: 2E:117   Date: 3/16/1804   RcCt: 14 May 1804
Philip SOUDER and John SLATER (Exors of Anthony SOUDER dec'd) of Ldn to Peter FRYE of Ldn. B/S of 2 tracts totaling 176 3/4ac, adj Jacob STONEBURNER. Wit: Jacob ?[in German], Philip SOUDER Jr, Isaac LAROWE, name in German.

Bk:Pg: 2E:119   Date: 11/16/1786   RcCt: 12 Oct 1801
Archibald JOHNSTON of Ffx [also signed by Jerremiah JOHNSTON] to Richard CRUPPER of Ldn. B/S of 156ac, adj Bryan FAIRFAX, Col. Francis PEYTON, John WALKER. Wit: Benja'n DOWNS, Burr POWELL, Jno. HARRISON, Wm. BRONAUGH Jr.

Bk:Pg: 2E:122   Date: 11/22/1803   RcCt: 14 May 1804
Archibald JOHNSTON & wife Jemimiah to Richard CRUPPER. CoE for above 156*ac*. Wit: Francis PAYTON, Burr POWEL.

Bk:Pg: 2E:123   Date: 19 Feb 1801   RcCt: 14 May 1804
John Dalrymple ORR & wife Lucinda of PrWm to Gen. Henry LEE of Wstm. B/S - on 19 Oct 1741 two tracts on Goose Ck were granted to Capt William AYLETE, one for 609*ac* and one for 200*ac* which he passed one to daughter Mrs. Mary LEE wd/o Col. Thomas Ludwell LEE dec'd of StafVa, Mary conveyed to Dr. John Dalrymple ORR and he passed 11*ac* to Isaac GOUCHNOUER of Ldn and 205*ac* to Burr POWELL; 19 Feb 1801 selling 636*ac* to LEE. Wit: Benj. Grayson ORR, Stes. Thon. MASON, Leven POWELL, Thos. SWANN.

Bk:Pg: 2E:129   Date: 3/17/1804   RcCt: 14 May 1804
John SLATER & wife Catharine of Ldn to Philip SOUDER of Ldn. B/S of 89*ac*, adj Jacob FAWLEY, nr the school house. Wit: Jacob ?, Isaac LAROWE, ?

Bk:Pg: 2E:131   Date: 4/10/1804   RcCt: 14 May 1804
Samuel RITCHIE & wife Rachel of Ldn to Eneas GARRETT of FrdkMd. B/S of 157*ac* on Dutchman Run, adj Conrod ROLER, John George's Mill. Wit: Wm. H. HARDING, John H. CANBY, Edward McDANIEL, Richard CONER.

Bk:Pg: 2E:133   Date: 4/14/1804   RcCt: 14 May 1804
Ferdinando FAIRFAX of JeffVa to Eneas GARRETT of FrdkMd. B/S of 69½*ac* on SE side of Short hill in Shannondale. Wit: Edward McDANIEL, Thos. D. STEVENS, Thomas STEVENS, John H. CANBY.

Bk:Pg: 2E:135   Date: 4/14/1804   RcCt: 14 May 1804
Ferdinando FAIRFAX of JeffVa to Thomas Darnel STEPHENS of Ldn. B/S of 155½*ac* in Piedmont, adj William HOUGH, Jonath LODGE, Edward McDANIEL, Richard BROWN, William WILDMAN. Wit: John H. CANBY, Edward McDANIEL, Thomas STEPHENS, Wm. H. HARDING.

Bk:Pg: 2E:138   Date: 4/10/1804   RcCt: 14 May 1804
William ELLZEY & wife Frances of Ldn to Samuel RITCHIE of Ldn. B/S of 157*ac* on E side of Dutchman Run, adj Conrod ROLER, John GEORGE. Wit: Wm. H. HARDING, Jno. H. CANBY, Edward McDANIEL, Nisban? CUMER.

Bk:Pg: 2E:140   Date: 5/10/1804   RcCt: 14 May 1804
William GREGG (Exor of Samuel GREGG dec'd) of Ldn to James NIXON of Ldn. B/S of 158*ac* farm of Samuel GREGG, adj Jas. ROACH, Uriah WILLIAMS, Joseph TRIBBY, Nicholas SAUNDERS now dec'd, Jas. McILHANY. Wit: Jonas POTTS, Samuel CARR, Joseph WILKINSON.

Bk:Pg: 2E:141   Date: 7/16/1803   RcCt: 14 May 1804
Richard Bland LEE & wife Elizabeth of Sully in Ffx to Ferdinando FAIRFAX of JeffVa. B/S of 2325*ac* on S fork of Cattocton Creek, adj Israel THOMPSON, Patrick McGAVICK, Luke SMALLWOOD, John NICKLING, Charles LAWSON, John HOUGH, Isaac SIDDLE, John MARTIN, John

HOUGH, Jas. HAMILTON, George SHAFFER, James NIXON, Samuel EVANS. Wit: W. DENEAL, Bern'd CARTER, Francis ADAMS.

Bk:Pg: 2E:146　Date: 2/11/1804　RcCt: 14 May 1804
Ferdinando FAIRFAX of JeffVa to David LACY of Ldn. B/S of 182¾ac on road from Wtfd to Thompson's Mill, adj Sandford RAMEY. Wit: Wm. H. HARDING, Jno. H. CANBY.

Bk:Pg: 2E:148　Date: 11/3/1803　RcCt: 14 May 1804
William A. BINNS of Ldn to brother Charles BINNS of Ldn. PoA for survey due by writ of wright brought by Jno. ALEXANDER.

Bk:Pg: 2E:148　Date: 4/25/1804　RcCt: 15 May 1804
Thomas A. HEREFORD & wife Margaret to William WOODY. CoE for lot in Lsbg. Wit: Burr POWELL, William BRONAUGH.

Bk:Pg: 2E:149　Date: 5/15/1804　RcCt: 15 May 1804
Joshua DANIEL of Ldn. DoE for Negro man Sharper age 40y. Wit: Jno. HENRY, Timothy HIXON, Jacob BAUGH.

Bk:Pg: 2E:150　Date: 5/15/1804　RcCt: 15 May 1804
Robert FULTON of Ldn. DoE for Samuel JACKSON. Wit: Sampson BLINCOE, Henry LONG, G. W. BLINCOE.

Bk:Pg: 2E:151　Date: 3/24/1804　RcCt: 15 May 1804
Ferdinando FAIRFAX of Shannon hill in JeffVa to Andrew COPELAND of Ldn. Mortgage on 202¾ac. Wit: W. H. HARDING, Saml. H. YOUNG, Thos. LESLIE, Jno H. CANBY.

Bk:Pg: 2E:152　Date: 3/30/1804　RcCt: 10 Apr 1804
John GEORGE to Enos GARRETT of FrdkMd. Agreement - conveys 1ac to GARRETT adj farm GARRETT purchased of Samuel RITCHIE on Dutchman Run; GARRETT conveys to George 1ac partly covered by George's mill pond, adj Christopher FEARSNER. Wit: W. ELLZEY, Wm. H. HARDING, Simon SHOVER, Jno GEORGE, Saml RITCHIE Jr.

Bk:Pg: 2E:154　Date: 1/10/1804　RcCt: 15 May 1804
David LACEY & wife Sarah of Ldn to John SCHOOLY Jr. of Ldn. B/S of 10ac Lot #1 on survey by Robert BRADEN on Kittocton Mt nr Lsbg. Wit: Samuel HOUGH, William HOLMES.

Bk:Pg: 2E:156　Date: 1/4/1804　RcCt: 15 May 1804
David LACEY & wife Sarah of Ldn to Mungo DYKES of Lsbg. B/S of 9ac Lot #4 on survey by Robert BRADEN on Cattocton Mt nr Lsbg. Wit: Francis TRIPLETT, Mary WADE, John DRANE.

Bk:Pg: 2E:158　Date: 1/8/1789　RcCt: 15 May 1804
Henry Astley BENNETT to Peter DOWE. B/S of Negro girl Nancy age 10y for 15y period then she is emancipated; John COLVILLE of Ffx at time of his death had a number of slaves and considerable personal estate; COLVILLE devised all to Earl of Tankerville and the Earl to BENNETT and now slave girl to DOWE.

Bk:Pg: 2E:160   Date: 1/4/1804   RcCt: 15 May 1804
David LACEY & wife Sarah of Ldn to Francis TRIPLETT of Lsbg. B/S of
9ac Lot #7 on survey by Robert BRADEN on Catocton Mt nr Lsbg. Wit: S.
BLINCOE, G. W. BLINCOE, George FICHTER.

Bk:Pg: 2E:162   Date: 1/2/1804   RcCt: 15 May 1804
David LACEY & wife Sarah of Ldn to Barton LUCAS of Lsbg. B/S of 10ac
Lot #2 on survey by Robert BRADEN on Catocton Mt nr Lsbg. Wit:
Joseph BEARD, Anthony LAMBAG, Obadiah CLIFFORD.

Bk:Pg: 2E:164   Date: 5/28/1804   RcCt: 15 May 1804
Isaac BALL of Ldn to Rubin HIXON and Cornelious SHAWEEN of Ldn.
B/S of 81 perches of land, adj the Great Road from the Mill formerly Ball's
to Isaac Steer's Mill; this lot is conveyed by HIXON and SHAWEEN for
the purpose of a school house for the use of the following subscribers and
successors: Jno. MARTIN, Jno. HALL, Jacob SHIVELY, Thomas LACEY,
Nathan BALL, George FULTON, Jno McNEIL, Thomas DAVIS, Peter
HICKMAN, Jno. SHAVER, Frederick COOPER, James CAMPBELL,
Jacob RUCE, Daniel DAVIS, Michael BOGART, Geo VINCEL, Farling
BALL, Farling BALL Jr., Adam HOUSHOLDER Jr., and said HIXON &
SHAWEEN. Wit: William HIXON, Jacob DAVIS, Solomon DAVIS.

Bk:Pg: 2E:166   Date: 1/6/1804   RcCt: 15 May 1804
David LACEY & wife Sarah of Ldn to John McCORMICK of Lsbg. B/S of
9ac Lot #3 on survey by Robert BRADEN on Catocton Mt nr Lsbg. Wit:
Giles TILLETT, Joseph KNOW.

Bk:Pg: 2E:168   Date: 10/12/1803   RcCt: 14 May 1804
George Fairfax LEE and John Tasker CARTER of WstmVa to Archibald
McVICAR of Ldn. B/S of 220ac, adj Leven LUKET, Silas ROSE. Wit: Geo.
CARTER, Josh'a DANNIEL, Thomas FOUCHE, Joseph BEARD, Jno.
MATTHIAS.

Bk:Pg: 2E:171   Date: 1/2/1804   RcCt: 15 May 1804
David LACEY & wife Sarah of Ldn to George FEICHTER of Lsbg. B/S of
9ac Lot #6 on survey by Robert BRADEN on Catoctan Mt nr Lsbg. Wit: S.
BLINCOE, G. W. BLINCOE, Francis TRIPLETT.

Bk:Pg: 2E:173   Date: 7/18/1803   RcCt: 15 May 1804
Thomas SIM & wife Kitty of Lsbg to Samuel MURREY of Lsbg. B/S of Lot
#52 in Lsbg. Wit: C. BINNS, Martin CORDELL, Patrick H. DOUGLAS,
Chas. BENNETT, Jno. ROSE.

Bk:Pg: 2E:177   Date: 5/1/1804   RcCt: 14 May 1804
William LITTLEJOHN of Ldn to Josiah MOFFETT of Ldn. B/S of Lot #46
on Cornwall St in Lsbg, adj James HAMILTON. Wit: C. BINNS, Isaac
HARRIS, Jas. HAMILTON.

Bk:Pg: 2E:178   Date: 5/15/1804   RcCt: 15 May 1804
Thomas N. BINNS of Ldn. DoE for Negro man Thomas GALLOWAY age
40y.

Bk:Pg: 2E:179   Date: 6/11/1804   RcCt: 11 Jun 1804
Thos. N. FIELDS, Wm. JONES, Archibald McVICAR, Temple SMITH & Jno. LINTON. Bond on FIELDS as Constable of Ldn.

Bk:Pg: 2E:180   Date: 7/9/1804   RcCt: 9 Jul 1804
William LITTLEJOHN of Ldn to Robert PERFECT of Ldn. B/S of 1ac lot #32 in Lsbg.

Bk:Pg: 2E:182   Date: 3/14/1804   RcCt: 12 Apr 1804
John McIVER (Admr dbn of William SMITH dec'd of Alexandria, DC) to Samuel MURRAY of Lsbg. B/S of small lot on main road leading through Loudoun St in Lsbg, adj Lot #57 now occupied by Charles GULLATT, same lot conveyed by Jno. HEREFORD & wife to SMITH. Wit: Jno. SCHOOLEY Jr., Jas. CAVAN Jr., Isaac HARRIS, David ENGLISH.

Bk:Pg: 2E:185   Date: 6/9/1804   RcCt: 9 Jul 1804
Richard PURCY & wife Elizabeth of Lsbg to Daniel DOWLING of Lsbg. B/S of lot in Lsbg formerly the property of Henry McCABE, adj Martin CORDELL, John DRISH. Wit: Samuel MURRAY, Francis H. PEYTON.

Bk:Pg: 2E:188   Date: 11/15/1803   RcCt: 9 Jul 1804
William SIMPSON of Ldn to Richard PRESGRAVES. Trust using 3 negroes PRESGRAVES hired, farm and household items, for land where SIMPSON now lives. Wit: Jno. LOVE, Wm. PRESGRAVES, George HALL.

Bk:Pg: 2E:189   Date: 8/27/1803   RcCt: 9 Jul 1804
Sebastian LOSH & wife Jane to Patrick McINTYRE. Agreement - to rent McINTYRE 2 lots in Lsbg. Wit: Christopher ROPER, Jno. MATTHIAS, Joseph T. NEWTON.

Bk:Pg: 2E:191   Date: 11/1/1803   RcCt: 9 Jul 1804
George Emley GOFF & wife Mary to Richard PURDY. CoE for sale of Lot #12 in Lsbg. Wit: Robert CAMPBELL, Jno. GOLD.

Bk:Pg: 2E:192   Date: 3/6/1804   RcCt: 9 Jul 1804
John MANSFIELD & wife Mary of Ldn to Richard PURDY of Lsbg. B/S of part of lot formerly of Henry McCABE, adj Martin CORDELL on main road from Lsbg to Noland's Ferry. Wit: S. BLINCOE, G. W. BLINCOE, Eli OFFUTT, Jno. ALEXANDER, Saml MURRAY.

Bk:Pg: 2E:196   Date: 7/7/1804   RcCt: 9 Jul 1804
Asa MOORE of Wtfd to Thos. PHILLIPS of Wtfd. B/S of small lot adj MOORE.

Bk:Pg: 2E:198   Date: 8/26/1803   RcCt: 9 Jul 1804
William BETTS & wife Mary of Grason Co VA to Asa MOORE of Wtfd. B/S of 50ac, adj Jno. HAMILTON.

Bk:Pg: 2E:200   Date: 1/27/1804   RcCt: 9 Jul 1804
George BRENT & wife Mary of StafVa to Col. Leven POWELL of Ldn. B/S of 480ac, adj William P. BAYLY, Jno. BAYLY, Col. Leven POWELL, Burr POWELL, Jno. P. POWELL, William HALE. Wit: Walter S. BELT, Edwin

C. MONCURE, Benjn WILLIAMS, Henry WOODROW, Matth NORMAN, Richd Bland LEE, Jno. MONCURE, E. MASON.

Bk:Pg: 2E:204   Date: 9/8/1803   RcCt: ___
Thos. D. STEPHENS & wife Mary to Josiah WHITE. CoE for sale of 9 3/8ac in Hllb. Wit: James McILHANY, James HAMILTON.

Bk:Pg: 2E:205   Date: 3/19/1804   RcCt: 9 Jul 1804
William NOLAND of Ldn to Samuel CLAPHAM of Ldn. B/S of 21ac. Wit: Thos. NOLAND, Jno. MATTHIAS, James JOHNSON Jr.

Bk:Pg: 2E:207   Date: 12/19/1803   RcCt: 4 Aug 1804
Jonathan EDWARDS of Ldn to Edward B. EDWARDS of Ldn. BoS for Negro boy Dennis abt 12 or 13y old. Wit: Leven POWELL, Jno. LINTON.

Bk:Pg: 2E:208   Date: 8/3/1804   RcCt: 13 Aug 1804
Spencer BALL of PrWm [signed for by Fleet SMITH] to Dr. Thomas SIM of Lsbg. BoS for Negro man Jesse. Wit: Wm. H. TRIPLETT, Jno. W. COOKE.

Bk:Pg: 2E:209   Date: 6/29/1804   RcCt: 10 Sep 1804
Thomas HARRISON Jr. & wife Mary of PrWm to Colin AULD of Alexandria, DC. B/S of 150ac for part conveyed to HARRISON by Tobert MILLIGAN. Wit: B. DADE, W. SEATON, Jno. NEILE.

Bk:Pg: 2E:211   Date: 9/8/1804   RcCt: 10 Sep 1804
Thos. D. STEPHENS & wife Mary Eleaner of Ldn to Josiah WHITE Jr. of Ldn. B/S of 3/8ac, part of 5/8ac (2/8ac conveyed to son Jno. B. STEVENS), adj James ROACH. Wit: Jas. HAMILTON, David GOODWIN, Thos. HOUGH, Mahlon ROACH, Levi HOLE.

Bk:Pg: 2E:214   Date: 9/10/1804   RcCt: 10 Sep 1804
Saml RITCHEY of Ldn to Enas GARRETT. Deed of assignment.

Bk:Pg: 2E:215   Date: 3/24/1804   RcCt: 10 Sep 1804
Ferdinando FAIRFAX and William B. PAGE of JeffVa to William THOMPSON of Ldn. B/S of 64¾ac in Shannondale, adj Nancy WILLIAMS, William EVANS, Thomas LESLIE, Nicholas TUCKER. Wit: Saml. W. YOUNG, Andrew COPELAND, Thos. LESLIE, Wm. H. HARDING.

Bk:Pg: 2E:218   Date: 9/10/1804   RcCt: 10 Sep 1804
John IDAN & wife Hannah of Ldn to Mahlon BALDWIN of Ldn. B/S of 64ac on Goose Creek.

Bk:Pg: 2E:221   Date: 5/9/1804   RcCt: 10 Sep 1804
Edward HATFIELD of PA to Conrad NEAR of Ldn. A/L of 100ac. Wit: Nicholas OSBORN, Abraham OSBORN, Andrew MYERS.

Bk:Pg: 2E:223   Date: 4/7/1804   RcCt: 10 Sep 1804
Abraham OSBORNE & wife Rachel & daughter Mary of Ldn to Samuel Wade YOUNG of Ldn. B/S of leased 100ac in ShelP. Wit: Josiah WHITE Jr., Thos. WHITE, Edward CUNARD Sr.

Bk:Pg: 2E:228   Date: 9/10/1804   RcCt: 10 Sep 1804
James SINCLAIR & wife Mary of Ldn [signed as SINKLER] to Joseph DANIEL of Ldn. B/S of 150*ac* on Little River.

Bk:Pg: 2E:229   Date: 9/10/1804   RcCt: 10 Sep 1804
Peter RITCHIE & wife Elizabeth of Ldn to Jacob FAWLEY of Ldn. B/S of 105 7/8*ac* Lot #12 on Paynes & Summers survey on Cotoctin, formerly leased by Joseph FIRESTONE, adj Michael SHEIK, Peter FRY, Philip HUFF. Wit: Henry HUFF, John FOWLY, Josiah MOFFETT.

Bk:Pg: 2E:231   Date: 5/1/1804   RcCt: 10 Sep 1804
John FAWLEY & wife Margrett of Ldn to John WEIST. B/S of 4½*ac* on S side of Roach's Mill road. Wit: Cornelius SHAWEEN, John McNEEL, George FULTON, Henry HUFF, Jacob FAWLEY.

Bk:Pg: 2E:234   Date: 9/10/1804   RcCt: 10 Sep 1804
Peter RITCHIE & wife Elizabeth of Ldn to Michael SHEIK of Ldn. B/S of 13*ac*, Lot #12 on Payne & Sommers Survey formerly Catoctan Manor but now Tankerville. Wit: Henry HUFF, Josiah MOFFETT, Jno. FOWLEY.

Bk:Pg: 2E:236   Date: 7/9/1804   RcCt: 10 Sep 1804
George FORTNEY & wife Susannah of Lsbg to Daniel DOWLING of Lsbg and Thomas JANNEY of Alexandria, DC (copartners in firm of Daniel Dowling & Co). B/S of lot on W end of Lsbg and N side of Market St. Wit: Francis H. PEYTON, Samuel MURRAY, Martin KITZMILLER.

Bk:Pg: 2E:237   Date: 2/11/1805   RcCt: 12 Feb 1805
Daniel EMREY & wife Yenaith? of Ldn to Jno. DAVIS of Ldn. B/S of 150*ac*.

Bk:Pg: 2E:239   Date: 4/16/1804   RcCt: 10 Sep 1804
Wilson Cary SELDEN & wife Eleanor of Ldn to William CARR of Ldn. B/S of 76*ac* on Tuskarora. Wit: Isaac HARRIS, Jas. HAMILTON, B. HOUGH, Samuel MURREY, Fra. H. PEYTON.

Bk:Pg: 2E:240   Date: 5/1/1802   RcCt: 10 Sep 1804
William HOUGH, Samuel HOUGH & Mahlon HOUGH of Ldn as Exors of John HOUGH dec'd to Isaac STEER of Ldn. B/S of 325*ac*, adj Ebenezer GRUBB, William HOUGH, road to German Settlement, Jacob WINE, Anthony CUNARD, William PAXON, Conrad WERTZ. Wit: Jas. MOORE, Jonah HOUGH, Asa MOORE, Thos. PHILLIPS, Edward CUNARD Sr., Josiah WHITE Jr., Jesse TALBOTT.

Bk:Pg: 2E:243   Date: 5/1/1802   RcCt: 10 Sep 1804
William HOUGH, Samuel HOUGH and Mahlon HOUGH of Ldn (Exors of John HOUGH dec'd) to Asa MOORE of Ldn. B/S of 104¾*ac* on Kittocton Creek, adj Ebenezer GRUBB, Conrod WERTZ, Jacob SHIBELEY. Wit: Jas. MOORE, Daniel STONE, Thos. PHILLIPS, Jonah HOUGH, Edward CUNARD Sr, Josiah WHITE Jr., Thos. PHILLIPS, Jesse TALBOTT.

Bk:Pg: 2E:246   Date: 3/24/1804   RcCt: 10 Sep 1804
Ferdinando FAIRFAX of Shannon hill, JeffVa to Samuel Wade YOUNG of Ldn. B/S of revisionary right title of 77*ac* for lot leased to Morris DAVIS in Shannondale, adj James NELSON, Andrew COPELAND, Mrs. Hannah

FEARST, Wm. EVANS, Wm. THOMPSON. Wit: Wm. H. HARDING, Thos. LESLIE, Andrew COPELAND, Wm. THOMPSON.

Bk:Pg: 2E:248   Date: 3/24/1804   RcCt: 10 Sep 1804
Ferdinando FAIRFAX & Wm. Byrd PAGE of JeffVa to Samuel M. YOUNG of Ldn. B/S of revisionary right title of 128*ac*, adj Michael LONG, William GRUBB, Robert MORRISS, John WOLFCAIL, Conrad DARR. Wit: Wm. H. HARDING, Thos. LESLIE, And'w COPELAND, Wm. THOMPSON.

Bk:Pg: 2E:256   Date: 2/25/1804   RcCt: 10 Sep 1804
[signed by] Hugh BARR and Wm. BARR to George and Adam BARR. Assignment - 100*ac* George BARR dec'd possessed which he purchased of Thomas MOORE and had his bond of conveyance and George died intestate but intended his sons George, Thomas & Adam should have the land. Wit: A. GIBSON, Jas. BATTSON, Jesse McVEIGH, Jas. HAGARMAN, Joseph PATTERSON.

Bk:Pg: 2E:257   Date: 4/21/1803   RcCt: 9 May 1804
Alexander ODEN of CamP to Ariss BUCKNER of CamP. B/S of 54½*ac*, part of larger tract divided among several heirs of his father. Wit: Hezekiah ODEN, John KIMBLER, Joseph BLINCOE, Phillip PALMER.

Bk:Pg: 2E:259   Date: 4/12/1804   RcCt: 10 Sep 1804
Samuel Wade YOUNG & wife Ruth of Ldn to Thomas HOUGH of Ldn. B/S of 128*ac* adj Jno. EVANS, Morris DAVIS, Thos. HOUGH & Ebenezer WILSON; and 77*ac* adj James NELSON, Andrew COPELAND, Mrs. Hannah FEARCIS, Wm. EVANS, William THOMPSON & James NELSON. Wit: Wm. H. HARDING, Josiah WHITE Jr., Thos. WHITE, Jno. H. CANBY, Jno. LYONS, Johnston CLEVELAND.

Bk:Pg: 2E:263   Date: 6/11/1804   RcCt: 10 Sep 1804
Robert McCORMICK of Ldn to Samuel DUNKIN of Ldn. B/S of 26*ac* adj Samuel.

Bk:Pg: 2E:264   Date: 4/9/1804   RcCt: 10 Sep 1804
William H. PEAKE, John PEAKE, Sally PEAKE, Mary PEAKE, Elizabeth FOWKE, Thos. PEAKE & George PEAKE of Ldn to David FULTON. BoS for Negro boy Juba. Wit: Wm. FOWKE, Mahlon FULTON.

Bk:Pg: 2E:265   Date: 9/10/1804   RcCt: 10 Sep 1804
Mary TAYLOR of Ldn to Thos. FOUCH & Israel LACEY of Ldn. Trust for 124*ac*.

Bk:Pg: 2E:267   Date: 2/10/1804   RcCt: 9 Jul 1804
Nathaniel CRAWFORD & wife Sarah of PrG to Samuel DUNKIN of Ldn. B/S of 88½*ac*, adj Isaac COGIL, Joseph HOGUE, Isaac BROWN, Samuel SMITH Jr. Wit: Wm. ELLZEY, Thos. SWANN, Joseph LEWIS Jr., Saml HEPBURN, David CRAWFORD.

Bk:Pg: 2E:271   Date: 2/15/1804   RcCt: 10 Sep 1804
Jno. Tasker CARTER and George Fairfax LEE of Mt. Pleasant, WstmVa to Mary TAYLOR. B/S of 124*ac*, adj Robert CARTER Jr, Joseph JONES. Wit: George CARTER, Nathaniel BUTLER, Willoughby NEWTON, Spencer BALL, Henry L. YEATMAN.

Bk:Pg: 2E:273   Date: 12/19/1803   RcCt: 10 Sep 1804
James SINCLAIR & wife Mary of Ldn to Jno. SINCLAIR of Ldn. B/S of
54ac on little river of Goose Creek, adj James SINCLAIR, James
MERCER. Wit: Wm. SINCLAIR, Traverse GEORGE, Wm. GEORGE, Ely
GIBSON, Jas. HIXON.

Bk:Pg: 2E:275   Date: 9/11/1804   RcCt: 11 Sep 1804
Christopher ROSE of Ldn to Thomas FOUCH and Israel LACEY of Ldn.
Trust to secure payment of ROSE's purchase from Jno. T. CARTER and
George F. LEE.

Bk:Pg: 2E:277   Date: 2/15/1804   RcCt: 8 Oct 1804
Jno. Tasker CARTER and George Fairfax LEE of Mt. Pleasant, WstmVa
to Christopher ROSE of Ldn. B/S of 182ac, adj Archibald McVICAR. Wit:
George CARTER, Nathaniel BUTLER, Willoughby NEWTON, Spencer
BALL, Henry L. YEATMAN.

Bk:Pg: 2E:281   Date: 5/4/1804   RcCt: 14 May 1804
Ferdinando FAIRFAX of Shannon hill, JeffVa to Joseph LEWIS Jr. of Ldn.
B/S of 4713ac of Piedmont, adj Pateson WRIGHT, Patrick McGAVICK,
Jonah THOMPSON, Jonathan LODGE, Samuel EVANS, James NIXON,
George SHAFFER, Jas. HAMILTON, Benjamin STEERE, Thomas
PHILLIPS. Wit: Geo. W. HUMPHREY, Wm. STEPHENSON, I.
SANDERS, Wm. H. HARDING, Phillip FITZHUGH.

Bk:Pg: 2E:285   Date: 4/28/1804   RcCt: 10 Oct 1804
John LEWIS of Ldn to Isaac RICHARDS of Ldn. BoS for cow and
household items. Wit: Wm. CHAMBLIN.

Bk:Pg: 2E:286   Date: 3/28/1804   RcCt: 8 Oct 1804
Jno. TURLEY & wife Mary of Ldn to Reubin HUTCHINSON of PrWm. B/S
of 174ac on branches of broad run, adj Joseph LACEY. Wit: Geo. NEALE,
Sampson TURLEY, Job RACE.

Bk:Pg: 2E:288   Date: 3/29/1804   RcCt: 8 Oct 1804
Jno TURLEY of Ldn to Reuben HUTCHINSON of PrWm. Release for
above land. Wit: Geo NEALE, Sampson TURLEY, Job RACE.

Bk:Pg: 2E:290   Date: 3/3/1804   RcCt: 8 Oct 1804
Jno. SINCLAIR of Sullivan Co TN to George SINCLAIR of Ldn. B/S of
John's share of land held by Mary SINCLAIR (m. Israel SEARS) as her
right of dower from marriage with Jno. SINCLAIR the elder, father to seller
Jno. Wit: Joseph STEERE, Isaac LARROWE, Jno. SWORD, Hannah
STEERE.

Bk:Pg: 2E:292   Date: 9/25/1804   RcCt: 8 Oct 1804
Leven POWELL & wife Sarah of Ldn to Richd Bland LEE of Ffx. B/S of
500ac, adj lands of William HALE, Wm. P. BAYLEY & Burr POWELL, for
purpose of holding the title until LEE made the payment, which has now
been done. Wit: A. GIBSON, Burr POWELL, Henry BRAWNER, Thos. A.
HEREFORD.

Bk:Pg: 2E:293   Date: 8/15/1804   RcCt: 8 Oct 1804
Richard LEE & wife Elizabeth of Ffx to Leven LUCKETT of Ldn. B/S of
420¾ac, adj Richd CRUPPER, Leven LUCKETT, James GUN. Wit: Noble
BEVERIDGE, A. GIBSON, Mesheck LACEY, Jas. BATTSON, Hugh
ROGERS, Leven POWELL, Burr POWELL.

Bk:Pg: 2E:295   Date: 9/28/1804   RcCt: 8 Oct 1804
Richard Bland LEE & wife Elizabeth of Ffx to Burr POWELL of Ldn. B/S of
259¼ac, adj John BATTSON. Wit: Francis ADAMS, Jno KEENE.

Bk:Pg: 2E:299   Date: 7/20/1804   RcCt: 8 Oct 1804
Jno. Peyton HARRISON & wife Elizabeth of StafVa to Richd Bland LEE of
Ldn. B/S of 570ac, adj Leven LUCKETT, Richard CRUPPER. Wit: Burr
POWELL, Thos. SIM, Wm. CHILTON, Leven POWELL, Hancock
EUSTAU, Saml H. PEYTON.

Bk:Pg: 2E:302   Date: 9/20/1804   RcCt: 8 Oct 1804
Richard Bland LEE & wife Elizabeth of Ffx to William WILLIAMSON of
Fqr. B/S of 218 5/8ac, adj Burr POWELL. Wit: Francis ADAMS, John
KEENE.

Bk:Pg: 2E:305   Date: 6/12/1804   RcCt: 8 Oct 1804
Jas. CLAYPOOLE & wife Sibbe of Fqr to George TAVENOR of Ldn. B/S
of 89ac, adj Wm. BROWN. Wit: Blackstone JANNY, Stacy TAYLOR, Jno.
HAMILTON, Joseph VANDEVANTER.

Bk:Pg: 2E:307   Date: 6/12/1804   RcCt: 8 Oct 1804
Jas. CLAYPOOLE & wife Sibbe of Fqr to George TAVENOR of Ldn. B/S -
Fauquier Ct chancery suit of Mar 1804 between plt Jas. CLAYPOOL and
def Esther WILLIS, Spencer WILLIS, Seth WILLIS, Isaac WILLIS, Rachel
WILLIS, Susannah WILLIS, Edward WILLIS, Wm. WILLIS, Lydia WILLIS
& Hannah PRICE the legatees of Joel WILLIS dec'd and Isaac WILLIS
Exor of Joel's estate, suit said def must convey to plt all lands Joseph
CLAYPOOLE & wife Ann conveyed by lease to Joel WILLIS less 100ac
WILLIS sold to TAVENOR leaving 113ac, now sold to TAVENOR. Wit:
Bleackston JANNY, Stacy TAYLOR, Jno HAMILTON, Joseph
VANDEVENTER.

Bk:Pg: 2E:311   Date: 5/14/1804   RcCt: 8 Oct 1804
Mahlon COMBS & wife Sarah of Ldn to Joseph GARRETT and Joseph
BURROUGHS as trustees for the Baptist Society of the Northfork Meeting
House. B/S of land on which Northfork meeting house stands. Wit:
Edward COE, Conrod LICKEY, Walter POWER, Wm. WILKISON.

Bk:Pg: 2E:312   Date: 6/1/1804   RcCt: 8 Oct 1804
William CULLISON of Ldn to Leven HARL & daughter Jamima HARL.
Jamima bond as apprentice to CULLISON until she is 18y old on 16 Mar
1813, to do spinning and sewing for the family and teach her to read and
write, since CULLISON is aged she could be willed to another person.
Wit: Chas. VEALE, Wm. VEALE, Jno. VEALE.

Bk:Pg: 2E:314   Date: 6/1/1804   RcCt: 8 Oct 1804
Jeremiah CULLISON of Ldn to Leven HARL, sons James HARL &
Tompson HARL of Ldn. James & Tompson bind themselves to
CULLISON until each reaches 21y (James on 23 Oct 1812 and Tompson
on 29 Nov 1821) and as CULLISON is old they can be willed to someone
else. Wit: Chas. VEALE, Wm. VEALE, Jno. VEALE.

Bk:Pg: 2E:316   Date: 10/18/1804   RcCt: 8 Oct 1804
Absalom HAWLEY of Ldn to George KILLGORE of Ldn. BoS for horses
and feed. Wit: James LEWIS, Christopher SKILLMAN.

Bk:Pg: 2E:317   Date: 9/26/1804   RcCt: 8 Oct 1804
Wm. B. HARRISON, Chas. LEWIS and Absalom HAWLEY as
commissioners appointed by Ct to George KILLGORE of Ldn. B/S of 40ac
with mill - by decree of 14 Jun 1804 of plt George KILLGORE and
defendents widow Rebekah FOX & George Killgore FOX, Martenea B.
FOX, Ann H. FOX, Elizabeth FOX & Jane FOX infant children of Jas. FOX
dec'd decreed land and mill of George KILLGORE be sold. Wit: Stephen
BEARD, Vincent L. LEWIS, Newton B. COCKERILL, Thos. E. MINOR.

Bk:Pg: 2E:319   Date: 3/23/1804   RcCt: 8 Oct 1804
William MOXLEY & wife Sally of PrWm to William CARR of Ldn. B/S of
17½ac, near Carolina Road adj Samuel MURRAY. Wit: Obadiah
CLIFFORD, James HAMILTON, Alexander COUPER Jr., Samuel
MURRAY.

Bk:Pg: 2E:322   Date: 10/7/1802   RcCt: 12 Oct 1802
Joseph GIBSON (s/o Isaac) of Ldn to Isaac GIBSON of Alexandria, DC.
B/S of Joseph's share of the following - Isaac GIBSON the elder died
some time ago on 260 acre tract where he lived and law prescribes 1/3
goes to widow Hesther as her dower and the remainder be divided
amongst his children William, Joseph, Moses, Isaac, Alice, Rachel,
Elizabeth and Samuel. Wit: Jno. GIBSON, Amos GIBSON, Thos. WREN.

Bk:Pg: 2E:324   Date: 3/17/1804   RcCt: 14 May 1804
Jeremiah McVEIGH & wife Sarah of Ldn to William BLAKELY of Ldn. B/S
of 14¾ac, part of Jno. ROMINE dec'd division amongst heirs. Wit: Ben
GRAYSON, Wm. BRONAUGH, Wm. WOODFORD, Alexr INNES.

Bk:Pg: 2E:327   Date: 4/5/1804   RcCt: 8 Oct 1804
Thos. HIRST & wife Anne of Wtfd to James RUSSELL of Wtfd. B/S of lots
#3 and #4 in Wtfd, adj Mahlon JANNY, William HOUGH. Wit: Jas.
MOORE, Danl. STONE, Israel H. THOMPSON, Jno. Henry DOLEMAN,
Chas. BENNETT, Jas. HAMILTON.

Bk:Pg: 2E:330   Date: 9/11/1804   RcCt: 11 Sep 1804
Ferdinando FAIRFAX of JeffVa to Hannah MILLER of Ldn. B/S of
revisionary interest in 3ac in Piedmont, adj Jonah THOMPSON, Joseph
LEWIS, where Hannah now resides.

Bk:Pg: 2E:332   Date: 9/10/1804   RcCt: 8 Oct 1804
Ferdinando FAIRFAX and William Byrd PAGE of JeffVa by their attorney
Wm. H. HARDING to Thos. HUMPHREY of Ldn. B/S of 134½ac, on NW

side of Short Hill in Shannondale, adj Joseph BEAL, Robert WHITE, Nicholas TUCKER, Andrew COPELAND, Thos. HOUGH. Wit: Thos. HOUGH, Joseph DANIEL, Charles HUMPHREY, Mahlon ROACH, Wm. ELLZEY.

Bk:Pg: 2E:334   Date: 8/25/1804   RcCt: 8 Oct 1804
Hannah, Betsy, Nancy and Sally DEHAVEN of Scott Co KY to Jacob DEHAVEN of Scott Co KY. PoA to receive their legacies from Jno. S'CLAIR to his daughter Mary DEHAVEN also dec'd (they are her heirs).

Bk:Pg: 2E:336   Date: 10/8/1804   RcCt: 8 Oct 1804
Hannah, Betsy, Nancy & Sally DEHAVEN of Scott Co KY by attorney in fact Jacob DEHAVEN to Samuel SINCLAIR of Ldn. B/S of undivided share descended to their mother from the estate of Jno. SINCLAIR dec'd, being part of the lands held by Mary SINCLAIR wd/o Jno SINCLAIR as her dower. Wit: Isaac LARROW.

Bk:Pg: 2E:337   Date: 8/13/1804   RcCt: 8 Oct 1804
Josiah CRAVEN of Ldn to Abner CRAVEN of Ldn. B/S of Josiah's full share from father Thos. CRAVEN dec'd. Wit: Aaron SANDERS, John LITTLEJOHN, Thos. WILKERSON, Isaac LARROWE.

Bk:Pg: 2E:339   Date: 2/19/1802   RcCt: 13 Sep 1802
Thos. PURSELL & wife Lydia of Ldn to Thos. LESLIE of Ldn. B/S of 30 perches and buildings, in Gap of Short hill on turnpike road, adj David SMITH, Thos. LESLIE. Wit: Aaron SANDERS, Saml. RUSSELL, Thos. HOUGH.

Bk:Pg: 2E:341   Date: 6/13/1804   RcCt: 8 Oct 1804
Wm. Hough CRAVEN of PrWm to Abner CRAVEN of Ldn. B/S of Wm.'s full share from father Thos. CRAVEN dec'd. Wit: Aaron SANDERS, Jas. SANDERS, Josiah CRAVEN, Jos. CRAVEN.

Bk:Pg: 2E:343   Date: 9/10/1804   RcCt: 8 Oct 1804
Jonas POTTS of Lsbg to Samuel CLAPHAM of Lsbg and George TAVENDER Admr and Jemima HOLLINGSWORTH widow & relict of Jno. HOLLINGSWORTH dec'd. B/S - HOLLINGSWORTH had land in trust to Jas. HEATON, Jonas POTTS and Robert BRADEN with agreement they sell the land and pay Richard ROACH dec'd heirs; HOLLINGSWORTH died in 1803; BRADEN and HEATON sold land to Jonas POTTS; before final sale Jemima claimed 1/3 of sale as her dower; CLAPHAM given deed of trust for 300ac. Wit: Saml. CARR, Chas. SHEPHERD, Thos. SWANN.

Bk:Pg: 2E:347   Date: 6/8/1804   RcCt: 9 Oct 1804
Samuel H. WHEELER & wife Ann of MontMd to Tilghman HILLARY & wife Ann of PrG. B/S of 296ac, part of tract purchased by Clement WHEELER which by Clement's will was to be divided between Samuel H. WHEELER & Ann HILLARY the wife of Tilghman HILLARY. Wit: Lawrence C. NEALE, Richard BEALL.

Bk:Pg: 2E:350   Date: 11/8/1803   RcCt: 7 Dec 1803 and 10 Dec 1804
George GRAHAM and Jno. GRAHAM by his attorney George GRAHAM
Exors of Richard GRAHAM dec'd and Jane GRAHAM the widow to Jno.
MYERS of Ldn. B/S - George GRAHAM contracted with Matthew
HARRISON in 1799 to sell him ½ac lot in Lsbg of the estate of Richard
GRAHAM, HARRISON built an office & stable on the lot and then sold it
to Jno. MYERS but MYERS never received a deed; now transferring the
deed. Wit: Andrew RAMSAY, Jas. LARIMER, Jno. WATERS.

Bk:Pg: 2E:352   Date: 6/24/1804   RcCt: 10 Dec 1804
Jno. IREY & wife Sarah of Ldn to Abel DAVIS of Ldn. B/S of 19ac on
Crooked Run, adj George FAIRHURST, James HATCHER. Wit: Gideon
DAVIS, George FAIRHIRST, Jno. BOLON, Isaiah POTTS.

Bk:Pg: 2E:354   Date: 12/10/1804   RcCt: 10 Dec 1804
Jno. IREY & wife Sarah of Ldn to Eli JANNEY of Ldn. B/S of 66 perches
on Crooked Run, adj Hamilton ROGERS. Wit: Gideon DAVIS, Blackston
JANNEY, Abel DAVIS, Thos. JANNEY.

Bk:Pg: 2E:356   Date: 12/1/1804   RcCt: 10 Dec 1802
Price JACOBS & wife Sarah of Ldn to Swithen NICHOLS of Ldn. B/S of
62ac, adj Reubin TRIPLETT, Jno. O'NEALE.

Bk:Pg: 2E:358   Date: 12/10/1804   RcCt: 10 Dec 1804
James LOVE & wife Susannah of Ldn to Philip FRY of Ldn. B/S of 188ac,
adj Spencer PEW, Jno. BALDWIN, Elisha MARKS, Peter HAND. Wit: Sn.
BLINCOE, Saml. DONOHOE, Christian SAGER.

Bk:Pg: 2E:259   Date: 6/16/1804   RcCt: 10 Dec 1804
Jno. McGEATH of Ldn to James MOORE and Dr. Isaac HOUGH of Ldn.
Trust - to secure debt due to James McILHANY, trust on 120ac adj
Stephen SCOTT, Murto SULLIVAN, Wm. HOUGH, Jesse TAYLOR, Wm.
WRIGHT, Joshua DANIEL. Wit: Thos. PHILLIPS, Wm. HAMILTON, Israel
H. THOMPSON, Richd GRIFFITH.

Bk:Pg: 2E:361   Date: 3/10/1804   RcCt: 10 Dec 1804
George Fairfax LEE of WstmVa to Hugh QUINLAN of WstmVa. B/S of
300ac on Goose Creek adj George CARTER and now occupied by Wm.
FIELDS as tenant for life. Wit: Jno. RAWAN, Mary CURTIS, Wm. C.
CHANDLER, Chs. R. THOMPSON, Thos. CHANDLER, Daniel CRABB,
Richd B. JOHNSTON.

Bk:Pg: 2E:363   Date: 6/30/1804   RcCt: 10 Dec 1804
James PRYOR of Hllb to Enos BEST of Ldn. Trust on 2 story house on S
side of main st in Hllb now occupied by PRYOR to secure debt. Wit:
Mahlon HOUGH, Charles HUMPHREY.

Bk:Pg: 2E:364   Date: 5/24/1804   RcCt: 10 Oct 1804
Jonah THOMPSON & wife Margaret and Richd VEITCH & wife Elizabeth
of Alexandria, DC to Amos THOMPSON of Ldn. B/S of 372ac on broad
run old church tract. Memo - if THOMPSON should be evicted by an older
& better title his money will be refunded. Wit: C. THOMPSON, Israel P.
THOMPSON, Jno. McIVER, R. J. TAYLOR, Thos. SWANN, John

SHREVE, Ann THOMPSON, Ann Eliz ALRICKS, Cuthbt. POWELL, Jacob HOFFMAN.

Bk:Pg: 2E:369   Date: 3/15/1804   RcCt: 10 Sep 1804
Jonah THOMPSON and Richd VEITCH of Alexandria, DC to Amos THOMPSON & wife Jane of Ldn. Mortgage for purchase of 372*ac*. Wit: Jas. CAVAN Jr., Saml MURRAY, Jno. SCHOOLEY Jr., Jno. McIVER.

Bk:Pg: 2E:373   Date: 11/14/1804   RcCt: 10 Dec 1804
Michael RUSE of Ldn to James HAMILTON of Ldn. A/L of 100*ac*. Wit: Isaac HOUGH, Jas. NIXON, Mary W. McFARLING.

Bk:Pg: 2E:374   Date: 7/24/1804   RcCt: 10 Dec 1804
Jesse TAYLOR & wife Ruth of Ldn to Jno. A. BINNS of Ldn. B/S of 2*ac*, adj Conard VERTS. Wit: Zarl? REE, Catharine ROOSE, Samuel WARD, Wm. BURGETT, Chas. BENNETT, James HAMILTON.

Bk:Pg: 2E:377   Date: 11/29/1804   RcCt: 10 Dec 1804
Wm. SIDDLE & wife Sarah of Ldn to William WILKISON of Ldn. B/S of 16*ac*. Wit: Joseph GARRETT, Aaron RAWLINGS, Samuel TODD.

Bk:Pg: 2E:379   Date: 8/21/1804   RcCt: 10 Dec 1804
Jacob SHRY & wife Catharine, Moses PILCHER & wife Sarah and Joshua LEE & wife Theodocia to Wm. WARFORD. B/S of shares SHRY, PILCHER & LEE received under will of Abraham WARFORD dec'd. Wit: Israel LACEY, Wm. COOKE, Jno. BLAKER.

Bk:Pg: 2E:380   Date: 12/10/1804   RcCt: 10 Dec 1804
Wm. WILKISON & wife Sarah of Ldn to Wm. SIDDLE of Ldn. B/S of 16*ac*. Wit: Joseph FOX, Saml. TODD.

Bk:Pg: 2E:382   Date: 12/5/1804   RcCt: 10 Dec 1804
Conrod VERTS & wife Barbary of Ldn to Jno. A. BINNS of Ldn. B/S of water BINNS plans to take out of original bed to use in his mill race. Wit: Saml WARD, Adam WERTS, Christner VERTS.

Bk:Pg: 2E:383   Date: 5/26/1804   RcCt: 10 Dec 1804
Ferdinando FAIRFAX of JeffVa to Thos. HOUGH of Ldn. B/S of 96½*ac* in Shannondale, adj Andrew COPELAND, Saml WADE, Jno. CAMPBELL, Jonathan MATTHEWS. Wit: Jno. H. CANBY, Edward CUNARD Sr., George MILLER, Wm. H. HARDING.

Bk:Pg: 2E:385   Date: 9/18/1804   RcCt: 10 Dec 1804
Edward CUNARD Sr. & wife Judith of Ldn to Thos. HOUGH of Ldn. B/S of Lots 1, 2, 3 & 4 in Hllb – ½*ac*, 3¼*ac*, 1*ac* & 17 perches. Wit: David GOODWIN, James HAMILTON, Mahlon ROACH, Stacy TAYLOR.

Bk:Pg: 2E:389   Date: 12/10/1804   RcCt: 10 Dec 1804
Sebastian WOOFTER of Ldn to Price JACOBS of Ldn. Mortgage on 59*ac*.

Bk:Pg: 2E:390   Date: 4/23/1804   RcCt: 10 Dec 1804
Wm. S. BELT of Ldn to daughter Elizabeth W. HARWOOD. Gift of Negro woman Elcy, boy Otho, cow, furniture. Wit: Wm. Smith BELT Jr., Richd HARWOOD, Middleton BELT.

Bk:Pg: 2E:391   Date: 12/10/1804   RcCt: 10 Dec 1804
Noah JOHNSON & wife Rachel of Ldn to Timothy TAYLOR of Ldn. B/S of 30ac, on road from Snickers Gap to Israel JANNEY, adj Samuel RUSSELL. Wit: Wm. BRONAUGH, Stacy TAYLOR, Abraham SILCOTT.

Bk:Pg: 2E:393   Date: 11/16/1804   RcCt: 10 Dec 1804
Edmond LOVETT of Ldn to James LOVE of Ldn. B/S of 115ac, adj Thos. HUGHS, Henry NICHELS, Richard BROWN. Wit: R. BRADEN, Abner WILLIAMS, Jno. BROWN, David REECE.

Bk:Pg: 2E:395   Date: 11/16/1804   RcCt: 10 Dec 1804
Edmond LOVETT of Ldn to Jas. LOVE of Ldn. Mortgage for 115ac. Wit: R. BRADEN, Abner WILLIAMS, Jno. BROWN, David REECE.

Bk:Pg: 2E:396   Date: 6/6/1804   RcCt: 10 Dec 1804
David LACEY & wife Sarah of Ldn to Robert PERFECT of Ldn. B/S of 9ac. Wit: Sampson BLINCOE, G. W. BLINCOE, Eli OFFUTT.

Bk:Pg: 2E:398   Date: 8/20/1804   RcCt: 10 Dec 1804
John REIGOR of Lsbg to Jane Reigor DAVIS w/o Henry M. DAVIS of Lsbg. Gift of Negro girl Sall abt 8y old. Wit: Sampson BLINCOE, David LOVETT, Thos. WILKINSON.

Bk:Pg: 2E:399   Date: 8/20/1804   RcCt: 10 Dec 1804
Jno. REIGOR & wife Peggy of Lsbg to Jane R. DAVIS w/o Henry M. DAVIS of Lsbg. Gift (in consideration of the natural love) of lot adj Thos. WILKERSON and towards the market house with King St. Wit: Jno. McCORMICK, Sn. BLINCOE, Jno BARRET.

Bk:Pg: 2E:400   Date: 8/17/1804   RcCt: 10 Sep 1804
Thos. BLINCOE to son Joseph BLINCOE. Gift of Negro boy Elleck. Wit: Mark BLINCOE, Saml. A. THOMPSON, Jno. SMITH.

Bk:Pg: 2E:401   Date: 12/10/1804   RcCt: 10 Dec 1804
David LACEY & wife Sarah to Barton LUCAS. CoE for sale of 1Cac. Wit: Leven POWELL, Armistead LONG, Wm. NOLAND.

Bk:Pg: 2E:402   Date: 12/10/1804   RcCt: 10 Dec 1804
David LACEY & wife Sarah of Ldn to Mungo DYKES. CoE for sale of 9ac. Wit: Leven POWELL, Armistead LONG, William NOLAND.

Bk:Pg: 2E:403   Date: 12/10/1804   RcCt: 10 Dec 1804
David LACEY & wife Sarah to Francis TRIPLETT. CoE for sale of 9¾ac. Wit: Leven POWELL, Armistead LONG, Wm. NOLAND.

Bk:Pg: 2E:406   Date: 12/6/1804   RcCt: 10 Dec 1804
Jonah THOMPSON & wife Margarett of Alexandria, DC to Alexander SUTHERLAND of Ldn. B/S of 775ac (formerly of Israel THOMPSON dec'd) on fork of Catocton Creek, and 19ac. Wit: Leven POWELL, Jacob HOFFMAN, Cuthbert POWELL.

Bk:Pg: 2E:411   Date: 12/6/1804   RcCt: 10 Dec 1804
Jonah THOMPSON of Alexandria, DC to Alexander SUTHERLAND & wife Nancy of Ldn. Mortgage for above land. Wit: Samuel MURRAY, Obadiah CLIFFORD.

Bk:Pg: 2E:416   Date: 8/14/1804   RcCt: 10 Dec 1804
James SANDERS (s/o Jno) of Ldn to Aaron SANDERS of Ldn. B/S of
James' equal share of 501*ac* devised to him & brother by his father Jno.
SANDERS dec'd. Wit: Isaac LARROWE, Edward SOMMERS, Edwd
SLATER, Jno. SANDERS, Moses SANDERS.

Bk:Pg: 2E:418   Date: 9/20/1804   RcCt: 10 Dec 1804
Peter FARNANDIS of Ldn to Jacob GOOLLEY of Hardy Co VA. B/S of
FARNANDIS' interest in estate of Thos. GOOLEY dec'd (married widow
Amelia GOOLEY), includes Negroes Gerard, Rachael, Charlotte &
Matilda, farm animals and household items. Wit: George SHIVELY,
Joseph TIMMS, James TIMMS.

Bk:Pg: 2E:419   Date: 5/25/1804   RcCt: 10 Dec 1804
John COTTON of Ldn to William COTTON of Ldn: PoA. Wit: Josiah
MOFFETT Jr., Minor SMITH, Jacob BENNON.

Bk:Pg: 2E:420   Date: 8/1/1804   RcCt: 10 Dec 1804
Chas. Fenton MERCER of Lsbg to Matthew RUST of Ldn. B/S of land on
little river purchased of heirs of James MERCER dec'd by Stephen
Thomson MASON now dec'd, land bequeathed to him by father James
MERCER now of record in Spotsylvania Co. Wit: Solomon BETTON,
Francis TRIPLETT, Burr POWELL.

Bk:Pg: 2E:423   Date: 8/1/1804   RcCt: 10 Dec 1804
Charles Fenton MERCER of Lsbg to Matthew RUST of Ldn. Mortgage for
above land. Wit: Burr POWELL, Solo. BETTON, Francis TRIPLETT.

Bk:Pg: 2E:426   Date: 10/26/1804   RcCt: 10 Dec 1804
John Fenton MERCER to Charles Fenton MERCER. PoA for land sales.
Wit: George ROUSSEAU, Sollomon BETTON, Matthew RUST, Wm. H.
ROUSSEAU.

Bk:Pg: 2E:427   Date: 7/11/1796   RcCt: 10 Dec 1804
Jno. Fenton MERCER of Ldn to Solomon BETTON now resident of Ldn.
B/S of 500*ac* in Green Co KY, granted to James MERCER in
consideration of Military warrants N1924 issued 1787 as devisee of
Alexander DICK dec'd. Wit: Jno. T. BROOKE, Lan. TALEOFERROR, R.
BROOKE, Israel LACEY, Joseph LEWIS Jr., Cuthbert POWELL,
Townshend L. PEYTON.

Bk:Pg: 2E:428   Date: 12/10/1804   RcCt: 10 Dec 1804
Thos. DAVIS & wife Rebecca of Ldn to Rachel WHITE of Ldn. B/S of 5*ac*
where DAVIS now lives. Wit: Thos. WHITE, Jno DAVIS, Margaret DAVIS.

Bk:Pg: 2E:430   Date: 4/7/1804   RcCt: 10 Dec 1804
Thos. Ludwell LEE of Ldn and Landon CARTER of RichVa (Exors of
George CARTER dec'd late of StafVa) to Ignatius ELGIN of Ldn. B/S of
82*ac,* adj Benjamin H. CANBY, Samuel DONOHOE, lease of John
DONOHOE. Wit: Benj. SHRIEVE, Jno. CAVAN, Samuel DONOHOE,
Henry JENKINS, Jno. MATTHIAS, Thos. SIM, Jno. LITTLEJOHN, Wm. B.
HARRISON, C. BINNS.

Bk:Pg: 2E:432   Date: 4/7/1803   RcCt: 4 May 1804
Thos. Ludwell LEE of Ldn and Landon CARTER of RichVa (Exors of George CARTER dec'd late of StafVa) to Samuel DONOHOE of Ldn. B/S of 83½ac, adj John WILDMAN's lease, Ignatius ELLGIN. Wit: John CAVAN, Ignatius ELLGIN, Henry JENKINS, Benjamin DEWELL, Thos. SIM, Jno. LITTLEJOHN, Wm. B. HARRISON, C. BINNS.

Bk:Pg: 2E:435   Date: 4/7/1803   RcCt: 10 Dec 1804
Thos. Ludwell LEE of Ldn and Landon CARTER of RichVa (Exors of George CARTER dec'd late of StafVa) to Benjamin SHREVE of Ldn. B/S of 130¼ac. Wit: Ignatius ELGIN, Samuel DONOHOE, Henry JENKINS, Benj DEWELL, Jno. MATTHIAS, Thos. SIM, Jno. LITTLEJOHN, Wm. B. HARRISON, Chas. BINNS.

Bk:Pg: 2E:437   Date: 4/7/1803   RcCt: 10 Dec 1804
Thos. Ludwell LEE of Ldn and Landon CARTER of RichVa (Exors of George CARTER dec'd late of StafVa) to Benjamin SHREVE of Ldn. B/S of 60ac, adj William CHILTON, junction of Foxes Mill road and turnpike road. Wit: Ignatius ELGIN, Samuel DONOHOE, Henry JENKINS, Benjamin DEWELL, Jno. MATTHIAS, Thos. SIM, Jno. LITTLEJOHN, Wm. B. HARRISON, C. BINNS.

Bk:Pg: 2E:440   Date: ___   RcCt: 10 Dec 1804
Thos. Ludwell LEE & wife of Ldn to William SMITH of Ldn. B/S of 214ac below Goose Creek. Wit: A. CLIFFORD, Jas. HAMILTON, Alexr COUPER Jr.

Bk:Pg: 2E:442   Date: 8/29/1804   RcCt: 10 Sep 1804
Ferdinando FAIRFAX and Wm. Byrd PAGE to Wm. Hanby HARDING. PoA for sale in Valley of Shannon Dale. Wit: Westwood T. MASON, Charles C. LITTLE, Wm. STROTHER, R. Bland LEE, Thos. SWANN.

Bk:Pg: 2E:443   Date: 12/1/1804   RcCt: 10 Dec 1804
Aquila LANHAM of MontMd to Zadok LANHAM of MontMd. B/S of 116ac where Walter LANHAM now lives and sold by Zadok to Nathaniel MOSS. Wit: Thos. JONES, Willy JANES, Joseph BLINCOE.

Bk:Pg: 2E:444   Date: 9/28/1804   RcCt: 11 Dec 1804
Ferdinando FAIRFAX and William Byrd PAGE of JeffVa by their attorney Wm. H. HARDING to David LOVETT and Thos. LESLIE of Ldn. B/S of 306ac in Shannondale where Robert WHITE and William THOMPSON now live, adj Joseph BEAL, Thos. HUMPHREY. Wit: Notley C. WILLIAMS, Joshua OSBURN, Thos. GREGG, Wm. OSBURN.

Bk:Pg: 2E:447   Date: 9/28/1804   RcCt: 10 Dec 1804
Ferdinando FAIRFAX and William Byrd PAGE of JeffVa by attorney Wm. H. HARDING to David LOVETT and Thos. LESLIE of Ldn. Release of 112½ac held by lease of Mahlon HOUGH, adj Joseph BEAL, Col. Thos. HUMPHREY late, William THOMPSON, Thos. LESLIE. Wit: Notley C. WILLIAMS, Joshua OSBURN, Thos. GREGG, Wm. OSBURN.

Bk:Pg: 2E:449 Date: ___ RcCt: 11 Dec 1804
Thos. LESLIE of Ldn to Ruth GREGG of Ldn. B/S of ¼ac in Hllb, adj
Thos. HIPBURN.

Bk:Pg: 2E:451 Date: 4/7/1803 RcCt: 11 Dec 1804
Jonah THOMPSON & Jacob HOFFMAN of Alexandria, DC and Benjamin
COMEGYS of BaltMd to Presley SAUNDERS of Ldn. B/S of 500ac. Wit:
Jas. CALHOUN, Craven P. THOMPSON, Thos. SWANN, R. J. TAYLOR,
Joseph SMITH.

Bk:Pg: 2E:455 Date: 12/12/1804 RcCt: 14 Jan 1805
Jno. THRELKELD & wife Elizabeth of Washington Co., DC to Whitson
BIRDSALL of Ldn. B/S of 155ac abt 7 miles from Lsbg & near Matthew
Rust Mill. Wit: Daniel REINTZEL.

Bk:Pg: 2E:456 Date: 1/14/1805 RcCt: 14 Jan 1805
George TAVENOR & wife Tobitha Ldn to Richard TAVENOR of Ldn. B/S
of 202ac, adj George TAVENOR on main road from the Cross Roads to
Lsbg. Wit: Jesse JANNEY, Stephen KERRICK, Isaac TAVENNER.

Bk:Pg: 2E:458 Date: 11/8/1804 RcCt: 14 Jan 1805
George Fairfax LEE of WstmVa to Hugh QUINLAN of WstmVa. B/S of
1500ac on Goose Creek. Wit: Allen S. DOZIER, Chas. C. RICE, Nelson
R. DOZIER, New Year BRANSON, Jno. PEAKE.

Bk:Pg: 2E:460 Date: 8/9/1804 RcCt: 14 Jan 1805
Sarah PHILLIPS of Ldn to Ezekil CHAMBLIN of Land. A/L of 100ac on W
side of Short Hill to Israel THOMPSON as Guardian of Sarah PHILLIPS
(for lives of Sarah, Jenkins & Saml PHILIPS, children of Benjamin
PHILLIPS dec'd). Wit: Wm. H. HARDING, Thos. LESLIE, David LOVETT.

Bk:Pg: 2E:462 Date: 11/12/1804 RcCt: 14 Jan 1805
William ELLIOTT of Ldn to William CARR of Ldn. B/S of lot on west street
between Loudoun & Market St in Lsbg, adj Joseph SMITH, Peter DOWE,
Presbyterian Church. Wit: Obadiah CLIFFORD, Alexr COUPER Jr., Wm.
A. BINNS.

Bk:Pg: 2E:463 Date: 12/31/1804 RcCt: 14 Jan 1805
William ESKRIDGE of Ldn to Charles ESKRIDGE. BoS for a horse. Wit:
Thos. E. MINOR, Alexander BEACH.

Bk:Pg: 2E:464 Date: 11/13/1804 RcCt: 10 Dec 1804
Moses DILLON & wife Rebecca of Ldn to Isaac NICHOLS Sr. of Ldn.
Trust on 319ac conveyed as gift DILLON by his father James DILLON, adj
William BEANS, Jno. SMITH. Wit: Stacy TAYLOR, Sarah TAYLOR, Ruth
TAYLOR, P. F. MARBLE.

Bk:Pg: 2E:467 Date: 1/6/1804 RcCt: 10 Sep 1804
Edward DORSEY of Wtfd to Hugh LEMON of Wtfd. B/S of 1ac nr Wtfd.
Wit: James MOORE, Thos. PHILLIPS, Thos. HIRST.

Bk:Pg: 2E:468   Date: 11/29/1803   RcCt: 13 Feb 1804
Jno. ODEN & wife Margaret of Fqr to Ariss BUCKNER of Ldn. B/S of 57*ac* in CamP inherited from his father. Wit: Charles LEWIS, Israel LACEY, Hezekiah ODEN, Thos. BEVERIDGE, Jacob ISH.

Bk:Pg: 2E:471   Date: 11/14/1804   RcCt: 14 Jan 1805
Isaac LEWIS & wife Nancy of Ldn to Nathaniel MOSS of Ldn. B/S of 89½*ac*, on S side of road of Moss' meeting house, adj Bernard MANN, Col. Leven POWELL, James LEWIS, Thos. FRANCIS. Wit: Benj GRAYSON, Wm. BRONAUGH, Daniel THOMAS, Stephen MOSS.

Bk:Pg: 2E:475   Date: 1/14/1805   RcCt: 14 Jan 1805
Benjamin B. THORNTON and Matthew HARRISON to Jno. WILDMAN. BoS for Negroes Mariah & Patt.

Bk:Pg: 2E:476   Date: 11/3/1804   RcCt: 11 Dec 1804
Charles McKNIGHT of Alexandria, Washington DC to Presly SAUNDERS of Ldn. Release of mortgage on 500*ac* on Goose Creek. Wit: Thos. SWANN, R. J. TAYLOR, R. BRADEN, Joseph SMITH.

Bk:Pg: 2E:477   Date: 11/6/1804   RcCt: 11 Dec 1804
Daniel DOWLING & wife Kitty of Lsbg to Cloe GREENE of Lsbg. B/S of lot, formerly property of Henry McCABE, adj Martin CORDELL on main road from Lsbg to Nolands Ferry, Jno. DRISH. Wit: Jno. CAVAN, Wm. WOODDY, Charles BINNS, Francis H. PEYTON, Samuel MURRAY.

Bk:Pg: 2E:480   Date: 1/11/1805   RcCt: 15 Jan 1805
Daniel DOWLING & wife Kitty of Alexandria, DC to Thos. JANNEY of Alexandria, DC. B/S of Lot #3 on Loudoun St in Lsbg, adj Obadiah CLIFFORD. Wit: Jas. CAVAN Jr., Presley SANDERS, Jno. MATTHIAS.

Bk:Pg: 2E:482   Date: 2/9/1805   RcCt: 11 Feb 1805
Mahlon HOUGH & wife Mary of Ldn to Edward CUNARD Sr. of Ldn. B/S of 2*ac* on Kittocton Creek in the Gap of the short hill, adj meeting house lot. Wit: Mahlon MORRIS, Wm. THOMPSON, Jno. CUNARD, Henry CUNARD.

Bk:Pg: 2E:485   Date: 10/27/1804   RcCt: 11 Feb 1805
Samuel BEAL & wife Rebekah of Ldn to Thos. BEAL of Ldn. B/S of 99*ac* on broad run near the German church, adj Jno. WITTIMAN, Peter HICKMAN. Wit: Edward CUNARD Sr., Wm. THOMPSON, Thos. BEAL.

Bk:Pg: 2E:486   Date: 10/27/1804   RcCt: 11 Feb 1805
Thomas LASLIE of Ldn to Samuel BEAL of Ldn. B/S of 99*ac* on Broad Run near German church, adj Jno. WITTIMAN, Lawrence MINK, Peter HICKMAN. Wit: Joseph POTTS, Phillip BEAL, Wm. THOMPSON, Thos. HOUGH.

Bk:Pg: 2E:488   Date: 9/1/1803   RcCt: 11 Feb 1805
Thos. HOUGH & wife Mary of Ldn to Margaretha SANDERS of Ldn. B/S of 119*ac* on beaverdam branch, adj William HOUGH, Joseph WILKINSON, Eustis ARNOLD. Wit: Stacy TAYLOR, Notley C. WILLIAMS, Joel OSBURN, Wm. H. HARDING.

Bk:Pg: 2E:490   Date: 2/11/1805   RcCt: 11 Feb 1805
William HARRISON & Wm. B. HARRISON. Bond on William ROSE as
Constable.

Bk:Pg: 2E:491   Date: 7/26/1804   RcCt: 11 Feb 1805
Jas. McILHANY, Jonas POTTS and Asa MOORE as commissioners to
sell land of Jno. JANNEY dec'd to James BRADFIELD of Ldn. B/S of ¾ac
lot in Hllb. Wit: Jos. LEWIS Jr, Thos. LESLIE, Amos JANNEY, Westwood
T. MASON.

Bk:Pg: 2E:492   Date: 7/26/1804   RcCt: 11 Feb 1805
Jas. McILHANY, Jonas POTTS and Asa MOORE as commissioners to
sell land of Jno. JANNEY dec'd to Jas. BRADFIELD of Ldn. B/S of 45
perches in Hllb. Wit: Jos. LEWIS Jr., Thos. LESLIE, Amos JANNY,
Westwood T. MASON.

Bk:Pg: 2E:494   Date: 7/26/1804   RcCt: 11 Feb 1805
James McILHANY, Jonas POTTS and Asa MOORE as commissioners to
sell land of Jno. JANNEY dec'd to Joseph LEWIS. B/S of 60ac.

Bk:Pg: 2E:495   Date: 8/22/1804   RcCt: 11 Feb 1805
George TAVENOR Jr. & wife Martha of Ldn to Jno. HANDY of Ldn.
Mortgage on 102ac on W fork of Goose Creek, adj daughters of Joseph
BATES (Catharine, Susanna and Ann and their husbands Alexander
BERNETT, Jno. RANDOLPH and Jas. GILL), Richd BROWN. Wit: Jacob
BROWN, Jas. CRAVEN, Rees JUREY, Wm. H. HANDEY.

Bk:Pg: 2E:499   Date: 12/29/1804   RcCt: 11 Feb 1805
Abner WILLIAMS & wife Mary of Ldn to Josiah CRAVEN of Ldn. B/S of lot
in Wtfd where Thos. HIRST now lives, adj Asa MOORE. Wit: Josh'a
DANIEL, M. SULLIVAN, Jas. BALL.

Bk:Pg: 2E:500   Date: 1/12/1804   RcCt: 11 Feb 1805
Ferdinando FAIRFAX and William Byrd PAGE of JeffVa by attorney Wm.
H. HARDING to Edward CUNNARD of Ldn. B/S of 4ac on N side of Short
Hill in Shannondale, adj James McILHANY, Mason HOUGH. Wit: Josiah
PATTY, David LOVETT, Thos. HOUGH.

Bk:Pg: 2E:502   Date: 1/10/1805   RcCt: 11 Feb 1805
Ferdinando FAIRFAX and Wm. Byrd PAGE of JeffVa by attorney Wm. H.
HARDING to David LOVETT of Ldn. B/S of 131ac, adj Nicholas TUCKER,
Thos. HUMPHREY, Ezekiel POTTS. Wit: Wm. OSBURN Josiah PATTY,
Craven OSBURN, Joshua OSBURN, Edwd CUNARD, Thos. HOUGH.

Bk:Pg: 2E:504   Date: 2/15/1805   RcCt: 11 Feb 1805
Josiah CRAVEN & wife Elizabeth of Ldn to Mortho SULLIVAN of Ldn. B/S
of part of lot in Wtfd sold by Abner WILLIAMS to CRAVENS. Wit: Isaac
LAROWE, Jonas POTTS, Sanford WREN.

Bk:Pg: 2E:505   Date: 5/10/1804   RcCt: 11 Feb 1804
Leah MONTEITH (w/o James MONTEITH dec'd), Enos MONTEITH &
wife Elenor of StafVa to William VICKERS of Ldn. B/S of 120ac on Goose
Creek, adj Mason FRENCH, James WARNELL. Wit: Jno. SINCLAIR,

Jacob REEDER, Wm. RUSSELL, Burr POWELL, Francis PEYTON, A. GIBSON, Francis PEYTON.

Bk:Pg: 2E:509 Date: 6/14/1804 RcCt: 11 Feb 1805
Jno. SEAGER & wife Eve of Ldn to George SEAGER Sr. of Ldn. B/S of 88ac, adj George SHOVER, widow VENBUSKIRK. Wit: Adam SHOVER, ? [name in German], Jacob HEFFNER.

Bk:Pg: 2E:510 Date: ___ RcCt: 11 Feb 1805
Mahlon HOUGH & wife Polly [signed as Mary] of Hllb to Thos. EDMONDSON & Isaac EDMONDSON, merchant & copartners of BaltMd. B/S of 93ac of Scotland tract on NW fork of Goose Creek. Wit: Lewis ELLZEY, Stacy TAYLOR, Notley C. WILLIAMS.

Bk:Pg: 2E:513 Date: 2/11/1805 RcCt: 11 Feb 1805
Margaret McILHANY (wd/o James McILHANY dec'd) to Samuel GREGG. Relinquishment of dower - releases all interest she has to title.

Bk:Pg: 2E:514 Date: 12/6/1804 RcCt: 11 Feb 1805
Samuel MURRAY & wife Betsey of Lsbg to Joseph SMITH of AlexVa. B/S of lot adj Lsbg on main road through Loudoun St, adj Joseph HUNT, Joseph SMITH. Wit: David ENGLISH, Isaac HARRIS, Geo HEAD, Jno. ROSE, Fra. H. PEYTON.

Bk:Pg: 2E:516 Date: 6/13/1804 RcCt: 12 Feb 1805
Robert W. KIRK & wife Sarah of Alexandria, DC to Alexander SUTHERLAND of Lsbg. B/S of lot on E side of King St and N side of Royal St in Lsbg. Wit: R. HOOE, Joseph SMITH, Thos. SWANN, R. J. TAYLOR.

Bk:Pg: 2E:518 Date: 8/29/1804 RcCt: 12 Feb 1805
Thos. LESLIE & wife Ann of Hllb to Christopher BURNHOUSE of Ldn. B/S of 54½ac lots #21 & #22 on Short Hill, adj John CUMMINGS, Jno. STAGERSFIELD, Peter SANDERS. Wit: Wm. H. HARDING, Wm. JAY, Jno. MARTAIN Jr., Notley C. WILLIAMS, Stacy TAYLOR.

Bk:Pg: 2E:521 Date: 5/26/1804 RcCt: 10 Dec 1804
Ferdinando FAIRFAX of JeffVa to Edward CUNARD of Ldn. B/S of 60ac, lot #3 on plat of Short Hill, adj Conrad FARR. Wit: Jno. H. CANBY, Wm. H. HARDING, George MILLER.

Bk:Pg: 2E:522 Date: 11/15/1803 RcCt: 12 Feb 1805
Ferdinando FAIRFAX of JeffVa to David LACEY of Ldn. Mortgage for 229½ac "Mountain farm". Wit: Wm. H. HARDING, Wm. MAINES, Asa HARRIS.

Bk:Pg: 2E:224 Date: 6/6/1804 RcCt: 11 Sep 1804
James CAVAN Jr. (Admr of Patrick CAVAN dec'd of Lsbg) to George ROWAN of Lsbg. LS of 1ac James HEREFORD leased to Patrick CAVANS renewable forever. Wit: Obadiah CLIFFORD, Jas. HAMILTON, D. DOWLING.

Bk:Pg: 2E:527   Date: 2/11/1804   RcCt: 12 Feb 1805
Wm. H. HARDING and Ferdinando FAIRFAX of Jefferson to David
LACEY of Ldn. Trust of several bonds. Wit: Jno. H. CANBY.

Bk:Pg: 2E:528   Date: 2/12/1805   RcCt: 12 Feb 1805
Jno. PYOTT to Samuel MURRAY. Reassignment of lease - William
MORLAN to Isaac WRENN in 1777, transferred his right to PYOTT in
1800.

Bk:Pg: 2E:529   Date: 2/11/1805   RcCt: 12 Feb 1805
Samuel MURRAY & wife Betsey of Ldn to Jno. PYOTT of Ldn. B/S of
70ac on road from Lsbg to Russes Mill. Wit: Jno. ROSE, Fra. H.
PEYTON.

Bk:Pg: 2E:532   Date: 10/29/1804   RcCt: 12 Feb 1805
Samuel MURREY & wife Betsey of Lsbg to William HOLMES of Ldn. B/S
of 80ac, adj George NIXON. Wit: Wm. WHALEY, Isaac HARRIS, Jno.
CARTER, Fras. H. PEYTON, Jno. ROSE.

Bk:Pg: 2E:544   Date: 6/5/1804   RcCt: 11 Sep 1804
Peter BOSS of Lsbg to Samuel MURRAY and Jonas POTTS of Lsbg.
Trust using Lot #12 in Lsbg. Wit: Geo. EMREY, Richard BROWN, Isaac
HATCHER.

Bk:Pg: 2F:001   Date: 12 Jun 1804   RcCt: 12 Feb 1805
James CAVAN Jr. (Admr of Patrick CAVAN dec'd of Lsbg) to Thomas N.
BINNS. A/L of 1ac.

Bk:Pg: 2F:003   Date: 7 Apr 1803   RcCt: 12 Sep 1803
Ferdinando FAIRFAX of Shannon Hill, JeffVa to Thomas LESLIE of Ldn.
B/S of 56½ac adj Jno. CUMMINGS. Wit: C. BINNS, Jno. A. BINNS, Wm.
H. HARDING.

Bk:Pg: 2F:005   Date: 14 Jan 1805   RcCt: 14 Jan 1805
John WILDMAN & wife Eleanor of Lsbg to Thos. JANNEY of AlexVa. B/S
of Lot #7 in Lsbg. Wit: F. H. PEYTON, Jas. CAVAN Jr., Armistead LONG.

Bk:Pg: 2F:008   Date: 14 Jan 1805   RcCt: 12 Feb 1805
John A. BINNS. Writ of adquoddamnum – to assess damages which may
be sustained by erecting (on 8 Feb 1805) a water grist mill on Catocton
through his plantation. Subscribers: Reubin SCHOOLEY, Jacob SANDS,
Israel H. THOMPSON, Thomas PHILLIPS, Jno. McGEATH, Sandford
RAMEY, Moses COLWELL, Rich'd GRIFFITH, Patrick McGAVACK, Elijah
MYERS, Abner WILLIAMS, Anthony WRIGHT.

Bk:Pg: 2F:010   Date: 22 Jan 1805   RcCt: 13 Feb 1805
Francis H. PEYTON & wife Frances of Ldn to Leven LUCKETT of Ldn.
B/S of ___ ac on Brush Creek in Ohio. Wit: Armistead LONG, Samuel
MURRAY, Joshua HICKMAN Jr.

Bk:Pg: 2F:013   Date: 24 Apr 1804   RcCt: 10 Sept 1804
Jno. GREGG and Rich'd. THATCHER (Exors. of Timothy HOWELL dec'd
of Ldn) to John LOVE. B/S of 190ac adj old school house, Wm. DANIELS.
Wit: Stacy TAYLOR, George BROWN, James HEATON, Wm. BEST.

Bk:Pg: 2F:015   Date: 4 Sep 1804   RcCt: 8 Apr 1805
James HIXSON & wife Sarah, Daniel VERNON & wife Rebekah, Abner
GIBSON, Elia GIBSON, Levi GIBSON & Thos. GIBSON of Ldn to David
GIBSON of Ldn. B/S of 202¾ac (of Thos. GIBSON dec'd). Wit: Noble
BEVERIDGE, Peter MYERS, Mesheck LACEY.

Bk:Pg: 2F:017   Date: 28 Mar 1805   RcCt: 8 Apr 1805
Levi GIBSON (s/o Thos. GIBSON dec'd) & wife Mary of Ffx to David
GIBSON of Ldn. B/S of 202¾ac. Wit: Leven POWELL, Burr POWELL,
Noble BEVERIDGE, Mesheck LACY.

Bk:Pg: 2F:021   Date: 4 Sep 1804   RcCt: 8 Apr 1805
David GIBSON of Ldn to Burr POWELL of Ldn. Trust for above 202¾ac.
Wit: Peter MYERS, Noble BEVERIDGE, Mesheck LACEY, Leven D.
POWELL.

Bk:Pg: 2F:023   Date: 27 Mar 1805   RcCt: 9 Apr 1805
Burr POWELL & wife Catherine of Ldn to Jacob STONEBURNER of Ldn.
B/S of 149ac adj Edward MUD, Leven POWELL, Daniel REES. Wit: Hugh
ROGERS, Samuel HENDERSON, Henry BRAWNER, Francis PEYTON,
Leven POWELL.

Bk:Pg: 2F:026   Date: 15 Mar 1805   RcCt: 8 Apr 1805
Jno. THRELKELD of Washington Co DC to Casper JOHNSON & Jno.
WILSON of Ldn. B/S of 322ac. Wit: Thos. CORCORAN, Geo. FENWICK.

Bk:Pg: 2F:027   Date: 10 Feb 1804   RcCt: 14 May 1804
Nathaniel CRAUFORD/CRAWFORD of PrG & wife Sarah to William
CARTER of Ldn. B/S of 177ac adj Isaac COGILL, Joseph SMITH. Wit:
Wm. ELLZEY, Thos. SWANN, Jos. LEWIS Jr., Saml. HEPBURN, David
CRAUFORD.

Bk:Pg: 2F:030   Date: 16 Nov 1804   RcCt: 9 Apr 1805
Isaac LEWIS of Ldn to Susannah BUTCHER of Ldn. PoA for sale of grice
& foaling mills which Thos. FRANCIS bought of Jacob LEWIS. Wit:
Benj'a. SINGLETON, Collin CARTER, David W. MORRIS, James LEWIS.

Bk:Pg: 2F:031   Date: 15 Mar 1805   RcCt: 9 Apr 1805
Jno. PAYNE, Henry M. DAVIS & Presley SANDERS. Bond on PAYNE as
Constable. Wit: Jno. PAYNE, Henry M. DAVIS, Westwood T. MASON.

Bk:Pg: 2F:032   Date: 31 Dec 1804   RcCt: 9 Apr 1805
Isaiah MYERS (s/o Jonathan & Mary MYERS dec'd) & wife Alice of
Harrison Co Va to Thomas PHILIPS of Wtfd. B/S of 154¾ac adj Elijah
MYERS, Abner WILLIAMS, Jonathan MYERS. Wit: Asa MOORE, Hugh
LEMON, Daniel STONE, Joseph BOND.

Bk:Pg: 2F:034   Date: 12 Sep 1804   RcCt: 9 Apr 1805
Joseph SMITH, John LITTLEJOHN & Stephen COOKE (court appointed
commissioners for Jesse TAYLOR) to William TAYLOR of Lsbg. B/S of
westernmost part of Lot #24 in Lsbg. Wit: Jas. MILES, David CONLIN,
Joseph SHIELDS, Thos. N. BINNS, Jos. BEARD, S. COOK, Ben H.
CANBY.

Bk:Pg: 2F:036   Date: 5 Jan 1805   RcCt: 9 Apr 1805
William NOLAND of Ldn to Thos. NOLAND of FrdkMd. B/S of 60½ac adj
where Enoch THOMAS formerly lived. Wit: Wm. LUCKETT, Saml.
LUCKETT, Clarissa LUCKETT.

Bk:Pg: 2F:037   Date: 22 Feb 1804   RcCt: 9 Apr 1805
Thomas FRANCIS of Ldn to Joseph CARR of Ldn. Trust for payment from
FRANCIS to Jacob LEWIS using 54ac. Wit: Wm. BRONAUGH, Benj'a.
GRAYSON, George FRENCH, Thos. FRED, Joshua FRED.

Bk:Pg: 2F:039   Date: 31 Aug 1804   RcCt: 9 Apr 1805
Gustavus Richard BROWN & wife Margaret of Charles Co Md to William
GRAHAM of PrWm. B/S of 250¾ac Lot #1 in PrWm chancery suit dated
Apr 1800 of Catesby GRAHAM vs. William & Jean GRAHAM. Wit: Jno. M.
GANT, Caleb HAWKINS.

Bk:Pg: 2F:042   Date: 11 Aug 1804   RcCt: 9 Apr 1805
Jno. MITCHEL of Ldn to Jno. TIMMS of Ldn. BoS for negro boy Moses
abt 6y old b. Va. Wit: Wm. B. HARRISON, Wm. B. HARRISON Jr.

Bk:Pg: 2F:043   Date: 5 Apr 1805   RcCt: 9 Apr 1805
John JANNEY & wife Elizabeth of AlexVa to Alexander SUTHERLAND of
Lsbg. B/S of ½ac Lot #4 in Lsbg. Wit: Thos. SWANN, Thos. JANNEY, R.
J. TAYLOR, Joseph SMITH.

Bk:Pg: 2F:047   Date: 1 May 1804   RcCt: 10 Dec 1804
Thomas Atwood DIGGS (eldest s/o Ann the only ch/o George ATWOOD)
of PrG to Edmond JENNINGS of Ldn. B/S of 422ac adj Smidley's
Meadow on E side of Short Hill. Wit: Wm. CHILTON, G. W. BLINCOE,
Wm. T. STURMAN.

Bk:Pg: 2F:049   Date: 18 Mar 1805   RcCt: 9 Apr 1805
Thomas Atwood DIGGS of PrG to Edmund JENNINGS of Ldn: New
boundaries for above land. Wit: Thos. N. BINNS, L. D. POWELL, Geo. W.
BLINCOE, Francis TRIPLETT, Henry S. COOKE, Charles Fenton
MERCER.

Bk:Pg: 2F:053   Date: 30 Mar 1805   RcCt: 9 Apr 1805
Jacob STONEBURNER of Ldn to Leven POWELL Jr. Trust of 150ac
STONEBURNER purchased from Burr POWELL & wife. Wit: Hugh
ROGERS, Samuel HENDERSON, Henry BRAWNER.

Bk:Pg: 2F:055   Date: 22 Aug 1804   RcCt: 9 Apr 1805
John HANDY & wife Given of Ldn to George TAVENNER Jr. B/S of 102ac
on NW fork of Goose Creek, adj Richard BROWN. Wit: Jacob BROWN,
Jas. CRAVEN, Rees JUREY, Wm. H. HANDEY, Wm. ELLZEY, Wm.
BRONAUGH.

Bk:Pg: 2F:059   Date: 8 Feb 1805   RcCt: 9 Apr 1805
Thos. REECE & wife Gerry/Janey/Jane to Benjamin JAMES. B/S of 10ac
in CamP adj Phillip PALMER, Benjamin JAMES. Wit: Emmor REECE,
Moses JAMES, Abel JAMES.

Bk:Pg: 2F:060   Date: 10 Apr 1805   RtCt 9 Apr 1805
Dan'l. DOWLING & wife Kitty to Thos. JANNEY. CoE for lot in Lsbg. Wit: Samuel MURREY, Obadiah CLIFFORD.

Bk:Pg: 2F:061   Date: 24 Apr 1804   RcCt: 10 Sep 1804
John LOVE of Ldn to Stacy TAYLOR of Ldn. Trust using 190*ac* for debt to Jno. GREGG. Wit: Jesper POULSON, Jas. HEATON, Saml. LEARD.

Bk:Pg: 2F:064   Date: 11 Dec 1804   RcCt: 9 Apr 1805
Wm. TAYLOR of Lsbg to John BOYD of Ldn. B/S of part of Lot #24 in Lsbg. Wit: Francis TRIPLETT, Jno. NEWTON, Dan'l. TRIPLETT.

Bk:Pg: 2F:066   Date: 18 Sep 1803   RcCt: 9 Apr 1805
Thos. Ludwell LEE of Ldn & Landon CARTER Jr of RichVa (Exors of George CARTER dec'd of StafVa) to John WILDMAN of Ldn. B/S of 178*ac* previously leased to WILDMAN, adj Samuel DONOHOE. Wit: Jno. LITTLEJOHN, Jno. McCORMICK, Saml. HOUGH, Jno. MATTHIAS.

Bk:Pg: 2F:068   Date: 18 Sep 1803   RcCt: 9 Apr 1805
John WILDMAN & wife Eleanor of Ldn to Thos. Ludwell LEE & Landon CARTER Jr. S/L of above 178*ac*. Wit: Obadiah CLIFFORD, Samuel MURREY, Jno. MATTHIAS.

Bk:Pg: 2F:071   Date: 18 Sep 1803   RcCt: 10 Apr 1805
Thos. Ludwell LEE of Ldn & Landon CARTER Jr of RichVa (Exors of George CARTER dec'd of StafVa) to Thos. SWANN of AlexVa. B/S of 178*ac*. Wit: Jno. McCORMICK, Jno. LITTLEJOHN, Saml. HOUGH, Jno. MATTHIAS.

Bk:Pg: 2F:074   Date: 8 Apr 1805   RcCt: 9 Apr 1805
Thos. Ludwell LEE of Ldn & Landon CARTER Jr of RichVa (Exors of George CARTER dec'd of StafVa) to Thos. SWANN of AlexVa. B/S of 248*ac*, 492*ac* & 1010*ac*. Wit: Jno. McCORMICK, Jno. LITTLEJOHN, Samuel HOUGH, Jno. MATTHIAS.

Bk:Pg: 2F:078   Date: 18 Sep 1803   RcCt: 10 Apr 1805
Thos. Ludwell LEE of Ldn & Landon CARTER Jr of RichVa (Exors of George CARTER dec'd of StafVa) to Matthew HARRISON of PrWm. B/S of 54*ac*. Wit: Jno. LITTLEJOHN, Samuel HOUGH, Jno. MATHIAS, Wm. MAINS.

Bk:Pg: 2F:080   Date: 18 Sep 1804   RcCt: 10 Apr 1805
Thos. Ludwell LEE of Ldn & Landon CARTER Jr of RichVa (Exors of George CARTER dec'd of StafVa) to Barnett HOUGH of Ldn and Jno. Thos. RICKELS & William NEWTON of AlexVa. B/S of 30*ac*. Wit: Jno. McCORMICK, Jno. LITTLEJOHN, Samuel HOUGH, Jno. MATHIAS.

Bk:Pg: 2F:083   Date: 9 Apr 1805   RcCt: 10 Apr 1805
Thos. SWANN & wife Jane of AlexVa to Landon CARTER of RichVa. B/S of 248*ac* and 498*ac*.

Bk:Pg: 2F:086   Date: 9 Apr 1805   RcCt: 10 Apr 1805
Thos. SWANN & wife Jane B. of AlexVa to Thos. L. LEE of Ldn. B/S of 1010*ac*.

Bk:Pg: 2F:088   Date: 9 Apr 1805   RcCt: 10 Apr 1805
Josiah MOFFETT & wife Rachel to Landon CARTER of RichVa. B/S of
377*ac*. Wit: Stephen COOKE, Samuel HOUGH, Jno. MATTHIAS.

Bk:Pg: 2F:090   Date: 16 Aug 1804   RcCt: 10 Apr 1805
William LITTLEJOHN of Ldn to Presley CORDELL of Lsbg. B/S of ___*ac*
adj Lsbg, Benjamin H. CANBY. Wit: Westwood T. MASON, Jonas
POTTS, Hervey M. DAVIS.

Bk:Pg: 2F:091   Date: 4 Mar 1805   RcCt: 13 May 1805
Richard Bland LEE & wife Eliza of Ffx to Stephen DONALDSON of Ldn.
B/S of 309¾*ac* adj Nicholas HYCHEW, John CLOISE, John
RICHARDSON, Peter WARNER. Wit: Thos. Lud. LEE, Thos. DARNE Jr.,
Philip SNYDER, Geo. W. BLINCOE, C. BINNS, L. D. POWELL, Fleet
SMITH, Jno. JACKSON, R'd. RATCLIFF.

Bk:Pg: 2F:095   Date: 5 Mar 1805   RcCt: 13 May 1805
Stephen DONALDSON & wife Susannah of Ldn to Richard Bland LEE of
Ffx. Mortgage on above land. Wit: Stacy TAYLOR, Notley C. WILLIAMS,
Geo. W. BLINCOE, C. BINNS, L. D. POWELL, Fleet SMITH.

Bk:Pg: 2F:098   Date: ___ 1804   RcCt: 13 May 1805
John McELDREY & wife Ann (formerly Ann SINCLAIR) before of Ldn now
of Knox Co Tn to Samuel SINCLAIR of Ldn. B/S of 36*ac* Ann inherited
from father Jno. SINCLAIR dec'd. Also Ann's share of 110*ac* (from widow
Mary SINCLAIR now dec'd, who intermarried Israel SEARS) not yet
divided.

Bk:Pg: 2F:100   Date: 5 Apr 1805   RcCt: 13 May 1805
Sarah PAXON (wd/o James PAXON dec'd) and William SIDDAL & wife
Sarah of Ldn to Richard GRIFFITH of Ldn. B/S of 17*ac* adj Jonathan
MYERS' heirs. Wit: Wm. S. NEALE, Jno. McGEATH, Wm. PAXON, Abner
WILLIAMS, Chas. BENNETT, Armistead LONG.

Bk:Pg: 2F:103   Date: 14 Dec 1804   RcCt: 13 May 1805
Thomas HATCHER & wife Bebe of Ldn to James HATCHER of Ldn. B/S
of 11*ac* adj George HATCHER. Wit: Margery HATCHER, Thos.
HATCHER Jr.

Bk:Pg: 2F:106   Date: 13 Mar 1805   RcCt: 13 May 1805
Noah HATCHER & wife Rachel of Ldn to Whitson BIRDSALL of Ldn. B/S
of 150*ac* adj Mercer BROWN, Stacy TAYLOR. Wit: Stacy TAYLOR,
James BROWN, Thos. GREGG.

Bk:Pg: 2F:108   Date: 4 May 1805   RcCt: 13 May 1805
William WENNER & wife Magdalena of Ldn to Jacob KEARN of Ldn. B/S
of 111¼*ac* [also given as 110¼*ac*] Lot #9 in Payne & Summers Survey.
Wit: Adam SHOVER, Peter STUCK, Josiah MOFFETT.

Bk:Pg: 2F:110   Date 17 Mar 1805   RcCt: 13 May 1805
Mahlon HOUGH & wife Mary of Ldn to Joseph GRIFFITH of Ldn. B/S of
¼*ac* Lot #7 in Gap of Short Hill. Wit: Edward CUNARD Sr., Mahlon
MORRIS, Chas. HUMPHREY, George S. HOUGH.

Bk:Pg: 2F:112   Date: 13 Mar 1805   RcCt: 13 May 1805
Whitson BIRDSALL of Ldn to Noah HATCHER of Ldn. Trust on 150*ac*.
Wit: Stacy TAYLOR, James BROWN, Thomas GREGG.

Bk:Pg: 2F:114   Date: 16 Mar 1805   RcCt: 13 May 1805
John BURCHETT & wife Nancy (d/o George HATCHER s/o Wm.
HATCHER dec'd) of Ldn to Joseph TAVENNER of Ldn. B/S of Nancy's
1/3 share of George's land. Wit: Stacy TAYLOR, Jesse SILCOTT, Jno.
TOBIN, John PANCOAST, Notley C. WILLIAMS.

Bk:Pg: 2F:117   Date: 18 Dec 1804   RcCt: 13 May 1805
Mahlon HOUGH & wife Mary of Ldn to Jonah HOUGH of Ldn. B/S of
38*ac*. Wit: Stacy TAYLOR, Mary MORRIS, Peter P. PLANKETT, Geo. S.
HOUGH, Notley C. WILLIAMS.

Bk:Pg: 2F:120   Date: 13 Apr 1805   RcCt: 13 May 1805
William BEANS & wife Hannah of Ldn to Noah HATCHER of Ldn. B/S of
150*ac* adj James DILLON. Wit: Stacy TAYLOR, Timothy TAYLOR, David
GOODEN, Nicholas OSBURN, Samuel HUGHES.

Bk:Pg: 2F:121   Date: 10 Apr 1805   RcCt: 13 May 1805
Noah HATCHER & wife Rachel of Ldn to William BEANS of Ldn. Trust on
above 150*ac*. Wit: Stacy TAYLOR, Nicholas OSBURN, Timothy TAYLOR.

Bk:Pg: 2F:123   Date: 9 Mar 1805   RcCt: 13 May 1805
John SOUTHARD & wife Martha (d/o Jno. ROMINE dec'd) of FrdkVa to
William BLAKELY of Ldn. B/S of 14*ac* adj Martin OVERFIELD. Wit: Stacy
TAYLOR, Notley C. WILLIAMS, Jas. TUCKER, Theophilus HOFF.

Bk:Pg: 2F:126   Date: 13 May 1805   RcCt: 13 May 1805
Samuel CLAPHAM & wife Elizabeth of Ldn to David BEATTY of Ldn. B/S
of 15*ac* adj Charles SHEPHERD. Wit: Johnston CLEVELAND, Wm.
NOLAND.

Bk:Pg: 2F:128   Date: 13 May 1805   RcCt: 13 May 1805
William ROBERTS & wife Ellenor of Ldn to Joseph DANIEL of Ldn. B/S of
10*ac* on E side of Kittocton Mt.

Bk:Pg: 2F:130   Date: 22 Apr 1805   RcCt: 13 May 1805
Sarah FAIRFAX of GrB to Joseph BEAL of Ldn. LS of 100*ac* in ShelP
originally L/L to under age David SMITH (s/o Henry SMITH dec'd) of Ldn
by his Guardian Jno. SMITH and Joseph & Jesse SMITH (s/o Thos.
SMITH) on 13 Feb 1786 but never recorded. Wit: Wm. H. HARDING,
Edward CUNNARD?, Joseph CANLEY, Nancy A. HARDING.

Bk:Pg: 2F:137   Dated 4 May 1805   RcCt: 13 May 1805
William ELLZEY & wife Frances Hill to Samuel RITCHEY. CoE for sale of
150*ac*. Wit: Albert RUSSELL, James HAMILTON.

Bk:Pg: 2F:138   Date: 8 Apr 1805   RcCt: 13 May 1805
William SPENCER & wife Sarah of Ldn to David YOUNG of Ldn. B/S of
139*ac* adj Elisha YOUNG, Jno. YOUNG, Jas. CRAIG. Wit: Jno.
SPENCER, Jno. YOUNG, Abijah JANNEY, Wm. YOUNG.

Bk:Pg: 2F:139, 141   Date: 4 Sep 1771   RcCt: 14 Nov 1771, 13 May 1805
Wagner Thomas PHILLIPS of Ldn to Jenkin PHILLIPS of Ldn. L/R of 208*ac* adj John PHILLIPS, William HARRIS, Ben SUBASTON. Wit: Benjamin BURSON, Thos. PHILIPS, Jos. BURSON.

Bk:Pg: 2F:146   Date: 10 Oct 1804   RcCt: 13 May 1805
James HIXSON & wife Sarah of Ldn to David GIBSON & Daniel VERNON of Ldn. B/S of 3*ac* adj Lsbg on Little River with race. Wit: Phil'o R. LANE, Ely GIBSON, Abijah SANDS, Leven POWELL, Burr POWELL.

Bk:Pg: 2F:150   Date: 19 Apr 1805   RcCt: 13 May 1805
Michael SHEIK & wife Catharine of Ldn to Jacob FAWLEY of Ldn. B/S of 13*ac* Lot #12 in Payne & Summers Survey of Catoctin Manor formerly L/L to Joseph FIRESTONE, adj Peter FRY. Wit: Chas. BENNETT, Jno. HAMILTON, William WOLF, Wm. SHAFAR.

Bk:Pg: 2F:153   Date: 25 Mar 1805   RcCt: 13 May 1805
James RATTIKEN & wife Susannah of Ldn to Benjamin STEER of Ldn. B/S of 20*ac* on Catoctin Mt adj Elijah MYERS. Wit: Lambert MYERS, Abner WILLIAMS, Jno. WILLIAMS.

Bk:Pg: 2F:155   Date: 12 Apr 1805   RcCt: 13 May 1805
Willam CARTER & wife Margaret of Ldn to Isaac & Samuel NICHOLS of Ldn. B/S of 177*ac*. Wit: Ben GRAYSON, William BRONAUGH, Wm. GRAYSON.

Bk:Pg: 2F:158   Date: 7 Apr 1805   RcCt: 13 May 1805
Lewis NEILL and Jno. McPHERSON (Exor of Joseph NEILL dec'd of Frdk) to Isaac STEER of Ldn. Bond on 325*ac* adj Ebenezer GRUBB, William HOUGH.

Bk:Pg: 2F:160   Date: 1 May 1805   RcCt: 13 May 1805
Bertand EWELL of Ldn to Philip EVERHEART. BoS for negro girl Sophia. Wit: Wm. WENNER, Christian EVERHEART written in German.

Bk:Pg: 2F:161   Date: 3 Apr 1805   RcCt: 13 May 1805
Abiel JENNERS & wife Deborah of Ldn to Jno. LITTLEJOHN, Charles BINNS & Robert BRADEN of Ldn. Trust using 358*ac* for debt to Jno. HAMILTON. Wit: Sanford RAMEY, Jno. DODD Jr., Jonah TAVENOR.

Bk:Pg: 2F:164   Date: 6 Nov 1804   RcCt: 13 May 1805
Joshua CHILTON & wife Nancy of Md to Samuel MURRAY of Lsbg. B/S of ½*ac* Lot #49 in Lsbg adj Methodist meeting house. Wit: Wm. BRONAUGH, Francis H. PEYTON, Jno. CAVANS.

Bk:Pg: 2F:167   Date: 26 Dec 1804   RcCt: 14 May 1805
Joseph PERRY to James PATTON. BoS for horses and cow. Wit: Danl. BYRN, Rachel WELLS.

Bk:Pg: 2F:168   Date: 24 Jan 1805   RcCt: 13 May 1805
Richard CONNER of Ldn. DoE for slave Rachel abt 12y & d/o free black man Dubbin & wife Nancy (formerly CONNER's property), was a gift to

daughter Mrs. Samuel MORAN, but Dubbin bought her freedom. James MOORE, Rt. BRADEN, C. BITZER.

Bk:Pg: 2F:169   Date: 5 Nov 1804   RcCt: 13 May 1805
Thomas BEALE (going to OH) to Edward CUNNARD of Ldn. PoA. Wit: S. BLINCOE, Stacy TAYLOR, Notley C. WILLIAMS.

Bk:Pg: 2F:171   Date: 17 Apr 1805   RcCt: 13 May 1805
John CUMMINGS & wife Jane of Ldn to Robert BRADEN of Ldn. B/S of 32ac part of Lot #20. Wit: Joseph BRADEN, Jno. LINDSAY, Jos. BRADEN Jr.

Bk:Pg: 2F:172   Date: 25 Apr 1805   RcCt: 13 May 1805
Amos JANNEY (Admr of Abel JANNEY dec'd of Ldn) to Robert BRADEN of Ldn. B/S of 60ac on E side of Short Hill adj Edmund JENNINGS, Adam HOUSEHOLDER dec'd & 68ac. Wit: Isaac HOUGH, James HAMILTON, Jonathan CUNARD, Nathan CUNARD.

Bk:Pg: 2F:174   Date: 25 Apr 1805   RcCt: 13 May 1805
Amos JANNEY (Admr of Abel JANNEY dec'd of Ldn) to Edmund JENNINGS of Ldn. B/S of 70ac on E side of Short Hill, adj Robert BRADEN. Wit: Isaac HOUGH, James HAMILTON, Jonathan CUNARD, Nathan CUNARD.

Bk:Pg: 2F:176   Date: 6 Apr 1805   RcCt: 13 May 1805
Mahlon HOUGH & wife Mary of Ldn to Archibald YOUNG of Ldn. B/S of 108ac adj Thos. WHITE at Scotland Mills, Caleb GREGG. Wit: Stacy TAYLOR, Thos. HUMPHREY, Notley C. WILLIAMS.

Bk:Pg: 2F:180   Date: 9 Apr 1805   RcCt: 13 May 1805
Sarah CAVAN & Joshua BAKER of Wtfd to Presley SAUNDERS Jr. of Lsbg. B/S of Lot #50 in Lsbg. Wit: Thos. PHILLIPS, Jno. WILLIAMS, David GOODWIN.

Bk:Pg: 2F:182   Date: 13 May 1804   RcCt: 13 May 1805
Vincent KEITH & wife Beaulah of Ldn to Thomas MARKS of Ldn. B/S of 19ac adj Andrew REED.

Bk:Pg: 2F:183   Date: 1 Apr 1805   RcCt: 13 May 1805
Mahlon JANNEY of Ldn to Lewis KLEIN of Wtfd. B/S of Lot #5 in new addition of Wtfd. Wit: Jacob BAUGH, Wm. PAXON, John V'DEVENTER, Jno. WILLIAMS.

Bk:Pg: 2F:185   Date: 9 Apr 1805   RcCt: 13 May 1805
Thos. Ludwell LEE of Ldn & Landon CARTER Jr. of RichVa (Exors of George CARTER dec'd of StafVa) to Stephen COOK of Ldn. B/S of 37ac adj Samuel LOVE. Wit: Samuel HOUGH, Jno. LITTLEJOHN, M. HARRISON, Jno. MATHIAS.

Bk:Pg: 2F:187   Date: 3 May 1805   RcCt: 13 May 1805
William LITTLEJOHN of Ldn to William WOODY of Ldn. B/S of 148½ perches.

Bk:Pg: 2F:189   Date: 13 May 1805   RcCt: 13 May 1805
Stacy JANNEY & wife Hannah of Ldn to Wilse POSTON of Ldn. B/S of
47*ac* adj George RUST, Peter LEIPLEY. Wit: Notly C. WILLIAMS, Stacy
TAYLOR, Mahlon GREGG.

Bk:Pg: 2F:191   Date: 13 May 1805   RcCt: 13 May 1805
Joseph BENTLEY & wife Catharine (d/o Alexr. McINTYRE) of Ldn to
Michael SHRYOCK of Ldn. B/S of ½ of Lot #36 in Lsbg. Wit: Samuel
MURRAY, Obadiah CLIFFORD, Jas. HAMILTON.

Bk:Pg: 2F:194   Date: 9 Apr 1805   RcCt: 13 May 1805
Presley SANDERS Jr. & wife Mary of Lsbg to Thos. PHILLIPS of Wtfd.
Trust of Lot #58 in Lsbg to cover debt with Sarah CAVAN & Joshua
BAKER. Wit: Jas. CAVAN Jr., Obadiah CLIFFORD, Samuel MURREY.

Bk:Pg: 2F:199   Date: 13 May 1805   RcCt: 13 May 1805
Enos GARRETT & wife Elenor of Ldn to John BOURSETT of Ldn. B/S of
69½*ac* on SE side of Short Hill. Wit: Johnston CLEVELAND, Jas.
HAMILTON, Thos. CONNER.

Bk:Pg: 2F:202   Date: 25 Apr 1805   RcCt: 13 May 1805
Israel LACEY (acting Exor of William EVANS dec'd of Ldn) to Nathan
SKINNER & Peter SKINNER. B/S of land conveyed to Jno. EVANS father
of William, subject to dower of widow Martha EVANS. Wit: Wm. COOKE,
Armistead T. MASON, R. H. LITTLE, Francis B. WHITING, Joseph
JONES Jr., Elias LACEY, Nich's PEERS.

Bk:Pg: 2F:203   Date: 13 May 1805   RcCt: 13 May 1805
Obediah CLIFFORD, Jonas POTTS & Jno. SCHOOLEY (Commissioners
of Ldn) to Benjamin B. THORNTON of Ldn. B/S of ½ of Lot #8 in Lsbg.

Bk:Pg: 2F:205   Date: 13 May 1805   RcCt: 13 May 1805
Benjamin B. THORNTON of Ldn to John JACOBS of Ldn. Mortgage on
above lot. Wit: O. CLIFFORD, Jno. SCHOOLEY J., Jonas POTTS.

Bk:Pg: 2F:207   Date: 4 May 1805   RtCt; 13 May 1805
Edmund JENNINGS & wife Seney of Ldn to Moses MILLER of Ldn. B/S of
14*ac* on E side of Short Hill adj Robert BRADEN. Wit: Peter MILLER, Jas.
McFARLIN, Jaco MILLER.

Bk:Pg: 2F:209   Date: 13 May 1805   RcCt: 13 May 1805
Benjamin BRADFIELD & wife Rachel of Ldn to William CHAMBLIN of
Ldn. B/S of 98*ac* adj John CHAMBLING.

Bk:Pg: 2F:211   Date: 13 May 1805   RcCt: 13 May 1805
Benjamin BRADFIELD & wife Rachel of Ldn to John CHAMBLIN of Ldn.
B/S of 98*ac* adj William CHAMBLIN.

Bk:Pg: 2F:213   Date: 8 May 1805   RcCt: 13 May 1805
Leven POWELL & wife Sarah of Ldn to Thomas FRANCIS of Ldn. B/S of
1*ac*.

Bk:Pg: 2F:214   Date: 11 Feb 1805   RcCt: 13 May 1805
Mahlon COMBS & wife Sarah of Ldn to John McCORMICK of Ldn. B/S of
133*ac* in Berkley Co. Wit: Jno. LITTLEJOHN, A. B. T. MASON, Wm.
MAINS, Wilson C. SELDON, Obadiah CLIFFORD.

Bk:Pg: 2F:217   Date: 19 Apr 1805   RcCt: 13 May 1805
Charles DRISH & wife Susanna of Ldn to Henry M. DAVIS of Ldn. B/S of
½*ac* Lot #41 in Lsbg. Wit: Christopher ROPER, Martin CORDELL,
Charles HORSKINSON.

Bk:Pg: 2F:219   Date: 29 Nov 1803   RcCt: 13 Feb 1804
William BROWN of WstmVa to Edward CARTER of Ldn. B/S of 36*ac* adj
Robert FULTON. Wit: Noble BEVERIDGE, Rawleigh CHINN, Burr
POWELL.

Bk:Pg: 2F:220   Date: ___ 1805   RcCt: 13 May 1805
Presley CORDELL & wife Amelia of Ldn to John McCORMICK of Ldn.
B/S of land adj Benjamin T. CANBY on Market St Lsbg. Wit: Samuel
MURREY, James HAMILTON.

Bk:Pg: 2F:222   Date: 28 May 1803   RcCt: 12 Dec 1803
William BROWN (by attorney Wm. Jett BROWN of WstmVa) to Robert
FULTON of Ldn. B/S of 125*ac* adj Robt. M. POWELL. Wit: Burr POWELL,
George LOVE, Wm. HALE, Samuel HENDERSON, Thos. VIOLETT,
Thos. TRIPLETT.

Bk:Pg: 2F:224   Date: 19 Nov 1804 Fayette Co PA   RcCt: 14 May 1805
Deposition: Carrie Nicholas OSBORN has been an inhabitant of ShelP in
Ldn for 46y last past & within a few years after he settled there Wm.
MARTIN settled on Alexandria Rd 1m from the Gap of Short Hill and
OSBORN saw and conversed with MARTIN who now lives in the vicinity
of Union Town Borough, Fayette Co Pa.

Bk:Pg: 2F:224   Date: 19 Nov 1804 Fayette Co PA   RcCt: 14 May 1805
Deposition: Henry BEESON in 1766 or 1y sooner became intimately
acquainted with Wm. MARTIN who then lived 1m from the Gap of Short
Hill on Alexandria Road and in 1767 BEESON married Mary MARTIN one
of his daughters. BEESON visited MARTIN up to 1776 when MARTIN
moved his family to Union Town in Redstone Settlement.

Bk:Pg: 2F:225   Date: 25 Dec 1804   RcCt: 14 May 1805
Robert WHITE this day paid to renew the lease granted by Geo. Wm.
FAIRFAX to Wm. MARTIN but was refused by Wm. H. HARDING agent
for Mrs. Sarah FAIRFAX. Wit: George NORTH, Gersham KEYES, Alexr.
WHITE.

Bk:Pg: 2F:225   Date: 2 Apr 1805   RcCt: 14 May 1805
Robert WHITE this day paid to renew the lease granted by Geo. Wm.
FAIRFAX to Wm. MARTIN but was refused by Jno. H. CANBY agent of
Mrs. Sarah FAIRFAX. Wit: Wm. H. HARDING, Humphrey GUYNN.

Bk:Pg: 2F:226   Date: 27 Mar 1805   RcCt: 14 May 1805
Ludwell LEE to daughters Mary Ann LEE & Eliza Armistead LEE (both
<21y, paid by Thos. DARNE Jr.). Trust of negroes Peggy d/o old Phil &

her children George Rippon & Father; Jenny d/o old Phil & her son Phil to Mary; Sack & her children Daniel & Charity; & Molly & her children Joel Ned & Venus to Eliza.

Bk:Pg: 2F:227   Date 29 Jun 1805   RcCt: 8 Jul 1805
Hugh DOUGLASS, Mathew HARRISON, Abraham B. T. MASON, Wm. ELLZY, Chs. BINNS and Wm. CHILTON. Bond on DOUGLASS as Sheriff of Ldn to collect officers fees. Wit: Geo. W. BLINCOE.

Bk:Pg: 2F:229   Date: 8 Jul 1805   RcCt: 8 Jul 1805
Hugh DOUGLASS, Mathew HARRISON, Abm. B. T. MASON, Wm. ELLZY, Chs. BINNS & Wm. CHILTON. Bond on DOUGLASS as Sheriff of Ldn to collect levies. Wit: G. W. BLINCOE.

Bk:Pg: 2F:230   Date: 8 Jul 1805   RcCt: 8 Jul 1805
Hugh DOUGLASS, Mathew HARRISON, Abm. B. T. MASON, Wm. ELLZY, Chs. BINNS & Wm. CHILTON. Bond on DOUGLASS as Sheriff of Ldn to collect taxes. Wit: Geo. W. BLINCOE.

Bk:Pg: 2F:232   Date: 15 Mar 1805   RcCt: 8 Jul 1805
Storekeeper Timothy WHELAN dec'd late of Baltimore Md devised ½ of property to brother James WHELAN of Baltimore and ½ to sisters Margaret, Catherine, Winefred and Judith WHELAN then of Ireland. James died immediately after Timothy and Judith is also dead. Widow Margaret WHELAN otherwise DUNN and spinster Catherine WHELAN now reside in Durrow, Kilkenny Co Ireland; Whinefred now wife of Jeremiah PHELAN resides at Bullygeehin, Queens Co Ireland. PoA to Maurice DELANY of Baltimore. Wit: John SULLIVAN, Dennis PHELAN, Edw'd. PHELAN.

Bk:Pg: 2F:237   Date: 2 Apr 1794   RcCt: 8 Jul 1805
Jonas POTTS of Ldn to James McILHANY of Ldn. B/S of 140ac on N Kittoctain adj Ezekiel POTTS. Wit: Samuel HOUGH, Amos JANNEY, George GRAHAM, William HOUGH 3rd.

Bk:Pg: 2F:238   Date: 4 Jun 1805   RcCt: 8 Jul 1805
William WARFORD & wife Hannah of Ldn to Joshua LEE of Ldn. B/S of 50ac adj Abraham WARFORD. Wit: Henry M. DAVIS, J. HARDING, Charles E. POWELL.

Bk:Pg: 2F:240   Date: 2 Jan 1805   RcCt: 14 May 1805
Benjamin H. CANBY of Lsbg to Daniel DUTY of Ldn. Mortgage on lot adj Lsbg that CANBY purchased from Exor of Israel THOMPSON. Wit: Samuel MURREY, John LITTLEJOHN, Simon JENKINS.

Bk:Pg: 2F:242   Date: 11 Mar 1805   RcCt: 8 Jul 1805
Whitson BIRDSALL & wife Rachel of Ldn to Edmund LOVETT of Ldn. B/S of 156ac on Goose Creek. Wit: Abner WILLIAMS, Jesse JANNEY, James BRADFORD.

Bk:Pg: 2F:244   Date: 13 Apr 1805   RcCt: 8 Jul 1805
John Taliaferro BROOKE & James Mercer GARNETT (Admr of James MERCER dec'd) to Charles Fenton MERCER of Ldn. B/S of 768ac on Little River to Ashby's Gap, adj Moses DILLON, Matthew RUST, John

SINCLAIR, Joseph DANIEL, Matthew ADAMS. Wit: Hazlewood FARISH, Zachariah LUCUS, William FISDALL, John MINOR, John W. GREEN.

Bk:Pg: 2F:247   Date: 8 Jul 1805   RcCt: 8 Jul 1805
Mahlon JANNEY of Ldn to Israel H. THOMPSON of Ldn. B/S of ½ac of 2 lower lots adj Wtfd. Wit: Rich'd NORWOOD, Terrence FIGH, Abner MOORE.

Bk:Pg: 2F:249   Date: 14 Dec 1792   RcCt: 8 Jul 1805
Richard FREEMAN. Col of slaves Mosses, Ben & Rachel.

Bk:Pg: 2F:249   Date: 8 Jul 1805   RcCt: 8 Jul 1805
Hugh DOUGLAS, Matthew HARRISON, Abraham B. T. MASON, Wm. ELLZEY, Chs. BINNS & Wm. CHILTON. Bond on DOUGLASS as Sheriff to pay officers.

Bk:Pg: 2F:251   Date: 3 Jan 1805   RcCt: 13 Aug 1805
Ferdinando FAIRFAX & wife Eliz. B. FAIRFAX of JeffVa to Richard Bland LEE of Ffx. B/S of 309¾ac nr Kittoctan Creek adj Mrs. Ann PEYTON, James McILHANEY. Wit: Geo. NORTH, Abram DAVENPORT, Wm. GIBBS, Moses WILSON Jr., James McENDREE.

Bk:Pg: 2F:254   Date: 5 Sep 1805   RcCt: 9 Sep 1805
Israel PHILLIPS of Ldn to David LOVETT & Lewis ELLZEY of Ldn and Joshua OSBURN (owed debt by PHILLIPS) of Ldn. Trust using land in Harrison Co (Hester PHILLIPS inherited from James McILHANEY, then gift to Israel). Wit: Stephen DONALDSON, Thomas GREGG, Thomas DORRELL.

Bk:Pg: 2F:257   Date: 11 May 1805   RcCt: 9 Sep 1805
John SPENCER of Wood Co Va to John HOUPP of Ldn. B/S of 120ac adj William SMALLEY, John HOUGH. Wit: Elias W. LITTELL, Nathaniel POLEN, And'w. REDMOND, Benjamin JAMES, Benj. REDMOND, Charles STEWART.

Bk:Pg: 2F:259   Date: 22 Aug 1805   RcCt: 9 Sep 1805
John HOFF & wife Mary of Ldn to Andrew REDMOND of Ldn. B/S of 150ac adj William COKE, Nathaniel PEGG. Wit: Benjamin JAMES, Nathaniel POLEN, Benj. Redwood.

Bk:Pg: 2F:262   Date: 3 Apr 1805   RcCt: 9 Sep 1805
Benjamin GRAYSON & wife Nancy of Ldn to John RICHARDS of Ldn. B/S of 183¼ac on road to John Gibson's Mill, adj Leven POWELL, James TORBERT, William RICHARDS. Wit: Wm. BRONAUGH, Saml. BOGGESS, Abner HUMPHREY, Edw'd McDANIEL, Burr POWELL.

Bk:Pg: 2F:265   Date: 3 Apr 1805   RcCt: 9 Sep 1805
Benjamin GRAYSON & wife Nancy of Ldn to William RICHARDS of Ldn. B/S of 121¼ac adj Henry CARTER, John RICHARDS. Wit: Wm. BRONAUGH, Saml. BOGGESS, Abner HUMPHREY, Edw'd McDANIEL, Burr POWELL.

Bk:Pg: 2F:268   Date: 2 Jun 1804   RcCt: 9 Sep 1805
Jacob WALTMAN & wife Margaret of Ldn to Jacob BECKLEY of Ldn. B/S
of 22*ac* adj Henry KEEZEY nr Great Dutchman. Wit: Jos. LEWIS Jr., Burr
POWELL.

Bk:Pg: 2F:271   Date: 13 Apr 1805   RcCt: 9 Sep 1805
Richard CRUPPER & wife Ann of Ldn to Levin LUCKETT. B/S of 10½*ac*.
Wit: Robert DAGG, Samuel HENDERSON, Noble BEVERIDGE, Meshock
LACEY.

Bk:Pg: 2F:273   Date: 9 Sep 1805   RcCt: 9 Sep 1805
David POTTS Sr. of Ldn to George ABEL of Ldn. B/S of 2*ac*.

Bk:Pg: 2F:274   Date: 28 Jun 1805   RcCt: 9 Sep 1805
Joseph LEWIS Jr. of Ldn to Susannah SMITH of Ldn. B/S of 50*ac*. Wit:
Frederick SLATES, 2 names in German.

Bk:Pg: 2F:276   Date: 23 Feb 1805   RcCt: 9 Sep 1805
Mahlon HOUGH of Ldn to John FOUNDLING of Ldn. B/S of 26 poles adj
Thos. LESLIE. Wit: John B. STEVENS, Mahlon MORRIS, Thos. HOUGH.

Bk:Pg: 2F:278   Date: 2 Apr 1805   RcCt: 9 Sep 1805
John HAMILTON & wife Winefred of Ldn to Abiel JENNERS of Ldn. B/S
of 358*ac* (2 lots) where HAMILTON now lives, adj Robert BRADEN,
Charles BENNETT, Old Schoolhouse, Abner WILLIAMS, James RICE.
Wit: R. BRADEN, Sanford RAMEY, John DODD Jr., Jonah TAVENNER.

Bk:Pg: 2F:281   Date: 27 Apr 1805   RcCt: 9 Sep 1805
John HAMILTON & wife Winefred of Ldn to James RICE of Ldn. B/S of
71¼*ac* adj Abner WILLIAMS, William FOX. Wit: Richard GRIFFITH,
Jacob SANDS, Edw'd DARSEY, Abner MOORE, David GOODWIN.

Bk:Pg: 2F:283   Date: 13 Apr 1805   RcCt: 9 Sep 1805
John LAIDLER & wife Catherine Ann of Charles Co Md to James
HEATON of Ldn. B/S of 390*ac* adj Thomas HUMPHREY. Wit: Stacy
TAYLOR, Jesse JANNEY, Notley C. WILLIAMS, Nicholas OSBORN,
Timothy TAYLOR, Benjamin MEAD.

Bk:Pg: 2F:286   Date: ___   RcCt: 9 Sep 1805
Albert RUSSELL to William MORAN (wife Rebeccah MORAN, Gustavus
MORAN). L/L of 295*ac*. Wit: Samuel ADAMS, Richard ADAMS, Cloe
ADAMS, Mary ADAMS.

Bk:Pg: 2F:289   Date: 22 Aug 1805   RcCt: 9 Sep 1805
Lewis ELLZEY & wife Rosannah of Ldn to Albert RUSSELL of Ldn. B/S of
534*ac* on Broad Run at mouth of Horsepen Run. Wit: William HOSKINS,
Daniel PARRIS, S. Dorathy FOWKE, Jacob [in German], John
HOWDERSHELT, Stacy TAYLOR, Notley C. WILLIAMS.

Bk:Pg: 2F:293   Date: 13 Nov 1804   RcCt: 9 Sep 1805
James HAMILTON & wife Elizabeth of Ldn to Jacob WINE of Ldn. B/S of
134*ac* (from HAMILTON's Revolutionary right, where George SHAFFER
has L/L) adj John MARTIN. Wit: John V'DEVANTER, Isaac HOUGH,
James SAMPLE, Cha. BENNETT, Jno. ROSE.

Bk:Pg: 2F:296   Date: 9 Sep 1805   RcCt: 9 Sep 1805
Aaron SANDERS & wife Susannah of Ldn to John ROSE of Ldn. B/S of
2¼ac adj Hugh DOUGLAS.

Bk:Pg: 2F:298   Date: 6 Sep 1805   RcCt: 9 Sep 1805
James DUTTON of Ldn to William POLEN of Ldn. B/S of 49ac. Wit:
Reuben SETTLE, Nathaniel POLEN, John BLAKER.

Bk:Pg: 2F:301   Date: 13 Mar 1797   RcCt: 11 Sep 1797
Franklin PERRY of Ldn to Isaac HOUGH of Ldn. B/S of __ac adj Mrs.
Mary BRUSTER. John JACKSON Jr., Jno. S. PERRY, Peggy PERRY, J.
GILPIN, Thomas EVANS, Hugh CONN.

Bk:Pg: 2F:303   Date: 23 Mar 1805   RcCt: 9 Sep 1805
John MOORE & wife Sarah of Ldn to Joseph MOORE. B/S of part of
200ac adj John EVANS. Wit: Eden B. MOORE, Nicholas TAYLOR, Elias
LACEY, Spencer E. GIBSON, Elijah RITICOR.

Bk:Pg: 2F:304   Date: 6 May 1805   RcCt: 9 Sep 1805
Abijah SANDS (s/o Isaac SANDS dec'd) of Ldn to John ROBERTSON of
Ldn. Bond on sale of 150ac (1/7 part of 2 tracts). Wit: Jacob SANDS,
David ORISON, name in German.

Bk:Pg: 2F:305   Date: 21 Mar 1805   RcCt: 13 May 1805
William H. HARDING (Exor of John HANDY dec'd of JeffVa) to William
HOUGH of Ldn. B/S of 154½ac less 15ac sold to William GREGG, adj
Joseph JANNEY dec'd. Wit: John H. CANBY, Abnor WILLIAMS, Daniel
STONE, Thomas PHILLIPS.

Bk:Pg: 2F:308   Date: 24 Mar 1804   RcCt: 8 Oct 1804
Ferdinando FAIRFAX & William Byrd PAGE of JeffVa to Thomas LESLIE
of Ldn. B/S of 108ac adj Nancy WILLIAMS, Joseph BEAL, Nicholas
TUCKER, William THOMPSON. Wit: And'w COPELAND, Wm. H.
HARDING, Saml. W. YOUNG, William THOMPSON.

Bk:Pg: 2F:310   Date: 19 Apr 1804   RcCt: 9 Sep 1805
John P. HARRISON & wife Elizabeth of StafVa to Thomas ATWELL of
Ldn. B/S of 100ac adj James GUNN. Wit: John C. SHAR, James F.
HARRISON, Sarah A. HARRISON, Sethey HARRISON, Lev D. POWELL,
John UPP, A. GIBSON, Noble BEVERIDGE.

Bk:Pg: 2F:312   Date: 9 Sep 1805   RcCt: 9 Sep 1805
Janet DOW, Alexander DOW & Anna DOW of Ldn (heirs of Peter DOW
dec'd) to Gustavus ELLGIN of Ldn. B/S of 17½ac known as Musterfield nr
road to Potts Mill on Goose Creek. Wit: Francis ELGIN, Ignatius ELGIN,
Alexander TAYLOR.

Bk:Pg: 2F:314   Date: 9 Sep 1805   RcCt: 9 Sep 1805
Joseph ROBERTS & wife Sarah of Ldn to Jonah SANDS of Ldn. B/S of
28ac on Beaver Dam adj John BROWN, Stacy JANNEY, Eli NICHOLS.

Bk:Pg: 2F:316   Date: 9 Sep 1805   RcCt: 9 Sep 1805
Jonah SANDS & wife Esther of Ldn to Rachel SANDS & Abijah SANDS of
Ldn. B/S of 6ac adj Constantine HUGHESE, Ann CLEWS.

Bk:Pg: 2F:318   Date: 10 Jan 1805   RcCt: 9 Sep 1805
Ferdinando FAIRFAX of JeffVa to William ELLZEY of Ldn. B/S of 63¼ac.
Wit: John H. CANBY, Edw. McDANIEL, Rich'd H. HENDERSON, Edw'd
ADAMS, Edward CUNARD Sr., Jo. BLINCOE, Westwood F. MASON,
John McILHANEY Jr., Thomas WILKINSON.

Bk:Pg: 2F:321   Date: 7 Sep 1805   RcCt: 9 Sep 1805
Richard Bland LEE & wife Elizabeth of Ffx to Leven POWELL of Ldn. B/S
of 150ac adj Thaddius McCARTY. Wit: T. BLACKBURNE Jr., Theodorik
LEE, Wm. GUNNELL Jr., Francis ADAMS.

Bk:Pg: 2F:324   Date: 23 Aug 1804   RcCt: 9 Sep 1805
Jonas POTTS & wife Phoebe of Ldn to Joshua DANIEL of Ldn. B/S of
123ac on Cotactin Creek adj Catesby COCKE and 45ac adj Richard
WILLIAMS. Wit: Saml. CARR, Will. VESTAL, Robt. HAMILTON, John
CARSON.

Bk:Pg: 2F:326   Date: 25 Mar 1805   RcCt: 9 Sep 1805
Sarah FAIRFAX to Samuel EVANS of Ldn. Renewal of LS of 81ac L/L
(lives of Thomas HUTTON, wife Mary, son John) who transferred to
Israel THOMPSON, who transferred to Garlick STEGLAR, who
transferred to Samuel EVANS; Thomas & Mary HUTTON now dec'd,
EVANS appoints sons Jessey & Evan EVANS. Wit: William VERTZ, Jos.
BEARD, Thos. WILKINSON, Jonas POTTS, Joseph WILKINSON,
Benjamin STEER, Jonathan MARTOR.

Bk:Pg: 2F:329   Date: 25 Mar 1805   RcCt: 9 Sep 1805
Sarah FAIRFAX to William VIRTZ. Renewal of LS of 134ac L/L (lives of
Thomas HUTTON, wife Mary, son John) who transferred to Israel
THOMPSON, who transferred to VIRTZ with Wm. & son John VIRTZ in
place of Thomas & Mary HUTTON dec'd. Wit: Samuel EVANS, Jos.
BEARD, Thos. WILKINSON.

Bk:Pg: 2F:332   Date: 22 Mar 1805   RcCt: 9 Sep 1805
Sarah FAIRFAX to Jonathan McCARTY (son Jonathan) of Ldn. Renewal
of LS of 160ac adj Edward McDANIEL, Richard BROWN, Thomas
TREBBE, Amos BEANS, Andrew THOMPSON, Samuel CLENDENNING.
Wit: Edward McDANIEL, Wm. H. HARDING, John B. STEPHENS,
Benjamin STEER, Joseph WILKINSON, Samuel EVANS.

Bk:Pg: 2F:336   Date: 22 Mar 1805   RcCt: 9 Sep 1805
Sarah FAIRFAX to Jonathan McCARTY (son Jonathan) of Ldn. Renewal
of LS of 150ac L/L (lives of John NEWLAND, wife Elizabeth, son John, his
son Isaac NEWLAND) who transferred to Israel THOMPSON, who
transferred to McCARTY; Elizabeth & John NEWLAND are dec'd,
McCARTY and son in their stead. Wit: Wm. H. HARDING, Edward
McDANIEL, John B. STEVENS, Jonas POTTS, Benjamin STEER, Joseph
WILKINSON.

Bk:Pg: 2F:339   Date 24 Mar 1805   RcCt: 9 Sep 1805
Sarah FAIRFAX to Joseph WILKINSON (son William) of Ldn. Renewal of
LS of 150ac L/L (lives of Thomas LAMB, wife Affe, son Thomas LAMB)

who transferred to George DYKE, then to WILKINSON for lives of him, his son and Thomas LAMB Jr. Wit: Thomas WILKINSON, Walter BLACKWELL, Jos. WILLIAMS, Jonas POTTS, Benjamin STEER, Samuel EVANS.

Bk:Pg: 2F:341   Date: 14 May 1805   RcCt: 9 Sep 1805
Benjamin H. CANBY & wife Sarah of Ldn to Ignatius ELGIN of Ldn. B/S of 174ac on Secolon Run. Wit: Jno. MATHIAS, Jos. BEARD, Samuel HOUGH, Samuel MURREY, Obadiah CLIFFORD.

Bk:Pg: 2F:244   Date: 9 Sep 1805   RcCt: 19 Sep 1805
James NELSON of Ldn to Thomas LESLIE of Ldn. PoA.

Bk:Pg: 2F:345   Date: 14 May 1805   RcCt: 10 Sep 1805
William LITTLEJOHN of Ldn to James GARDENER of Lsbg. B/S of lot adj Presley CORDELL on Markett St. towards Loudoun St.

Bk:Pg: 2F:346   Date: 10 Jul 1805   RcCt: 10 Sep 1805
William LITTLEJOHN of Ldn to Josiah MOFFETT of Lsbg. B/S of 11ac adj Chas. BINNS.

Bk:Pg: 2F:348   Date: 3 Sep 1805   RcCt: 10 Sep 1805
William LITTLEJOHN of Ldn to Charles BINNS of Ldn. B/S of 3¾ac Lot #1 adj Poor House lot, 4½ac Lot #2 adj W corner of Lot #1, 4ac Lot #5 adj W corner of Lot #2.

Bk:Pg: 2F:349   Date: 10 Dec 1804   RcCt: 15 Jan 1805
Joseph SMITH, John LITTLEJOHN & Stephen COOKE (court appoint commissioner for Jesse TAYLOR) to Benjamin H. CANBY of Lsbg. B/S of lot on W end of Market St. adj William LITTLEJOHN. Wit: Jos. SMITH, Jno. MATHIAS, Wm. MAINS. James MILES, William CLINE, Joseph SHIELDS, Jos. BEARD, David ENGLISH, John BOYD.

Bk:Pg: 2F:351   Date: 29 Jan 1805   RcCt: 10 Sep 1805
Rev. John LITTLEJOHN & wife Monica of Ldn to Robert I. TAYLOR of AlexVa. B/S of 130ac adj William MEANS, Joshua DANIEL, Benjamin EDWARDS. Wit: Stephen COOKE, Jas. CAVAN Jr., Jo. BLINCOE, A. MORRISON.

Bk:Pg: 2F:353   Date: 20 Mar 1805   RcCt: 10 Sep 1805
Samuel MURREY of Lsbg to Wilson Carey SELDON of Ldn. B/S of part of Lot #12 on E side of King St. Wit: Wm. CHILTON, Wm. WOODDY, Charles GULLATT.

Bk:Pg: 2F:355   Date: 20 Mar 1805   RcCt: 10 Sep 1805
Wilson Carey SELDON & wife Nelly of Ldn to John DRISH cf Ldn. B/S of 195ac on road from Lsbg to Noland Ferry. Wit: Stephen COOKE, Samuel MURREY, Elizabeth NOLAND.

Bk:Pg: 2F:358   Date: 20 Mar 1805   RcCt: 10 Sep 1805
John DRISH & wife Eleanor of Ldn to Wilson C. SELDON of Ldn. Mortgage on above land. Wit: Stephen COOKE, Samuel MURREY, Joseph BENTLEY.

Bk:Pg: 2F:361   Date: 13? May 1805   RcCt: 10 Sep 1805
Joseph SMITH & wife Molly of AlexVa to William CARR of Ldn. B/S of part of lot on W side of West St between Loudoun & Market St. Wit: Geo. W. BLINCOE, Chs. BINNS, Charles THRIFT.

Bk:Pg: 2F:362   Date: 20 Feb 1805   RcCt: 11 Sep 1805
Walter TAYLOR of Ldn to Joseph HARDING of Ldn. BoS for negro woman Suck. Wit: Robert ROSE, William HARDEN.

Bk:Pg: 2F:363   Date: 11 Sep 1805   RcCt: 11 Sep 1805
Maurice DULANY (Exor of Timothy WHELANS dec'd) to Catherine WHELAN, Winefred WHELAN, Margarett DUNNE, Jer. PHELAN. Receipt.

Bk:Pg: 2F:364   Date: 27 Aug 1804   RcCt: 12 Sep 1805
George Fairfax LEE to William CHILTON. B/S of 640ac on Goose Creek between George CARTER and John T. CARTER. Wit: Hugh QUINLAN, Geo. MOORE, Willis GARNER, Chas. R. THOMPSON.

Bk:Pg: 2F:366   Date: 21 Feb 1805   RcCt: 12 Sep 1805
Commissioners Jonas POTTS, Obadiah CLIFFORD & George ROWAN of Ldn to William CARR of Ldn. B/S of part of Lot #8 in Lsbg owned by Jacob JACOBS dec'd. Wit: Wm. WOODDY, Jesse DAILEY, Benj'a SHREVE.

Bk:Pg: 2F:367   Date: 7 Sep 1805   RcCt: 14 Oct 1805
George SHULTS of Ldn to Peter RIDENBAUGH of Ldn. A/L of land on Potomac adj John WALTERS which Jacob SHOEMAKER leased to SHULTS.

Bk:Pg: 2F:369   Date: 14 Oct 1805   RcCt: 14 Oct 1805
Daniel SHOEMAKER of Ldn to Jacob COOPER of Ldn. A/L of ___. Wit: Sn. BLINCOE, Geo. W. BLINCOE, S. M. EDWARDS.

Bk:Pg: 2F:369   Date: 19 Mar 1805   RcCt: 13 May 1805
Thadeus McCARTY & wife Sarah of Ldn to Moses WILLSON of Ldn. B/S of 57ac on Goose Creek and Wancopin line. Wit: Burr POWELL, Leven LUCKETT, Geo. W. McCARTY.

Bk:Pg: 2F:372   Date: 19 Mar 1805   RcCt: 9 Sep 1805
Thadeus McCARTY & wife Sarah of Ldn to Jehu BURSON of Ldn. B/S of 52¾ac on Wancopin Branch. Wit: Burr POWELL, Leven LUCKETT, Geo. W. McCARTY.

Bk:Pg: 2F:374   Date: 6 Apr 1805   RcCt: 14 Oct 1805
John ALEXANDER to Mrs. Jane KENT. Terms for use of lands and house. Wit: John WALKER.

Bk:Pg: 2F:374   Date: 3 Apr 1804   RcCt: 14 May 1804
John NORTON & wife Mary Ann to John KILE. B/S of 81ac adj Nathaniel NORTON. Wit: Burr POWELL, Wm. BRONAUGH, Richard VANPELT.

Bk:Pg: 2F:377   Date: 24 Jul 1805   RcCt: 9 Sep 1805
John MOORE of Ldn to Elias LACEY of Ldn. B/S of 252½ac adj Jacob
ISH. Wit: Joseph MOORE, Elijah RITICOR, Cornelius SKINNER, Spencer
E. GIBSON.

Bk:Pg: 378   Date: 25 Mar 1805   RcCt: 14 Oct 1805
Farmer Thomas E. MINOR of Ldn to farmer William WHALEY of Ldn. BoS
for farm and household items; WHALEY is security for MINOR. Wit:
James McNATHAN, Johnston WHALEY.

Bk:Pg: 2F:380   Date: 18 Sep 1802   RcCt: 9 May 1803
James L. MITCHELL of Ldn to James HUTCHISON of PrWm. A/L of
158ac on Bull Run where MITCHELL now lives. Wit: Fred'k. ELGIN,
Moses PILCHER, Sampson HUTCHISON, George NEALE.

Bk:Pg: 2F:381   Date: 14 Oct 1805   RcCt: 14 Oct 1805
James Mercer GARNETT & John Taliaferro BROOKE (Admr of James
MERCER dec'd late of Fredericksburg Va) to Matthew ADAM. B/S of
253½ac on road from Little River to Ashby and Snickers Gaps.

Bk:Pg: 2F:383   Date: 14 Oct 1805   RcCt: 14 Oct 1805
Matthew ADAM to James Mercer GARNETT & John Taliaferro BROOKE
(Admr of James MERCER dec'd late of Fredericksburg Va). Mortgage on
above land.

Bk:Pg: 2F:384   Date: 19 Jul 1805   RcCt: 14 Oct 1805
Thomas LESLEY & wife Nancy of Ldn to John WEDOWMAN /
WITTOWMAN of Ldn. B/S of 9ac adj Peter VERTS. Wit: Josiah WHITE,
Tho. WHITE, William WRIGHT, Stacy TAYLOR, James HAMILTON.

Bk:Pg: 2F:386   Date: 9 Dec 1804   RcCt: 14 Oct 1805
Robert PARFECT & wife Jane of Ldn to Peter WHITING of Ldn. B/S of
142ac. Wit: William CHILTON, Johnston CLEVELAND, Alexander
SUTHERLAND, Robert HAMILTON, Charles LEWIS.

Bk:Pg: 2F:389   Date: 14 Oct 1805   RcCt: 14 Oct 1805
John BOWERSET of Ldn to Samuel BAKER of Ldn. B/S of 25ac on E
side of Short Hill. Wit: Adam SHOVER, George HUFF, name in German.

Bk:Pg: 2F:390   Date: 9 Aug 1805   RcCt: 14 Oct 1805
Farmer John CARTER Jr. of Ldn to farmer William HORSEMAN of Ldn.
BoS for negro girl Fanny, farm and household items; to cover debt. Wit:
John A. HARRIS, Johnston WHALEY, Alexander BEACH.

Bk:Pg: 2F:391   Date: 12 Mar 1805   RcCt: 14 Oct 1805
John TYLER to Mary, Isaac, William & Margaret WYCOFF (ch/o Abraham
WICOFF dec'd). B/S of 200ac (military warrant #3884) part of agreement
between Matthew HARRISON, John TYLER and Abraham WICOFF. Wit:
A. HARRISON, L. D. POWELL, Geo. W. BLINCOE.

Bk:Pg: 2F:394   Date: 21 Apr 1804   RcCt: 8 Oct 1804
James DILLON & wife Mary of Ldn to James LOVE of Ldn. B/S of 169ac
adj Spencer PEW, John BALDWIN, Elisha MARKS, Peter HAND. Wit:
Stacy TAYLOR, James McILHANEY, David GOODIN, Mosses DILLON.

Bk:Pg: 2F:397   Date: 12 Sep 1805   RcCt: 14 Oct 1805
Susannah HUMPHREY (Admr & w/o William HUMPHREY dec'd) to
Samuel HUMPHREY and Hannah HUMPHREY (ch/o William dec'd).
Receipt and release as Admr. Wit: Johnston CLEVELAND, Saml. LANE.

Bk:Pg: 2F:397   Date: 9 Apr 1805   RcCt: 14 Oct 1805
Thomas JANNEY & wife Sarah of AlexVa to Charles GULLATT of Lsbg.
B/S of ½ of Lot #3 in Lsbg. Wit: Jacob BAUGH, Obadiah CLIFFORD,
Fleet SMITH.

Bk:Pg: 2F:399   Date: 12 Oct 1805   RcCt: 14 Oct 1805
John Adam WOLF & wife Susannah of Ldn to William LONGSTRAW of
Ldn. B/S of 2ac on Great Dutchman adj Jacob BECKLY.

Bk:Pg: 2F:401   Date: 14 Oct 1805   RcCt: 14 Oct 1805
John Adam WOLF of Ldn to Jacob WALTMAN of Ldn. A/L of land in
Piedmont Manor with L/L to Frederick BELTS.

Bk:Pg: 2F:402   Date: 14 Oct 1805   RcCt: 14 Oct 1805
John Adam WOLF & wife Susannah of Ldn to Jacob WALTMAN of Ldn.
B/S of 20ac adj Henry KEENZE.

Bk:Pg: 2F:403   Date: 9 Sep 1805   RcCt: 14 Oct 1805
Nicholas GARRETT & wife Patty of Md to Thomas BURGEE of Md. B/S of
110ac. Wit: Jas. CAVANS Jr., John H. EVANS, Jno. MATHIAS, Greenly
HOWARD, M. BROWNING.

Bk:Pg: 2F:405   Date: 21 Feb 1805   RcCt: 9 Apr 1805
Jacob LEWIS (s/o Abraham LEWIS) & wife Lovey of Ldn to Thomas
FRANCIS of Ldn. B/S of 53ac adj James LEWIS. Wit: Wm. BRONAUGH,
Ben. GRAYSON, George FRENCH, Thomas FRED, Joshua FRED.

Bk:Pg: 2F:408   Date: 24 Sep 1805   RcCt: 14 Oct 1805
Jonathan CUNARD & wife Elizabeth of Ldn to Isaac HOUGH of Ldn. B/S
of 50ac. Wit: James HAMILTON, Mauduit YOUNG, Solomon JENKINS,
Joseph BRADEN Jr.

Bk:Pg: 2F:410   Date: 24 Sep 1805   RcCt: 14 Oct 1805
Isaac HOUGH of Ldn to James HAMILTON of Ldn. Trust of 50¾ac for
debt to Jonathan CUNARD. Wit: Edw'd McDANIEL, Mauduit YOUNG,
Joseph BRANDEN Jr., Joseph SANDS.

Bk:Pg: 2F:411   Date: 30 Sep 1803   RcCt: 17 Dec 1804/14 Oct 1805
John JAMESON & wife Elizabeth of Culpeper to Ferdinando FAIRFAX of
JeffVa. B/S of 400ac nr Lsbg. Wit: John D. ORR, David HUMPHREYS, G.
W. HUMPHREYS, George TATE, James GREEN Jr., Richard NORRIS.

Bk:Pg: 2F:414   Date: 8 Oct 1805   RcCt: 8 and 14 Oct 1805
Thomas OSBURNE of Ldn to Ferdinando FAIRFAX of JeffVa. Trust using
170½ac.

Bk:Pg: 2F:417   Date: 25 Apr 1805   RcCt: 14 Oct 1805
Robert BRADEN of Ldn to Isaac HOUGH of Ldn. B/S of 4ac adj Adam
GRUBB. Wit: Edmund JENINGS, James HAMILTON, Nathan CONARD.

Bk:Pg: 2F:418   Date: 1 Apr 1805   RcCt: 14 Oct 1805
Ezekiel CHAMBLIN of Ldn to David LOVETT of Ldn. B/S of L/L of 100ac
(on lives of Sarah PHILLIPS [Guardian is Israel THOMPSON], and Jenkin
& Samuel PHILIPS [s/o Benjamin PHILLIPS dec'd]). Wit: Edward
CUNARD Sr., Mahlon MORRIS, Samuel FERGUSON.

Bk:Pg: 2F:420   Date: ___ 1805   RcCt: 14 Oct 1805
George FORTNEY & wife Susannah of Lsbg to Jacob FORTNEY of Lsbg.
Mortgage using household items. Wit: Sn. BLINCOE, A. LANGLY, Amos
BOLTON.

Bk:Pg: 2F:422   Date: 19 Jul 1805   RcCt: 14 Oct 1805
James Mercer GARNETT & John Taliaferro BROOKE (Admr of James
MERCER dec'd late of Fredericksburg Va) to Moses DILLON of Ldn. B/S
of 300ac at foot of Bull Run Mt. Wit: Simon TRIPLETT, Joseph JONES
Jr., Mathew RUST.

Bk:Pg: 2F:425   Date: 12 Aug 1805   RcCt: 14 Oct 1805
Samuel TILLETT of Ldn to Jonas POTTS of Ldn. BoS for negro man John
age 35y for 3y then freed. Wit: Jas. HAMILTON, Chas. LEWIS.

Bk:Pg: 2F:426   Date: 13 May 1805   RcCt: 14 Oct 1805
Hugh QUINLAN of WstmVa to William BRONAUGH of Ldn. Trust for debt
to Samuel NICHOLS &c using 297ac "William Fields' lot". Wit: R. J.
TAYLOR, Jno. MATHIAS, Stacey TAYLOR, A. GIBSON.

Bk:Pg: 2F:427   Date: 9 Feb 1805   RcCt: 11 Sep 1805
Daniel DOWLING & wife Kitty of AlexVa to Thomas JANNEY of AlexVa.
Mortgage using Kitty's share of land the late Henry McCABE left to
children Harriet, John and above Kitty subject to dower of widow Jane
McCABE. Wit: John JANNEY, Joseph JANNEY, Obadiah CLIFFORD.

Bk:Pg: 2F:429   Date: 14 Oct 1805   RcCt: 15 Oct 1805
Smallwood MIDDLETON & wife Casander of Lsbg to William ELLIOTT of
Ldn. Mortgage using ¼ac of lot at N end of King St in Lsbg, farm and
household items. Wit: Sn. BLINCOE, Henry M. DAVIS, J. HARDING.

Bk:Pg: 2F:430   Date: 15 Mar 1805   RcCt: 15 Oct 1805
Sally, Mary, John & Thos. PEAKE to Anna B. WEST. BoS for negroes
George & Daniel and cattle. Wit: Jos. BEARD, John SHAW, Francis
STONE, John SHREVE.

Bk:Pg: 2F:430   Date: 15 Oct 1805   RcCt: 15 Oct 1805
Joseph LEWIS Jr. of Ldn to John BALL of Ldn. B/S of 97½ac in Piedmont
Manor formerly occupied by late Farling BALL dec'd.

Bk:Pg: 2F:431   Date: 11 Jun 1805   RcCt: 15 Oct 1805
John DRISH & wife Elenor of Ldn to John NIXON of Ldn. B/S of Lot #45 in
Lsbg. Wit: Thos. N. BINNS, Joseph BENTLEY, Daniel DOWLING.

Bk:Pg: 2F:432   Date: 11 Jun 1805   RcCt: 15 Oct 1805
Charles BINNS & William MAINS (Exor of Daniel LOSCH dec'd) to John
NIXON. B/S of 1ac lot on main road from Lsbg to Noland Ferry. Wit: Thos.
N. BINNS, G. W. BLINCOE, Leven D. POWELL.

Bk:Pg: 2F:433   Date: 15 Oct 1805   RcCt: 15 Oct 1805
George CARTER of Ldn to Edward COE of Ldn. B/S of 525*ac* (plat given) on Goose Creek.

Bk:Pg: 2F:435   Date: 8 Jul 1805   RcCt: 15 Oct 1805
Presley SANDERS Jr. & wife Mary of Lsbg to Jesse DAILEY of Lsbg. B/S of part of Lot #58 in Lsbg. Wit: Thomas SANDERS, Samuel MURREY, Fra. H. PEYTON.

Bk:Pg: 2F:437   Date: 15 Oct 1805   RcCt: 15 Oct 1805
Robert ARMISTEAD. Trust of land and slaves acquired thru marriage to late wife Lusinda Margaret to her child Armstead MASON for use by Robert's daus. Elizabeth & Mary. Slaves John, Esther and her 8 children Phanny, Joe, Lella, Duanna, Phillis, Phill, Frankey & Becca.

Bk:Pg: 2F:437   Date: 2 Mar 1805   RcCt: 15 Oct 1805
James McDONAUGH of Ldn to Jonas POTTS of Ldn. BoS for farm animals. Wit: James CAVANS Jr., Saml. CARR.

Bk:Pg: 2F:438   Date: 19 Jun 1805   RcCt: 9 Sep 1805
Ann PEYTON (wd/o Craven PEYTON dec'd) of AlexVa to Joshua & William OSBURNE of Ldn. A/L of 367*ac* L/L (now on lives of William, Craven & Valentine PEYTON) on Kotochton Creek adj Samuel JOHNSTON. Wit: Lewis ELLZEY, Charles CHAMBLIN, Joel OSBORNE, Jonah THOMPSON, R. J. TAYLOR, Thomas SWANN.

Bk:Pg: 2F:440   Date: 15 Oct 1805   RcCt: 15 Oct 1805
John LITTLEJOHN & wife Monica of Ldn to Thomas N. BINNS of Ldn. B/S of 66*ac* nr Lsbg.

Bk:Pg: 2F:441   Date: 15 Oct 1805   RcCt: 15 Oct 1805
Thomas N. BINNS of Ldn to John LITTLEJOHN. Mortgage on above land.

Bk:Pg: 2F:443   Date: 15 Oct 1805   RcCt: 15 Oct 1805
John BALL of Ldn to Joseph LEWIS Jr. of Ldn. Mortgage on 97½*ac*.

Bk:Pg: 2G:001   Date: 30 Sep 1805   RcCt: 9 Dec 1805
Ferdinando FAIRFAX & wife Elizabeth B. of JeffVa to Joshua OSBURNE of Ldn. B/S of 368*ac* in "Arcadia" tract adj Thos. OSBORNE, John HOUGH. Wit: Wm. H. HARDING, Geo. NORTH, Jacob H. MANNING.

Bk:Pg: 2G:003   Date: 6 Dec 1805   RcCt: 9 Dec 1805
Thomas HOUGH & wife Mary of Hllb to Mahlon ROACH of Hllb. B/S of 3*ac* on new road NE from Hllb to James ROACH's. Wit: John B. STEPHENS, Joseph HUNT, John HOCKLEY.

Bk:Pg: 2G:004   Date: 30 Jul 1805   RcCt: 9 Dec 1805
Charles J. LOVE of Ffx to Jeremiah HUTCHISON of Ldn. B/S of 46*ac* on Lsbg and Centreville Road. Wit: William HANBY, Benjamin HUTCHISON, Lewis AMBLAR, William AMBLAR, Jno. HUTCHISON.

Bk:Pg: 2G:005   Date: 30 Jul 1805   RcCt: 9 Dec 1805
Charles J. LOVE of Ffx to John HUTCHISON of Ldn. B/S of 132*ac*. Wit: J. HUTCHISON, Benjamin HUTCHISON, Lewis AMBLAR, William AMBLAR, William HAWLEY.

Bk:Pg: 2G:006   Date: 22 Nov 1805   RcCt: 9 Dec 1805
Patrick MILHOLLEN & wife Mary of Ldn to Thomas PHILIPS of Ldn. B/S
of 28½ac adj James RADICAN, Elizah MIERS. Wit: John WILLIAMS,
Reuben SCHOOLEY, Issachar SMITH.

Bk:Pg: 2G:007   Date: 16 Apr 1805   RcCt: 9 Dec 1805
Mahlon JANNEY of Ldn to James MOORE of Ldn. B/S of 29 perches Lots
#9 & #10 in new addition to Wtfd. Wit: Edw'd DORSEY, James RUSSELL,
Amos GIBSON.

Bk:Pg: 2G:008   Date: 1 Nov 1805   RcCt: 9 Dec 1805
Frederick STONEBURNER & wife Elizabeth of Ldn to John
STOUSEBURGER of Ldn. B/S of 90½ac. Wit: John HAMILTON, Francis
WHITELY, Enos GARRET, Chas. BENNETT.

Bk:Pg: 2G:010   Date: 13 Dec 1802   RcCt: 9 Dec 1806
John BAYLEY, William P. BAYLEY and George BAYLEY. Division of land
based on undetermined suit in court of Dumfries. William P. BAYLEY
given list #1 (825ac) where John BEVERIDGE, Joseph JACKSON,
Richard CRUPPER, Aquila BRISCOE, John BATSON & James BATSON
live. John BAYLEY given list #1 (814ac) where John WOOD, Hugh
ROGERS, Arther ROGERS, Thomas SEALOCKS, Joseph WEST,
Elizabeth BEATY & Thomas WILSON live. George BAYLEY given list #3
(825ac) where Jeremiah HAMPTON, Samuel SKINNER, Samuel
DISHMAN, Samuel DAVIS, Phillip FRY & Rawleigh CHINN live. Wit:
Robert BAYLEY, Moses DOWDELL, Hugh ROGERS, James BATTSON.

Bk:Pg: 2G:012   Date 28 Nov 1805   RcCt: 9 Dec 1805
Eneas GARRET & wife Elenor of Ldn to Frederick STONEBURNER of
Ldn. B/S of 157ac on Dutchman Run. Wit: John STOUSEBERGER, John
HAMILTON, Chas. BENNETT.

Bk:Pg: 2G:014   Date: 16 Apr 1805   RcCt: 9 Dec 1805
Mahlon JANNEY of Ldn to Edward DORSEY of Ldn. B/S of 33 perches
Lot #6 and part of #7 in new addition to Wtfd. Wit: James MOORE, James
RUSSELL, Amos GIBSON.

Bk:Pg: 2G:015   Date: 9 Dec 1805   RcCt: 9 Dec 1805
Enos GARRETT of Ldn to Frederick STONEBURNER of Ldn. A/L of ___.
Wit: Geo. W. BLINCOE.

Bk:Pg: 2G:016   Date: 28 Aug 1805   RcCt: 10 Sep 1805
Isaac BALL of Ldn to James HAMILTON & Robert BRADEN. Trust to
secure payment for fees due court & Edward McDANIEL from Farling
BALL dec'd using 5ac and 109ac. Wit: Geo. W. BLINCOE, John HENRY,
Mungo DYKES, S. M. EDWARDS.

Bk:Pg: 2G:018   Date: 24 Jun 1803   RcCt: 12 Dec 1805
William, Samuel & Mahlon HOUGH (Exors of John HOUGH dec'd) of Ldn
to Ebenezer GRUBB of Ldn. B/S of 267ac on Kittoctan Creek, adj Wm.
HOUGH Jr., Thomas HOUGH, Jacob SHIVELY. Wit: Walker REID, G. W.
BLINCOE, Sn. BLINCOE, Mahlon ROACH, Edward CUNNARD Sr., Thos.
HOUGH, Thomas PHILLIPS, David POTTS, Bayn SMALLWOOD.

Bk:Pg: 2G:020   Date: 27 Apr 1804   RcCt: 8 Oct 1804
Nicholas OSBURNE & wife Margaret of Ldn to Ebenezer GRUBB of Ldn. B/S of 325ac. Wit: James McILHANEY, Thos. WHITE, David LOVETT, Thos. HOUGH, Josiah WHITE Jr., Bayn SMALLWOOD.

Bk:Pg: 2G:021   Date: 21 May 1805   RcCt: 9 Dec 1805
Thomas SIM of Ldn to William HOLMES of Ldn. B/S of 9ac adj Thomas SWANN, Dr. Thomas SIM. Wit: Thos. N. BINNS, Lee D. POWELL, Thompson MASON.

Bk:Pg: 2G:022   Date: __ Nov 1805   RcCt: 9 Dec 1805
John SLACK of Ldn to Joseph LEWIS Jr. of Ldn. A/L of __ac L/L. Wit: Peter MILLER Jr., William MILLER, Peter MILLER.

Bk:Pg: 2G:023   Date: 14 Nov 1805   RcCt: 9 Dec 1805
John SLACK & wife Elizabeth of Ldn to Joseph LEWIS Jr. of Ldn. B/S of 4ac in Piedmont adj Joseph SMITH, Henry Joseph FRY. Wit: Peter MILLER Jr., William MILLER, Peter MILLER.

Bk:Pg: 2G:024   Date: 7 Dec 1805   RcCt: 9 Dec 1805
Samuel RUST (s/o George RUST dec'd) of Ldn to friend Capt. George RUST of Ldn. PoA for sale of 180ac in WstmVa. Wit: William FOWKE, Saml. BOGGESS, Wm. CLEVELAND.

Bk:Pg: 2G:025   Date: 10 May 1804   RcCt: 8 Oct 1804
Benjamin DRAKE of Ldn to Jonathan McCARTER of Ldn. B/S of 70ac adj Benjamin GRAYSON, Joseph FRED. Wit: Saml. BOGGESS, Thomas DRAKE Jr., Abner HUMPHREY, Phinehas THOMAS, Thos. FRED.

Bk:Pg: 2G:027   Date: 12 Nov 1796   RcCt: 9 Dec 1805
Gustavus Richard BROWN & wife Margaret of Md to William GRAYHAM, Catesby GRAHAM & Jane GRAHAM (joint devisees and tenants of lands of late mother Elizabeth GRAHAM) of PrWm. B/S of 1198ac on Goose Creek. Wit: Thomson MASSON, Thomas MASSON, John HOOFMAN, John SPENCER, Phillip SHEPPARD, Daniel McCARTY, Henry SUTTLE.

Bk:Pg: 2G:030   Date: 7 Nov 1805   RcCt: 9 Dec 1805
Simeon PANCOAST of Ohio Co Va to Joseph PANCOAST of Belmont Co Oh. PoA for sale of his share of land of Israel PANCOAST dec'd of Ldn.

Bk:Pg: 2G:031   Date: 9 Dec 1805   RcCt: 9 Dec 1805
James CAVAN Jr. (Admr of Patrick CAVAN dec'd of Lsbg) to George FITCHER of Ldn. A/L of 4ac Lot #30 leased by CAVAN of James HEREFORD.

Bk:Pg: 2G:033   Date: 9 Dec 1805   RcCt: 9 Dec 1805
George NIXON & wife Ann of Ldn to Mary FITZSIMMONS of Ldn. B/S of 2ac. Wit: John LITTLEJOHN, William RHODES, John W. STONE.

Bk:Pg: 2G:034   Date: 19 Nov 1805   RcCt: 9 Dec 1805
Robert OWENS & wife Elenor of Ldn to Abner CRAVEN of Ldn. B/S of __ac undivided tract of land where Thomas CRAVEN died seized & Abner now lives. Wit: John LITTLEJOHN, Aaron SANDERS, John ROSE, Wm. SMITH, John TAVENOR?

Bk:Pg: 2G:036   Date: 31 Jul 1805   RcCt: 9 Dec 1805
Ferdinando FAIRFAX & William Byrd PAGE of JeffVa to Thomas JAMES
of Ldn. B/S of 91¾ac in Shannondale on SE side of Blue ridge where
James now lives. Wit: John H. CANBY, Joshua OSBURN, Joel OSBURN,
Thos. LESLIE.

Bk:Pg: 2G:037   Date: 7 Apr 1803   RcCt: 14 Oct 1805
Thomas Ludwell LEE of Ldn & Landon CARTER of RichVa (Exors of
George CARTER dec'd of Stafford) to Benjamin DEWELL of Ldn. B/S of
107ac adj Benjamin H. CANBY, Nich's. GARRETT. Wit: Jno. MATTHIAS,
Obadiah CLIFFORD, Thos. FOUCH, Samuel DONOHOE, John LYONS,
John B. RATHIE, Thomas HETHERLY.

Bk:Pg: 2G:039   Date: 27 Aug 1804   RcCt: 10 Dec 1805
John Tasker CARTER (br/o George CARTER) of WstmVa to George
Fairfax LEE of WstmVa. B/S of 640ac on Goose Creek. Wit: Charles R.
THOMPSON, Hugh QUINLAN, Daniel GARNER.

Bk:Pg: 2G:041   Date: 15 Jan 1805   RcCt: 8 Apr 1805
Samuel GRIFFITH to Jacob WALTMAN Sr. BoS for farm and household
items. Wit: Sn. BLINCOE, Martin CORDELL, Joseph BURSON.

Bk:Pg: 2G:042   Date: 11 Dec 1805   RcCt: 13 Jan 1806
Benjamin THORNTON to Matthew HARRISON. BoS (as security to
James DAWSON) for slaves Wabro commonly called Warbler, 2 women
each of the name Lucy David commonly called Davy, Maney a negro
woman and boy James commonly called Jim. Wit: Wm. LITTLEJOHN,
Robt. ARMISTEAD, John H. CANBY, Thos. WILKINSON.

Bk:Pg: 2G:043   Date: 27 Oct 1804   RcCt: 13 Jan 1806
Thomas LESLIE of Ldn to Samuel BEAL of Ldn. B/S of 99ac on Broad
Run adj John WITTEMAN nr German Church, Peter HICKMAN. Wit:
Josiah POTTS, Philip BEAL, William THOMPSON, Thos. HOUGH, Stacy
TAYLOR, James HAMILTON.

Bk:Pg: 2G:045   Date: 25 Oct 1805   RcCt: 13 Jan 1806
John LOVING & wife Elizabeth, Arminger LILLY & wife Rebeckah and
Strother CRAWFORD & wife Nancy of Fluvanna Co VA to Joshua
HUTCHISON of Ffx. B/S of undivided shares of land of late Benjamin
HUTCHISON dec'd of Ldn on Elk Licking Run. Wit: John DAVIS, Elijah
HUTCHISON, John BRAGG, Elizabeth HUTCHISON, Lewis AMBLAR.

Bk:Pg: 2G:047   Date: 10 Jan 1806   RcCt: 13 Jan 1806
John A. BINNS & wife Duanna of Ldn to Enos WILLIAM. B/S of 119ac.
Wit: Josh DANIEL, John RAWLINGS, John HAMILTON, Jno. ROSE.

Bk:Pg: 2G:049   Date: 13 Jan 1806   RcCt: 13 Jan 1806
Rheuben SCHOOLEY of Ldn to James BALL of Ldn. B/S of 7½ac on
Kittocton Mt adj Richard GRIFFITH, Patrick MILHOLLAN.

Bk:Pg: 2G:050   Date: Feb 1804   RcCt: 13 Jan 1806
John HIRST & Jesse HIRST. Bond on Thomas HIRST & wife Ann for sale
of land in Ohio [devised to Ann by father Stephen T. MASON] to Stephen
WILSON. Wit: Bernard TAYLOR, Abijah JANNEY.

Bk:Pg: 2G:050   Date: 12 Dec 1805   RcCt: 13 Jan 1806
Leven POWELL & wife Sarah of Ldn to James GRADY of Ldn. B/S of
161½ac adj Joseph REED. Wit: Wm. BRONAUGH, Leven POWELL.

Bk:Pg: 2G:052   Date: 4 Jun 1805   RcCt: 13 Jan 1806
Samuel CLAPHAM of Ldn to Benjamin PRICE of Ldn. B/S of ½ac Lot #48
in Lsbg. Wit: Saml. LUCKETT, Josiah MOFFETT, Saml. SINCLAIR.

Bk:Pg: 2G:053   Date: 12 Dec 1805   RcCt: 13 Jan 1806
John BAILEY of Ldn to James CHANNEL of Ldn. B/S of 148¾ac adj
Jeremiah HAMPTON, Elizabeth BEATY. Wit: A. GIBSON, Thomas
ATTWELL, Hugh ROGERS, Thos. BISCOE, Meshech LACEY, Jesse
McVEIGH.

Bk:Pg: 2G:055   Date: 12 Dec 1805   RcCt: 13 Jan 1806
John BAYLEY of Ldn to Jesse McVEIGH of Ldn. B/S of 150½ac from land
of Pierce BAYLY dec'd devised to William P., John, and George BAYLEY.
Wit: A. GIBSON, Adam BARR, Thos. ATTWELL, Jas. CHANNEL,
Mesheck LACEY, Thos. BISCOE, Hugh ROGERS.

Bk:Pg: 2G:056   Date: 2 Dec 1805   RcCt: 2 Dec 1805
Stephen G. ROSSELL/ROSZEL & wife Mary of FredVa to Nathan
LITTLER of FredVa. B/S of 115ac on Great Road from Snicker's Gap to
Centreville.

Bk:Pg: 2G:058   Date: 13 Jan 1806   RcCt: 13 Jan 1806
James HAMILTON of Ldn to Charles CRIMM of Ldn. B/S 29ac. Wit:
Jacob CRIM, Fanny McGEATH, Francis WITELY.

Bk:Pg: 2G:059   Date: 3 Jun 1805   RcCt: 13 Jan 1806
Peter SANDERS & wife Ann of Ldn to Margaret Sanders of Ldn. B/S of
Peter's 1/7 share of 275ac from father Nicholas SANDERS dec'd, and 1/7
part of lease lot where Margaret now lives. Wit: John HAMILTON, James
HAMILTON, Joseph BRADEN Jr., Isaac HOUGH.

Bk:Pg: 2G:261   Date: 13 Jan 1806   RcCt: 13 Jan 1806
John HAMILTON of Ldn. DoE of mulatto man George PEARSONS.

Bk:Pg: 2G:261   Date: 13 Jan 1806   RcCt: 13 Jan 1806
John NIXON of Ldn. DoE of negro fellow Isaac abt 43y old. Wit: Saml. M.
EDWARDS, Eli OFFUTT.

Bk:Pg: 2G:062   Date: 24 Sep 1805   RcCt: 14 Oct 1805
Lydia HOUGH (wd/o John HOUGH dec'd) of Ldn to Jonathan CUNARD of
Ldn. B/S of 50¾ac willed Lydia by father Isaac HOLLINGSWORTH. Wit:
James HAMILTON, Mauduit YOUNG, Isaac HOUGH, Solomon JENKINS.

Bk:Pg: 2G:063   Date: 27 Mar 1804   RcCt: 14 Jan 1806
Robert William KIRK & wife Sarah of AlexVa to Jacob FORTNEY of
AlexVa. B/S of lot on western edge of Lsbg on Loudoun St. adj Martin
KITZMILLER. Wit: Tho. SWANN, R. J. TAYLOR, Arch McCLEAN.

Bk:Pg: 2G:065   Date: 22 Jun 1805   RcCt: 15 Jan 1806
Michael BELL (Lt in GrB Navy, s/o William BELL & wife Julia, grand
nephew of widow Ann BATES dec'd, grandson of Elizabeth BELL) to John

WEATHERBURN, William GREETHAM & John DEVREUX of Balt. PoA on 538ac in PrWm and slave & household items devised under will of Lovell JACKSON dec'd. Wit: Jno. Warren PAGET, Nathl. STEVENS. Lists certificates: christening 14 Feb 1755 of Michael s/o William & Julia BELL at Swalwell; burial 2 Apr 1759 of William BELL at Swalwell; burial 3 Feb 1774 of Elizabeth wife of Fewster TEASDALE at Rylon Parish; burial May 1797 of widow Anne BATES at Parish of Saint Nicholas in Newcastle upon Tyne. Extensive certifications from England.

Bk:Pg: 2G:072   Date: 7 Nov 1805   RcCt: 15 Jan 1806
John WEATHERBURN, William GREETHAM & John DEVREUX of Balt to John LITTLEJOHN. PoA for above.

Bk:Pg: 2G:073   Date: 9 May 1804   RcCt: 13 Jan 1806
Thomas Ludwell LEE of Ldn & Landon CARTER of RichVa (Exors of George CARTER dec'd of Stafford) to Benjamin SHREEVE of Ldn. B/S of 165ac. Wit: John LITTLEJOHN, John McCORMICK, Samuel HOUGH, Jno. MATHIAS.

Bk:Pg: 2G:075   Date: 10 Dec 1805   RcCt: 15 Jan 1806
Benjamin B. THORNTON of Lsbg to Anthony HUFFMAN. For Sampson BLINCOE as his security, BoS for negro man Daniel. Wit: Wm. CHILTON.

Bk:Pg: 2G:076   Date: 14 Jan 1806   RcCt: 15 Jan 1806
John GIST of Ldn to Thomas GIST Jr. BoS for negro man Charles, woman Luce and 2 children Alfred & Harry, boy Arther, farm and household items, to be divided among John's children Thomas Jr., Rector and Violett when Violett is of age. Wit: Sn. BLINCOE.

Bk:Pg: 2G:077   Date: 7 Nov 1803   RcCt: 10 Sep 1804
Thomas Ludwell LEE of Ldn & Landon CARTER of RichVa (Exors of George CARTER dec'd of Stafford) to Hezekiah WAID of Ldn. B/S of 98¼ac. Wit: Thos. L. LEE, Johnston CLEVELAND, Jno. MATHIAS, Silas WHERRY, Alfred POWELL.

Bk:Pg: 2G:079   Date: 10 Feb 1806   RcCt: 10 Feb 1806
William DULIN (Exor of Edward DULIN dec'd) of Ldn to Hugh DOUGLAS of Ldn. B/S of 150ac adj Thompson MASON. Wit: Sampson BLINCOE, A. MORRISON, Charles BINNS, Isaac LARROWE.

Bk:Pg: 2G:080   Date: 22 Aug 1805   RcCt: 10 Feb 1806
Walter S. BELT to William S. BELT Sr. BoS for negro woman Mary with her children Nancy & Diana. Wit: Middleton BELT.

Bk:Pg: 2G:080, 84   Date: 18 Jun 1788   RcCt: 9 Feb 1789
Thomas HAGUE, Samuel HAGUE & Israel THOMPSON (Exors of Francis HAGUE dec'd) of Ldn to William HOUGH of Ldn. B/S and release of 406ac. Wit: James MOORE, Thos. MOORE Jr., Asa MOORE, John HOUGH 3rd, John HIRST, John BUTCHER, Abel JANNEY, Israel JANNEY.

Bk:Pg: 2G:086   Date: 22 Jan 1806   RcCt: 10 Feb 1806
Samuel BEAL & wife Rebeccah to Thomas BEAL. CoE for sale of 99ac. Wit: Stacy TAYLOR, N. C. WILLIAMS.

Bk:Pg: 2G:087   19 Nov 1805   RcCt: 10 Feb 1806
Joseph BEAL of Ldn to Edward CONARD & William RUSSELL of Ldn.
PoA, BEAL going to Ohio. Wit: John McCLUN, James THOMPSON,
Samuel BEAL.

Bk:Pg: 2G:089   Date: 15 Aug 1805   RcCt: 10 Feb 1806
Jonah THOMPSON, Richard GRIFFITH & wife Nancy, William
HAMILTON & wife Elizabeth, Israel Hague THOMPSON, John
VANDEVANTER & wife Pleasents and Sarah THOMPSON (heirs of
Samuel THOMPSON dec'd) to Thomas HOUGH of Ldn. A/L of 109*ac.*
Wit: William SMITH, Isaac LARROWE, Wm. WOODDY, Levi HOLE, Wm.
HOUGH, Jonas POTTS, Wm. PAXON, James PRYOR.

Bk:Pg: 2G:091   Date: 10 Feb 1806   RcCt: 10 Feb 1806
Jesse TAYLOR of Ldn to Timothy HIXON of Ldn. B/S of 8¼*ac* nr road to
Fairfax Meeting House to Thomas Taylor's Mill.

Bk:Pg: 2G:092   Date: 10 Feb 1806   RcCt: 10 Feb 1806
Stephen Thatcher & wife Alice of Ldn to Edward CUNARD Jr. of Ldn. B/S
of 1*ac* nr foot of Blue Ridge. Wit: Josiah MOFFETT, Thos. HUMPHREY,
Abner HUMPHREY.

Bk:Pg: 2G:094   Date: 2 Apr 1805   RcCt: 13 May 1805
Peter RIDENBAUGH & wife Margaret of Ldn to Enos GARRETT of Ldn.
B/S of 88*ac* adj George SHULTZ, Michael EVERHART. Wit: James
HAMILTON, Terrence FIGH, Henry HUFF, Thos. CONNER, Johnston
CLEVELAND.

Bk:Pg: 2G:096   Date: 12 Oct 1805   RcCt: 10 Feb 1806
Benjamin GRAYSON (s/o Capt. Benjamin GRAYSON dec'd) & wife
Nancy of Ldn to Abner HUMPHREY of Ldn. B/S of 100*ac* adj William
COX, James CARTER. Wit: William FOWKE, Thomas DRAKE Jr., John
McFARLING, Leven POWELL, Wm. BRONAUGH.

Bk:Pg: 2G:099   Date: 10 Feb 1806   RcCt: 10 Feb 1806
Andrew HESSER of Ldn to William, Jane, James & Hugh THOMPSON
(ch/o Sarah THOMPSON dec'd) of Ldn. B/S of 136*ac* adj Mahlon
HOUGH, Robert WHITE, Andrew COPELAND. Wit: Timothy TAYLOR,
Isaac WHITE, Josiah MOFFETT.

Bk:Pg: 2G:100   Date: 10 Feb 1806   RcCt: 10 Feb 1806
William McFARLAND & wife Rebecca of Ldn to Price JACOBS of Ldn.
B/S of 2*ac*. Wit: Wm. H. HANDEY, Moses GULICK, Constantine
HUGHES.

Bk:Pg: 2G:102   Date: 4 Feb 1806   RcCt: 10 Feb 1806
Ferdinando FAIRFAX & William Byrd PAGE of JeffVa to John CONARD
of Ldn. B/S of 130*ac* adj Peter DIMORY, Levi PRINCE, John WOOLF,
Paulser DERREY. Wit: James RUSSELL, Peter DEMERY, J. HARDING,
John DEMORY.

Bk:Pg: 2G:104   Date: 3 Feb 1806   RcCt: 10 Feb 1806
Ferdinando FAIRFAX & William Byrd PAGE of JeffVa to John DEMORY
of Ldn. B/S of 137¼ac adj George SMITH. Wit: James RUSSELL, Peter
DEMERY, John CONARD, Robert RUSSELL.

Bk:Pg: 2G:106   Date: 3 Feb 1806   RcCt: 10 Feb 1806
Ferdinando FAIRFAX & William Byrd PAGE of JeffVa to James RUSSELL
of Ldn. B/S of 131ac. Wit: John CONARD, John DEMORY, J. HARDING,
Robert RUSSELL, Peter DEMERY.

Bk:Pg: 2G:108   Date: 10 Apr 1805   RcCt: 10 Feb 1806
Thomas Ludwell LEE of Ldn & Landon CARTER of RichVa (Exors of
George CARTER dec'd of Stafford) to Stephen COOK of Ldn. B/S of __ac
to give way to sale made by late Geo. CARTER to Samuel LOVE. Wit:
John CARTER, Robert CARTER, George MEANS, Charles TUTT,
Charles Fenton MERCER.

Bk:Pg: 2G:110   Date: 5 Nov 1805   RcCt: 10 Feb 1806
Anthony OSBORN of Trunable Co Oh to James RUSSELL of Ldn. PoA
for debts, and income from estate of Henry DURFLINGER dec'd. Wit:
Edward CUNARD Sr., John WOOLFCALE, name in German.

Bk:Pg: 2G:110   Date: 26 Jul 1805   RcCt: 10 Feb 1806
Mahlon JANNEY of Ldn to Joseph TALBOTT of Ldn. B/S of 4¾ac nr main
road from Wtfd to Lsbg. Wit: James MOORE, R. BRADEN, John
WILLIAMS, Richard GRIFFITH, Timothy HIXON.

Bk:Pg: 2G:112   Date: 10 Dec 1805   RcCt: 13 Jan 1806
William SHREEVE & Benjamin SHREEVE (heirs of Benj. SHREEVE
dec'd) of Ldn. Lands of Benj. SHREEVE dec'd to be divided among sons
William, Benj., Joshua & Abner. Wm. buying Benj. share. Wit: John
LITTLEJOHN, Geo. W. BLINCOE, Chas. THRIFT.

Bk:Pg: 2G:113   Date: 10 Feb 1806   RcCt: 10 Feb 1806
William LITTLEJOHN of Ldn to Benjamin PRICE of Ldn. B/S of Lot #19 in
Lsbg.

Bk:Pg: 2G:114   Date: 8 Feb 1806   RcCt: 10 Feb 1806
Jacob MILLER, Vallentine MILLER, John MILLER, Christian MILLER Jr.,
Adam MILLER, Elizabeth MILLER of Ldn (and Jacob MILLER & wife
Catherine, Christian RUNAMUS and Jacob RUNAMUS children & heirs of
Mary RUNAMUS who was d/o Christian MILLER Sr. of JeffVa) to George
MILLER of Ldn. B/S of 6ac adj David POTTS, Ebenezer GRUBB, George
ABEL; with Mary MILLER widow of Christian receiving 1/3 of income
during her lifetime. Wit: James RUSSELL, John CONARD, Robert
RUSSELL.

Bk:Pg: 2G:116   Date: 8 Feb 1806   RcCt: 10 Feb 1806
Jacob MILLER, Vallentine MILLER, John MILLER, Christian MILLER Jr.,
Adam MILLER, Elizabeth MILLER of Ldn (and Jacob MILLER & wife
Catherine, Christian RUNAMUS and Jacob RUNAMUS children & heirs of
Mary RUNAMUS who was d/o Christian MILLER Sr. of JeffVa) to George
MILLER of Ldn. B/S of 111½ac adj Ebenezer GRUBB; with provision as

above for widow Mary MILLER. Wit: James RUSSELL, John CONARD, Robert RUSSELL.

Bk:Pg: 2G:118   Date: 8 Feb 1806   RcCt: 10 Feb 1806
Jacob MILLER, Vallentine MILLER, John MILLER, George MILLER, Adam MILLER, Elizabeth MILLER of Ldn (and Jacob MILLER & wife Catherine, Christian RUNAMUS and Jacob RUNAMUS children & heirs of Mary RUNAMUS who was d/o Christian MILLER Sr. of JeffVa) to Christian MILLER of Ldn. B/S of 213*ac* with provision as above for widow Mary MILLER. Wit: James RUSSELL, John CONARD, Robert RUSSELL.

Bk:Pg: 2G:120   Date: 8 Feb 1806   RcCt: 8 Feb 1806
Jacob MILLER, Christian MILLER, John MILLER, George MILLER, Adam MILLER, Elizabeth MILLER of Ldn (and Jacob MILLER & wife Catherine, Christian RUNAMUS and Jacob RUNAMUS children & heirs of Mary RUNAMUS who was d/o Christian MILLER Sr. of JeffVa) to Valentine MILLER of Ldn. B/S of 213*ac*. Wit: James RUSSELL, John CONARD, Robert RUSSELL.

Bk:Pg: 2G:122   Date: 29 Oct 1804   RcCt: 10 Dec 1804
Sebastian WOOFTER & wife Mary of Ldn to Price JACOBS of Ldn. B/S of 59*ac* on Beaverdam. Wit: Ben GRAYSON, Wm. BRONAUGH, Daniel ONEAL.

Bk:Pg: 2G:125   Date: 22 Jan 1806   RcCt: 10 Feb 1806
Hugh HOLMES & wife Elizabeth of FrdkVa to Dr. Isaac HOUGH of Ldn. B/S of 153*ac* lot in Piedmont Manor now in possession of Mrs. Abigail HAUKS wd/o John HAUKS for L/L adj Daniel SHOEMAKER, Geo. MULL, James HAMILTON; 97¾*ac* lot in Piedmont Manor now in possession of James McKEMIE under L/L adj Samuel UNDERWOOD, Daniel SHOEMAKER, Michael ROOSE. Wit: John H. NORTON, Robert MACKEY, Corn'l. BALDWIN.

Bk:Pg: 2G:127   Date: 1 Sep 1803   RcCt: 10 Feb 1806
Hugh HOLMES & wife Elizabeth of Winchester to Isaac HOUGH of Ldn. B/S of 160*ac* in Piedmont Manor now in possession of Joseph WILKINSON under L/L adj John HOUGH, Michael COOPER, Rheuben HIXON. Wit: Obed. WAITE, Levi JAMES, Mary R. CARY.

Bk:Pg: 2G:130   Date: 2 Oct 1803   RcCt: 10 Feb 1806
Dr. Isaac HOUGH & wife Fanny of Ldn to Hugh HOLMES of Winchester. Mortgage on above 160*ac*. Wit: Obed WAITE, Mary R. CARY, Levi JAMES, Presley WILLIAMS, Saml. HOUGH, Stephen CLAYTON.

Bk:Pg: 2G:132   Date: 22 Jan 1806   RcCt: 10 Feb 1806
Isaac HOUGH & wife Fanny of Ldn to Hugh HOLMES of Winchester. Mortgage on above 153*ac* & 97¾*ac*. Wit: John H. NORTON, Robert MACKEY, Corn'ls. BALDWIN.

Bk:Pg: 2G:134   Date: 15 Oct 1805   RcCt: 10 Feb 1806
Alexander SUTHERLAND & wife Ann of Lsbg to Jonah THOMPSON of AlexVa. B/S of 775*ac* former property of Israel THOMPSON dec'd; also 19*ac*. Wit: Leven POWELL, Thos. Lud LEE, Thos. FOUCH.

Bk:Pg: 2G:139   Date: 9 Jul 1805   RcCt: 10 Feb 1806
Sanford WRENN. Col for negro woman Hoate & children Sela abt 9y, Lucy abt 2y & Jerry abt 3y, property of his wife.

Bk:Pg: 2G:139   Date: 4 Feb 1806   RcCt: 10 Feb 1806
William WILSON of AlexVa to William TAYLOR of Lsbg. B/S of ½ac "Still House Lot" opposite Edmund DENNY on Market St in Lsbg. Wit: R. S. TAYLOR, Wm. TAYLOR, Jesse T. RAMSAY.

Bk:Pg: 2G:141   Date: 7 Apr 1803   RcCt: 13 Feb 1804
Henry NEUSCHWANGER of Ldn and John CONARD Jr. of Ldn to Ferdinando FAIRFAX of JeffVa. Trust on 122½ac. Wit: Thos. LESLIE, Edward CUNARD, Wm. H. HARDING, Sanford RAMEY.

Bk:Pg: 2G:144   Date: 20 Jul 1805   RcCt: 9 Dec 1805
Jonas POTTS & Asa MOORE (commissioners to sell estate of John JANNY dec'd) to Thomas LESLIE of Ldn. B/S of ¼ac on Kittocton Creek below Pursel's Mill Dam. Wit: Wm. H. HARDING, Thomas PHILLIPS, Saml. CARR, John NEWTON, Lewis ELLZEY.

Bk:Pg: 2G:146   Date: 3 Feb 1806   RcCt: 11 Feb 1806
John SURGNOR (s/o Hugh SURGNOR) of Ldn apprentices himself to Aaron DIVINE of Lsbg to learn trade of boot and shoemaker for 7y. Wit: John BOGUE, Jesse PHILLIPS, Edward RINKER.

Bk:Pg: 2G:147   Date: 7 Apr 1803   RcCt: 11 Feb 1806
Thomas Ludwell LEE of Ldn & Landon CARTER of RichVa (Exors of George CARTER dec'd of Stafford) to Wilson Cary SELDON of Ldn. B/S of 206ac. Wit: John McCORMICK, John LITTLEJOHN, Samuel HOUGH, Jno. MATHIAS.

Bk:Pg: 2G:150   Date: 24 Aug 1805   RcCt: 11 Feb 1806
James CAVAN Jr. (Admr of Patrick CAVAN dec'd) of Lsbg to John DORRELL of Ldn. A/L to James HEREFORD of 1ac adj John LITTLEJOHN. Wit: John H. EVANS, Samuel HOUGH, John SHAW.

Bk:Pg: 2G:153   Date: 31 Jul 1805   RcCt: 11 Feb 1806
Ferdinando FAIRFAX & William Byrd PAGE of JeffVa to Thomas OSBURN of Ldn. B/S of 170½ac adj Thomas JAMES, Jesse HOWELL. Wit: John H. CANBY, Joshua OSBURN, Joel OSBURN, Thos. LESLIE.

Bk:Pg: 2G:155   Date: 11 Feb 1806   RcCt: 11 Feb 1806
Francis TRIPLETT & wife Elizabeth of Ldn to James GARNER of Ldn. B/S of 9ac Lot #7. Wit: Isaac LAROWE.

Bk:Pg: 2G:157   Date: 8 Jul 1805   RcCt: 11 Feb 1806
Henry TAYLOR of Ldn to Robert WHEELER of Ldn. BoS for farm and household items. Wit: Geo. McCABE, Israel WILLIAMS.

Bk:Pg: 2G:158   Date: 18 Jun 1804   RcCt: 11 Feb 1806
Samuel MURREY of Lsbg to Joseph HUNT of Lsbg. LS of lot on upper end of Loudoun St opposite Geo. Fortney's Smith Shop.

Bk:Pg: 2G:160   Date: 9 Nov 1805   RcCt: 5 Dec 1805
Isaac RITCHEY Jr. & wife Margaret of Ldn to Jacob WERTZ of Ldn. B/S of 102¼ac adj Adam KOONTS, Jacob BAKER. Wit: Henry HUFF, Terence FIGH, John SHAFFER, Chas. THRIFT.

Bk:Pg: 2G:163   Date: 8 Feb 1806   RcCt: 11 Feb 1806
Henry M. DAVIS & wife Catharine of Lsbg to Charles DRISH & wife Susannah of Lsbg. Release – original contract stated ½ac but should have been ¼ac next to Thomas SANDERS which DAVIS sold to James RUSSELL. Wit: Sn. BLINCOE, William DRISH, John DRISH, Samuel MURREY, John LITTLEJOHN.

Bk:Pg: 2G:166   Date: 25 Jan 1806   RcCt: 11 Feb 1806
Henry M. DAVIS of Lsbg, Catharine ANSELL of Ldn, and Leonard ANSELL of Ldn. Marriage intended for Henry and Catharine; she entitled as a child to part of estate of Lenoard ANSELL Sr.; they agree that once they die her right goes to their children, and if none, to survivors in fee simple. Wit: John FICHTER, John FRY, Melher ANCEL.

Bk:Pg: 2G:169   Date: 25 Jan 1806   RcCt: 11 Feb 1806
Henry M. DAVIS of Lsbg, Catharine ANSELL of Ldn, and Leonard ANSELL of Ldn. Contract for upcoming marriage – lot in Lsbg where Leonard ANSELL now lives which was conveyed to his dec'd wife Jane R. DAVIS shortly after their marriage by John REIGER & wife Margaret, lot in trust for use of Catharine until she dies, then back to Leonard. Wit: John FICHTER, John FRY, Melher ANCEL.

Bk:Pg: 2G:170   Date: 11 Feb 1804   RcCt: 11 Feb 1806
Thomas MOORE & wife Mary of MontMd to Mary __ and Hugh, Thomas, George, Adam, William, Sarah & John BARR (heirs of George BARR dec'd of Ldn). B/S of 110ac adj Thaddeus McCARTY on Goose Creek. Wit: Jno. THOMAS 3rd, John BURGESS.

Bk:Pg: 2G:173   Date: 7 Apr 1803   RcCt: 11 Feb 1806
Thomas Ludwell LEE of Ldn & Landon CARTER of RichVa (Exors of George CARTER dec'd of Stafford) to Wilson Cary SELDON of Ldn. B/S of 231ac adj Samuel LOVE, John WILDMAN, Alexander McMICHEN. Wit: Stenphen [Stephen] COOKE, John McCORMICK, John LITTLEJOHN, Samuel HOUGH, John MATHIAS.

Bk:Pg: 2G:175   Date: 12 Feb 1806   RcCt: 12 Feb 1806
Levi HOLE & wife Mariam of Ldn, Major HUNT of Ldn and William HOMES & Daniel LOVETT of Ldn. Trust on 47ac in Katacton Mt. adj Thomas CARR, Charles McMANAMIES. Wit: William PAXSON, Timothy HIXON.

Bk:Pg: 2G:177   Date: 10 Feb 1806   RcCt: 12 Feb 1806
Samuel & Isaac NICHOLS. Receipt of payment from Peter BOSS of Lsbg for trust on house belonging to S. P. BOSS. Wit: Samuel MURREY.

Bk:Pg: 2G:177   Date: 2 Feb 1801   RcCt: 11 Feb 1806
William GEORGE of Lee Co Va to Isaac STEER of Ldn. PoA. Wit: Josias CLAPHAM, John CARTER Jr.

Bk:Pg: 2G:178   Date: 12 Feb 1806   RcCt: 12 Feb 1806
William MAINS. DoE for slave James WINTER. Wit: Isaac LARROWE.

Bk:Pg: 2G:178   Date: 2 Apr 1805   RcCt: 9 Sep 1806
Isaac GRIFFITH of Ldn to Samuel CLAPHAM of Ldn. Mortgage on
270¾ac on Catocton Creek. Wit: Isaac LARROWE, John DAVIS, Thomas
DAVIS.

Bk:Pg: 2G:180   Date: 15 Oct 1805   RcCt: 16 Apr 1806
William LITTLEJOHN of Ldn to James GARNER of Ldn. B/S of 5½ac Lot
#6 adj Charles BINNS' Lot #5. Wit: John LITTLEJOHN.

Bk:Pg: 2G:182   Date: 18 Sep 1803   RcCt: 15 Apr 1806
James CROSS of Ldn to Thomas Ludwell LEE of Ldn & Landon CARTER
of RichVa (Exors of George CARTER dec'd of Staf). Mortgage on
153¾ac. Wit: Chas. TUTT, Jno. MATHIAS, John CAVAN.

Bk:Pg: 2G:184   Date: 16 Apr 1806   RcCt: 16 Apr 1806
Benjamin H. CANBY & wife Sarah of Lsbg to John LITTLEJOHN of Ldn.
B/S of 2ac adj Matthew WEATHERBY on Carolina Rd. Wit: Samuel
MURREY, Obadiah CLIFFORD.

Bk:Pg: 2G:188   Date: 16 Apr 1806   RcCt: 16 Apr 1806
John LITTLEJOHN & wife Monica of Ldn to Benjamin H. CANBY of Lsbg.
B/S of 1ac nr Caroline Road. Wit: Samuel MURREY, Obadiah
CLIFFORD.

Bk:Pg: 2G:188   Date: 8 Apr 1804   RcCt: 14 Apr 1806
Jno. Stone MARLOW. DoI of negroes Nicholas age 26y, Jerry age 27,
Kitty age 8y, Polly age 5y, Sally abt 5y, Phoebe age 3y & Anne abt 4
months.

Bk:Pg: 2G:189   Date: 9 Mar 1806   RcCt: 14 Apr 1806
Westwood T. MASON. DoI of negro Elias and woman Easter both abt 17y
and b. in Md, brought to Va within the past 60 days.

Bk:Pg: 2G:189   Date: 15 Oct 1805   RcCt: 14 Apr 1806
Daniel McCARTY (grandson of Daniel McCARTY the Elder dec'd of Ffx)
& wife Matilda Margaret SNOWDEN of Ffx, Elias JANNEY & James
KEITH Jr. of AlexVa and John ROBERTS & Samuel G. GRIFFITH of
AlexVa (merchants & partners under Robert & Griffith). McCARTY
indebted to Roberts & Griffith; trust from JANNEY & KEITH using 305ac
McCarty's Island in Potomac. Wit: Wm. WASHINGTON, Jonathan
FOSTER, Jas. KEITH, R. J. TAYLOR, Geo. YOUNGS, John W.
ASHTON, Rich'd H. HENDERSON.

Bk:Pg: 2G:195   Date: 12 May 1804   RcCt: 14 Apr 1806
Ferdinando FAIRFAX of JeffVa to Jacob EMERY of Ldn. B/S of 49ac Lot
#25 on SE side of Short Hill in Shannondale. Wit: Wm. H. HARDING,
Charles CONNER, Geo. HITE, Charles LEWIS, Johnston CLEVELAND,
Fleet SMITH.

Bk:Pg: 2G:196 Date: 28 Feb 1806 RcCt: 16 Apr 1806
Jonas POTTS & wife Phoebe and Jacob BAUGH & wife Mary of Ldn to John JANNEY of AlexVa. B/S of 1¾ac, 40ac, & 8ac on Limestone Run. Wit: Thos. SWANN, Samuel HOUGH, Chas. THRIFT, Saml. CARR.

Bk:Pg: 2G:202 Date: 12 Nov 1805 RcCt: 15 Apr 1806
Edward DENNY & wife Elizabeth of AlexVa to Charles BINNS of Ldn. B/S of ½ac Lot #26 in Lsbg. Wit: Jas. CAVAN Jr., Patrick H. DOUGLAS, John CAVAN.

Bk:Pg: 2G:203 Date: 17 Jul 1779 RcCt: 15 Apr 1806
William HATCHER of Ldn. DoE for negro Rose abt 25y old. Wit: John HUST, William HATCHER Jr., Mary HATCHER.

Bk:Pg: 2G:204 Date: 13 Apr 1806 RcCt: 15 Apr 1806
Charles Fenton MERCER of Ldn per will of father James MERCER dec'd late of Fredericksburg Va. DoE for negroes Granville & Matilda ch/o Hannah, Molly <20y d/o Esther and Bella d/o Milly, __ ch/o Bella born since death of James.

Bk:Pg: 2G:205 Date: 9 Apr 1806 RcCt: 15 Apr 1806
Thomas CHINN Jr. of Ldn to Burr POWELL of Ldn. Trust to secure payment to Noble BEVERIDGE, using negro boy Armistead aged 17y. Wit: Mesheck LACEY, Rich'd COCHRAN, Charles GIBBS.

Bk:Pg: 2G:208 Date: 1 Apr 1806 RcCt: 15 Apr 1806
Thomas JANNEY & wife Sarah to Charles GULLATT. CoE for sale of Lot #3 in Lsbg. Wit: Elisha C. DICK, Peter WISE Jr.

Bk:Pg: 2G:207 Date: 26 Mar 1806 RcCt: 15 Apr 1806
Thomas JANNEY & wife Sarah of AlexVa to Stacy HAINES of Ldn. B S of 26ac. Wit: John D. BROWN, G? MANN?, Alex'r WILLIAMS, Elisha C. DICK, Peter WISE Jr.

Bk:Pg: 2G:209 Date: 28 Aug 1805 RcCt: 15 Apr 1806
Jacob KEYLOR/CAYLOR of Ldn to Adam SHOVER of Ldn. Mortgage of 4ac on SE side of Short Hill in Piedmont. Wit: Jacob HEFFNER, Caty HEFFNER, Luesie MILLER.

Bk:Pg: 2G:211 Date: 20 Mar 1806 RcCt: 15 Apr 1806
Elizabeth PURCEL and John ROBERTSON. Marriage contract – gives ROBERTSON slave woman Winny & boy William, then to her next of kin after her death. Wit: John MINES, Thomas Moral LEE.

Bk:Pg: 2G:212 Date: 2 Nov 1805 RcCt: 15 Apr 1806
James LEWIS (s/o Abraham LEWIS dec'd) & wife Sarah of Ldn to Nathaniel MOSS of Ldn. B/S of 96ac adj Thomas FRANCIS, Col. Leven POWELL. Wit: William GLASSCOCK, Thomas ANDERSON, Stephen MOSS, Ben. GRAYSON.

Bk:Pg: 2G:213 Date: 12 Oct 1805 RcCt: 14 Oct 1805
Thomas DRAKE Sr. of Ldn to William BRONAUGH. Trust for payment to Benjamin GRAYSON using 100ac on Beaverdam adj James CARTER,

heirs of Benjamin BARTON dec'd. Wit: William FOWKE, John McFARLING, Abner HUMPHREY.

Bk:Pg: 2G:214   Date: 15 Apr 1806   RcCt: 15 Apr 1806
Hannah OSBURNE of Ldn bound to Joel OSBURNE for her share of 150ac as wd/o Richard OSBURNE dec'd. Wit: Morris OSBURNE, Richard OSBURNE, Mary OSBURN.

Bk:Pg: 2G:215   Date: 13 Apr 1806   RcCt: 15 Apr 1806
Elias THRASHER of Ldn to George SAGER Sr. of Ldn. Mortgage using 103ac nr Peter Hickman's Smith Shop. Wit: Alex. SUTHERLAND, William SCHOOLEY, Levy PRINCE.

Bk:Pg: 2G:218   Date: 14 Apr 1806   RcCt: 15 Apr 1806
Phineas THOMAS of Ldn to James HATCHER of Ldn. Trust using 116ac adj Joseph JANNEY, James GRADY, Joshua BOTTS. Wit: Solomon HOGUE, Israel JANNEY, Jane JANNEY.

Bk:Pg: 2G:221   Date: 24 Dec 1792   RcCt: 15 Apr 1806
Frederick ELLGAN. Col for unnamed slaves.

Bk:Pg: 2G:221   Date: 1 Apr 1806   RcCt: 15 Apr 1806
David LOVETT of Ldn to Joseph GOURLEY of Ldn. B/S of 103ac adj Joseph LOVETT. Wit: Joseph LOVETT, Daniel EACHES, Joseph GORE.

Bk:Pg: 2G:222   Date: 15 Apr 1806   RcCt: 15 Apr 1806
Aaron SANDERS of Ldn: DoE for Thomas RESPESS paid by RESPESS. Wit: S. BLINCOE, Benj'a SHREEVE.

Bk:Pg: 2G:223   Date: ___   RcCt: 15 Apr 1806
Peter WARRICK & daughter Sarah bound to Thomas GORE to pay for Sarah's freedom. Sarah's children are Marcus, Cortney & Peper. List receipts of payments beginning 22 Apr 1791. DoE dated 15 Apr 1806. Wit: Isaac LARROW, S. BLINCOE, Sam. M. EDWARDS.

Bk:Pg: 2G:225   Date: 2 Jan 1806   RcCt: 15 Apr 1806
Agreement between that John DRISH reserves use of well from part of Lot #45 in Lsbg he sold to John CARR. Wit: John H. EVANS, Jno. MATHIAS, Jos. BEARD.

Bk:Pg: 2G:225   Date: 23 Dec 1805   RcCt: 15 Apr 1806
Henry WALKER of Ldn to Thomas LESLIE of Ldn. BoS for farm animals. Wit: James HAMILTON, David LOVETT.

Bk:Pg: 2G:226   Date: 15 Apr 1806   RcCt: 15 Apr 1806
Israel H. THOMPSON & wife Ann of Wtfd to Benjamin H. CANBY of Lsbg. B/S of 2ac nr town spring of Lsbg. Wit: W. S. NEALE, Timothy HIXON, Terence FIGH.

Bk:Pg: 2G:227   Date: 15 Apr 1806   RcCt: 15 Apr 1806
George SAGER Sr. & wife Mary Elizabeth of Ldn to Elias THRASHER of Ldn. B/S of 1213ac nr Peter Hickman's Smith Shop; and 88ac adj George SHOVER. Wit: Alex. SUTHERLAND, William SCHOOLEY, Levy PRINCE.

Bk:Pg: 2G:229 Date: 14 Apr 1806 RcCt: 15 Apr 1806
Hannah OSBURN of Ldn to Morriss OSBURN of Ldn. B/S of 44ac on NW fork of Goose Creek. Wit: Joel OSBURN, Thomas OSBURN, Samuel PURSELL.

Bk:Pg: 2G:231 Date: 1 Mar 1806 RcCt: 15 Apr 1806
Joseph SMITH & wife Mary of AlexVa to Samuel CLAPHAM of Ldn. B/S of part of Lot #15 in Lsbg. Wit: Isaac HARRIS, Samuel MURREY, Jesse DAILEY, Jacob HOFFMAN, John McKINNEY.

Bk:Pg: 2G:233 Date: 15 Mar 1805 RcCt: 15 Apr 1806
John A. BINNS of Ldn agrees that negro George (whom he set free) may have wife Moll and any children so long as he takes them far away from the state to prevent harboring BINNS' other negroes. Wit: Enoch FRANCIS, John MORRISON.

Bk:Pg: 2G:234 Date: 2 Jan 1806 RcCt: 15 Apr 1806
John DRISH & wife Elenor of Lsbg to John CARR Jr. of Ldn. B/S of Lot #45 in Lsbg. Wit: John H. EVANS, Jos. BEARD, Jno. MATHIAS, Armistead LONG, Obadiah CLIFFORD.

Bk:Pg: 2G:236 Date: 26 Mar 1806 RcCt: 15 Apr 1806
David LOVETT (s/o Daniel LOVETT dec'd) of Ldn to Joseph LOVETT of Ldn. B/S of 46½ac on S fork of Beaverdam. Wit: Thomas FRANCIS, Thos. LESLIE, Edmund LOVETT.

Bk:Pg: 2G:237 Date: 21 Jan 1806 RcCt: 15 Apr 1806
George TAVENAR & Jonathan LODGE affirmed that Jno. WILDMAN with L/L of 150ac in Ldn is alive and well. John DODD & Mahlon TAYLOR of Ldn affirm they saw on 3 Mar last at Tavern of Thomas WILKINSON in Lsbg WILDMAN give money to Wm. H. HARDING & John H. CANBY agents for Sarah FAIRFAX to renew lease to Wm. WILDMAN Sr.

Bk:Pg: 2G:238 Date: 28 Mar 1806 RcCt: 15 Apr 1806
Mrs. Easter EDWARDS. Col for unnamed slaves.

Bk:Pg: 2G:238 Date: 12 Nov 1805 RcCt: 15 Apr 1806
Charles BINNS & wife Hannah of Lsbg to Samuel MURREY & Fleet SMITH of Lsbg. Trust for debt owed Edward DENNY of AlexVa using ½ac Lot #26 in Lsbg. Wit: Patrick H. DOUGLAS, Jas. CAVAN, John CAVAN.

Bk:Pg: 2G:242 Date: 7 Apr 1803 RcCt: 15 Apr 1806
Wilson Cary SELDON of Ldn to Thomas Ludwell LEE of Ldn & Landon CARTER of RichVa (Exors of George CARTER dec'd of Staf). Mortgage on 430ac. Wit: Richard H. LOVE, Jno. MATHIAS, John E. COOKE.

Bk:Pg: 2G:244 Date: 30 Dec 1805 RcCt: 15 Apr 1806
Saml TRENARY & wife Mary of FrdkVa to William HUMMER of Ldn. B/S of ½ac on main road from Lsbg to AlexVa

Bk:Pg: 2G:246 Date: 15 Apr 1806 RcCt: 16 Apr 1806
Joshua GORE & wife Sarah of Ldn to James CARRUTHERS of Ldn. B/S of 74ac adj William HOLMES, Daniel WHITE, Ashur CLAYTON, William MORELAND. Wit: Israel JANNEY, David JANNEY, Jonathan JANNEY.

Bk:Pg: 2G:248   Date: 8 Feb 1806   RcCt: 16 Apr 1806
Joshua GORE & wife Sarah of Ldn to Daniel WHITE of Ldn. B/S of 19*ac*
adj James CARUTHERS. Wit: Israel JANNEY, Jane JANNEY, Jonathan
JANNEY, Daniel JANNEY.

Bk:Pg: 2G:250   Date: ___ 1806   RcCt: 16 Apr 1806
Bricklayer William WRIGHT & wife Ann of Ldn to Jacob BAUGH of Ldn.
B/S of Lot #26 in Lsbg. Wit: John LITTLEJOHN, Fra. H. PEYTON.

Bk:Pg: 2G:253   Date: 14 Apr 1806   RcCt: 16 Apr 1806
James BATSON & wife Hannah of Ldn to Nancy FOUCH (wd/o Isaac
FOUCH dec'd), Mary HALLING and Elizabeth HALLING. B/S of Lot #41 in
Mdbg.

Bk:Pg: 2G:254   Date: 8 Apr 1805   RcCt: 8 Apr 1805
Alexander SUTHERLAND & wife Nancy (signed as Anne) of Lsbg to
Joseph BEARD of Lsbg. B/S of part of Lot #4 in Lsbg. Wit: Willy JANES,
Benj'a PRICE, Jas. HAMILTON, Samuel MURREY, Obadiah CLIFFORD.

Bk:Pg: 2G:257   Date: 13 Apr 1806   RcCt: 12 May 1806
Richard BOND. DoI for slaves Henry a low mulatto woman between 2 or 3
[23?] & 30y of age, her child Calvert abt 7 months, John a mulatto lad abt
16y old, Southen a mulatto lad between 9 & 10y, and Edith a woman abt
22y old.

Bk:Pg: 2G:258   Date: 9 Apr 1806   RcCt: 12 May 1806
Leven POWELL of Mdbg to Richard COCHRAN of Mdbg. LS of ½ac Lot
#13 in Mdbg. Wit: Noble BEVERIDGE, Tho. CHUNN Jr., William M.
POWELL, Meshek LACEY.

Bk:Pg: 2G:260   Date: 22 Feb 1806   RcCt: 12 May 1806
William HOUGH & wife Elenor of Ldn to John WILLIAMS of Ldn. B/S of lot
in Wtfd adj Flemon PATTERSON, John WILLIAMS, Thomas HAGUE. Wit:
Daniel STONE, Thomas PHILLIPS, Joseph BOND, William H. HOUGH.

Bk:Pg: 2G:261   Date: 1 Apr 1806   RcCt: 12 May 1806
John, Samuel & Mahlon HOUGH (Exors of John HOUGH dec'd) of Ldn to
William PAXSON of Ldn. B/S of 208*ac* on Kittoctin Creek adj Edward
STONE, Anthony WRIGHT, Patterson WRIGHT, Anthony CUNARD,
Isaac STEER, Jesse TAYLOR, William HOUGH. Wit: Daniel STONE, W.
S. NEALE, Edward STONE, David GOODWIN, Timothy HIXON, Nathan
BALL, Edward DORSEY.

Bk:Pg: 2G:263   Date: 22 Apr 1806   RcCt: 12 May 1806
William HOLMES & wife Abigail of Ldn to Levi WHITE of Ldn. B/S of 1*ac*
on Secolon adj Daniel WHITE. Wit: Josias HALL, Daniel WHITE, Jacob
SCANDIETT.

Bk:Pg: 2G:265   Date: 9 May 1806   RcCt: 12 May 1806
John BAYLY (s/o Pierce BAYLEY) of Ldn to William P. BAYLY of Ldn.
B/S of 69½ac nr Mdbg on road from AlexVa to Winchester, adj Hugh
ROGERS. Wit: Geo. BAYLY, Saml. BUCK, Marcus BUCK.

Bk:Pg: 2G:267   Date: 12 Sep 1804   RcCt: 12 Sep 1804
Ferdinando FAIRFAX of JeffVa to Samuel CLENDENING of Ldn. B/S of
99*ac* in Piedmont adj Jonah THOMPSON, Joseph LEWIS, Andrew
THOMPSON.

Bk:Pg: 2G:269   Date: 24 Feb 1806   RcCt: 12 May 1806
John WILLIAMS & wife Lydia of Ldn to Patrick McFADDIAN of Ldn. B/S of
40 perch lot in Wtfd (1 lot purchased from Exors of Joseph JANNEY and 1
purchased from William HOUGH) adj Flemon PATTERSON. Wit: W. S.
NEALE, Wm. GOODWIN, Joseph BURGOYNE.

Bk:Pg: 2G:270   Date: 9 May 1806   RcCt: 12 May 1806
William P. BAYLY & wife Mary L. of StafVa to John BATTSON of Ldn. B/S
of 157½*ac* by Fauquier Road at Little River adj James BATTSON. Wit:
Samuel HENDERSON, Jesse McVEIGH, Burr POWELL, A. GIBSON,
James BATTSON.

Bk:Pg: 2G:272   Date: 9 May 1806   RcCt: 12 May 1806
William P. BAYLY & wife Mary L. of StafVA to James BATTSON of Ldn.
B/S of 121*ac* by Fauquier Road at Little River adj John BATTSON. Wit:
Burr POWELL, John BATTSON, Samuel HENDERSON, A. GIBSON,
Jesse McVEIGH.

Bk:Pg: 2G:274   Date: 23 Mar 1806   RcCt: 12 May 1806
Presley SANDERS & wife Mary of Lsbg to Ignatius NORRIS of Lsbg. B/S
of lot in Lsbg adj Back St, James GREENLEASE. Wit: S. BLINCOE,
Benj'a B. THORNTON, Benj'a MOFFETT, Fra. H. PEYTON, Obadiah
CLIFFORD.

Bk:Pg: 2G:276   Date: 14 Mar 1806   RcCt: 12 May 1806
William WOODY & wife Nancy of Lsbg to Henry CLAGETT of Culpeper.
B/S of part of Lot #14 in Lsbg between Samuel MURREY & Barnet
HOUGH. Wit: Sn. BLINCOE, Saml. BOGGESS, Wm. MAINS.

Bk:Pg: 2G:278   Date: 1 Apr 1806   RcCt: 12 May 1806
Caleb GREGG & wife Hannah of Ldn to Charles CHAMBLIN of Ldn. B/S
of 114*ac* adj George BROWN, Mahlon GREGG. Wit: Stacy TAYLOR,
Joshua OSBURN, Lewis ELLZEY, Thos. LESLIE, William NOLAND.

Bk:Pg: 2G:281   Date: 2 Apr 1806   RcCt: 12 May 1806
James MOORE of Ldn to William PAXSON of Ldn. B/S of 2*ac* now in
possession of Robert WRIGHT, adj Anthony WRIGHT, Patterson
WRIGHT. Wit: Thomas PHILLIPS, W. S. NEALE, Edward STONE, James
CURTIS.

Bk:Pg: 2G:282   Date: 15 Feb 1806   RcCt: 12 May 1806
Mahlon MORRIS & wife Catharine of Ldn to David SMITH of Ldn. B/S of
2*ac* in Gap of Short Hill below Pursel's Mill Dam. Wit: Wm. HARNED,
Edward CUNARD Sr., Thomas HEPBURN.

Bk:Pg: 2G:285   Date: 15 Feb 1806   RcCt: 12 May 1806
Mahlon MORRIS & wife Catharine of Ldn to David SMITH of Ldn. B/S of
¾*ac* at Hllb at S side of Great Road adj James BRADFIELD. Wm.
HARNED, Edward CUNARD Sr., Thomas HEPBURN.

Bk:Pg: 2G:287   Date: 13 Apr 1806   RcCt: 12 May 1806
Samuel Wade YOUNG & wife Ruth of Ldn to Thomas DAVID of Ldn. B/S
of 63¾ac on W side of Short Hill adj Abraham OSBURN, William GRUBB,
Michael LONG. Wit: Stacy TAYLOR, James H. HAMILTON, James
HAMILTON, Mahlon MORRIS.

Bk:Pg: 2G:290   Date: 5 Nov 1796   RcCt: 12 May 1806
Leven POWELL of Ldn to Saml. HENDERSON of Ldn. LS of ½ac Lots
#25 & #19 in Mdbg. Wit: Robt. DAGG, two names in German.

Bk:Pg: 2G:292   Date: 14 Apr 1806   RcCt: 12 May 1806
Henry HOWELL of Ldn to Stacy TAYLOR. Trust for debt to Benjamin
MEREDITH of Belmont Co Oh using 6ac. Wit: John H. McCABE, Sydnor
BAILEY, Tho. WHITE.

Bk:Pg: 2G:295   Date: 28 Apr 1806   RcCt: 12 May 1806
Miss Elizabeth GREEN (a resident of Va for 16y). Col for negro woman
Fanny (who was in Md until the 19th or 20th of this month) and her children
Henry abt 12y, Mary abt 10y, Milky abt 8y & David abt 3y.

Bk:Pg: 2G:295   Date: 24 Feb 1806   RcCt: 12 May 1806
Patrick MILHOLLEN of Ldn to Flemon PATTISON of Ldn. B/S of lot in
Wtfd adj Flemon. Wit: W. S. NEALE, Richard GRIFFITH, Mos.
CALDWELL, Patrick McFADIAN.

Bk:Pg: 2G:297   Date: 1 Mar 1806   RcCt: 12 May 1806
Stephen McPHERSON & wife Sarah of Ldn to James McGEATH & John
ASH of Ldn. B/S of 12ac nr Quaker Rd adj Samuel NICHOLS, Samuel
PEUGH. Wit: Leven POWELL, Mos. B. SPEAKE, A. GIBSON.

Bk:Pg: 2G:298   Date: 1 Mar 1806   RcCt: 12 May 1806
James McGEATH & John ASH of Ldn to Burr POWELL of Ldn. Trust for
debt to Stephen McPHERSON using above land. Wit: Leven POWELL,
Mos. B. SPEAKE, A. GIBSON.

Bk:Pg: 2G:300   Date: 12 May 1806   RcCt: 12 May 1806
James TREYHERN & wife Dinah and Sarah TREYHERN of Ldn to
Anthony SWICK of Ldn. B/S of 24ac on Beaverdam.

Bk:Pg: 2G:302   Date: 28 Mar 1806   RcCt: 12 May 1806
Leven POWELL Sr. of Ldn to Aaron GRANT of Ldn. LS of ½ac Lot #11 in
Mdbg. Wit: Andrew SMARR, A. GIBSON, Mos. B. SPEAKE.

Bk:Pg: 2G:303   Date: 14 Feb 1806   RcCt: 12 May 1806
Mahlon JANNEY of Ldn to Leven POWELL of Ldn. B/S of 600ac adj
Benjamin GRAYSON, John EDMONDSON, William RUST, John
CARLYLE; land descended from Ann JANNEY to Mahlon. Wit: John
WILLIAMS, Richard GRIFFITH, Wm. HOUGH.

Bk:Pg: 2G:305   Date: 27 Mar 1804   RcCt: 13 May 1806
Robert William KIRK & wife Sarah to Jacob FORTENEY. CoE for sale of
land. Wit: George TAYLOR, Alexr. SMITH.

Bk:Pg: 2G:307   Date: 8 Dec 1805   RcCt: 13 May 1806
Ludwell LEE of Ldn and William SMITH of Ldn. Exchange of 7ac.

Bk:Pg: 2G:310   Date: 1 Nov 1805   RcCt: 14 May 1806
Henry M. DAVIS of Lsbg to John REIGOR of Lsbg. BoS of household items. Wit: William BEATY, Henry GLASSGOW.

Bk:Pg: 2G:310   Date: 14 Apr 1806   RcCt: 14 May 1806
John ALEXANDER & wife Elizabeth of Ldn to son Charles Barnes ALEXANDER of Ldn. Gift of slaves Jack, Dick, Moses, George, Lewis, Molly, her daughter Sall, and Sally. Also horses. Wit: Walter TAYLOR, Thomas SQUIRS, Mahlon BEWLY.

Bk:Pg: 2G:311   Date: 10 Apr 1806   RcCt: 14 May 1806
Solomon HOGE (attorney for Harmon COX of Randolph Co NC) of Ldn to Phineas THOMAS of Ldn. Surrender of 274½ac nr Round Hill. Wit: James HATCHER, Israel JANNEY, Jane JANNEY.

Bk:Pg: 2G:313   Date: 14 May 1806   RcCt: 14 May 1806
Benjamin B. THORNTON to Jacob HOWDERSHELL. BoS for negro girl Ruth abt 9y old. Wit: John SHAW, A. MORRISON.

Bk:Pg: 2G:314   Date: 18 Mar 1806   RcCt: 14 May 1806
David SMALLEY & wife Mary of Ldn to James ALLEN of Ldn. B/S of 100ac. Wit: Israel LACEY, Chas. LEWIS, Jos. LEWIS, Joshua LEE, William WARFORD, Jeremiah RIDDLE.

Bk:Pg: 2G:318   Date: 25 Apr 1806   RcCt: 14 May 1806
Benjamin H. CANBY & wife Sarah of Ldn to Jesse DAILEY of Ldn. B/S of 4ac adj James McNELLEDGE. Wit: Wm. WOODDY, William CLINE, Jos. BEARD, Jos. ALEXANDER, Samuel MURREY.

Bk:Pg: 2G:321   Date: 19 Apr 1806   RcCt: 14 May 1806
Benjamin H. CANBY & wife Sarah of Lsbg to William WOODDY. B/S of ½ac lot on Royal St in Lsbg. Wit: Jos. BEARD, James McNELLAGE, William CLINE, J. ALEXANDER, Samuel MURREY.

Bk:Pg: 2G:323   Date: 19 Apr 1806   RcCt: 14 May 1806
Benjamin H. CANBY & wife Sarah of Ldn to James McNELLAGE of Ldn. B/S of __ac on Carolina Rd between James McNELLAGE & Ben'n. WOODLEY. Wit: Wm. WOODY. William CLINE, Jos. BEARD, J. ALEXANDER, Samuel MURREY.

Bk:Pg: 2G:326   Date: 22 Dec 1804   RcCt: 11 Sep 1805
George ROWAN of Lsbg to Thomas N. BINNS of Lsbg. A/L of 1ac Lot #5. Wit: Jno. MATHIAS, Jas. HAMILTON, John H. EVANS.

Bk:Pg: 2G:329   Date: 1 Jan 1806   RcCt: 14 Jul 1806
Samuel & Hannah HUMPHRIES to Susannah HUMPHRIES. Gift of slaves Bray, Matt, Dick, Ruth, Lucy, Fan, Reuben, Charles & Harry. Wit: William PRESGRAVES, Henry JONES.

Bk:Pg: 2G:329   Date: 3 Jan 1806   RcCt: 14 Jul 1806
Johnston LACY of Ldn to William PEYTON of Ldn. BoS for farm and household items. Wit: W. TAYLOR Jr.

Bk:Pg: 2G:330   Date: 22 Oct 1805   RcCt: 14 Jul 1806
Ferdinando FAIRFAX of JeffVa to Jacob WINE of Ldn. B/S of 21¾ac in
Piedmont nr Kittoctin Creek adj Patterson WRIGHT, Ellen POULTNEY.
Wit: Joseph CRANE, John B. HENRY, Diederick SCHULTZE.

Bk:Pg: 2G:332   Date: 14 Jul 1806   RcCt: 14 Jul 1806
Mungo DYKES & wife Ann of Ldn to Thomas CARR of Ldn. B/S of ½ac lot
adj Lot #17 in Lsbg. Wit: Jas. CAVAN Jr., John H. EVANS, Saml. CARR,
Armistead LONG, Saml. CLAPHAM.

Bk:Pg: 2G:334   Date: 3 Feb 1806   RcCt: 14 Jul 1806
Bertrand EWELL & wife Kitty of Lsbg to Francis TRIPLETT of Lsbg. Trust
to Samuel MURREY, John McCORMICK & Sampson BLINCOE using lot
in Lsbg where EWELL now lives. Wit: Samuel HOUGH, John NEWTON,
Daniel DOWLING, Fra. H. PEYTON, Samuel MURREY.

Bk:Pg: 2G:338   Date: 14 Nov 1805   RcCt: 9 Dec 1805
James LEWIS Jr. of Ldn to Peter MILLER of Ldn. B/S of 125½ac adj
George COOPER, Jacob EMERY, Joseph SMITH. Wit: Jno. SLACK,
Peter MILLER Jr., William MILLER.

Bk:Pg: 2G:340   Date: 12 Jul 1806   RcCt: 14 Jul 1806
Samuel TILLETT of Ldn to Thomas MOSS of Ldn. B/S of 13ac adj road to
Adams Mill. Wit: Robert SANGSTER.

Bk:Pg: 2G:342   Date: 14 Jul 1806   RcCt: 15 Jul 1806
John Fenton MERCER to Andrew LEWIS of Mason Co and Charles
Fenton MERCER of Ldn. PoA for sale of land on Ohio River.

Bk:Pg: 2G:342   Date: 16 Sep 1805   RcCt: 15 Jul 1806
Henry M. DAVIS & wife Jane of Lsbg to James RUSSELL of AlexVa. B/S
of ½ac between lot of Charles DRISH now occupied by Thomas
McGEATH and lot of Thomas SANDERS. Wit: C. BINNS, Sn. BLINCOE,
S. M. EDWARDS, Samuel MURREY, Obediah CLIFFORD.

Bk:Pg: 2G:345   Date: 1 May 1806   RcCt: 15 Jul 1806
Elias THRASHER. Col for slave woman Nan abt 30y, Tom age 15y,
Rachel age 10y, Mill age 8y, Jim age 6y, Phill age 4y & Will age 2m
brought into Va on 3 Apr last.

Bk:Pg: 2G:345   Date: 21 May 1796   RcCt: 13 Jan 1806
Attorney Matthew HARRISON to Tomizin ELLZEY & Marmeduke
BECKWITH (surviving Exors of Lewis ELLZEY dec'd). B/S of Goose
Creek land between Daniels Mill and Kilgores. Wit: Thomas HARRISON
Jr., J. W. WIGGINTON, Danl. BRENT, Wm. LANE 3rd, Danl. PALMER,
Peter JETT Jr., William BISHOP Sr., Jeremiah COCKERILL Jr., George
NEWMAN.

Bk:Pg: 2G:347   Date: 16 Aug 1802   RcCt: 13 Jan 1806
Tomazin ELLZEY (surviving Exor of Lewis ELLZEY dec'd) to Attorney
Matthew HARRISON of Dumfries. B/S of above land.

Bk:Pg: 2G:349   Date: 21 May 1804   RcCt: 13 Aug 1806
Armistead Tho'n. MASON. Col of negro servant Bill age abt 18y from Md, brought into Va within the last 60 days.

Bk:Pg: 2G:350   Date: 10 Mar 1802   RcCt: 8 Sep 1806
Abiel JENNERS. Col of unnamed slaves.

Bk:Pg: 2G:350   Date: 3 Oct 1803   RcCt: 8 Sep 1806
Ferdinando FAIRFAX of JeffVa to Ezekiel POTTS of Ldn. B/S of 185½ac where Ailce SMITH lately lived, adj James McILHANEY. Wit: John McILHANEY, Edward CUNARD, James McILHANEY, Wm. H. HARDING, Lewis ELLZEY.

Bk:Pg: 2G:352   Date: 6 Mar 1806   RcCt: 8 Sep 1806
Ferdinando FAIRFAX & William Byrd PAGE to Thomas BACKHOUSE. B/S of 254ac adj William EVANS, John EVANS, Robert HERRON. Wit: John ANDERSON, Curtis GRUBB, William HICKMAN.

Bk:Pg: 2G:354   Date: 21 Mar 1804   RcCt: 8 Sep 1806
Abiel JENNERS & wife Deborah of Ldn to James McILHANEY of Ldn. B/S of 400ac -2 tracts in occupation of George WARNER & Peter WARNER in "Arcadia" adj William OSBURNE, Stephen DONALDSON. Wit: Lewis ELLZEY, Otho H. W. LUCKETT, John HAMILTON.

Bk:Pg: 2G:356   Date: ___ 1806   RcCt: 8 Sep 1806
Samuel CLENDENING of Ldn to John McILHANEY Jr. of Ldn. B/S of 99ac on N branch of Kittoctan Creek where CLENDENING now lives, adj Jonah THOMPSON, Joseph LEWIS, Andrew THOMPSON. Wit: Thomas LOVE, Jonathan W. CARTER, William CLENDENING.

Bk:Pg: 2G:357   Date: 2 Sep 1806   RcCt: 8 Sep 1806
James BRADFIELD & wife Ruth of Ldn to William HARNED of Hllb. B/S of ¾ac lot in Hllb where HARNED now lives, formerly of John JANNEY dec'd. Wit: James HAMILTON, Stacey TAYLOR, Benj. BRADFIELD, N. DAVISSON.

Bk:Pg: 2G:360   Date: 8 Sep 1806   RcCt: 8 Sep 1806
William SMITH (s/o Henry SMITH dec'd, br/o David SMITH) of Ldn to Isaac BROWN of Ldn. B/S of 46ac adj James BURSON, Henry PLASTER.

Bk:Pg: 2G:361   Date: 9 Apr 1806   RcCt: 8 Sep 1806
Thomas LESLIE & wife Annie of Ldn to Amos BEANS of Ldn. B/S of 87ac in Piedmont adj Andrew THOMPSON. Wit: N. DAVISSON, George S. HOUGH, Stacy TAYLOR, Josiah WHITE Jr., James HAMILTON.

Bk:Pg: 2G:364   Date: 8 Sep 1806   RcCt: 8 Sep 1806
William SMITH of Ldn to Henry PLASTER of Ldn. B/S of 92ac adj Isaac BROWN.

Bk:Pg: 2G:366   Date: 11 Aug 1806   RcCt: 8 Sep 1806
William CRAIG & wife Deborah of Ldn to Isaac & Samuel NICHOLS of Ldn. B/S of 42ac on NW fork of Goose Creek adj Jacob BROWN. Wit:

Joseph SHIELDS, Isaac NICHOLS, name in German, Johnston CLEVELAND, Wm. BRONAUGH.

Bk:Pg: 2G:369   Date: 8 Sep 1806   RcCt: 8 Sep 1806
Thomas LOVE of Ldn to David GOODEN and Noah HATCHER of Ldn. Trust of 49ac adj Jesper POULSON, Thomas HUGHES.

Bk:Pg: 2G:371   Date: 8 Sep 1806   RcCt: 8 Sep 1806
David GOODWIN of Ldn to Thomas LOVE of Ldn. B/S of 49ac adj Jesper POULSON, Jesse SILLCOTT.

Bk:Pg: 2G:373   Date: 10 Jan 1806   RcCt: 8 Sep 1806
William Barton HUNGERFORD (Admr of Charles HUNGERFORD dec'd) to James COPELAND. BoS for negro Brice age 18y old abt Christmas last. Wit: Thomas LOVE, Isaac LAROWE.

Bk:Pg: 2G:373   Date: 8 Mar 1806   RcCt: 8 Sep 1806
Nathan SPENCER & wife Ann of Ldn to Stephen WILSON of Ldn. B/S of 172ac on NW fork of Goose Creek adj John HEAD, Benjamin DANIEL, Thomas GREGG. Wit: Stacy TAYLOR, Benj'a BRADFIELD, Stephen C. ROSZEL, Samuel NICHOLS, Samuel RUSSEL, Notley C. WILLIAMS.

Bk:Pg: 2G:376   Date: 13 Mar 1806   RcCt: 8 Sep 1806
Evan EVANS of Ldn to son William EVANS. A/L of 100ac between Short Hill & Blue Ridge with L/L on lives of William EVANS, Isaac IVANS & Josiah EVANS. Wit: Charles HUMPHREY, Margaret HUMPHREY, Lee HUMPHREY.

Bk:Pg: 2G:378   Date: 3 Apr 1806   RcCt: 8 Sep 1806
Farmer Jacob BAKER & wife Catharine of Ldn to farmer Jacob WIRTS of Ldn. B/S of 100ac. Wit: N. Davisson, James HAMILTON, Peter STUCK, John SLATER, Thos. JOHNSTON 3rd, Enos GARRETT, John HAMILTON.

Bk:Pg: 2G:381   Date: __ Mar 1806   RcCt: 8 Sep 1806
James CAMPBELL & wife Mary of Ldn to Amos JANNEY of Ldn. B/S of 96½ac on Broad Run adj John BALL, Michael BOGER. Wit: Philip BYRNES, Mahlon JANNEY, Adam HOUSEHOLDER, James WHITE, John HAMILTON, James HAMILTON.

Bk:Pg: 2G:384   Date: 24 Jan 1806   RcCt: 8 Sep 1806
Isaac HOUGH & wife Fanny of Ldn to Francis McKEMIE of Ldn. B/S of 97¾ac in Piedmont Manor with L/L to James McKEMIE, adj Saml. UNDERWOOD, Daniel SHUMAKER, Michael RUSE, James NIXON. Wit: James HAMILTON, Joseph BRADEN Jr., Ric'd ROACH, Richard GRIFFITH.

Bk:Pg: 2G:387   Date: 12 Jun 1806   RcCt: 8 Sep 1806
Isaac HOUGH & wife Fanny of Ldn to John NICKLIN of Monongalia Co Va. B/S of land in Fairfax Co. Wit: James HAMILTON, N. DAVISSON, Fanny McGEATH, Richard GRIFFITH.

Bk:Pg: 2G:389   Date: 24 Feb 1806   RcCt: 8 Sep 1806
Patrick McFADIAN & wife Margrea of Ldn to Patrick MILHOLLEN of Ldn. B/S of lot in Wtfd adj Flemon PATTERSON. Wit: W. S. NEALE, Richard GRIFFITH, Mos. COLDWELL.

Bk:Pg: 2G:391   Date: 7 Mar 1806   RcCt: 8 Sep 1806
George SHEWMAKER & wife Barbary of Ldn to Moses MILLER of Ldn. B/S of 22ac adj John JACKSON, Jacob EMERY. Wit: Isaac MILLER, Daniel SHOEMAKER, Jacob MILLER, James HAMILTON, Richard GRIFFITH.

Bk:Pg: 2G:394   Date: 20 Jun 1806   RcCt: 8 Sep 1806
Joseph CARR & wife Delia of Ldn to John FLEMING of Ldn. B/S of ½ac in Upperville on side of Turnpike Rd. Wit: Wm. BRONAUGH, David FULTON, Wm. GRANT, Ben. GRAYSON.

Bk:Pg: 2G:397   Date: 11 Apr 1806   RcCt: 8 Sep 1806
Joseph CARR of Ldn to Jacob IDEN of Ldn. B/S of ¼ac on S side of Turnpike Rd passing Ashby's Gap opposite Carr's Grist Mill, adj John WEEDON. Wit: Ezar DILLON, James RUST, William M. POWELL, Thomas DRAKE.

Bk:Pg: 2G:399   Date: 16 May 1806   RcCt: 8 Sep 1806
James NELSON (by attorney Thomas LESLIE) to Charles HUMPHREY of Ldn. A/L of 125ac. Wit: Thos. HUMPHREY, David LOVETT, Abel MARKS.

Bk:Pg: 2G:400   Date: 31 Mar 1806   RcCt: 8 Sep 1806
Charles THRIFT of Ldn to William THRIFT of Ldn. Mortgage of 154ac on Tuscarora where William now lives. Wit: S. BLINCOE, Josiah MOFFETT, George DOWNS.

Bk:Pg: 2G:402   Date: 5 Sep 1806   RcCt: 8 Sep 1806
Albert RUSSELL & wife Ann of Ldn to Leven POWELL Jr. of Ldn. B/S of 534ac on Broad Run, 170ac on Beaverdam branch and 5ac. Wit: W. ELLZEY, Chas. LEWIS.

Bk:Pg: 2G:405   Date: 2 Sep 1806   RcCt: 8 Sep 1806
James BRADFIELD & wife Ruth of Ldn to James HAMILTON of Hllb. B/S of 45 perches bought from Joseph JANNEY dec'd on S side of Turnpike Rd. Wit: James HAMILTON, Stacy TAYLOR, Benjamin BRADFIELD, N. DAVISSON.

Bk:Pg: 2G:409   Date: 11 Aug 1806   RcCt: 8 Sep 1806
David JOHNSTON of Ldn to Jacob SHIVELY of Ldn. BoS for farm animals. Wit: Samuel MURREY, William CARR.

Bk:Pg: 2G:410   Date: 6 Sep 1805   RcCt: 9 Sep 1805
Isaac RICHARDS & wife Deborah of Ldn to John RALPH of Ldn. B/S of 2ac on road leading to Ebenezer Meeting House, adj Thomas DRAKE Sr, Benjamin BARTON. Wit: Wm. BRONAUGH, Ben. GRAYSON, David MAILEN.

Bk:Pg: 2G:413   Date: 18 Jun 1806   RcCt: 8 Sep 1806
Benjamin H. CANBY & wife Sarah of Ldn to Joshua RILEY of Ldn. B/S of lot in Lsbg adj Lots #65 & #66. Wit: Jno. MYERS, Jos. BEARD, Fra. H. PEYTON, O. CLIFFORD.

Bk:Pg: 2G:415   Date: 18 Jun 1806   RcCt: 8 Sep 1806
Joshua REILEY of Lsbg to Benjamin H. CANBY of Lsbg and Samuel MURREY, Francis TRIPLETT & Alexander SUTHERLAND. Trust on above land. Wit: Jos. BEARD, Jno. MYERS, Fra. H. PEYTON, O. CLIFFORD.

Bk:Pg: 2G:418   Date: 1 Apr 1806   RcCt: 12 May 1806
John McILHANEY Jr. of Ldn to Samuel CLENDENING of Ldn and William CLENDENING & William NIXON of Ldn. Trust using 96ac on N Kittockton adj Jonah THOMPSON, Jonathan M. CARTER, Andrew THOMPSON. Wit: Thomas LOVE, Jonathan N. CARTER, Thos. HOUGH, Thos. WHITE.

Bk:Pg: 2G:420   Date: 11 Jun 1806   RcCt: 8 Sep 1806
John BAYLY of Ldn to Elizth BEATY of Ldn. B/S of 151½ac adj Jeremiah HAMPTON, John BURK. Wit: Thos. BISCOE, Jas. CHANNEL, Jesse McVEIGH, Leven POWELL Jr., A. GIBSON.

Bk:Pg: 2G:422   Date: ___ 1806   RcCt: 8 Sep 1806
Robert PARFECT & wife Jane of Ldn to Charles BINNS of Ldn. B/S of 1ac allowing Robert NEWTON & wife Ann to occupy in trust (after dec'd their <21y children John Cunningham NEWTON, Elizabeth Lee NEWTON & Robert Cunningham NEWTON). Wit: Fleet SMITH, B. H. CANBY.

Bk:Pg: 2G:425   Date: 8 Sep 1806   RcCt: 8 Sep 1806
John BURSON & wife Catherine of Ldn to Samuel DUNKIN of Ldn. B/S of 50ac on N branch of Beaverdam adj Benjamin BURSON, Jonathan BURSON, James BURSON.

Bk:Pg: 2G:426   Date: 31 May 1806   RcCt: 8 Sep 1806
Thomas LOVE of Ldn to Benjamin DANIEL & wife Jane of Ldn. B/S of 162ac on N Kittockton Creek adj James COPELAND. Wit: Obed PEIRPOINT, James COPELAND, William PEACOCK, Jehu HOLLINGSWORTH.

Bk:Pg: 2G:429   Date: 31 May 1779   RcCt: 8 Sep 1806
Bazel STONESTREET. Col of slaves Cate, Patiance, Rachel & Nace from Md.

Bk:Pg: 2G:429   Date: 14 Apr 1806   RcCt: 8 Sep 1806
George TAVENER & wife Tabitha of Ldn to Jonah TAVENNER of Ldn. B/S of 97ac on Beaverdam adj Richard TAVENER, John BROWN, William BROWN. Wit: Jesse JANNEY, Jonah SANDS, Thomas GREGG.

Bk:Pg: 2G:431   Date: 14 Apr 1806   RcCt: 8 Sep 1806
Stacy JANNEY & wife Hannah of Ldn to Jesse JANNEY of Ldn. B/S of 1 rood. Wit: George TAVENNER, Jonah SANDS, Jonah TAVENNER.

Bk:Pg: 2G:433   Date: 5 Sep 1806   RcCt: 8 Sep 1806
Leven POWELL of Ldn to Edmund DENNY of AlexVa. LS of part of Lot #22 in Mdbg.

Bk:Pg: 2G:434   Date: ___ 1802   RcCt: 10 May 1802
David DAVIS & wife Pamela to Peter OATYER of Ldn. B/S of 71ac and 21ac. Wit: J. E. O. LEE, John CARTER, John VERE.

Bk:Pg: 2G:435   Date: 3 Sep 1806   RcCt: 9 Sep 1806
James CURTIS of Ldn to James SAUNDERS of Lsbg. BoS for slaves women Lucy & her daughters woman Sena & girl Phillis (rec. from marriage to present wife the late Mary HUNGERFORD who rec. from her father Charles HUNGERFORD). Wit: George HAMMAT, Josiah MOFFETT Sr., Saml. M. EDWARDS, Eli OFFUTT.

Bk:Pg: 2G:437   Date: 3 Sep 1806   RcCt: 9 Sep 1806
James SANDERS of Lsbg to Fleet SMITH of Lsbg. Trust using above slaves Lucy, Sena & Phillis. Wit: Eli OFFUTT, Saml. M. EDWARDS, Jonah MOFFETT Sr.

Bk:Pg: 2G:439   Date: 28 May 1806   RcCt: 9 Sep 1806
Enos GARRETT & wife Elenor to Joseph LEWIS Jr. of Ldn. B/S of 88½ac adj David MULL, George SHULTZ, Michael EVERHARD. Wit: Thos. TRIBBEY, Aaron GARROTT, Samuel BEAL.

Bk:Pg: 2G:440   Date: __ Sep 1806   RcCt: 9 Sep 1806
Joseph LEWIS Jr. of Ldn to Enos GARROTT of Ldn. B/S of 124ac adj Thomas HUGHS, Amos BEANS, Thomas TRIBBY and 158ac on S fork of Katockton L/L to Thos. TRIBBY adj Amos BEANS, Jos. THOMSON, Richard BROWN. Wit: S. BLINCOE, Geo. W. BLINCOE, R. BRADEN.

Bk:Pg: 2G:442   Date: 9 Sep 1806   RcCt: 9 Sep 1806
Joseph LEWIS Jr. of Ldn to Robert BRADEN of Ldn. B/S of 26¼ac adj Adam MILLER, David AXLINE.

Bk:Pg: 2G:444   Date: 6 Sep 1806   RcCt: 8 Sep 1806
Nancy FOUCH, Mary HAWLING, Elizabeth HAWLING, John HAWLING & Sarah FOUCH and Daniel FOUCH (reps of Hannah HAWLING dec'd who was d/o & rep of John SINCLAIR dec'd) to their brother William HAWLING. B/S of 25ac Lot #11 on HAWLING division and 6ac part of dower. Wit: Burr POWELL, A. GIBSON, Ths. BISCOE, Thos. FOUCH, Isaac HAWLING, William FOUCH.

Bk:Pg: 2G:446   Date: 12 Aug 1806   RcCt: 10 Sep 1806
Benjamin B. THORNTON & wife Hannah of Lsbg to Matthew HARRISON. Trust using negro children Lorinda, Charlotte, Harriet & Priscilla.

Bk:Pg: 2G:447   Date: 25 Aug 1804   RtCt; 10 Sep 1804
Joshua DANNIEL of Ldn to Jonas POTTS of Ldn. Release of mortgage from indenture of 1799. Wit: Asa MOORE, Mahlon JANNEY Jr., James RUSSELL, William CLINE.

Bk:Pg: 2G:450   Date: 26 Aug 1806   RcCt: 10 Sep 1806
Jonas POTTS & wife Phebe of Ldn to Samuel ADAMS of Ldn. B/S of
300*ac* on Goose Creek. Wit: Chars. GULLATT, John CARR Jr., Samuel
DONOHOE, Albert RUSSELL, Thos. SIM.

Bk:Pg: 2G:452   Date: 4 Sep 1806   RcCt: 10 Sep 1806
Samuel ADAMS & wife Catharine of Ldn to Jonas POTTS of Ldn.
Mortgage on above land. Wit: Jno. MATHIAS, John H. EVANS, Albert
RUSSEL, Richard GRIFFITH.

Bk:Pg: 2G:455   Date: 6 Sep 1806   RcCt: 8 Sep 1806
Samuel MURREY of Lsbg to partners & traders Jonas POTTS & Samuel
CARR. LS of part of Lot #12 in Lsbg. Wit: Jas. CAVAN Jr., Benj'n
SHREVE, S. WHERRY.

Bk:Pg: 2G:459   Date: 14 May 1803   RcCt: 10 Oct 1803
John D. ORR & wife Lucinda of JeffVa and Thomas LANG & wife of NY to
Burr POWELL of Ldn. B/S of 244¾*ac*. Wit: Noble BEVERIDGE, John
UPP, Daniel VERNON, Thomas ATWELL, James ARMSTRONG, Martin
BRENT, Jesse McVEIGH.

Bk:Pg: 2G:461   Date: 14 May 1803   RcCt: 10 Oct 1803
John D. ORR & wife Lucinda of JeffVa and Thomas LANG & wife ___ of
NY to John IDEN of Ldn. B/S of 636½*ac* on Goose Creek. Wit: Burr
POWELL, Noble BEVERIDGE, John UPP, Thomas ATWELL, Daniel
VERNON, James ARMSTRONG, Martin BRENT, Jesse McVEIGH.

Bk:Pg: 2G:464   Date: 8 Sep 1806   RcCt: 13 Oct 1806
James LEWIS & wife Sarah of Shelby Co Ky to Nathaniel MOSS of Ldn.
B/S of 96*ac* adj Thomas FRANCIS. Wit: Alex'r. REID, Isaac WHITACRE,
Chs. LYNCH.

Bk:Pg: 2G:467   Date: 10 Oct 1806   RcCt: 13 Oct 1896
Thomas HEPBURN & wife Elizabeth of Ldn to William CLENDENING of
Ldn. B/S of ½*ac* lot on N side of Main St in Hllb adj Joseph TRIBBE,
Thomas LESLIE, Ruth GREGG. Wit: John B. STEPHENS, Thos.
HOUGH, Mahlon ROACH.

Bk:Pg: 2G:469   Date: 13 Oct 1806   RcCt: 13 Oct 1806
William HUTCHISON & wife Mary of Ldn to Reuben HUTCHISON of
PrWm. B/S of 200*ac* bequeathed from Joseph HUTCHISON dec'd, adj
Pierce BAYLY dec'd. Wit: Nathan HUTCHISON.

Bk:Pg: 2G:471   Date: 22 May 1806   RcCt: 13 Oct 1806
Thomas FRED & wife Elizabeth of Ldn to Enoch FURR of Ldn. B/S of
85*ac* (devised from Joseph FRED dec'd) adj Joshua FRED, Joseph
FRED, Thomas A. HEREFORD. Wit: Minor FURR, George RUST, Abel
PALMER, Wm. FURR.

Bk:Pg: 2G:473   Date: ___ 1805   RcCt: 13 Oct 1806
Peter CARR & wife Mary and Maria WILSON of Ldn and Henry L.
WILLSON of Hampshire Co Va (ch/o of John WILSON dec'd) to Jesse
HIRST of Ldn. B/S of 47*ac* adj John PIGGOTT. Wit: Jo'n. PEIRPOINT,

Stephen DONALDSON, Israel POOL, John CARR, Samuel MURREY, Obadiah CLIFFORD.

Bk:Pg: 2G:476   Date: 13 Jan 1806   RcCt: 13 Oct 1806
Wheatman LEATH & wife Cloe of Ldn to William VICKERS of Ldn. B/S of 30*ac* on Goose Creek. Wit: John SINCLAIR, Ezer. DILLON, William GEORGE, Leven LUCKETT, Leven POWELL, Jesse McVEIGH.

Bk:Pg: 2G:479   Date: 12 Oct 1806   RcCt: 13 Oct 1806
Peter STONE & wife Mary of Ldn to John BOWERSETT of Ldn. B/S of 2*ac* on Broad Run adj Samuel BAKER. Wit: James HAMILTON, Richard GRIFFITH, Thomas PHILIP, Philip BYRNES.

Bk:Pg: 2G:481   Date: 2 Sep 1806   RcCt: 13 Oct 1806
Lewis ELLZEY & wife Rosannah of Ldn to James BRADFIELD of Ldn. B/S of 190*ac* on NW fork of Goose Creek adj Bradfield's Mill. Wit: Stacy TAYLOR, James HAMILTON, N. DAVISSON, James H. HAMILTON.

Bk:Pg: 2G:484   Date: 6 Sep 1806   RcCt: 13 Oct 1806
Lewis ELLZEY and Nathaniel DAVISSON of Ldn to James BRADFIELD. Bond on above land due to dower of Margaret McILHANEY (wd/o James McILHANEY). Wit: Stacy TAYLOR, James HAMILTON.

Bk:Pg: 2G:485   Date: 15 Aug 1806   RcCt: 13 Oct 1806
Patrick CAVAN Jr. (Admr of Patrick CAVAN dec'd) to Joseph BURSON of Ldn. A/L of 10*ac* originally from James HEREFORD dec'd to Patrick dec'd. Wit: Jno. MATTHIAS, Alex. SUTHERLAND, Thos. WILKINSON.

Bk:Pg: 2G:487   Date: 13 Oct 1806   RcCt: 13 Oct 1806
Joseph BURSON of Ldn to Catharine EMERY of Ldn. A/L of 10*ac* above. Wit: Isaac LAROWE, C. BINNS, Saml. M. EDWARDS.

Bk:Pg: 2G:489   Date: 26 Mar 1804   RcCt: 10 Apr 1804
Solomon DAVIS of FrdkMd to Benjamin PRICE of Ldn. B/S of 164*ac* on main rd to Nolands ferry. Wit: W. NOLAND, Isaac GRIFFITH, Thomas CHILTON, Amos VEAL.

Bk:Pg: 2G:490   Date: 13 Oct 1806   RcCt: 13 Oct 1806
John SCHOOLEY Jr. & wife Elizabeth of Ldn to Patrick McINTYRE of Ldn. B/S of 10*ac* Lot #1 on Kittocton Mt.

Bk:Pg: 2G:493   Date: 17 Sep 1806   RcCt: 13 Oct 1806
Joseph LEWIS Jr. of Ldn to Philip FRYE of Ldn. B/S of 112½*ac* in Piedmont Manor adj John JACKSON, George COOPER, Peter STONE. Wit: name in German, Mary FRY, Peter MILLER.

Bk:Pg: 2G:495   Date: 17 Sep 1806   RcCt: 13 Oct 1806
Philip FRYE of Ldn to Joseph LEWIS Jr. of Ldn. Mortgage on above land under L/L to William BAKER. Wit: name in German, Mary FRY, Peter MILLER.

Bk:Pg: 2G:496   Date: 31 May 1806   RcCt: 8 Sep 1806
Thomas LOVE, John LOVE, Sarah LOVE, Elizabeth LOVE, Benjamin DANIEL & wife Jane and Hannah LOVE Jr. (ch/o James LOVE Sr. dec'd) of Ldn to brothers James and Samuel LOVE. B/S of 162*ac* on N

Kittockton Creek adj Josiah WHITE, William RUSSELL. Wit: Obed PIERPOINT, James COPELAND, William PEACOCK, John HOLLINGSWORTH, Jehu HOLLINGSWORTH.

Bk:Pg: 2G:499   Date: 25 Jun 1806   RcCt: 13 Oct 1806
John ALEXANDER of Ldn to Charles Barnes ALEXANDER of Ldn. B/S of __ac.

Bk:Pg: 2G:501   Date: 14 May 1806   RcCt: 13 Oct 1806
Joseph BENTLEY & wife Catharine (d/o Alexander McINTYRE dec'd) of Ldn and Sebastian LOSCH & wife Jane (wd/o Alex. McINTYRE) to Alexander SUTHERLAND of Ldn. B/S of 2ac on Tuskorora nr Lsbg. Wit: Jas. CAVAN Jr., Thos. SIM, Corn's. SKINNER Jr., Stephen COOKE, Samuel MURREY, Obadiah CLIFFORD.

Bk:Pg: 2G:504   Date: 24 Mar 1806   RcCt: 15 Apr 1806
Henry POTTERFIELD & wife Elizabeth of Ldn to Elias THRASHER. B/S of 45¼ac. Wit: John HAMILTON, Chas. BENNETT, Adam STREAM.

Bk:Pg: 2G:507   Date: 27 Jan 1806   RcCt: 14 Oct 1806
Thomas BEALE & wife Ann of Trumbull Co Oh to Robert BRADEN of Ldn. B/S of 99ac on Broad Run adj John WITTERMAN nr German Church, John MARTIN, Laurence MINK, Peter HICKIMAN. Wit: Calvin AUSTIN, Alex'r. SUTHERLAND, Caleb PALMER.

Bk:Pg: 2G:510   Date: 8 Oct 1806   RcCt: 14 Oct 1806
William A. ROGERS & wife Susanna (late BAYLY, d/o Pierce BAYLY the Elder dec'd) to William P. BAYLY. B/S of land descended to Pierce BAYLY the younger who died intestate and descended to the eldest who was Susanna.

Bk:Pg: 2G:511   Date: ___   RcCt: 14 Oct 1806
William THRIFT of Ldn to Charles THRIFT of Ldn. Bond and B/S of 154ac on Tuskarora from father. Wit: Sn. BLINCOE, Benj'n. B. THORNTON, Simon A. BINNS.

Bk:Pg: 2G:513   Date: 28 Feb 1806   RcCt: 14 Oct 1806
Edward MORRIS of Ldn to William ORE of Ldn. BoS for farm and household items. Wit: Daniel MULLIN, James MAGAHA.

Bk:Pg: 2G:514   Date: 28 Oct 1806   RcCt: 8 Dec 1806
Maurice DULANY of Balt to Edward PHELAN late of Abbyleix in Queens Co Ireland but at the time of Balt. Letter of Attorney: Timothy WHELAN dec'd of Ldn devised ½ of his estate of brother James WHELAN and ½ to sisters (Margaret, Judith, Catharine & Winnefred). Brother James WHELAN died shortly after Timothy and Maurice DELANY is sole Exor. Winnefred m. Jeremiah PHELAN now of Ballguhin, Queens Co Ireland. Timothy's estate had many debts. Margaret now widow Margaret DUNN lives in Durrow, Kilkenny Co Ireland. The following debts are listed: Thomas DAVIS, Philip BYRNES, Robbin HOWELL, Joseph LILLY, Jacob LONG, Danl. MILLER, Henry SHORTS Jr., Ben PRINS, Philip HAITER, John BYRNEHOUSE, Jeremiah BYRNES, John DEMERY, Henry KEUNTS, Thomas BATEMAN, Peter BELT, Isaac EVANS, Philip NEAR,

Thomas THOMPSON, Oliver McCLUER, Samuel McFARM?, Henry ADAMS, Cornelius SHOHER, Jacob AXLINE, Isaac MILLER, Peter WEDDEY, Samuel LILE, John FILLER, Jesse JAMES, John BAILLEY.

Bk:Pg: 2H:001   Date: 17 Mar 1792   RcCt: 11 Sep 1799
William LEE of James City Co to Thomas ROOKARD (Robert Carter ROOKARD s/o Nancy ROOKARD, John BENTLEY s/o John & Lydia BENTLEY) of Ldn. L/L of 145*ac* in CamP. Wit: Elijah HUTCHISON, Jno. HUTCHISON, Chs. STEUART, Reuben HUTCHISON. LS then assigned to George NEALE by Thomas & Sarah ROOKARD. Wit: Asael OWENS, James NEALE, Jno. POWELL.

Bk:Pg: 2H:004   Date: 1 Sep 1806   RcCt: 13 Oct 1806
Sarah THOMPSON of Ldn to Israel H. THOMPSON of Ldn. A/L of Lots #9, #10 & #11 in Wtfd. Wit: James MOORE, Daniel STONE, Joseph BOND.

Bk:Pg: 2H:005   Date: 1 Dec 1806   RcCt: 9 Dec 1806
James ROACH & wife Elizabeth of Ldn to son Mahlon ROACH of Ldn. B/S of lot where Mahlon now lives in Hllb adj Thomas HOUGH, Josiah WHITE Jr.

Bk:Pg: 2H:007   Date: 16 Jun 1806   RcCt: 8 Dec 1806
Margaret, Catharine, Winnefred & Judith WHELAN (d/o Timothy WHELAN dec'd, sisters of James WHELAN dec'd) to Edward PHELAN. PoA. [see 2G:515]

Bk:Pg: 2H:012   Date: 21 Nov 1806   RcCt: 8 Dec 1806
Thomas CRAVEN to Abner CRAVEN. B/S of Thomas' share of estate of father Thomas CRAVEN dec'd. Wit: C. BINNS, Isaac LAROWE, Eli OFFUTT, Saml. M. EDWARDS.

Bk:Pg: 2H:014   Date: 4 Nov 1806   RcCt: 8 Dec 1806
John SLACK & wife Elizabeth to Joseph LEWIS Jr. CoE for sale of 4*ac*. Wit: Wm. BRONAUGH, Stephen C. ROSZEL.

Bk:Pg: 2H:015   Date: 12 May 1806   RcCt: 8 Dec 1806
John Thomas RICKETTS & wife Mary of Ffx to William NEWTON of AlexVa. B/S of half of Ricketts, Newton and Co. including lot in AlexVa & plantation between Goose Creek & Lsbg where Joseph T. NEWTON now lives. Wit: James BLOXHAM, Peter W. LUNGSTRASS, William SIMMONS, Geo. HULLS, Geo. YOUNGS, Thos. SWANN, James H. BLAKE, R. J. TAYLOR.

Bk:Pg: 2H:026   Date: 26 Nov 1806   RcCt: 8 Dec 1806
Given HANDY (Admr of John HANDY dec'd) of Ldn to George TAVENNER Jr. of Ldn. Release on 102*ac*. Wit: Isaac LARROWE, Wm. H. HANDY, Patrick H. DOUGLAS, C. BINNS, Eli OFFUTT, Saml. M. EDWARDS.

Bk:Pg: 2H:030   Date: 26 Nov 1806   RcCt: 8 Dec 1806
George TAVENER Jr. & wife Martha (signed Patty) of Ldn to Samuel GREGG of Ldn. B/S of 113*ac* on W fork of Goose Creek adj Richard

BROWN. Wit: C. BINNS, Eli OFFUTT, Saml. M. EDWARDS, Isaac LAROWE, John LITTLEJOHN, Samuel MURREY.

Bk:Pg: 2H:034   Date: 26 Nov 1806   RcCt: 8 Dec 1806
Samuel GREGG & wife Hannah of Ldn to George TAVENER Jr. B/S of 190*ac*. Wit: C. BINNS, Eli OFFUTT, Saml. M. EDWARDS, Isaac LAROWE, John LITTLEJOHN, Samuel MURREY.

Bk:Pg: 2H:038   Date: 12 Mar 1806   RcCt: 14 Jul 1806
Owen WILLIAMS (s/o John WILLIAMS dec'd of Ldn) & wife Rodia of Hampshire Co Va to Elice WILLIAMS of Ldn. B/S of John's ¾*ac* land except the share of son Daniel WILLIAMS who has been at sea for some time. Wit: David EVELAND, Robert WAID, Wm. MAINS.

Bk:Pg: 2H:040   Date: 6 Jun 1806   RcCt: 8 Dec 1806
David WILSON of Ldn to Benjamin WHITE (agent for David WHITE & George SMITH Admrs of David WHITE dec'd of Adams Co Pa). B/S of 54*ac*. Wit: Fleet SMITH, Jas. SAUNDERS, Saml. M. EDWARDS.

Bk:Pg: 2H:041   Date: 6 Jun 1806   RcCt: 8 Dec 1806
Benjamin WHITE (agent for David WHITE & George SMITH Admrs of David WHITE dec'd of Adams Co Pa) to John DOWNS of FrdkMd. B/S of 54*ac*. Wit: Fleet SMITH, Jas. SAUNDERS, Saml. M. EDWARDS.

Bk:Pg: 2H:043   Date: 24 Jan 1804   RcCt: 8 Dec 1806
Edmund Jennings LEE & wife Sally of AlexVa to Thomas SWANN of AlexVa. Trust of 500*ac* "Haws Farm" nr Lsbg at present held by Dr. Stephen COOKE as tenant.

Bk:Pg: 2H:048   Date: 10 May 1806   RcCt: 8 Dec 1806
Isaac MILLER of Ldn to Joseph SMITH of Ldn. BoS for farm and household items. Wit: Martin SACKMAN, Cathrena SMITH, name in German.

Bk:Pg: 2H:051   Date: 17 Sep 1806   RcCt: 14 Nov 1806
George LEWIS & wife Violett of Ldn to Israel LACEY of Ldn. B/S of 374¼*ac* on Gum Spring Road. Wit: Armistead LONG, William NOLAND, Jos. BEARD, John SHAW.

Bk:Pg: 2H:055   Date: 15 Nov 1806   RcCt: 8 Dec 1806
Thomas Ludwell LEE & wife Fanny of Ldn to William SMITH of Ldn. B/S of 214*ac* on Rocky branch of Goose Creek. Wit: Obadiah CLIFFORD, David STEUART, Armistead LONG, Ludwell LEE.

Bk:Pg: 2H:059   Date: 5 Jun 1806   RcCt: 8 Dec 1806
John McGEATH of Ldn to Thomas PHILLIPS & William PAXON of Ldn. Trust for bond to Samuel WRIGHT using 100*ac*, adj Stephen SCOTT, Murto SULLIVAN, William WRIGHT, William HOUGH. Wit: Richard GRIFFITH, James MOORE, William S. NEALE.

Bk:Pg: 2H:063   Date: 22 Feb 1805   RcCt: 8 Dec 1806
Asa MOORE of Wtfd to John A. BINNS of Ldn. B/S of 69½*ac* adj Jacob SHIBLEE, Conrad WERTZ, Cornelius SHAW. Wit: C. BINNS, Thos. N. BINNS, L. D. POWELL.

Bk:Pg: 2H:065   Date: 1 Nov 1805   RcCt: 12 May 1806
Asa MOORE of Wtfd to John WILLIAMS of Wtfd. B/S of 2 lots in Wtfd (Lot # not given). Wit: William S. NEALE, Mahlon JANNEY Jr., William HOUGH Jr., Stephen BALL, Jonas POTTS.

Bk:Pg: 2H:068   Date: 7 Aug 1806   RcCt: 8 Dec 1806
Joseph LEWIS Jr. of Ldn to Otho H. W. LUCKETT of Ldn. B/S of 180¼ac adj Michael BOGER, Church lot, George MANN. Wit: Sally GRAHAM, Walter GRAHAM, Geo. FISHER, John H. CANBY, Jas. CAVAN Jr., R. BRADEN.

Bk:Pg: 2H:070   Date: 7 Aug 1806   RcCt: 8 Dec 1806
Otho H. W. LUCKETT & wife Elizabeth of Ldn to Joseph LEWIS Jr. of Ldn. Mortgage of above land in Piedmont Manor. Wit: Walter GRAHAM, Geo. FISHER, Sally GRAHAM, John H. CANBY, Jas. CAVAN Jr., R. BRADEN, Ch. BENNETT, Saml. CLAPHAM.

Bk:Pg: 2H:075   Date: 8 Sep 1806   RcCt: 8 Dec 1806
Samuel RITCHIE of Ldn to Frederick SLATES of Ldn. BoS for negro Bet abt 18y old with infant child 7m. Wit: ?, Wm. D. POWERS, John GEORGE.

Bk:Pg: 2H:076   Date: 12 Nov 1806   RcCt: 8 Dec 1806
John BOWERSETT of Ldn to Peter RICKARD of Ldn. B/S of 22¼ac on Short Hill adj William BAKER. Wit: ?, Joh[n?] GROVES.

Bk:Pg: 2H:078   Date: 6 Jan 1803   RcCt: 8 Dec 1806
John H. HARWOOD. Col for unnamed slaves.

Bk:Pg: 2H:079   Date: 25 Nov 1806   RcCt: 9 Dec 1806
Obediah CLIFFORD & wife Betsey of Lsbg to Samuel MURREY, Armistead LONG & William CHILTON of Lsbg. Mortgage of lot on Loudoun & Royal Sts in Lsbg for debt to Samuel CLAPHAM & Charles BINNS. Wit: John LITTLEJOHN, Eben POTTER, B'd. HOUGH.

Bk:Pg: 2H:083   Date: 18 Jun 1806   RcCt: 9 Dec 1806
Wm. Fitzhugh CARTER of Ffx to Mary LYNE of Ldn. BoS for negro girl Jane abt 10y or 11y a slave for life. Wit: Robt. LYNE, Wm. LYNE, William ANDROES, Sanford LYNE.

Bk:Pg: 2H:083   Date: 11 Oct 1806   RcCt: 9 Dec 1806
Albert RUSSELL & wife Ann Frances Harris of Ldn to John BAYLY of Ldn. B/S of 368ac [small plat]. Wit: Zepharah POSY?, William MARSHALL, J. H. PEYTON, Levi DOUGLAS, Thomas VANHORNE, Johnston CLEVELAND, Chas. LEWIS.

Bk:Pg: 2H:090   Date: 12 Jan 1807   RcCt: 12 Jan 1807
Isaac LAROWE of Ldn to Thomas B. BEALL of DC. B/S of 5½ac adj John OXLEY.

Bk:Pg: 2H:092   Date: 25 Oct 1806   RcCt: 12 Jan 1807
James McPHERSON (s/o Steven McPHERSON) & wife Elizabeth of Ldn to John GIBSON of Ldn. B/S of 94ac on Pantherskin branch adj James

GIBSON, John DULIN. Wit: Ben. GRAYSON, Jos. CARR, James RUST, Wilse POSTON.

Bk:Pg: 2H:096   Date: 18 Oct 1806   RcCt: 12 Jan 1807
Nathaniel MOSS & wife Nancy of Ldn to Daniel THOMAS of Ldn. B/S of 58*ac.* Wit: Ben GRAYSON, Vincent MOSS, Stephen MOSS, Daniel PORTER, Jos. CARR.

Bk:Pg: 2H:100   Date: 10 Jan 1807   RcCt: 12 Jan 1807
Joseph TALBOTT & wife Jane of Ldn to Thomas LACEY of Ldn. B/S of 4¾*ac* on N side of Balls Run nr road from Wtfd to Lsbg adj William HOUGH. Wit: Timothy HIXON, Sanford RAMEY, William SCHOOLEY, Richard GRIFFITH, Chas. BENNETT.

Bk:Pg: 2H:104   Date: 10 Sep 1806   RcCt: 12 Jan 1807
Thomas MILHOLLEN (br/o John MILHOLLEN dec'd) of Bath Co Va to Patrick MILHOLLEN of Ldn. B/S of 35¾*ac.* Wit: W. S. NEALE, M. SULLIVAN, John HENRY, John McGEATH, Terence FIGH.

Bk:Pg: 2H:106   Date: 12 Jan 1807   RcCt: 12 Jan 1807
William HOUGH Jr. & wife Jane of Ldn to William SMITH of Ldn. A/L of 139*ac* L/L (lives of Easter SCATTERDAY, son John SCATTERDAY, Samuel CRAIG s/o Samuel CRAIG). Wit: John H. CANBY, Edw. McDANIEL, Benjamin KNIGHT.

Bk:Pg: 2H:109   Date: 10 Jan 1807   RcCt: 12 Jan 1807
William HOUGH & wife Eleanor of Ldn to Asa MOORE of Ldn. B/S of 12*ac* on W side of Kittoctan Creek adj Mahlon JANNEY, James MOORE. Wit: Samuel GOVER, Thos. PHILIPS, Joseph TALBOTT, James MOORE.

Bk:Pg: 2H:112   Date: 10 Jan 1807   RcCt: 12 Jan 1807
Mahlon JANNEY of Wtfd to Asa MOORE of Wtfd. B/S of 10500 sq ft lot on W side of main st in Wtfd adj James MOORE. Wit: James MOORE, Jos. TALBOTT, Samuel GOVER, Thomas PHILLIPS.

Bk:Pg: 2H:114   Date: 12 Jan 1807   RcCt: 13 Jan 1807
Charles CRIM of Ldn to John WITTERMAN of Ldn. B/S of 29*ac* on E side of Short Hill. Wit: Edw. McDANIEL, Jos. BRADEN, Leven STEVENS, R. BRADEN.

Bk:Pg: 2H:116   Date: 29 Aug 1799   RcCt: 14 Oct 1799
Thomas CHAPMAN & wife Sally of Ldn to Robert BRADEN of Ldn. B/S of 25*ac* (devised by John EBLIN dec'd). Wit: James McILHANEY, Jos. BRADEN, Isaac VANDEVANTER, John HAMILTON.

Bk:Pg: 2H:120   Date: 26 Apr 1805   RcCt: 9 Sep 1805
William SMITH & wife Hannah of Ldn to Mary SPOONT of Lsbg. B/S of Lot #54 and part of lot adj John McCORMICK in Lsbg. Wit: Hugh DOUGLAS, Fra. H. PEYTON, Jas. CAVAN Jr.

Bk:Pg: 2H:125   Date: 1 Apr 1806   RcCt: 12 Jan 1807
Thomas GREGG (grandson of Thomas GREGG dec'd) & wife Hannah of Ldn to Robert McCULLAH of Ldn. Trust of part of 69*ac* devised to widow

Mary GREGG for life being 14 3/8*ac* (Joseph GREGG, Samuel GREGG, Josiah GREGG and Dinah GREGG now Dinah RODGERS wife of Hamilton ROGERS and Thomas GREGG's part of legacy left Levy GREGG dec'd). Wit: Wm. BRONAUGH, Joseph HAINS, Thomas EWERS, Stacy TAYLOR.

Bk:Pg: 2H:129   Date: 1 Apr 1806   RcCt: 13 Oct 1806
Samuel GREGG & wife Hannah, Thomas GREGG & wife Sarah, Joseph GREGG & wife Mary, Josiah GREGG & wife Margaret and Hamilton ROGERS & wife Dinah of Ldn to Thomas GREGG of Ldn. B/S of the above shares from 14 3/8*ac*. Wit: Wm. BRONAUGH, Joseph HAINS, Thomas EWERS, Stacy TAYLOR.

Bk:Pg: 2H:134   Date: 12 Jan 1807   RcCt: 12 Jan 1807
James CARRUTHERS of Ldn to Josiah HALL of Ldn. B/S of 90 sq poles on NW corner of land CARRUTHERS now lives on, adj Richard WHITE dec'd, William HOMBS. Wit: Daniel WHITE, Daniel LOVETT.

Bk:Pg: 2H:135   Date: 6 Sep 1806   RcCt: 12 Jan 1807
James BRADFIELD & wife Ruth to Lewis ELLZEY of Ldn. B/S of 55½*ac* at top of Short Hill. Wit: James HAMILTON, Stacy TAYLOR, Benj'a BRADFIELD, N. DAVISSON.

Bk:Pg: 2H:139   Date: 10 Jun 1806   RcCt: 13 Jan 1807
John ALEXANDER of Ldn to son Charles Barnes ALEXANDER. Gift of slaves Abraham, Old James & Betsy, also farm and household items. Wit: Fleet SMITH, James RUST, Geo. W. BLINCOE.

Bk:Pg: 2H:140   Date: 10 Jun 1806   RcCt: 13 Jan 1807
John ALEXANDER to daughter Penelope Barnes ALEXANDER. Gift of slaves James, Tom, Davy, Christopher, Niney, Betsey, Lavenia, Judy and Peggy, also farm and household items. Wit: Chas. P. TUTT, Jos. TUTT, Charles B. ALEXANDER.

Bk:Pg: 2H:141   Date: 14 Jun 1806   RcCt: 13 Jan 1807
Jonas POTTS & wife and Jacob BAUGH & wife of Ldn to Colin AULD of AlexVa. Trust for debt to John RAMSEY using 90*ac* abt 4 miles from Lsbg. Wit: Saml. CARR, John H. EVANS, W. M. LITTLEJOHN, Wm. COOKE, John CAVAN.

Bk:Pg: 2H:144   Date: 21 Jun 1806   RcCt: 9 Dec 1806
Cornelius SHAWEN & wife Mary of Ldn to Aaron SAUNDERS of Ldn. Trust for SAUNDERS as security in debt to Timothy HIXON using 41*ac*. Wit: Isaac LAROWE, John SAUNDERS, James CURTIS.

Bk:Pg: 2H:147   Date: 18 Jun 1806   RcCt: 13 Jan 1807
Daniel DUTY to Benjamin Hough CANBY of Lsbg. Relinquishment of mortgage of lot in Lsbg. Wit: Fra. H. PEYTON, Jos. BEARD, John MYERS, O. CLIFFORD.

Bk:Pg: 2H:150   Date: 12 Jan 1807   RcCt: 14 Jan 1807
Francis H. PEYTON (heirs at law of Dade PEYTON dec'd of Lsbg) & wife Frances to William LITTLEJOHN and John Hough CANBY of Lsbg. B/S of 1000*ac* on W ford of Parish Creek in Adams Co Oh (½ of Military Warrant

#3235). Wit: Jas. CAVAN Jr., John PAYNE, Thomas WILKINSON, Leven LUCKETT, William NOLAND.

Bk:Pg: 2H:155   Date: 16 Aug 1806   RcCt: 9 Dec 1806
Henry M. DAVIS & wife Catharine of Lsbg to Aaron SAUNDERS of Ldn. Trust for payment to Deputy Sheriff Benjamin SHREVES as security using 1/9 share of land from Leonard ANSELL dec'd to his children. Wit: Samuel MURREY, Thomas SIM, Sampson BLINCOE.

Bk:Pg: 2H:159   Date: 15 Oct 1806   RcCt: 14 Jan 1807
Armistead T. MASON to Majr. Fleet SMITH. BoS for mulatto boy Billy JACKSON. Wit: Armistead LONG, John LITTLEJOHN.

Bk:Pg: 2H:160   Date: 9 Feb 1807   RcCt: 9 Feb 1807
Jonas JANNEY of Ldn to George TAVENER of Ldn. Release of trust on 142*ac*. Wit: C. BINNS, Isaac LAROWE, Saml. M. EDWARDS.

Bk:Pg: 2H:164   Date: 11 Sep 1805   RcCt: 14 Oct 1805
Thos. Ludwell LEE of Ldn and Landon CARTER of Richmond Co VA as Exors of George CARTER dec'd late of Stafford Co. VA to Thomas HETHERLY of Ldn. B/S of 1*ac* on SW side of Loudoun St Lsbg. Wit: John LYONS, John B. RATHY, Jno. MATHIAS.

Bk:Pg: 2H:167   Date: 7 Apr 1803   RcCt: 14 Oct 1803
Thos. Ludwell LEE of Ldn and Landon CARTER of Richmond Co VA as Exors of George CARTER dec'd late of Stafford Co. VA to Nicholas GARRETT of Md. B/S of 110*ac*. Wit: Edward MUSE, Henry JENKENS, Mark WOOD, John LYONS, John B. RATHY, Jno. MATHIAS.

Bk:Pg: 2H:171   Date: 24 Jan 1807   RcCt: 9 Feb 1807
Bernard CREMAR of Ldn to Bernard MANN. BoS for farm and household items. Wit: Jas. Lewin GIBBS Jr., Thomas MURPHEY, Mahlon FULTON.

Bk:Pg: 2H:173   Date: 2 Jan 1807   RcCt: 9 Feb 1807
Benjamin B. THORNTON to John DRISH. BoS for mulatto woman Lucey. Statement from A. MORRISON stating he has no objection to the sale. Wit: Benj'a SHREVE.

Bk:Pg: 2H:175   Date: 9 Feb 1808[7]   RcCt: 9 Feb 1807
Abner CRAVEN & wife Sarah to Isaac LAROWE. B/S of Sarah CRAVEN's share of land from her father John SINCLAIR dec'd held by his widow Mary who married Israel SEARS.

Bk:Pg: 2H:177   Date: 9 Feb 1808[7]   RcCt: 9 Feb 1807
Isaac LAROWE of Ldn to Edith SINCLAIR and Abner CRAVEN (Admr of Samuel SINCLAIR dec'd). B/S of land that fell to Sarah CRAVEN w/o Abner as in deed above.

Bk:Pg: 2H:179   Date: 22 Nov 1806   RcCt: 9 Feb 1807
John MOORE dec'd. Division of land to Nancy RITACIE (and Elijah RITTEKER) and Sally RUSSELL, each given 100*ac* [gives plat & full description] by Francis PEYTON, John TYLER.

Bk:Pg: 2H:181   Date: 31 Oct 1806   RcCt: 9 Feb 1807
Jacob LEWIS of Ky to Leven POWELL of Ldn. PoA to collect funds from
Thomas FRANCIS. Wit: John DORRELL, Noble BEVERIDGE, Rich'd
COCKRAN, Meshek LACEY.

Bk:Pg: 2H:182   Date: 8 Dec 1806   RcCt: 9 Feb 1807
John LOVE of Ldn to William DANIEL & Benjamin DANIEL of Ldn. B/S of
106½ac (from will of William DANIEL dec'd). Wit: Stacy TAYLOR, George
BROWN, Samuel PURSEL.

Bk:Pg: 2H:185   Date: 26 Dec 1806   RcCt: 9 Feb 1807
Phinehas THOMAS of Ldn to John THOMAS of Ldn. B/S of 150ac adj
Joseph JANNEY, William LODGE, Samuel PALMER. Wit: Matthias
HAYS, Jacob THOMAS, Evan THOMAS.

Bk:Pg: 2H:187   Date: 4 Feb 1807   RcCt: 9 Feb 1807
Daniel CASEY of Ldn to Robert BRADEN of Ldn. BoS for farm and
household items. Wit: Isaac HOUGH, John B. STEVEN, James CASEY.

Bk:Pg: 2H:190   Date: 5 Oct 1806   RcCt: 12 Jan 1807
Bertrand EWELL of Lsbg to Fleet SMITH and Armistead LONG of Lsbg.
Trust for debt to merchants James HORTON & John CLARKE of Balt of 2
parts of Lot #35 in Lsbg. Wit: Josiah MOFFETT, Daniel DOWLING, Saml.
M. EDWARDS.

Bk:Pg: 2H:195   Date: 17 Nov 1806   RcCt: 9 Feb 1807
Albert RUSSELL & wife Ann F. H. of Ldn to Catesby GRAHAM of Fqr. B/S
of 692 2/3ac (from patent of Pres. Thomas JEFFERSON). Wit: Jno.
BAYLY, Thomas MARSHALL, Leven POWELL Jr., Wm. Grayson ORR,
Levi DOUGLAS, Thomas VANHORNE.

Bk:Pg: 2H:199   Date: 26 Nov 1806   RcCt: 8 Dec 1806
George TAVENER Jr. & wife Martha (signed Patty) of Ldn to Burr
POWELL of Ldn. Trust for debt to Given HANDY (Admr of John HANDY
dec'd) using 190ac. Wit: C. BINNS, Eli OFFUTT, Saml. M. EDWARDS,
Isaac LAROWE, John LITTLEJOHN, Samuel MURREY.

Bk:Pg: 2H:204   Date: 9 Sep 1806   RcCt: 12 Dec 1806
Thomas MILHOLLEN of Bath Co Va to Richard GRIFFITH & Moses
CALDWELL of Ldn. Trust for debt to Patrick MILHOLLEN for Jonathan
MILHOLLEN's part of his brother John's estate using 1000ac + Grist Mill
in Bath Co. Wit: Joseph TALBOTT, Joshua HENRY, W. S. NEALE.

Bk:Pg: 2H:207   Date: 9 Feb 1807   RcCt: 9 Feb 1807
Lindores LUCAS of Ldn to Jacob WALTMAN of Ldn. BoS for negro man
Giles age 24y. Wit: Chs. VEALE, Barton LUCAS, C. BINNS, Isaac
LAROWE.

Bk:Pg: 2H:208   Date: 17 Oct 1804   RcCt: 11 Feb 1806
Jacob STONEBURNER & wife Barbara of Ldn to John HAMILTON of
Ldn. B/S of 102ac at mouth of Tasner's branch. Wit: Francis WHITELY,
William BALL, Cullep STONEBURNER, Burr POWELL, Wm.
BRONAUGH.

Bk:Pg: 2H:213   Date: 5 Sep 1806   RcCt: 13 Jan 1807
Bertrand EWELL of Lsbg to Fleet SMITH of Lsbg. Trust for debt to merchants Jacob & William BALTZELL of Balt using slave girl Daphne abt 14y and Belinda abt 12y old. Wit: John H. McCABE, John NEWTON.

Bk:Pg: 2H:216   Date: 21 Jan 1807   RcCt: 10 Feb 1807
Charles P. TUTT of Ldn to Thomas SWANN of AlexVa. Mortgage on household items and slave man Jack abt 27y, Hannah abt 45y, Martha & her children James, Betty and young one unnamed.

Bk:Pg: 2H:219   Date: 10 Feb 1807   RcCt: 10 Feb 1807
Jonas POTTS, John SCHOOLEY & Obadiah CLIFFORD (appt. com. to sell property of Jacob JACOBS dec'd) to Benjamin SHREVE. B/S of Lot #8 in Lsbg.

Bk:Pg: 2H:221   Date: 14 Jan 1807   RcCt: 11 Feb 1807
William WOODDY & wife Nanny of Lsbg to Jesse DAILEY of Lsbg. B/S of ½ac adj Lsbg on Royal St. Wit: John LITTLEJOHN, Samuel MURREY, John WOODDY.

Bk:Pg: 2H:225   Date: 29 Oct 1804   RcCt: 16 Jan 1805
William LITTLEJOHN of Ldn to James GARDINER of Ldn. B/S of 6ac nr Lsbg adj Poor House, Giles TILLETT, Charles BINNS. Wit: John H. EVANS, Willey JANES, Jonas POTTS.

Bk:Pg: 2H:227   Date: 14 Apr 1807   RcCt: 15 Apr 1807
Jesse HIRST & wife Mary of Ldn to widow Eliza & John ZIMMERMAN (Admr of Henry ZIMMERMAN dec'd of AlexVa). B/S of 47ac. Children of Henry ZIMMERMAN dec'd are Eliza, John, Jacob, George <21y, Catharine <21y, Adam <21y, Henry <21y & Samuel <21y Zimmerman and Susanna SIMPSON.

Bk:Pg: 2H:230   Date: 10 Apr 1807   RcCt: 13 Apr 1807
Samuel CLAPHAM & wife Elisa of Ldn to John STOUTSEBERGER of Ldn. B/S of 100ac of "Western Mountain Land" adj Henry TAYLOR, Thomas JOHNSTON. Wit: John HAMILTON, Tho. JOHNSON 3rd, Thomas SCHLEY, William NOLAND.

Bk:Pg: 2H:233   Date: 23 Mar 1807   RcCt: 14 Apr 1807
Elisha GREGG & wife Martha of Ldn to son George GREGG of Ldn. Gift of 100ac on Limestone Run adj Isaac LAROWE. Wit: Isaac LAROWE.

Bk:Pg: 2H:234   Date: 17 Oct 1806   RcCt: 15 Apr 1807
Elijah COE of Ldn to John WOOLFCAIL Sr. of Ldn. L/L (lives of Elijah, wife Ann & son Hezekiah COE) of lot in ShelP between short hill and blue ridge adj Samuel YOUNG, Jonathan MATTHEWS, John CAMPBELL, John MILLER. Wit: Saml. W. YOUNG, James H. HAMILTON, John WOLFCALE Jr., Chs. BINNS, Isaac LAROWE, Chas. ELGIN.

Bk:Pg: 2H:238   Date: 14 Jan 1807   RcCt: 16 Apr 1807
Isaac & Samuel NICHOLS. Receipt for payment from Peter BOSS on trust of land in Lsbg. Wit: Phebe NICHOLS.

Bk:Pg: 2H:238   Date: 22 Nov 1806   RcCt: 15 Apr 1807
Burr POWELL & wife Catharine of Ldn to Daniel REES of Ldn. B/S of
25¼*ac*. Wit: Jno. B. SPEAKE, Thomas RUSSELL, Samuel N. GALLIHER.

Bk:Pg: 2H:240   Date: 13 Oct 1806   RcCt: 16 Apr 1807
George WARNER & wife Sarah of Ldn to Robert BRADEN of Ldn. B/S of
14*ac*. Wit: Tho. HOUGH, William DODD, Thomas D. STEVENS, Leven
STEVENS, Josiah WHITE, Jos. WILDMAN.

Bk:Pg: 2H:242   Date: 13 Oct 1807   RcCt: 16 Apr 1807
Thomas HOUGH & wife Mary of Ldn to George WARNER of Ldn. B/S of
186*ac* adj William BROWN. Wit: Thomas D. STEVENS, William DODD,
Leven STEVENS, R. BRADEN, Josiah WHITE, Joshua WILDMAN, Stacy
TAYLOR, Lewis ELZEY.

Bk:Pg: 2H:245   Date: 11 Apr 1807   RcCt: 16 Apr 1807
Charles Fenton MERCER (heir of James MERCER dec'd) of Ldn to John
SINCLAIR of Ldn. B/S of 30*ac* on Little River adj Matthew RUST, Joseph
DANIEL.

Bk:Pg: 2H:247   Date: 11 Apr 1807   RcCt: 16 Apr 1807
Charles Fenton MERCER (heir of James MERCER dec'd) of Ldn to
Joseph DANIEL of Ldn. B/S of 20*ac* adj James HIXON, Thomas
OWSLEY.

Bk:Pg: 2H:249   Date: 9 Apr 1807   RcCt: 16 Apr 1807
Isaac NICHOLS & wife Rebecca of Ldn to Moses DILLON of Ldn.
Relinquishment of mortgage. Wit: Abdon DILLON, Stacy TAYLOR, John
TRIBBEY.

Bk:Pg: 2H:250   Date: 16 Apr 1807   RcCt: 16 Apr 1807
Moses DILLON & wife Rebecca of Ldn to Isaac NICHOLS of Ldn. B/S of
145*ac* on Kittocton Creek adj Israel HOWELL, William HOWELL, Samuel
PURSEL, Abdon DILLON. Wit: Stacy TAYLOR, Abdon DILLON, John
TRIBBEY.

Bk:Pg: 2H:253   Date: 16 Sep 1806   RcCt: 16 Apr 1807
Obediah CLIFFORD of Lsbg to Thomas DARNE of Ldn. Trust for debt to
Ludwell LEE & Stephen COOKE as security using lot adj Presbyterian
Meeting House, negro woman Mary, farm and household items. Wit:
Alex'r. COUPER Jr., Tho. SANDERS, John SHAW.

Bk:Pg: 2H:255   Date: 14 Oct 1806   RcCt: 16 Apr 1807
John BALL & wife Susan of Ldn to Henry HOUGH of Ldn. B/S of 100*ac*
on Broad Run at mouth of Balls Mill Tail and 97½*ac*. Wit: John MATHIAS,
Jas. CAVAN Jr., Thos. WILKINSON.

Bk:Pg: 2H:257   Date: 12 Apr 1806   RcCt: 12 May 1806
George BARR & Adam BARR of Ldn to William P. HALE of Fqr. B/S of
30*ac* nr Wancapin Branch. Wit: Abner GIBSON, Jesse McVEIGH, Peter
MYERS, Samuel HENDERSON.

Bk:Pg: 2H:259   Date: 10 Jan 1807   RcCt: 14 Apr 1807
William SMITH & wife Sarah of Ldn to Jonathan SWIFT of AlexVa. B/S of 214*ac* on Rocky branch. Wit: John LITTLEJOHN, Samuel MURREY, Isaac HARRIS.

Bk:Pg: 2H:263   Date: 24 Oct 1806   RcCt: 11 May 1807
Col. Leven POWELL of Ldn to Leven POWELL Jr. of Mdbg. B/S of 5*ac* & 10 1/6*ac* lots on both sides of Mdbg Meeting House.

Bk:Pg: 2H:265   Date: 13 Jan 1807   RcCt: 11 May 1807
John DEMERY of Ldn to Jacob VERTS of Ldn. BoS for negro wench abt 20y girl abt 6y old. Wit: James VEER, J. HARDING, Saml. McPHERSON.

Bk:Pg: 2H:266   Date: 12 Nov 1806   RcCt: 11 May 1807
William HUTCHISON & wife Nancy to Reuben HUTCHISON. CoE for sale of land. Wit: Israel LACEY, Ariss BUCKNER.

Bk:Pg: 2H:267   Date: 21 Nov 1806   RcCt: 11 May 1807
Samuel GIBSON (s/o Isaac GIBSON dec'd of Ldn) to James BOYLES of Ldn. B/S of 32½*ac* (part of 260*acc* Isaac purchased from Alice GIBSON). Wit: Thomas WRENN, John LOGAN, Israel HICKS.

Bk:Pg: 2H:269   Date: 1 Jan 1807   RcCt: 11 May 1807
Moses GIBSON Jr. (s/o Isaac GIBSON dec'd) & wife Betsey W. of Ldn to James BOYLES of Ldn. B/S of 32½*ac* [see 2H:267]. Wit: Thos. WRENN, Amos DENHAM, Samuel GIBSON, Ben. GRAYSON, Joseph CARR.

Bk:Pg: 2H:272   Date: 27 Jan 1807   RcCt: 11 May 1807
John THRELKELD of DC to John EBLEN of Roan Co Tn. B/S of __*ac* adj William WHITE. Wit: Danl. REINTZEL.

Bk:Pg: 2H:275   Date: 11 May 1807   RcCt: 11 May 1807
John SPENCER (Exor of Nathan SPENCER dec'd) of Ldn to Stephen WILSON of Ldn. B/S of 183*ac* adj John SPENCER, Benjamin BRADFIELD.

Bk:Pg: 2H:277   Date: 31 Mar 1807   RcCt: 11 May 1807
Jacob AXLINE & wife Catharine of Ldn to Anthony CONNARD of Ldn. B/S of Catharine's 1/5 share of land of George MOUL & Daniel MOUL dec'd. Wit: Philip H. MOUL, Philip HUFF, Joshua McGEATH.

Bk:Pg: 2H:279   Date: 17 Sep 1806   RcCt: 20 Oct 1806
Daniel McCARTY & wife Matilda of Ffx to Thomas SWANN of AlexVa. Trust for debt to Robert T. HOOE & Co. using land nr Potomac. Wit: B. BRASHEARS, Edward SOMMERS, Thomas PEAKE.

Bk:Pg: 2H:283   Date: 15 Apr 1807   RcCt: 11 May 1807
Nathan HUTCHISON & wife Hannah to Susannah HUMPHREY. B/S of Hannah's child's portion of 2 lots of father William HUMPHREY dec'd. Wit: Israel LACEY, Ariss BUCKNER, Chas. LEWIS.

Bk:Pg: 2H:286   Date: 6 Feb 1807   RcCt: 11 May 1807
Jacob FILLER of Ldn to Adam SHOVER, William WINNER & John SANBOWER of Ldn. BoS for farm and household items. Wit: Benjamin SHREVE, Henry HUFF, Chas. ELGIN.

Bk:Pg: 2H:287   Date: 9 Mar 1807   RcCt: 11 May 1807
Moses MILLER & wife Christiana of Ldn to Stiles JACKSON of Ldn. B/S of 22*ac* on Broad Run adj John JACKSON, Jacob EMERY. Wit: W. S. NEALE, Richard GRIFFITH, John JACKSON.

Bk:Pg: 2H:290   Date: 25 Apr 1807   RcCt: 11 May 1807
John HEAD & wife Elizabeth of Ldn to Stephen WILSON of Ldn. B/S of 60*ac* on NW fork of Goose Creek. Wit: Lewis ELLZEY, Jesse SILCOTT, Thomas GREGG, John H. CANBY, John H. EVANS, Samuel MURREY, F. H. PEYTON.

Bk:Pg: 2H:293   Date: __ May 1807   RcCt: 11 May 1807
Thomas SIM of Ldn to Jacob WALTMAN. BoS for negro Tom and Jesse each abt 36y old. Wit: S. BLINCOE.

Bk:Pg: 2H:294   Date: 28 Nov 1806   RcCt: 11 May 1807
John SPENCER & wife Phebe of Wood Co Va to Israel LACEY, Stephen BEARD & Charles LEWIS of Ldn. Trust for debts to Cuthbert POWELL using 101*ac* where James H. BRADSHAW now lives, adj Benjamin JAMES nr road from Gumspring to Little River Meeting house and 51*ac* on branch of Broad Run. Wit: Robert J. TAYLOR, Thomas SWANN, Thos. W. POWELL, Leven POWELL.

Bk:Pg: 2H:297   Date: 11 May 1807   RcCt: 11 May 1807
William P. HALE of Fqr to James KINCHELOE to Fqr. B/S of ½*ac* Lot #17 in Mdbg.

Bk:Pg: 2H:299   Date: 30 Mar 1807   RcCt: 11 May 1807
Jacob G. PEARCE of Amherst Co Va to Sally VANHORN of Ldn. Gift of negro girl Gracey. Wit: Thomas VANHORN, William WALKER, Richard WILSON.

Bk:Pg: 2H:300   Date: 12 Aug 1803   RcCt: 12 Dec 1803
Dorcas CLAPHAM (wd/o Josias CLAPHAM) to Samuel CLAPHAM (s/o Josias). B/S of her widow's interest in estate. Wit: Saml. LUCKETT, William DULIN.

Bk:Pg: 2H:301   Date: 12 Aug 1803   RcCt: 12 Dec 1803
Dorcas CLAPHAM (wd/o Josias CLAPHAM) to Samuel CLAPHAM (s/o Josias). B/S of her $1000 annuity. Wit: Saml. LUCKETT, William DULIN.

Bk:Pg: 2H:301   Date: 12 Aug 1803   RcCt: 12 Dec 1803
Dorcas CLAPHAM to Samuel CLAPHAM. B/S of negroes Gin or Jinny daughter to Flora, Cibbey, Basil, his wife Hannah and their children Winney, Sam, Barbara & Jesse (bequeathed to her from late husband's estate); gives up rights to all negroes except girl Kit. Wit: Saml. LUCKETT, William DULIN.

Bk:Pg: 2H:302   Date: 11 May 1807   RcCt: 11 May 1807
Charles Fenton MERCER (Admr of James MERCER dec'd) to Moses DILLON of Ldn. Relinquishment of mortgage. Wit: Isaac LAROWE, Saml. M. EDWARDS, Eli OFFUTT.

Bk:Pg: 2H:304   Date: 2 Jan 1807   RcCt: 9 Feb 1807
Robert C. NEWTON of Ldn to John NEWTON. BoS for farm and
household items. Wit: C. BINNS.

Bk:Pg: 2H:305   Date: 21 Apr 1808[7]   RcCt: 11 May 1807
Henry HUFF of Ldn to John BALL of Ldn. B/S of 100*ac* on Broad Run at
mouth of Balls Mill Tail and 97½*ac*. Wit: John HALL, Isaac HOUGH, John
SLATER, Tunis TITUS, John McKEMIE.

Bk:Pg: 2H:307   Date: 24 Oct 1806   RcCt: 11 May 1807
Jesse JOHNSTON & wife Susannah (late Susannah BUTCHER Exor of
John BUTCHER dec'd) of Ky to Benjamin GRAYSON of Ldn. PoA. Wit:
Thomas BARTON, John KENDRICKS Jr., Benjamin GRAYSON Jr.

Bk:Pg: 2H:308   Date: 23 Apr 1807   RcCt: 11 May 1807
Leonard ANSELL & wife Susannah of Ldn to Aaron SANDERS and
Sampson BLINCOE of Ldn. Trust for debt to SANDERS, using 1/9th share
of land of Leonard ANSELL dec'd to BLINCOE. Wit: Nicholas FRY, Martin
ANSELL, Margaret SPRING.

Bk:Pg: 2H:311   Date: 7 May 1807   RcCt: 11 May 1807
Robert PARFECT & wife Jane of Ldn to Charles BINNS of Ldn. B/S of 1a
adj BINNS allowing L/L of Robert NEWTON & wife Ann (children John
Cunningham, Elizabeth Lee & Robert Cummingham NEWTON all <21y)
to occupy. Wit: Eli OFFUTT, Saml. M. EDWARDS, George HAMMAT.

Bk:Pg: 2H:314   Date: 13 Mar 1806   RcCt: 8 Sep 1807
George SWANK & wife Margaret of Ldn and John SLACK & wife
Elizabeth of Ldn to John SHAVER of Ldn. B/S of their shares of 121*ac*
from land of John SWANK dec'd who died intestate (children are Philip
Michael, Margaret, Catharine, Susan and George SWANK and Elizabeth
SWANK who married John SLACK, dower to widow Catharine SWANK).
Wit: John HAMILTON, James HAMILTON, Philip EVERHART.

Bk:Pg: 2H:318   Date: 26 Oct 1806   RcCt: 11 May 1807
John SEIVER & wife Polley (d/o John SWANK) of Rockingham Co Va to
John SHAVER of Ldn. B/S of Polley's share of father's land (see 2H:314).
Wit: James HAMILTON, Richard GRIFFITH, George SHUMAKER, Simon
SHUMAKER.

Bk:Pg: 2H:321   Date: 5 Mar 1806   RcCt: 9 Sep 1806
Philip SWANK & wife Margaret, Michael SWANK, Margaret SWANK,
Catharine SWANK and John TRITIPEAU & wife Susan of Ldn to John
SHAVER of Ldn. B/S of their shares of father's land (see 2H:314). Wit:
John HAMILTON, Adam SHOVER, James HAMILTON, Saml.
PEIRPOINT, Francis WHITELY, William ALT, name in German.

Bk:Pg: 2H:326   Date: 11 Sep 1805   RcCt: 9 Dec 1805
Thomas Ludwell LEE of Ldn & Landon CARTER of RichVA (Exor of
George CARTER dec'd of StafVa) to William SMITH of Ldn. B/S of 2*ac* on
N side of Loudoun St in Lsbg. Wit: John LYONS, John B. RATHIE, Jno.
MATHIAS.

Bk:Pg: 2H:329   Date: 22 Apr 1807   RcCt: 12 May 1807
Elijah RITTAKER/RITICOR & wife Nancy (d/o John MOORE dec'd) of Ldn
to Jacob ISH of Ldn. B/S of 5 1/8*ac* on Old Turnpike Road nr Ish's house.
Wit: John TYLER, Israel LACEY, J. H. SCHOLFIELD.

Bk:Pg: 2H:332   Date: 5 Jan 1807   RcCt: 12 May 1807
Joseph JANNEY & wife Mary of Ldn to Phinehas THOMAS of Ldn. B/S of
5¾*ac* on Lsbg Rd adj John HESSKETT. Wit: Jacob THOMAS, Amos
JANNEY, Matthias HAYS?

Bk:Pg: 2H:334   Date: 17 Mar 1806   RcCt: 8 Sep 1806
Joseph JONES (s/o Joseph JONES dec'd of Ldn) to James SWART of
Ldn. B/S of 283½*ac* on Little River. Wit: Jno. BAYLY, Charles B.
ALEXANDER, Elijah RITICOR.

Bk:Pg: 2H:337   Date: 21 Oct 1806   RcCt: 12 May 1807
William H. HARDING & wife Ann ALEX'R of JeffVa to Dr. Thomas SIM of
Lsbg. B/S of 171¼*ac*. Wit: John H. CANBY, Chas. LOBB, Wm. Byrd
PAGE, John D. ORR, Wm. LITTLEJOHN.

Bk:Pg: 2H:340   Date: 12 May 1807   RcCt: 12 May 1807
William Butler HARRISON & wife Penelope of Ldn to William ELLZEY of
Ldn. B/S of a 1641*ac* ELLZEY is entitled to of 3 tracts (500*ac*, 1730*ac* &
826 1/3a on little Miami River) granted Penelope by Mil. War. #3630 &
#3631.

Bk:Pg: 2H:342   Date: 12 May 1807   RcCt: 12 May 1807
William Butler HARRISON & wife Penelope of Ldn to William ELLZEY of
Ldn. B/S of a 307 9/13*ac* ELLZEY is entitled to of 1000a granted to
HARRISON by Mil War #1774.

Bk:Pg: 2H:344   Date: 1 Sep 1806   RcCt: 12 May 1807
Thomas SANDERS of Lsbg to John PAYNE of Lsbg. B/S of ¼*ac* or
easternmost ½ of Lot #42 in Lsbg. Wit: Samuel HOUGH, Daniel
DOWLING, James GARNER.

Bk:Pg: 2H:346   Date: 23 Apr 1807   RcCt: 13 May 1807
Aaron SANDERS of Ldn to Leonard ANSELL of Ldn. B/S of 1/9 of land of
Leonard ANSELL dec'd conveyed in trust to SAUNDERS by Henry M.
DAVIS & wife Catharine. Wit: S. BLINCOE, Nicholas FRY, Martin
ANSELL.

Bk:Pg: 2H:348   Date: 23 Mar 1807   RcCt: 13 May 1807
John DRISH & wife Eleanor of Ldn to Sarah MURRAY (d/o Samuel &
Betsey MURREY) of Ldn. B/S of lot at end of King St in Lsbg between
Joseph GORE and Martin CORDELL. Wit: Isaac HARRIS, W. JANES,
George HAMMAT, Presly CORDELL.

Bk:Pg: 2H:350   Date: 16 Apr 1807   RcCt: 16 Apr 1807
John A. BINNS & wife Dewanner of Ldn to Charles BINNS of Ldn. B/S of
704*ac* on little Miami River in Ohio.

Bk:Pg: 2H:353   Date: 16 Apr 1807   RcCt: 16 Apr 1807
John A. BINNS & wife Dewanner of Ldn to William ELLZEY of Ldn. B/S of
441ac on little Miami River in Ohio.

Bk:Pg: 2H:355   Date: 20 May 1807   RcCt: 13 Jul 1807
Charles THRIFT of Ldn to William THRIFT of Ldn. Mortgage using negro
man Aleck. Wit: Saml. M. EDWARDS, Eli OFFUTT, Chas. ELGIN.

Bk:Pg: 2H:356   Date: 14 Apr 1807   RcCt: 13 Jul 1807
Benjamin B. THORNTON of Ldn to John HAWLING of Ldn. BoS for negro
Westward abt 2y old. Release of claim by A. MORRISON. Wit: Isaac
LAROWE, Saml. M. EDWARDS, Eli OFFUTT.

Bk:Pg: 2H:357   Date: 8 Jul 1807   RcCt: 13 Jul 1807
Anthony AMOND of Ldn to Peter HICKMAN of Ldn. B/S of 203ac on
Catocton adj Conrod SHAVER. Wit: John HAMILTON, Henry HUFF, John
STOUSEBERGER, John STEEFLER Jr., Gasper TROUT.

Bk:Pg: 2H:360   Date: 26 Nov 1806   RcCt: 11 May 1807
David JAMES of Ldn to Augustine LOVE of Ldn. Release of mortgage.
Wit: Simon TRIPLETT, John SINCLAIR, Jesse HARRIS, Geo. LOVE.

Bk:Pg: 2H:362   Date: 24 Jun 1807   RcCt: 13 Jul 1807
Augustine LOVE & wife Mary of Ldn to Daniel BROWN of Ldn. B/S of
36ac. Wit: Saml. BOGGESS, Timothy TAYLOR, Matthew RUST, Simon
TRIPLETT, Stephen C. ROSZEL.

Bk:Pg: 2H:365   Date: 27 Nov 1806   RcCt: 13 Jul 1807
Augustine LOVE & wife Mary of Ldn to David JAMES of Ldn. B/S of
192¼ac on road from Browns Mill to Beaverdam. Wit: Simon TRIPLETT,
John SINCLAIR, Jesse HARRIS, Geo. LOVE, Wm. BRONAUGH.

Bk:Pg: 2H:369   Date: 8 May 1807   RcCt: 13 Jul 1807
Mary (Molley) Ann LUCKETT, Samuel N. LUCKETT & wife Patience,
William M. LUCKETT, Craven LUCKETT, Elizabeth N. LUCKETT & Mary
D. LUCKETT of Jefferson Co Ky (widow & legal reps of John M.
LUCKETT dec'd) to Philip H. LUCKETT of Ldn. PoA for sale of Lsbg lot to
William CHILTON. Wit: Wm. LITTLEJOHN, James DENNY, Saml. N.
LUCKETT.

Bk:Pg: 2H:371   Date: 11 Jul 1807   RcCt: 13 Jul 1807
Mary (Molley) Ann LUCKETT, Samuel N. LUCKETT & wife Patience,
William M. LUCKETT, Craven LUCKETT, Elizabeth N. LUCKETT & Mary
D. LUCKETT of Jefferson Co Ky (widow & legal reps of John M.
LUCKETT dec'd) to William CHILTON of Ldn. B/S of ½ac lot on Cornwall
St in Lsbg. Wit: Samuel MURREY, O. CLIFFORD, Joseph KNOX.

Bk:Pg: 2H:374   Date: 18 Jun 1807   RcCt: 13 Jul 1807
Jonas POTTS and Obadiah CLIFFORD of Ldn to James DAWSON of
Lsbg. Trust for debt DAWSON owes to Roberts & Griffith of DC using
brick house & lot in Lsbg. Wit: John HANBY, Thos. WILKINSON, John H.
EVANS, Isaac LAROWE, Saml. M. EDWARDS, Jas. CAVAN Jr.

Bk:Pg: 2H:377   Date: 8 Jun 1807   RcCt: 13 Jul 1807
James DAWSON (free negro) & wife Polly of Lsbg to Peter F. MARBLE of
Lsbg. B/S of lot on Loudoun St in Lsbg adj James & John CAVAN as heirs
of Patrick CAVAN dec'd. Wit: Thos. FOUCH, Samuel MURREY, Jonas
POTTS, John CAVAN.

Bk:Pg: 2H:382   Date: 10 Aug 1807   RcCt: 10 Aug 1807
Benjamin GRAYSON, William BRONAUGH, James HEATON, Matthew
RUST & Stacy TAYLOR. Bond on GRAYSON as Sheriff to collect levies.

Bk:Pg: 2H:383   Date: 10 Aug 1807   RcCt: 10 Aug 1807
Benjamin GRAYSON, William BRONAUGH, James HEATON, Matthew
RUST & Stacy TAYLOR. Bond on GRAYSON as Sheriff to collect officers
fees.

Bk:Pg: 2H:383   Date: 10 Aug 1807   RcCt: 10 Aug 1807
Benjamin GRAYSON, William BRONAUGH, James HEATON, Matthew
RUST & Stacy TAYLOR. Bond on GRAYSON as Sheriff to collect taxes.

Bk:Pg: 2H:386   Date: 10 Aug 1807   RcCt: 11 Aug 1807
Receipts for prisoners in jail under Sheriff Hugh DOUGLAS: John HOUCH
assignee of Jacob HOUCH agt. Saml. HOUGH. Edward CUNNARD
assignee of Jacob SHOPE agt. Saml. HOUGH. Eleazer THOMAS at the
suit of THOMPSON & others trustees of O. CLIFFORD.

Bk:Pg: 2H:386   Date: 8 Jun 1807   RcCt: 14 Sep 1807
George TAVENER & Joseph WHITE (Exors of George NIXON dec'd) of
Ldn to William CARR of Ldn. B/S of 84ac on NW fork of Goose Creek adj
Edward COE. Wit: John NEWTON, Edward RINKER, Francis TRIPLETT.

Bk:Pg: 2H:388   Date: 28 Aug 1804   RcCt: 9 Apr 1805
Ferdinando FAIRFAX of JeffVa to Joseph LEWIS Jr. of Ldn. B/S of 310ac
adj Edward McDANIEL, Joseph THOMPSON, Richard BROWN, Thomas
TREBBE, Samuel CLENDENNING, Jonah THOMPSON, Hannah
MILLER, Jonathan LODGE. Wit: Richard Bland LEE, Wm. H. HARDING,
Wm. GIBBS.

Bk:Pg: 2H:391   Date: 4 Oct 1805   RcCt: 10 Feb 1806
Ebenezer WILSON & wife Hannah of Ldn to Thomas LESLIE of Va. B/S
of 75½ac on S side of Blue Ridge adj Wm. JONES. Wit: Jacob
BARTHOLOMEW, Thomas KIDWELL, Jane WILSON, Jeremiah BYRNE,
Wm. H. HARDING, Wm. B. HARRISON, Alex'r DOWE.

Bk:Pg: 2H:394   Date: 14 Sep 1807   RcCt: 14 Sep 1807
David POTTS of Ldn to George ABLE of Ldn. B/S of 2ac at between the
Hills.

Bk:Pg: 2H:395   Date: 17 Aug 1807   RcCt: 14 Sep 1807
Thomas LYNE & wife Mary of Fluvanna Co Va to William LYNE of Ldn.
B/S of lands of Thomas LYNE dec'd. Wit: William HUTCHISON, Jeremiah
HUTCHISON 3rd, Timothy LYNE, John PALMER, Lewis HUTCHISON,
Robt. LYNE, Sandford LYNE.

Bk:Pg: 2H:396   Date: ___ 1807   RcCt: 14 Sep 1807
Isaac RICHARDS & wife Deborah of Ldn to David THARP of Ldn. B/S of
1ac on road leading to Ebenezer Meeting House, adj John RALPH.

Bk:Pg: 2H:398   Date: 12 Sep 1807   RcCt: 14 Sep 1807
John WOLFCALE & wife Beulah of Ldn to Samuel EVANS of Ldn. B/S of
¼ac where WOLFCAILE now resides in Hllb. Wit: Joseph TRIBBEY,
William CLENDENING, Samuel CLENDENING.

Bk:Pg: 2H:399   Date: 10 Jun 1807   RcCt: 14 Sep 1807
Jesse HARRIS & wife Margaret of Ldn to friend Augustine LOVE. PoA for
income from Exors of George NIXON dec'd. Wit: Traves WREN, William
HARRIS, Richard VANPELT.

Bk:Pg: 2H:400   Date: 11 Apr 1807   RcCt: 11 Sep 1807
Nicholas OSBURN & wife Elizabeth of Ldn to James COCKRANE of Ldn.
B/S of 100ac on NW fork of Goose Creek adj Abel MARKS, John
BROWN, James HEATON. Wit: Tholemeah RHODES, Charles
BENNETT Jr., James GRADY, Stacy TAYLOR, Notley C. WILLIAMS.

Bk:Pg: 2H:403   Date: 2 Feb 1807   RcCt: 14 Sep 1807
Samuel (signed as Edward) SPENCER & wife Alice of JeffVa to Benjamin
BRADFIELD of Ldn. B/S of 9ac adj Benjamin MEAD, Stephen WILSON,
Nathan SPENCER. Wit: Edward CUNARD Sr., Edmond SPENCER,
Thomas SHUBRIDGE, Lewis ELLZEY, Jacob HROESIN, Stacey
TAYLOR.

Bk:Pg: 2H:407   Date: 31 Aug 1807   RcCt: 14 Sep 1807
Lukner MIDDLETON of Ldn to son Studley Middleton of Ldn. Gift of
Lukner's rights to estate of his son John lately dec'd, Studley to support
Lukner in old age. Wit: Leven POWELL, A. GIBSON, Amos JOHNSTON,
Noble BEVERAGE.

Bk:Pg: 2H:408   Date: 2 Aug 1807   RcCt: 14 Sep 1807
Jonathan TAYLOR & wife Ann of Mt Pleasant Township, Jefferson Co
Ohio to Jonas JANNEY of Ldn. B/S of 309ac adj William WEST, Thomas
GREGG. Wit: Mary GRUBB, George JAMES, Mary HOBSON.

Bk:Pg: 2H:410   Date: 27 Feb 1807   RcCt: 14 Sep 1807
David Fensall BEALL of Ldn to William BEST of Ldn. BoS for negro
woman Dinah abt 23y old and her 4 month old child. Wit: Giles CRAVEN,
Thomas BEST, Edward CUNARD Jr.

Bk:Pg: 2H:411   Date: 1 Feb 1806   RcCt: 14 Jul 1806
John SPENCER of Wood Co Va to Isaac WYCKOFF of Ldn. B/S of 24ac
on Gumspring Rd adj George STEVENS. Wit: Benjamin JAMES,
Cornelius WYCKOFF, Eden B. MOORE.

Bk:Pg: 2H:413   Date: 4 Apr 1807   RcCt: 14 Sep 1807
George RICHTER & wife Susanna of Ldn to Anthony CUNARD of Ldn.
B/S of Susanna's 1/5 share of lands of George MOUL & Daniel MOUL
dec'd. Wit: George HUFF, John TODHUNTER, Isaac LAROWE, Philip H.
MOUL.

Bk:Pg: 2H:414   Date: 7 Mar 1807   RcCt: 11 May 1807
William JAY & wife Anna of Ldn to Moses MILLER of Ldn. B/S of 88*ac* adj George SHOEMAKER Jr., Henry Joseph FRYE, Peter VERTZ, Jeremiah PURDOM. Wit: Chas. BENNETT, Richard GRIFFITH, Thomas PHILLIPS, Pateson WRIGHT.

Bk:Pg: 2H:417   Date: 14 Sep 1807   RcCt: 14 Sep 1807
Joseph SMITH & wife Margaret of Ldn to Philip COOPER of Ldn. B/S of 51¼*ac* adj Peter VIRTS, John WITTERMAN.

Bk:Pg: 2H:419   Date: 14 Sep 1807   RcCt: 14 Sep 1807
Joshua OSBURN of Ldn to William CARTER of Ldn. B/S of 43*ac*.

Bk:Pg: 2H:421   Date: 3 Jul 1807   RcCt: 14 Sep 1807
Enos GARROTT & wife Elenor of Ldn to Thomas TRIBBY of Ldn. B/S of 158*ac* in Piedmont adj Richard BROWN. Wit: Lewis ELLZEY, Stacy TAYLOR, Amos BEANS.

Bk:Pg: 2H:425   Date: 10 Aug 1807   RcCt: 10 Aug 1807
Stacy TAYLOR, George NICKOLS, Thomas LESLIE & Stephen C. ROSZEL. Bond on TAYLOR as Coroner

Bk:Pg: 2I:001   Date: 2 Jul 1807   RcCt: 14 Sep 1807
Thomas TRIBBY & wife Ruth of Ldn to Enos GARROTT of Ldn. Mortgage on land where TRIBBY resides. Wit: Stacy TAYLOR, Lewis ELLZEY, Amos BEANS, James TRIBBY.

Bk:Pg: 2I:004   Date: 10 Jan 1807   RcCt: 12 Jan 1807
Leven POWELL of Mdbg to Amos JOHNSTON of Mdbg. LS of ½*ac* Lot #16 in Mdbg. Wit: Leven POWELL Jr., A. GIBSON, John UPP.

Bk:Pg: 2I:007   Date: 8 Jun 1807   RcCt: 14 Sep 1807
Hugh HOLMES & wife Elizabeth of Winchester to Mary HIXON. B/S of 204*ac* in Piedmont Manor where Rheuben HIXON lately lived and died, adj Joseph WILKINSON, John HALL (formerly Balls Mill Lot), Geo. MULL. Wit: William PAXSON, Wm. MAINS, Fleet SMITH.

Bk:Pg: 2I:009   Date: 8 Jun 1807   RcCt: 13 Jul 1807
Mary HIXON of Piedmont Manor to Hugh HOLMES of Winchester. Mortgage on above land. Wit: Wm. MAINS, Wm. PAXSON, Fleet SMITH.

Bk:Pg: 2I:012   Date: __ Mar 1807   RcCt: 14 Sep 1807
Jonathan HUNTER to Frederick DARFLINGER. A/L of 219*ac*. Wit: S. BLINCOE, John PAYNE, George HAMMAT.

Bk:Pg: 2I:014   Date: 14 Sep 1807   RcCt: 14 Sep 1807
John WITTERMAN of Ldn to Henry Jos. FRYE of Ldn. B/S of 14¼*ac* on E side of Short Hill.

Bk:Pg: 2I:015   Date: 7 Sep 1807   RcCt: 14 Sep 1807
Stacy TAYLOR of Ldn to John LOVE of Ldn. Release of trust due Exors of Timothy HOWELL dec'd.

Bk:Pg: 2I:016   Date: 19 May 1807   RcCt: 13 Jul 1807
Enoch FRANCIS & wife Nancy of Ldn to Joseph T. NEWTON of Ldn. B/S
of 400ac on W side of Goose Creek. Wit: John SHAW, Jno. MATHIAS,
John CAVAN, Armistead LONG, Saml. MURREY.

Bk:Pg: 2I:021   Date: 13 Nov 1806   RcCt: 13 Jul 1807
William NEWTON of AlexVa to Enoch FRANCIS of Ldn. B/S of 400ac on
W side of Goose Creek [detailed plat]. Wit: Isaac LAROWE, Jos. T.
NEWTON, Thomas BOLTON, A. FAW, George GILPIN.

Bk:Pg: 2I:028   Date: 4 Jun 1807   RcCt: 14 Sep 1807
Elijah JAMES of Ldn to Charles HUMPHREY of Ldn and Jesse
MATTHEWS of FrdkMd. BoS for household items. Wit: Thomas CATON,
Jonathan MATTHEWS, Israel YOUNG, Isaac LAROWE, Saml. M.
EDWARDS.

Bk:Pg: 2I:029   Date: 9 Feb 1807   RcCt: 14 Sep 1807
Joseph HOLMES & wife Elizabeth of Ldn to Abel DAVIS of Ldn. B/S of 12
roods of land. Wit: Gideon DAVIS, George IDEN, Jonathan MILBURN Jr.

Bk:Pg: 2I:031   Date: 14 Sep 1807   RcCt: 14 Sep 1807
George TAVENER Jr. & wife Martha (signed Patty) of Ldn to Hamilton
ROGERS of Ldn. B/S of 60ac.

Bk:Pg: 2I:033   Date: 14 Sep 1807   RcCt: 14 Sep 1807
George TAVENER Jr. & wife Martha (signed Patty) of Ldn to Joseph
TAVENER of Ldn. B/S of 41ac.

Bk:Pg: 2I:035   Date: 14 Sep 1807   RcCt: 14 Sep 1807
George TAVENER Jr. & wife Martha (signed Patty) of Ldn to George
TAVENER Sr. of Ldn. B/S of 94ac adj Hamilton ROGERS.

Bk:Pg: 2I:038   Date: 14 Sep 1807   RcCt: 14 Sep 1807
Joseph TAVENER & wife Ann of Ldn to George TAVENER Sr. of Ldn.
B/S of 18ac on road leading to Wtfd adj Stacy JANNEY, Samuel GREGG.
Wit: Stephen KERRICK, Samuel MEAD, Hamilton ROGERS.

Bk:Pg: 2I:040   Date: __ Sep 1808[7]   RcCt: 14 Sep 1807
Hamilton ROGERS & wife Dinah of Ldn to Stacy TAYLOR & Robert
BRADEN of Ldn. Trust for debt to George TAVENER Sr. using 60ac
(conveyed to Rogers by George TAVENER Jr.). Wit: Saml. M.
EDWARDS.

Bk:Pg: 2I:044   Date: 14 Sep 1807   RcCt: 14 Sep 1807
Joseph TAVENER & wife Ann of Ldn to Stacy TAYLOR & Robert
BRADEN of Ldn. Trust for debt to George TAVENER Sr. using 41ac
(conveyed to TAVENER by George TAVENER Jr.). Wit: Saml. M.
EDWARDS.

Bk:Pg: 2I:048   Date: 9 Mar 1807   RcCt: 14 Sep 1807
Robert BRADEN of Ldn to Isaac HOUGH of Ldn. B/S of 2 lots conveyed
to BRADEN & James HAMILTON by Isaac BALL in trust; HAMILTON
having died. Wit: Saml. BOGGESS, Abiel JENNERS, Leven STEVENS,
John H. CANBY.

Bk:Pg: 2I:051   Date: 14 Sep 1807   RcCt: 14 Sep 1807
Hamilton ROGERS & wife Dinah of Ldn to Gideon DAVIS of Ldn. B/S of
41*ac*. Wit: Saml. MEAD, Stephen KERRICK, Joseph HOLMES.

Bk:Pg: 2I:053   Date: 14 Sep 1807   RcCt: 14 Sep 1807
Gideon DAVIS & wife Nancy of Ldn to Joshua GORE & John IRY of Ldn.
Trust for bond to Hamilton ROGERS 41*ac* adj Eli JANNEY, Joseph
HOLMES. Wit: Samuel MEAD, Stephen KERRICK, Joseph HOLMES.

Bk:Pg: 2I:057   Date: 8 Jun 1807   RcCt: 14 Sep 1807
George TAVENER & Joseph WHITE (Exors of George NIXON dec'd) of
Ldn to Edward COE of Ldn. B/S of 81*ac* on NW fork of Goose Creek on
road from Moses Dillon's Mill to Mdbg adj William CARR. Wit: Francis
TRIPLETT, John NEWTON, Edward RINCHER.

Bk:Pg: 2I:059   Date: 3 Mar 1807   RcCt: 14 Sep 1807
William TAYLOR of Lsbg to William CARR of Ldn. B/S of 1*ac* on Market
St in Lsbg.

Bk:Pg: 2I:061   Date: 21 Aug 1805   RcCt: 15 Apr 1806
Hiland CROWE & wife of Ldn to Hamilton ROGERS of Ldn. B/S of 4½*ac*
on Crooked Run. Wit: Jesse JANNEY, Robert EDELIN, John HUFF,
Stacy TAYLOR.

Bk:Pg: 2I:064   Date: 14 Sep 1801   RcCt: 13 Sep 1802
Lewis SUDDATH of Ffx to John Babtist RATHIE of Ldn. A/L of L/L (to
Benjamin THOMAS) of 124*ac*. Wit: John CLEVELAND, Rhodham
SIMPSON, Hardage SMITH, Jno. D. BELL, Benjamin JACKSON.

Bk:Pg: 2I:066   Date: 15 Jun 1807   RcCt: 14 Sep 1807
Daniel TRIPLETT of Ldn to Isaac VANDEVANTER of Ldn. BoS for negro
Charlotte abt 26y old. Wit: John McCORMICK, Joseph VANDEVANTER.

Bk:Pg: 2I:067   Date: 26 Nov 1806   RcCt: 15 Sep 1807
Thomas TRIPLETT & wife Elizabeth (d/o John SANDERS dec'd s/o
James SANDERS dec'd) of Amherst Co Va to William Temple Thompson
MASON of FrdkMd. B/S of 150*ac* leased land. Wit: Rich'd H.
HENDERSON, James RUST, Eli OFFUTT, Jos. BURRUS, David S.
GARLAND.

Bk:Pg: 2I:070   Date: 14 Jul 1806   RcCt: 15 Sep 1807
A. MORRISON. States he has no interest in the slaves of Benjamin
THORNTON except for deed with MORRISON as his security in
obligation to John RAMSAY.

Bk:Pg: 2I:071   Date: 13 Feb 1806   RcCt: 16 Sep 1807
George HEAD & wife Liddy of Ldn to Charles DRISH of Ldn. B/S of lot in
Lsbg in line of Presbyterian Meeting house lot. Wit: Samuel MURREY,
Isaac HARRIS, Joseph HUNT.

Bk:Pg: 2I:072   Date: 15 May 1807   RcCt: 16 Sep 1807
Barnett HOUGH & wife Louisa of Lsbg to William NEWTON of AlexVa.
Mortgage of 179*ac* with merchant & saw mill. Wit: W. JANES, Charles G.
EDWARDS, Jas. CAVAN Jr., John ROSE, Thos. FOUCH.

Bk:Pg: 2I:077   Date: 10 Sep 1796   RcCt: 12 Sep 1796
Ferdinando FAIRFAX of Berkley Co Va to Jonah THOMPSON & William
HOUGH (Exors of Israel THOMPSON dec'd). B/S of 14*ac* adj George
NIXON. Wit: Sandford REMEY, James MILTON, Nehemiah GARISON.

Bk:Pg: 2I:079   Date: 26 Jun 1807   RcCt: 12 Oct 1807
Mahlon JANNEY of Wtfd to Mahlon MYERS of Ldn. B/S of lot on upper
end of main St in Wtfd adj Ann BALL. Wit: James MOORE, John
VANDEVANTER, Pateson WRIGHT.

Bk:Pg: 2I:081   Date: 7 Feb 1807   RcCt: 12 Oct 1807
John STEERE of Sullivan Co Tn to brother Isaac STEERE Jr. of Ldn. B/S
of 250*ac* in Harrison Co Va (late property of brother Joseph STEERE
dec'd deeded to John by James COCKINN & wife Temperance of
Harrison Co on 8 Jan 1802). Wit: Saml. CLAPHAM, Isaac STEERE,
Thomas STEERE.

Bk:Pg: 2I:082   Date: 9 Sep 1805   RcCt: 12 Oct 1807
Joseph DANIEL & wife Tacy of Ldn to Isaac VANDERVANTER of Ldn.
B/S of 58½*ac* on Kittoctan Mt. Wit: Jonas POTTS, Wm. MAINS, R.
BRADEN, Jos. BRADEN, Burr POWELL, Leven LUCKETT.

Bk:Pg: 2I:086   Date: 28 Apr 1807   RcCt: 12 Oct 1807
Thomas KEENE of Ldn to John HUTCHISON of PrWm. LS of 5*ac* in
CamP on E side of Bull Run. Wit: John FULTON, Silas HICKERSON,
Jacob DAYMUD, Reuben HUTCHISON, Sampson HUTCHISON.

Bk:Pg: 2I:088   Date: 27 Jun 1807   RcCt: 12 Oct 1807
Mahlon MYERS of Ldn to Jonas POTTS & John VANDEVANTER of Wtfd.
Trust for debt to Patterson WRIGHT using lot on upper end of main St in
Wtfd adj Ann BALL. Wit: James MOORE, Edw'd DORSEY, James
RUSSELL.

Bk:Pg: 2I:091   Date: 25 Jun 1807   RcCt: 14 Sep 1807
John ERSKINE of Ldn to William GREGG of Ldn. B/S of 173*ac*. Wit:
Joshua DANIEL, Aaron SANDERS, John McNEIL, Timothy HIXON.

Bk:Pg: 2I:093   Date: 3 Dec 1805   RcCt: 12 Oct 1807
Catesby GRAHAM & Jane/Jean GRAHAM (d/o Catesby COCKE) of Fqr
to Leven POWELL of Ldn. B/S of 496a part of "black oak thicket". Wit:
Thomas CHILTON, Blackwell CHILTON, Adam ROSE, Jno.
TURBERVILLE, Jos. CHILTON, Thomas CHILTON, Wm. CHILTON,
Saml. CHILTON, William STEWART.

Bk:Pg: 2I:096   Date: 7 May 1807   RcCt: 12 Oct 1807
John STOUTSEBERGER & wife Margaret of Ldn to Peter
STONEBURNER of Ldn. B/S of 90½*ac*. Wit: John HAMILTON, 3 names
in German, William NOLAND.

Bk:Pg: 2I:100   Date: 7 May 1807   RcCt: 12 Oct 1807
Peter STONEBURNER & wife Susanna of Ldn to Simon AGA of Ldn. B/S
of 90½*ac* adj Martin AGA, Levi PRINCE. Wit: John HAMILTON, John
STOUSEBERGER, name in German, William NOLAND.

Bk:Pg: 2I:104   Date: 30 Sep 1807   RcCt: 12 Oct 1807
Moses MOSS, John MOSS, Lela MOSS, William MOSS, Elijah MOSS, Vincent MOSS, Daniel MOSS, Stephen MOSS, William WILLIAMSON & wife Sara, and Daniel THOMAS & wife Mary (heirs of Nathaniel MOSS dec'd) to Vincent MOSS. PoA. Wit: Jacob EVELAND, John WILSON, Burr POWELL, Leven LUCKETT, A. GIBSON.

Bk:Pg: 2I:106   Date: 15 Apr 1807   RcCt: 12 Oct 1807
Moses DILLON & wife Rebeckah of Ldn to William HOUGH of Ldn. B/S of 173*ac* adj Samuel PURSEL, Isaac NICHOLS, Israel HOWELL. Wit: Wm. POWELL, Jesse JANNEY, W. SMITH, Giles CRAVEN.

Bk:Pg: 2I:108   Date: 15 Apr 1807   RcCt: 12 Oct 1807
William HOUGH & wife Jane of Ldn to Moses DILLON of Ldn. Trust on above 173*ac*. Wit: Jesse JANNEY, William SMITH, Wm. POWELL, Giles CRAVEN.

Bk:Pg: 2I:111   Date: 12 Oct 1807   RcCt: 12 Oct 1807
John A. BINNS of Ldn to Jacob WINE of Ldn. B/S of 4*ac* adj Reuben HIXON dec'd.

Bk:Pg: 2I:113   Date: 3 Jul 1807   RcCt: 13 Jul 1807
Enos GARROTT & wife Elenor of Ldn and Thomas HUGHES & wife Sarah of Ldn. Exchange 124*ac* on S fork of Kittocton Creek lately occupied by Amos BEANS for 130*ac*. Wit: Stacy TAYLOR, Lewis ELLZEY, Amos BEANS, James TRIBBY.

Bk:Pg: 2I:119   Date: 6 Oct 1807   RcCt: 12 Oct 1807
Wilson C. SELDON & wife Nelly of Ldn to William JOHNSTON of Ldn. B/S of 1*ac* lot on N side of Markett St in Lsbg. Wit: Presley CORDELL, W. JANES, John SAUNDERS, Obadiah CLIFFORD, Samuel MURREY.

Bk:Pg: 2I:122   Date: 10 Aug 1807   RcCt: 16 Sep 1807
Jonah THOMPSON & William HOUGH (Exors of Israel THOMPSON dec'd) to Hugh DOUGLAS of Ldn. B/S of 100*ac* adj Moses COLDWELL. Wit: John A. BINNS, Alex'r DOW, Francis TRIPLETT, John LYONS.

Bk:Pg: 2I:125   Date: 12 Oct 1807   RcCt: 12 Oct 1807
Trustees George TAVENER, Jesse JANNEY & Robert BRADEN of Ldn to farmer William SMITH of Ldn. B/S of 150*ac* on Kittocton Creek leased for 5 lives to William WILDMAN.

Bk:Pg: 2I:127   Date: 9 Oct 1807   RcCt: 12 Oct 1807
John HESKETT & wife Milley of Ldn to Phinehas THOMAS of Ldn. B/S of 52*ac* adj James GRADY. Wit: Stephen JANNEY, Valentine FORD, Aaron JANNEY.

Bk:Pg: 2I:130   Date: 8 Oct 1807   RcCt: 12 Oct 1807
Thomas GREGG & wife Sarah of Ldn to Negro Harry of Ldn. B/S of 2*ac*. Wit: Stacy TAYLOR, Stephen C. ROSZELL, John MARKS.

Bk:Pg: 2I:134   Date: 4 Apr 1807   RcCt: 12 Oct 1807
Mary TAYLOR of Ldn to Elizabeth HARDEN & William HARDEN of Ldn.
B/S of 124*ac*. Wit: Christopher ROSE, Archibald McVICKER, Henry
TAYLOR.

Bk:Pg: 2I:136   Date: 2 Oct 1807   RcCt: 12 Oct 1807
Joseph SMITH of Ldn to Jacob WALTMAN of Ldn. Mortgage of lot in
Piedmont Manor conveyed to SMITH by Joseph LEWIS Jr. except 51
1/8*ac*. Wit: Jos. LEWIS Jr., Emanuel WALTMAN, John WALTMAN.

Bk:Pg: 2I:137   Date: 12 Oct 1807   RcCt: 12 Oct 1807
William PAXON & wife Jane of Ldn to John VANDEVANTER of Ldn. B/S
of Lots #16 & #17 in new addition to Wtfd. Wit: Sam. LUCKETT, Jas.
SAUNDERS, John WORSELEY.

Bk:Pg: 2I:139   Date: 14 Aug 1807   RcCt: 12 Oct 1807
William H. HARDING & wife Ann Alex'r of JeffVa to Sandford RAMEY of
Ldn. B/S of 148*ac* on Broad Run adj James CAMPBELL, Michael
BOGAR. Wit: John H. CANBY, John SAUNDERS, Washington MAINS,
John VANDEVANTER, Arch'd. MAINS, John D. ORR, Wm. Byrd PAGE.

Bk:Pg: 2I:143   Date: 10 Apr 1807   RcCt: 12 Oct 1807
Benjamin CANBY & wife Sarah of Lsbg to Matthew RUST of Ldn. B/S of
241*ac* on Beaverdam adj James BUCKLY, Robt CARTER. Wit: Steph.
COOKE, Stacy TAYLOR, Chas. F. MERCER.

Bk:Pg: 2I:148   Date: 10 Apr 1807   RcCt: 12 Oct 1807
Matthew RUST & wife Patty of Ldn to Moses DILLON of Ldn. B/S of
241*ac*. Wit: Francis PEYTON, Simon TRIPLETT, Leven LUCKETT.

Bk:Pg: 2I:152   Date: 12 Apr 1807   RcCt: 12 Oct 1807
Moses DILLON & wife Rebecca of Ldn to Matthew RUST of Ldn.
Mortgage of 241*ac*. Wit: Stacy TAYLOR, Steph. COOKE, Chs. Fenton
MERCER.

Bk:Pg: 2I:157   Date: 26 Jun 1807   RcCt: 12 Oct 1807
Moses DILLON & wife Rebecca of Ldn to Matthew RUST of Ldn. B/S of
1½*ac* on Little River at foot of Bull Run Mt. Wit: Stacy TAYLOR, Charles
Fenton MERCER, Lewis ELLZEY, Timothy TAYLOR.

Bk:Pg: 2I:161   Date: 11 Apr 1807   RcCt: 12 Oct 1807
Moses DILLON & wife Rebecca of Ldn to Benjamin CANBY of Ldn.
Mortgage of 241*ac*. Wit: Steph. COOKE, Stacy TAYLOR, Chs. Fenton
MERCER.

Bk:Pg: 2I:165   Date: 11 Jun 1806   RcCt: 12 Oct 1807
Abiel JENNERS & wife Deborah of Ldn to Samuel BROOKE of
Georgetown DC. B/S of 358*ac* in possession of William COCKING, adj
James RICE, Robert BRADEN, Charles BENNETT. Wit: Wm. MAINS, N.
DAVISSON, Wm. COCKING, Thos. WILKINSON, Leven LUCKETT,
Thos. SIM.

Bk:Pg: 2I:169   Date: 18 May 1807   RcCt: 14 Sep 1807
William THRIFT & wife Hannah of Ldn to Charles THRIFT of Ldn. B/S of
100*ac*. Wit: George ELGIN, Gusta's. ELGIN, Thos. HETHERLY, Steph
COOKE, Samuel MURREY.

Bk:Pg: 2I:173   Date: ___ 1807   RcCt: 14 Sep 1807
William THRIFT & wife Hannah of Ldn to Charles THRIFT of Ldn. B/S of
154*ac* on SW side of Tuskorora. Wit: Gusta's. ELGIN, Thos. HETHERLY,
Gustavus ELGIN Jr., Steph COOKE, Samuel MURREY.

Bk:Pg: 2I:177   Date: 30 Apr 1807   RcCt: 12 Oct 1807
Philip EVERHEART of Ldn to John HALL of Ldn. BoS for negro girl
Sophia abt 18y old. Wit: John MARTIN.

Bk:Pg: 2I:178   Date: 14 Apr 1807   RcCt: 15 Sep 1807
Francis HAGUE & wife Mary of Ffx Ct. House to Benjamin Hough CANBY
of Lsbg. B/S of ½ of HAGUE's lot on W side of Carolina Road on S side of
Lsbg. Wit: Chas. BENNETT, Joseph CARR, Robert HAMILTON.

Bk:Pg: 2I:181   Date: 13 Mar 1807   RcCt: 13 Oct 1807
John Thomas RICKETTS & wife Mary of Ffx and William NEWTON & wife
Jane of AlexVa to Wilson Cary SELDON of Ldn. B/S of 128*ac* on
Potomac and 13*ac* nr Edwards Rd (total given as 141½*ac*). Wit: Thos.
SWANN, Edm'd DENNEY, Saml. SMITH, Geo. W. BALL, Thomson
MASON, James H. BLAKE, A. FEW, John McKINNEY.

Bk:Pg: 2I:187   Date: ___ 1807   RcCt: 13 Oct 1807
Wilson Cary SELDON & wife Nelly of Ldn to Aaron SANDERS of Ldn. B/S
of 103*ac* on Potomac except 1*ac*.

Bk:Pg: 2I:190   Date: 15 Sep 1807   RcCt: 14 Oct 1807
William LITTLEJOHN of Ldn to James GARDNER of Lsbg. B/S of lot in
Lsbg adj Thomas WILKINSON.

Bk:Pg: 2I:192   Date: 10 Aug 1807   RcCt: 14 Sep 1807
John HENRY Jr. of Ldn to John CUMMINGS of Ldn. A/L of L/L to Joshua
KNOWLS of 100*ac* in CamP adj John SCHOOLEY, Nathan
NEIGHBOURS, George SCATTERDAY, William WILDMAN, Jonathan
MAYERS. Wit: Saml. M. EDWARDS, Isaac LAROWE, C. BINNS.

Bk:Pg: 2I:195   Date: 12 Jul 1807   RcCt: 15 Sep 1807
William HOUGH & wife Eleanor of Wtfd to Stephen COOKE of Lsbg. B/S
of Grist Mill and adj land on Goose Creek. Wit: Samuel MURREY, W. C.
SELDEN, Chs. Fenton MERCER, John R. COOKE.

Bk:Pg: 2I:201   Date: 17 Jul 1807   RcCt: 14 Dec 1807
Wilson Carey SELDON & wife Nelley of Ldn to Ignatius NORRIS of Ldn.
B/S of 1*ac* at Market & Cornwall Sts in Lsbg. Wit: Wilson C. SELDEN,
Jno. MATHIAS, Alex'r SUTHERLAND, Patrick H. DOUGLAS, Samuel
MURREY, John LITTLEJOHN.

Bk:Pg: 2I:204   Date: 10 Nov 1807   RcCt: 14 Dec 1807
Sarah FAIRFAX to George MULL of Ldn. Renewal of lease of 120*ac* L/L
on (David MULL, wife Margaret, son David MULL), David & Margaret are

now dec'd, so Sarah FAIRFAX and son George MULL now in their stead. Wit: H. G. SAUNDERS, John SPANGLER, Thos. WILKINSON.

Bk:Pg: 2I:207   Date: 5 Nov 1806   RcCt: 14 Dec 1807
John ALEXANDER of Ldn to Bertrand EWELL of Ldn. B/S of __ac ALEXANDER purchased from BUTCHER. Wit: Jos. BEARD, John H. EVANS, John SHAW.

Bk:Pg: 2I:209   Date: 13 Oct 1807   RcCt: 14 Dec 1807
Rebecca SCHOLFIELD Sr., John SCHOLFIELD, William SCHOLFIELD & wife Hannah of Ldn to Elias LACEY of Ldn. B/S of 233ac on Carolina Rd adj Jacob ISH. Wit: Nathaniel SKINNER, James SWARTS, Wm. M. BAYLY, Jonathan H. SCHOLFIELD, Cornelius SKINNER, Israel LACEY, Ariss BUCKNER.

Bk:Pg: 2I:213   Date: 6 Dec 1806   RcCt: 9 Feb 1807
Joseph DANIEL, Benjamin DANIEL & Samuel DANIEL (Exors of William DANIEL dec'd) of Ldn to John LOVE of Ldn. B/S of 106½ac. Wit: Stacy TAYLOR, George BROWN, Samuel PURSEL.

Bk:Pg: 2I:215   Date: 9 Nov 1807   RcCt: 14 Dec 1807
John SANDERS (s/o John SANDERS dec'd, br/o James SANDERS) of Ldn and Aaron SANDERS of Ldn (s/o John SANDERS dec'd). John dec'd left 501ac on Potomac, Aaron bought land of James, John will now have 154ac and Aaron 346ac. Wit: Jas. SAUNDERS, A. SUTHERLAND, Jno. MATHIAS.

Bk:Pg: 2I:220   Date: 27 Nov 1807   RcCt: 14 Dec 1807
Philip FULKERSON of Ldn to Christian NISWANGER. Mortgage using farm and household items, land where FULKERSON lives. Wit: Jos. CARR, Danl. MASON, Joseph BALDWIN.

Bk:Pg: 2I:221   Date: 2 Sep 1807   RcCt: 14 Dec 1807
Edward DORSEY & wife Maria of Ldn to Josiah CRAVEN of Ldn. B/S of part of Lot #6 in new addition of Wtfd. Wit: Chs. BENNETT, Richard GRIFFITH, Terence FIGH, Sanford RAMEY.

Bk:Pg: 2I:224   Date: 11 Jul 1807   RcCt: 14 Dec 1807
Stephen COOKE & with Catharine of Ldn to William HOUGH of Ldn. Mortgage of lots on Goose Creek [see 2I:195]. Wit: Charles Fenton MERCER, Samuel MURREY, W. C. SELDEN, John R. COOKE, Armistead LONG.

Bk:Pg: 2I:231   Date: 20 Apr 1807   RcCt: 14 Dec 1807
George GIBSON of Ldn to brother John GIBSON Jr. of Ldn (sons of Joseph GIBSON dec'd). B/S of 1/7 share of 272ac. Wit: Ben GRAYSON, Joseph CARR, James RUST.

Bk:Pg: 2I:233   Date: ___ 1807   RcCt: 14 Dec 1807
Peter OATYER of Ldn to Colley McATTEE of Ldn. LS of 71ac L/L (lives of Elizabeth & Catharine SCHRY). Wit: Saml. M. EDWARDS.

Bk:Pg: 2I:236   Date: 5 Dec 1807   RcCt: 14 Dec 1807
Jacob BAUGH of Ldn to Aaron SAUNDERS of Ldn. Trust for debts to
SAUNDERS, Charles SHEPPARD, John UPPDYKE, David BAILS &
Joseph SMITH using farm and household items. Wit: Jas. SAUNDERS,
Jno. MATHIAS, Fleet SMITH, S. BLINCOE, Chas. THRIFT.

Bk:Pg: 2I:239   Date: 5 Dec 1807   RcCt: 14 Dec 1807
Jacob BAUGH & wife Mary of Ldn to Aaron SAUNDERS of Ldn. Trust for
debts as listed in 2I:236 using 600a & 1280a nr Knoxville Tn. Wit: Jas.
SAUNDERS, Jno. MATHIAS, Fleet SMITH, S. BLINCOE, Chas. THRIFT.

Bk:Pg: 2I:243   Date: 21 Oct 1807   RcCt: 15 Dec 1807
Benjamin DEWELL & wife Barbary of Ldn to Ignatius ELGIN of Ldn. B/S
of 107ac on Secolon Branch adj Benjamin H. CANBY, Nicholas
GARRETT. Wit: William Y. STURMAN, Saml. M. EDWARDS, Isaac
LAROWE, John LITTLEJOHN, Obadiah CLIFFORD.

Bk:Pg: 2I:247   Date: 1 Dec 1807   RcCt: 15 Dec 1807
Jacob BAUGH & wife Mary of Ldn to Fleet SMITH of Lsbg. B/S of part of
Lot #22 in Lsbg now part of estate of Daniel LOSCH dec'd. Wit: C.
BINNS, Saml. M. EDWARDS, Chas. ELGIN, Wilson Cary SELDEN,
Samuel MURREY.

Bk:Pg: 2I:250   Date: 27 Apr 1807   RcCt: 16 Dec 1807
Walter POWER of Ldn to Samuel BOGGESS of Ldn. Trust for debt to
William BRONAUGH using horse. Wit: Thos. WILKINSON, Robert
WILSON, John ORRISON.

Bk:Pg: 2I:251   Date: 2 Feb 1807   RcCt: 11 Jan 1808
Enos MONTEITH & wife Elenor of StafVa to James WORNALD of Ldn.
B/S of 83ac on Goose Creek previously leased to WORNALD. Wit:
William BERRY, William VICKERS, John SINCLAIR, Wheatman LEATH,
Richard CARTER, Burr POWELL, Jesse McVEIGH, Mason FRENCH, A.
GIBSON, Leven POWELL, Jonathan CARTER.

Bk:Pg: 2I:254   Date: 5 Jan 1808   RcCt: 11 Jan 1808
Enos MONTEITH & wife Elenor of StafVa to Jonathan CARTER of Ldn.
B/S of 218ac (2 lots leased by James MONTEITH and held by Richard
CARTER & John NEWLIN). Wit: Burr POWELL, Leven POWELL, Jesse
McVEIGH, A. GIBSON, Mason FRENCH, James WORNALD.

Bk:Pg: 2I:257   Date: 5 Jan 1808   RcCt: 11 Jan 1808
Enos MONTEITH & wife Elenor of StafVa to Mason FRENCH of Ldn. B/S
of 150ac on Goose Creek. Wit: Burr POWELL, Leven POWELL, Jesse
McVEIGH, A. GIBSON, Wm. VICKERS. Jonathan CARTER, James
WORNALD.

Bk:Pg: 2I:260   Date: 16 May 1804   RcCt: 11 Feb 1805
John McILHANY of Ldn to Mahlon MORRIS of Ldn. B/S of 28ac SE side
of NE end of Short Hill. Wit: Josiah WHITE Jr., Thos. LESLIE, David
LOVETT.

Bk:Pg: 2I:262   Date: 20 Jun 1807   RcCt: 11 Jan 1808
Mahlon MORRIS & wife Catharine of Ldn to James H. HAMILTON of Ldn.
B/S of 28ac on SE side of Short Hill. Wit: Stacy TAYLOR, Lewis ELLZEY,
Thos. HOUGH, David GOODWIN.

Bk:Pg: 2I:265   Date: 5 Oct 1807   RcCt: 11 Jan 1808
Ferdinando FAIRFAX of JeffVa to Adam SHOVER & Philip SANDER as
trustees of German Presbyterian Church. B/S of 3ac in Piedmont Manor
on road from John George's Mill to Luckett's Ferry. Wit: Nich's. ROPER,
William HICKMAN, Simon SHOEMAKER, John GEORG Jr., William
BAKER.

Bk:Pg: 2I:267   Date: 23 Feb 1804   RcCt: 14 May 1807
Noble BEVERIDGE & Mesheck LACEY to Burr POWELL. Trust for debt
to Thomas CHINN Sr. using 200ac. Wit: A. GIBSON, Daniel VERNON,
James BATTSON, Leven D. POWELL.

Bk:Pg: 2I:269   Date: 14 Sep 1807   RcCt: 11 Jan 1808
John NIXON of Ldn to Thomas JACOBS of Ldn. B/S of 1ac on E side of
road from N end of King St Lsbg to Nolands Ferry.

Bk:Pg: 2I:271   Date: 13 Jun 1807   RcCt: 11 Jan 1808
Carter BEVERLEY & wife Jane of Culpeper Co to Joseph LEWIS Jr. of
Ldn. Mortgage of 992ac on Kittockton Creek adj Thomas D. STEVENS.
Wit: Thomas SWANN, Thomas SIM, Wilson C. SELDEN, William
NOLAND.

Bk:Pg: 2I:272   Date: 24 Aug 1807   RcCt: 11 Jan 1808
Thomas OWENS of Ldn to William SMITH of Ldn. BoS for farm and
household items. Wit: Pressley SAUNDERS Jr., John F. SAPPINGTON.

Bk:Pg: 2I:273   Date: 31 Mar 1807   RcCt: 14 Sep 1807
William BRONAUGH of Ldn to Richard VANPELT of Ldn. Mortgage of
118ac. Wit: Stephen C. ROSZELL, Daniel BONNELL, Ben GRAYSON.

Bk:Pg: 2I:274   Date: 31 Mar 1807   RcCt: 12 Oct 1807
Richard VANPELT & wife Elizabeth of Ldn to William BRONAUGH of Ldn.
B/S of 118ac. Wit: Step C. ROSZELL, Daniel BONNELL, Benj.
GRAYSON.

Bk:Pg: 2I:276   Date: 31 May 1807   RcCt: 11 Jan 1808
Amos FOX of Ldn to Henry BROWN of Ldn. BoS for horse. Wit: Jesse
FOX, Mary FOX.

Bk:Pg: 2I:277   Date: 20 Jun 1807   RcCt: 11 Jan 1808
Josiah MOFFETT & wife Rachel of Ldn to Josiah MOFFETT Jr. & Robert
MOFFETT of Ldn. B/S of 138ac, 38acc & 40ac. Wit: C. BINNS, Saml. M.
EDWARDS, Chas. THRIFT, Armistead LONG, Fra. H. PEYTON.

Bk:Pg: 2I:280   Date: 22 Jun 1807   RcCt: 11 Jan 1808
Josiah MOFFETT Jr. & Robert MOFFETT of Ldn to Josiah MOFFETT of
Ldn. Mortgage on 138ac, 38ac & 40ac. Wit: C. BINNS, Saml M.
EDWARDS, Chas. THRIFT, Eli OFFUTT.

Bk:Pg: 2I:282   Date: 11 Jan 1809[8]   RcCt: 11 Jan 1808
Josiah MOFFETT Jr. & Robert MOFFETT of Ldn to Josiah MOFFETT Sr. of Ldn. Bond on above land. Wit: C. BINNS, Saml. M. EDWARDS, Eli OFFUTT, Chas. THRIFT.

Bk:Pg: 2I:283   Date: 11 Jan 1809[8]   RcCt: 11 Jan 1808
Josiah MOFFETT Jr. & Robert MOFFETT of Ldn to Josiah MOFFETT Sr. of Ldn. Bond on above land. Wit: C. BINNS, Saml. M. EDWARDS, Eli OFFUTT, Chas. THRIFT.

Bk:Pg: 2I:283   Date: 3 Jul 1807   RcCt: 12 Oct 1807
Enos GARRETT & wife Elenor of Ldn to Thomas HUGHES to Stacey TAYLOR, Edmond JENINGS & Lewis ELLZEY of Ldn and Thomas HUGHES & wife Sarah of Ldn. Trust – GARRETT and HUGHES exchanged lots and GARRETT owes HUGHES wheat. Wit: Amos BEANS, James TRIBBEY, Thos. TRIBBEY.

Bk:Pg: 2I:286   Date: 11 Jan 1808   RcCt: 11 Jan 1808
Isaac STEERE & Thomas STEERE (Admr of John STEERE dec'd) to Isaac STEERE Sr. Release of Admr. Wit: L. ELLZEY.

Bk:Pg: 2I:286   Date: 23 Sep 1807   RcCt: 11 Jan 1808
Andrew HOSPITAL & wife Mary of Ldn to Henry GLASSGOW of Lsbg. B/S of Lot #54 in Lsbg. Wit: Steph COOKE, Samuel MURREY.

Bk:Pg: 2I:288   Date: 11 Jan 1808   RcCt: 11 Jan 1808
Henry GLASSGOW & wife Catharine of Lsbg to Andrew HOSPITAL & wife Mary (formerly Mary SPOONT) of Lsbg and Robert BRADEN & George TAVENDER Sr. of Ldn. Trust for Lot #54 in Lsbg.

Bk:Pg: 2I:290   Date: 18 Apr 1799   RcCt: 11 Jan 1808
Thomas Crandall WELLS. Col from Md for slaves Jane abt 20y, Nancy abt 3y, and Tom abt 8 months old.

Bk:Pg: 2I:290   Date: 19 Dec 1807   RcCt: 11 Jan 1808
Joseph ROBISON to Mrs. Sarah SMITH. Receipt for full claim agst estate of Nathaniel SMITH, Sarah SMITH and agrees to will of Temple SMITH of Hartford NC of 18 Apr 1807. Wit: Celia KELLEY, Richard KEEN, Jacob ISH, Eli OFFUTT, Saml. M. EDWARDS, Minor SMITH.

Bk:Pg: 2I:291   Date: 9 Jan 1807   RcCt: 11 Jan 1808
William PATTERSON & wife Abigail, Jacob BAXTER & wife Lydda, Jacob DEHAVEN & wife Nancy, John LOWREY & wife Hannah and William JONES & wife Mary of Scott Co Ky to William DULIN of Ldn. B/S of 224¾ac from estate of Charles BELL dec'd of Ldn.

Bk:Pg: 2I:294   Date: 14 Nov 1807   RcCt: 12 Jan 1808
William MANN and Charles Fenton MERCER (comm. for suit of Richard CHESTER and William MASTERMAN exors of Daniel MILDRED dec'd agst Samuel HOUGH, Lewis ELLZEY, and Mahlon HOUGH) to Henry CLAGETT of Lsbg. B/S of one lot with 2 tenements on King St Lsbg adj Thomas SANDERS and lot on Loudoun St part of Samuel HOUGH's. Wit: Jas. SAUNDERS, John SAUNDERS, Fleet SMITH, Chs. F. MERCER.

Bk:Pg: 2I:297   Date: 14 Nov 1807   RcCt: 12 Jan 1808
Henry CLAGETT of Lsbg to Richard CHESTER & William MASTERMAN
(Exor of Daniel MILDRED dec'd). Mortgage on above land.

Bk:Pg: 2I:298   Date: 8 Jan 1808   RcCt: 12 Jan 1808
William TAYLOR to Charles DRISH. B/S of "Old Gallows Lot" in Lsbg
where first gallows was erected, now occupied by Mrs. GARDNER wife of
Joseph GARDNER. Wit: S. BLINCOE, Isaac LAROWE, Saml. M.
EDWARDS.

Bk:Pg: 2I:299   Date: 10 Apr 1807   RcCt: 12 Jan 1808
Lewis ELLZEY of Ldn to sister Salley ELLZEY of Ldn. Gift of negro
woman Flora (he bought from Abiel JENNERS) & her 3 children Henry,
Jem & Virgie.

Bk:Pg: 2I:300   Date: 13 Mar 1807   RcCt: 12 Jan 1808
Robert William KIRK (s/o James KIRK dec'd) & wife Sarah of
Germantown Pa to Isaac HARRIS of Ldn. B/S of 13ac "Kirks Meadow" adj
Lsbg. Wit: John PATTERSON, Jacob MAYLAND.

Bk:Pg: 2I:303   Date: 13 Jan 1808   RcCt: 18 Jan 1808
Jonas POTTS of Wtfd to Samuel CARR of Lsbg. A/L of ½ of Lot #12 on
King St Lsbg.

Bk:Pg: 2I:305   Date: 26 Jan 1808   RcCt: 12 Apr 1808
Benjamin WOODLEY & wife Elizabeth of Ldn to George HAMMAT of Ldn.
B/S of ½ of lot conveyed to WOODLEY by Matthew WEATHERLEY, adj
Benjamin SHREVE on road from Lsbg to Haymarket. Wit: Isaac
LAROWE, Eli OFFUTT, Saml. M. EDWARDS.

Bk:Pg: 2I:308   Date: 26 Mar 1808   RcCt: 12 Apr 1808
Josiah MOFFETT of Ldn to Charles BINNS of Ldn. B/S of 4ac on road
from Market St to John Williams' blacksmith shop. Wit: Eli OFFUTT, Benj.
SHREVE, Chas. ELGIN, Saml. M. EDWARDS, Isaac LAROWE.

Bk:Pg: 2I:309   Date: 21 Jan 1808   RcCt: 12 Apr 1808
John NEWTON of Lsbg and Charles BINNS (Guardian of Harriet
McCABE orphan of Henry McCABE dec'd). Marriage contract. Wit: Eli
OFFUTT, Rich'd H. HENDERSON, Saml. M. EDWARDS.

Bk:Pg: 2I:311   Date: 6 Feb 1808   RcCt: 12 Apr 1808
Ignatius NORRIS & wife Mary of Ldn to William AUSTINE of Ldn. B/S of
lot in Lsbg on Back St adj James GREENLEASE. Wit: Jesse DAILEY,
Thomas SANDERS, Isaac HARRIS, Saml. M. EDWARDS, Isaac
LAROWE, Eli OFFUTT, Samuel MURREY, Francis H. PEYTON.

Bk:Pg: 2I:313   Date: 22 Mar 1808   RcCt: 12 Apr 1808
Asa MOORE of Wtfd to Hugh LEMON of New Market FrdkMd. B/S of lot
in Wtfd adj Flemon PATTERSON, John F. SAPPINGTON, Leven
SMALLWOOD. Wit: John McGEATH, James MOORE, John F.
SAPPINGTON.

Bk:Pg: 2I:314   Date: 31 Mar 1808   RcCt: 12 Apr 1808
Leven POWELL & wife Sarah of Ldn to Robert M. POWELL & Daniel
EACHES of Ldn. B/S of 8*ac* on Goose Creek.

Bk:Pg: 2I:316   Date: 2 Mar 1805   RcCt: 13 May 1805
George TAVENER & wife Martha (signed Patty) of Ldn to Richard
OSBURN of Ldn. B/S of 122*ac* nr grist road from Israel JANNEY to Lsbg.
Wit: Stacey TAYLOR, Notley C. WILLIAMS, John OSBURNE, John
OSBURNE.

Bk:Pg: 2I:319   Date: 12 Apr 1808   RcCt: 12 Apr 1808
Richard OSBURN & wife Polly of Ldn to John OSBURN of Ldn. B/S of
107*ac* where John now lives, adj Ezekiel POTTS, Edward POTTS.

Bk:Pg: 2I:320   Date: 25 Feb 1808   RcCt: 12 Apr 1808
Anthony CONARD & wife Mary of Ldn to Isaac STEER of Ldn. B/S of
87*ac* on Kittockton Creek, adj Patterson WRIGHT. Wit: Jno. MATTHIAS,
Rich'd NORWOOD, Wm. WRIGHT.

Bk:Pg: 2I:322   Date: 23 Nov 1807   RcCt: 7 Dec 1807
Silas GARRETT of Franklin Co Va to Robert McCULLOCH of Ldn. B/S of
100*ac* adj Thomas GARRETT Jr, Abel GARRETT, Benjamin GARRETT.
Wit: Daniel BROWN, John FORBES, John ARTHUR, Peter BOOTH,
Robert PARLEY, Peter BARNARD Jr.

Bk:Pg: 2I:323   Date: 30 Nov 1807   RcCt: 12 Apr 1808
Charles BRASHEARS of Ldn to daughter Rachel who m. Christopher
ATCHER. Gift of negro Pegg age 16y to 17y. Wit: Wm. WRIGHT, Daniel
MOORE, John PHILLIPS.

Bk:Pg: 2I:324   Date: 13 Apr 1808   RcCt: 12 Apr 1808
Joseph HATCHER & Jesse HATCHER of Ldn to Joseph TAVENER of
Ldn. B/S of 66*ac* bought from sister Nancy (George HATCHER who d. 12
Nov last was devisee of William HATCHER dec'd; George's children were
Joseph, Jesse & Nancy who m. John BURCHETT).

Bk:Pg: 2I:326   Date: 13 Apr 1808   RcCt: 13 Apr 1808
Joseph HATCHER & wife Hannah of Ldn to Jesse HATCHER of Ldn. B/S
of 66a [see 2I:324].

Bk:Pg: 2I:328   Date: 22 Jan 1808   RcCt: 13 Apr 1808
Sampson TURLEY Jr. & wife Sally of Ldn to Stephen BEARD of Ldn. B/S
of 200*ac* on Broad Run. Wit: Alex SUTHERLAND, Joseph BEARD, Fleet
SMITH, Newton B. COCKRILLE, Charles LEWIS, Ariss BUCKNER.

Bk:Pg: 2I:330   Date: 3 Mar 1807   RcCt: 13 Apr 1807
Stephen BOWEN to Alex'r BOWEN. A/L of 120a in Ldn and Fqr, adj. John
VILOTT, John CARTER, Amos DENHAM. Wit: Saml. HARRIS, Turner
WREN, William WREN.

Bk:Pg: 2I:331   Date: 8 Apr 1808   RcCt: 13 Apr 1808
Edward COE of Ldn to Moses DILLON of Ldn. Mortgage on 172*ac*. Wit:
Rich'd H. HENDERSON, Gustavus HARRISON, Ben H. CANBY.

Bk:Pg: 2I:332   Date: 14 Sep 1807   RcCt: 13 Apr 1808
David LACEY & wife Sally to Mary CAIN. B/S of 8ac. Wit: S. BLINCOE, Ben. H. CANBY, Fleet SMITH, Jas. SAUNDERS.

Bk:Pg: 2I:333   Date: 9 Apr 1808   RcCt: 13 Apr 1808
William HOUGH & wife Elenor and Asa MOORE of Ldn to Henry LONG of Ldn. B/S of lot in Wtfd. Wit: Jos. TALBOTT, Hugh THOMPSON, Ralph SMITH, Benjamin HOUGH, Chas. BENNETT, Richard GRIFFITH.

Bk:Pg: 2I:335   Date: 7 Apr 1808   RcCt: 13 Apr 1808
Edward COE of Ldn to Benjamin H. CANBY of Ldn. Mortgage of 243ac. Wit: Richard H. HENDERSON, Gustavus HARRISON, Thos. L. MOORE.

Bk:Pg: 2I:337   Date: 1 Sep 1807   RcCt: 14 Apr 1808
William DAVIS of PrWm to Timothy TAYLOR of Ldn. BoS of horse. Wit: James FIELD, William BURK.

Bk:Pg: 2I:338   Date: 26 Oct 1807   RcCt: 14 Apr 1808
Joseph BENTLEY & wife Catharine of Lsbg to Thomas MORALLEE & wife Sarah of Lsbg. B/S of Lot #36 in Lsbg. Wit: John PAYNE, Daniel DOWLING, John CARR, Wm. B. HARRISON, Samuel MURREY.

Bk:Pg: 2I:340   Date: 13 Feb 1808   RcCt: 9 May 1808
John ROSE & wife of Ldn to Hugh DOUGLAS of Ldn. B/S of land in dispute between ROSE and James BALL under whom DOUGLAS claims. Wit: Saml. M. EDWARDS, Jesse TIMMS, D. MOFFETT, Isaac LAROWE.

Bk:Pg: 2I:341   Date: 2 May 1808   RcCt: 9 May 1808
Sarah BUSSELL of Ldn to Jacob ISH of Ldn. B/S of 66ac on Little River bequeathed to Sarah by John MOORE dec'd. and 34ac "Woodland Lot". Wit: John TYLER, Sampson HUTCHISON, Elijah RETICOR, John E. THOMPSON.

Bk:Pg: 2I:343   Date: ___ 180_   RcCt: 9 May 1808
William ROBERTS & wife Eleanor of Ldn to Richard BROWN. B/S of 171ac on Tuskarora where ROBERTS now lives.

Bk:Pg: 2I:345   Date: 14 Dec 1807   RcCt: 9 May 1808
William PAXSON & wife Jane/Jean of Ldn to Frederick COOPER of Ldn. B/S of 57¾ac on Catockton adj Anthony SOUDERS, George MANN, Daniel LONG. Wit: John VANDEVANTER, Richard GRIFFITH, William HAMILTON, Terrence FIGH.

Bk:Pg: 2I:347   Date: 5 Nov 1807   RcCt: 9 May 1808
Jacob FILLER Sr. of Ldn to Frederick FILLER, Bolser FILLER & Jacob FILLER Jr. of Ldn. BoS for all moveable property in house and on lot where Jacob FILLER Sr. now lives. Wit: Adam SHOVER, Washington JOHNSON, George EBERTS, Valentine BANTZ.

Bk:Pg: 2I:348   Date: ___ 1808   RcCt: 9 May 1808
Stephen WILSON & wife Martha of Ldn to Blackstone JANNEY of Ldn. B/S of 20½ac adj William HATCHER, Mary WILSON.

Bk:Pg: 2I:349, 351   Date: 8 Feb 1808   RcCt: 9 May 1808
Stephen WILSON & wife Martha of Ldn to John SPENCER of Ldn. B/S of
3*ac* on NW fork of Goose Creek.

Bk:Pg: 2I:351   Date: 8 Feb 1808   RcCt: 9 May 1808
Stephen WILSON & wife Martha of Ldn to John SPENCER of Ldn. Trust
using 183*ac* which Nathan SPENCER dec'd died possessed of.

Bk:Pg: 2I:352   Date: 9 Nov 1807   RcCt: 9 May 1808
Henry LEE of WstmVa to Richard B. LEE of Ffx. LS of 1200*ac* on
Potomac in occupation of Ludwell LEE, also 150*ac* Lower Island in
Potomac now occupied by Baldwin DADE, also 75*ac* Pepper Island in
Potomac occupied by Ludwell LEE & Richard B. LEE. Wit: Burdett
ESKRIDGE, Walt. MUSE, Thos. YEATMAN, Fanny POPE, Jos. LEWIS
Jr., Joseph WHEATONG, Jesse MOORE, F. FAIRFAX, Edm. J. LEE, R.
J. TAYLOR, Alexander MOORE.

Bk:Pg: 2I:354   Date: 8 Nov 1806   RcCt: 13 Jul 1807
Nicholas TUCKER of Ldn to James THOMPSON, Jane THOMPSON &
Hugh THOMPSON of Ldn. A/L of 100*ac* in ShelP where TUCKER now
lives adj David LOVETT, Thomas LEWIS between Short Hill and Blue
Ridge. Wit: Mahlon ROACH, Josiah WHITE Jr., James PRYOR.

Bk:Pg: 2I:356   Date: 6 May 1808   RcCt: 9 May 1808
Thomas & Daniel DARFLINGER (Exor of Henry DARFLINGER dec'd) of
Ldn to John CLICE of Ldn. B/S of 97*ac* between Short Hill and Blue
Ridge. Wit: Edward CUNARD Sr., Samuel NEER, James NEER.

Bk:Pg: 2I:359   Date: 13 Apr 1808   RcCt: 9 May 1808
Issachar BROWN of Ldn to Stacey TAYLOR of Ldn. Trust for debt to
Theophilus HOFF 63*ac* adj Jane HUMPHREY, James HEATON, John
BROWN. Wit: Wm. BRONAUGH, Ben GRAYSON, Abner HUMPHREY.

Bk:Pg: 2I:361   Date: 8 Apr 1808   RcCt: 9 May 1808
Abner HUMPHREY & wife Mary of Ldn to James HEATON of Ldn. B/S of
10*ac* adj John BROWN. Wit: Wm. BRONAUGH, Stacy TAYLOR, Ben
GRAYSON.

Bk:Pg: 2I:363   Date: 29 Apr 1808   RcCt: 9 May 1808
Abner HUMPHREY & wife Mary of Ldn to Issachar BROWN of Ldn. B/S
of 63*ac* adj Jane HUMPHREY, James HEATON, John BROWN. Wit: Wm.
BRONAUGH, Stacey TAYLOR, Ben GRAYSON.

Bk:Pg: 2I:366   Date: 30 Jan 1808   RcCt: 9 May 1808
Nancy DAVISON, Lewis ELLZEY & wife Rosanna, John McILHANY Jr.,
Elizabeth McILHANY, Solomon DAVIS & wife Mary and Cecelia, James,
Louisa & Mortimer McILHANY by Guardian Margaret McILHANY (of
James McILHANY dec'd) to Josiah WHITE of Ldn. B/S of 150*ac* where
WHITE now lives. Wit: Stacy TAYLOR, N. C. WILLIAMS, John WHITE,
Robert WHITE, Mahlon ROACH, Josiah WHITE Jr., Josabed WHITE.

Bk:Pg: 2I:369   Date: 18 Apr 1808   RcCt: 9 May 1808
Peter F. MARBLE now of Lsbg to Charles GULLATT of Lsbg. B/S of lot adj James & John CAVAN on Loudoun St. Wit: Jno. MATTHIAS, John H. EVANS, Jas. CAVAN Jr.

Bk:Pg: 2I:372   Date: 20 Apr 1808   RcCt: 9 May 1808
Henry LONG & wife Rebekah of Ldn to Mortho SULLIVAN of Ldn. B/S of lot in Wtfd. Wit: Joshua HENRY, William STEERE, W. S. NEALE, Chas. BENNETT, John HAMILTON.

Bk:Pg: 2I:374   Date: 6 Apr 1808   RcCt: 9 May 1808
Abdon DILLON & wife Ann, Moses DILLON & wife Rebekah Mary DILLON widow of James DILLON dec'd of Ldn to Thomas KENT of Ldn. B/S of 30ac adj George BURSON, Peter HANN. Wit: Stacey TAYLOR, Lewis ELLZEY, Dennis G. JONES, Henry SMITH.

Bk:Pg: 2I:377   Date: 4 Apr 1808   RcCt: 9 May 1808
Robert LITTLE of PrWm to Reuben SETTLE. BoS for negro boy Thomas. Wit: Daniel SETTLE, Job RACE.

Bk:Pg: 2I:378   Date: 27 Jan 1808   RcCt: 9 May 1808
John PAYNE of Ldn to William WINNER of Ldn. BoS for negro girl Harriot abt 13y old. Wit: Isaac LAROWE, Saml. M. EDWARDS.

Bk:Pg: 2I:379   Date: 10 Dec 1807   RcCt: 9 May 1808
Price JACOBS of Ldn to John PANCOAST of Ldn. Trust using 59ac on Beaverdam Creek, 12ac & 2ac. Wit: Joshua PANCOAST, Samuel NICHOLS, John PANCOAST.

Bk:Pg: 2I:380   Date: 8 Jan 1808   RcCt: 9 May 1808
Elizabeth McILHANY (distributee of James MCILHANY dec'd) of Ldn to Rachel WHITE. B/S of 142¾ac adj Jonah THOMPSON, James NIXON, Thomas DAVIS, Rachel WHITE. Wit: John BEATY, Samuel COOK, Thomas DAVIS.

Bk:Pg: 2I:382   Date: 9 May 1807   RcCt: 9 May 1808
Benjamin MEAD & wife Ann of Ldn to Josiah HALL & Mary BEATY of Ldn. B/S of 221ac. Wit: Stacey TAYLOR, Lewis ELLZEY, Leven D. POWELL, Saml. BOGGESS.

Bk:Pg: 2I:385   Date: 21 Apr 1808   RcCt: 9 May 1808
William J. DUTY of Fayette, Lexington Co Ky to Daniel DUTY of Ldn. B/S of rights to estate of father Thomas DUTY dec'd.

Bk:Pg: 2I:386   Date: 21 Jan 1804   RcCt: 10 Sep 1804
Joseph JANNEY of AlexVa (s/o John JANNEY dec'd of Ldn) to John JANNEY of AlexVa. Mortgage to cover debt to John of 300ac from father upon death of widow Hannah JANNEY. Wit: William SHREVE, John LLOYD, Henry COOPER, Jonas POTTS, Daniel LUKE, John WILLIAMS.

Bk:Pg: 2I:389   Date: 23 Apr 1808   RcCt: 9 May 1808
James RATIKEN & wife Susannah of Ldn to James NIXON of Ldn. B/S of 145ac adj Joseph COX dec'd. Wit: Samuel MURREY, Fra. H. PEYTON,

William HALL, Geo. W. BALL, Jas. CAVAN, Jno. MATTHIAS, A.
SUTHERLAND, William SCHOOLEY, James GARNER.

Bk:Pg: 2I:391   Date: 1 Apr 1808   RcCt: 9 May 1808
Moses DILLON & wife Rebecca of Ldn to Edward COE of Ldn. B/S of
241*ac* adj Israel COMBS. Wit: John LITTLEJOHN, Rich'd H.
HENDERSON, Benj. H. CANBY, Samuel MURREY.

Bk:Pg: 2I:393   Date: __ Aug 1807   RcCt: 9 May 1808
William HARNED & wife Margaret of Hllb to James H. HAMILTON,
George S. HOUGH & Thomas HOUGH of Hllb. Trust for debt to Lewis
ELLZEY using lot in Hllb formerly of John JANNEY dec'd. Wit: Joseph
HOWELL, David LOVETT, Samuel BEALLE.

Bk:Pg: 2I:395   Date: 10 Apr 1807   RcCt: 9 May 1808
William HARNET (Admr of Job THOMAS dec'd of Hllb) to Rosannah
ELLZEY of Ldn. BoS for negro Sarah abt 35y old. Wit: James H.
HAMILTON, Saml. W. YOUNG.

Bk:Pg: 2I:396   Date: 2 May 1808   RcCt: 9 May 1808
Ann FREEMAN & Alexander SMITH to William HUMMER. A/L of 100*ac*.
Wit: Johnston CLEVELAND, John JEFFERSON, William WHALEY, Mark
BLINCOE, Joseph DOUGLASS.

Bk:Pg: 2I:398   Date: 6 Jan 1808   RcCt: 9 May 1808
William HUMMER (Admr of Thomas EVANS dec'd) to Samuel NEWMAN
& wife Rhoda (formerly widow Rhoda EVANS). Receipt and
relinquishment of all claims against estate. Wit: Abiel JENNIERS, William
RIGHT, John KEENE, James B. LANE.

Bk:Pg: 2I:398   Date: 12 Nov 1803   RcCt: 9 Jan 1804
Ferdinando FAIRFAX of JeffVa to Henry PLITCHER of Ldn. LS of 25*ac*
on Short Hill adj Michael EVERHEART, Peter RIDENBAUGH. Wit: John
D. ORR, J. SAUNDERS, Wm. H. HARDING, John H. CANBY, Abiel
JENNIERS, Alex. JEURY.

Bk:Pg: 2I:400   Date: 8 Jan 1808   RcCt: 9 May 1808
Burr POWELL & wife Catharine of Ldn to Jehu BURSON of Ldn. B/S of
45*ac* on Wankapin branch adj Peter TOWARMAN. Wit: Leven POWELL,
Leven LUCKETT.

Bk:Pg: 2I:402   Date: 9 May 1808   RcCt: 10 May 1808
Thomas N. BINNS (s/o Charles BINNS dec'd) of Ldn to William
BRONAUGH. Trust for debt to Sheriff Benjamin GRAYSON using 545*ac*
adj George NICKSON. Wit: Stacey TAYLOR, James RUST, John H.
CANBY, Thomas LOVE.

Bk:Pg: 2I:404   Date: 14 Aug 1804   RcCt: 10 May 1808
Joseph SMITH & wife Mary of AlexVa to Thomas WILKINSON of Lsbg.
B/S of lot in Lsbg adj Lot #12. Wit: Samuel MURREY, Obadiah
CLIFFORD.

Bk:Pg: 2I:407   Date: 17 Feb 1808   RcCt: 10 May 1808
James LEITH & wife Sarah to Robert M. POWELL & Daniel EACHES.
B/S of 5ac on Goose Creek. Wit: Burr POWELL, Fleet SMITH, Samuel
BOGGESS, B. E. WILLS, Leven POWELL.

Bk:Pg: 2I:409   Date: 14 Feb 1808   RcCt: 10 May 1808
James LEITH & wife Sarah of Ldn to Daniel EACHES of Ldn. B/S of 50ac
on Goose Creek adj Robert POWELL. Wit: Burr POWELL, Fleet SMITH,
Saml. BOGGESS, B. E. WILLS, Leven POWELL.

Bk:Pg: 2I:412   Date: 14 Jan 1805   RcCt: 14 Jan 1805
John WILDMAN & wife Eleanor of Lsbg to Benjamin B. THORNTON of
Lsbg. B/S of lot in Lsbg late property of Jacob JACOBS on Loudoun St.
Wit: Jas. CAVAN Jr., Francis H. PEYTON, Armistead LONG.

Bk:Pg: 2I:415   Date: 2 Apr 1808   RcCt: 11 May 1808
John DORRELL & wife Peggy of Ldn to George WAGLEY of Ldn. B/S of
½ of Lot #3 where DORRELL now lives. Wit: John LITTLEJOHN, Samuel
LITTLEJOHN, John W. STONE.

Bk:Pg: 2I:417   Date: 25 Jan 1808   RcCt: 13 Apr 1808
John BROWN to Edward RINKER & wife Sally. Release of mortgage. Wit:
C. BINNS, Saml. M. EDWARDS, Eli OFFUTT.

Bk:Pg: 2I:417   Date: 11 Jan 1808   RcCt: 11 Jul 1808
James DAWSON & wife Polly of Ldn to Colin AULD of AlexVa. Trust for
debt to John RAMSEY using lot on Loudoun St in Lsbg lately used by
DAWSON as a tavern. Wit: John CAVAN, John H. EVANS, Alex.
LANGLEY.

Bk:Pg: 2I:420   Date: 30 Jan 1808   RcCt: 1 Jul 1808
Sheriff Benjamin GRAYSON of Ldn to George HAMMAT of Ldn. B/S of
11ac nr Lsbg.

Bk:Pg: 2I:421   Date: 8 Jun 1808   RcCt: 11 Jul 1808
Benjamin H. CANBY, Samuel MURREY, Francis TRIPLETT & Alexander
SUTHERLAND of Ldn to Joshua RILEY of Ldn. Release of trust on lot in
Lsbg. Wit: Saml. M. EDWARDS, John NEWTON, Isaac HARRIS.

Bk:Pg: 2I:424   Date: 9 Feb 1808   RcCt: 9 Mar 1808
Thomas MILHOLLEN of Bath Co Va (br/o John MILHOLLEN dec'd of Ldn,
for himself & Jonathan MILHOLLEN of Champaign Co OH) to brother
Patrick MILHOLLEN. Release.

Bk:Pg: 2I:425   Date: 30 Nov 1807   RcCt: 11 Jan 1808
Peter GLASSCOCK & wife Ann of Fqr to Leven POWELL of Ldn. B/S of
209ac adj Elizabeth BAKER. Wit: Burr POWELL, Jos. CARR, Jno. B.
ARMISTEAD, William WILLIAMSON, Elias PORTER.

Bk:Pg: 2I:428   Date: 27 Feb 1808   RcCt: 9 May 1808
John WILKINSON & wife Mary (d/o Joseph NEILL dec'd) of Lsbg to
Martin KITZMILLER of Ldn. Mortgage using 240ac in Jefferson Co Ky nr
Salt River. Wit: Jacob FADELEY, Edward DAWES, Jacob TAWNER.

Bk:Pg: 2K:001   Date: 12 Nov 1803   RcCt: 13 Feb 1804
Ferdinando FAIRFAX & William B. PAGE of JeffVa to Peter TEMERY of
Ldn. B/S of 122¼ac adj Jacob ROPP, Balser DERRY. Wit: John D. ORR,
J. SAUNDERS, Wm. H. HARDING, John H. CANBY, Abiel JENNIERS,
Alexander YOUNG.

Bk:Pg: 2K:002   Date: 17 Aug 1808   RcCt: 12 Sep 1808
James CAVAN Jr. (Admr of Patrick CAVAN dec'd of Lsbg) to Benjamin H.
CANBY of Ldn. A/L of 5ac adj John LITTLEJOHN. Wit: Barton LUCAS,
Jno. MATTHIAS, John SHAW.

Bk:Pg: 2K:005   Date: 24 Aug 1808   RcCt: 12 Sep 1808
Catharine EMERY of Ldn and Joseph BURSON to Benjamin H. CANBY.
A/L of 10ac. Wit: Joshua DANNIEL, John MARTS, Joseph GREEN.

Bk:Pg: 2K:007   Date: 7 Sep 1808   RcCt: 12 Sep 1808
William DANIEL of Ldn to Benjamin DANIEL of Ldn. B/S of half of land
held in partnership together. Wit: Stacey TAYLOR, George BROWN,
Samuel HUGHES.

Bk:Pg: 2K:008   Date: 4 Apr 1808   RcCt: 12 Sep 1808
Joshua GORE Jr. and Mark GORE. Partition of 175ac from father
Thomas GORE dec'd. Wit: Stacy TAYLOR, Thomas GREGG, Samuel
REED, Robert BRYSON.

Bk:Pg: 2K:010   Date: 4 Apr 1808   RcCt: 12 Sep 1808
Mark GORE of Ldn to Thomas GREGG of Ldn. B/S of 87ac on Kittockton
Creek adj Lewis ELLZEY, Joshua GORE. Wit: Stacy TAYLOR, Joshua
GORE, Robert BRYSON, Samuel REED.

Bk:Pg: 2K:012   Date: 26 Apr 1808   RcCt: 12 Sep 1808
James RATIKEN of Ldn to Joshua PUSEY, Asa MOORE & Thomas
PHILLIPS [firm of Joshua Pusey & Co.] of Ldn. B/S of 140ac adj Patrick
McHOLLAND, John SCHOOLEY. Wit: James MOORE, Rich'd
NORWOOD, Leven SMALLWOOD, Saml. PEIRPOINT.

Bk:Pg: 2K:013   Date: 23 Apr 1808   RcCt: 12 Sep 1808
Asa MOORE and Abner WILLIAMS & wife of Ldn to Benjamin STEERE of
Ldn. B/S of 57ac adj Joshua DANNIEL, Thomas PHILLIPS. Wit: Joshua
HENRY, Isaac E. STEER, Alex'r SANDERSON.

Bk:Pg: 2K:015   Date: __ Feb 1808   RcCt: 12 Sep 1808
Presley SAUNDERS Jr. & wife Mary of Ldn to William AUSTINE of Ldn.
B/S of part of Lot #50 on Back St in Lsbg. Wit: Pressley CORDELL,
Thomas McCOWATT, Chars. GULLATT, Wm. BRONAUGH, Lewis
ELLZEY.

Bk:Pg: 2K:017   Date: 13 May 1808   RcCt: 12 Sep 1808
Joseph LEWIS Jr. of Ldn to Jacob EMERY of Ldn. B/S of 88ac adj John
AXLINE, Philip EVERHEART. Wit: R. BRADEN, Catharine EMREY,
Christiana EMREY.

Bk:Pg: 2K:018   Date: 13 Apr 1808   RcCt: 12 Sep 1808
Jonas POTTS of Ldn to Samuel CLAPHAM of Ldn. Trust for CLAPHAM
as security using lot in Wtfd where POTTS now lives. Wit: John
JACKSON, John FRYE, Isaac STEERE.

Bk:Pg: 2K:019   Date: 9 Apr 1808   RcCt: 12 Sep 1808
Benjamin RUST & wife Hannah of Fqr to Israel HICKS of Ldn. B/S of
253ac in Ldn & Fqr adj Col. John THORNTON, William FITZHUGH. Wit:
Joshua WRIGHT, Thos. COATS, Tomzin PORTER, James COLLINGS,
Wm. BRONAUGH, Jos. CARR.

Bk:Pg: 2K:022   Date: 9 Apr 1808   RcCt: 12 Sep 1808
Benjamin RUST & wife Hannah of Fqr to Isaiah HICKS of Ldn. B/S of
253ac on Painther Skin branch in Ldn & Fqr adj Israel HICKS, William
FITZHUGH. Wit: Joshua WRIGHT, Thomas COATS, Tomzen PORTER,
James COLLINS, Wm. BRONAUGH, Jos. CARR.

Bk:Pg: 2K:025   Date: 12 Sep 1808   RcCt: 12 Sep 1808
Basil STONESTREET of Ldn to daughter the wife of Joseph BLINCOE of
Ffx. Loan of negroes Ellick, Patience, Will & Jem and farm and household
items. Wit: Rich'd H. HENDERSON, Thos. L. MOORE.

Bk:Pg: 2K:025   Date: 23 Nov 1806   RcCt: 11 May 1808
Charles BELL (s/o Charles BELL dec'd, br/o Abigail PATTERSON, Lydda
BAXTOR, Nancy DEHAVEN, Charles BELL, Hannah LOWRY, Mary
JONES, Elizabeth BELL) of Ldn to William DULIN of Ldn. B/S of 224¾ac
adj Enoch THOMAS, George RAZOR, Mary NOLAND. Wit: Saml.
LUCKETT, Wm. SMITH, Wm. WILLIAMS, N. LUCKETT, Samuel COCKE.

Bk:Pg: 2K:027   Date: 19 May 1808   RcCt: 12 Sep 1808
Thomas & Daniel DARFLINGER (Exors of Henry DARFLINGER dec'd) of
Ldn to James H. HAMILTON of Hllb. B/S of 147ac between Blue Ridge &
Short Hill adj Ebenezer GRUBB. Wit: Thos. LESLIE, I. N. HOOK, Thomas
GREGG.

Bk:Pg: 2K:030   Date: 11 Mar 1808   RcCt: 12 Sep 1808
Thomas NOLAND of FrdkMd to Samuel LUCKETT of Ldn. B/S of 70½ac
& 2¾ac. Wit: William NOLAND, Saml. CLAPHAM, Philip LUCKETT.

Bk:Pg: 2K:032   Date: 3 May 1808   RcCt: 12 Sep 1808
Andrew SMARR of Ldn to Joseph VANMETRE of Hardy Co VA. BoS for
horse. Wit: Wm. CHILTON.

Bk:Pg: 2K:033   Date: 1 Apr 1808   RcCt: 12 Sep 1808
Deposition: Thomas MARKS age 51y said nr 30y ago he was shown a
tree by his brother Elisha MARKS said to be the corner of his property
next to John DAVIS, Thomas showed the place on 31 Dec last to Jasper
POULSON, Thomas HUGHES, stone was now there and POULSON who
now owns the land and HUGHES said the land was DAVIS'. Wit: Stacy
TAYLOR.

Bk:Pg: 2K:033   Date: 2 Apr 1808   RcCt: 9 Sep 1808
Deposition: William BEANS age 67y abt 20y ago he was acquainted with
the corner of land of John DAVIS [see 2K:033]. Wit: Stacy TAYLOR.

Bk:Pg: 2K:034 Date: 12 Mar 1808 RcCt: 12 Sep 1808
Moses DILLON & wife Rebekah of Ldn to Amos FERGUSON of Ldn. B/S
150*ac*. Wit: Stacy TAYLOR, Lewis ELLZEY, James LOVE.

Bk:Pg: 2K:036 Date: 1 Apr 1808 RcCt: 12 Sep 1808
Ludwell LEE & wife Eliza to Johnston CLEVELAND. B/S of 250*ac*. Wit:
Steph COOKE, Edm. J. LEE, Thomas DARNE Jr., Obadiah CLIFFORD.

Bk:Pg: 2K:038 Date: 21 Jan 1808 RcCt: 12 Sep 1808
Isaac HOUGH of Ldn to James HAMILTON heirs, John HANKS heirs,
George MULL, Joseph WILKINSON, Joseph POSTON, George
SHUMAKER, Francis McKEMEY, Jacob COOPER, John HOUGH,
Jeremiah PURDOM, Simon SHUMAKER, John STATLER and Daniel
SHOMAKER Jr. of Ldn. B/S of 1*ac* in Piedmont Manor adj Michael
COOPER. Wit: Jos. McGEATH, Abiel JENNERS, Peter STONE, Jos.
TRIBBY.

Bk:Pg: 2K:040 Date: 24 Aug 1808 RcCt: 12 Sep 1808
Sarah/Sally ELLZEY of Ldn to sister-in-law Rosannah ELLZEY w/o
brother Lewis ELLZEY of Ldn. Gift of slave Flora & her children Henry,
Jim & Virgil. Wit: Jno. BAYLEY, Saml. TILLETT.

Bk:Pg: 2K:041 Date: 16 May 1808 RcCt: 11 Jul 1808
Baker JOHNSON of FrdkMd to Thomas JOHNSON of FrdkMd. B/S of 1/5
share [other shares owned by Henry LEE & Henry Astly BENNET, Jonas
CLAPHAM, Thomas, James, Baker & Roger JOHNSON] of 1310½*ac*
Potowmack Iron Furnace. Wit: Otho LAURENCE, Joshua JOHNSON,
Geo. JOHNSON.

Bk:Pg: 2K:042 Date: 13 Apr 1808 RcCt: 11 Jul 1808
Roger JOHNSON of FrdkMd to Thomas & James JOHNSON of FrdkMd.
B/S of shares of Potowmack Iron Furnace [see 2K:041]. Wit: Ferd.
FAIRFAX, Saml. CLAPHAM, Geo. JOHNSON, Richard JOHNSON.

Bk:Pg: 2K:043 Date: 2 Jun 1808 RcCt: 11 Jul 1808
Thomas & James JOHNSON of FredkMd to Roger JOHNSON of
FredkMd. B/S of iron ore to use at Roger Johnson's Furnace nr mouth of
Monocasy. Wit: Geo. JOHNSON, Richard JOHNSON, Wm. T.
JOHNSON.

Bk:Pg: 2K:045 Date: 18 May 1808 RcCt: 12 Sep 1808
Jacob BAUGH & wife Mary to John JANNY. CoE for sale of land. Wit:
Samuel MURREY, John LITTLEJOHN.

Bk:Pg: 2K:046 Date: 19 Apr 1808 RcCt: 12 Sep 1808
Samuel BROOK of Washington Co Territory of Columbia to John
WORLSEY of Ldn. B/S of 2 lots totaling 358*ac* adj Robert BRADEN,
James RATEKIN, Charles BENNETT. Wit: Thos. HERTY, Robt KING,
Robert BRENT.

Bk:Pg: 2K:049 Date: 13 Mar 1801 RcCt: 13 Apr 1801/ 12 Sep 1808
Samuel & Mahlon HOUGH (Exors of John HOUGH dec'd) of Ldn to Jacob
WINE of Ldn. Re-lease of land. Wit: Alex. SUTHERLAND, John H.
CANBY, Thos. HOUGH, B. HOUGH, Isaac HOUGH, Patterson WRIGHT.

Bk:Pg: 2K:052   Date: 9 May 1808   RcCt: 11 Jul 1808
Fanny LEE (Exor of Thomas Ludwell LEE late of Coten) to Peter
OATYER of Ldn. B/S of 416ac adj Hugh CALDWELL. Wit: Edm. J. LEE,
R. B. VOSS, Thomas DARNE Jr., Allen READ, Isaac HARRIS.

Bk:Pg: 2K:054   Date: 16 Apr 1808   RcCt: 12 Sep 1808
Isreal COMBS of Ldn to Elisha JANNY of Ldn. B/S of 150ac on
Beaverdam. Wit: Abraham SKILLMAN, John TREBBY, Hendley
SIMPSON, Elie MILLAN.

Bk:Pg: 2K:055   Date: 13 Aug 1808   RcCt: 12 Sep 1808
William SMITH. Nominates sons Jonas & John SMITH as renewable lives
on L/L on former property of William WILDMAN now dec'd.

Bk:Pg: 2K:055   Date: 12 Sep 1808   RcCt: 12 Sep 1808
Peter GLASSCOCK & wife Ann to Leven POWELL. CoE for sale of
209ac. Wit: Jno. B. ARMISTEAD, Elies EDMONDS Jr.

Bk:Pg: 2K:056   Date: 13 Jul 1808   RcCt: 12 Sep 1808
Presley SAUNDERS & wife Mary of Ldn to James SAUNDERS of Lsbg.
B/S of part of Lot #50 on Loudoun St in Lsbg. Wit: Jno. MATTHIAS, Thos.
EDWARDS, Robt ROBERTSON, James SAUNDERS, Thomas AWBREY,
Evritt SANDERS.

Bk:Pg: 2K:059   Date: 16 Jul 1808   RcCt: 12 Sep 1808
James SAUNDERS of Lsbg to Sampson BLINCOE of Lsbg. B/S of part of
Lot #50 on Loudoun St in Lsbg. Wit: Thos. WILKINSON, Warner
HUGHES, Andrew GARDNER, Matthew MITCHELL, George HEAD,
William DRISH.

Bk:Pg: 2K:060   Date: 25 Jun 1808   RcCt: 12 Sep 1808
David CONNER & wife Martha (d/o John WILLIAM dec'd) of Ldn to Ellis
WILLIAMS of Ldn. B/S of 1/7 of 30ac where wd/o John WILLIAMS dec'd
lives & 1/7 of adj ¾ac. Wit: Saml. CARR, Obadiah CLIFFORD, Eli
OFFUTT, John CARR, Jno. ROSE.

Bk:Pg: 2K:063   Date: 12 Sep 1808   RcCt: 13 Sep 1808
Robert PARFECT & wife Jane of Ldn to Samuel Murrey EDWARDS of
Ldn. B/S of 1ac (Lots #32 & #41) on W side of Lsbg adj Poorhouse lot on
Market St. Wit: Samuel MURREY, Joseph CARR.

Bk:Pg: 2K:066   Date: 13 Sep 1808   RcCt: 13 Sep 1808
Richard H. HENDERSON and Nathan KING of Ldn. Agreement for
HENDERSON to free Negro Tom (late the property of John
ALEXANDER) after 10y if Nathan keeps Tom in Va. Wit: Tho. L. MOORE.

Bk:Pg: 2K:066   Date: 1 Sep 1808   RcCt: 14 Sep 1808
Thomas SIM & wife Harriet of Ldn to Thomas SWANN & wife Jane of
AlexVa. Mortgage of land nr Lsbg. Wit: Henry S. COOKE, John
NEWTON, Arthur NELSON, W. C. SELDEN, Burr POWELL.

Bk:Pg: 2K:071   Date: 12 Aug 1808   RcCt: 15 Sep 1808
Thomas SWANN & wife Jane of AlexVa to Thomas SIM of Ldn. B/S of
178ac. Wit: Richard H. LOVE, Wilson Cary SELDEN, Richd. M. SCOTT.

Bk:Pg: 2K:073   Date: 15 Mar 1808   RcCt: 13 Apr 1808
William CARR & wife Margaret of Ldn to Samuel HOUGH (Exor of Edward STABLER dec'd). B/S of 17½ac nr Caroline Rd adj William CARR. Thos. SANDERS, A. SUTHERLAND, Jno. MATTHIAS.

Bk:Pg: 2K:075   Date: 18 Jul 1808   RcCt: 10 Oct 1808
John BROWN Sr. & wife Sarah of Ldn to Isaac BROWN of Ldn. B/S of 114ac adj George BROWN, Abel MARKS. Wit: Hugh DOUGLAS, Step C. ROSZELL, Saml. BOGGESS, Chas. CHAMBLIN.

Bk:Pg: 2K:076   Date: 15 Mar 1808   RcCt: 10 Oct 1808
John BALL & wife Susannah of Ldn to William ELLZEY of Ldn. Trust for debt to George KILGORE using 100ac & 97½ac. Wit: Jno. MATTHIAS, Jas CAVAN Jr., John A. BINNS, Samuel HOUGH, Wm. MAINS.

Bk:Pg: 2K:079   Date: 17 Feb 1808   RcCt: 10 Oct 1808
Robert M. POWELL & wife Elizabeth of Ldn to Daniel EACHES of Ldn. B/S of ½ of 50ac lot. Wit: Burr POWELL, William BRONAUGH, William VICKERS, Leven LUCKETT.

Bk:Pg: 2K:081   Date: 14 Apr 1808   RcCt: 10 Oct 1808
Leven POWELL of Ldn to William BRONAUGH of Ldn. B/S of 11ac. Wit: A. GIBSON, John UPP, John KIPHEART, Noble BEVERAGE, Mesheck LACEY, Leven LUCKETT.

Bk:Pg: 2K:083   Date: 8 Oct 1808   RcCt: 10 Oct 1808
Jehu BURSON of Ldn to William P. HALE of Ldn. Mortgage on 30ac on Wancapin branch. Wit: Joseph BURSON, Moses WILSON, William MANKIN.

Bk:Pg: 2K:084   Date: 8 Oct 1808   RcCt: 10 Oct 1808
William P. HALE of Ldn to Jehu BURSON of Ldn. B/S of 30ac adj Moses WILSON. Wit: Joseph BURSON, Moses WILSON, William MANKIN.

Bk:Pg: 2K:085   Date: 26 Aug 1808   RcCt: 10 Oct 1808
Henry CLAGETT & wife Julia of Ldn to Thomas SAUNDERS of Ldn. B/S of part of lot on N side of Loudoun St Lsbg. Wit: Jno. MATTHIAS, John H. EVANS, John PAYNE, John LITTLEJOHN, Saml. MURREY.

Bk:Pg: 2K:088   Date: 17 Sep 1807   RcCt: 10 Oct 1808
Joseph LEWIS Jr. and Philip FITZHUGH to Joseph TIDBALL. B/S of 203ac "Clifton" estate by Burr POWELL & Joseph CARR as result of a suit. Wit: A. GIBSON, John BATTSON, John UPP, Thos. BISCOE, Zophas JOHNSTON, John DULIN.

Bk:Pg: 2K:090   Date: 12 Apr 1808   RcCt: 10 Oct 1808
Hugh LEMON & wife Rachel of FrdkMd to John F. SAPPINGTON of Wtfd. B/S of lot in Wtfd adj Flemon PATTERSON. Wit: Eli OFFUTT, Saml. M. EDWARDS, Isaac LAROWE, Jno. ROSE, John VANDEVANTER.

Bk:Pg: 2K:092   Date: 21 May 1808   RcCt: 11 Jul 1808
Joseph HAINS & wife Maria (late Maria HANDY) of Ldn to William H. HANDY of Ldn. B/S of share of land & mill of father John HANDY dec'd

(deed to Given HANDY & children). Wit: Stacey TAYLOR, Wm.
ESKRIDGE, Step C. ROSZELL.

Bk:Pg: 2K:095   Date: 10 Oct 1807   RcCt: 10 Oct 1808
Benjamin PRICE & wife Sarah of Ldn to Thomas CHILTON of Ldn. B/S of
10*ac* adj Marg't SINCLAIR.

Bk:Pg: 2K:096   Date: 25 Aug 1807   RcCt: 10 Oct 1808
Elizabeth BAYLY. Received from father Montjoy BAYLY (appointed
Guardian) full portion of estate of Uncle Joseph BAYLY dec'd. Wit:
Armis'd T. MASON, A. B. T. MASON, John T. MASON Jr.

Bk:Pg: 2K:097   Date: 25 Aug 1807   RcCt: 10 Oct 1808
Eleanor BAYLY. Received from father Montjoy BAYLY (appointed
Guardian) full portion of estate of Uncle Joseph BAYLY dec'd. Wit:
Armis'd T. MASON, A. B. T. MASON, John T. MASON Jr.

Bk:Pg: 2K:097   Date: ___ 1808   RcCt: 10 Oct 1808
Wilson Carey SELDON & wife Nelly of Ldn to Thomas SWANN of AlexVa.
B/S of 483*ac*. Wit: Thos. SIM, Burr POWELL.

Bk:Pg: 2K:101   Date: 29 Aug 1805   RcCt: 10 Oct 1808
William ELLZEY & wife Francis Hill of Ldn to Lewis ELLZEY & wife
Rosannah of Ldn. B/S of all land Lewis became entitled to as reps of
James McILHANY dec'd. If they die without issue goes to Rosannah's
brothers James, Mortimer & John McILHANY Jr. Wit: Ben GRAYSON,
Wm. GRAYSON, James HEATON. Albert RUSSELL, Chas. LEWIS.

Bk:Pg: 2K:103   Date: 23 Aug 1805   RcCt: 11 Feb 1806
Lewis ELLZEY & wife Rosannah (d/o James McILHANY who d. 16 Sep
1804, widow Margaret) of Ldn to William ELLZEY of Ldn. B/S of land from
James. Wit: Stacy TAYLOR, James HEATON, Notley C. WILLIAMS.

Bk:Pg: 2K:106   Date: 3 Oct 1808   RcCt: 10 Oct 1808
Joseph LEWIS Jr. of Ldn to Joseph TIDBALL of Winchester, FrdkVa. B/S
of 68*ac* formerly Ball's Mill (Farling dec'd) now under L/L to John HALL.

Bk:Pg: 2K:107   Date: 3 Mar 1807   RcCt: 13 Jul 1807
John Thomas RICKETTS & wife Mary of Ffx and William NEWTON & wife
Jane B. of AlexVa to Barnett HOUGH of Ldn. B/S of 30*ac*. Wit: Thos.
SWANN, Edm'd DENNY, Saml. SMITH, Geo. W. BALL.

Bk:Pg: 2K:113   Date: 26 Jan 1808   RcCt: 10 Oct 1808
Abner SHREVE (s/o Benjamin SHREVE dec'd of Ldn) of Bedford Co Va
to Benjamin SHREVE of Ldn. B/S of ¼ share from father's will. Wit:
Robert MOFFETT, William MEAD, Alexander WHITELY.

Bk:Pg: 2K:114   Date: 14 Nov 1806   RcCt: 12 Apr 1808
Commissioners William MANN & Charles Fenton MERCER to Thomas
SANDERS of Lsbg. B/S of lot and house in Lsbg formerly of Samuel
HOUGH at corner of Loudoun & King Sts. Wit: Jas. SAUNDERS, Thos.
DARNE Jr., Fleet SMITH.

Bk:Pg: 2K:116   Date: ___ 1808   RcCt: 10 Oct 1808
Solomon LITTLETON, Jacob BAUGH, John KEPHEART, Thomas
KEPHEART & Jacob KEPHEART. Bond on sale to John PAYNE land of
Godfrey KEPHEART dec'd (to children Lenora & Kitty KEPHEART <21y).
Wit: Saml. MURREY, Jno. ROSE, Jas. CAVAN Jr., Barton LUCAS.

Bk:Pg: 2K:117   Date: 7 Oct 1807   RcCt: 10 Oct 1808
James SAUNDERS Jr. & wife Sarah (d/o John SAUNDERS dec'd) of
Fleming Co Ky to Presly SAUNDERS Jr. of Ldn. B/S of Sarah's share of
estate.

Bk:Pg: 2K:120   Date: 11 Oct 1808   RcCt: 11 Oct 1808
Fielding MARQUIS of Ldn to William B. HARRISON of Ldn. B/S of farm
and household items and interest in 123ac leased land – for benefit of his
wife Rebeccah and children Catharine & Thomas Harrison MARQUIS.

Bk:Pg: 2K:121   Date: 7 Mar 1808   RcCt: 11 Oct 1808
Josiah MOFFETT Sr. of Ldn to Simon BINNS of Ldn. BoS for cow. Wit:
Chas. THRIFT, Gust. ELGIN Jr.

Bk:Pg: 2K:122   Date: 5 Dec 1807   RcCt: 12 Apr 1808
Daniel BROWN & wife Rachel of Ldn to Reuben TRIPLETT of Ldn.
Mortgage of 80ac with water grist and saw mill on Goose Creek. Wit:
Simon TRIPLETT, Wm. H. TRIPLETT, Catherine TRIPLETT, Alice
TRIPLETT.

Bk:Pg: 2K:124   Date: ___ Mar 1807   RcCt: 11 Oct 1808
George ROSE of Fairfield Co Oh formerly of Ldn & wife Jane (formerly
Jane BOYD an heir of Thomas BOYD dec'd of Ldn) to Aaron SANDERS
of Ldn. PoA. Wit: Isaac LAROWE, Saml. M. EDWARDS.

Bk:Pg: 2K:125   Date: 3 Mar 1806   RcCt: 13 Oct 1806
Michael BOGAR & wife Elizabeth of Ldn to Daniel DAVIS of Ldn. B/S of
5ac adj Isaac BALL. Wit: I. BALL, John McNEEL, Thomas DAVIS, William
JAY, James HAMILTON, Richard GRIFFITH.

Bk:Pg: 2K:128   Date: 10 Aug 1808   RcCt: 10 Oct 1808
Presley SAUNDERS Jr. & wife Mary of Ldn to Presley SAUNDERS Sr. of
Ldn. B/S of 1/9 share of 140ac (James SAUNDERS Jr & wife Sarah's
share from John SAUNDERS dec'd). Wit: John LITTLEJOHN, Samuel
MURREY, William AUSTIN.

Bk:Pg: 2K:131   Date: 11 Oct 1808   RcCt: 11 Oct 1808
Joseph LEWIS Jr. of Ldn to Carter BEVERLY of Culpeper. Re-mortgage
of 25ac.

Bk:Pg: 2K:133   Date: 1 Jul 1808   RcCt: 11 Oct 1808
Joseph LEWIS Jr. of Ldn to Peter R. BEVERLEY late of Rockbridge Co
Va. Mortgage of 203ac adj Moses GIBSON, John VILETT, Leven
POWELL. Wit: Carter BEVERLEY, Jno. B. GIBSON, Munford
BEVERLEY, G. GRAY Jr.

Bk:Pg: 2K:134   Date: 10 Oct 1807   RcCt: 11 Oct 1808
Sheriff Hugh DOUGLAS (acting Admr of John MOORE dec'd) to Charles Fenton MERCER of Ldn. B/S of 336*ac* adj Joseph & John MOORE, Sarah RUSSELL.

Bk:Pg: 2K:137   Date: 12 Dec 1808   RcCt: 12 Dec 1808
Daniel EACHES & wife Mary and Joseph GORE of Ldn to Amos HIBBS of Ldn. B/S of 46*ac* adj Robert McCORMACK, Samuel SMITH, Hezekiah Guy's Mill.

Bk:Pg: 2K:138   Date: 9 Dec 1808   RcCt: 12 Dec 1808
John THOMAS & wife Leah of Ldn to Benjamin PALMER of Ldn. B/S of 9*ac* adj John HEARTLEY, Judeth BOTTS, Samuel PALMER. Wit: Jacob THOMAS, John WARFORD, Vincent SANDFORD.

Bk:Pg: 2K:140   Date: 28 Nov 1808   RcCt: 12 Dec 1808
Robert McCULLAH & wife Mary of Ldn to Stephen McPHERSON of Ldn. B/S of 100*ac* adj Thomas, Benjamin and Abel GARRETT. Wit: Stacey TAYLOR, Step C. ROSZEL, Abner BAILES.

Bk:Pg: 2K:142   Date: 25 Apr 1808   RcCt: 12 Dec 1808
John ADAMS of Ldn to Henry BROWN of Ldn. BoS for horses. Wit: David ALEXANDER

Bk:Pg: 2K:143   Date: 10 Dec 1808   RcCt: 12 Dec 1808
Barnett HOUGH & wife Louisa of Lsbg to William WOODY of Lsbg. B/S of part of Lot #57 in Lsbg. Wit: C. BINNS, Jno. MATTHIAS, Isaac HARRIS, Hugh DOUGLAS, Leven LUCKETT, Saml. CLAPHAM.

Bk:Pg: 2K:145   Date: 12 Dec 1808   RcCt: 12 Dec 1808
William WOODY & wife Elizabeth of Lsbg to Charles BINNS & John MATTHIAS of Ldn. Trust for debt to Henry CLAGETT of Lsbg using lots on N side of Loudoun St in Lsbg adj Mrs. DONOHOE and Charles GULLAT. Wit: Isaac HARRIS, Charles G. EDWARDS, Wm. B. HARRISON.

Bk:Pg: 2K:147   Date: __ Dec 1808   RcCt: 12 Dec 1808
Henry SMITH & wife Sarah of Ldn to William STALKUP of Columbiana Co Oh. B/S of 80*ac* on Kittocton Creek on main road from Thomas HUMPHRIES to Lsbg adj James BEST, John LOVE.

Bk:Pg: 2K:148   Date: 18 Aug 1808   RcCt: 12 Dec 1808
Henry SMITH & wife Sarah of Ldn to John LOVE of Ldn. B/S of 26*ac* on NW fork of Goose Creek adj William STALLCUP. Wit: William DANIEL, Reed POULTON, John JURDAN.

Bk:Pg: 2K:150   Date: 12 Dec 1808   RcCt: 12 Dec 1808
Cornelius WYNKOOP & wife Cornela of Ldn to Andrew CAMPBELL of Ldn. B/S of 140*ac*. Wit: Isaac LAROWE, Saml. M. EDWARDS, Mat. WETHERBY.

Bk:Pg: 2K:151   Date: 12 Dec 1808   RcCt: 12 Dec 1808
Andrew CAMPBELL & wife Jane of Ldn to Cornelius WYNKOOP of Ldn.
B/S of 100*ac* on Beaverdam adj Matthew RUST. Wit: Isaac LAROWE,
Saml. M. EDWARDS, Mat WETHERBY.

Bk:Pg: 2K:153   Date: 12 Dec 1808   RcCt: 12 Dec 1808
Andrew CAMPBELL & wife Jane of Ldn to Cornelius WYNKOOP of Ldn.
Mortgage on 104*ac* [2K:151 states 100*ac*]. Wit: Isaac LAROWE, Saml. M.
EDWARDS, Mat WETHERBY.

Bk:Pg: 2K:154   Date: 13 Oct 1808   RcCt: 12 Dec 1808
Armistead LONG of Ldn and Mary GRAY (signed Polley) w/o Daniel
GRAY to Daniel F. STROTHER of Culpeper. B/S (Mary relinquish her
right of Dower to land in Campbell Co to Long) in trust for Mary negroes
Patrick, Jack, Nancy & Jane, farm and household items. Wit: C. BINNS,
Saml. M. EDWARDS, Eli OFFUTT.

Bk:Pg: 2K:155   Date: 12 Dec 1808   RcCt: 12 Dec 1808
James TRAHERN of Ldn to Isaac NICHOLS Jr. of Ldn. B/S of 25*ac* on N
fork of Beaverdam adj John ASH. Wit: John SINCLAIR, George JANNEY,
Isaac WALTER.

Bk:Pg: 2K:157   Date: 28 May 1808   RcCt: 12 Dec 1808
Elizabeth ALEXANDER of Ldn to daughter Penelope Barnes
ALEXANDER (d/o John ALEXANDER). B/S of negroes James, Judeth &
Peggy. Wit: Thomas FOUCH, Thomson FOUCH, William FOUCH.

Bk:Pg: 2K:157   Date: 2 Nov 1808   RcCt: 12 Dec 1808
John HAMILTON. Receipt of payment from John WORSLEY of balance
for which Abiel JENNIERS executed trust on farm where WESLEY
[WORSLEY] now lives. Wit: Wm. COPELAND.

Bk:Pg: 2K:158   Date: ___ 1808   RcCt: 12 Dec 1808
John LITTLEJOHN, Charles BINNS & Robert BRADEN of Ldn to Abiel
JENNIERS of Ldn. Release of trust for purchase of 358*ac* from John
HAMILTON. Wit: Saml. M. EDWARDS, Wm. MAINS, Charles BENNETT
Jr.

Bk:Pg: 2K:160   Date: 17 Apr 1808   RcCt: 12 Dec 1808
Elizabeth BOYD of Ldn to Joseph LOVETT of Ldn. B/S of 128 1/8*ac* on
Beaverdam adj William GALLIHER, James REED. Wit: Jesse McVEIGH,
Hugh RODGERS, Hamilton ROGERS, Daniel EACHES, James
STEPHENS, Felix TRIPLETT, George HILL.

Bk:Pg: 2K:161   Date: 12 Dec 1808   RcCt: 13 Dec 1808
John HISKETT of Ldn to John HISKETT Jr. BoS for negro man Rob, farm
and household items. Wit: Saml. M. EDWARDS, Eli OFFUTT.

Bk:Pg: 2K:162   Date: 12 Oct 1808   RcCt: 13 Dec 1808
Thomas CHILTON & wife Susanna of Ldn to Benjamin PRICE of Ldn. B/S
of 5*ac*. Wit: Isaac LAROWE, Eli OFFUTT, Saml. M. EDWARDS.

Bk:Pg: 2K:164   Date: 21 Sep 1807   RcCt: 13 Dec 1808
Rawleigh COLSTON & wife Elizabeth of Berkeley Co Va to Given HANDY wd/o John HANDY dec'd and his legal reps William H. HANDY, Maria HAINES late HANDY, Hannah HANDY, John C. HANDY & Eli H. HANDY of Ldn. B/S of 592½ac on Goose Creek [detailed plat given]. Wit: Samuel CRESWELL, David W. DAVIS, Daniel YOUNG, Edward COLSTON, William RIDDLE, Phil. VADENBUSCH.

Bk:Pg: 2K:170   Date: 3 Apr 1807   RcCt: 12 Oct 1808
Benjamin PURDOM to Jacob HOUSER. A/L of lot where HOUSER now lives. Wit: John WILLIAMS, Joseph TALBOTT, William BRANNAM.

Bk:Pg: 2K:171   Date: 5 Mar 1806   RcCt: 8 Sep 1806
Catharine SWANK wd/o John SWANK dec'd of Ldn to John SHAVOR of Ldn. B/S of all land of late husband. Wit: John HAMILTON, Adam SHOVER, James HAMILTON, Saml. PEIRPOINT.

Bk:Pg: 2K:172   Date: 5 Nov 1807   RcCt: 9 Jan 1809
John HAMILTON & wife Winifred to Abiel JENNEIRS. CoE for sale of 358ac. Wit: Saml. CLAPHAM, William NOLAND.

Bk:Pg: 2K:173   Date: 10 Nov 1808   RcCt: 9 Jan 1809
John CHEW. Col of slaves Charlotte and Hiram from DC.

Bk:Pg: 2K:174   Date: 7 Mar 1808   RcCt: 11 Oct 1808
Elizabeth TUSTIMER wd/o Jacob TUSTIMER dec'd of Ldn to John TUSTIMER, John YOUNKIN, Jacob ADAMS, Daniel MAY, Charles TUSTIMER, Daniel WOLFORD & Michael STREAM. Release of dower rights. Wit: Adam SHOVER, John STOUSEBERGER, Jas. CAVAN Jr., name in German.

Bk:Pg: 2K:175   Date: 7 Mar 1808   RcCt: 11 Oct 1808
Elizabeth TUSHTIMER wd/o Jacob TUSHTIMER dec'd of Ldn to John TUSHTIMER of Rockingham Co Va, John YOUNKIN of Turkeyfoot Twnshp Somerset Co PA, Jacob ADAMS of Southampton Twnshp Bedford Co Pa, Daniel MAY of Bedford Co Pa, Charles TUSHTIMER of Rockingham Co Va, Daniel WOLFORD of Southampton Twnshp Bedford Co Pa & Michael STREAM of Ldn. A/L of 103½ac. Wit: Adam SHOVER, John STOUSEBERGER, Jas. CAVAN Jr., name in German.

Bk:Pg: 2K:177   Date: 22 Feb 1808   RcCt: 9 Jan 1809
Daniel & Mary WOLFORD of Southampton Twnshp Bedford Co Pa to Michael STREAM of Ldn. PoA. wit: Jeremiah JAMES, Luke FETTER.

Bk:Pg: 2K:178   Date: 22 Feb 1808   RcCt: 9 Jan 1809
Jacob & Lorey ADAMS of Southampton Twnshp Bedford Co Pa to Michael STREAM of Ldn. PoA. Wit: Jeremiah JAMES, Luke FETTER.

Bk:Pg: 2K:179   Date: 12 Oct 1808   RcCt: 9 Jan 1809
John ROBERTS of Ldn to son Henry ROBERTS. Gift of lease lot where John lives & 2 other lots, negro woman Sook & her children Linney & Chloe?, farm and household items. Wit: Jeremiah SLACK, Adrian Lane SWARTS, Florence McCARTY.

Bk:Pg: 2K:180   Date: 14 Dec 1808 FrdkMd   RcCt: 9 Jan 1809
Eleanor NOLAND w/o Thomas NOLAND. Relinquishes dower rights to
151½ac sold to Samuel CLAPHAM. Wit: Henry KULM, Peter
BUCKHART.

Bk:Pg: 2K:181   Date: 1 Jun 1808   RcCt: 10 Oct 1808
Joseph TIDBALL & wife Jane of Winchester FrdkMd to Joseph LEWIS Jr.
of Ldn. B/S of 203ac "Clifton Mill". Wit: W. ELLZEY, Jno. MATTHIAS,
Saml. CLAPHAM, Thos. SWANN, Philip NELSON, William DAVISON.

Bk:Pg: 2K:183   Date: 7 Oct 1807   RcCt: 9 Jan 1809
William SMITH & wife Hannah of Ldn to John NIXON of Ldn. B/S of Lot
#54 in Lsbg. Wit: William NOLAND, Saml. CLAPHAM, Saml. LUCKETT.

Bk:Pg: 2K:185   Date: 9 Jan 1806   RcCt: 9 Jan 1809
Alexander SUTHERLAND & wife Ann to John NIXON. B/S of 1ac adj
Lsbg. Wit: B. HOUGH, Thos. SANDERS, Daniel DOWLING.

Bk:Pg: 2K:186   Date: 7 Jul 1808   RcCt: 9 Jan 1809
John MILLER Jr., Daniel SMITH, Joseph Saunders LEWIS & John
Clement STOKER (assignees of John MILLER Jr.) of PhilPa to Thomas
SWANN of AlexVa. B/S of lot nr Lsbg. Wit: Jno. TREMELLS Jr., George
REESE Jr.

Bk:Pg: 2K:189   Date: 25 Jul 1803   RcCt: 14 Dec 1803
James DAWSON of Lsbg to Robert PARFECT of Ldn. B/S of ¼ac at E
end of Lsbg on S side of Market St. Wit: Alex'r SUTHELAND, W. C.
SELDEN, John EVANS.

Bk:Pg: 2K:190   Date: 7 Apr 1808   RcCt: 9 May 1808
Nicholas WYCKOFF and Eden B. MOORE & wife Hannah of Ldn to
Cornelius WYCKOFF (s/o Nicholas) of Ldn. B/S of 97ac adj John
SPENCER, Vincent LEWIS and 24¼ac adj Vincent LEWIS. Wit: Willis
LEGG, Micajah TRIPLETT, Charles LEWIS.

Bk:Pg: 2K:192   Date: 26 Dec 1808   RcCt: 9 Jan 1809
Robert PARFECT & wife Jane of Ldn to Ignatius NORRIS of Ldn.
Mortgage of ¼a lot in Lsbg. Wit: C. BINNS, Saml. M. EDWARDS, Isaac
LAROWE.

Bk:Pg: 2K:194   Date: 20 Jan 1808   RcCt: 12 Dec 1808
Joseph JONES (s/o Joseph JONES dec'd) of Ldn to Charles Fenton
MERCER of Ldn. Trust for debts using leased land. Wit: Job RACE, Israel
LACEY.

Bk:Pg: 2K:197   Date: 9 Jan 1809   RcCt: 9 Jan 1809
William HUMMER & wife Rachel to Enoch FRANCIS. B/S of ½ac on road
from Lsbg to AlexVa. Wit: Geo. W. BLINCOE, Thos. N. BINNS, Wm.
CHILTON.

Bk:Pg: 2K:198   Date: 31 Dec 1808   RcCt: 13 Feb 1809
William P. BAYLY & wife Mary L. to James BATTSON. CoE for sale of
121ac. Wit: Hancock EUSTACE, Urn. BRENT Jr.

Bk:Pg: 2K:200   Date: 31 Dec 1808   RcCt: 13 Feb 1809
William P. BAYLY & wife Mary L. to John BATTSON. CoE for sale of
157½ac. Wit: Hancock EUSTACE, Urn. BRENT Jr.

Bk:Pg: 2K:201   Date: 11 Feb 1809   RcCt: 13 Feb 1809
Leven POWELL of Mdbg to John UPP of Mdbg. LS of part of Lot #23 in
Mdbg. Wit: A. GIBSON, Peter MYERS, Leven D. POWELL.

Bk:Pg: 2K:203   Date: 22 Oct 1807   RcCt: 14 Dec 1807
Whetman LEITH of Ldn to William VICKERS of Ldn. Mortgage of 100ac.
Wit: Amos JOHNSON, B. E. WILLS, Gustavus HARRISON, Burr
POWELL.

Bk:Pg: 2K:205   Date: 20 Feb 1808   RcCt: 12 Sep 1808
Patrick MORELAND of Ldn to son James MORELAND. Gift of negro
woman Priscilla, boy John, girl Maria, and household items. Wit: John
POTTS, Thomas HALL Jr., Lee COCKELL.

Bk:Pg: 2K:206   Date: 19 Apr 1808   RcCt: 9 May 1808
Moses DILLON & wife Rebeckah of Ldn to Henry SMITH of Ldn. B/S of
10ac adj Stacy TAYLOR. Wit: Abdon DILLON, Dennis G. JONES, Reed
POULTON, William STALLCUP, Stacy TAYLOR, Lewis ELLZEY.

Bk:Pg: 2K:209   Date: 1 Dec 1808   RcCt: 13 Feb 1809
Isaac & Samuel NICKOLS. Receipt for payment from Peter BOSS for
trust on lot where BOSS lives in Lsbg. Wit: Isaac HATCHER.

Bk:Pg: 2K:209   Date: 13 Feb 1809   RcCt: 13 Feb 1809
Daniel EACHES of Ldn to William BRONAUGH of Ldn. Trust for debt to
Isaac & Samuel NICKOLLS using 196ac. Wit: ?, Daniel C. BOSS.

Bk:Pg: 2K:210   Date: 19 Sep 1809   RcCt: 13 Feb 1809
Jonas POTTS of Ldn to Mahlon JANNEY of Ldn. Mortgage 67ac with grist
mill. Wit: James MOORE, W. S. NEALE, Thomas PHILIPS.

Bk:Pg: 2K:213   Date: 3 Jun 1807   RcCt: 13 Feb 1809
John RAMSEY & wife Clarissa of AlexVa to Colin AULD of AlexVa. B/S of
440ac on Travers' Branch adj Mary BOLAN and 314ac. Wit: Abram FAW,
Robert YOUNG.

Bk:Pg: 2K:216   Date: 30 Jun 1808   RcCt: 13 Feb 1809
Matthew WETHERBY of Ldn and James CRAINE of Ldn. Agreement –
transfers rights from marriage with Jane McFARLING wd/o John
McFARLING dec'd from m. contracted of 12 Jun 1804 in Fqr. Wit: Wm.
CHILTON, Noble BEVEREDGE, Richard H. HENDERSON, John
LITTLEJOHN.

Bk:Pg: 2K:218   Date: 11 Mar 1808   RcCt: 14 Feb 1809
Willy JANES of Lsbg to Fleet SMITH of Lsbg. Trust for several debts in
Balt using farm and household items.

Bk:Pg: 2K:221   Date: 22 Oct 1808   RcCt: 10 Apr 1809
Samuel BERKLEY Sr. of Ldn to Minor FURR of Ldn. Bond on lease of
58ac. Wit: Saml. BERKLEY Jr., Lewis LEWIS, Josias MURRAY.

Bk:Pg: 2K:223   Date: 22 Oct 1808   RcCt: 10 Apr 1809
Samuel BERKLEY Sr. & Thomas BERKLEY of Ldn to Minor FURR of
Ldn. Bond using 1*ac* "Trap" lot now in possession of Thomas. Wit: Saml.
BERKLEY Jr., Lewis LEWIS, Josias MURRAY. Wit: Saml. BERKLEY Jr.,
Josias MURRAY, Lewis LEWIS.

Bk:Pg: 2K:224   Date: 10 Apr 1809   RcCt: 11 Apr 1809
William RHODES & wife Mary of Columbiana Co Oh to Henry CLAGETT
of Lsbg. B/S of 248*ac* adj Broken Hills. Wit: S. BLINCOE, James
GARNER, Rich'd H. HENDERSON.

Bk:Pg: 2K:226   Date: 10 Apr 1809   RcCt: 11 Apr 1809
Henry CLAGETT of Ldn to William RHODES of Columbiana Co Oh.
Mortgage on 248*ac*. Wit: S. BLINCOE, James GARNER, Rich'd H.
HENDERSON.

Bk:Pg: 2K:228   Date: 15 Mar 1809   RcCt: 15 Mar 1809
Robert BRADEN & George TAVENDER Sr. of Ldn to Henry GLASSGOW
of Lsbg. Release of lot on N side of Market St Lsbg.

Bk:Pg: 2K:229   Date: 26 Aug 1808   RcCt: 11 Apr 1809
Henry CLAGETT & wife Julia of Ldn to John DRISH of Ldn. B/S of lot in
Lsbg. Wit: Jno. MATTHIAS, Isaac HARRIS, Danl. DOWLING, John
LITTLEJOHN, Saml. MURREY.

Bk:Pg: 2K:231   Date: 11 Aug 1797   RcCt: 14 Aug 1797
Theodorick LEE & wife Catharine of Berkeley to Benjamin MITCHELL of
Ldn. B/S of 260*ac* where MITCHELL now lives on Flat Lick Run. Wit:
James BLINCOE, Thomas BLINCOE Jr., Henry CLOWES, W. C.
SELDEN, Tho. SWANN, Isaac LAROWE, Benj'a SHREVE.

Bk:Pg: 2K:234   Date: 26 Aug 1808   RcCt: 11 Apr 1809
John DRISH of Ldn to Presley CORDELL and John MATTHIAS of Ldn.
Trust for debts to Henry CLAGETT using lot in Lsbg. Wit: Isaac HARRIS,
D. DOWLING, David RICKETTS.

Bk:Pg: 2K:236   Date: 25 Aug 1808   RcCt: 11 Apr 1809
Joseph SMITH of Ldn to Samuel SMITH of Ldn. BoS for farm and
household items.

Bk:Pg: 2K:237   Date: 3 Nov 1808   RcCt: 8 May 1809
Samuel PALMER Sr. of Ldn to Jacob SILCOTT of Ldn. B/S of 74*ac* on
Beaverdam adj Richard RICHARDS. Wit: Wm. WOODFORD, Jeremiah
SANDFORD Jr., John CHEW, Vincent SANFORD.

Bk:Pg: 2K:239   Date: 1 Mar 1809   RcCt: 8 May 1809
David MULL & wife Mary of Ldn to John BOOTH Jr. of Ldn. B/S of ½*ac*
adj James BOOTH. Wit: Edmund JENINGS, John GEORGE, name in
German.

Bk:Pg: 2K:241   Date: 8 May 1809   RcCt: 8 May 1809
Israel LACEY, Stephen BEARD & Charles LEWIS of Ldn to Benjamin
JAMES of Ldn. B/S of 101*ac* adj Ben. JAMES on road from Gumspring to
Little River Meeting house, and 152*ac* adj James LEWIS, Daniel & Hugh

THOMAS; conveyed to LACEY, BEARD & LEWIS as security for John
SPENCER for debt to Cuthbert POWELL. Wit: Johnston CLEVELAND,
Darby B. BYRN, James McKIM.

Bk:Pg: 2K:242   Date: 7 Jul 1808   RcCt: 8 May 1809
John SPENCER. Receipt for above transaction. Wit: Israel LACEY, Benj.
REDMOND.

Bk:Pg: 2K:242   Date: 14 Nov 1808   RcCt: 8 May 1809
Colin AULD of AlexVa to John RAMEY of AlexVa. B/S of 90ac abt 4m
from Lsbg; was in trust from Jonas POTTS and Jacob BAUGH.

Bk:Pg: 2K:245   Date: 17 Sep 1808   RcCt: 12 Dec 1808
Reuben TRIPLETT & wife Peggy of Ldn to Leven POWELL of Ldn. B/S of
54¾ac on Beaverdam. Wit: Burr POWELL, Wm. BRONAUGH, Fanny
TRIPLETT, Gustavus HARRISON.

Bk:Pg: 2K:247   Date: 5 Dec 1808   RcCt: 8 May 1809
Betsy TIBBS of Dumfries to Peggy CARR of Dumfries. B/S of 5000 to
6000ac in Stafford, 2000ac in PrWm, 500ac in PrWm, 900ac in Ldn; with
Peggy CARR relinquishing her dower from late husband was agreed by
late husband of Betsy TIBBS by William CARR now dec'd and John
CARR now dec'd to grant annuity to Peggy which ends. Wit: Wm. A. G.
DADE, Thomas A. SMITH, George WILLIAMS.

Bk:Pg: 2K:249   Date: 13 May 1808   RcCt: 12 Dec 1808
William MARTIN Sr. of Ldn to Andrew MARTIN Sr. of Ldn. A/L of 50ac adj
George CHILTON. Wit: Wm. BRONAUGH, Nicholas KILE, John MARTIN.

Bk:Pg: 2K:251   Date: 27 Sep 1808   RcCt: 12 May 1809
Michael EBLIN & wife Rebekah of Ldn to Daniel EACHES & Joseph
GORE of Ldn. B/S of 63ac adj Thomas GREGG, Joseph HOGUE, John
LEMING, Jos. BROWN. Wit: Burr POWELL, Leven LUCKETT, Wm.
BRONAUGH.

Bk:Pg: 2K:254   Date: 20 Mar 1808   RcCt: 8 May 1809
Burr POWELL & wife Catharine of Ldn to Fielding LYNN of Ldn. B/S of
51ac. Wit: Leven POWELL, Leven LUCKETT, John L. BERKLEY.

Bk:Pg: 2K:256   Date: 10 Apr 1809   RcCt: 11 Apr 1809
Jesse JANNEY of Ldn to Bernard TAYLOR of Ldn. B/S of 10ac adj Abdon
DILLON, Iden TAYLOR. Wit: Fleet SMITH, Edward CUNNARD, Eli
OFFUTT.

Bk:Pg: 2K:258   Date: 12 Oct 1808   RcCt: 8 May 1809
George S. HOUGH of Ldn to Thomas LESLIE of Ldn. Trust using farm
and household items. Wit: William HISKETT, Mahlon HOUGH.

Bk:Pg: 2K:259   Date: 17 Dec 1808   RcCt: 8 May 1809
David SMITH of Ldn to Samuel CLENDENING Sr. of Ldn. B/S of 2 lots in
Hllb. Wit: James H. HAMILTON, Jonathan MATTHEWS, Samuel
CLENDENING Jr.

Bk:Pg: 2K:261   Date: 8 May 1809   RcCt: 8 May 1809
William HORSEMAN of Ldn to Joseph HORSEMAN of Ldn. A/L of 100ac.
Wit: Johnston CLEVELAND, William ESKRIDGE, John KEENE, William
WHALEY.

Bk:Pg: 2K:262   Date: 16 Mar 1809   RcCt: 8 May 1809
Peter RICKARD & wife Elizabeth of Ldn to Jacob WALTMAN of Ldn. B/S
of Elizabeth's 1/5 share of land of father Jacob EVERHEART dec'd. Wit:
Jos. LEWIS Jr., William WENNER, name in German.

Bk:Pg: 2K:264   Date: 10 Dec 1808   RcCt: 9 May 1809
John LOGAN & wife Alice (d/o Isaac GIBSON dec'd) of Ldn to James
BOLES of Ldn. B/S of John's 1/8 share of 260ac in Ldn & Fqr of father
Isaac. Wit: Wm. BRONAUGH, John MITCHELL, Amos WRIGHT, John
BUCHANAN, Joseph CARR.

Bk:Pg: 2K:267   Date: 1 Apr 1809   RcCt: 8 May 1809
Joshua OSBURN of Ldn to Joel OSBURN of Ldn. B/S of 8ac "Arcadia"
land adj Thomas OSBURN.

Bk:Pg: 2K:268   Date: 8 May 1809   RcCt: 8 May 1809
Joab OSBURN of Ldn to Joel OSBURN of Ldn. B/S of 46ac at foot of Blue
Ridge adj Thomas HUMPHREY, Hannah OSBURN.

Bk:Pg: 2K:269   Date: 2 Apr 1809   RcCt: 8 May 1809
Joab OSBURN of Ldn. Bond to Joel OSBURN of Ldn to make sufficient
title to 150ac the dower land of Hannah OSBURN wd/o Richard OSBURN
dec'd. Wit: Thomas OSBURN, Mary OSBURN, William PACK.

Bk:Pg: 2K:270   Date: 23 Sep 1808   RcCt: 9 Jan 1809
Mahlon JANNEY of Wtfd to James MOORE of Wtfd. B/S of Lot #8 in new
addition to Wtfd. Wit: Joseph TALBOTT, David JANNEY, Joseph LACEY.

Bk:Pg: 2K:272   Date: 8 May 1809   RcCt: 8 May 1809
Bernard TAYLOR & wife Sarah of Ldn to Walter KERRICK of Ldn. B/S of
4ac adj Samuel IDEN.

Bk:Pg: 2K:273   Date: 12 Nov 1808   RcCt: 8 May 1809
Joseph CARR & wife Delia of Ldn to John WRIGHT of Ldn. B/S of 25ac
adj William SUDDITH. Wit: Sydnor BAILEY, Wm. BRONAUGH, Step C.
ROSZELL, Rich'd CLARK.

Bk:Pg: 2K:276   Date: 15 Sep 1802   RcCt: 8 May 1809
John KEPHART (Admr of Godfrey KEPHEART dec'd) and Jacob
KEPHART (a distributee). Agreement on transfer of rights to estate. Wit:
George MILNER, James BOYD.

Bk:Pg: 2K:277   Date: 1 Apr 1809   RcCt: 8 May 1809
Daniel DUTY of Loudoun (abt to remove to Ky) to James CHILTON of
Ldn. PoA. Sampson BLINCOE, Charles SMITH.

Bk:Pg: 2K:277   Date: 22 Apr 1809   RcCt: 8 May 1809
Henry SMITH & wife Sarah of Ldn to Mahlon TAYLOR & Giles CRAVEN
of Ldn. Trust for debt to William BEANS using 10ac adj Stacey TAYLOR,

Samuel IDEN. Wit: Thomas ODEN, Benj. BRADFIELD, Samuel IDEN, Stacy TAYLOR, Steph C. ROSZELL.

Bk:Pg: 2K:281   Date: 6 May 1809   RcCt: 8 May 1809
Henry TAYLOR & wife Ann of Ldn to John STOUTSEBUGER of Ldn. B/S of 30ac on Katockton adj Peter STONEBURNER, Andrew SPRING, Adam CORDELL. Wit: John HAMILTON, William NOLAND. Wit: John HAMILTON, William NOLAND.

Bk:Pg: 2K:283   Date: 8 May 1809   RcCt: 8 May 1809
Thomas FOUCH & Israel LACEY of Ldn to Joshua PANCOAST of Ldn. B/S of 182½ac adj Archibald McVICKERS. Wit: Rich'd H. HENDERSON, Jno. MATHIAS, John S. MARLOW.

Bk:Pg: 2K:285   Date: 8 May 1809   RcCt: 8 May 1809
Michael STREAM & wife Elizabeth (late DURSHTIMER) of Ldn to John Stone MARLOW of Ldn. B/S of 103½ac Eliz.'s 1/7 share of estate of Jacob DURSHEMER dec'd. Wit: Jas. CAVAN Jr., Jno. MATTHIAS, Wm. SMITH.

Bk:Pg: 2K:287   Date: 7 Mar 1808   RcCt: 9 Jan 1809
Daniel WOLFORD & wife Mary of Southampton Twnshp Bedford Co Pa to John Stone MARLOW of Ldn. B/S of 103½ac Mary's 1/7 share of estate of Jacob TUSHSHIMER dec'd. Wit: James CHAMBERS, Isaac JONES, Jacob ADAMS Jr.

Bk:Pg: 2K:290   Date: ___ 1809   RcCt: 9 May 1809
Dr. Thomas SIM & wife Harriott of Ldn to James SANDERS of Ldn. B/S of Lot #52 in Lsbg. Wit: John LITTLEJOHN, Samuel MURREY, Jas. HAMILTON.

Bk:Pg: 2K:292   Date: 20 Jun 1808   RcCt: 9 May 1809
Henry M. DAVIS of Shenandoah late of Ldn to Fleet SMITH of Lsbg. PoA to rent out house after 25 Dec, now occupied by Edward DAWES on King St. Wit: Middleton BELT, Warner W. WHITING.

Bk:Pg: 2K:293   Date: 9 May 1809   RcCt: 9 May 1809
Francis TRIPLETT Sr. of Lsbg to merchant George PRICE of Balt. B/S of part of Lot #31 in Lsbg.

Bk:Pg: 2K:295   Date: 11 Feb 1809   RcCt: 9 May 1809
Wilson Cary SELDON of Ldn to William WRIGHT of Ldn. B/S of 117ac. Wit: John MATTHIAS, Henry S. COOKE, Mark WOOD.

Bk:Pg: 2K:296   Date: 17 Mar 1809   RcCt: 12 Jun 1809
Moses MILLER & wife Christiana of Ldn to Joseph LEWIS Jr. of Ldn. B/S of 14ac adj Robert BRADEN. Wit: George SHUMAKER, Betsey SHUMAKER, Caty SHUMAKER.

Bk:Pg: 2K:298   Date: 24 Sep 1808   RcCt: 8 May 1809
Thomas BERKLEY (s/o William BERKLEY dec'd) & wife Ann of Ldn to James NICHOLS of Ldn. B/S of 64ac adj Thomas HUMPHREY, Jonathan PALMER. Wit: Joseph THOMAS, George THOMAS, Minor FURR, Ben GRAYSON.

Bk:Pg: 2K:300   Date: 24 Sep 1808   RcCt: 12 Jun 1809
Thomas BERKLEY (s/o William BERKLEY dec'd) & wife Ann of Ldn to
Samuel MASSIE of Ldn. B/S of 74*ac* adj Richard HATCHER. Wit: Joseph
THOMAS, George THOMAS, Minor FURR, Ben GRAYSON.

Bk:Pg: 2K:302   Date: 24 Sept 1808   RcCt: 12 Jun 1809
Thomas BERKLEY (s/o William BERKLEY dec'd) & wife Ann of Ldn to
Samuel MASSIE of Ldn. B/S of 100*ac* adj Thomas KIRKPATRICK,
Edward SNICKERS. Wit: Joseph THOMAS, George THOMAS, Minor
FURR, Ben GRAYSON.

Bk:Pg: 2K:303   Date: 4 Apr 1809   RcCt: 12 Jun 1809
Mahlon JANNEY of Ldn to Patterson WRIGHT of Ldn. B/S of Lots #4 & #5
& ½ of #3 in Wtfd. Wit: W. S. NEALE, Levi JAMES, John F.
SAPPINGTON, Jacob JACOBS.

Bk:Pg: 2K:305   Date: 17 Feb 1809   RcCt: 12 Jun 1809
Andrew GARNER of Ldn to Robert BRADEN of Ldn. BoS for farm and
household items. Wit: John CASEY, Arthur GARNER.

Bk:Pg: 2K:306   Date: 7 Sep 1808   RcCt: 14 Dec 1808
Hannah WHITING (Exor of P. B. WHITING dec'd) to Margaret COWAN
(Exor of Alexander COWAN dec'd). Mortgage of 148*ac*. Wit: Beverly
WHITING, Fran WHITING, Francis W. WASHINGTON, Warner WHITING.

Bk:Pg: 2K:307   Date: 28 Jan 1809   RcCt: 12 Jun 1809
Jacob HOUSER of Ldn to Peter MILLER Sr, Abiel JENNEIRS, Cornelius
SHAWEN, Peter MILLER Jr. and Moses MILLER (trustees of Episcopal
Church Methodist). B/S of 1*ac* adj George MULL where there is now a
Methodist Meeting house. Wit: Isaac HOUGH, Wm. COPELAND, Styles
JACKSON.

Bk:Pg: 2K:308   Date: 13 Apr 1809   RcCt: 12 Jun 1809
George KILGORE & wife Martenna of Ldn to Elisha PHELPS & Daniel
LEE (Exors of Eli PHELPS dec'd of FrdkVa). B/S of 40*ac* adj Goose
Creek. Wit: Eli OFFUTT, Fleet SMITH, Saml. M. EDWARDS, W. ELLZEY.

Bk:Pg: 2K:309   Date: 9 Jun 1809   RcCt: 12 Jun 1809
Charles CARTER of FrdkVa to Peter R. BEVERLY of FrdkVa. B/S of
166½*ac* adj Michael SHAFFER, Christian RUSE, 93*ac* now in possession
of Michael MILLER adj David AXLINE, John JACKSON, 96½*ac* in
possession of Michael MILLER, 197*ac* in possession of John JACKSON.
Wit: Thos. HAMILTON, Lourena PHILLIPS, Kenze HARDY, Reuben
STROTHER.

Bk:Pg: 2K:312   Date: 24 May 1809   RcCt: 13 Jun 1809
John THRELKELD of Georgetown DC to heirs of William JONES & wife
Sarah of Ldn. B/S of 403*ac* adj Isaac HUGHES. Wit: Thomas PETER,
Rich'd PARROTT, W. S. BELT Jr.

Bk:Pg: 2K:314   Date: 10 Aug 1808   RcCt: 10 Aug 1808
Benjamin GRAYSON & William BRONAUGH. Bond on GRAYSON as
Sheriff to collect levy. Wit: Isaac LAROWE.

Bk:Pg: 2K:315   Date: 24 Feb 1808   RcCt: 13 Jun 1809
John McILHANY Jr. & wife Harriott of Ldn to Elizabeth McILHANY of Ldn (both are heirs of James McILHANY dec'd). B/S of land John inherited. Wit: Thos. NICHOLS, Rosannah ELLZEY, Lewis ELLZEY, Margaret McILHANY, Stacy TAYLOR.

Bk:Pg: 2K:317   Date: 1 Dec 1808   RcCt: 10 Jul 1809
John FILLER of Ldn to John SAGER of Ldn. BoS for farm and household items. Wit: Adam KENDALL, Jacob CRUMBAKER.

Bk:Pg: 2K:318   Date: 10 Jun 1809   RcCt: 10 Jul 1809
James DAWSON of Lsbg to Fleet SMITH & Aaron SANDERS of Ldn. Trust for debt to merchant Joseph SMITH of AlexVA using lot in Lsbg where DAWSON lives. Wit: Samuel M. EDWARDS, Alex. COUPER Jr., Francis TRIPLETT.

Bk:Pg: 2K:321   Date: 14 Aug 1809   RcCt: 14 Aug 1809
Philip EVERHART of Ldn to Joseph SMITH of Ldn. B/S of 38ac adj Philip COOPER, Peter VERTS. Wit: Peter WERTZ, R. BRADEN, Christian RUSE.

Bk:Pg: 2K:323   Date: 14 Jun 1809   RcCt: 14 Aug 1809
Joseph SMITH & wife Margaret of Ldn to Philip EVERHART of Ldn. B/S of 102¼ac adj Phillip COOPER, Peter VERTS. Wit: L. ELLZEY, Stacy TAYLOR, Samuel MURREY.

Bk:Pg: 2K:324   Date: 14 Aug 1809   RcCt: 14 Aug 1809
William VICKERS of Ldn to Wheatman LEATH of Ldn. Release of mortgage. Wit: Samuel M. EDWARDS.

Bk:Pg: 2K:326   Date: ___ 1809   RcCt: 14 Aug 1809
Nathan LITTLER & wife Rebecca of FrdkVa to Jacob SMITH of Ldn. B/S of 115ac on great road from Snickers Gap to Centreville adj Joseph GARRETT, Lovewell JACKSON. Wit: Stacy TAYLOR, Lewis ELLZEY.

Bk:Pg: 2K:328   Date: 1 Jun 1809   RcCt: 14 Aug 1809
John B. STEVENS & wife Sarah Ann of Ldn to Robert BRADEN of Ldn. B/S of 3/8ac lot in Hllb. Wit: Stacy TAYLOR, Lewis ELLZEY.

Bk:Pg: 2K:331   Date: 14 Aug 1809   RcCt: 14 Aug 1809
Charles BENNETT, Ludwell LEE, Saml CLAPHAM, Aaron SANDERS, John ROSE, Johnston CLEVELAND, Sandford REMY, John A. BINNS, Jas. HEATON & Stacey TAYLOR. Bond on BENNETT as Sheriff to collect taxes.

Bk:Pg: 2K:332   Date: 14 Aug 1809   RcCt: 14 Aug 1809
Charles BENNETT, Ludwell LEE, Saml CLAPHAM, Aaron SANDERS, John ROSE, Johnston CLEVELAND, Sandford REMY, John A. BINNS, Jas. HEATON & Stacey TAYLOR. Bond on BENNETT as Sheriff to collect levies.

Bk:Pg: 2K:333   Date: 14 Aug 1809   RcCt: 14 Aug 1809
Charles BENNETT, Ludwell LEE, Saml CLAPHAM, Aaron SANDERS, John ROSE, Johnston CLEVELAND, Sandford REMY, John A. BINNS,

Jas. HEATON & Stacey TAYLOR. Bond on BENNETT as Sheriff to collect officer fees.

Bk:Pg: 2K:334   Date: 4 Feb 1809   RcCt: 12 Jun 1809
Samuel GARRETT & wife Abigal of Ldn to Robert BRADEN of Ldn. B/S of 10ac (Abigal's legacy). Wit: John BRADEN, John SMITH, John CASEY, Thomas STEVENS.

Bk:Pg: 2K:335   Date: 14 Aug 1809   RcCt: 14 Aug 1809
James H. HAMILTON & wife Margaret of AlexVa to John A. MARMADUKE of Hllb. B/S of lot where MARMADUKE now lives. Wit: William ELLZEY, Robert BRADEN.

Bk:Pg: 2K:337   Date: 14 Aug 1809   RcCt: 14 Aug 1809
List of Prisoners in jail of Sheriff Benjamin GRAYSON: Richard HOLLINGSHEAD for horse stealing, James MALONE for ditto, James SULLIVAN for burglary, debtor Mahlon COMTZ, Viney WORKMAN as insane.

Bk:Pg: 2K:338   Date: 8 Jun 1809   RcCt: 14 Aug 1809
Ann LEWIS of Franklin Co Ky (Exor & wd/o Thomas LEWIS dec'd) to Joseph CARR of Ldn. PoA, right of dower to 350ac in husband sold to Leven LUCKETT.

Bk:Pg: 2K:339   Date: 15 Jun 1809   RcCt: 14 Aug 1809
Thomas Brook BEALL of DC to Anna ROSE of Ldn. B/S of 309ac on E side of Catoctan Mt. except ¼ac for Oxley burying ground, Adj John ROSE, Henry STEVENS, Everett OXLEY, John OXLEY, Isaac LAROWE. Wit: J. G. McDONALD, Thomas C. HODGES, Alex. McCORMICK.

Bk:Pg: 2K:341   Date: ___ 1808   RcCt: 19 Aug 1809
John PAYNE & wife Rosannah of Lsbg to Solomon LITTLETON & wife Margaret, Jacob BAUGH & wife Mary, John KEPHEART, Thomas KEPHEART, Jacob KEPHEART, Lenora KEPHEART & Kitty KEPHEART of Ldn. Mortgage of 89ac. Wit: Samuel MURREY, Jas. CAVAN Jr., Barton LUCAS.

Bk:Pg: 2K:343   Date: 25 Mar 1809   RcCt: 14 Aug 1809
Jonah THOMPSON of AlexVa & James MOORE of Ldn (Exors of Israel THOMPSON dec'd of Ldn) to Richard CHILTON of Ldn. A/L of Lots #9, #10 & #11 in Wtfd. Wit: George S. HOUGH, Levi JAMES, R. BRADEN, Wm. HAMILTON, Leven SMALLWOOD.

Bk:Pg: 2K:346   Date: 3 Sep 1807   RcCt: 14 Aug 1809
John BOGUE of Ldn to Ludwell LEE of Ldn, Edmund J. LEE & Charles ALEXANDER of AlexVa. Trust for debt to Frances ALEXANDER (Admr of Charles ALEXANDER dec'd) using 114ac. Wit: Robt. J. TAYLOR, Henry MOORE, Colin AULD.

Bk:Pg: 2K:349   Date: 29 Jul 1809   RcCt: 19 Aug 1809
Formation of a relief Fire Company: Samuel MURREY, Jacob FADLEY, William AUSTIN, John CARNEY, Thomas MYERS, Henry GLASSGOE, Rich'd H. HENDERSON, John PAYNE, Jas. HAMILTON, Francis TRIPLETT Sr., Patrick McINTYRE, Henry CLAGETT, Thomas

SANDERS, John SHAW, John McCORMICK, C. BINNS, S. BLINCOE, P. CORDELL, Thomas MORALLEE, Jos. BEANS, Isaac HARRIS, B'd HOUGH, G. HEAD, Jno. MYERS, Daniel McCALSTER, Eli OFFUTT, Alex'r COUPER Jr., Samuel CARR, Robt. HAMILTON, Thomas McCOWAT, J. WRIGHT, A. SUTHERLAND, Aron DIVINE, Fleet SMITH, Edward DAVIS, John COOPER, Benjamin DORIN, William DRISH Jr., Henry OSWALD, Jesse DAILEY, James GARNER, Matt'w MITCHEL, William WOODDY, Geo. POTTER, Charles GULLATT, Martin KITZMILLER, John POTTER, Samuel M. EDWARDS, Charles DRISH, Joseph BENTLY, John DRISH Sr., Martin CORDELL, John HAMMERLY, John MYERS Jr., Chas. P. TUTT, James CAVAN Jr., Thomas L. MOORE, William CHILTON, Chas. F. MERCER, Daniel GRAY, John NEWTON, Robt. ROBERTSON, Nich's PEERS, H. PEERS, Stoughton GANTT, Robt. R. HOUGH, Thomas HOUGH, W. TAYLOR, Samuel HOUGH, Garrett HOUGH, Thomas F. JENKINS, John W. EVANS, John LITTLEJOHN, Thomas N. BINNS, John J. HARDING, John McCABE, D. MOFFETT, Jos. FEAGANS, James SANDERS, John S. CRANWELL, Daniel DOWLING, Jos. WILDMAN Jr., Chas. G. ESKRIDGE.

Bk:Pg: 2K:350   Date: 17 Oct 1800   RcCt: 11 May 1801
Philip PHILLER & wife Mary of Ldn to John SANBOWER of Ldn. B/S of 107a Lot #19 in Catocton Manor adj John BARRACK. Wit: Fleet SMITH, John DAVIS, G. E. CORDELL, Jon'a FOUCH.

Bk:Pg: 2K:352   Date: 25 May 1809   RcCt: 11 Sep 1809
Thomas HOUGH & wife Anne of Ldn to Rachel WHITE of Ldn. B/S of 47¼ac on SE side of Short Hill in Shanondale. Wit: John McKEMIE, Thomas DAVIS, John DAVIS, Lewis ELLZEY, Joshua OSBURN, Josiah WHITE, Geo. S. HOUGH.

Bk:Pg: 2K:354   Date: 9 Sep 1809   RcCt: 11 Sep 1809
Wilse POSTON of Ldn to daughter Elizabeth POSTON. Gift of negro girl Hannah abt 15y old purchased of William BRONAUGH, household items. Wit: Samuel BOGGESS, James RUST, Wm. RUST.

Bk:Pg: 2K:355   Date: 13 Feb 1809   RcCt: 11 Sep 1809
Ferdinando ONEALE of Ldn to Andrew SMARR of Ldn. Trust for debt to James STEPHENSON using farm animals. Wit: Menan COE.

Bk:Pg: 2K:357   Date: 13 Feb 1808   RcCt: 11 Sep 1809
Elias ODEN & wife Sarah of Fqr to Joshua HUTCHISON of Ffx. B/S of 25ac. Wit: Johnston CLEVELAND, Chas. LEWIS, Vin't L. LEWIS, Thos. STONESTREET.

Bk:Pg: 2K:358   Date: 11 Sep 1809   RcCt: 11 Sep 1809
Francis PIERPOINT Sr. of Ldn to Samuel PIERPOINT of Ldn. B/S of lot in Wtfd.

Bk:Pg: 2K:360   Date: 11 Sep 1809   RcCt: 11 Sep 1809
David LACEY & wife Sarah of Ldn to Nathaniel MANNING of Ldn. B/S of 156ac on road from Wtfd to Thompson's Mill, adj James MOORE,

Sandford REMEY. Wit: Isaac LAROWE, Edward CUNNARD, John BROWN, Benjamin MEAD, Saml. M. EDWARDS.

Bk:Pg: 2K:362   Date: 27 Mar 1809   RcCt: 11 Sep 1809
Peter TOWPERMAN of Ldn to John CONNARD of Ldn. A/L of 150*ac*. Wit: John NEAR, George SMITH, Philip D. DERRY.

Bk:Pg: 2K:362   Date: 4 Apr 1809   RcCt: 12 Jun 1809
Mahlon JANNEY of Ldn to Patrick McGAVOCK of Ldn. B/S of ¼*ac* Lot #6, Lot #2 & ½ of Lot #3 in Wtfd. Wit: W. S. NEALE, John McGEATH, Pateson WRIGHT.

Bk:Pg: 2K:364   Date: 17 Sep 1808   RcCt: 9 Jan 1809
Mahlon JANNEY & wife Sarah of Ldn to Jonas POTTS of Ldn. B/S of 67*ac* with Grist Mill. Wit: James MOORE, W. S. NEALE, Thomas PHILLIPS.

Bk:Pg: 2K:365   Date: 18 Apr 1809   RcCt: 11 Sep 1809
Mahlon JANNEY of Ldn to Samuel GOVER of Ldn. B/S of lot in Wtfd. Wit: Asa MOORE, John F. SAPPINGTON, John WILLIAMS, W. S. NEALE, Joseph TALBOTT.

Bk:Pg: 2K:367   Date: 16 Apr 1808   RcCt: 12 Sep 1808
Jonah SANDS & wife Hester, Abijah SANDS, Rachel SANDS, Thomas OWENS & wife Bathsheba of Ldn and Joseph SANDS & wife Tamer (ch/o Jesse SANDS dec'd) to John ROBERTSON of Ldn. B/S of 100*ac* on road from Fairfax Meeting House to Taylor's Mill adj William BROWN, Joshua DANNIEL. Wit: John HAMILTON, William WINNER, Chas. BENNETT.

Bk:Pg: 2K:370   Date: ___ 1808   RcCt: 10 Oct 1808
Solomon LITTLETON & wife Margaret, Jacob BAUGH & wife Mary, John KEPHEART, Thomas KEPHEART, Jacob KEPHEART, Lenora KEPHEART & Kitty KEPHEART of Ldn to John PAYNE of Lsbg. B/S of 89*ac* below Goose Creek. Wit: Jno. ROSE, Saml. MURREY, John LITTLETON, Jas. CAVAN Jr., Barton LUCAS.

Bk:Pg: 2K:374   Date: 17 Jan 1809   RcCt: 11 Sep 1809
John CARR (grandson of John CARR dec'd) of Ldn to Elizabeth MARTIN wife of David MARTIN. B/S of 20¼*ac*. Wit: Jno. MATTHIAS, Isaac LAROWE, Saml. M. EDWARDS, Eli OFFUTT.

Bk:Pg: 2K:376   Date: 2 May 1809   RcCt: 11 Sep 1809
Michael BELL of GrB to Gabriel McGEATH of Ldn. B/S of 116*ac*. Wit: Step C. ROSZEL, Benjamin WALKER, John VANHORN.

Bk:Pg: 2K:377   Date: 2 May 1809   RcCt: 11 Sep 1809
Michael BELL of GrB to Benjamin WALKER of Ldn. B/S of 169*ac*. Wit: John VANHORN, Step C. ROSZELL, Gabriel MEGEATH.

Bk:Pg: 2K:379   Date: 21 Jun 1809   RcCt: 11 Sep 1809
John WEST of Ldn to Samuel NICKOLS & Company of Ldn. Mortgage of 33*ac*. Jesse NALLY, Uriah FOX, Swithen NICKOLS.

Bk:Pg: 2K:383   Date: 7 Jun 1808   RcCt: 11 Sep 1809
James DAWSON & wife Polley of Lsbg to Alexander SUTHERLAND of
Lsbg. B/S of 1ac Lots #69 & #70 in Lsbg. Wit: Robert R. HOUGH, Corn's
SKINNER Jr.

Bk:Pg: 2K:385   Date: 10 May 1809   RcCt: 11 Sep 1809
David LACEY & wife Sarah of Ldn to John ROSE of Ldn. B/S of Lot #43 in
Lsbg. Wit: Eli OFFUTT, Saml. M. EDWARDS, James COLEMAN Jr.,
Thos. N. BINNS, Thos. F. JENKINS.

Bk:Pg: 2K:387   Date: 13 Mar 1809   RcCt: 11 Sep 1809
John WRIGHT of Ldn to Saml NICKOLS & Company. Mortgage of 25a.
Wit: Jonas JANNEY, Israel JANNEY, Israel JANNEY Jr.

Bk:Pg: 2K:390   Date: 5 Sep 1809   RcCt: 11 Sep 1809
Joseph LONGLEY Jr. summons has been issued for John LOGAN to
justify his conduct towards Joseph's son Edward who is bound to LOGAN
as apprentice as shoe and bootmaker. Wit: Joseph CARR, Joseph
LONGLEY Sr.

Bk:Pg: 2K:390   Date: 11 Sep 1809   RcCt: 11 Sep 1809
Commissioners Stephen C. ROSZELL, John BROWN & Thomas GREGG
to Howell DAVIS of Ldn. B/S of 7ac land of George VANANDER dec'd
(suit by Ambrose D. CURTIS & wife Nancy against George's children
Catharine VANANDER, Polly COUNTS, Jane VANANDER & Peggy
VANANDER and Thomas VANANDER dec'd children John, Eby & Nancy
VANANDER).

Bk:Pg: 2K:393   Date: 9 Oct 1809   RcCt: 9 Oct 1809
Conrad DARR of Ldn to Richard GRUBB of Ldn. A/L of __. Wit: John H.
CANBY, Jonas POTTS, Ebenezer GRUBB.

Bk:Pg: 2K:394   Date: 7 Oct 1809   RcCt: 9 Oct 1809
Sarah JONES, Jonathan JONES & wife Barbary, George JONES & wife
Eve, William HUNT & wife Mary & Wealthy JONES (heirs of William
JONES dec'd of JeffVa) to William PAXSON of Ldn. B/S of 3ac & 5ac.
Wit: Jno. MORGAN, Samuel PAXSON, George SMALLWOOD, Charles
W. OGDEN.

Bk:Pg: 2K:396   Date: 23 Sep 1809   RcCt: 9 Oct 1809
Sarah FAIRFAX to Simon SHOEMAKER (Exor of George SHOEMAKER
Sr). Renewal of LS of 200ac adj Bartholomew SHOEMAKER. Wit: Moses
MILLER, Henry Joseph FRY, William GILPIN.

Bk:Pg: 2K:398   Date: 22 Sep 1809   RcCt: 9 Oct 1809
Sarah FAIRFAX to Henry Joseph FRY and Moses MILLER of Ldn.
Renewal of LS. Wit: John JACKSON, William BRUMERETCH, William
SIMSON.

Bk:Pg: 2K:400   Date: 22 Sep 1809   RcCt: 9 Oct 1809
Sarah FAIRFAX to Peter COMPHER. Renewal of LS of 125ac. Wit: Jacob
BAUGH, John BOYD, Thos. LESLIE.

Bk:Pg: 2K:402   Date: 21 Sep 1809   RcCt: 9 Oct 1809
Sarah FAIRFAX to Jacob HOUSER. Renewal of LS of 140*ac*. Wit: Lewis M. BAYLY, Henry PEERS, Robert R. HOUGH.

Bk:Pg: 2K:404 Date: 21 Sep 1809   RcCt: 9 Oct 1809
Sarah FAIRFAX to Mary HIXON (w/o Reuben HIXON). Renewal of LS of 150*ac*. Wit: John McCORMACK, Charles BENNETT Jr., Wm. B. WRIGHT.

Bk:Pg: 2K:406   Date: 6 Jun 1809   RcCt: 9 Oct 1809
Thomas GREGG of Ldn to Samuel NICKOLS & Company. Mortgage of 87*ac*. Wit: Swithen NICHOLS, Charity NICHOLS.

Bk:Pg: 2K:409   Date: 20 Mar 1809   RcCt: 9 Oct 1809
John NEWTON of Ldn to daughter Elizabeth STROTHER w/o Anthony STROTHER of JeffVa. Gift of negro woman Suck. Wit: Samuel M. EDWARDS, Fleet SMITH.

Bk:Pg: 2K:410   Date: 20 Mar 1809   RcCt: 9 Oct 1809
John NEWTON of Ldn to son Joseph T. NEWTON of Ldn. Gift of negro man Bob. Wit: Samuel M. EDWARDS, Fleet SMITH.

Bk:Pg: 2K:411   Date: 20 Mar 1809   RcCt: 9 Oct 1809
John NEWTON of Ldn to son Joseph T. NEWTON of Ldn. Gift of slaves Ben, Philip, Mark, Cloke, Tom, David, farm and household items & 369*ac* in exchange for support for John and daughter Mary T. NEWTON of AlexVa. Wit: Samuel M. EDWARDS, Fleet SMITH. Wit: Samuel M. EDWARDS, Isaac LAROWE, Eli OFFUTT, Thomas H. JENKINS.

Bk:Pg: 2K:412   Date: 20 Mar 1809   RcCt: 9 Oct 1809
John NEWTON of Ldn to son Benjamin NEWTON of StafVa. Gift of Negro Nace. Wit: Samuel M. EDWARDS, Fleet SMITH.

Bk:Pg: 2K:412   Date: 20 Mar 1809   RcCt: 9 Oct 1809
John NEWTON of Ldn to daughter Martha WISE w/o George WISE of DC. Gift of Negro Charlotte. Wit: Samuel M. EDWARDS, Fleet SMITH.

Bk:Pg: 2K:413   Date: 20 Mar 1809   RcCt: 9 Oct 1809
John NEWTON of Ldn to son Augustine NEWTON of AlexVa. Gift of negro George. Wit: Samuel M. EDWARDS, Fleet SMITH.

Bk:Pg: 2K:414   Date: 20 Mar 1809   RcCt: 9 Oct 1809
John NEWTON of Ldn to daughter Mary T. NEWTON. Gift of negro Rose. Wit: Samuel M. EDWARDS, Fleet SMITH.

Bk:Pg: 2K:415   Date: 20 Mar 1809   RcCt: 9 Oct 1809
John NEWTON of Ldn to daughter Mary T. NEWTON. Gift of negro Rose. Wit: Samuel M. EDWARDS, Fleet SMITH.

Bk:Pg: 2K:415   Date: 20 Mar 1809   RcCt: 9 Oct 1809
John NEWTON to Joseph T. NEWTON. PoA. Wit: Saml. M. EDWARDS, Isaac LAROWE, Eli OFFUTT, Thos. F. JENKINS.

Bk:Pg: 2K:416   Date: 2 Jan 1806   RcCt: 9 Oct 1806
George BEALL. Col for slave woman Teanor, boys James, Aaron & Henry, girls Amme, Seller, Sophia & Polly.

Bk:Pg: 2K:416   Date: 26 Sep 1809   RcCt: 9 Oct 1809
Sarah FAIRFAX to John STADLER. Renewal of LS of 140*ac*. Wit: Jacob CRIMM, Henry PEERS, Nich's PEERS.

Bk:Pg: 2K:418   Date: 1 Mar 1809   RcCt: 11 Sep 1809
James KINCHOLOE of Fqr to Elizabeth BOYDE of Ldn. B/S of Lots #17 & #23 where James DAVIS last resided, totaling 1*ac*. Wit: Jesse McVEIGH, Andrew SMARR, Silas BEATTY, Felix TRIPLETT, A. GIBSON, Leven D. POWELL, James STEPHENSON.

Bk:Pg: 2K:420   Date: 21 May 1809   RcCt: 9 Oct 1809.
William POWELL Ldn to Vincent L. LEWIS of Ldn. Trust for debt to Charles POWELL using farm and household items. Wit: Philip PALMER, Edw'd KELLEY, Thomas STONESTREET.

Bk:Pg: 2K:421   Date: 25 Sep 1809   RcCt: 9 Oct 1809
Sarah FAIRFAX to Jacob WALTMAN (Admr of Jacob EVERHEART dec'd). Renewal of LS of 150*ac*. Wit: Bazil DEVER, John WINNER, Jacob WALTMAN Jr.

Bk:Pg: 2K:423   Date: 9 Oct 1809   RcCt: 9 Oct 1809
Frederick TARFLINGER of Ldn to Adam MILLER of Ldn. A/L of 219*ac*. Wit: Eli OFFUTT, Isaac LARAWE, Saml. M. EDWARDS.

Bk:Pg: 2K:424   Date: 20 Jul 1809   RcCt: 9 Oct 1809
William PATTERSON & wife Abigail, Jacob BAXTER & wife Lydia, Jacob DEHAVEN & wife Nancy, John LOWREY & wife Hannah and William JONES & wife Mary of Scott Co Ky to William DULIN. CoE for Mary JONES.

Bk:Pg: 2K:426   Date: 2 May 1809   RcCt: 9 Oct 1809
Ellender JENKINS of Ldn to daughter Ansey JENKINS of Ldn. Gift of furniture. Wit: Elisha TIMMS, George SHIVELLEY, Elizabeth JENKINS.

Bk:Pg: 2K:427   Date: 20 Jun 1809   RcCt: 9 Oct 1809
Presley SAUNDERS Jr. & wife Mary of Ldn to Jesse DAILEY of Lsbg. B/S of part of Lot #58 in Lsbg. Wit: John LITTLEJOHN, Samuel MURREY, James SAUNDERS.

Bk:Pg: 2K:429   Date: 3 Jun 1809   RcCt: 9 Oct 1809
Wm. POWELL. Receipt for payment from Chas. POWELL for negro girl Agg. Wit: Thos. STONESTREET, Philip PALMER.

Bk:Pg: 2K:430   Date: __ Dec 1808   RcCt: 9 Oct 1809
Presley SAUNDERS Jr. & wife Mary of Ldn to William AUSTINE of Lsbg. B/S of part of Lot #58 and part of lot SAUNDERS purchased from Sally CRAVEN & Joshua BAKER. Wit: John LITTLEJOHN, Samuel MURREY, James SAUNDERS.

Bk:Pg: 2K:432   Date: 13 Apr 1805   RcCt: 9 Oct 1809
Thomas HARRISON Jr & wife Mary to Colin AULD. CoE in PrWm for sale of 150*ac*. Wit: Jno. MACRAE, David BOYLE.

Bk:Pg: 2K:433   Date: 10 Oct 1809   RcCt: 10 Oct 1809
John PAYNE & wife Rosannah to Solomon LITTLETON & wife Margaret,
Jacob BAUGH & wife Mary, John, Thomas, Jacob, Lenora & Kitty
KEPHEART. CoE for sale of 79ac. Wit: Samuel MURREY, Steph C.
ROSZELL.

Bk:Pg: 2K:434   Date: 10 Jun 1793 Frederick   RcCt: 10 Oct 1809
Capt. John ROSE. Col for unnamed slaves.

Bk:Pg: 2L:001   Date: 14 Aug 1809   RcCt: 10 Oct 1809
Isaac HOUGH & wife Fanny to John ROSE, Cornelius SHAWEN, Peter
MILLER Sr., Peter MILLER Jr., and Moses MILLER (trustees of Methodist
Episcopal Church). B/S of 1ac adj George MULL. Wit: John HAMILTON,
R. BRADEN.

Bk:Pg: 2L:003   Date: 14 Feb 1809   RcCt: 10 Oct 1809
David MARTIN & wife Elizabeth, James McMANAMAN & wife Mary
(wives are d/o John CARR 2nd dec'd) to William CARR and John WADE.
Release. Wit: Jno. MATTHIAS, Wm. ROBERTS, John DRISH.

Bk:Pg: 2L:005   Date: 13 Nov 1809   RcCt: 13 Nov 1809
Thomas WEST of Ohio (Admr of Nathaniel WEST dec'd of Ldn) to James
NICKOLS of Ldn. PoA. Wit: Saml. M. EDWARDS.

Bk:Pg: 2L:006   Date: 14 Nov 1807   RcCt: 12 Dec 1808
Stephen DONALDSON & wife Susanna of Ldn to Samuel GREGG,
Stephen C. ROSSELL and John LITTLEJOHN of Ldn. Trust 309ac on S
end of Short Hill and slaves Harry, Dick, Minn, Easter & child Isaac, Diner,
Enoch, Eady, Hannah & Harry the younger and wagon and cattle. Wit:
James RUST, Wm. STURMAN, Saml. M. EDWARDS, John TYLER, Ths.
FOUCH, Samuel MURREY.

Bk:Pg: 2L:009   Date: 14 Nov 1809   RcCt: 14 Nov 1809
Samuel GREGG, Stephen C. ROSSELL and John LITTLEJOHN (trustees
of Stephen DONALDSON) of Ldn to Morris OSBURN of Ldn. B/S of
317ac where DONALDSON now lives.

Bk:Pg: 2L:011   Date: 14 Nov 1807   RcCt: 13 Jan 1808
Thomas SANDERS of Lsbg to Richard CHESTER & William
MASTERMAN (Exors of Daniel MILDRED dec'd). Mortgage of lot in Lsbg
on Loudoun & King Sts. Wit: Will CHELTON, John LITTLEJOHN, Charles
Fenton MERCER, Thos. EDWARDS.

Bk:Pg: 2L:013   Date: 16 Nov 1809   RcCt: 16 Nov 1809
Exors of Daniel MILDRED dec'd to Thomas SAUNDERS. Release of
mortgage. Wit: S. BLINCOE.

Bk:Pg: 2L:013   Date: 10 Oct 1809   RcCt: 18 Nov 1809
John PAYNE & wife Rosannah of Lsbg to Quintin BAIN of Georgetown.
B/S of 89ac adj Enoch FRANCIS. Wit: C. BINNS, S. BLINCOE, Saml. M.
EDWARDS, Samuel MURREY, Step C. ROSZEL.

Bk:Pg: 2L:016   Date: 15 Feb 1809   RcCt: 11 Dec 1809
Thomas RHODES & wife Sarah of Belmont Co Oh to William RHODES of Columbiana Co Oh. B/S of 200ac adj Kittockton Mt. Wit: Thos. THOMPSON, Joseph RHODES, Edmond VAUGH.

Bk:Pg: 2L:019   Date: 17 Jan 1809   RcCt: 11 Dec 1809
John CARR of Ldn to Mary McMANAMY wife of James McMANAMY of Ldn. B/S of 20¼ac adj Elizabeth MARTIN. Wit: Jno. MATTHIAS, Saml. M. EDWARDS, Eli OFFUTT, Isaac LAROWE.

Bk:Pg: 2L:021   Date: 9 Dec 1809   RcCt: 11 Dec 1809
Mahlon COMBS & wife Sarah of Ldn to Eli MILLAN of Ldn. B/S of 4½ac adj William SUDDITH, John GIBSON. Wit: C. BINNS, William DRISH, Saml. M. EDWARDS, Thomas F. JENKINS.

Bk:Pg: 2L:023   Date: 19 Aug 1809   RcCt: 11 Dec 1809
Joseph LOVETT & wife Naomi of Ldn to William GALLAHER, David GALLAHER, Joseph LOVETT Jr., Samuel DUNKIN, Robert FULTON, Thomas VIOLETT & William LEATH (trustees of Methodist Episcopal Church). B/S of 1ac adj William GALLAHER. Wit: Wm. BRONAUGH, Daniel EACHES, Jacob SMITH, Step. C. ROSZELL.

Bk:Pg: 2L:027   Date: 13 Apr 1809   RcCt: 11 Dec 1809
Walter LANHAM & wife Caroline of Ldn to Samuel BOGGESS. Trust for debt to George RUST Sr & Joseph REED as security, using 192 2/3ac. Wit: Ben GRAYSON, James WAUGH, Jas. L. GIBB Sr., Joseph CARR.

Bk:Pg: 2L:030   Date: 11 Nov 1809   RcCt: 11 Dec 1809
Sandford CONNELLY of Shelby Co Ky (Guardian to heirs of James LYNE dec'd) to William LYNE of Ldn. B/S of 80ac (from estate of Thomas LYNE dec'd). Wit: Martin SETTLE, Daniel FOX, Henry SETTLE, Jonas FOX, Henry SETTLE Jr.

Bk:Pg: 2L:030   Date: 22 Mar 1809   RcCt: 11 Dec 1809
Joseph LOVETT & Samuel SMITH (Exors of Robert McCORMICK dec'd of Ldn) to William HARNED of Ldn. B/S of 65ac on Beaverdam adj Amos HIBBS, Isaac COWGILL, Samuel DUNKIN, Joseph GOURLEY. Wit: Joseph EACHES, Gourley REEDER.

Bk:Pg: 2L:032   Date: 24 Mar 1809   RcCt: 11 Dec 1809
William HARNED of Ldn to Joseph LOVETT & Samuel SMITH (Exors of Robert McCORMICK dec'd of Ldn). Mortgage on above land. Wit: Joseph EACHES, Gourley REEDER.

Bk:Pg: 2L:037   Date: 2 Sep 1809   RcCt: 11 Dec 1809
William M. LITTLEJOHN of Ldn to John Nickolas KLINE of Ldn. B/S of ½ac Lot #10 in Littlejohn addition to Lsbg.

Bk:Pg: 2L:039   Date: 5 May 1809   RcCt: 11 Dec 1809
David POTTS of Ldn to Jonas POTTS of Ldn, William POTTS of Ohio, Ann BACKHOUSE of JeffVa, and Jane POTTS of Ldn (all heirs of Ezekiel POTTS dec'd of Ldn, widow Elizabeth POTTS). Partition of land between Short Hill and Blue Ridge. Wit: Edward POTTS, William THOMPSON, Jno. MATTHIAS.

Bk:Pg: 2L:042   Date: 5 May 1809   RcCt: 11 Dec 1809
David, Jonas and William POTTS (s/o Ezekiel POTTS dec'd of Ldn) and
Ann BACKHOUSE & Jane POTTS (d/o Ezekiel POTTS dec'd of Ldn)
Agreement concerning negroes. Wit: Edward POTTS, William
THOMPSON, Jno. MATTHIAS.

Bk:Pg: 2L:044   Date: 9 Dec 1809   RcCt: 11 Dec 1809
David POTTS, Jonas POTTS & wife Martha, William POTTS & wife
Isabella to Ann BACKUS & Jane POTTS. Mortgage of David's 195*ac* &
Jonas' 185½*ac* & William's 158*ac*. Wit: Isaac LAROWE, William
THOMPSON, Edward POTTS.

Bk:Pg: 2L:047   Date: 3 Jun 1809   RcCt: 11 Dec 1809
Terance FIGH of Ldn to John F. SAPPINGTON of Ldn. BoS for horse,
bedding, and trunk. Wit: Joseph TALBOTT, John VANDEVANTER.

Bk:Pg: 2L:048   Date: 20 Nov 1809   RcCt: 11 Dec 1809
Thomas A. HEREFORD of Mdbg to Andrew SMARR of Mdbg. B/S of Lots
#39 & #40 in Mdbg. Wit: Burr POWELL, Jesse McVEIGH, A. GIBSON,
Hugh SMITH.

Bk:Pg: 2L:049   Date: 11 Dec 1809   RcCt: 11 Dec 1809
William HOUGH & wife Eleanor of Ldn to Jonas POTTS of Ldn. B/S of 2
lots in Wtfd adj Potts Mill.

Bk:Pg: 2L:051   Date: 1 Jul 1809   RcCt: 11 Dec 1809
John WORSLEY of Ldn to Jane COCKING of DC. Mortgage of land
WORSLEY bought from Samuel BROOK. Wit: Wm. COCKING, Will'm
BLANCHARD, Jno. UNDERWOOD.

Bk:Pg: 2L:052   Date: 13 Jul 1809   RcCt: 11 Dec 1809
John CAVAN Jr. of Lsbg to Thomas JANNEY of AlexVa. Mortgage of ½ of
Lot #24 in Lsbg. Wit: William CLINE, Jos. BEARD, Jno. MATTHIAS.

Bk:Pg: 2L:055   Date: 14 Nov 1809   RcCt: 12 Dec 1809
Abraham WINNING (s/o Margaret) of Ldn to John SANBOWER of Ldn.
Trust for debt to Adam SHOVER 39*ac*. Wit: Jas. CAVAN Jr., A.
SUTHERLAND, John CAVAN, George McCABE, William MILLS, Jacob
HEFFNER.

Bk:Pg: 2L:058   Date: 1 Jan 1810   RcCt: 8 Jan 1810
Daniel EACHES of Ldn to Robert M. POWELL of Ldn. B/S of 8*ac* on
Goose Creek. Wit: Wm. POWELL, Wm. TRIPLETT, Wm. H. POWELL.

Bk:Pg: 2L:060   Date: 8 Jan 1810   RcCt: 8 Jan 1810
Daniel EACHES of Ldn to Margaret & Mary VICKERS (d/o William
VICKERS) of Ldn. B/S of ¼*ac* Lot #2 on S side of main st in Millsville. Wit:
Isaac LAROWE.

Bk:Pg: 2L:061   Date: 4 Nov 1809   RcCt: 8 Jan 1810
William LITTLEJOHN of Ldn to James GARDNER of Ldn. B/S of Lots #44
& #45 in Littlejohn's addition of Lsbg.

Bk:Pg: 2L:063   Date: 6 Jan 1810   RcCt: 8 Jan 1810
Silas BURSON of Columbiana Co Oh to George BURSON of Ldn (both s/o Benjamin BURSON dec'd). B/S of 154*ac* adj Joseph BURSON. Wit: Joshua GORE, Samuel NICKOLS.

Bk:Pg: 2L:064   Date: 8 Jan 1810   RcCt: 8 Jan 1810
George BURSON of Ldn to Benjamin GRAYSON of Ldn. Trust for debt to Samuel NICKOLS using 154*ac*. Wit: Joshua GORE, Samuel NICKOLS.

Bk:Pg: 2L:066   Date: 26 Sep 1809   RcCt: 8 Jan 1810
Sarah FAIRFAX to Thomas DAVIS. Renewal of LS on 150*ac*. Wit: John DAVIS.

Bk:Pg: 2L:068   Date: 8 Apr 1805   RcCt: 8 Jul 1805
Mahlon JANNEY & wife Sarah of Ldn to Israel H. THOMPSON of Ldn. B/S of ¾*ac* lot in Wtfd. Wit: Thomas PHILLIPS, James MOORE, John WILLIAMS, Abner MOORE.

Bk:Pg: 2L:069   Date: 23 Dec 1809   RcCt: 8 Jan 1810
Benjamin McCOY of Ldn to Alexander McMAKEN of Ldn. BoS of negro Letty abt 45 or 50y old, farm and household items. Wit: Martin CORDEL, John BROWN.

Bk:Pg: 2L:071   Date: 3 Jun 1809   RcCt: 8 Jan 1810
Isaac PHILLIPS of Ldn to William SCHOOLEY of Ldn. BoS for farm and household items. Wit: John HAMMERLEY, Wm. WOODY, John GREEN.

Bk:Pg: 2L:072   Date: 20 Sep 1809   RcCt: 11 Dec 1809
Mahlon JANNEY & wife Sarah of Ldn to William HOUGH of Ldn. B/S of lot in Wtfd adj Jonas POTTS. Wit: Reuben SCHOOLEY, Levi JAMES, Reuben SCHOOLEY Jr., W. S. NEALE.

Bk:Pg: 2L:074   Date: 20 Sep 1809   RcCt: 11 Dec 1809
William HOUGH & wife Eleanor of Ldn to Mahlon JANNEY of Ldn. B/S of lot in Wtfd adj Asa MOORE. Wit: Levi JAMES, Reuben SCHOOLEY, Reuben SCHOOLEY Jr., Wm. S. NEALE.

Bk:Pg: 2L:076   Date: 8 Jun 1809   RcCt: 8 Jan 1810
Joseph TIDBALL & wife Jane of Winchester to Archibald MAGILL of Winchester and John BALL of Ldn and Susannah BALL (w/o John). B/S of ½ of Balls Mill, Susannah transferred her rights to Paddies Pond in FrdkVa. Wit: Edward McGUIRE, James M. MARSHALL.

Bk:Pg: 2L:083   Date: 18 Oct 1808   RcCt: 8 Jan 1810
Malcher ANSILL of Kenaway Co Va to brother Leonard ANSILL of Ldn. PoA for interest in estate of father Leonard ANSILL dec'd of Ldn. Wit: Timothy HIXON, John HAMILTON, Thomas AWBREY, Isaac STEERE, Aaron SANDERS.

Bk:Pg: 2L:084   Date: 8 Jan 1810   RcCt: 9 Jan 1810
John DRISH & wife Eleanor to John CARR Jr. Correction of mistake in deed.

Bk:Pg: 2L:084   Date: 12 Sep 1809   RcCt: 12 Feb 1810
Peter RICHARD & wife Elizabeth of Ldn to Daniel HOUSEHOLDER of Ldn. B/S of 22¼ac adj George VINCELL, Amos JANNEY, Samuel BAKER. Wit: Benj. SHREVE, Chs. ELGIN, Jno. ROSE, Samuel MURREY.

Bk:Pg: 2L:087   Date: 26 Jan 1810   RcCt: 12 Feb 1810
Joshua LEE & wife Theodocia of Ldn to James ALLEN of Ldn. B/S of 72ac adj David SMALLEY. Wit: John SINCLAIR, Wilson ATHEY, Mason DUNCAN.

Bk:Pg: 2L:089   Date: 8 Feb 1810   RcCt: 12 Feb 1810
Richard OSBURN of Ldn to Isreal JANNEY of Ldn. B/S of 42ac adj Israel Janney's Mill Creek. Wit: James MOORE, Jonathan JANNEY, Lot JANNEY.

Bk:Pg: 2L:091   Date: 8 Feb 1810   RcCt: 12 Feb 1810
Richard OSBURN of Ldn to Joshua GORE of Ldn. B/S of 77ac adj Israel Janney's tail race, Solomon HOGE. Wit: James MOORE, Jonathan JANNEY, Lot JANNEY.

Bk:Pg: 2L:094   Date: 13 May 1809   RcCt: 12 Feb 1810
Mary GREGG of Ldn to John BEAVERS of Ldn. A/L of lot in Manor of Leeds. Wit: Henry BROWN, Jesse ATWELL, John MUDD, John ADAMS.

Bk:Pg: 2L:095   Date: 31 Jan 1807   RcCt: 14 Sep 1807
John EBLIN & wife Ann of Roan Co Tn to William WHITE of Ldn. B/S of 18ac on Kittockton Mt. nr Secolin, adj John NIXON, James CARUTHERS, Daniel WHITE. Wit: Jesse JANNEY, Stacey JANNEY, Levi MILBURN, Saml. ESKRIDGE, Daniel WHITE.

Bk:Pg: 2L:097   Date: 8 May 1809   RcCt: 12 Feb 1810
William RHODES & wife Mary to Henry CLAGGETT. CoE for sale of 248ac. Wit: Alex'r SNODGRASS, Joseph SPRINGER.

Bk:Pg: 2L:099   Date: 14 Aug 1809   RcCt: 14 Aug 1809
Benjamin GRAYSON & William GRAYSON. Bond on Benjamin as Sheriff to collect levy. Wit: C. BINNS.

Bk:Pg: 2L:099   Date: 10 Feb 1810   RcCt: 12 Feb 1810
Asa MOORE, Mahlon JANNEY & Abner WILLIAMS of Ldn to Thomas LACEY of Ldn. B/S of lot on SW side of main st in Wtfd. Wit: Daniel STONE, Josiah CRAVEN, James MOORE.

Bk:Pg: 2L:101   Date: 19 Mar 1809   RcCt: 12 Feb 1810
James McGIRTH (signed McGATH) of Ldn and Mary McGIRTH, Stephen McGIRTH and William H. HANDY & wife Eleanor. Agreement – James received 64ac and renounced any claim from estate of James McGIRTH dec'd. Wit: Wm. BRONAUGH, Step G. ROSZEL.

Bk:Pg: 2L:101   Date: 13 Mar 1809   RcCt: 12 Feb 1810
Mary McGIRTH, Stephen McGIRTH (signed McGEATH) and William H. HANDY & wife Eleanor of Ldn to James McGIRTH of Ldn. B/S of 64ac on

Beaverdam [see above]. Wit: Wm. BRONAUGH, Step C. ROSZEL, James FOX.

Bk:Pg: 2L:103   Date: 1 Nov 1809   RcCt: 12 Feb 1810
Leven LUCKETT (Exor of Francis H. PEYTON) to Joshua LEE. B/S of 200ac on Broad Run adj John BAYLY. Wit: Jno. MATTHIAS, Henry DUNCAN, Wilson ATHEY.

Bk:Pg: 2L:105   Date: 1 Nov 1809   RcCt: 12 Feb 1810
Joshua LEE to Leven LUCKETT. Mortgage on above 200ac. Wit: Jno. MATTHIAS, Wilson ATHEY, Henry DUNCAN.

Bk:Pg: 2L:107   Date: 29 Jul 1809   RcCt: 12 Feb 1810
William COLEMAN of Ldn to James COLEMAN Jr. of Ldn. Trust using negro woman Joan abt 50y, girl Mary abt 12y, girl Mary abt 10y for use Keturah KEENE w/o John KEENE late of Ffx. Wit: Lane SMITH, John COLEMAN, Frances COLEMAN, Jas. B. LANE, Henry SUMMERS.

Bk:Pg: 2L:109   Date: 12 Feb 1810   RcCt: 12 Feb 1810
Asa MOORE of Wtfd to Leven SMALLWOOD of Wtfd. B/S of lot in Wtfd adj. John F. SAPPINGTON.

Bk:Pg: 2L:111   Date: 19 Jan 1810   RcCt: 12 Feb 1810
Timothy LYNE & wife Mary of Logan Co Ky to William JAMES of Ldn. B/S of 58ac from Thomas LYNE dec'd. Wit: Lewis HUTCHISON, Reuben SETTLE, Jeremiah HUTCHISON Jr., Deen JAMES, Joseph FOX, William LYNE.

Bk:Pg: 2L:113   Date: 20 Jan 1810   RcCt: 12 Feb 1810
Timothy LYNE & wife Mary of Logan Co Ky to Reuben SETTLE of Ldn. B/S of Timothy's interest in widow's dower from land of Thomas LYNE dec'd. Wit: Willam JAMES, William LYNE, Deen JAMES, Jeremiah HUTCHISON Jr., Lewis HUTCHISON, Amos FOX.

Bk:Pg: 2L:114   Date: 21 Oct 1809   RcCt: 12 Feb 1810
Jonathan CARTER of Ldn to John NEWLIN of Ldn. B/S of 109ac on Goose Creek which NEWLIN now leases. Wit: John SINCLAIR, Thomas NICKOLS, William VICKER.

Bk:Pg: 2L:116   Date: 20 Feb 1808   RcCt: 12 Feb 1810
Elizabeth McILHANY of Ldn to John McILHANY Jr. & wife Harriot of Ldn. Exchange of lands from James McILHANY dec'd. Wit: Thos. NICKOLS, John WHITE, Rosannah ELLZEY, Lewis ELLZEY, Margaret McILHANY, Saml. BOGGESS.

Bk:Pg: 2L:118   Date: 5 Dec 1809   RcCt: 12 Feb 1810
Benjamin GRAYSON & wife Nancy of Ldn to Elizabeth QUEEN of Ldn. B/S of 20ac adj Enoch FURR Sr., Joshua FRED. Wit: Benjamin GRAYSON Jr., John W. B. GRAYSON, George M. GRAYSON, Wm. BRONAUGH, J. F. FOWKE, Joseph CARR.

Bk:Pg: 2L:121   Date: 24 Mar 1809   RcCt: 11 Dec 1809
William MAINS & wife Mary of Ldn to Archibald MAINS of Ldn. B/S of 328¾ac. Wit: John LITTLEJOHN, John McCORMICK, Robert PARFECT.

Bk:Pg: 2L:123   Date: 1 Oct 1809   RcCt: 12 Feb 1810
William TAYLOR of Lsbg to John S. CRANWELL of Lsbg. B/S of ½ac Lot #40 in Lsbg. Wit: Presley SAUNDERS Jr., Joseph EDWARDS, John RATCLIFFE.

Bk:Pg: 2L:125   Date: 1 Oct 1809   RcCt: 12 Feb 1810
John S. CRAMWELL of Lsbg to William TAYLOR of Lsbg. Trust on above land. Wit: Presley SAUNDERS Jr., Joseph EDWARDS, John RATCLIFFE.

Bk:Pg: 2L:129   Date: 15 Sep 1809   RcCt: 12 Feb 1810
Andrew GARNER of Ldn to Isaac LAROWE & Jonas POTTS of Ldn. Trust for several debts using farm and household items. Wit: Fleet SMITH, Eli OFFUTT, Saml. M. EDWARDS.

Bk:Pg: 2L:130   Date: 3 Apr 1809   RcCt: 14 Mar 1809 [10?]
George MANN Sr to John MANN. B/S of 103ac on road from Dutch Mill to Roaches. Wit: William CHILTON, Isaac LAROWE, S. BLINCOE.

Bk:Pg: 2L:133   Date: 13 Feb 1810   RcCt: 13 Feb 1810
James McMANAMAN & wife Mary of Ldn to John CARR of Ldn. B/S of 19ac adj David MARTIN. Wit: Jno. MATHIAS, Saml. CARR, Thos. CARR.

Bk:Pg: 2L:135   Date: 5 May 1804   RcCt: 10 Dec 1804
John P. HARRISON & wife Elizabeth of StafVa to Burr POWELL of Ldn. B/S of 22ac. Wit: Mesheck LACEY, Noble BEVERIDGE, Thomas ATWELL, Henry BROWN, Jesse McVEIGH.

Bk:Pg: 2L:137   Date: 24 Jun 1808   RcCt: 12 Mar 1810
Carter BEAVERLY/BEVERLY & wife Jane of Culpeper to Peter Randolph BEAVERLY of Culpeper. B/S of 2000ac. Wit: Edmund EDRINGTON, Wm. ALCOKE, George MILLS, R. B. VOSS, Jos. LEWIS Jr., Mumford BEVERLEY, John B. GIBSON, Jas. GRAY Jr.

Bk:Pg: 2L:140   Date: 20 Jun 1809   RcCt: 10 Feb 1810
William WEST of Chester Co Pa and Samuel WEST of Delaware Co Pa (Exors of brother William WEST dec'd of Delaware Co Pa) to brother John WEST of Ldn. B/S of 183ac where John now dwells. Wit: Israel JANNEY, Mahlon TAYLOR, George TAVENER.

Bk:Pg: 2L:143   Date: 12 Mar 1809   RcCt: 12 Mar 1810
Barnett HOUGH & wife Louisa of Lsbg to James GREENLEASE of Ldn. B/S of part of Lot #57 in Lsbg. Wit: Saml. CLAPHAM, Saml. MURREY.

Bk:Pg: 2L:146   Date: 9 Jun 1809   RcCt: 12 Mar 1810
Burr POWELL & wife Catherine of Ldn to Ezekiel MOUNT. B/S of 75ac adj Fielding LYNN, David JAMES. Wit: A. GIBSON, John MARTIN, Michael PLASTER, Leven POWELL, Leven LUCKETT.

Bk:Pg: 2L:150   Date: 4 Jun 1809   RcCt: 12 Mar 1810
John KEYTH & wife Sarah (late Sarah TORBERT) and Thomas TORBERT to John TORBUT. B/S of their share (as sister & brother) of 100ac from estate of Samuel TORBERT dec'd of Ldn. Wit: James

PUCKETT, Vincent KEITH, Richard NUTT, Leven POWELL, A. GIBSON, Ben GRAYSON, Joseph CARR.

Bk:Pg: 2L:156   Date: 7 Mar 1810   RcCt: 12 Mar 1810
James McARTOR & wife Mary of Ldn to Barnett HOUGH, John LITTLEJOHN & Samuel CARR. Trust of William CARR for 197½ac. Wit: Ths. L. MOORE.

Bk:Pg: 2L:159   Date: 7 Mar 1810   RcCt: 12 Mar 1810
William CARR of Ldn to James McARTOR of Ldn. B/S of 100ac at mouth of Ball's Mill tail &97½ac. Wit: John LITTLEJOHN, Thomas L. MOORE, Daniel LOVETT.

Bk:Pg: 2L:162   Date: 16 Sep 1809   RcCt: 13 Feb 1810
Charles TURSHIMER & wife Catherine and John TURSHIMER & wife Magdalene of Rockingham Co Va to Adam SHOVER of Ldn. PoA for sale of land in Ldn. Wit: Giles TURLEY, George DOVE.

Bk:Pg: 2L:163   Date: 14 Jun 1809   RcCt: 12 Feb 1810
Isaac BROWN of Ldn bound to John BROWN of Ldn for 30ac. Wit: Wm. CHILTON, John MARKS, George NICKOLS.

Bk:Pg: 2L:165   Date: 7 Apr 1809   RcCt: 13 Mar 1810
James LEITH of Ldn to Gregory NOLAND. LS of 100ac where NOLAND now lives. Wit: Burr POWELL, H. SMITH, Ammon HEREFORD.

Bk:Pg: 2L:167   Date: 13 Mar 1810   RcCt: 14 Mar 1810
William ELLZEY & wife Frances Hill of Ldn to Jacob WALTMAN of Ldn. B/S of 122¾ac on Dutchman Run adj John GEORGE, Frederick STEELE. Wit: Thomas McCOWAT, Wm. B. HARRISON, Hen. GLASSGOW, John McCORMACK.

Bk:Pg: 2L:170   Date: 14 Oct 1809   RcCt: 8 Apr 1809 [10?]
Whetman LEITH of Ldn to Edward CARTER of Ldn. B/S of 78ac on Goose Creek adj William VICKERS. Wit: Hugh SMITH, A. GIBSON, Jesse McVEIGH, William McVICKERS.

Bk:Pg: 2L:173   Date: 14 Mar 1810   RcCt: 15 Mar 1810
Thomas HETHERLY & wife Mary of Ldn to Jonathan FOUCH of Ldn. B/S of lot nr Lsbg adj Basel HALL. Wit: Jno. MATHIAS, Stacy HANES, John HANES.

Bk:Pg: 2L:175   Date: 16 Aug 1809   RcCt: 15 Mar 1810
Thomas HETHERLY & wife Mary of Ldn to Bazel HALL of Ldn. B/S of part of lot on S side of Loudoun St in Lsbg. Wit: A. SUTHERLAND, John CAVANS, Isaac KENT.

Bk:Pg: 2L:177   Date: 19 Jan 1805   RcCt: 10 Sep 1805
John CLINE and David CLINE (ch/o David CLINE Sr. dec'd) & wife Jane of Ldn to William CLINE of Ldn. B/S of lot adj Lsbg that father purchased of Henry McCABE. Wit: C. BINNS, Samuel MURREY, Samuel HOUGH, Barten LUCAS, Pat'k McINTYRE, Obediah CLIFFORD.

Bk:Pg: 2L:181   Date: 20 Sep 1808   RcCt: 13 Dec 1808
John H. SMITH of Lsbg to Fleet SMITH of Lsbg. Mortgage of 250*ac*. Wit:
John H. EVANS, Jas. CAVAN Jr., Saml. CARR.

Bk:Pg: 2L:184   Date: 4 Apr 1810   RcCt: 10 Apr 1810
Daniel MAY & wife Elizabeth of Bedford Co Pa to Adam SHOVER of Ldn.
PoA for sale of land formerly belonging to Jacob TUSTHIMER.

Bk:Pg: 2L:186   Date: 10 Apr 1810   RcCt: 10 Apr 1810
Michael BELL of GrB to John VANHORN of Ldn. B/S of 240*ac* on
Beaverdam.

Bk:Pg: 2L:189   Date: 7 Apr 1810   RcCt: 9 Apr 1810
Henry CLAGETT & wife Julia of Ldn to John POTTER of Ldn. B/S of lot
on King St Lsbg adj Thomas SANDERS. Wit: Samuel MURREY, B.
HOUGH, Isaac HARRIS, John LITTLEJOHN.

Bk:Pg: 2L:193   Date: 9 Mar 1810   RcCt: 10 Apr 1810
George PRICE of Balt to William NOLAND of Ldn. B/S of part of Lot #30
in Lsbg. Wit: Charles BINNS, Isaac LAROWE, Fleet SMITH, Jonas
SMITH, Jonas POTTS.

Bk:Pg: 2L:195   Date: 8 Mar 1810   RcCt: 9 May 1810
Solomon HOGE & wife Mary of Ldn to Nathan BROWN of Ldn. B/S of
30*ac* adj John BROWN, John QUEEN. Wit: Joshua GORE, Israel
JANNEY, David JANNEY, John BROWN, Stacy TAYLOR, Joshua
OSBURN.

Bk:Pg: 2L:199   Date: 8 Mar 1810   RcCt: 9 May 1810
Solomon HOGE & wife Mary of Ldn to Israel JANNEY of Ldn. B/S of 32*ac*
adj Israel JANNEY, Joshua GORE. Wit: Joshua GORE, David JANNEY,
Nathan BROWN, John BROWN, Stacy TAYLOR, Joshua OSBURN.

Bk:Pg: 2L:203   Date: 16 Feb 1810   RcCt: 9 Apr 1810
John HAMILTON & wife Winefred to James RICE. CoE for sale of 71¼*ac*.
Wit: Saml. CLAPHAM, John S. MARLOW.

Bk:Pg: 2L:205   Date: 12 Mar 1810   RcCt: 10 Apr 1810
Burr POWELL of Ldn to Jacob STONEBURNER of Ldn. Release of trust.

Bk:Pg: 2L:205   Date: 9 Mar 1810   RcCt: 10 Apr 1810
William P. HALE to John BURSON. Release of mortgage. Wit: Burr
POWELL, A. GIBSON, William MANKIN, George BARR.

Bk:Pg: 2L:206   Date: 10 Apr 1810   RcCt: 10 Apr 1810
James TRAHERN of Ldn to James BROWN of Ldn. B/S of 17*ac* adj
Anthony SWICK.

Bk:Pg: 2L:208   Date: 2 Apr 1810   RcCt: 10 Apr 1810
Daniel & David FARNSWORTH of Ldn to Samuel FARNSWORTH of Ldn.
B/S of 20*ac* adj Joseph THOMAS, Hannah WILLIAMS, John
FARNSWORTH. Wit: John COOPER, Jesse THOMAS, John
FARNSWORTH.

Bk:Pg: 2L:211   Date: 21 Mar 1810   RcCt: 10 Apr 1810
Frederick William RICE of Lsbg to William WOODY of Lsbg. B/S of house & lot to preserve it for the heirs of Cath'e McCaleb RICE now dec'd in GrB when they arrive here. Wit: Joseph HUNT, Reuben SCHOOLY, David WOODY.

Bk:Pg: 2L:213   Date: 11 Sep 1809   RcCt: 14 May 1810
George MILLER & wife Nancy of FrdkVa to Thomas A. TIDBALL of Winchester. B/S of 40ac with grist & saw mill previously owned by Joseph TIDBALL & wife Jane for trust to Joseph. Wit: Griffin TAYLOR, Wm. CASTLEMAN, John McDONALD, Michael POWER.

Bk:Pg: 219   Date: 29 Mar 1810   RcCt: 14 May 1810
Joshua DANIEL & wife Jane to Jonas POTTS. CoE for sale of 300ac. Wit: John A. BINNS, R. BRADEN.

Bk:Pg: 2L:220   Date: 12 Jan 1793   RcCt: 14 May 1810
Bazel STONESTREET. Col for slaves Penelope, Jeremiah, Amelia Ann & Moses from Md.

Bk:Pg: 2L:221   Date: 20 Dec 1809   RcCt: 14 May 1810
Burr POWELL & wife Catherine of Ldn to Edward MUD (free black man). B/S of 9ac adj Daniel REES. Wit: A. GIBSON, John BOYD, Hugh SMITH.

Bk:Pg: 2L:224   Date: 24 Jan 1810   RcCt: 14 May 1810
Samuel CLAPHAM of Ldn to John JOHNSON of Ldn. B/S of 400ac in Ldn called "Kentuck". Wit: Henry BANTZ, George A. WATERS, John JECKEN.

Bk:Pg: 2L:226   Date: 6 Jan 1810   RcCt: 14 May 1810
Thomas ATWELL & wife Sytha of Ldn to Hugh WYLEY of Ldn. B/S of 6ac nr Middleburg Road. Wit: Hugh SMITH, Andrew SMARR, Hugh WYLIE Jr., George Washington McCARTY, Moses WILSON, Thos. A. DENNIS, Leven LUCKETT, Hugh RODGERS, Burr POWELL.

Bk:Pg: 2L:230   Date: 23 Feb 1810   RcCt: 14 May 1810
John BUCHANAN of Ldn to Sydnor BAILY & John GIBSON Jr. of Ldn. Trust for debt to Joseph CARR using 1000ac. Wit: Danl. MASON, John FLEMING, Joseph BALDWIN.

Bk:Pg: 2L:233   Date: 14 May 1810   RcCt: 14 May 1810
Joshua GORE Jr. of Ldn to Stacy TAYLOR of Ldn. Trust for debt to Isaac N. HOOK using 87ac adj Martha POLTON, Thomas GREGG. Wit: Calven THATCHER, John BISHOP, Hannah GORE.

Bk:Pg: 2L:236   Date: 4 Oct 1809   RcCt: 14 May 1810
Charles J. LOVE & wife Fanny of Ffx to Martha ODEN & heirs of Thomas ODEN dec'd. B/S of 100ac in "Grimes Tract" adj John HUTCHISON. Wit: Humph. PEAKE, Lewis HUTCHISON, Joshua HUTCHISON, J. HUTCHISON Jr., Benjemin HUTCHISON.

Bk:Pg: 2L:240   Date: 14 Apr 1810   RcCt: 14 May 1810
Mathias SMITLY of Ldn to Jacob SMITH of Ldn. A/L of land on
Dutchmans Run in ShelP. Wit: John THOMAS, Benjamin PERRY, Jacob
VANS?, Lucy WIRTZ.

Bk:Pg: 2L:243   Date: 16 Feb 1810   RcCt: 14 May 1810
Joel OSBURN & wife Massey of Ldn to Richard OSBURN of Ldn. B/S of
46*ac*. Wit: Stacy TAYLOR, Joshua OSBURN, James HEATON, Henly
BOGGESS.

Bk:Pg: 2L:247   Date: 16 Feb 1810   RcCt: 14 May 1810
Joel OSBURN & wife Massey of Ldn to Richard OSBURN of Ldn. B/S of
158*ac* adj Joshua OSBURN, Thomas HUMPHREY [150*ac* from Hannah
OSBURN wd/o Richard OSBURN dec'd]. Wit: Stacy TAYLOR, James
HEATON, Joshua OSBURN, Hanley BOGGESS.

Bk:Pg: 2L:252   Date: 2 Apr 1810   RcCt: 14 May 1810
Notley C. WILLIAMS & wife Frances D. of Ldn to Joel OSBURN of Ldn.
B/S of 4½*ac* adj Thomas HUMPHREY, James HEATON. Wit: Morris
OSBURN, Nicholas OSBURN, Stacy TAYLOR, Joshua OSBURN.

Bk:Pg: 2L:256   Date: 2 Mar 1810   RcCt: 14 May 1810
James COCHRAN & wife Sarah of Ldn to Joel OSBURN of Ldn. B/S of
100*ac* on NW fork of Goose Creek, adj John BROWN, James HEATON,
Abel MARKS. Wit: Stacy TAYLOR, James JACKSON, William FINCH,
Joshua OSBURN.

Bk:Pg: 2L:260   Date: 14 May 1810   RcCt: 14 May 1810
Nicholas OSBURNE of Ldn to Joel OSBURN of Ldn. B/S of 1*ac* adj Abel
MARKS, Joel OBSURN. Wit: N. C. WILLIAMS, Richard BROWN, Francis
TRIPLETT Jr.

Bk:Pg: 2L:262   Date: 12 Feb 1810   RcCt: 14 May 1810
Mark GORE of Ldn to Thomas GREGG and Stacy TAYLOR, Joshua
OSBURNE & Lewis ELLZEY of Ldn. Trust for joint bond of GORE &
GREGG using leased land GORE bought from John WOLFCALE Sr. Wit:
William RUST, Jas. RUST, Nicholas OSBURN.

Bk:Pg: 2L:265   Date: 22 Feb 1810   RcCt: 14 May 1810
Lewis ELLZEY & wife Rosanna of Ldn to Henly BOGGESS of Ldn. B/S of
128*ac* adj Elizabeth REED, Thos. GREGG and 68*ac* Rosanna's share of
estate of James McILHANY dec'd. Wit: Stacy TAYLOR, Joshua
OSBURNE, Nicholas OSBURN, Thomas GREGG.

Bk:Pg: 2L:269   Date: 7 Mar 1810   RcCt: 14 May 1810
William TAYLOR of Ldn to Aaron DIVINE of Lsbg. LS of lot on King St
Lsbg. Wit: S. BLINCOE, George FECHTER, George HAMMET.

Bk:Pg: 2L:271   Date: 12 Sep 1809   RcCt: 12 Feb 1810
John QUICK of Ldn to Sanford RAMEY of Ldn. Mortgage using land
QUICK purchased of Anthony CUNNARD where Joseph BURSON now
lives. Wit: S. BLINCOE, Joseph HUNT.

Bk:Pg: 2L:273   Date: 7 May 1810   RcCt: 14 May 1810
William BRONAUGH & wife Jane of Ldn to William H. HANDEY of Ldn.
B/S of 10ac. Wit: Ben GRAYSON, Step C. ROSZELL.

Bk:Pg: 2L:277   Date: 27 Jul 1809   RcCt: 14 May 1810
Charles B. ALEXANDER of Ldn to Josiah HALL of Ldn. B/S of 2ac. Wit:
Jno. MATHIAS, John DRISH, S. BLINCOE.

Bk:Pg: 2L:279   Date: 18 Apr 1810   RcCt: 14 May 1810
John HALL of Ldn to Adam HOUSEHOLDER of Ldn. Release of
mortgage. Wit: Cornelious SHAVER, John VANDEVANTER, W. S.
NEALE.

Bk:Pg: 2L:280   Date: 18 Apr 1810   RcCt: 14 May 1810
Adam HOUSHOLDER of Ldn to John HALL of Ldn. Release of mortgage.
Wit: Cornelious SHAVER, John VANDEVANTER, W. S. NEALE.

Bk:Pg: 2L:281   Date: 10 Mar 1810   RcCt: 14 May 1810
Charles Fenton MERCER of Ldn to James SWART of Ldn. B/S of
116½ac devised from father Judge MERCER. Wit: Wm. COOE, Wm. M.
SMITH, John DAYMUD.

Bk:Pg: 2L:283   Date: 19 Dec 1809   RcCt: 14 May 1810
Samuel DORSETT of Ldn to John HUGULY of Ldn. BoS for negro
Emmely abt 8y old.

Bk:Pg: 2L:284   Date: 10 Mar 1810   RcCt: 14 May 1810
Samuel MASSY & wife Catherine, Samuel FARNSWORTH & Jonathan
FARNSWORTH (heirs of Adonijah FARNSWORTH dec'd) of Ldn to John
FARNSWORTH of Ldn. B/S of 30ac (dower right of Hannah BOND wd/o
Adonijah) at foot of Blue Ridge. Wit: Joshua OSBURN, N. C. WILLIAMS,
Joseph THOMAS.

Bk:Pg: 2L:288   Date: ___ 1810   RcCt: 14 May 1810
William ELLZEY as trustee for George KILGORE to John BALL. Release
in sale of 100ac & 97½ac from BALL to KILLGORE.

Bk:Pg: 2L:290   Date: 14 Nov 1809   RcCt: 14 May 1810
Anthony CUNNARD of Ldn to Levi PRINCE of Ldn. A/L of 200ac. Wit:
Chas. THRIFT, Geo. HUFF, Samuel SPENCER.

Bk:Pg: 2L:292   Date: __ May 1810   RcCt: 14 May 1810
Levin HAYS alias POWELL & wife Elizabeth of Ldn to John T. MASON of
Washington Co Md, William ELLZEY & Armstead T. MASON of Ldn. Trust
for sale of 100ac to Mathew HARRISON dec'd & wife Patty. Wit: Stacy
TAYLOR, Lewis ELLZEY, Sarah SANDS.

Bk:Pg: 2L:297   Date: 14 May 1810   RcCt: 14 May 1810
William PIGGOTT & wife Mary of Ldn to Stephen WILSON of Ldn. B/S of
85ac on NW fork of Goose Creek.

Bk:Pg: 2L:299   Date: 14 May 1810   RcCt: 14 May 1810
John MURPHEY & wife Ann (d/o William CHAMBERS dec'd) of Ldn to
Jacob WALTMAN of Ldn. B/S of 200ac (where William lived, as heir in

law of father William CHAMBERS, who claimed in right of wife Anne CHAMBERS from her father Robert BOOTH dec'd).

Bk:Pg: 2L:301   Date: 2 Jun 1800   RcCt: 14 May 1810
John L. BERKLEY of Ldn to Steven BEARD of Ldn. LS of lot on road from Mountain (or Little River) Meeting house to Gumspring. Wit: Wm. B. HARRISON, Vincent DAVIS, John LINTON.

Bk:Pg: 2L:303   Date: 12 Apr 1810   RcCt: 14 May 1810
Thomas HETHERLY & wife Mary of Ldn to James WINTERS of Ldn. B/S of ¼ac lot in Lsbg. Wit: Saml. M. EDWARDS, Richard H. HENDERSON, French S. GRAY, John LITTLEJOHN, Samuel MURREY.

Bk:Pg: 2L:306   Date: 13 Nov 1806   RcCt: 14 Jul 1807
John ALEXANDER & wife Elizabeth of Ldn to Richard B. ALEXANDER of PrWm. B/S of 150ac adj George CARTER, William COTTON, Jno. ALEXANDER. Wit: Pat'k. McINTYRE, Mathew ADAMS, Chas. P. TUTT, Thomas CRAVEN.

Bk:Pg: 2L:309   Date: 18 Jun 1796   RcCt: 14 May 1810
Hannah & Morris OSBURN (Admr of Richard OSBURN dec'd the son of John OSBURN dec'd). Receipt of payment from William OSBURN. Wit: Thomas OSBURN, Joel OSBURN.

Bk:Pg: 2L:309   Date: 28 Apr 1810   RcCt: 14 May 1810
Washington JOHNSON & wife Elizabeth of FrdkMd to John SMITH of Ldn. B/S of 128¼ac adj William WENNER, Adam SHOVER. Wit: Henry HUFF, Saml. CLAPHAM, John HAMILTON.

Bk:Pg: 2L:313   Date: 20 May 1810   RcCt: 14 May 1810
Henry HOUGH & wife Mary of Ldn to John BALL of Ldn. B/S of 100ac on Broad Run at mouth of Balls Mill tail and adj 97½ac. Wit: John HAMILTON, George HUFF, John STOUSEBERGER, John A. BINNS.

Bk:Pg: 2L:317   Date: 17 Oct 1807   RcCt: 9 May 1808
John STONE & wife Barbara of Ldn to William WOLF of Ldn. B/S of 50¾ac. Wit: Cha. BENNETT, John HAMILTON, John WOLF, Mathias SYFERT.

Bk:Pg: 2L:321   Date: 27 Feb 1810   RcCt: 13 Mar 1810
John BOYD of Ldn to Richard H. HENDERSON of Ldn. B/S of house & lot now occupied by Dr. Patrick DOUGLAS. Wit: Saml. M. EDWARDS, Isaac LAROWE, George HAMMAT.

Bk:Pg: 2L:322   Date: 25 Nov 1809   RcCt: 11 Dec 1809
Elizabeth LUCKETT (wd/o Thomas H. LUCKETT dec'd) and Thomas H. LUCKETT the youngest son of FrdkMd to Saml CLAPHAM of Ldn. B/S of 182½ac adj Col. Josias CLAPHAM. Wit: Peter BURKHART, Fred'k. HEIBELY, Wm. MICHAEL, John RIGNEY, John FRITCHIE.

Bk:Pg: 2L:328   Date: 13 Apr 1810   RcCt: 14 May 1810
James COLEMAN of Ffx to son William COLEMAN of Ldn. Gift of 150ac on Broad Run adj George KILGORE. Wit: James COLEMAN Jr., John COLEMAN, Thomas COLEMAN.

Bk:Pg: 2L:329   Date: 9 Mar 1810   RcCt: 14 May 1810
Adam HOUSHOLDER & wife Sarah of Ldn to widow Susannah
HOUSHOLDER of Ldn. B/S of 36½ac (Adam's 1/5 share from land of
father Adam HOUSHOLDER Sr. dec'd, dower of Susannah). Wit: John
HAMILTON, Edmond JENINGS, R. BRADEN, Michael RICHARDS, John
A. BINNS.

Bk:Pg: 2L:333   Date: 20 Jan 1810   RcCt: 14 May 1810
John YOUNKIN & wife Catherine of Turkey Foot Twnshp Somerset Co Pa
to Adam SHOVER of Ldn. PoA for sale of land adj John VINSEL, Jacob
FAWLEY & Lawrence AWMAN formerly of Jacob TUSHTIMER dec'd. Wit:
name in German, John ARMSTRONG.

Bk:Pg: 2L:335   Date: 19 Oct 1809   RcCt: 14 May 1810
John BALL & wife Susanna of Ldn to William CARR of Ldn. B/S of 100ac
& 97½ac. Wit: Eli OFFUTT, Saml. M. EDWARDS, Peter CARR, Saml.
CLAPHAM, Samuel MURREY.

Bk:Pg: 2L:339   Date: 14 May 1810   RcCt: 14 May 1810
William CARR of Ldn to John BALL of Ldn. B/S of 2ac adj Balls Mill tract,
Isaac HOUGH.

Bk:Pg: 2L:341   Date: 16 Feb 1810   RcCt: 15 May 1810
John CAVAN of Lsbg to Richard H. HENDERSON of Lsbg. B/S of lot on
Market St. Wit: Jno. MATHIAS, Benj. PRICE, A. SUTHERLAND.

Bk:Pg: 2L:342   Date: 7 May 1810   RcCt: 15 May 1810
Benjamin H. CANBY & wife Sarah of Ldn to Peter BOSS of Ldn. B/S of
1¼ac adj Lsbg, Jacob TOWNER, Jesse DAILEY, Joshua RILEY. Wit:
John LITTLEJOHN, A. SUTHERLAND, Thos. MORALLE, Samuel
MURREY.

Bk:Pg: 2L:345   Date: 15 May 1810   RcCt: 15 May 1810
Charles BINNS, Isaac LAROWE & Benj'n SHREVE. Bond on BINNS to
build addition to Clerks office on Courthouse. Wit: Saml. M. EDWARDS.

Bk:Pg: 2L:346   Date: 1 Dec 1809   RcCt: 8 Jan 1810
James SAUNDERS to Charles Fenton MERCER. B/S of lot on Cornwall &
Back Sts Lsbg adj Methodist Meeting House. Wit: John LITTLEJOHN,
Fayette BALL, John F. MERCER.

Bk:Pg: 2L:348   Date: 15 May 1810   RcCt: 15 May 1810
Patrick McINTYRE (s/o Alex. McINTYRE dec'd of Lsbg) & wife Polly of
Ldn to Wilson Cary SELDON of Ldn. B/S of 4ac. Wit: Jno. MATHIAS.

Bk:Pg: 2L:350   Date: 20 Mar 1810   RcCt: 14 May 1810
William NOLAND to Thomas JOHNSON of FrdkMd & son James
JOHNSON of Ldn. Release. Wit: Jacob DILLENGER.

Bk:Pg: 2L:351   Date: 25 Nov 1809   RcCt: 11 Jun 1810
Thomas HUMPHREY & wife Mary of Ldn to Abel MARKS, Hannah
Osburn CRAVEN (wd/o William OSBURNE dec'd), Landon OSBURN,
Nicholas OSBURN, James COCKRAN, Samuel Daniel MARCUS, Jonah
HUMPHREY, Isaac BROWN, James CURRELL, George BROWN (of

John), Charles CHAMBLIN, Jesse HOWELL, John CAMPBELL, Amos HAGUE, Thomas OSBURNE & Joshua OSBURNE of Ldn. B/S of ¼ac adj Thomas HUMPHREY. Wit: Philip THOMAS, Edward CUNARD Jr., Thomas WHITE, Nathan NICKOLS.

Bk:Pg: 2L:354   Date: 14 Jun 1810   RcCt: 11 Jun 1810
Thomas HUMPHREY of Ldn to William HOWELL of Ldn. LS of __ac.

Bk:Pg: 2L:356   Date: 12 Jan 1808   RcCt: 11 Jun 1810
Otho H. W. LUCKETT & wife Elizabeth of Ldn to Joseph LEWIS Jr. of Ldn. B/S of 180¼ac adj Michael BOGUE, George MASON. Wit: Fleet SMITH, Rich'd H. HENDERSON, Benj. SHREVE.

Bk:Pg: 2L:359   Date: 20 Jan 1810   RcCt: 11 Jun 1810
Joseph GILBERT of Dumfries, PrWm to Isaac HARRIS of Lsbg. B/S of 3ac on Tuskarora Run on S side of Lsbg adj James KIRK.

Bk:Pg: 2L:361   Date: 24 Apr 1810   RcCt: 11 Jun 1810
Mahlon JANNEY of Wtfd to Patrick McGAVACK of Ldn. B/S of lot in Wtfd adj Lot #6. Wit: Abiel JENNERS, Levi JAMES, Wm. S. NEALE.

Bk:Pg: 2L:363   Date: 10 Apr 1810   RcCt: 11 Jun 1810
John VANHORNE & wife Sarah of Ldn to James BROWN of Ldn. B/S of 99ac. Wit: John LITTLEJOHN, James SHEPHERD, Stephen DONALDSON, Samuel DODD, Wm. BRONAUGH, Step C. ROSZELL.

Bk:Pg: 2L:367   Date: 18 Apr 1810   RcCt: 11 Jun 1810
John VANHORNE & wife Sarah of Ldn to Armistead LONG & William BRONAUGH. Trust for debt to Michael BELL using 240ac on Beaverdam. Wit: Stephen DONALDSON, Jno. MATTHIAS, John DRISH, Wm. BRONAUGH, Step C. ROSZEL.

Bk:Pg: 2L:371   Date: 11 Jun 1810   RcCt: 11 Jun 1810
Joseph LEWIS Jr. of Ldn to George COOPER of Ldn. Release of mortgage.

Bk:Pg: 2L:372   Date: 11 Jun 1810   RcCt: 11 Jun 1810
Joseph LEWIS Jr. of Ldn to Michael EVERHART of Ldn. Release of mortgage.

Bk:Pg: 2L:373   Date: 11 Jun 1810   RcCt: 11 Jun 1810
Joseph LEWIS Jr. of Ldn to Christian RUSE of Ldn. Release of mortgage.

Bk:Pg: 2L:374   Date: 11 Jun 1810   RcCt: 11 Jun 1810
Joseph LEWIS Jr. of Ldn to Peter COMPHER of Ldn. Release of mortgage.

Bk:Pg: 2L:375   Date: 17 May 1810   RcCt: 11 Jun 1810
Joseph LEWIS Jr. of Ldn to Philip EVERHEART of Ldn. B/S of 10ac in Piedmont Manor. Wit: Michael FLYNN, Jacob COTUNFOLL?, Michael EVERHART.

Bk:Pg: 2L:377   Date: 17 May 1810   RcCt: 11 Jun 1810
Joseph LEWIS Jr. of Ldn to Michael EVERHEART of Ldn. B/S of two 10ac lots in Piedmont Manor. Wit: Philip EVERHART, Michael FLYNN, Jacob COTUNFULL?.

Bk:Pg: 2L:379   Date: 16 May 1810   RcCt: 11 Jun 1810
Joseph LEWIS Jr. of Ldn to William WINNERS of Ldn. B/S of 10ac lot in
Piedmont Manor. Wit: Jacob WALTMAN, Philip EVERHART, George ? [in
German].

Bk:Pg: 2L:380   Date: 16 May 1810   RcCt: 11 Jun 1810
Joseph LEWIS Jr. of Ldn to George COOPER of Ldn. B/S of 10ac lot in
Piedmont Manor. Wit: Jacob WALTMAN, William WENNER, Philip
EVERHART.

Bk:Pg: 2L:382   Date: 8 Jun 1810   RcCt: 11 Jun 1810
Joseph LEWIS Jr. of Ldn to Michael BOGER of Ldn. B/S of 180¼ac in
Piedmont Manor occupied by John B. RATHIE adj Church lot. Wit: Elias
THRASHER, Melinda THRASHER, Henson THRASHER.

Bk:Pg: 2L:384   Date: 8 Jun 1810   RcCt: 11 Jun 1810
Michael BOGER of Ldn to Joseph LEWIS Jr of Ldn. Mortgage of 180¼ac
in Piedmont Manor occupied by John B. RATHIE. Wit: Elias THRASHER,
Melinda THRASHER, Henson THRASHER.

Bk:Pg: 2L:385   Date: 1 Sep 1809   RcCt: 11 Jun 1810
John DANIEL of Ldn to Charles Fenton MERCER of Ldn. BoS for farm
and household items. Wit: Wm. COOKE.

Bk:Pg: 2L:389   Date: 9 Mar 1810   RcCt: 11 Jun 1810
Michael COOPER & wife Catherine of Ldn to Peter COOPER of Ldn. B/S
of 13ac in Piedmont adj George MULL, Schoolhouse. Wit: John
HAMILTON, R. BRADEN, Adam HOUSHOLDER, David AXLINE, Michael
RICHARDS.

Bk:Pg: 2L:392   Date: 11 Jun 1810   RcCt: 11 Jun 1810
Joseph LEWIS Jr. of Ldn to Michael EVERHEART of Ldn. Assignment of
mortgage of Christian EVERHEART for land in Piedmont Manor.

Bk:Pg: 2L:394   Date: 18 Jun 1804   RcCt: 11 Dec 1804
Joseph LEWIS Jr. of Ldn to Margaret SAUNDERS of Ldn. B/S of 144ac in
Piedmont Manor adj Archibald MORRISON, Daniel SHOEMAKER, Jacob
SHOEMAKER, George SHOEMAKER, Charles CRIM. Wit: James
McILHANY, Elizabeth McILHANY, Mary McILHANY, John McILHANY Jr.,
John H. EVANS, Jonas POTTS.

Bk:Pg: 2L:396   Date: 26 Mar 1810   RcCt: 11 Jun 1810
Lewis ELLZEY & wife Rosannah of Ldn to David LOVETT of Ldn. B/S of
55½ac adj Mahlon HOUGH, Andrew COPELAND, William THOMPSON.
Wit: Joseph GARRETT, Stephen GARRETT, Stacy TAYLOR, Thomas
GREGG, Samuel MURREY, Fra. H. PEYTON.

Bk:Pg: 2L:399   Date: 20 Aug 1808   RcCt: 11 Jun 1810
Lewis ELLZEY & wife Rosannah of Ldn to David LOVETT of Ldn. B/S of
55½ac on N side of Short Hill nr Hllb & two lots on NW fork of Goose
Creek called Harts & Carlisles lotts containing 183½ac. Wit: Fra. H.
PEYTON, Samuel MURRAY, Charles G. EDWARDS, Stacy TAYLOR,
Joshua OSBURN.

Bk:Pg: 2L:403   Date: 9 Jun 1810   RcCt: 11 Jun 1810
Isaac HOUGH & wife Fanny of Ldn to widow Margaret SAUNDERS of Ldn. B/S of 50¾ac adj James HAMILTON dec'd, Michael COOPER, Lydia HOUGH. Wit: John A. BINNS, Robt. BRADEN.

Bk:Pg: 2L:405   Date: 9 Jun 1810   RcCt: 11 Jun 1810
Isaac HOUGH & wife Fanny of Ldn to Jacob HOUSER of Ldn. B/S of 153ac adj Daniel SHOEMAKER, Jacob SHUMAKER, Geo. MULL, Peter COOPER, James HAMILTON. Wit: John A. BINNS, Robt. BRADEN.

Bk:Pg: 2L:408   Date: 9 Jun 1810   RcCt: 11 Jun 1810
Jacob HOUSER & wife Abigail of Ldn to Margaret SANDERS of Ldn. B/S of 4ac. Wit: John A. BINNS, Robt. BRADEN.

Bk:Pg: 2L:411   Date: 9 Jun 1810   RcCt: 11 Jun 1810
Jacob HOUSER & wife Abigail of Ldn to Peter COOPER of Ldn. B/S of ¾ac adj Schoolhouse lot. Wit: John A. BINNS, Robt. BRADEN.

Bk:Pg: 2L:414   Date: 9 Jun 1810   RcCt: 11 Jun 1810
Jacob HOUSER of Ldn to Robert BRADEN & Levi JAMES (trustees for Dr. Isaac HOUGH). Trust 153ac adj Daniel SHOEMAKER, Jacob SHOEMAKER, Geo. MULL, Peter COOPER.

Bk:Pg: 2L:417   Date: 9 Jun 1810   RcCt: 11 Jun 1810
William MARTIN Jr. & wife Agnes of Ldn to Elijah ANDERSON of Ldn. B/S of 119ac adj James WORNALD, heirs of Joseph LANE dec'd, William MARTIN Sr. Wit: Stacy TAYLOR, Ben GRAYSON, Saml. BOGGESS.

Bk:Pg: 2L:421   Date: 10 Feb 1804   RcCt: 8 Jul 1805
Nathaniel CRAWFORD & wife Sarah of PrG to William MARTIN of Ldn. B/S of 133ac "Batterland" adj Joseph CARR, Charles GREEN. Wit: W. ELLZEY, Thos. SWANN, Jos. LEWIS Jr.

Bk:Pg: 2L:422   Date: 2 Jun 1810   RcCt: 11 Jun 1810
Major HUNT, William HOLMES & Daniel LOVETT of Ldn to Meriam HOLE (Admr of Levi HOLE dec'd) of Ldn. Release of trust. Wit: Saml. M. EDWARDS, Rich'd H. HENDERSON, Isaac LAROWE. [see 2L:526]

Bk:Pg: 2L:424   Date: 28 May 1810   RcCt: 12 Jun 1810
Richard ADAMS of Ldn to Francis ELGIN of Ldn. Trust for sale of farm and household items for use of Rebecca ADAMS (w/o Richard, d/o Francis).

Bk:Pg: 2L:425   Date: 9 Nov 1806   RcCt: 12 Jun 1810
George CARTER. Receipt of payment from Stephen COOKE. Wit: Wm. SMITH, Jesse TIMMS.

Bk:Pg: 2L:425   Date: 13 Mar 1801   RcCt: 11 May 1801
James HEREFORD to William BLINSTONE commonly called William McCABE. LS of 1ac on road from William Means Mill to Lsbg. Wit: Jas. HAMILTON, Samuel HOUGH, Samuel CARR.

Bk:Pg: 2L:427   Date: 8 Jan 1810   RcCt: 14 Jun 1810
John MYERS & wife Charlotte of Lsbg to Jacob FADELEY of Lsbg. B/S of Lot #_ in Lsbg on S side of Royal St. Wit: Samuel MURREY, Wm. B. HARRISON, Jno. MATTHIAS.

Bk:Pg: 2L:429   Date: 7 Jul 1810   RcCt: 9 Jul 1810
Stephen COOKE & wife Catharine of Ldn to John Rogers COOKE. Gift of land on Goose Creek adj Col. Thomas LEE dec'd, Henry LAFAVER.

Bk:Pg: 2L:431   Date: 23 Feb 1810   RcCt: 9 Jul 1810
Henly BOGGESS of Ldn. Bound to Lewis ELLZEY of Ldn using 3 tracts of land. Wit: Joshua OSBURN, Stacy TAYLOR.

Bk:Pg: 2L:432   Date: 15 Aug 1810   RcCt: 15 Aug 1810
Edward RINKER Jr., John McCORMACK & James CAVAN Jr. Bond on RINKER as Constable. Wit: Saml. M. EDWARDS.

Bk:Pg: 2L:433   Date: 15 Aug 1810   RcCt: 15 Aug 1810
Thomas MORALLE, William WOODY & James GARNER. Bond on MORALLE as Constable. Wit: Saml. M. EDWARDS.

Bk:Pg: 2L:433   Date: 15 May 1810   RcCt: 13 Aug 1810
Thomas DRAKE Sr & wife Uree of Ldn to Jacob DRAKE of Ldn. B/S of 327ac adj James CARTER, Benjamin BARTON, John RALPH, Isaac RICHARDS, Abner HUMPHREY.

Bk:Pg: 2L:436   Date: 12 Mar 1810   RcCt: 13 Aug 1810
Enoch FRANCIS & wife Nancy of Ldn to Casper ECKERT of Ldn. B/S of 119ac adj Casper ECKART. Wit: Jno. MATHIAS, Timothy HIXSON, Wm. GILMORE, Steph COOKE, Samuel MURREY.

Bk:Pg: 2L:439   Date: 12 Mar 1810   RcCt: 13 Aug 1810
Casper ECKART & wife Ann of Ldn to William DULIN & Isaac STEER. Trust for bonds to Enoch FRANCIS using 119ac. Wit: Jno. MATTHIAS, Timothy HIXSON, Wm. GILMORE, Steph COOKE, Samuel MURREY.

Bk:Pg: 2L:443   Date: 10 Aug 1810   RcCt: 13 Aug 1810
Frederick William LONGSTRAWS & wife Charity of Ldn to Susannah SMITH of Ldn. B/S of 2ac nr Dutchman Run. Wit: Simon SHUMAKER, Jacob WALTMAN, Geo. HUFF.

Bk:Pg: 2L:445   Date: 11 Aug 1810   RcCt: 13 Aug 1810
Isaac HOUGH of Ldn to John AXLINE of Ldn. B/S of 4ac.

Bk:Pg: 2L:446   Date: 20 Mar 1810   RcCt: 9 Jul 1810
Charles & John HELM to William MORAN. A/L of 202ac. Wit: Benjamin MITCHELL, Peter HELM, Thomas FOUCH, Chas. LEWIS, Chas. B. ALEXANDER, Vin't L. LEWIS.

Bk:Pg: 2L:448   Date: 14 Apr 1810   RcCt: 13 Aug 1810
Timothy TAYLOR & wife Achsah of Ldn to George TAVENNER Jr. of Ldn. B/S of 19ac on NW fork of Goose Creek. Wit: Stacy TAYLOR, Martin N. McDANIEL, Nicholas OSBURN, Jno. WEST.

Bk:Pg: 2L:451   Date: 13 Aug 1810   RcCt: 13 Aug 1810
Jacob DRAKE of Ldn to William BRONAUGH of Ldn. Trust for debt to
Benjamin GRAYSON using 327*ac*. Wit: John McCORMICK.

Bk:Pg: 2L:453   Date: 15 Dec 1809   RcCt: 13 Aug 1810
Ludwell LEE & wife Eliza of Ldn to Bazil STONESTREET of Ldn. B/S of
151 9/10*ac* adj John MITCHELL, William PRESSGRAVES. Wit: Joshua
HUTCHISON, Levi WHALEY, John D. NEEDHAM.

Bk:Pg: 2L:455   Date: 13 Aug 1810   RcCt: 13 Aug 1810
Robert CUMMINGS, John CUMMINGS & Thomas GREGG. Bond on
Robert CUMMINGS as Constable. Wit: Saml. M. EDWARDS.

Bk:Pg: 2L:455   Date: 22 Mar 1810   RcCt: 13 Aug 1810
Ludwell LEE of Ldn to Miss Elizabeth LEE of Jefferson. Mortgage of
1480*ac* "Belmont" tract on road from Lsbg to AlexVA adj heirs of George
LEE, heirs of Col. Thomas Ludwell LEE dec'd, Jonathan SWIFT, Enoch
FRANCIS. Wit: Richard Bland LEE, Thomas DARNE Jr., William LEE, Th.
GREGG Jr.

Bk:Pg: 2L:458   Date: 7 Jun 1810   RcCt: 13 Aug 1810
William SUDDITH of Ldn to Edward COE, Joseph GARRETT, Hamilton
ROGERS, William WILKISSON & Joseph DANIEL (trustees of North Fork
Baptist Meeting). B/S of 2 roods of land. Wit: Thomas GHEEN, John
MUDD, John WRIGHT.

Bk:Pg: 2L:460   Date: 13 Aug 1810   RcCt: 13 Aug 1810
William SUDDITH of Ldn to Henry BROWN of Ldn. B/S of 13*ac* on N fork
of Goose Creek adj David ALEXANDER.

Bk:Pg: 2L:463   Date: __ May 1810   RcCt: 13 Aug 1810
William HOMES & wife Abigail (late HUGHS), Joseph HOMES & wife
Elizabeth (late HUGHS), Samuel CRAIG & wife Mary (late HUGHS),
George DULICK & wife Sally (late HUGHS), Gideon DAVIS & wife Nancy
(late HUGHS), Warner HUGHS, Mathew HUGHS & Patty HUGHS of Ldn
to Isaac HUGHES of Ldn. B/S of 250*ac* (from Isaac HUGHS dec'd) adj
Daniel WHITE, George NIXON, William JONES. Wit: Mahlon TAYLOR, C.
BINNS, Saml. M. EDWARDS, Isaac LAROWE, Burr POWELL, Step. C.
ROSZELL.

Bk:Pg: 2L:468   Date: 13 Aug 1810   RcCt: 14 Aug 1810
Charles BENNETT, Samuel CLAPHAM, James HEATON, John ROSE,
Notly C. WILLIAMS, Stephen C. ROSZELL, Thos. GREGG, William
ELLZEY & Ludwell LEE. Bound to James COLEMAN Jr. President of the
Overseers of the Poor of Ldn for BENNETT as Sheriff to collect the poor
rate.

Bk:Pg: 2L:470   Date: 29 Nov 1803   RcCt: 9 Apr 1804
Abraham Barnes Thompson MASON to Westwood Thompson MASON
and William Temple Thompson MASON (all s/o Thompson MASON
dec'd). Division of land, A. B. T. given 662½*ac*, W. T. given 568*ac*, and W.
T. T. given 757*ac*. Wit: Jno. MATTHIAS, Richard ALLISON, Dennis
COLE, Thos. FLOWERS, Robt. DRAKE Jr.

Bk:Pg: 473   Date: 23 Jun 1810   RcCt: 14 Aug 1810
Thomas N. BINNS to Henry MILTON. BoS for negro mage Cato (bought from John MILTON dec'd). Wit: Jesse TIMMS.

Bk:Pg: 2L:474   Date: 13 Aug 1810   RcCt: 14 Aug 1810
Charles BENNETT, Samuel CLAPHAM, James HEATON, John ROSE, Thomas GREGG, William ELLZEY, Ludwell LEE, Sandford RAMEY, and Robert BRADEN. Bond on BENNETT as Sheriff to collect taxes. Wit: Saml. M. EDWARDS.

Bk:Pg: 2L:474   Date: 14 Aug 1810   RcCt: 14 Aug 1810
Charles BENNETT, Samuel CLAPHAM, James HEATON, John ROSE, Thomas GREGG, William ELLZEY, Ludwell LEE, Sandford RAMEY, and Robert BRADEN. Bond on BENNETT as Sheriff to collect levies. Wit: Saml. M. EDWARDS.

Bk:Pg: 2L:474   Date: 14 Aug 1810   RcCt: 14 Aug 1810
Charles BENNETT, Samuel CLAPHAM, James HEATON, John ROSE, Thomas GREGG, William ELLZEY, Ludwell LEE, Sandford RAMEY, and Robert BRADEN. Bond on BENNETT as Sheriff to collect officers fees. Wit: Saml. M. EDWARDS.

Bk:Pg: 2L:477   Date: 13 Aug 1810   RcCt: 14 Aug 1810
Commissioners Edmund J. LEE & Richard HENDERSON to David LACEY of Ldn. B/S of 475¾ac as directed in suit of Willam LANE vs. Thomazin ELLZEY & Sally LANE (Exors of William LANE dec'd). Wit: Jos. E. ROWLES, Jesse GOVER, Chas. BENNETT.

Bk:Pg: 2L:478   Date: 24 Oct 1805   RcCt: 9 Dec 1805
Joseph BELLE & Edward CUNARD (Exors of Jonathan CUNARD dec'd) of Ldn to Elizabeth JACOBS of Ldn. B/S of 38ac between Blue Ridge and Short Hill. Wit: James HAMILTON, Anthony CUNNARD, John CAMPBELL, James MOORE, George ABEL.

Bk:Pg: 2L:480   Date: 27 Dec 1809   RcCt: 15 Aug 1810
John DRISH & wife Eleanor of Ldn to John HAMERLY of Ldn. B/S of part of lot nr Lsbg. Wit: Jno. MATTHIAS, Barton LUCAS, William DRISH, Wm. B. HARRISON, John LITTLEJOHN.

Bk:Pg: 2L:483   Date: 1 Jul 1810   RcCt: 14 Aug 1810
William DENEALE & wife Sybel of Ldn to Francis M. HOLLAND of BaltMd. B/S of 19½ac "Halley Field" tract left to Sybel by Col. George WEST of Ldn. Wit: Rich'd H. HENDERSON, Edm. J. LEE, Jonah THOMPSON.

Bk:Pg: 2L:486   Date: 16 Aug 1810   RcCt: 16 Aug 1810
Mortho SULLIVAN of Ldn to Sampson BLINCOE of Lsbg. BoS for negro boy Adam. Wit: D. MOFFETT, John HOUGH, Wm. WOODY.

Bk:Pg: 2K:486   Date: 16 Aug 1810   RcCt: 16 Aug 1810
James DONAUGH of Ldn to John T. MASON Jr. of Ldn. B/S of all farm and household items on small farm nr Lsbg where DONAUGH lives. Wit: Robt. ARMISTEAD, Geo. dela TRIPELLIERE.

Bk:Pg: 2L:488   Date: 17 Aug 1810   RcCt: 17 Aug 1810
George HAMMAT, Isaac LAROWE & Benjamin SHREVE. Bond on
HAMMAT as Constable. Wit: Saml. M. EDWARDS.

Bk:Pg: 2L:489   Date: 10 Sep 1810   RcCt: 10 Sep 1810
Alexander SUTHERLAND of Lsbg to Joseph BEARD of Lsbg. LS of lot on
E side of King St Lsbg.

Bk:Pg: 2L:492   Date: 24 Aug 1810   RcCt: 10 Sep 1810
William STALLCUP & wife Rebeca of Columbiana Co Oh to Samuel
RUSSELL of Ldn. B/S of 80ac on Kittockton Creek on main road from
Thomas HUMPHREY to Lsbg, adj John LOVE, Samuel PURCEL, James
BEST. Wit: Stacy TAYLOR, James LOVE, Samuel BEAL, Giles CRAVEN,
Thomas SANDS, Henry SMITH.

Bk:Pg: 2L:493   Date: 6 Mar 1810   RcCt: 11 Jun 1810
Mahlon JANNEY of Wtfd to Joseph TALBOTT of Wtfd. B/S of ¼ac adj
James MOORE. Wit: W. S. NEALE, Wm. FARISS, Joseph LACEY.

Bk:Pg: 2L:494   Date: 28 Aug 1810   RcCt: 10 Sep 1810
Stephen WILSON & wife Martha of Ldn to Richard COPELAND of Ldn.
B/S of 25ac. Wit: James COPELAND, Rufus UPDIKE, Elizabeth WILSON.

Bk:Pg: 2L:496   Date: 28 Aug 1810   RcCt: 10 Sep 1810
Richard COPELAND & wife Elizabeth of Ldn to David POTTS of Ldn. B/S
of 2ac adj Ezekiel POTTS. Wit: Joshua OSBORNE, Thomas NICKOLS,
John WHITE. Stacy TAYLOR.

Bk:Pg: 2L:497   Date: 1 Jan 1810   RcCt: 10 Sep 1810
James PATTERSON of Ldn to Sydnor BAYLEY of Ldn. Trust for debt to
Joseph CARR using farm and household items. Wit: George GIBSON,
Robert PATTERSON, Daniel MASON, John MITCHELL, James
RIDGEWAY.

Bk:Pg: 2L:498   Date: 1 Aug 1810   RcCt: 10 Sep 1810
John THOMAS of Ldn to James RUST & John PANCOAST of Ldn. Trust
for debt to PANCOAST using 140ac adj Joseph JANNEY, William
LODGE, Samuel PALMER. Wit: John PANCOAST, Sr., John GREGG Jr.,
Joshua PANCOAST.

Bk:Pg: 2L:500   Date: ___ 1808   RcCt: 10 Sep 1810
George FAWLEY (heir of John FAWLEY dec'd) to brothers John & Jacob
FAWLEY (Admrs of John FAWLEY dec'd). PoA. Wit: David ORISON,
John WEAST, James ATWOOD.

Bk:Pg: 2L:501   Date: 10 Sep 1810   RcCt: 10 Sep 1810
John MADDEN & wife Mary of Ldn to John WENNER of Ldn. B/S of
200ac (devised Ann CHAMBERS w/o William CHAMBERS dec'd by her
father Robert BOOTH). Wit: Jacob WALTMAN, John GEORGE, George
SHAFFER.

Bk:Pg: 2L:502   Date: 10 Mar 1809   RcCt: 10 Sep 1810
William P. BAYLY & wife Mary L. of StafVa to William WILLIAMSON of
Ldn. B/S of 123ac on E side of Fauquier road adj John BATSON and

E. MASON, Benj. TOLSON, William WALLER Jr., Walter
.J.

Bk:Pg: 2L:504   Date: 1 Dec 1809   RcCt: 12 Feb 1810
John WOLFCAILE Sr. of Trumball Co Oh to Mark GORE of Ldn. B/S of
100ac L/L (lives of Elijah COE, wife Ann dec'd, son Hezekiah COE). Wit:
Samuel SPENCER, Peter GIDEON, Jesse EVANS.

Bk:Pg: 2L:507   Date: 1 Sep 1810   RcCt: 10 Sep 1810
Mark GORE of Ldn to Mahlon MORRIS of Ldn. B/S of 100ac where
William JENKINS now lives between Short Hill & Blue Ridge, adj Samuel
W. YOUNG, Jonathan MATTHEWS, John CAMPBELL, John MILLER.
Wit: George GIDEON, Peter GIBSON, John POTTS.

Bk:Pg: 2L:510   Date: 14 May 1810   RcCt: 15 May 1810
Jonah THOMPKINS of JeffVa to Elizabeth SADLER of Ldn. B/S of lot nr
Lsbg. Wit: Jas. HAMILTON, Nancy THOMAS, George HAMMAT.

Bk:Pg: 2L:511   Date: 8 Sep 1810   RcCt: 10 Sep 1810
John PIGGOTT & wife Phebe of Ldn to William PIGGOTT of Ldn. B/S of
100ac adj William NICKOLS, Jesse HIRST, Bernard TAYLOR. Wit: Isaac
NICKOLS, Samuel NICKOLS.

Bk:Pg: 2L:513   Date: 16 Apr 1810   RcCt: 10 Sep 1810
William P. HALE of Mason Co Va to Andrew SMARR of Ldn. B/S of 88ac
on Goose Creek adj Daniel BROWN. Wit: Leven POWELL Jr., Hugh
SMITH, Burr POWELL, Jesse McVEIGH, Noble BEVERAGE, James
STEPHENSON, Felix TRIPLETT.

Bk:Pg: 2L:514   Date: 8 Sep 1810   RcCt: 10 Sep 1810
Vincent SANDFORD (attorney for father Jeremiah SANDFORD Sr. of Ga)
to Louis LYDER of Ldn. B/S of 150ac nr Blue Ridge adj William LODGE,
Joseph JANNEY, William WOODFORD. Wit: Edward CUNARD Jr.,
Jonathan BRADFIELD, Wm. WOODFORD.

Bk:Pg: 2L:516   Date: 21 Jun 1810   RcCt: 10 Sep 1810
Samuel FARNSWORTH of Ldn to Joseph THOMAS of Ldn. B/S of 20ac.
Wit: Edward CUNARD Jr., John COOPER, David FARNSWORTH.

Bk:Pg: 2L:517   Date: 12 May 1810   RcCt: 18 Sep 1810
Andrew SMARR & wife Lydia of Ldn to Adam BARR of Ldn. B/S of 88ac
on Goose Creek adj Daniel BROWN. Wit: Burr POWELL, Thos. WEEKS,
A. GIBSON, Leven POWELL.

Bk:Pg: 2L:521   Date: 5 Jul 1810   RcCt: 10 Sep 1810
John RAMSEY & wife Clarissa of AlexVa to John JANNEY of AlexVA. B/S
of 80ac. Wit: John LITTLEJOHN, Samuel MURREY, John NEWTON,
Colin AULD.

Bk:Pg: 5L:525   Date: 26 May 1810   RcCt: 10 Sep 1810
William HORSEMAN of Ldn to Hannah HORSEMAN (w/o Joseph
HORSEMAN) of Ldn. BoS for child slave George. Wit: John A. HARRISS,
William HUMMER Jr.

Bk:Pg: 5L:526   Date: 1 Mar 1804 PrG   RcCt: 11 Jun 1810
Samuel HEPBURNE and David CRANFURD as Justices of the Peace.
Item that should have gone on page 422.

Bk:Pg: 2M:001   Date: 8 Sep 1810   RcCt: 10 Sep 1810
Louis LYDER of Ldn to Vincent SANFORD attorney for Jeremiah
SANFORD Sr. Trust for debt using 150*ac*. Wit: Edward CUNNARD Jr.,
Jonathan BRADFIELD, Wm. WOODFORD.

Bk:Pg: 2M:002   Date: 12 Jul 1810   RcCt: 10 Sep 1810
Jeremiah SANFORD of Hancock Co Ga to Vincent SANFORD of Ldn.
PoA for sale of 150*ac*. Wit: Berkeley SANFORD, Benjamin SANFORD.

Bk:Pg: 2M:004   Date: 30 Aug 1810   RcCt: 10 Sep 1810
John SPENCER & wife Lydia of Ldn to Giles CRAVEN of Ldn. B/S of
210*ac* on NW fork of Goose Creek, adj Stephen WILSON.

Bk:Pg: 2M:007   Date: 10 Sep 1810   RcCt: 10 Sep 1810
Giles CRAVEN & wife Lydia of Ldn to John SPENCER of Ldn. Trust of
210*ac*.

Bk:Pg: 2M:009   Date: 10 Sep 1810   RcCt: 10 Sep 1810
Giles CRAVEN & wife Lydia of Ldn to Benjamin WHITE of Ldn. B/S of
25*ac* adj David BALES, Josiah HALL. Wit: Samuel MEAD.

Bk:Pg: 2M:011   Date: 10 Sep 1810   RcCt: 10 Sep 1810
Giles CRAVEN & wife Lydia of Ldn to Thomas HUGH & Elias HUGHES of
Ldn. B/S of 69*ac* adj David BALES, Benjamin WHITE. Wit: Samuel
MEAD.

Bk:Pg: 2M:014   Date: 10 Sep 1810   RcCt: 10 Sep 1810
Giles CRAVEN & wife Lydia of Ldn to David BALES of Ldn. B/S of 40*ac*.
Wit: Samuel MEAD, Elias HUGHES.

Bk:Pg: 2M:017   Date: 30 Apr 1810   RcCt: 10 Sep 1810
James COLEMAN of Ffx to son James COLEMAN Jr. of Ldn. Gift of
150*ac*. Wit: John COLEMAN, Thomas COLEMAN, Samuel COLEMAN.

Bk:Pg: 2M:020   Date: 21 May 1810   RcCt: 10 Sep 1810
William SUDDITH of Ldn to Isaac NICKOLS & Samuel NICKOLS of Ldn.
B/S of 6*ac* adj Henry BROWN. Wit: Isaac HATCHER, David YOUNG,
Evan NICHOLS, Warner HUGES.

Bk:Pg: 2M:023   Date: 13 Jun 1810   RcCt: 16 Aug 1810
Joseph GRIFFITH & wife Elizabeth of Ldn to George BINNS (black man)
of Ldn. B/S of ¼*ac*. Wit: James COLEMAN Jr., Thomas GREGG, Edward
CUNARD.

Bk:Pg: 2M:025   Date: 7 Sep 1810   RcCt: 10 Sep 1810
William WOODFORD & wife Elizabeth of Ldn to Edward CUNARD Jr. of
Ldn. B/S of 9*ac* adj William BROWN, Stephen THATCHER, John
MARKS. Wit: Edward RINCKER, John THOMAS, John MARKES.

Bk:Pg: 2M:027   Date: 10 Sep 1810   RcCt: 10 Sep 1810
Jesse HIRST & wife Mary of Ldn to George TAVENER of Ldn. B/S of land
in Columbiana Co Oh. Wit: Bernard TAYLOR, Hamilton ROGERS.

Bk:Pg: 2M:029   Date: 10 Sep 1810   RcCt: 10 Sep 1810
Jesse HIRST & wife Mary of Ldn to George TAVENER of Ldn. B/S of land
in Columbiana Co Oh. Wit: Bernard TAYLOR, Hamilton ROGERS.

Bk:Pg: 2M:032   Date: 28 Apr 1810   RcCt: 13 Aug 1810
John DAVIS & wife Elizabeth of Columbiana Co Oh to Samuel CLAPHAM
of Ldn. B/S of 270¾ac on Catocton Creek, adj Anthony AMONDS. Wit:
Daniel EMERY, John HAMILTON, John SMITH, James HOOK, Wm.
NOLAND.

Bk:Pg: 2M:037   Date: 10 Sep 1810   RcCt: 10 Sep 1810
George NIXON & wife Ann of Ldn to Presley SANDERS of Ldn. B/S of
land on road from Lsbg to Nolands Ferry, adj John NIXON, Thomas
JACOBS.

Bk:Pg: 2M:039   Date: 16 Feb 1810   RcCt: 10 Sep 1810
William VICKERS & wife Anne of Ldn to James CARTER of Ldn. B/S of
50ac on Goose Creek. Wit: Jesse McVEIGH, Burr POWELL, A. GIBSON,
Hugh SMITH.

Bk:Pg: 2M:042   Date: 2 Jan 1804   RcCt: 8 Apr 1806
Thomas ATWELL & wife Sithe of Ldn to Thomas DENNIS of Ldn. B/S of
51ac on road from Mdbg to Colston's Mill. Wit: Burr POWELL, James
BATTSON, Thomas CHINN, Jesse McVEIGH, Isaiah JONES, Francis
PEYTON.

Bk:Pg: 2M:047   Date: 28 Apr 1810   RcCt: 10 Sep 1810
Solomon HOGE & wife Mary of Ldn to Joshua GORE of Ldn. B/S of 25ac
adj John BROWN, Israel JANNEY, Joshua GORE. Wit: Thomas GORE,
Jesse HOGE, Samuel HOGE.

Bk:Pg: 2M:050   Date: 28 Apr 1810   RcCt: 10 Sep 1810
Samuel CLAPHAM & wife Elizabeth of Ldn to Edward MARLOW of Ldn.
B/S of 170¾ac adj Anthony AMONDS. Wit: John HAMILTON, Daniel
EMERY, James HOOK, John SMITH, William NOLAND.

Bk:Pg: 2M:056   Date: 28 Dec 1803   RcCt: 8 Oct 1810
Samuel OLDHAM & wife Nancy, Thomas SHEARMAN & wife Mary,
Joseph SHEARMAN, Hugh BAILY & wife Sarah, James MITCHELL &
wife Susanna (sons and daughters of Joseph SHEARMAN dec'd of
Lancaster Co) to Rawleigh CHINN of Ldn. B/S of 400ac. Wit: James
BALL, Jno. CARPENTER, C. TAPSCOOT, Robert CHINN, Rich'd
MITCHELL.

Bk:Pg: 2M:062   Date: 28 Sep 1810   RcCt: 8 Oct 1810
Jeremiah SANFORD & wife Ada of Ldn to William CARTER. B/S of 37ac
adj Abner HUMPHREY, John HATCHER. Wit: Burr POWELL, John
WILKINSON, John HATCHER, Wm. B. POWELL, Ben GRAYSON, Wm.
BRONAUGH.

Bk:Pg: 2M:068   Date: __ Aug 1810   RcCt: 8 Oct 1810
George BROWN & wife Mary of Ldn to James COCHRAN of Ldn. B/S of
166½ac on NW fork of Goose Creek adj Mahlon GREGG, Abel MARKS.
Wit: Stacy TAYLOR, Ruth TAYLOR, Joshua OSBURN, James CURRELL.

Bk:Pg: 2M:073   Date: 28 Sep 1810   RcCt: 8 Oct 1810
Jeremiah SANFORD & Ada of Ldn to John WILLIAMS of Ldn. B/S of 1*ac*
adj Jacob HUMPHREY. Wit: Burr POWELL, William CARTER, John
WILKINSON, John HATCHER.

Bk:Pg: 2M:077   Date: 28 Sep 1810   RcCt: 8 Oct 1810
Jeremiah SANFORD & Ada of Ldn to John WILKINSON of Ldn. B/S of
40*ac* adj John WILLIAMS, Jacob HUMPHREY. Wit: Burr POWELL,
William CARTER, John HATCHER, H. B. POWELL, Ben GRAYSON,
Wm. BRONAUGH.

Bk:Pg: 2M:082   Date: 232 Jun 1810   RcCt: 8 Oct 1810
Isaac STEERE & wife Rebekah and Thomas STEERE of Ldn to William
BROWN of Ldn. B/S of 295*ac*. Wit: John HAMILTON, David GOODWIN.

Bk:Pg: 2M:085   Date: 28 Sep 1810   RcCt: 8 Oct 1810
Jeremiah SANFORD & wife Ada of Ldn to John HATCHER of Ldn. B/S of
20*ac*. Wit: Burr POWELL, William CARTER, John WILKINSON, H. B.
POWELL.

Bk:Pg: 2M:089   Date: 29 May 1810   RcCt: 8 Oct 1810
George STOVIN late of AlexVa now of Clayworth, Nottingham Co GrB to
Charles STOVIN of Ldn. PoA. Wit: Adam DICKENS.

Bk:Pg: 2M:095   Date: 28 Sep 1810   RcCt: 8 Oct 1810
Thomas HUGHES & wife Sarah of Ldn to Mahlon TAYLOR & William
NICKOLS of Ldn. Trust for debt to Isaac NICKOLS using 78*ac* adj Joseph
POULSON. Wit: Stacy TAYLOR, Joshua OSBURN, I. N. HOOK.

Bk:Pg: 2M:101   Date: 8 Sep 1810   RcCt: 8 Oct 1810
William WOOLF & wife Susanna of Ldn to Peter HECKMAN of Ldn. B/S
of 53¾*ac*. Wit: Isaac LAROWE.

Bk:Pg: 2M:105   Date: 1 Oct 1810   RcCt: 8 Oct 1810
William EDDY & wife Wealthy of JeffVa to William PAXON of Ldn. B/S of
8*ac*. Wit: James MOORE, Thomas PHILLIPS, Ralph SMITH, Joseph
TALBOTT.

Bk:Pg: 2M:107   Date: 10 Sep 1810   RcCt: 8 Oct 1810
James CHAMBERS of Ldn to John WENNER of Ldn. B/S of 30*ac* (from
200*ac* devised to Ann CHAMBERS w/o William CHAMBERS, d/o Robert
BOOTH dec'd). Wit: David GOODWIN, Wm. PAXSON, Michael
EVERHART.

Bk:Pg: 2M:110   Date: 17 Mar 1810   RcCt: 8 Oct 1810
Joseph TRIBBY & wife Ruth of Ldn to Evan EVANS of Ldn. B/S lot on N
side of Turnpike Road in Gap of short hill in Hllb, adj Isiah WHITE, William
CLENDENING. Wit: James COPELAND, David LOVETT, William
CLENDENING.

Bk:Pg: 2M:112   Date: 28 Sep 1810   RcCt: 8 Oct 1810
Burr POWELL (Exor of Leven POWELL dec'd) to Jeremiah SANFORD.
B/S of 101*ac* adj Jonathan BURSON, Abner HUMPHREY. Wit: William
CARTER, John WILKINSON, John HATCHER, H. B. POWELL.

Bk:Pg: 2M:115   Date: 5 Oct 1810   RcCt: 8 Oct 1810
Joseph LEWIS Jr. of Ldn to George COOPER of Ldn. B/S of 14*ac* adj
Robert BRADEN, George MULL.

Bk:Pg: 2M:117   Date: 14 May 1810   RcCt: 8 Oct 1810
Isaac HUGHES & wife Sarah of Ldn to Joseph HOLMES of Ldn. B/S of
28*ac* adj Joseph WHITE, William WHITE, Howell DAVIS.

Bk:Pg: 2M:121   Date: 21 Jun 1810   RcCt: 8 Oct 1810
John Taliferro BROOKE & James Mercer GARNETT (Admrs of James
MERCER dec'd) to Solomon BETTON of Ldn. B/S of 200*ac* adj Jonathan
CARTER, 266*ac*, 233*ac*, and 198½*ac*. Wit: William NOLAND, William F.
LUCKETT, Wm. COOKE, Alexander LACY.

Bk:Pg: 2M:125   Date: 1 Apr 1810   RcCt: 8 Oct 1810
Thomas LOVE & wife Sarah to Samuel HUGHES of Ldn. B/S of 49*ac* adj
Jesper POULSTON, Thomas HUGHES, Jesse SILCOTT. Wit: Samuel
RUSSELL, Thomas HUGHES, Stacy TAYLOR, Joshua OSBURN, Isaac
N. HOOK.

Bk:Pg: 2M:131   Date: 22 Jun 1810   RcCt: 8 Oct 1810
Edward MUD (free black) of Ldn to James RUST & John PANCOAST of
Ldn. B/S of 9*ac* adj Burr POWELL, Daniel REES. Wit: John GREGG Jr.,
Joshua PANCOAST, John PANC[O]AST Jr.

Bk:Pg: 2M:135   Date: 20 Jul 1810   RcCt: 8 Oct 1810
Jonah THOMPSON & wife Margaret, Richard VEITCH & wife Elizabeth of
AlexVa to James SAUNDERS of AlexVa & John LAIRD of Georgetown.
B/S of 400*ac* adj Benjamin JAMES, John SPENCER Jr.

Bk:Pg: 2M:141   Date: 25 Nov 1800   RcCt: 8 Dec 1800
Enoch THOMAS of Ldn to William DULIN of Ldn. B/S of 1*ac* adj Wm.
NOLAND. Wit: Josias CLAPHAM, Isaac STEERE, William GEORGE.

Bk:Pg: 2M:142   Date: 4 Aug 1810   RcCt: 8 Oct 1810
Isaac HOUGH & wife Fanny of Ldn to Robert BRADEN of Ldn. B/S of
160*ac* adj John HOUGH dec'd, Lydia HOUGH, Mich'l COOPER, Rhubin
HIXON dec'd. Wit: John BRADEN, Mahlon JANNEY Jr., Stephen BALL,
Joseph BRADEN, John A. BINNS, John HAMILTON.

Bk:Pg: 2M:147   Date: 7 Apr 1810   RcCt: 8 Oct 1810
Amos FERGUSON & wife Rebecca of Ldn to John SINCLAIR & Daniel
VERNON. Trust for debt to James LOVE using 150*ac*. Wit: Thomas
NICHOLS, Thomas HARDESTY, Thomas CHINN Jr., Wm. RUST.

Bk:Pg: 2M:150   Date: 8 Oct 1810   RcCt: 8 Oct 1810
Anthony CONNARD & wife Mary of Ldn to firm of Isaac & Samuel
NICKOLS and Wm. NICKOLS of Ldn. B/S of 117*ac*. Wit: John WILLIAMS,
Samuel WRIGHT, Joseph TALBOTT.

Bk:Pg: 2M:154   Date: 6 Dec 1806   RcCt: 8 Oct 1810
William MARTIN Jr. of Ldn to Nathaniel CRAWFORD of PrG. Mortgage
133*ac*. Receipt of 13 Jul 1810 from Sarah B. CRAWFORD (Exor of

Nathaniel CRAWFORD dec'd) for full payment. Wit: Lewis ELZEY, Jonathan CARTER, Richard CARTER.

Bk:Pg: 2M:158   Date: 17 Mar 1810   RcCt: 8 Oct 1810
Catharine BERKLEY, Malinda BERKLEY, Marmadake BERKLEY, Robert HOSKINS & wife Matilda (late BERKLEY) of Jefferson Co Ky to Hugh BERKLEY of Jefferson Co Ky. PoA concerning estate of John BERKLEY dec'd.

Bk:Pg: 2M:161   Date: 8 Oct 1810   RcCt: 8 Oct 1810
Catharine BERKLEY, Malinda BERKLEY, Marmadake BERKLEY, Robert HOSKINS & wife Matilda (late BERKLEY) of Jefferson Co Ky (ch/o Ann BERKLEY who was Ann KEEN before her marriage, d/o Richard KEEN dec'd, sister of John KEEN) to James TILLETT of Ldn. B/S of 130*ac* adj Mrs. Alice ELLZEY, Richard KEEN.

Bk:Pg: 2M:164   Date: 12 May 1810   RcCt: 8 Oct 1810
Samuel ARNETT of Clark Co Ky to Aaron BURSON & John DUNCAN of Ldn. PoA of property left by Samuel ARNETT dec'd of Ldn.

Bk:Pg: 2M:167   Date: May 1810   RcCt: 8 Oct 1810
William SUDDUTH age 44y. Affadivit: elderly Thomas ARNETT & SUDDUTH settled in Clarke Co Ky 18y ago last March and ARNETT had a boy <21y he claimed as a son. ARNETT died abt 2y past and he and SUDDUTH lived within ¾ mile of each other. The Samuel ARNETT in above deed is one named in will of Thomas ARNETT. Also affidavit of Rob. SCOBY age 34y and James DUNCAN.

Bk:Pg: 2M:171   Date: 14 Nov 1807   RcCt: 12 Jan 1808
Henry CLAGETT of Lsbg to Richard CHESTER & William MASTERMAN (Exors of Daniel MILDRED dec'd surviving partner of Mildred & Roberts) Trust of lot in Lsbg on King St adj Thomas SANDER.

Bk:Pg: 2M:174   Date: May 1810   RcCt: 9 Oct 1810
Receipt of payment of mortgage by Henry CLAGETT.

Bk:Pg: 2M:174   Date: 12 May 1810   RcCt: 8 Oct 1810
Samuel ARNETT (s/o Thomas ARNETT dec'd) of Clarke Co Ky to Aaron BURSON & John DUNCAN of Ldn. BoS for all personal estate & money from father.

Bk:Pg: 2M:177   Date: 7 Jul 1810   RcCt: 12 Nov 1810
Daniel EACHES of Ldn to William VICKERS of Ldn. B/S of 50*ac*. Wit: Isaac FRY, Gourley REEDER, Jarvett GARNER.

Bk:Pg: 2M:179   Date: 10 Jul 1810   RcCt: 12 Nov 1810
William NOLAND & wife Catharine of Ldn to John J. HARDING of Ldn. B/S of part of Lot #31 in Lsbg. Wit: Saml. CLAPHAM, John HAMILTON.

Bk:Pg: 2M:183   Date: 2 Jun 1810   RcCt: 12 Nov 1810
Miriam HOLE (widow & Admr of Levi HOLE dec'd) & Ann and Ruth HOLE (ch/o Levi HOLE dec'd) to Major HUNT of Ldn. B/S of 2*ac*. Wit: William HOLMES, David SMITH, Joseph WILSON, Thomas GREGG, John TILLEY, Jno. SMITH.

Bk:Pg: 2M:186   Date: 12 Oct 1810   RcCt: 12 Nov 1810
Peter R. BEVERLY & wife Lovely of Culpeper to John CUMMINGS of
Ldn. B/S of 111¾ac adj John NICKLIN, Rich'd WILLET. Wit: William
CHILTON, Samuel MURREY, Wm. B. HARRISON, Robert BRADEN.

Bk:Pg: 2M:190   Date: 12 Oct 1810   RcCt: 12 Nov 1810
Peter R. BEVERLY & wife Lovely of Culpeper to John CUMMINGS of
Ldn. B/S of 127¼ac adj William SMITH, Richard CONNER, Davis RUSE,
Mathew BEANS, William SMITH. Wit: William CHILTON, Samuel
MURREY, Wm. B. HARRISON, Robert BRADEN.

Bk:Pg: 2M:195   Date: 12 Oct 1810   RcCt: 12 Nov 1810
Peter R. BEVERLY/BEAVERLY & wife Lovely of Ffx to Robert BRADEN
of Ldn. B/S of 172¾ac adj Jonah THOMPSON, Edward McDANIEL,
Thomas STEVENS, William SMITH, John CUMMINGS, John NICKLIN,
William VERTZ. Wit: Wm. CHILTON, Samuel MURREY, William B.
HARRISON, John CUMMINGS.

Bk:Pg: 2M:200   Date: 12 Nov 1810   RcCt: 12 Nov 1810
Peter R. BEVERLY/BEAVERLY & wife Lovely of Ffx to Robert BRADEN
of Ldn. B/S of 2ac under L/L adj Joseph BRADEN, for purpose of building
a meeting house or church & burying ground. Wit: Willam CHILTON,
Samuel MURREY, Wm. B. HARRISON, Charles BINNS.

Bk:Pg: 2M:202   Date: 30 Oct 1810   RcCt: 12 Nov 1810
Nicholas HARPER of Ldn to sons Walter HARPER of Ldn & Nicholas
HARPER Jr of Ffx. BoS for negro Tom over 40y, George abt 27y, Cager
abt 21y, Adam under 16y, Susannah over 50y, Vance abt 30y, James abt
10y, Ally abt 7y, Philip abt 5y, Linder abt 3y, Agga abt 19y & her daughter
Lucy 19 days old, farm and household items. Wit: John PHILPOTT,
Smallwood C. MIDDLETON, George FLING, Thomas JENKINS.

Bk:Pg: 2M:204   Date: 27 Feb 1810   RcCt: 13 Mar 1810
Daniel BROWN of Ldn to Fleet SMITH & Thomas GREGG of Ldn. Trust
for debt to John LLOYD of AlexVa using land with grist mill on Goose
Creek.

Bk:Pg: 2M:209   Date: 24 Oct 1810   RcCt: 12 Oct [Nov?] 1810
John CUMMINGS of Ldn to Charles Fenton MERCER of Ldn. Trust for
debt to Peter R. BEVERLY using 127ac. Wit: R. BRADEN.

Bk:Pg: 2M:213   Date: 4 Jun 1810   RcCt: 12 Nov 1810
Stephen Westley ROSZELL & wife Catharine to Stephen Chilton
ROSZELL. B/S of 100ac on Beaverdam adj "British property" of Benjamin
WALKER, heirs of James MEGEATH. Wit: Alexander WAUGH, Mary
JENKINS, Joseph FRYE, John LITTLEJOHN, William BRONAUGH.

Bk:Pg: 2M:217   Date: 12 Nov 1810   RcCt: 12 Nov 1810
Jesse TIMMS & George CARTER. Bond on TIMMS as Commissioner of
Revenue. Wit: Samuel M. EDWARDS.

Bk:Pg: 2M:218   Date: 25 Feb 1803   RcCt: 12 Nov 1810
Lewis ELLZEY to William ELLZEY. All accounts between Guardian &
ward are settled. Wit: William CHILTON.

Bk:Pg: 2M:219   Date: 12 Nov 1810   RcCt: 12 Nov 1810
Timothy TAYLOR & Joshua OSBURNE. Bond on TAYLOR as
Commissioner of Revenue. Wit: Samuel M. EDWARDS.

Bk:Pg: 2M:220   Date: 29 Oct 1810   RcCt: 12 Nov 1810
Abraham B. T. MASON of Ldn to George W. BALL, John MATHIAS &
Fleet SMITH of Ldn. Trust for debt to merchants Frederick
LINDENBERGER & Co. of BaltMd using 662½. Wit: French S. GRAY,
John POTTER, James B. LANE, Jno. MATHIAS, Samuel M. EDWARDS.

Bk:Pg: 2M:226   Date: 12 Nov 1810   RcCt: 13 Nov 1810
John NEWTON & wife Harriot of Lsbg to William JOHNSON of Ldn. B/S
of ½ac lot in Lsbg. Wit: Wm. B. HARRISON, John LITTLEJOHN.

Bk:Pg: 2M:231   Date: 13 Nov 1810   RcCt: 13 Nov 1810
Price JACOBS, Timothy TAYLOR & David LOVETT of Ldn to John
HATCHER of Ldn. Bond for HATCHER as security for Catharine JACOBS
(w/o Price, late Catharine CAMBLING) as Admr of William CAMBLING
dec'd with TAYLOR & LOVETT as counter security. Wit: Samuel M.
EDWARDS.

Bk:Pg: 2M:232   Date: 13 Nov 1810   RcCt: 13 Nov 1810
Lewis ELLZEY of Ldn to Sheriff Charles BENNETT of Ldn. B/S of all
property and claims, by act of insolvency.

Bk:Pg: 2M:234   Date: 6 Oct 1809   RcCt: 13 Nov 1810
Enoch FRANCIS & wife Nancy to Simon Alexander BINNS (br/o John A.
BINNS) of Ldn. B/S of ¾ac on road from Lsbg to AlexVa where James
THOMAS now lives. Wit: John DULIN, Betey BARRACROFT. Polley
LAYCOCK.

Bk:Pg: 2M:236   Date: 23 Jun 1810   RcCt: 8 Oct 1810
Solomon BETTON & wife Lucinda of Ldn to Burr POWELL of Ldn. B/S of
266ac Lot #2. Wit: Henry D. HALE, Leven D. POWELL, Thos. INGRAM,
Humphrey B. POWELL, Thomas A. DENNIS, Francis PEYTON, Leven
LUCKETT.

Bk:Pg: 2M:241   Date: 23 Jun 1810   RcCt: 8 Oct 1810
Solomon BETTON & wife Lucinda of Ldn to Owen SULLIVAN of Fqr. B/S
of 233ac Lot #3. Wit: Thomas A. DENNIS, Thomas INGRAM, Leven D.
POWELL, Henry D. HALE, Humphrey B. POWELL, Francis PEYTON,
Leven LUCKETT.

Bk:Pg: 2M:247   Date: 8 Jul 1810   RcCt: 13 Nov 1810
Lewis ELLZEY of Ldn to William ELLZEY of Ldn. B/S of 2 lots in trust from
Henly BOGGESS. Wit: Joshua OSBURN, James COLEMAN, Samuel
BOGGESS.

Bk:Pg: 2M:249   Date: 10 Sep 1810   RcCt: 13 Nov 1810
Thomas PHILIPS of Wtfd as trustee of Sarah CAVAN & Joshua BAKER
to Sampson BLINCOE of Lsbg. Release of trust on part of Lot #58 in
Lsbg. Wit: Thomas MORALLEE, Henry CLAGETT, Thos. SANDERS.

Bk:Pg: 2M:251 Date: 7 Sep 1807 RcCt: 14 Nov 1810
Thomas PURSEL dec'd. Division among widow and children by
commissioners appt in chancery 13 Jan 1807. Lot #1 of 24ac to Samuel
PURCEL Jr. nr Kittockton adj James COPELAND, William RUSSELL,
Thomas HOUGH. Lots #2 of 8ac & #6 of 19ac to Samuel, John, Joseph &
Thomas PURSELL. Lot #3 of 12½ac to Nancy RUSSEL. Lot #4 of 17ac to
Valentine PURSEL. Lot #7 of 16ac to Lydia PURSEL Jr. Lot #8 of 17ac to
Polly PURSEL. Lot #9 of 17ac to George PURSEL. Lots #10 of 13ac & #5
of 4ac to Pleasant PURSEL. [plat given] Divisors: David SMITH, James
COPELAND, Wm. RUSSELL, Edward CUNNARD Sr.

Bk:Pg: 2M:258 30 Sep 1809 RcCt: 14 Nov 1810
Dower of widow of William JONES dec'd of Ldn with residue to children.
Lot #1 of 120ac to widow. Lot #2 of 61ac to John JONES. Lot #3 of 71ac
to Martha wife of Sampson BLINCOE. Lot #4 of 8ac & #5 of 32ac to Philip
JONES. Lot #6 of 35½ac to Rich'd JONES. Lot #7 of 24ac & #8 of 7ac to
Thomas JONES. Lots #9 of 5ac & #10 of 27ac to Elizabeth JONES. Lot
#11 of 48ac to William JONES. Divisors: Thomas FOUCH, Abner
WILLIAMS, Samuel ADAMS.

Bk:Pg: 2M:262 Date: 20 Apr 1810 RcCt: 14 Nov 1810
Richard PURDY & wife Elizabeth of Orange Co to John A. W. SMITH of
Warrenton. Trust for debt to Thomas JANNEY & Co and Joseph JANNEY
of AlexVa using part of Lot #12 in Lsbg; also house & lott at Fqr
courthouse and Purdy's shoemakers shop. Wit: James HAMETT, Gideon
JOHNSTON, Jno. KEMPER.

Bk:Pg: 2M:268 Date: 5 Dec 1804 RcCt: 9 Apr 1805
Daniel DOWLING & wife Catharine (Kitty) of Ldn to Obadiah CLIFFORD
of Ldn. B/S of part of Lot #3 in Lsbg. Wit: Samuel MURREY, Francis H.
PEYTON, James HAMILTON.

Bk:Pg: 2M:272 Date: ___ 1810 RcCt: 14 Nov 1810
Murtho SULLIVAN, R. H. HENDERSON & Westwood Y. MASON. Bond
on SULLIVAN as Commission of Revenue. Wit: Isaac LAROWE.

Bk:Pg: 2M:273 Date: 14 Nov 1810 RcCt: 14 Nov 1810
Quinton BAIN of Lsbg to Enoch FRANCIS of Lsbg. B/S of 89ac below
Goose Creek. Wit: G. M. MOSS, F. S. GRAY, John KIPHEART.

Bk:Pg: 2M:276 Date: 15 Nov 1810 RcCt: 15 Nov 1810
William B. HARRISON, Charles LEWIS & Absolom HAWLEY of Ldn to
George KILGORE of Ldn. B/S of 40ac & mill (land in dispute between
KILGORE and heirs of James FOX dec'd – widow Rebecca, children
George Kilgore, Ann H., Martenet B., Elizabeth & Jane FOX).

Bk:Pg: 2M:281 Date: 15 Nov 1810 RcCt: 15 Nov 1810
Tunis TITUS & wife Jane of Hampshire Co Va to John TORBERT of Ldn
(both devisees of brother Samuel TORBERT dec'd). B/S of 1/9 share of
100ac. Wit: Samuel M. EDWARDS.

Bk:Pg: 2M:284   Date: 30 Apr 1810   RcCt: 16 Nov 1810
Thomas SHEARMAN & wife Molly and Ann OLDHAM of Lancaster Co
(ch/o Joseph SHEARMAN late of Lancaster) to Rawleigh CHINN of Ldn.
B/S of 700*ac*. Wit: James BALL, Jno. CARPENTER, Rich'd MITCHELL,
Robt. CHINN, Wm. B. MITCHELL.

Bk:Pg: 2M:289   Date: 14 Mar 1806   RcCt: 12 May 1806
William BRONAUGH trustee of Thomas HEREFORD to William WOODY.
Release of trust. Wit: Sampson BLINCOE, Samuel BOGGESS, Wm.
MAINS.

Bk:Pg: 2M:291   Date: 7 Apr 1810   RcCt: 10 Apr 1810
Mary BARR (wd/o George BARR dec'd), George BARR, Adam BARR &
wife Pretious of Ldn to Walter LANGLEY of Ldn. B/S of 40*ac* on Goose
Creek. Wit: Burr POWELL, Leven POWELL, Hugh SMITH, William
MANKIN, Moses WILSON, John A. BINNS.

Bk:Pg: 2M:297   Date: 26 Oct 1810   RcCt: 10 Dec 1810
Ferdinando FAIRFAX of JeffVa & William Byrd PAGE of FrdkVa to
Thomas LESLIE of Ldn. B/S of 107*ac*. Wit: Ebenezer GRUBB, John
CONARD, Peter DEMERY, Edward DOWLING.

Bk:Pg: 2M:300   Date: 26 Oct 1810   RcCt: 10 Dec 1810
Ferdinando FAIRFAX of JeffVa & William Byrd PAGE of FrdkVa to
Thomas LESLIE of Ldn. B/S of 120*ac*. Wit: John CONARD, David
POTTS, Edward DOWLING, Ebenezer GRUBB.

Bk:Pg: 2M:302   Date: 26 Oct 1810   RcCt: 10 Dec 1810
Ferdinando FAIRFAX of JeffVa & William Byrd PAGE of FrdkVa to John
CONARD of Ldn. B/S of 276*ac* in Shannondale adj Peter DEMORY, John
DEMORY. Wit: Ebenezer GRUBB, David POTTS, Peter DEMORY,
Edward DOWLING.

Bk:Pg: 2M:305   Date: 26 Oct 1810   RcCt: 10 Dec 1810
Ferdinando FAIRFAX of JeffVa & William Byrd PAGE of FrdkVa to Peter
DEMORY of Ldn. B/S of 130*ac* in Shannondale adj Peter DEMORY. Wit:
John CONARD, David POTTS, Ebenezer GRUBB, Edward DOWLING.

Bk:Pg: 2M:308   Date: 26 Oct 1810   RcCt: 10 Dec 1810
Ferdinando FAIRFAX of JeffVa & William Byrd PAGE of FrdkVa to
Ebenezer GRUBB of Ldn. B/S of 231*ac* where John HESS (holds LS of
109*ac*) & Henry COUNCE live. Wit: John CONARD, David POTTS, Peter
DEMORY, Edward DOWLING.

Bk:Pg: 2M:312   Date: 26 Oct 1810   RcCt: 10 Dec 1810
Ferdinando FAIRFAX of JeffVa & William Byrd PAGE of FrdkVa to Adam
GRUBB of Ldn. B/S of 105*ac* adj John POTTS, John MILLER. Wit: John
CONARD, David POTTS, Peter DEMORY, Edward DOWLING.

Bk:Pg: 2M:315   Date: 26 Oct 1810   RcCt: 10 Dec 1810
Ferdinando FAIRFAX of JeffVa & William Byrd PAGE of FrdkVa to Cath.
NIEUCEWANGER of Ldn. B/S of 78*ac*. Wit: John CONARD, David
POTTS, Edward DOWLING, Peter DEMORY, Ebenezer GRUBB, J.
HARDING, Nick's ROPER.

Bk:Pg: 2M:318   Date: 6 Oct 1810   RcCt: 10 Dec 1810
Ferdinando FAIRFAX of JeffVa & William Byrd PAGE of FrdkVa to
Edward DOWLING of Ldn. B/S of 103ac adj John CAMPBELL, Jonathan
MATHEWS, Richard GRUBB. Wit: John CONARD, David POTTS, Peter
DEMORY, Ebenezer GRUBB.

Bk:Pg: 2M:321   Date: 8 Dec 1810   RcCt: 10 Dec 1810
Edward DOWLING of Ldn to Thomas GREGG & Jonas POTTS (s/o
Ezekiel POTTS) of Ldn. Trust for debt to Jonas POTTS using 103ac.

Bk:Pg: 2M:323   Date: 23 Jun 1810   RcCt: 10 Dec 1810
John HAMILTON of Ldn to Isaac STEERE & Thomas STEERE of Ldn.
Mortgage of 224ac for bonds to William BROWN.

Bk:Pg: 2M:326   Date: 27 Sep 1809   RcCt: 11 Dec 1809
William REDWOOD of Ldn to Ludwell LEE of Ldn. B/S of 30ac on S side
of road from Lsbg to AlexVa, adj Enoch FRANCIS. Wit: Henson
JOHNSON, John D. NEEDHAM, Thomas DARNE Jr.

Bk:Pg: 2M:328   Date: 19 May 1810   RcCt: [Dec 1810?]
James CAMPBELL & wife Ruth of Ldn to William CLAYTON of Ldn. B/S
of 15ac on side of Blue Ridge (warrant #2244 issued 9 Aug 1797). Wit:
Martin OVERFIELD, George Hawkins ALLDER, John BRAIDY, Stacy
TAYLOR, Notley C. WILLIAMS.

Bk:Pg: 2M:332   Date: 4 May 1802   RcCt: 13 Dec 1802
William CAMMELL/CAMPBELL & wife Mary of FrdkVa to Benjamin
JAMES of Ldn. B/S of 215ac adj Thomas ODEN, Rachel COLCLOUGH.
Wit: Andrew REDMOND, Moses JAMES, Abel JAMES, John GILT,
Joseph GAMBLE, George REED.

Bk:Pg: 2M:336   Date: 10 Dec 1810   RcCt: 10 Dec 1810
John EBLIN & wife of Roan Co Tn to James GREENLEASE of Ldn. B/S
of 136ac adj William WHITE.

Bk:Pg: 2M:339   Date: 13 Oct 1810   RcCt: 10 Dec 1810
William McFARLING of Ldn to James CAMPBELL of Ldn. B/S of 25ac adj
William LUDWELL. Wit: George Hawkins ALLDER, John BRAIDY,
Edward CUNNARD Jr.

Bk:Pg: 2M:341   Date: 24 Jun 1810   RcCt: 10 Dec 1810
Henry LEE Jr. of WstmVa to Ludwell LEE of Ldn. B/S of 500ac on
Potomac. Wit: John D. NEEDHAM, Richard H. LEE, Thomas DARNE Jr.,
Henson JOHNSON.

Bk:Pg: 2M:343   Date: 14 Aug 1797   RcCt: 12 Feb 1798
Joseph JANNEY & John JANNEY Jr. (Exor of Joseph JANNEY dec'd)
and William HOUGH of Ldn to Murty SULLIVAN of Ldn. B/S of 4½ac on
road to Noland's Ferry adj Elizabeth SCOTT. Wit: Robert BRADEN,
James MOORE, Asa MOORE.

Bk:Pg: 2M:345   Date: 10 Dec 1810   RcCt: 10 Dec 1810
John HESKETT of Ldn to Stephen C. ROSZEL of Ldn. Trust for debt to
John PANCOAST Jr. 109ac & 51ac. Wit: Samuel NICKOLS.

Bk:Pg: 2M:348   Date: 27 Nov 1810   RcCt: 10 Dec 1810
Cornelius VANDEVANTER (s/o Isaac VANDEVANTER dec'd) of Ldn to
Joseph VANDEVANTER of Ldn. B/S of 130*ac* (Abram DAVIS has set up
a claim on part of land). Wit: R. BRADEN, Jonathan HEATON, Isaac
VANDEVANTER.

Bk:Pg: 2M:350   Date: 28 Nov 1810   RcCt: 10 Dec 1810
Joseph VANDEVANTER of Ldn to Robert BRADEN & Charles BENNETT
Jr. of Ldn. Trust for debt to Cornelius VANDEVANTER using above land.
Wit: R. BRADEN, Jonathan HEATON, Isaac VANDEVANTER.

Bk:Pg: 2M:352   Date: 8 Sep 1810   RcCt: 10 Dec 1810
Mahlon COMBS & wife Sarah of Ldn to William WILKINSON of Ldn. Trust
of land adj North fork Baptist Meeting House. Wit: John TRIPLETT,
Francis TRIPLETT Jr., Samuel TODD.

Bk:Pg: 2M:353   Date: 7 Dec 1810   RcCt: 10 Dec 1810
Stacy TAYLOR of Ldn to Issacher BROWN of Ldn. Release of mortgage
on 63*ac*.

Bk:Pg: 2M:355   Date: 17 Aug 1810   RcCt: 10 Dec 1810
Mahlon COMBS & wife Sarah of Ldn to Edward COE, Joseph GARRET,
Hamilton ROGERS, William WILKINSON & Joseph DANIEL (trustees of
North Fork Baptist Church) of Ldn. B/S of 1*ac* adj meeting house lot. Wit:
James MEGEATH, Peyton POWELL, Evan WILKISON.

Bk:Pg: 2M:357   Date: 24 May 1810   RcCt: 10 Dec 1810
Eli MELLON/MALIN & wife Elizabeth of Ldn to Mahlon COMBS of Ldn.
B/S of 4½*ac*. Wit: John SINCLAIR, John MUDD, Joseph DANIEL.

Bk:Pg: 2M:358   Date: 14 Nov 1810   RcCt: 10 Dec 1810
William PIGGOTT & wife Mary of Ldn to Enos POTTS of Ldn. B/S of 17*ac*
adj David SMITH, road leading to Abijah Janney's Mill, David BELL. Wit:
Stephen ETON, James BOLON, Lydia POTTS.

Bk:Pg: 2M:361   Date: 4 May 1810   RcCt: 10 Dec 1810
William PIGGOTT & wife Mary of Ldn to Stephen WILSON of Ldn. B/S of
85*ac* on SW fork of Goose Creek.

Bk:Pg: 2M:363   Date: 26 Aug 1810   RcCt: 12 Nov 1810
James BRADFIELD & wife Ruth of Ldn to Thomas SANDS of Ldn. B/S of
6*ac* on NW fork of Goose Creek. Wit: Stacy TAYLOR, Joshua OSBURN,
Joseph HOUGH.

Bk:Pg: 2M:367   Date: 8 Jan 1811   RcCt: 14 Jan 1811
Wilson Carey SELDEN & wife Nelly to Aron SANDERS. CoE for sale of
103*ac*. Wit: Jno. ROSE, John LITTLEJOHN.

Bk:Pg: 2M:368   Date: 17 Jul 1810   RcCt: 14 Jan 1811
Joseph SHEARMAN, Thomas SHEARMAN & Ann OLDHAM (heirs of
Joseph SHEARMAN dec'd of Lancaster Co) to Rawleigh CHINN of Ldn.
B/S of 400*ac*. Wit: Martin SHEARMAN, Ezekiel SHEARMAN, Thomas
MITCHELL, Chichester TAPSCOTT, John SEWARD, Wm. B. MITCHELL,
Thomas ARMSTRONG.

Bk:Pg: 2M:372   Date: 18 Jul 1810   RcCt: 14 Jan 1811
John B. STEVENS & wife Sarah of Ldn to Thomas D. STEVENS of Ldn.
B/S of lot in Hllb on S side of turnpike road adj Richard COPELAND.
Wit: James McDANIEL, Jehu HOLLINGSWORTH, Archibald McDANIEL,
Stacy TAYLOR, R. BRADEN.

Bk:Pg: 2M:375   Date: 28 Apr 1810   RcCt: 14 Jan 1811
John DULIN & wife Rebecca of Ldn to Robert ROBERTSON of Ldn. B/S
of Lot #10 in Lsbg. Wit: John LITTLEJOHN, Samuel MURREY, John
KIPHART.

Bk:Pg: 2M:378   Date: 14 Jan 1811   RcCt: 14 Jan 1811
David LACEY & wife Sarah of Ldn to Charles BENNETT Jr. of Ldn. B/S of
160ac on road from David LACY to Wtfd. Wit: Sanford RAMY, John
WORSLEY, Samuel M. EDWARDS, Isaac LAROWE, John A. BINNS,
Robert BRADEN.

Bk:Pg: 2M:381   Date: 29 May 1810   RcCt: 14 Jan 1811
Stacy TEMPLER of Ldn to James TEMPLER. BoS (James as security on
note to William MORGAN) of farm and household items. Wit: Sampson
BLINCOE, J. RILEY, Saml. LAYCOCK.

Bk:Pg: 2M:382   Date: Date: 7 Jan 1811   RcCt: 14 Jan 1811
John CUMMINGS & wife Jane of Ldn to Joseph BRADEN of Ldn. B/S of
239ac in Piedmont adj Wm. SMITH, Rob. BRADEN, John NICHLIN,
Rich'd WILLETT, Mathew BEANS. Wit: Robert CUMMINGS, Jacob
BAUGH, Thos. D. STEVENS, John B. STEVENS, David LOVETT, Stacy
TAYLOR, Robert BRADEN.

Bk:Pg: 2M:385   Date: 17 Oct 1810   RcCt: 14 Jan 1811
Owen WILLIAMS & wife Rodah to Ellis WILLIAMS. CoE for share of land
from father John WILLIAMS dec'd. Wit: Jacob JENKINGS, James
CAUDY.

Bk:Pg: 2M:387   Date: 31 Dec 1810   RcCt: 14 Jan 1811
William HOUGH of Ldn to Joseph TALBOTT of Ldn. B/S of lot in Wtfd adj
Flemon PATTISON. Wit: W. S. NEALE, Eleanor HOUGH, Elizabeth
SCHOOLLY.

Bk:Pg: 2M:388   Date: 15 Oct 1810   RcCt: 14 Jan 1811
Elizabeth LEWIS & Hector P. LEWIS (Exors of Thomas LEWIS dec'd) of
Fayette Co Ky to Asa K. LEWIS. PoA for mortgage by Hugh DOUGLAS,
land in Ffx leased to Timothy CARRINGTON, and Potomac Canal Co
stock.

Bk:Pg: 2M:390   Date: 29 Nov 1810   RcCt: 14 Jan 1811
Elizabeth LEWIS, Hector P. LEWIS & Asa K. LEWIS (Exors of Thomas
LEWIS dec'd) to Hugh DOUGLAS of Ldn. Release of mortgage. C.
BINNS, F. S. GRAY, Saml. M. EDWARDS.

Bk:Pg: 2M:392   Date: 12 Sep 1795   RcCt: 14 Jan 1811
Geo. Wm. FAIRFAX of Ffx to Lewis REASE of Ldn. LS of 125ac on SW
fork of Kittoctan adj Jonathan MIRES. Wit: David MULL, William
LAYCOCK, Wm. WILDMAN.

Bk:Pg: 2M:394   Date: 5 Jan 1811   RcCt: 14 Jan 1811
Daniel HAINS & wife Mary, Joseph HAINS & wife Maria of Fqr to Jozabed WHITE of Ldn. B/S of 36ac on S side of Kittocton Creek (20ac leased to Robert BRADEN). Wit: Chandler PEYTON, James PICKETT.

Bk:Pg: 2M:397   Date: 14 Jan 1811   RcCt: 14 Jan 1811
Jonah THOMPSON of AlexVa & James MOORE (Exors of Israel H. THOMPSON of Ldn) to David JANNEY of Ldn. B/S of lot in Wtfd. Wit: Wm. ELLZEY, Wm. ESKRIDGE, G. CARTER.

Bk:Pg: 2M:399   Date: 11 Feb 1811   RcCt: 11 Feb 1811
Thomas KENT of Ldn to son Isaac KENT and his children Thomas, Sarah, John, Smith & Milley KENT. B/S of 10ac adj Isaac KENT, George BURSON. Wit: Isaac LAROWE.

Bk:Pg: 2M:401   Date: 11 Feb 1811   RcCt: 11 Feb 1811
John WILKINSON & wife of Ldn to Daniel EACHES of Ldn. Trust for debt to Samuel & Isaac NICKOLS using 40ac. Wit: Isaac LAROWE, Saml. M. EDWARDS, Benj'n. SHREVE.

Bk:Pg: 2M:403   Date: __ Oct 1810   RcCt: 11 Feb 1811
Asahel TOMKINS & wife Nancy of Belmont Co Oh to Elizabeth SADLER of Ldn. B/S of lot nr Lsbg left Asahel by his dec'd mother. Wit: Wm. AUSTIN, Jas. HAMILTON, Saml. HAMILTON.

Bk:Pg: 2M:404   Date: 12 Oct 1810   RcCt: 11 Feb 1811
Peter R. BEVERLY & wife Lovely of Ffx to Patrick McGARVICK/McGARRICK of Ldn. B/S of 150ac in Piedmont on road from Wtfd to Thompson's Mill. Wit: Wm. CHILTON, Samuel MURREY, Wm. B. HARRISON, R. BRADEN.

Bk:Pg: 2M:407   Date: 11 Feb 1811   RcCt: 11 Feb 1811
John DRAIN & wife Ann (signed Nancy) of Ldn to Daniel TRIPLETT of Ldn. B/S of part of Lot #56 in Lsbg. Wit: Wm. B. HARRISON, Samuel MURREY.

Bk:Pg: 2M:409   Date: 3 Sep 1810   RcCt: 11 Feb 1811
David ALEXANDER of Ldn to Samuel GREGG of Ldn. B/S of 5ac on NW fork of Goose Creek. Wit: Samuel TODD, Joseph RANDELL, Jas. M. GARETT.

Bk:Pg: 2M:411   Date: 8 Feb 1811   RcCt: 11 Feb 1811
Sanford LYNE of Ldn to Reuben SETTLE of Ldn. B/S of 31ac.

Bk:Pg: 2M:412   Date: 30 Apr 1804   RcCt: 8 Oct 1804
Amos JANNEY & wife Grace (Admr of father Abel JANNEY dec'd) of Ldn to Adam GRUBB of Ldn. B/S of 113ac. Wit: James ROACH, Nathan CONARD, Ebenezer GRUBB, Mahlon ROACH.

Bk:Pg: 2M:414   Date: 10 Sep 1810   RcCt: 11 Feb 1811
William P. BAYLEY & wife Mary L. of StafVa to Peggy & Kitty HEREFORD (d/o Margaret dec'd) of Fqr. B/S of 300ac on edge of Ldn & Fqr adj James BATTSON. Wm. WALLER Jr., Math. NORMAN, Charles

W. WALLER, Charles MIFLIN, Benj'n TOLSON, Hancock EUSTACE, Thos. NORMAN.

Bk:Pg: 2M:417   Date: 14 Jan 1811   RcCt: 11 Feb 1811
Swithin NICKOLS & wife Rebeckah of Ldn to Jonathan REED of Ldn. B/S of 62*ac* on Beaverdam. Wit: Moses BROWN, James HATCHER, Jesse LEWELLEN, Stacy TAYLOR, Step C. ROSZEL.

Bk:Pg: 2M:419   Date: 11 Feb 1811   RcCt: 11 Feb 1811
William EVENS of Ldn to Charles ELLGIN of Ldn for use of Thomas LESLIE of Ldn. Trust using 75*ac*. Wit: William VIRTS, Edw. MARGINNIS, Timothy TAYLOR.

Bk:Pg: 2M:421   Date: 11 Feb 1811   RcCt: 11 Feb 1811
William EVANS of Ldn to Thomas LESLIE of Ldn. B/S of 75*ac*, part of lease lot where LESLIE now lives. Wit: Charles ELGIN, William VERTS, Edw. MARGINNIS.

Bk:Pg: 2M:422   Date: 11 Feb 1811   RcCt: 11 Feb 1811
Thomas LESLIE of Ldn to Robert BRADEN of Ldn. B/S of 7*ac* adj John WITTEMAN.

Bk:Pg: 2M:423   Date: 11 Feb 1811   RcCt: 12 Feb 1811
David AXLINE & Jacob VERTZ (commissioners suit of Michael EVERHART assee. Philip EVERHEART Guardian of Solomon EVERHART) to William EVERHART of Ldn. B/S of 96¾*ac*.

Bk:Pg: 2M:424   Date: 25 Jun 1810   RcCt: 10 Sep 1810
Capt. William TAYLOR late of Lsbg now of Ldn to Dr. Henry CLAGETT of Lsbg. B/S of lot on Market St Lsbg. Wit: James CAVAN Jr., John POLTON?, A. SUTHERLAND.

Bk:Pg: 2M:426   Date: 24 Jan 1811   RcCt: 12 Feb 1811
James GARNER & wife Margaret of Ldn to William JOHNSON & Joseph HUNT of Ldn. Trust using 9*ac* Lot #7. Wit: Thos. N. BINNS, Mark WOOD, Daniel GRAY.

Bk:Pg: 2M:427   Date: 7 Sep 1810   RcCt: 12 Feb 1811
David LACEY to Elias LACEY and Richard H. HENDERSON & Samuel M. EDWARDS, all of Ldn. Trust using 80*ac*. Ths. L. MOORE, Jesse GOVER, George HAMMAT, C. BINNS, G. M. MOSS, John A. BINNS, F. S. GRAY.

Bk:Pg: 2M:429   Date: 8 Nov 1806   RcCt: 12 Feb 1811
John Tasker CARTER of WstmVa to William CHILTON of Ldn. Release. Wit: John CAMPBELL, Wm. C. CHANDLER.

INDEX

James, 158
John, 232
Thomas, 251
ARNETT
Samuel, 11, 245
Thomas, 245
ARNOLD
Eustis, 110
ARRETT
Samuel, 15
ARTHUR
John, 189
ASH
John, 150, 203
ASHFORD
Aaron, 15
Jane, 88
John, 39, 63
Michael, 88
William, 88
ASHTON
Henry, 10
John W., 144
ATCHER
Christopher, 78, 189
Cornelius, 78, 92
Rachel, 189
ATHEY
Hezekiah, 69
Wilson, 223, 224
ATTWELL
Thomas, 137
ATWELL
Jesse, 223
Sithe, 242
Sytha, 228
Thomas, 126, 158,
225, 228, 242
ATWOOD
George, 115
James, 239
AULD
Colin, 5, 62, 97, 165,
194, 206, 208,
218, 240
Collin, 213
AULT

William, 72, 81, 84
AUSTIN
Calvin, 160
William, 201, 213,
253
AUSTINE
Austine, 218
William, 188, 195
AWBREY
Charity, 83
Henry, 82, 83, 91
Richard, 87
Samuel, 82, 83
Thomas, 82, 83,
198, 222
AWMAN
Lawrence, 232
AXLEY
Clare, 68
AXLIN
Josh, 3
AXLINE
Adam, 38
Catharine, 36, 170
David, 56, 66, 67,
157, 211, 234,
254
Henry, 36
Jacob, 25, 56, 66,
161, 170
John, 26, 37, 45, 56,
67, 195, 236
AYLET
William, 9
AYLETE
William, 93
AYLETT
William, 21, 45

B

BACKHOUSE
Ann, 220, 221
Thomas, 153
BACKUS
Ann, 221
BACON
Asa, 44, 58

BAILES
Abner, 202
BAILEY
John, 137
Sydnor, 150, 209
BAILLEY
John, 161
BAILS
David, 185
BAILY
Hugh, 242
Sarah, 242
Sydnor, 228
BAIN
Quintin, 219
Quinton, 248
BAKER
Catharine, 36, 154
Christener, 36
David, 34, 36
Elizabeth, 42, 50,
194
Jacob, 36, 50, 63,
143, 154
Josh, 32
Joshua, 31, 33, 91,
120, 121, 218,
247
Philip, 34, 36
Samuel, 34, 36, 130,
159, 223
William, 28, 36, 66,
159, 163, 186
BALDWIN
Cornelius, 141
John, 12, 104, 130
Joseph, 184, 228
Mahlon, 68, 97
BALES
David, 241
BALL
Ann, 180
Anna, 71
Burges, 88
Burgess, 18
Farling, 7, 11, 17,
27, 35, 66, 69, 71,

74, 83, 95, 132,
134
Fayette, 232
George W., 183,
193, 200, 247
I., 83
Isaac, 16, 28, 35,
71, 83, 87, 95,
134, 178, 201
James, 7, 26, 30,
32, 71, 76, 84,
111, 136, 190,
242, 249
John, 71, 83, 132,
133, 154, 169,
172, 199, 222,
230, 231, 232
Mary, 7, 11
Nathan, 7, 11, 14,
69, 71, 95, 148
Ruth, 7, 76
Spencer, 48, 97, 99,
100
Stephen, 71, 83,
163, 244
Susan, 169
Susanna, 232
Susannah, 199, 222
William, 167
BALLMER
Barbara, 25
Michael, 1, 25
BALTZELL
Jacob, 168
William, 168
BANTZ
Henry, 228
Valentine, 190
BARNARD
Peter, 189
BARNERD
A., 64
BARNS
Elizabeth, 8
Frances, 8
BARR

Adam, 99, 137, 143,
169, 240, 249
George, 99, 143,
169, 227, 249
Hugh, 99, 143
John, 143
Mary, 249
Pretious, 249
Sarah, 143
Thomas, 143
William, 99, 143
BARRACK
John, 214
BARRACROFT
Betey, 247
BARRET
John, 106
BARTHOLOMEW
Jacob, 175
BARTON
Benjamin, 19, 21,
25, 146, 155, 236
Thomas, 172
BATEMAN
Thomas, 160
BATES
Ann, 111, 137
Catharine, 111
Jesse, 65
Joseph, 111
Susanna, 111
BATSON
Hannah, 148
James, 22, 85, 134,
148
John, 134, 239
BATTERLAND, 235
BATTSON
James, 33, 70, 99,
101, 134, 149,
186, 205, 242,
253
John, 101, 149, 199,
206
BAUGH
Jacob, 13, 52, 54,
83, 94, 120, 131,

145, 148, 165,
185, 197, 201,
208, 213, 215,
216, 219, 252
Mary, 83, 145, 185,
197, 213, 215,
219
BAXTER
Jacob, 187, 218
Lydda, 187
Lydia, 218
BAXTOR
Lydda, 196
BAYER
John, 1
BAYLER
G. Wythe, 27
BAYLES
Benjamin, 92
BAYLEY
George, 134, 137
John, 134, 137, 197
Mary, 8
Mary L., 253
Pierce, 8, 148
Robert, 134
Sydnor, 239
William P., 100, 134,
137, 253
BAYLY
Eleanor, 200
Elizabeth, 200
George, 148
John, 96, 148, 156,
163, 167, 173,
224
Joseph, 200
Lewis M., 217
Mary L., 149, 205,
206, 239
Montjoy, 200
Peirce, 46
Pierce, 137, 158,
160
Susanna, 160
William M., 184

William P., 96, 148,
149, 160, 205,
206, 239
Z., 56
BEACH
Alexander, 109, 130
BEAL
Joseph, 103, 108,
118, 126, 139
Philip, 136
Phillip, 110
Rebeccah, 138
Rebekah, 110
Samuel, 110, 136,
138, 139, 157,
239
Thomas, 110, 138
BEALE
Ann, 160
Thomas, 120, 160
BEALL
David F., 176
George, 217
Richard, 103
Thomas B., 12, 79,
163, 213
BEALLE
Samuel, 193
BEANS
Amos, 127, 153,
157, 177, 181,
187
Hannah, 38, 118
James, 23, 36
Joseph, 214
Mathew, 246, 252
Ruth, 31, 36
William, 31, 38, 109,
118, 196, 209
BEARD
Joseph, 50, 69, 73,
77, 79, 95, 114,
127, 128, 132,
146, 147, 148,
151, 156, 162,
165, 184, 189,
221, 239

Stephen, 102, 171,
189, 207
Steven, 231
BEATTY
David, 29, 118
Silas, 218
Thomas, 52
BEATY
David, 48
Elizabeth, 134, 137,
156
John, 192
Mary, 192
Silas, 70
William, 151
BEAVERLY
Carter, 225
Jane, 225
Peter R., 225
BEAVERS
John, 223
Robert, 9
Samuel, 9
BECKLEY
Jacob, 125
BECKLY
Jacob, 131
BECKWITH
Lewis, 63
Marmeduke, 152
BEESON
Henry, 122
Mary, 122
BELL
Charles, 48, 62, 187,
196
David, 251
Elizabeth, 137, 196
John D., 179
Julia, 137
Michael, 137, 215,
227, 233
Peter, 25
Will, 88
William, 88, 90, 137
BELLE
Joseph, 238

BELT
Middleton, 105, 138,
210
Nancy, 29
Peter, 160
W. S., 211
Walter S., 96, 138
William S., 29, 77,
105, 138
BELTS
Frederick, 56, 131
Peter, 33, 50
BELTZ
Frederick, 29, 38
Peter, 33
BENNET
Henry A., 197
BENNETT
Charles, 11, 15, 17,
18, 24, 27, 40, 54,
69, 79, 87, 95,
102, 105, 117,
119, 125, 134,
160, 163, 164,
176, 177, 182,
183, 184, 190,
192, 197, 203,
212, 215, 217,
231, 237, 238,
247, 251, 252
Henry A., 71, 94
Stout, 9
BENNON
Jacob, 107
BENTLEY
Catharine, 121, 160,
190
John, 161
Joseph, 14, 61, 121,
128, 132, 160,
190
Lydia, 161
BENTLY
Caleb, 21
Joseph, 86, 214
BERKELEY
John L., 7, 8

John, 121
BOUSALL
John, 53
BOWEN
Alexander, 189
Stephen, 189
BOWERSET
John, 130
BOWERSETT
John, 159, 163
BOYD
Elizabeth, 88, 90,
   203
James, 88, 90, 209
Jane, 88, 201
John, 63, 88, 90,
   116, 128, 216,
   228, 231
John W., 88
Nancy, 88
Polly, 88
Samuel, 51
Sinah, 88
Thomas, 88, 90, 201
William, 88, 90
BOYDE
Elizabeth, 218
BOYLE
David, 218
BOYLES
James, 170
BRADEN
John, 213, 244
Joseph, 120, 131,
   137, 154, 164,
   180, 244, 246,
   252
R., 44, 106, 110,
   125, 140, 157,
   163, 164, 169,
   180, 195, 212,
   213, 219, 228,
   232, 234, 246,
   251, 252, 253
Robert, 37, 39, 40,
   71, 87, 91, 92, 94,
   95, 103, 119, 120,

121, 125, 131,
134, 157, 160,
164, 167, 169,
178, 181, 182,
187, 197, 203,
207, 210, 211,
212, 213, 235,
238, 244, 246,
250, 251, 252,
253, 254
BRADFIELD
Benjamin, 21, 25,
   29, 121, 153, 154,
   155, 165, 170,
   176, 210
Benjamine, 26
James, 4, 25, 29,
   69, 71, 77, 111,
   149, 153, 155,
   159, 165, 251
Jonathan, 26, 240,
   241
Rachel, 21, 121
Ruth, 4, 69, 153,
   155, 165, 251
BRADFORD
James, 123
BRADLEE
Newton, 10
BRADSHAW
James H., 171
BRAGG
John, 136
BRAIDY
John, 250
BRAND
Phebe, 47
Thomas, 47
BRANDEN
Joseph, 131
BRANNAM
William, 204
BRANTOP
William, 14
BRASHEARS
B., 170
Charles, 189

James, 26
Rachel, 189
BRAUFF
Jacob, 82
Rebeckah, 82
BRAWNER
Henry, 64, 100, 114,
   115
BRENOR
Barbara, 36
George, 36
BRENT
Charles, 22
Daniel, 152
George, 96
Martin, 55, 64, 66,
   68, 70, 83, 85,
   158
Mary, 96
Robert, 197
Thomas, 49, 55, 64
Urn., 205, 206
BRETT
Margarett, 23
Ret, 23
BRICKEY
William, 48
BRISCOE
Aquila, 134
BRONAUGH
Jane, 230
Jeremiah W., 65
William, 11, 21, 28,
   32, 33, 39, 63, 65,
   70, 83, 92, 94,
   102, 106, 110,
   115, 119, 124,
   129, 131, 132,
   137, 139, 141,
   145, 154, 155,
   161, 165, 167,
   174, 175, 185,
   186, 191, 193,
   195, 196, 199,
   206, 208, 209,
   211, 214, 220,
   223, 224, 230,

233, 237, 242,
243, 246, 249
BROOK
Samuel, 197, 221
BROOKE
Edmond, 11
John T., 58, 107,
123, 130, 132,
244
R., 107
Samuel, 182
Thomas A., 82
BROWN
Andrew, 1, 76
Daniel, 73, 174, 189,
201, 240, 246
Dawson, 51, 64
Esther, 72
Fielden, 34
George, 18, 28, 31,
113, 149, 167,
184, 195, 199,
232, 242
Gustavus R., 115,
135
Henry, 58, 72, 186,
202, 223, 225,
237, 241
Isaac, 51, 64, 99,
153, 199, 226,
232
Issachar, 191
Issacher, 251
Jacob, 26, 111, 115,
153
James, 47, 117,
118, 227, 233
Jane, 1
John, 11, 30, 33, 72,
80, 91, 106, 126,
156, 176, 191,
194, 199, 215,
216, 222, 226,
227, 229, 232,
242
John D., 145
Joseph, 51, 208

Margaret, 115, 135
Mary, 31, 242
Mercer, 19, 31, 117
Moses, 254
Nathan, 227
Rachel, 201
Richard, 44, 45, 93,
106, 111, 113,
115, 127, 157,
162, 175, 177,
190, 229
Sarah, 199
William, 71, 72, 77,
85, 101, 122, 156,
169, 215, 241,
243, 250
William J., 77, 85,
122
BROWNING
M., 131
BRUMERETCH
William, 216
BRUSTER
Mary, 126
BRYSON
Robert, 195
BUCHANAN
John, 209, 228
BUCK
Marcus, 148
Samuel, 148
BUCKHART
Peter, 205
BUCKHILL
Elizabeth, 41
BUCKLY
James, 182
BUCKNER
Aris, 64
Ariss, 18, 40, 44, 59,
75, 99, 110, 170,
184, 189
Arris, 59
BUCKY
John, 46
BURCHETT
John, 118, 189

Nancy, 118, 189
BURGEE
Thomas, 131
BURGESS
John, 143
BURGETT
William, 105
BURGOYNE
Joseph, 149
BURK
John, 156
William, 39, 190
BURKETT
Elizabeth, 30
Henry, 30
BURKHART
Peter, 231
BURKLEY
John L., 39
BURNHOUSE
Christopher, 112
BURROUGHS
Joseph, 101
BURRUS
Joseph, 36, 179
BURSON
Aaron, 68, 245
Benjamin, 15, 68,
119, 156, 222
Catherine, 156
George, 192, 222,
253
James, 68, 153, 156
Jehu, 129, 193, 199
John, 68, 156, 227
Jonathan, 68, 156,
243
Joseph, 15, 25, 46,
68, 69, 119, 136,
159, 195, 199,
222, 229
Rebekah, 68
Silas, 222
BUSSELL
Sarah, 190
BUTCHER
John, 138, 172

Samuel, 16, 18
Susannah, 114, 172
BUTLER
Nathaniel, 99, 100
BYOTT
John, 76
BYRN
Daniel, 119
Darby B., 208
BYRNE
Jeremiah, 175
BYRNEHOUSE
John, 160
BYRNES
Ignatious, 28
Jeremiah, 160
Philip, 154, 159, 160
BYRNS
Ignatious, 57

C

CAIN
Mary, 190
CALDWELL
Hugh, 22, 198
Moses, 150, 167
Robert, 22
Sarah, 22
William, 22
CALHOUN
James, 109
CAMBLING
Catharine, 247
William, 247
CAMEL
William, 72
CAMHELLE
John, 48
CAMMELL
Mary, 250
William, 250
CAMPBEL
Jane, 203
CAMPBELL
Andrew, 12, 202, 203
D., 14

James, 7, 90, 95, 154, 182, 250
Jane, 12, 203
John, 9, 15, 16, 75, 83, 90, 105, 168, 233, 238, 240, 250, 254
Mary, 154
Robert, 96
Ruth, 250
Sarah, 9, 75
William, 250
CAMPBELL
Andrew, 203
CANBY
B. H., 156
Benjamin, 19, 182
Benjamin H., 11, 16, 19, 21, 34, 65, 67, 75, 76, 80, 107, 114, 117, 123, 128, 136, 144, 146, 151, 156, 165, 183, 185, 189, 190, 193, 194, 195, 232
Benjamin T., 122
Jno. H., 105
John H., 15, 35, 36, 37, 38, 48, 52, 62, 90, 93, 94, 99, 112, 113, 122, 126, 127, 136, 142, 147, 163, 164, 165, 171, 173, 178, 182, 193, 195, 197, 216
Sarah, 128, 144, 151, 156, 182, 232
CANLEY
Joseph, 118
CANON
Elizabeth, 86
CAREY
Samuel, 37

CARGILE
James, 41
CARGYLL
John, 22
CARLILE
John, 34
CARLYLE
John, 150
CARMICHAEL
Daniel, 77
CARNAHAM
Adam, 38
CARNEY
John, 213
CARNSWORTH
Henry, 24
CARPENTER
John, 242, 249
CARR
Delia, 155, 209
James, 80
John, 34, 146, 147, 158, 159, 190, 198, 208, 215, 219, 220, 222, 225
Joseph, 16, 18, 62, 72, 115, 155, 164, 170, 183, 184, 194, 196, 198, 199, 209, 213, 216, 220, 224, 226, 228, 235, 239
Margaret, 199
Mary, 158
Peggy, 208
Peter, 7, 34, 61, 77, 92, 158, 232
Samuel, 5, 13, 30, 39, 52, 83, 93, 103, 127, 133, 142, 145, 152, 158, 165, 188, 198, 214, 225, 226, 227, 235

Thomas, 2, 16, 78,
143, 152, 225
William, 2, 5, 25, 27,
79, 98, 102, 109,
129, 155, 175,
179, 199, 208,
219, 226, 232
CARRINGTON
Timothy, 252
CARRUTHERS
James, 44, 147, 165
CARSON
John, 127
CARTER
Bernard, 94
Charles, 1, 211
Collin, 114
Edward, 122, 226
G., 253
George, 2, 30, 54,
75, 78, 95, 99,
100, 104, 107,
108, 116, 120,
129, 133, 136,
138, 140, 142,
143, 144, 147,
166, 172, 231,
235, 246
Henry, 124
James, 139, 145,
236, 242
Jesse, 90
John, 24, 41, 113,
130, 140, 143,
157, 189
John C., 4
John T., 48, 95, 99,
100, 129, 136,
254
Jonathan, 16, 185,
224, 244, 245
Jonathan M., 156
Jonathan N., 156
Jonathan W., 153
Landon, 75, 107,
108, 116, 117,
120, 136, 138,

140, 142, 143,
144, 147, 166,
172
Margaret, 119
Morriss, 41
Richard, 185, 245
Robert, 1, 9, 45, 54,
99, 140, 182
W., 4
William, 55, 90, 114,
119, 177, 242,
243
William F., 163
CARUTHERS
James, 148, 223
CARY
Mary R., 141
CASEY
Daniel, 167
James, 167
John, 211, 213
CASTLE
George, 47
CASTLEMAN
William, 31, 228
CATON
Thomas, 178
CAUDY
James, 252
CAUSEY
William, 54
CAVAN
James, 2, 6, 25, 33,
38, 43, 52, 53, 54,
62, 73, 76, 77, 79,
80, 83, 84, 86, 96,
105, 110, 112,
113, 121, 128,
135, 142, 145,
147, 152, 158,
160, 163, 164,
166, 169, 174,
175, 179, 192,
193, 194, 195,
199, 201, 204,
210, 213, 214,

215, 221, 227,
236, 254
John, 2, 4, 11, 33,
38, 52, 53, 67, 75,
76, 77, 84, 107,
108, 110, 144,
145, 147, 165,
175, 178, 192,
194, 221, 232
Patrick, 2, 4, 6, 8, 9,
11, 12, 15, 19, 22,
25, 29, 32, 33, 44,
46, 47, 52, 53, 55,
56, 62, 65, 72, 76,
77, 79, 80, 84, 89,
112, 113, 135,
142, 159, 175,
195
Sarah, 2, 4, 8, 9, 25,
33, 76, 91, 120,
121, 247
CAVANS
James, 131, 133
John, 13, 119, 226
Patrick, 112
CAVINS
John, 13
CAYLOR
Jacob, 145
CHALFINT
Charles, 1
Robert, 1
CHAMBERLIN
Elijah, 38
CHAMBERS
Ann, 239, 243
Anne, 231
James, 210, 243
William, 72, 230,
231, 239, 243
CHAMBLIN
Charles, 11, 133,
149, 199, 233
Ezekiel, 109, 132
John, 121
William, 100, 121
CHAMBLING

John, 7, 49, 94
COLWELL
  Hugh, 41
  Moses, 30, 46, 113
  Sarah, 41
  William, 41
COMBS
  Andrew, 9
  Ann, 9
  Israel, 9, 193
  Isreal, 198
  Jane, 9
  John, 9
  Joseph, 35
  Mahlon, 9, 101, 122,
    220, 251
  Mary, 9
  Sarah, 9, 101, 122,
    220, 251
COMEGYS
  Benjamin, 109
COMPHER
  John, 30, 63
  Peter, 60, 74, 76,
    216, 233
COMTZ
  Mahlon, 213
CONARD
  Anthony, 13, 189
  Edward, 139
  John, 60, 61, 139,
    140, 141, 142,
    249, 250
  Mary, 189
  Nathan, 131, 253
CONER
  Richard, 93
CONLIN
  David, 114
CONN
  Hugh, 126
CONNARD
  Anthony, 13, 170,
    244
  John, 215
  Mary, 244
CONNELLY

Frances, 10
  John, 10
  Mary, 10
  Sandford, 10, 220
CONNER
  Charles, 3, 144
  David, 198
  Edward, 57
  Martha, 198
  Richard, 119, 246
  Samuel, 3
  Thomas, 121, 139
CONNOR
  Richard, 53
CONRAD
  Edward, 23
  Judith, 23
CONROD
  John, 59
COOE
  William, 230
COOK
  Henry, 77
  John, 77
  John E., 72
  S., 114
  Samuel, 192
  Stephen, 55, 79,
    120, 140
COOKE
  Catharine, 184, 236
  Henry S., 115, 198,
    210
  John E., 38, 147
  John R., 183, 184,
    236
  John W., 97
  Stephen, 114, 117,
    128, 143, 160,
    162, 169, 182,
    183, 184, 187,
    197, 235, 236
  William, 46, 105,
    121, 165, 234,
    244
COOMS
  Joseph, 65

COOPER
  Alexander, 52, 72,
    90
  Catherine, 234
  Frederick, 95, 190
  George, 66, 152,
    159, 233, 234,
    244
  Henry, 192
  Jacob, 129, 197
  John, 42, 214, 227,
    240
  Margaret, 52
  Michael, 60, 67, 69,
    77, 141, 197, 234,
    235, 244
  Peter, 234, 235
  Philip, 177, 212
  Phillip, 212
  Robert, 9
  Thomas, 42
COPELAND
  Andrew, 11, 94, 97,
    98, 99, 103, 105,
    126, 139, 234
  Elizabeth, 239
  James, 154, 156,
    160, 239, 243,
    248
  Richard, 23, 58, 239,
    252
  William, 10, 13, 203,
    211
CORCORAN
  Thomas, 114
CORDEL
  Martin, 222
CORDELL
  Adam, 210
  Amelia, 122
  Cordell, 110
  G. E., 214
  Martin, 70, 77, 84,
    86, 95, 96, 122,
    136, 173, 214
  P., 214

Thomas, 21
DAVIS
Abel, 19, 20, 104,
178
Abraham, 2, 3, 7
Abram, 251
Allen, 9
Amos, 1, 7
Catharine, 20, 143,
166, 173
Daniel, 95, 201
David, 6, 10, 27, 157
David W., 204
Edward, 72, 214
Elizabeth, 242
Evan, 43
Gideon, 19, 104,
178, 179, 237
Hannah, 2, 3
Henry M., 68, 84,
106, 114, 122,
123, 132, 143,
151, 152, 166,
173, 210
Hervey M., 117
Howell, 216, 244
Jacob, 95
James, 7, 218
Jane, 152
Jane R., 106, 143
John, 10, 11, 43, 64,
98, 107, 136, 144,
196, 214, 222,
242
Joseph, 8
Leah, 18
Margaret, 107
Mary, 191
Morris, 98, 99
Nancy, 179, 237
Nathan, 50
Pamela, 157
Parnella, 6, 27
Rebecca, 107
Samuel, 134
Solomon, 95, 159,
191

Thomas, 16, 18, 36,
45, 89, 95, 107,
144, 160, 192,
201, 214, 222
Vincent, 7, 231
William, 190
DAVISON
Nancy, 191
William, 205
DAVISSON
N., 153, 154, 155,
159, 165, 182
Nathaniel, 159
DAWES
Edward, 194, 210
DAWSON
James, 15, 89, 136,
174, 175, 194,
205, 212, 216
Polley, 216
Polly, 175, 194
W., 9
DAYLY
John, 87
DAYMUD
Jacob, 180
John, 230
DEA
George, 17
DEALEHUNT
John, 70
DEBELL
William, 21
DECK
Elisha C., 53
DEHAVEN
Betsy, 103
Hannah, 103
Jacob, 25, 26, 45,
48, 103, 187, 218
Mary, 103
Nancy, 48, 103, 187,
196, 218
Sally, 103
DELA TRIPELLIERE
George, 238
DELANY

Maurice, 123
DEMERY
John, 160, 170
Peter, 82, 139, 140,
249
DEMORY
John, 139, 140, 249
Peter, 249, 250
DENEAL
W., 94
DENEALE
G., 5
Sybel, 238
William, 5, 238
DENHAM
Amos, 29, 170, 189
DENNEY
Edmond, 183
Edmund, 45
Elizabeth, 45
DENNIS
Thomas, 242
Thomas A., 228, 247
DENNY
Edmond, 4, 20, 200
Edmund, 4, 54, 142,
157
Edward, 145, 147
Elizabeth, 145
James, 174
DENT
Thomas, 12, 17, 65
DERAM
Lee, 77
DERREY
Paulser, 139
DERRY
Balser, 195
Peter, 69, 74, 92
Philip, 26
Philip D., 215
Polser, 76
DEVER
Bazil, 218
DEVREUX
John, 138
DEWELL

Catharine, 248
D., 77, 112, 207
Daniel, 45, 52, 72,
  96, 98, 110, 116,
  132, 152, 167,
  173, 190, 205,
  207, 214, 248
Edward, 249, 250
Kitty, 110, 116, 132
DOWNES
Benjamin B., 28
DOWNS
Benjamin, 92
George, 155
John, 162
DOZIER
Allen S., 109
Nelson R., 109
DRADEN
George, 68
DRAIN
Ann, 253
John, 253
DRAKE
Benjamin, 135
Jacob, 236, 237
Robert, 237
Thomas, 135, 139,
  145, 155, 236
Uree, 236
DRANE
John, 94
DREAN
John, 10, 19, 28, 46,
  54, 55, 61, 79
Nancy, 28
DRISH
Charles, 10, 11, 20,
  53, 60, 61, 122,
  143, 152, 179,
  188, 214
Eleanor, 34, 84, 128,
  173, 222, 238
Elenor, 132, 147
Elioner, 27
Frederick, 60

John, 19, 27, 34, 35,
  45, 61, 62, 70, 79,
  80, 84, 86, 96,
  110, 128, 132,
  143, 146, 147,
  166, 173, 207,
  214, 219, 222,
  230, 233, 238
Nelly, 70, 79, 84, 86
Susanna, 10, 11, 60,
  122
Susannah, 143
William, 33, 143,
  198, 214, 220,
  238
DUEL
Benjamin, 79
DULANY
Maurice, 129, 160
DULICK
George, 237
Sally, 237
DULIN
Anne, 16
Charles, 16
Dulin, 164
Edward, 138
John, 6, 199, 247,
  252
Rebecca, 252
William, 14, 61, 62,
  81, 86, 138, 171,
  187, 196, 218,
  236, 244
DULING
Thadius, 59
DUNCAN
Henry, 224
James, 245
John, 245
Mason, 223
DUNHAM
French, 25
DUNKIN
Charles, 37
Joshua, 82

Samuel, 64, 99, 156,
  220
DUNLAP
John, 26
DUNN
Margaret, 123, 160
DUNNE
Margarett, 129
DURFLINGER
Henry, 140
DURHAM
John, 23
Lee, 45
DURSHEMER
Jacob, 210
DURSHTIMER
Elizabeth, 210
DUTTON
James, 126
DUTY
Daniel, 123, 165,
  192, 209
Thomas, 192
William J., 192
DYER
John, 53
Ruth, 68
DYKE
George, 68, 128
DYKES
Ann, 152
Mungo, 91, 94, 106,
  134, 152

E

EACHER
Daniel, 44
EACHES
Daniel, 16, 44, 73,
  146, 189, 194,
  199, 202, 203,
  206, 208, 220,
  221, 245, 253
Joseph, 220
Margaret, 221
Mary, 202
EAN

230, 237, 238,
246, 247, 253
ELLZY
William, 123
ELZEY
Lewis, 169, 245
EMERY
Catharine, 159, 195
Daniel, 242
Jacob, 45, 144, 152,
155, 171, 195
EMREY
Catharine, 195
Christiana, 195
Daniel, 98
George, 46, 61, 113
Jacob, 4
Margaret, 46, 61
Yenaith, 98
EMRY
Jacob, 66
ENERS
Richard, 59
ENGLEBUCHT
John, 27
Mary, 27
ENGLISH
David, 78, 96, 112,
128
John, 4
EPISCOPAL CHURCH
METHODIST, 211
ERSKINE
John, 180
ERSKINS
John, 81
ESKRIDGE
Burdet, 191
Charles, 40, 109
Charles G., 214
Samuel, 223
William, 109, 200,
209, 253
ETON
Stephen, 251
EUSTACE

Hancock, 205, 206,
254
EUSTAU
Hancock, 101
EVANS
David, 20, 22, 67
Eleazer, 56
Eleazor, 31
Eliazor, 29
Elizabeth, 22
Evan, 127, 154, 243
Griffith, 22
Hannah, 22
Isaac, 160
Jesse, 240
Jessey, 127
John, 5, 6, 22, 28,
30, 31, 53, 56, 67,
69, 79, 99, 121,
126, 153, 205
John H., 131, 142,
146, 147, 151,
152, 158, 165,
168, 171, 174,
184, 192, 194,
199, 227, 234
John W., 214
Josiah, 154
Martha, 121
Mary, 22, 29, 56
Rhoda, 63, 193
Samuel, 1, 58, 59,
94, 100, 127, 128,
176
Sarah, 22
Thomas, 126, 193
William, 97, 99, 121,
153, 154, 254
EVELAND
David, 162
Jacob, 181
EVELANE
David, 59
EVENS
William, 254
EVERHARD
Michael, 61, 157

EVERHART
Christian, 74
Daniel, 33
Jacob, 45
Michael, 74, 139,
233, 243, 254
Philip, 33, 38, 66,
172, 212, 233,
234
Solomon, 254
William, 254
EVERHEART
Christian, 69, 119,
234
Jacob, 209, 218
Michael, 69, 193,
233, 234
Philip, 119, 183,
195, 233, 254
EVERITT
Joseph, 80
EVERLY
Jacob, 36
Molly, 36
EVINS
John, 77
EWELL
Bertand, 119
Bertrand, 152, 167,
168, 184
Kitty, 152
EWERS
Barton, 81
Jonathan, 81
Thomas, 81, 165

F

FADELEY
Jacob, 19, 194, 236
FADELY
Jacob, 43, 77, 85
FADLEY
Jacob, 213
FAIDLEY
Jacob, 35
FAIRFAX
Ann, 39

George, 246
FLOWERS
Thomas, 89, 237
FLOYD
Enoch, 77
FLYNN
Michael, 233
FOLAY
George, 70
FORBES
John, 189
FORD
Valentine, 181
FORTENEY
Jacob, 150
FORTNEY
George, 77, 98, 132
Jacob, 132, 137
Susannah, 98, 132
FOSTER
Jonathan, 144
Mary, 67
FOUCH
Daniel, 43, 157
George, 43
Isaac, 43, 51, 148
Jonathan, 18, 22,
43, 51, 214, 226
Mary, 43
Nancy, 148, 157
Sarah, 43, 157
Susanna, 43
Thomas, 32, 36, 43,
51, 75, 85, 90, 99,
100, 136, 141,
157, 175, 179,
203, 210, 219,
236, 248
Thomson, 203
William, 157, 203
FOUCHE
Thomas, 95
FOUNDLING
John, 125
FOWKE
Elizabeth, 99
J. F., 224

S. Dorathy, 125
William, 19, 21, 82,
99, 135, 139, 146
FOWLER
William, 7
FOWLEY
John, 98
FOWLY
John, 98
FOX
A., 8
Amos, 8, 186, 224
Ann H., 102, 248
Daniel, 220
Elizabeth, 102, 248
George K., 102, 248
Hannah, 50
James, 10, 50, 102,
224, 248
Jane, 102, 248
Jesse, 186
Jonas, 220
Joseph, 26, 105,
224
Martenea B., 102
Martenet B., 248
Mary, 186
Rebecca, 248
Rebekah, 102
Uriah, 215
William, 8, 87, 125
FRANCIS
Enoch, 70, 71, 147,
178, 205, 219,
236, 237, 247,
248, 250
Mary, 10, 32, 82, 87
Nanch, 236
Nancy, 70, 178, 247
Nicholas, 52
Thomas, 10, 32, 72,
82, 87, 110, 114,
115, 121, 131,
145, 147, 158,
167
William, 91
FRANTZ

Nicholas, 1
FRAZIER
James, 64
FRED
Elizabeth, 158
Francis, 48
Joseph, 91, 135,
158
Joshua, 115, 131,
158, 224
Thomas, 48, 115,
131, 135, 158
FREDD
Joseph, 48
Joshua, 48
Sarah, 48
FREEMAN
Ann, 193
Richard, 82, 124
FRENCH
George, 115, 131
Mason, 111, 185
FRITCHIE
John, 231
FRY
Henry J., 37, 45, 70,
74, 135, 216
Isaac, 245
Jacob, 11
John, 2, 6, 143
Mary, 159
Nicholas, 172, 173
Peter, 98, 119
Philip, 104
Phillip, 134
FRYAR
Abigah, 23
FRYE
Henry, 66
Henry J., 91, 177
John, 196
Joseph, 246
Peter, 92
Philip, 159
FULKERSON
Philip, 184
FULTON

David, 99, 155
George, 83, 95, 98
John, 180
Mahlon, 99, 166
Robert, 94, 122, 220
FURR
Enoch, 82, 91, 158,
224
Minor, 72, 158, 206,
207, 210, 211
William, 158

G

GALLAHER
David, 220
William, 220
GALLIHER
Samuel N., 169
William, 51, 203
GALLOWAY
Thomas, 95
GAMBLE
Joseph, 250
GANT
John M., 115
GANTE
Edward, 49
GANTT
Daniel, 22
Stoughton, 214
GARDENER
James, 128
GARDINER
James, 168
GARDNER
Andrew, 198
James, 183, 221
Joseph, 40, 67, 188
GARETT
James M., 253
GARISON
Nehemiah, 180
GARLAND
David S., 179
GARNER
Andrew, 211, 225
Arthur, 211

Daniel, 136
James, 62, 77, 79,
142, 144, 173,
193, 207, 214,
236, 254
Jarvett, 245
John, 11
Lewis, 37
Margaret, 254
Rebekah, 11
Willis, 129
GARNETT
James M., 58, 123,
130, 132, 244
GARRET
Elenor, 134
Eneas, 134
Enos, 134
John, 35
Joseph, 251
Nicholas, 73
Thomas, 48
GARRETT
Abel, 13, 31, 47, 62,
189, 202
Abigal, 213
Able, 26
Anna, 31
Benjamin, 13, 189,
202
Benjamine, 26
Edward, 26, 92
Elenor, 121, 157,
187
Enas, 97
Eneas, 93
Enos, 91, 94, 121,
134, 139, 154,
157, 187
Henry, 31
John, 31, 47
Joseph, 26, 31, 35,
48, 101, 105, 212,
234, 237
Mary, 13
Nancy, 62

Nicholas, 131, 136,
166, 185
Patty, 131
Samuel, 213
Silas, 13, 31, 189
Stephen, 234
Thomas, 13, 26, 31,
189, 202
GARROT
William, 40
GARROTT
Aaron, 157
Elenor, 177, 181
Enos, 157, 177, 181
GEE
David, 70
William, 37, 67
GEEN
Thomas, 31
GEORG
John, 45, 50, 186
GEORGE, 138
Evan, 21
John, 12, 29, 32, 37,
74, 92, 93, 94,
163, 207, 226,
239
Traverse, 31, 37,
100
William, 31, 36, 37,
86, 100, 143, 159,
244
GHANT
Daniel, 90
Lucy, 90
GHEEN
Margaret, 47
Thomas, 26, 35, 47,
48, 237
GIBB
James L., 220
GIBBS
Charles, 145
James L., 166
John H., 11, 37
William, 124, 175
GIBSON

GOVER
  Jesse, 238, 254
  Samuel, 78, 164,
    215
GRADY
  Edward, 79
  Edward B., 12
  James, 12, 33, 57,
    79, 137, 146, 176,
    181
  Jane, 79
  Susannah, 79
  Ury, 79
GRAHAM
  Catesby, 22, 115,
    135, 167, 180
  Elizabeth, 135
  George, 104, 123
  Jane, 22, 104, 135,
    180
  Jean, 115
  John, 104
  Richard, 104
  Sally, 163
  Walter, 163
  William, 115
GRANT
  Aaron, 150
  William, 155
GRASON
  Benjamin, 63
GRAY
  Daniel, 203, 214,
    254
  F. S., 248, 252, 254
  French S., 231, 247
  G., 201
  James, 225
  Mary, 203
  William, 79
GRAYHAM
  William, 135
GRAYSON
  Anne, 16
  Benjamin, 16, 19,
    21, 42, 50, 65, 82,
    83, 91, 102, 110,

    115, 119, 124,
    131, 135, 139,
    141, 145, 150,
    155, 164, 170,
    172, 175, 184,
    186, 191, 193,
    194, 200, 210,
    211, 213, 220,
    222, 223, 224,
    226, 230, 235,
    237, 242, 243
  George M., 224
  John W. B., 224
  Nancy, 124, 139,
    224
  Sarah, 16
  Susanna, 16
  William, 119, 200,
    223
GRAYSON
  Benjamin, 191
GREEN
  Charles, 235
  Elisha, 52
  Elizabeth, 43, 150
  Hannah, 52
  James, 131
  John, 31, 50, 222
  John W., 124
  Joseph, 195
GREENE
  Cloe, 110
GREENFIELD
  Mary, 3
GREENLEASE
  James, 149, 188,
    225, 250
GREENUP
  Christopher, 16, 74,
    75
GREETHAM
  William, 138
GREGG
  Caleb, 120, 149
  Dinah, 165
  Elisha, 168
  Esther, 82

  George, 168
  Hannah, 149, 162,
    164, 165
  Jacob, 59
  John, 65, 113, 116,
    239, 244
  Joseph, 11, 81, 165
  Joshua, 11
  Josiah, 165
  Levy, 165
  Mahlon, 121, 149,
    242
  Margaret, 165
  Martha, 168
  Mary, 59, 81, 165,
    223
  Nathan, 47
  Ruth, 109, 158
  Samuel, 8, 19, 47,
    55, 82, 93, 112,
    161, 162, 165,
    178, 219, 253
  Sarah, 165, 181
  Stephen, 47
  Thomas, 8, 28, 33,
    47, 51, 59, 62, 64,
    82, 85, 108, 117,
    118, 124, 154,
    156, 164, 165,
    171, 176, 181,
    195, 196, 208,
    216, 217, 228,
    229, 234, 237,
    238, 241, 245,
    246, 250
  William, 42, 63, 93,
    126, 180
GRIFFETH
  Richard, 65
GRIFFITH
  Elizabeth, 241
  Evan, 78
  Isaac, 69, 144, 159
  James, 34
  Joseph, 117, 241
  Nancy, 139

John, 228
JEFFERSON
John, 193
Thomas, 167
JENINGS
Edmond, 187, 232
Edmund, 131, 207
JENKENS
Henry, 75, 166
JENKINGS
Jacob, 252
JENKINS
Ansey, 218
Benjamin, 57, 58
Elizabeth, 218
Ellender, 218
Henry, 34, 75, 107, 108
Mary, 246
Philip, 62
Simon, 123
Solomon, 131, 137
Thomas, 246
Thomas F., 214, 216, 217, 220
Thomas H., 217
William, 18, 57, 58, 74, 240
JENNEIRS
Abiel, 204, 211
JENNERS
Abiel, 43, 45, 61, 70, 81, 82, 119, 125, 153, 178, 182, 188, 197, 233
Deborah, 82, 119, 153, 182
JENNEY
John, 49
JENNIERS
Abiel, 193, 195, 203
JENNINGS
Charles, 64
Edmond, 115
Edmund, 115, 120, 121
Seney, 121

JENNY
Stacy, 55
JETT
Peter, 23, 152
S., 77
JEURY
Alexander, 193
JEWELL
George, 22
Mary, 22
JOHN,
Thomas, 23
JOHNS
Richard Weaver, 13
JOHNSON
Amos, 206
Archibald, 83
Baker, 197
Casper, 84, 114
Charles, 56
Elizabeth, 231
George, 197
Henson, 250
James, 50, 87, 97, 197, 232
Jane, 50
Jemimah, 83
John, 50, 228
Joshua, 197
Noah, 106
Rachel, 106
Richard, 197
Roger, 197
Thomas, 168, 197, 232
Washington, 190, 231
Wilfred, 53
William, 247, 254
William T., 197
JOHNSTON
Amos, 176, 177
Archibald, 28, 37, 92, 93
Barton, 24
David, 155
George, 10, 53

Gideon, 248
Hugh, 10
James, 14
Jemima, 37
Jemimiah, 93
Jeremiah, 92
Jesse, 172
John, 41
Richard B., 104
Samuel, 133
Susannah, 172
Thomas, 154, 168
William, 181
Zophas, 199
JONES
Barbary, 216
Charles T., 43
Dennis G., 192, 206
Elizabeth, 248
Eve, 216
George, 216
Henry, 80, 151
Isaac, 210
Isaiah, 242
John, 248
Jonathan, 216
Joseph, 99, 121, 132, 173, 205
Mary, 187, 196, 218
Philip, 248
Richard, 21, 248
Sarah, 211, 216
Stephen, 24
Thomas, 6, 10, 58, 108, 248
Thomas T., 14, 19, 24, 27, 32, 36, 46, 52
Thomas W., 20
Wealthy, 216
William, 13, 56, 80, 96, 175, 187, 211, 216, 218, 237, 248
JURDAN
John, 202
JUREY

Rees, 111, 115
Rus, 36

K

KEARN
Jacob, 117
KEEN
Ann, 245
John, 245
Richard, 7, 18, 26, 187, 245
Sarah, 26
Thomas, 8, 63
KEENE
John, 48, 58, 101, 193, 209, 224
Keturah, 224
Thomas, 180
KEENZE
Henry, 131
KEEZEY
Henry, 125
KEIL
John, 24
KEITH
Beaulah, 120
James, 144
Vincent, 120, 226
KELLEY
Celia, 187
Edward, 218
KELLY
Moses, 21
KEMP
John, 88, 90
Nancy, 88, 90
KEMPER
John, 248
KEN
David C., 4
KENDALL
Adam, 212
KENDRICKS
John, 172
KENT
Isaac, 15, 226, 253
Jane, 129

John, 253
Milley, 253
Sarah, 253
Smith, 253
Thomas, 192, 253
KENTUCK, 228
KEPHART
Jacob, 209
John, 209
KEPHEART
Godfrey, 201, 209
Jacob, 201, 213, 215, 219
John, 201, 213, 215, 219
Kitty, 201, 213, 215, 219
Lenora, 201, 213, 215, 219
Thomas, 201, 213, 215, 219
KERRICK
Stephen, 109, 178, 179
Thomas, 40
Walter, 209
KEUNTS
Henry, 160
KEYES
Gersham, 122
KEYLOR
Jacob, 61, 145
KEYTH
John, 225
Sarah, 225
KIDWELL
Thomas, 175
KILE
John, 24, 129
Nicholas, 24, 208
KILGORE
George, 199, 211, 230, 231, 248
Martenna, 211
KILLGORE
George, 102
KIMBLER

John, 99
KINCHELOE
James, 171
KINCHELOW
Elizabeth, 66
James, 66
KINCHOLOE
James, 218
KING
Daniel, 18
Elizabeth, 8
Frances, 8
Mountjoy, 18
Nathan, 198
Orsburne, 24
Robert, 197
KIPHART
Godfrey, 2
John, 40, 252
KIPHEART
Godfrey, 5
John, 199, 248
KIRK
James, 20, 72, 89, 188, 233
Robert, 53
Robert W., 87, 89, 112, 137, 150, 188
Sarah, 87, 89, 112, 137, 150, 188
KIRKBRIDE
Mahlon, 29, 31
KIRKPATRICK
Thomas, 211
KITSMILLER
George, 89
Martin, 72, 89
KITZMILLER
Martin, 27, 72, 77, 98, 137, 194, 214
KLEIN
Lewis, 120
KLEINHOFF
John, 55, 57
KLINE
John N., 220

KNIGHT
  Benjamin, 164
KNOW
  Joseph, 95
KNOWLS
  Joshua, 183
KNOX
  Joseph, 19, 85, 174
KOONTS
  Adam, 143
KULM
  Henry, 205

L

LACEY
  Amos, 5
  David, 46, 77, 84,
    94, 95, 106, 112,
    113, 190, 214,
    216, 238, 252,
    254
  Elias, 33, 121, 126,
    130, 184, 254
  Israel, 8, 31, 40, 46,
    56, 59, 62, 63, 99,
    100, 105, 107,
    110, 121, 151,
    162, 170, 171,
    173, 184, 205,
    207, 208, 210
  Joseph, 5, 100, 209,
    239
  Meshech, 137
  Mesheck, 38, 84,
    101, 114, 137,
    145, 186, 199,
    225
  Meshek, 148, 167
  Meshock, 125
  Sally, 190
  Sarah, 94, 95, 106,
    214, 216, 252
  Thomas, 95, 164,
    223
LACKLAND
  J., 3
LACY

Alexander, 244
David, 23, 94, 252
Israel, 56, 75
Johnston, 151
Mesheck, 54, 114
Samuel, 83
LAFAVER
  Henry, 236
LAIDLER
  Catherine Ann, 125
  John, 125
LAIRD
  John, 244
LAMAR
  William, 26
LAMB
  Affe, 127
  Thomas, 127
LAMBAG
  A., 77
  Anthony, 71, 95
LAMYON
  Thomas, 5
LANE
  Benedict M., 72
  Daniel C., 12
  Hardage, 1, 3, 8, 24,
    82
  James, 52
  James B., 193, 224,
    247
  Joseph, 8, 24, 31,
    32, 38, 40, 41, 44,
    235
  Phil'o R., 119
  Sally, 52, 238
  Samuel, 131
  Sarah, 8, 52
  Susanna, 52
  W. W., 46
  Will, 52
  William, 8, 152, 238
LANG
  Thomas, 30, 65, 158
LANGLEY
  Alexander, 32, 194
  Walter, 249

LANGLY
  A., 132
LANHAM
  Aaron, 23
  Aquila, 108
  Caroline, 220
  Elizabeth, 23
  Mary Ann, 23
  Sethe, 23
  Walter, 23, 108, 220
  Zadok, 108
LARAWE
  Isaac, 218
LAREW
  Isaac, 35
LARIMER
  James, 104
LAROWE
  Isaac, 26, 30, 36,
    38, 45, 79, 92, 93,
    111, 142, 154,
    159, 161, 162,
    163, 165, 166,
    167, 168, 171,
    174, 176, 178,
    183, 185, 188,
    190, 192, 199,
    201, 202, 203,
    205, 207, 211,
    213, 215, 217,
    220, 221, 225,
    227, 231, 232,
    235, 237, 239,
    243, 248, 252,
    253
LARROW
  Isaac, 72, 103, 146
LARROWE
  Isaac, 2, 3, 12, 19,
    28, 42, 52, 68, 69,
    70, 71, 78, 100,
    103, 107, 138,
    139, 144, 161
  James, 24
LASLIE
  Thomas, 110
LAURENCE

86, 102, 110, 130,
132, 144, 151,
155, 163, 170,
171, 189, 200,
205, 207, 214,
236, 248
Charles., 7
Daniel, 15
David, 15
Elizabeth, 252
George, 5, 8, 11, 17,
37, 65, 75, 162
Hector P., 252
Isaac, 31, 110, 114
J. H., 8
Jacob, 114, 115,
131, 167
James, 7, 8, 15,
102, 110, 114,
131, 145, 152,
158, 207
John, 15, 100
Joseph, 7, 9, 25, 60,
62, 66, 67, 68, 69,
74, 76, 80, 85, 91,
92, 99, 100, 102,
107, 111, 114,
125, 132, 133,
135, 149, 151,
153, 157, 159,
161, 163, 175,
182, 186, 191,
195, 199, 200,
201, 205, 209,
210, 225, 233,
234, 235, 244
Joseph S., 205
Lewis, 206, 207
Lovey, 131
Nancy, 110
Samuel W., 7
Sarah, 145, 158
Stephen W., 37
Thomas, 3, 16, 24,
44, 92, 191, 213,
252
Vincent, 205

Vincent L., 102, 214,
218, 236
Violett, 75, 162
William, 75, 81
William Y., 7
LICKEY
Conrod, 4, 101
LIGGETT
George W., 74
LIGHTFOOT
Philip, 60
LILE
Samuel, 161
LILLY
Arminger, 136
Joseph, 160
Rebeckah, 136
LINDENBERGER
Frederick, 247
LINDSAY
John, 120
Susanah, 92
LINTON
J., 40
John, 7, 25, 96, 97,
231
LITTELL
Elias W., 124
LITTLE
Charles, 5, 6, 26
Charles C., 108
R. H., 121
Robert, 192
LITTLEJOHN
John, 2, 3, 4, 6, 9,
14, 19, 22, 27, 28,
30, 33, 34, 35, 38,
40, 41, 43, 46, 49,
52, 53, 54, 55, 56,
61, 62, 63, 65, 72,
75, 76, 79, 80, 85,
103, 107, 108,
114, 116, 119,
120, 122, 123,
128, 133, 135,
138, 140, 142,
143, 144, 148,

162, 163, 166,
167, 168, 170,
183, 185, 193,
194, 195, 197,
199, 201, 203,
206, 207, 210,
214, 218, 219,
224, 226, 227,
231, 232, 233,
238, 240, 246,
247, 251, 252
Monica, 19, 30, 53,
54, 128, 133, 144
Samuel, 194
W. M., 165
William, 39, 53, 54,
71, 91, 95, 96,
117, 120, 128,
136, 140, 144,
165, 168, 173,
174, 183, 221
William M., 220
LITTLER
Nathan, 137, 212
Rebecca, 212
LITTLETON
Francis, 62
John, 215
Margaret, 213, 219
Margart, 215
Solomon, 201, 213,
215, 219
LLOYD
Edward, 32
John, 192, 246
LOBB
Charles, 173
LODGE
Jacob, 67
Jonath, 93
Jonathan, 100, 147,
175
William, 7, 18, 28,
167, 239, 240
LOGAN
Alice, 209
John, 170, 209, 216

William F., 244
William M., 174
LUCUS
  Zachariah, 124
LUDWELL
  William, 250
LUKE
  Daniel, 192
  John, 37
LUKET
  Leven, 95
LUNGSTRASS
  Peter W., 161
LUNSFORD
  Swanson, 29
LUPTON
  David, 81
LUSBY
  Elizabeth, 41
  Josiah, 41
LYDER
  Louis, 240, 241
LYLE
  Robert, 82
LYNCH
  Charles, 158
LYNE
  James, 59, 220
  Mary, 163, 175, 224
  Robert, 163, 175
  Sandford, 175
  Sanford, 163, 253
  Thomas, 175, 220, 224
  Timothy, 175, 224
  William, 163, 175, 220, 224
LYNN
  Fielding, 208, 225
LYONS
  Anne, 1
  John, 1, 29, 63, 99, 136, 166, 172, 181

M

MACKEY

Robert, 141
MACKY
  Robert, 77
MACRAE
  John, 218
MADDEN
  John, 239
  Mary, 239
MAGAHA
  James, 160
MAGILL
  Archibald, 22, 222
MAHONY
  James, 43
MAHUGH
  Benjamin, 2
MAILEN
  David, 155
MAINES
  William, 112
MAINS
  Archibald, 22, 52, 85, 182, 224
  Ellzey, 89
  Mary, 75, 76, 224
  Washington, 182
  William, 5, 14, 75, 76, 77, 83, 87, 92, 116, 122, 128, 132, 144, 149, 162, 177, 180, 182, 199, 203, 224, 249
MAJOR
  Samuel, 24
MALIN
  Eli, 251
MALONE
  James, 213
MAN
  George, 36, 38
  Hannah, 36
MANKIN
  William, 199, 227, 249
MANN
  Barbara, 41

Bernard, 110, 166
G., 145
George, 41, 49, 87, 163, 190, 225
John, 225
William, 187, 200
MANNING
  Jacob H., 133
  Nathaniel, 214
MANSFIELD
  John, 70, 84, 96
  Mary, 96
MARBLE
  P. F., 109
  Peter F., 175, 192
MARCUS
  Samuel D., 232
MARGINNIS
  Edward, 254
MARKES
  John, 241
MARKS
  Abel, 11, 28, 155, 176, 199, 229, 232, 242
  Elisha, 15, 79, 104, 130, 196
  John, 18, 49, 181, 226, 241
  Thomas, 57, 120, 196
MARLOW
  Edward, 242
  John S., 144, 210, 227
  Stone, 210
MARMADUKE
  John A., 213
MARQUIS
  Catharine, 201
  Fielding, 201
  Rebeccah, 201
  Thomas H., 201
MARSHALL
  James, 50
  James M., 222
  John, 32

Joseph, 50
Rachel, 50
Samuel, 50
Thomas, 32, 45, 61,
82, 167
William, 32, 82, 163
MARTAIN
John, 112
MARTIN
Agnes, 235
Andrew, 208
David, 215, 219, 225
Elizabeth, 215, 219,
220
John, 13, 26, 41, 52,
53, 57, 59, 74, 81,
89, 91, 93, 95,
125, 160, 183,
208, 225
Mary, 122
Robert, 55
William, 24, 85, 122,
208, 235, 244
MARTOR
Jonathan, 127
MARTS
John, 27, 195
MARY'S GROVE, 67
MASH
James, 12
Ruth, 12
MASON
A. B. T., 122, 200
Abraham B. T., 52,
54, 73, 89, 123,
124, 237, 247
Armistead, 200
Armistead T., 121,
153, 166, 200
Armstead, 133
Armstead T., 230
Armsted T., 73
Daniel, 184, 228,
239
E., 97, 240
George, 233

John T., 18, 73, 200,
230, 238
Sarah, 41, 52
Stephen T., 107,
136
Stephens T., 13, 14,
46
Stevens T., 30, 45,
93
Thompson, 26, 73,
135, 138, 237
Thomson, 52, 183
Westwood F., 127
Westwood T., 89,
108, 111, 114,
117, 144, 237
Westwood Y., 248
William T. T., 89,
179, 237
MASSEY
Lewis, 23
MASSIE
Samuel, 211
MASSON
Thomas, 135
Thomson, 135
MASSY
Catherine, 230
Samuel, 230
MASTER
Jared, 46
MASTERMAN
William, 187, 188,
219, 245
MATCHIN
Ann, 15
MATHEWS
Elizabeth, 58
Jonathan, 250
Richard, 58
MATHIAS
John, 2, 4, 5, 6, 11,
17, 21, 22, 23, 27,
32, 34, 46, 53, 62,
72, 75, 76, 80, 83,
87, 89, 90, 116,
120, 128, 131,

132, 138, 142,
143, 144, 146,
147, 151, 158,
166, 169, 172,
178, 183, 184,
185, 210, 225,
226, 230, 232,
236, 247
MATTHENY
Daniel, 33
Judith, 33
Thomas, 33
MATTHEW
Jonathan, 1
MATTHEWS
Jesse, 178
John, 22
Jonathan, 105, 168,
178, 208, 240
Sak, 68
Thomas, 16, 41, 54,
68
MATTHIAS
Ann, 52
Anne, 52
John, 17, 40, 52, 65,
95, 96, 97, 107,
108, 110, 116,
117, 136, 159,
189, 192, 193,
195, 198, 199,
202, 205, 207,
210, 215, 219,
220, 221, 224,
233, 236, 237,
238
MAUL
George, 25
MAUND
J., 30
J. J., 48
John J., 48
John T., 30
MAY
Daniel, 204, 227
Elizabeth, 227
MAYERS

Joseph, 197
Joshua, 170
Mary, 76
Stephen, 223
Thomas, 152
MCGIRTH
James, 223
Mary, 223
Stephen, 223
MCGORLICK
Patrick, 59
MCGRAW
Richard, 8, 39, 62
MCGUIRE
Edward, 222
MCHOLLAND
Patrick, 195
MCHULLAH
Robert, 59
MCILHANEY
James, 1, 4, 11, 24,
  25, 32, 34, 35, 36,
  47, 52, 53, 58, 60,
  73, 79, 89, 91,
  124, 130, 135,
  153, 159, 164
John, 3, 47, 89, 127,
  153, 156
Margaret, 25, 159
Nancy, 25
Peggy, 25
Rosannah, 25
MCILHANY
Cecelia, 191
Elizabeth, 191, 192,
  212, 224, 234
Harriot, 224
Harriott, 212
James, 67, 73, 93,
  97, 104, 111, 112,
  123, 191, 192,
  200, 212, 224,
  229, 234
John, 52, 185, 191,
  200, 212, 224,
  234
Louisa, 191

Margaret, 112, 191,
  200, 212, 224
Mary, 234
Mortimer, 191, 200
Rosannah, 200
MCILHEANY
John, 36
MCILROY
Daniel, 92
MCINTYRE
Alexander, 2, 53, 61,
  121, 160, 232
Jane, 160
Patrick, 29, 37, 43,
  45, 96, 159, 213,
  226, 231, 232
Polly, 232
MCIVER
John, 96, 104, 105
MCKAIG
Patrick, 1
MCKEMEY
Francis, 197
MCKEMIE
Francis, 154
James, 141, 154
John, 172, 214
MCKENDREE
John, 82
MCKIM
James, 208
MCKIMMEY
James, 87
MCKINNEY
John, 147, 183
MCKNIGHT
Charles, 110
MCLEAN
James, 53, 72
Martha, 72
MCLELAND
Alexander, 31
MCMAKEN
Alexander, 222
MCMANAMAN
James, 40, 219, 225
Mary, 219, 225

MCMANAMIES
Charles, 143
MCMANAMY
James, 220
Mary, 220
MCMANNAMY
Charles, 40
Jane, 40
MCMICHEN
Alexander, 143
MCMULLIN
Andrew, 12
MCNAB
James, 63
William, 18
MCNABB
James, 37
MCNATHAN
James, 130
MCNEALE
John, 69
MCNEEL
John, 98, 201
MCNEIL
John, 95, 180
S., 63
MCNELLAGE
James, 35, 151
MCNELLEDGE
James, 151
MCPHERSON
Elizabeth, 163
J. H., 23
James, 163
John, 119
Samuel, 170
Sarah, 150
Stephen, 21, 150,
  202
Steven, 163
MCVEIGH
Jeremiah, 102
Jesse, 29, 34, 36,
  55, 68, 70, 85, 99,
  137, 149, 156,
  158, 159, 169,
  185, 203, 218,

174, 175, 178,
179, 181, 183,
184, 185, 187,
188, 190, 192,
193, 194, 197,
199, 201, 207,
210, 212, 213,
215, 218, 219,
223, 225, 226,
227, 231, 232,
234, 236, 240,
246, 248, 252,
253
MURRY
Samuel, 55, 65, 70
MUSE
Battaile, 16
Edward, 166
Walt., 191
MUSTERFIELD, 126
MYARS
Ann, 44
MYERS
Alice, 114
Andrew, 97
Benjamin, 53, 62
Charlotte, 236
Eligah, 63
Elijah, 84, 113, 114,
119
Isaac, 19, 29, 37
Isaiah, 114
Jacob, 55
John, 70, 77, 104,
156, 165, 214,
236
Jonathan, 7, 13,
114, 117
Lambert, 84, 119
Mahlon, 180
Mary, 114
Peter, 68, 114, 206
Peters, 169
Thomas, 213

N

NALLY

Jesse, 215
NEALE
George, 100, 130,
161
James, 161
Lawrence C., 103
W. S., 146, 148,
149, 150, 155,
164, 167, 171,
192, 206, 211,
215, 222, 230,
239, 252
William S., 117, 162,
163, 222, 233
NEAR
Conrad, 97
Cunard, 26
John, 215
Philip, 160
NEEDHAM
John D., 237, 250
NEER
James, 191
Samuel, 191
NEGRO
Aaron, 217
Abraham, 71, 165
Adam, 6, 18, 78,
238, 246
Agg, 218
Agga, 246
Aleck, 174
Alfred, 90, 138
Ally, 246
Amasa, 71
Amelia Ann, 228
Amme, 217
Amy, 43
Ann, 65
Ann Minte, 30
Anne, 72, 88, 144
Anthony, 52, 55
Armistead, 145
Arther, 138
Barbara, 171
Barbary, 72
Basil, 171

Becca, 133
Beck, 12
Belinda, 168
Bella, 145
Ben, 47, 69, 124,
217
Benjamin, 78
Bet, 163
Betsey, 73, 165
Betsy, 165
Bett, 17
Betty, 15, 168
Bill, 153
Billy Jackson, 166
Bob, 15, 217
Bray, 151
Brice, 14, 154
Butler, 34, 35
Cager, 246
Calvert, 148
Carter, 50
Cate, 16, 156
Cato, 72, 238
Caty, 35
Charity, 122
Charles, 15, 31, 91,
138, 151
Charles Gibson, 14
Charlotte, 107, 157,
179, 204, 217
Charlotty, 71
Chloe, 12, 204
Christopher, 165
Cibbey, 171
Cloke, 217
Cortney, 146
Courtney, 73
Cyrus, 43
Daniel, 50, 122, 132,
138
Daphne, 50, 168
Darkes, 40
David, 16, 150, 217
Davy, 136, 165
Dealey, 80
Dennis, 53, 97
Diana, 138

Dick, 62, 151, 219
Dinah, 176
Diner, 219
Dolly, 7
Duanna, 133
Dubbin, 119
Dublin, 62
Eady, 219
Easter, 31, 144, 219
Edith, 148
Elcy, 105
Elias, 144
Elijah, 14
Eliza, 3
Elleck, 106
Ellender, 32
Ellick, 7, 196
Emily, 50
Emmely, 230
Enoch, 219
Esther, 35, 68, 133,
   145
Eve, 78
Fan, 151
Fanny, 65, 130, 150
Father, 122
Fillis, 14
Flora, 171, 188, 197
Francis, 78
Frankey, 133
Gabriel, 14
George, 65, 68, 71,
   132, 147, 151,
   217, 240, 246
George Pearsons,
   137
George Rippon, 122
Gerard, 107
Giles, 167
Gin, 171
Gracey, 171
Granville, 145
Greenberry, 43
Hannah, 13, 14, 15,
   65, 78, 145, 168,
   171, 214, 219
Harriet, 65, 157

Harriett, 31
Harriot, 192
Harriott, 91
Harry, 14, 78, 79,
   138, 151, 181,
   219
Henna, 14
Henney, 62
Henry, 148, 150,
   188, 197, 217
Hiram, 204
Hoate, 142
Isaac, 18, 137, 219
Jack, 40, 151, 168,
   203
Jacob, 50
James, 3, 6, 17, 18,
   62, 65, 88, 136,
   165, 168, 203,
   217, 246
James Hogins, 36
Jane, 14, 15, 163,
   187, 203
Jem, 188, 196
Jenny, 122
Jeremiah, 228
Jerry, 142, 144
Jess, 80
Jesse, 97, 171
Jim, 43, 152, 197
Jinny, 171
Jo, 41
Joan, 224
Joe, 7, 133
Joel, 65
Joel Ned, 122
John, 11, 47, 132,
   133, 148, 206
Joseph, 14
Juba, 99
Judah, 6, 18
Jude, 50
Judeth, 203
Judy, 165
Kit, 171
Kitty, 47, 144
Kity, 78

Lavenia, 165
Leana, 50
Lella, 133
Lemon, 50
Leonard Goings, 62
Letty, 50, 222
Lewis, 2, 151
Linder, 246
Linney, 204
Lizza, 50
Lorinda, 157
Luce, 138
Lucey, 166
Lucy, 14, 43, 142,
   151, 157, 246
Lucy David, 136
Lukey, 15
Mahlon, 35
Man, 6
Maney, 136
Marcus, 146
Maria, 206
Mariah, 110
Mark, 217
Marquis, 73
Martha, 168
Mary, 6, 18, 138,
   150, 169, 224
Mary Ann, 50
Matilda, 80, 107,
   145
Matt, 151
Milky, 150
Mill, 152
Milley, 7
Milly, 90, 145
Minn, 219
Mint, 17
Moll, 147
Molly, 5, 122, 145,
   151
Moses, 115, 151,
   228
Mosses, 124
Muler, 17
Nace, 156, 217
Nall, 21

O

OATYAR
Peter, 47
OATYER
Peter, 157, 184, 198
OAYER
Peter, 82
OBSURN
Joel, 229
ODEN
Alexander, 99
Elias, 214
Elizabeth, 40
Hezekiah, 99, 110
Hezikiah, 40
John, 110
Lydia, 44
Margaret, 110
Martha, 228
Sarah, 214
Thomas, 44, 59, 64,
80, 210, 228, 250
OFFUTT
Eli, 81, 96, 106, 137,
157, 161, 162,
167, 171, 172,
174, 179, 186,
187, 188, 194,
198, 199, 203,
208, 211, 214,
215, 216, 217,
218, 220, 225,
232
James, 34
OGDEN
Charles W., 216
OLD GALLOWS LOT,
188
OLDHAM
Ann, 249, 251
Nancy, 242
Samuel, 242
OMEHUNDRO
Thomas, 48
ONEAL
Daniel, 141
ONEALE

Ferdinando, 214
John, 82
O'NEALE
John, 104
ORANDURFF
Martha, 42
ORE
William, 160
ORENDURF
Martha, 73
ORISON
David, 126, 239
ORR
Benjamin G., 93
John D., 45, 53, 60,
93, 131, 158, 173,
182, 193, 195
Lucinda, 45, 93, 158
William G., 167
ORRISON
John, 185
OSBERN
Abner, 25
OSBORN
Abraham, 97
Anthony, 140
Carrie N., 122
Joshua, 16
Nicholas, 97, 125
OSBORNE
Abner, 11, 20
Abraham, 97
Joel, 133
Joshua, 16, 239
Mary, 97
Rachel, 97
Thomas, 133
OSBURN
Abner, 3, 11, 23, 24,
25, 26, 31, 34, 46
Abraham, 150
Craven, 111
Elizabeth, 176
Hannah, 57, 147,
209, 229, 231
Joab, 209

Joel, 11, 56, 57,
110, 136, 142,
147, 209, 229,
231
John, 21, 56, 57,
189, 231
Joshua, 108, 111,
124, 136, 142,
149, 177, 209,
214, 227, 229,
230, 234, 236,
242, 243, 244,
247, 251
Landon, 232
Mary, 28, 57, 146,
209
Massey, 229
Morris, 11, 28, 56,
219, 229, 231
Morriss, 147
Nicholas, 21, 118,
176, 229, 232,
236
Polly, 189
Richard, 10, 57, 189,
209, 223, 229,
231
Sarah, 56, 57
Thomas, 11, 28, 57,
142, 147, 209,
231
William, 43, 108,
111, 231
OSBURNE
Abner, 31
Hannah, 146, 232
Joel, 146
John, 189
Joshua, 133, 229,
233, 247
Margaret, 135
Morris, 146
Nicholas, 135, 229
Richard, 47, 146
Thomas, 131, 233
William, 133, 153,
232

PEAKOCK
John, 65
PEARCE
Jacob G., 171
PEARS
Griffith G., 26
PEARSONS
George, 137
PEERS
H., 214
Henry, 217, 218
Nicholas, 121, 214, 218
PEGG
Nathaniel, 46, 124
PEIRPOINT
Catrenah, 78
Francis, 78
Jo'n., 158
Joseph, 78
Obed, 156
Samuel, 172, 195, 204
PENDERGAS
James, 56
PENDERGRASS
James, 56
PERFECT
Robert, 96, 106
PERREY
Roger, 27
PERRY
Benjamin, 229
Franklin, 126
John S., 126
Joseph, 119
Peggy, 126
Roger, 27
PETER
Thomas, 211
PETERSON
Henry, 37
PEUGH
Samuel, 150
PEW
Samuel, 49

Spencer, 57, 58, 104, 130
PEYTON
Ann, 20, 124, 133
Burr, 83
Chandler, 253
Craven, 20, 133
Dade, 165
F. H., 113, 171
Frances, 113, 165
Francis, 28, 31, 46, 83, 84, 92, 112, 114, 166, 182, 242, 247
Francis H., 37, 67, 70, 73, 77, 80, 86, 87, 90, 96, 98, 110, 112, 113, 119, 133, 148, 149, 152, 156, 164, 165, 186, 188, 192, 194, 224, 234, 248
J. H., 163
Samuel H., 101
Townshead D., 37
Townshend L., 107
Valentine, 133
William, 133, 151
PHELAN
Dennis, 123
Edward, 123, 160, 161
Jer., 129
Jeremiah, 123, 160
Winnefred, 160
PHELPS
Eli, 211
Elisha, 211
PHILIP
Thomas, 159
PHILIPS
Benjamin, 4
Edmond, 5
Hannah, 16
Jenkin, 15, 16, 132
Jenkins, 109

Samuel, 109, 132
Thomas, 15, 16, 44, 63, 71, 91, 114, 119, 134, 164, 206, 247
PHILLER
Mary, 214
Philip, 214
PHILLIPS
Benjamin, 109, 132
Hester, 124
Isaac, 222
Israel, 124
James, 28
Jenkin, 119
Jesse, 142
John, 119, 189
Lourena, 211
Sarah, 109, 132
Thomas, 21, 30, 41, 42, 44, 49, 58, 91, 96, 98, 100, 104, 109, 113, 119, 120, 121, 126, 134, 142, 148, 149, 162, 164, 177, 195, 215, 222, 243
PHILPOTT
John, 246
PHINNALL
Stephen, 17
PICKETT
James, 253
PIERCE
Alice, 18
Delilah, 18
Griffith, 18
Samuel, 18
Thomas, 18
PIERPOINT
Francis, 214
Obed, 160
Samuel, 214
PIGGOTT
Ebenezer, 4
John, 4, 158, 240

Cuthbert, 45, 105,
106, 107, 171,
208
Elisha, 24
Elizabeth, 199
H. B., 243
Humphrey B., 247
John, 161
John P., 96
L. D., 115, 117, 130,
162
Lee D., 135
Leven, 11, 16, 25,
28, 33, 34, 36, 38,
40, 45, 54, 55, 56,
58, 59, 66, 82, 83,
85, 93, 96, 97,
100, 101, 106,
110, 114, 115,
119, 121, 124,
127, 137, 139,
141, 145, 148,
150, 155, 156,
157, 159, 167,
170, 171, 176,
177, 180, 185,
189, 193, 194,
198, 199, 201,
206, 208, 225,
226, 240, 243,
249
Leven D., 38, 85,
114, 126, 132,
186, 192, 206,
218, 247
Levin, 230
Peyton, 251
Robert, 194
Robert M., 85, 122,
189, 194, 199,
221
Sarah, 33, 58, 100,
121, 137, 189
Thomas W., 171
William, 47, 48, 65,
73, 92, 181, 218,
221

William B., 242
William H., 42, 50,
221
William M., 148, 155
POWER
Michael, 228
Walter, 101, 185
POWERS
William D., 163
PRESGRAVES
Richard, 96
William, 96, 151
PRESSGRAVES
William, 237
PRICE
Benjamin, 77, 86,
137, 140, 148,
159, 200, 203,
232
George, 210, 227
Hannah, 101
Sarah, 200
Thomas, 4
PRINCE
Levi, 139, 180, 230
Levy, 69, 146
Matthias, 69
PRINS
Ben, 160
PROBASCO
Elizabeth, 27, 30
Samuel, 12, 27, 30
PROBASCOE
Samuel, 11
PRYOR
James, 104, 139,
191
Silas, 47
PUCKETT
James, 226
PUE
Spencer, 12
PUGH
Samuel, 21
Spencer, 21, 65
PULLER
Joseph, 50

PURCEL
Elizabeth, 145
Samuel, 239, 248
PURCELL
Lydia, 24
Thomas, 24
PURCY
Elizabeth, 96
Richard, 96
PURDOM
Benjamin, 204
Jeremiah, 177, 197
PURDUM
Benjamin, 89
Jeremiah, 26, 35,
36, 37, 41, 56, 67,
74
PURDY
Elizabeth, 248
Richard, 84, 85, 86,
96, 248
PURNELL
Jesse R., 35
PURSEL
George, 248
Lidia, 73
Lydia, 3, 47, 248
Pleasant, 248
Polly, 248
Samuel, 167, 169,
181, 184
Thomas, 3, 47, 73,
248
Valentine, 248
PURSELL
John, 248
Joseph, 248
Lydia, 10, 20, 23,
24, 46, 47, 103
Samuel, 147, 248
Thomas, 10, 17, 20,
23, 24, 46, 47,
103, 248
PURSSELL
Thomas, 58
PUSEY
Joshua, 195

PUSEY & CO, 195
PYOT
  John, 80
PYOTT
  John, 113

Q

QUEEN
  Elizabeth, 224
  John, 36, 227
  Mary, 36
QUICK
  John, 229
QUINLAN
  Hugh, 104, 109,
    129, 132, 136

R

RACE
  Job, 7, 100, 192,
    205
RADICAN
  James, 14, 134
RALLS
  George, 8
RALPH
  John, 155, 176, 236
RAMEY
  Debby, 92
  Deborah, 40
  Jacob, 40, 92
  John, 208
  Sandford, 57, 84,
    94, 113, 182, 238
  Sanford, 34, 45, 57,
    59, 60, 119, 125,
    142, 164, 184,
    229
RAMSAY
  Andrew, 104
  Jesse T., 142
  John, 62, 65, 179
  P., 87
RAMSEY
  Clarissa, 206, 240

John, 165, 194, 206,
  240
William, 87
RAMY
  Sanford, 252
RANDALL
  Jones, 24
RANDELL
  Joseph, 253
RANDLE
  Annanias, 12
RANDOLPH
  John, 111
RATCLIFF
  Richard, 117
RATCLIFFE
  John, 225
RATEKIN
  James, 197
RATHIE
  John B., 136, 172,
    179, 234
RATHY
  John B., 166
RATIKEN
  James, 192, 195
  Susannah, 192
RATTIKEN
  James, 119
  Susannah, 119
RAWAN
  John, 104
RAWLINGS
  Aaron, 48, 105
  John, 136
RAY
  Benjamin, 23
  Eleanor, 23
RAZOR
  George, 25, 48, 196
READ
  Allen, 198
  Joseph, 12, 33
REAMY
  Sandford, 10
REASE
  Lewis, 252

Thomas, 11
REDMON
  Andrew, 8
REDMOND
  Andrew, 8, 40, 124,
    250
  Benjamin, 124, 208
REDWOOD
  Benjamin, 124
  William, 10, 250
REE
  Zarl, 105
REECE
  David, 106
  Emoor, 115
  Jane, 115
  Thomas, 115
REED
  Agness, 49
  Andrew, 120
  Elizabeth, 229
  George, 250
  Jacob, 10
  James, 203
  John, 56
  Jonathan, 57, 254
  Joseph, 10, 11, 49,
    137, 220
  Samuel, 195
  Stephen, 57
  Walker, 73
REEDER
  David, 46
  Gourley, 220, 245
  Jacob, 25, 55, 112
  William, 36, 51
REEPOLD
  Christian, 48
  George, 48
REES
  Daniel, 114, 169,
    228, 244
REESE
  George, 205
  Silas, 32
REID
  Agnes, 50

Alexander, 158
Joseph, 50
W., 64
Walker, 54, 64, 73,
  75, 77, 83, 134
William, 63
REIGER
John, 143
Margaret, 143
REIGOR
John, 14, 15, 48,
  106, 151
Margaret, 15
Margarett, 14
Peggy, 106
REILEY
David, 27
Joshua, 156
Martin, 27, 36
REILY
David, 36
REINTZEL
Daniel, 13, 109, 170
REINTZELL
Daniel, 4
REMEY
Sandford, 180, 215
REMY
Sandford, 212
RESPESS
Thomas, 146
RETICOR
Elijah, 190
RHODES
George, 83
Joseph, 220
Mary, 207, 223
Randolph, 17
Samuel, 17
Sarah, 220
Tholemeah, 176
Thomas, 220
William, 26, 135,
  207, 220, 223
RHORBACH
Adam, 1
RHORBACK

Adam, 29, 45
RICE
Catherine M., 91,
  228
Charles C., 109
Frederick W., 228
James, 3, 5, 125,
  182, 227
John, 27
RICHARD
Elizabeth, 223
Isaac, 19
Peter, 223
RICHARDS
Deborah, 155, 176
Isaac, 48, 100, 155,
  176, 236
John, 124
Mary, 90
Michael, 232, 234
Richard, 51, 90, 207
Samuel, 90
William, 124
RICHARDSON
John, 117
RICHEY
Isaac, 81
RICHEYES
Isaac, 29
RICHIE
Isaac, 11
Peter, 72
RICHTER
George, 176
Susanna, 176
RICKARD
Elizabeth, 209
Peter, 163, 209
RICKELS
John T., 116
RICKETTS
Benjamin, 53
David, 207
John T., 53, 161,
  183, 200
Mary, 161, 183, 200
Thomas, 5, 88

RICKEY
Peter, 76
RIDDLE
Jeremiah, 43, 151
William, 204
RIDENBAUGH
Margaret, 139
Peter, 61, 129, 139,
  193
RIDGEWAY
James, 239
RIEGER
John, 19
RIEGOR
John, 22
Margaret, 22
RIGHT
William, 193
RIGNEY
John, 231
RIGOR
John, 46
RILEY
J., 252
Joshua, 156, 194,
  232
RINCHER
Edward, 179
RINCKER
Edward, 241
RINE
George, 2, 79
RINKER
Edward, 46, 91, 142,
  175, 194, 236
Jeremiah, 18
Sally, 91, 194
RITACIE
Nancy, 166
RITCHEY
Isaac, 143
Margaret, 143
Samuel, 97, 118
RITCHIE
Elizabeth, 98
Isaac, 39, 68
Peter, 98

Rachel, 93
Samuel, 12, 39, 93,
  94, 163
RITCHTER
  John, 6
RITICOR
  Elijah, 126, 130, 173
  Nancy, 173
RITTAKER
  Elijah, 173
RITTEKER
  Elijah, 166
ROACH
  Edmund, 40
  Elizabeth, 161
  James, 3, 17, 24,
    40, 47, 53, 93, 97,
    133, 161, 253
  Mahlon, 17, 20, 47,
    52, 53, 67, 97,
    103, 105, 133,
    134, 158, 161,
    191, 253
  Richard, 40, 103,
    154
ROALER
  Conrod, 38
ROAN
  Catharine, 25
  John, 25
  Mary, 25
ROBERTS
  Charles, 46
  Eleanor, 190
  Ellenor, 118
  Griffith, 53
  Henry, 50, 71, 204
  John, 12, 144, 204
  Joseph, 126
  Rebecca, 12
  Sarah, 126
  Vandevanter, 89
  William, 2, 3, 5, 7,
    61, 83, 92, 118,
    190, 219
ROBERTS &
  GRIFFITH, 174

ROBERTSON
  John, 8, 52, 68, 126,
    145, 215
  Robert, 198, 214,
    252
ROBISON
  John, 16
  Joseph, 187
ROCKAFIELD
  Jonathan, 1
RODES
  George, 79
RODGERS
  Dinah, 165
  Hamilton, 20
  Hugh, 203, 228
ROGERS
  Arther, 134
  Arthur, 70
  Charles, 3
  Dinah, 165, 178, 179
  Hamilton, 8, 19, 20,
    21, 82, 104, 165,
    178, 179, 203,
    237, 241, 242,
    251
  Hugh, 101, 114,
    115, 134, 137,
    148
  Martha, 50
  Mary, 40
  Owen, 40
  Susanna, 160
  William A., 160
ROLER
  Conroad, 39
  Conrod, 44, 69, 93
  John, 43
ROLERS
  John, 29
ROLLER
  Conrad, 66
ROLLISON
  John, 62
ROMINE
  Daniel, 22

John, 22, 33, 91, 92,
  102, 118
Peter, 12, 22, 57, 58
Sarah, 22
ROOCE
  Michael, 52
ROOKARD
  Nancy, 161
  Robert C., 161
  Sarah, 46, 161
  Thomas, 46, 161
ROONEY
  Michael, 18
ROOSE
  Catharine, 105
  Michael, 141
ROPER
  Ann, 48, 86
  Catharine, 48
  Catherine, 86
  Christopher, 5, 6,
    21, 35, 48, 75, 77,
    86, 96, 122
  Nicholas, 82, 186,
    249
  Thomas, 48, 86
  William P., 5, 6, 25,
    48, 86
ROPP
  Jacob, 195
RORBAUGH
  Adam, 48
ROSE
  Adam, 180
  Anna, 79, 213
  Christopher, 100,
    182
  George, 63, 88, 90,
    201
  James, 63
  Jane, 63, 88, 90,
    201
  John, 12, 32, 49, 63,
    79, 85, 95, 112,
    113, 125, 126,
    135, 136, 179,
    190, 198, 199,

Aaron, 36, 68, 83,
103, 107, 126,
135, 146, 172,
173, 180, 183,
184, 201, 212,
222
Ann, 137
Aron, 251
Benjamin, 61
Cyrus, 60
Evritt, 198
Henry, 60
I., 92, 100
James, 77, 79, 103,
107, 157, 179,
184, 210, 214
John, 35, 107, 179,
184
Margaret, 36, 235
Margareta, 69
Margaretha, 110
Mary, 121, 133, 149
Moses, 107
Nicholas, 137
Peter, 112, 137
Presley, 25, 35, 63,
68, 110, 114, 121,
133, 149, 242
Susannah, 126
Thomas, 60, 133,
143, 152, 169,
173, 187, 188,
199, 200, 205,
214, 219, 227,
247
SANDERSON
Alexander, 195
SANDFORD
Jeremiah, 207, 240
Vincent, 202, 240
SANDS
Abijah, 119, 126,
215
Esther, 126
Hester, 215
Isaac, 8, 52, 68, 126

Jacob, 30, 63, 81,
113, 125, 126
Jesse, 215
Jonah, 8, 52, 55, 80,
126, 156, 215
Joseph, 8, 131, 215
Rachel, 68, 126, 215
Sarah, 230
Tamer, 215
Thomas, 239, 251
SANFORD
Ada, 242, 243
Benjamin, 241
Berkeley, 241
Jeremiah, 241, 242,
243
Vincent, 207, 241
SANGSTER
Robert, 152
SAPP
Vincent, 41
SAPPINGTON
John F., 186, 188,
199, 211, 215,
221, 224
SAUNDERS
Aaron, 32, 165, 166,
185
Cyrus, 76
H. G., 184
J., 193, 195
James, 157, 162,
182, 184, 185,
187, 190, 198,
200, 201, 218,
232, 244
John, 165, 181, 182,
187, 201
Margaret, 234, 235
Mary, 195, 198, 201,
218
Nicholas, 93
Presley, 109, 120,
198, 201, 218,
225
Presly, 110, 195,
201

Pressley, 186
Sarah, 201
Thomas, 199, 219
SCANDIETT
Jacob, 148
SCATTERDAY
Easter, 164
George, 183
John, 22, 24, 83,
164
Rebecca, 22
SCHELLGY
John H., 53
SCHLEY
Thomas, 168
SCHOLEFIELD
John, 56
Rebeckah, 56
Thomas, 56
SCHOLFIELD
Hannah, 184
J. H., 173
John, 81, 184
Jonathan H., 184
Rebecca, 184
William, 184
SCHOOLEY
Dorothy, 7
Elizabeth, 159
John, 16, 22, 46, 63,
71, 80, 86, 91, 96,
105, 121, 159,
168, 183, 195
Reuben, 71, 83,
134, 222
Reubin, 113
Rheuben, 136
Samuel, 7, 76
William, 146, 164,
193, 222
SCHOOLLY
Elizabeth, 252
SCHOOLY
John, 53, 94
Reuben, 228
Samuel, 53
SCHRIDLEY

William, 17
SHEPPARD
  Charles, 185
  Phillip, 135
SHEWMAKER
  Barbary, 155
  George, 155
SHIBELEY
  Jacob, 98
SHIBLEE
  Jacob, 162
SHIELDS
  Joseph, 114, 128,
    154
SHIVELLEY
  George, 218
SHIVELY
  George, 64, 82, 107
  Jacob, 95, 134, 155
SHLATZ
  Frederick, 45
SHOEMAKER
  Bartholomew, 216
  Daniel, 29, 45, 52,
    69, 87, 129, 141,
    155, 234, 235
  George, 35, 37, 45,
    67, 74, 76, 91,
    177, 216, 234
  Jacob, 45, 76, 129,
    234, 235
  John, 36
  Mary, 36
  Simon, 60, 66, 67,
    186, 216
SHOHER
  Cornelius, 161
SHOLFIELD
  William, 56
SHOMAKER
  Daniel, 197
  Elizabeth, 24
  Jacob, 24
  Simon, 24, 72
SHOPE
  Jacob, 91, 175
SHORTS

Henry, 160
SHOVER
  Adam, 18, 32, 37,
    112, 117, 130,
    145, 170, 172,
    186, 190, 204,
    221, 226, 227,
    231, 232
  George, 112, 146
  Simon, 68, 69, 94
SHOWER
  Adam, 12
SHREEVE
  Abner, 140
  Benjamin, 75, 138,
    140, 146
  Joshua, 140
  William, 140
SHREIVE
  Benjamin, 15, 20
SHREVE
  Abner, 200
  Benjamin, 14, 35,
    43, 61, 63, 64, 75,
    83, 84, 87, 108,
    129, 158, 166,
    168, 170, 188,
    200, 207, 223,
    232, 233, 239,
    253
  John, 105, 132
  William, 192
SHREVES
  Benjamin, 166
SHRIEVE
  Benjamin, 32, 107
SHRIEVES
  Benjamin, 18
SHRIVER
  Abraham, 85
SHRY
  Catharine, 105
  Jacob, 105
  Mathias, 47
SHRYOCK
  Michael, 121
SHUBRIDGE

Thomas, 176
SHULTS
  George, 129
SHULTZ
  George, 61, 139,
    157
SHUMAKER
  Betsey, 210
  Caty, 210
  Daniel, 154
  George, 172, 197,
    210
  Jacob, 60, 235
  Simon, 35, 67, 172,
    197, 236
SHUNK
  Isaac, 59
SIDDAL
  Sarah, 117
  William, 117
SIDDLE
  Isaac, 89, 93
  Sarah, 105
  William, 105
SILCOTT
  Abraham, 106
  Jacob, 51, 64, 207
  Jesse, 38, 118, 171,
    244
SILLCOTT
  Jesse, 154
SILMAN
  Wylless, 4
SIM
  Ariana, 52
  Harriet, 198
  Harriott, 210
  Kitty, 95
  Patrick, 52
  Thomas, 22, 28, 32,
    38, 49, 52, 54, 55,
    63, 64, 77, 79, 85,
    86, 95, 97, 101,
    107, 108, 135,
    158, 160, 166,
    171, 173, 182,

186, 198, 200,
210
Thomas L., 10
SIMM
Thomas, 65
SIMMONS
Catherine, 47
David, 47
William, 161
SIMMS
Charles, 55
SIMPSON
Hendley, 198
Henson, 63
Rhodham, 179
Susanna, 168
William, 96
SIMSON
William, 216
SINCLAIR
Ann, 117
Edith, 78, 166
George, 78, 100
James, 31, 37, 98,
100
John, 31, 37, 59, 78,
100, 103, 111,
117, 124, 157,
159, 166, 169,
174, 185, 203,
223, 224, 244,
251
Margaret, 200
Margarett, 78
Mary, 31, 98, 100,
103, 117, 166
Samuel, 78, 103,
117, 137, 166
William, 31, 37, 100
SINGLETON
Benjamin, 114
Hannah, 42, 50
Joshua, 42, 50
Samuel, 17
SINKLER
James, 98
SKILLMAN

Abraham, 63, 64,
69, 198
Catharine, 36
Christopher, 36, 69,
102
Heneriette, 36
John, 9, 36
SKILMAN
Abraham, 54
Violinda, 54
SKINNER
Cornelius, 3, 9, 56,
72, 81, 87, 130,
160, 184, 216
Jacob, 43
Nathan, 121
Nathaniel, 81, 184
Peter, 81, 121
Richard, 9
Samuel, 134
William, 56
SLACK
Elizabeth, 135, 161,
172
Enoch, 2
Jeremiah, 204
John, 26, 66, 70, 81,
135, 152, 161,
172
SLACUM
George, 54
SLATER
Catharine, 93
Edward, 107
John, 10, 92, 93,
154, 172
SLATES
Frederick, 29, 72,
125, 163
SLAUGHTER
Philip, 79
SMALLEY
David, 8, 42, 151,
223
Ezekiel, 42
Mary, 151

William, 37, 38, 42,
124
SMALLWOOD
Bayn, 134, 135
George, 216
Leven, 188, 195,
213, 224
Luke, 91, 93
Susannah, 11
SMALLY
Joshua, 42
SMARR
Andrew, 64, 70, 150,
196, 214, 218,
221, 228, 240
Lydia, 240
SMIDLEY
Mathias, 91
SMIDLEY'S
MEADOW, 115
SMITH
Aaron, 21
Ailce, 153
Alexander, 88, 89,
150, 193
Cathrena, 162
Charles, 77, 209
Daniel, 205
David, 10, 23, 49,
103, 118, 149,
153, 208, 245,
248, 251
Fleet, 5, 10, 13, 27,
29, 33, 40, 60, 61,
64, 70, 77, 78, 79,
86, 97, 117, 131,
144, 147, 156,
157, 162, 165,
166, 167, 168,
177, 185, 187,
189, 190, 194,
200, 206, 208,
210, 211, 212,
214, 217, 225,
227, 233, 246,
247

Basil, 196
Bazel, 156, 228
Bazil, 80, 237
Richard W., 30
Thomas, 30, 45, 82,
  214, 218
STOUSABERGER
John, 35
STOUSEBERGER
John, 74, 134, 174,
  180, 204, 231
Margeret, 74
STOUSEBURGER
John, 134
STOUSENBERGER
John, 39
STOUTSEBERGER
John, 168, 180
Margaret, 180
STOUTSEBUGER
John, 210
STOUTSENBARGER
John, 18, 48
STOVIN
Charles, 243
George, 243
STRAHAN
John C., 47
STREAM
Adam, 160
Elizabeth, 210
Michael, 204, 210
STREET
Jonas, 73
STROTHER
Anthony, 217
Daniel F., 66, 203
Elizabeth, 217
Reuben, 211
William, 108
STRUP
Mahlon, 72
STRUPE
Mary Ann, 87
Melcher, 87
STRUTS
Jonas, 17

STUCK
Peter, 45, 117, 154
STUMP
Jacob, 2
John, 26
Peter, 26, 30
STURMAN
William, 219
William T., 115
William Y., 185
SUBASTON
Benjamin, 119
SUDDATH
Lewis, 179
SUDDITH
William, 34, 58, 80,
  209, 220, 237,
  241
SUDDUTH
William, 245
SULLIVAN
James, 213
John, 123
M., 3, 111, 164
Mortho, 18, 84, 111,
  192, 238
Murtho, 20, 43, 63,
  248
Murto, 104, 162
Murty, 250
Owen, 247
SUMMERS
Henry, 224
John L., 23
SUNEFRANK
George, 1
SUNFRANK
Abraham, 33
SURGHNOR
Hugh, 19
SURGNOR
Hugh, 142
John, 142
SUTHELAND
Alexander, 205
SUTHERLAND

A., 26, 77, 184, 193,
  199, 214, 221,
  226, 232, 254
Alex, 189
Alexander, 6, 19, 25,
  28, 30, 33, 53, 80,
  106, 112, 115,
  130, 141, 146,
  148, 156, 159,
  160, 183, 194,
  197, 205, 216,
  239
Ann, 141, 205
Nancy, 30, 106, 148
SUTTLE
Henry, 135
SWAIN
Thomas, 2
SWAN
Thomas, 54
SWANK
Catharine, 172, 204
Elizabeth, 172
George, 68, 69, 172
John, 53, 172, 204
Margaret, 172
Michael, 172
Philip, 172
Philip M., 172
Polley, 172
Susan, 172
SWANN
Jane, 116, 198
Jane B., 116
Thomas, 3, 5, 10,
  14, 18, 21, 50, 55,
  58, 64, 73, 74, 84,
  85, 87, 89, 93, 99,
  103, 104, 108,
  109, 110, 112,
  114, 115, 116,
  133, 135, 137,
  145, 161, 162,
  168, 170, 171,
  183, 186, 198,
  200, 205, 207,
  235

200, 202, 209,
212, 213
Stacy, 3, 12, 20, 23,
24, 25, 26, 31, 34,
35, 38, 39, 40, 43,
46, 48, 56, 58, 59,
71, 90, 101, 105,
106, 109, 110,
112, 113, 116,
117, 118, 120,
121, 125, 130,
136, 138, 149,
150, 153, 154,
155, 159, 165,
167, 169, 175,
176, 177, 178,
179, 181, 182,
184, 186, 191,
195, 196, 197,
200, 206, 210,
212, 227, 228,
229, 230, 234,
235, 236, 239,
242, 243, 244,
250, 251, 252,
254
Thomas, 19
Timothy, 26, 29, 31,
39, 56, 57, 58, 90,
92, 106, 118, 125,
139, 174, 182,
190, 236, 247,
254
W., 151, 214
Walter, 52, 129, 151
William, 6, 11, 15,
19, 35, 38, 43, 60,
67, 70, 83, 114,
116, 142, 179,
188, 225, 229,
254
William R., 11, 14,
28, 32, 33, 38, 39,
43, 46, 50
William T., 70, 85
TEASDALE
Elizabeth, 138

Fewster, 138
TEBBS
W. P., 30
TEMERY
Peter, 195
TEMPLER
James, 252
Martha, 92
Stacy, 252
TERRY
James, 34
THACKER
Albin, 77
THARP
David, 176
THATCHER
Alice, 139
Calven, 228
Richard, 65, 113
Stephen, 139, 241
THOMAS
Benjamin, 3, 8, 179
Daniel, 8, 110, 164,
181, 208
David, 43
Eleazer, 175
Enoch, 115, 196,
244
Evan, 167
George, 210, 211
Hugh, 8, 208
Jacob, 167, 173,
202
James, 40, 247
Jesse, 227
Job, 193
John, 92, 143, 167,
202, 229, 239,
241
Joseph, 92, 210,
211, 227, 230,
240
Leach, 92
Leah, 202
Mary, 181
Nancy, 240
Philip, 57, 233

Phineas, 28, 91,
146, 151
Phinehas, 7, 135,
167, 173, 181
William, 12, 85
THOMPKINS
Jonah, 240
THOMPSON
___, 175
Amos, 5, 41, 65, 90,
104, 105
Andrew, 26, 59, 73,
89, 127, 149, 153,
156
Ann, 105, 146
C., 104
Charles R., 104,
129, 136
Craven P., 16, 109
Hugh, 139, 190, 191
Isaac, 19, 59
Israel, 16, 49, 59,
93, 106, 109, 123,
127, 132, 138,
141, 180, 181,
213
Israel H., 71, 102,
104, 113, 124,
139, 146, 161,
222, 253
Israel P., 104
James, 139, 191
James A., 48
James N., 48
Jane, 90, 105, 139,
191
John E., 190
Jonah, 5, 16, 20, 39,
59, 89, 100, 102,
104, 105, 106,
109, 133, 139,
141, 149, 153,
156, 175, 180,
181, 192, 213,
238, 244, 246,
253

Joseph, 16, 49, 76, 77, 175
Margaret, 104, 244
Margarett, 106
Samuel, 59, 139
Samuel A., 106
Sarah, 139, 161
Thomas, 16, 161, 220
William, 77, 97, 99, 108, 110, 126, 136, 139, 220, 221, 234
THOMSON
Joseph, 157
THORNTON
Anthony, 46
Benjamin, 80, 136, 179
Benjamin B., 110, 121, 138, 149, 151, 157, 160, 166, 174, 194
Hannah, 157
Jinny, 46
John, 14, 196
William, 4, 20, 22
THRASHER
Elias, 146, 152, 160, 234
Henson, 234
Melinda, 234
THRELKELD
Elizabeth, 109
Joel, 82
John, 4, 13, 80, 82, 109, 114, 170, 211
Jonathan, 82
Rebeckah, 82
Sarah, 82
THRIFT
Charles, 129, 140, 143, 145, 155, 160, 174, 183, 185, 186, 187, 201, 230

Hannah, 183
William, 155, 160, 174, 183
TIBBS
Betsy, 208
TIDBALL
Jane, 205, 222, 228
Joseph, 62, 199, 200, 205, 222, 228
Thomas A., 228
TILLETT
Giles, 53, 62, 95, 168
James, 245
Samuel, 3, 55, 78, 132, 152, 197
TILLEY
John, 245
TIMMS
Elisha, 64, 82, 218
James, 107
Jesse, 190, 235, 238, 246
John, 115
Joseph, 107
TITUS
Abner, 43
Francis, 54, 63, 83
Jane, 54, 63, 248
Tunis, 1, 172, 248
TOBIN
John, 118
TODD
Robert, 23
Samuel, 48, 105, 251, 253
TODHUNTER
John, 25, 176
TOLSON
Benjamin, 240, 254
TOMKINS
Asahel, 253
Marcy, 19
Nancy, 253
TOMLINSON
William, 9

TORBERT
James, 124
John, 248
Samuel, 57, 225, 248
Sarah, 225
Thomas, 225
TORBUT
John, 225
TOWARMAN
Peter, 193
TOWERMAN
Peter, 85
TOWNER
Jacob, 6, 77, 232
TOWPERMAN
Peter, 215
TRAHERN
James, 203, 227
TREBBE
Thomas, 127, 175
TREBBY
John, 198
TREMELLS
John, 205
TRENARY
Mary, 147
Samuel, 147
TREYHERN
Dinah, 150
James, 150
Sarah, 150
TREYHORN
William, 21
TRIBBE
Joseph, 158
TRIBBEE
John, 19
TRIBBEY
Charles, 36
James, 187
John, 169
Joseph, 34, 176
Thomas, 157, 187
TRIBBY
James, 177, 181
John, 35

William, 240, 253
WALTER
  Isaac, 203
WALTERS
  John, 129
WALTMAN
  Emanuel, 182
  Jacob, 1, 45, 48, 50,
    55, 66, 78, 90,
    125, 131, 136,
    167, 171, 182,
    209, 218, 226,
    230, 234, 236,
    239
  John, 182
  Margaret, 125
WARD
  Robert, 61
  Samuel, 17, 70, 71,
    105
WARFIELD
  Charles A., 62
WARFORD
  Abraham, 7, 23, 32,
    105, 123
  Hannah, 123
  John, 202
  William, 32, 105,
    123, 151
WARNELL
  James, 111
WARNER
  George, 153, 169
  Peter, 117, 153
  Sarah, 169
WARREN
  Jacob, 62
WARRICK
  Betsey, 73
  Courtney, 73
  Marquis, 73
  Nancy, 73
  Peter, 73, 146
  Sarah, 146
WARTERS
  Jonathan, 12
WASHINGTON

Ann, 51
Anne, 64
Bushrod, 51, 64
Francis W., 211
William, 144
WATERS
  George A., 228
  John, 104
WATSON
  Joseph, 7, 27
  Polly, 88, 90
  Thomas, 13
  William, 88, 90
WAUGH
  Alexander, 6, 9, 75,
    246
  James, 220
WEAST
  John, 239
WEATHERBURN
  John, 138
WEATHERBY
  Mathew, 19
  Matthew, 35, 43, 46,
    79, 144
WEATHERLEY
  Matthew, 188
WEAVER
  Philip, 92
WEDDEY
  Peter, 161
WEDOWMAN
  John, 130
WEEDON
  John, 155
WEEKS
  Thomas, 240
WEIST
  John, 98
WELFORD
  Robert, 4, 20, 22
WELLS
  Rachel, 119
  Thomas C., 34, 64,
    85, 187
WELMAN
  Michael, 44

WENNER
  John, 239, 243
  Magdalena, 117
  William, 117, 119,
    209, 231, 234
WERTS
  Adam, 105
WERTZ
  Conrad, 98, 162
  Conrod, 98
  Jacob, 143
  Peter, 212
WEST
  Anna B., 132
  Charles, 9, 24
  George, 7, 238
  John, 17, 30, 31, 65,
    215, 225, 236
  Joseph, 85, 134
  Margarett, 6
  Mary, 36, 62, 65
  Nathaniel, 219
  Sally, 9
  Samuel, 225
  Sybil, 6
  Thomas, 219
  William, 7, 39, 176,
    225
WETHERBY
  Mat, 62
  Matthew, 10, 202,
    203, 206
WHALEY
  Johnston, 130
  Levi, 237
  William, 1, 24, 64,
    113, 130, 193,
    209
WHALY
  Vincent, 55
WHEATONG
  Joseph, 191
WHEELER
  Ann, 103
  Clement, 103
  Robert, 142
  Samuel H., 103

WHELAN
Catharine, 160, 161
Catherine, 123, 129
James, 123, 160,
161
Judith, 123, 160,
161
Margaret, 123, 160,
161
Timothy, 123, 160,
161
Winefred, 123, 129
Winnefred, 160, 161
WHELANS
Timothy, 129
WHERRY
S., 158
Silas, 138
WHIP
Peter, 37
WHITACRE
Ann, 83
Benjamin, 23
Enoch, 34
Enock, 34
Isaac, 158
Joshua, 83
Thomas, 4
WHITE
Alexander, 122
Benjamin, 40, 162,
241
Daniel, 13, 44, 147,
148, 165, 223,
237
David, 62, 162
Isaac, 139
Isiah, 243
James, 45, 154
John, 64, 191, 224,
239
Jonah, 49
Josabed, 191
Joseph, 80, 83, 175,
179, 244
Josiah, 20, 23, 67,
89, 97, 98, 99,

130, 135, 153,
160, 161, 169,
185, 191, 214
Jozabed, 253
Levi, 148
Rachel, 1, 107, 192,
214
Richard, 7, 165
Robert, 40, 103,
108, 122, 139,
191
Thomas, 35, 97, 99,
107, 120, 130,
135, 150, 156,
233
William, 170, 223,
244, 250
WHITELY
Alexander, 200
Francis, 38, 56, 134,
167, 172
WHITING
Beverly, 211
Carlisle F., 5, 25
Carlyle F., 5, 6
Fran, 211
Francis B., 121
Hannah, 211
P. B., 211
Peter, 130
Sarah M., 25
Sarah M., 5, 6
Warner, 211
Warner W., 210
WHITMIRE
John, 1
Michael, 1
WHITMORE
Benjamin, 5
Esther, 28
Henry, 28
WICOFF
Abraham, 130
WIGGENTON
Richard Y., 60
WIGGINTON
J. W., 152

Mary, 60
Richard Y., 60
WILD
John, 57
WILDBAHN
Catharine, 15
Frederick, 15, 40
WILDMAN
Eleanor, 113, 116,
194
John, 29, 61, 77, 84,
108, 110, 113,
116, 143, 147,
194
Joseph, 169, 214
Joshua, 169
William, 44, 73, 93,
147, 181, 183,
198, 252
WILK
Francis, 7
Samuel, 7
WILKERSON
Thomas, 33, 103,
106
William, 26
WILKINSON
John, 51, 194, 242,
243, 253
Joseph, 67, 77, 93,
110, 127, 141,
177, 197
Mary, 194
Thomas, 35, 39, 46,
48, 52, 70, 75, 77,
79, 80, 86, 106,
127, 128, 136,
147, 159, 166,
169, 174, 182,
183, 184, 185,
193, 198
William, 2, 36, 62,
127, 251
WILKISON
Evan, 251
Sarah, 105
Thomas, 18

WINTERS
James, 231
WIRT
John, 84
WIRTS
Jacob, 154
John, 86
WIRTZ
Lucy, 229
WISE
George, 217
Martha, 217
Peter, 145
WITELY
Francis, 137
WITTEMAN
John, 136, 254
WITTERMAN
John, 66, 68, 160,
164, 177
WITTIMAN
John, 110
WOFTER
Boston, 28
WOLF
Abigail, 41
Abigal, 27
Adam, 70
Henry, 81
John, 27, 41, 231
John A., 131
Susannah, 131
William, 119, 231
WOLFCAIL
John, 99
WOLFCAILE
John, 240
WOLFCALE
Beulah, 176
John, 58, 168, 176,
229
WOLFORD
Daniel, 204, 210
Mary, 204, 210
WOLHARD
William, 82
WOLLARD

Aaron, 68
John, 69
Mary, 68
WOOD
John, 134
Mark, 166, 210, 254
WOODDY
John, 168
Nanny, 168
William, 83, 110,
128, 129, 139,
151, 168, 214
WOODEY
William, 78
WOODFORD
Elizabeth, 241
William, 18, 102,
207, 240, 241
WOODLAND LOT, 190
WOODLEY
Benjamin, 15, 19,
35, 151, 188
Elizabeth, 15, 35,
188
WOODROW
Henry, 97
WOODY
David, 228
Elizabeth, 202
Nancy, 149
William, 63, 75, 77,
94, 120, 149, 151,
202, 222, 228,
236, 238, 249
WOOFTER
Mary, 141
Sebastian, 105, 141
WOOLF
John, 139
Susanna, 243
William, 243
WOOLFCAIL
John, 168
WOOLFCALE
John, 140
WORKMAN
Viney, 213

WORLSEY
John, 197
WORNALD
James, 185, 235
WORSELEY
John, 182
WORSLEY
John, 203, 221, 252
WREN
Isaac, 76
James, 26
John, 76
Sanford, 111
Thomas, 102
Traves, 176
Turner, 76, 189
William, 189
WRENN
Hannah, 2, 3
Isaac, 113
John, 2, 3, 6
Sanford, 142
Thomas, 23, 170
Turner, 79
WRIGHT
Amos, 209
Ann, 148
Anthony, 57, 71, 84,
113, 148, 149
J., 214
John, 209, 216, 237
Joshua, 196
M., 48
Paterson, 71, 78
Pateson, 57, 59,
100, 177, 180,
215
Patson, 57
Patterson, 57, 58,
148, 149, 152,
180, 189, 197,
211
Peteson, 57
Robert, 149
Samuel, 162, 244

Other Books by Patricia B. Duncan:

1810-1840 Loudoun County, Virginia Federal Population Census Index
1860 Loudoun County, Virginia Federal Population Census Index
1870 Loudoun County, Virginia Federal Population Census Index

Abstracts From Loudoun County, Virginia Guardian Accounts:
Books A-H, 1759-1904

Abstracts Of Loudoun County, Virginia Register Of Free Negroes, 1844-1861

Clarke County, Virginia Will Book Abstracts
Books A - I (1836 - 1904) And 1a - 3c (1841 - 1913)

Fauquier County, Virginia Death Register, 1853 – 1896

Genealogical Abstracts From The Lambertville Press, Lambertville, New Jersey:
4 November 1858 (Vol. 1, Number 1) To 30 October 1861 (Vol. 3, Number 155)

Hunterdon County, New Jersey, 1895 State Census, Part I: Alexandria-Junction
Hunterdon County, New Jersey, 1895 State Census, Part II: Kingwood-West
Amwell

Index To Loudoun County, Virginia Land Deed Books A – Z, 1757 – 1800
Index To Loudoun County, Virginia Land Deed Books 2A – 2M, 1800 – 1810

Jefferson County, Virginia 1802-1813 Personal Property Tax Lists
Jefferson County, Virginia 1814-1824 Personal Property Tax Lists
Jefferson County, Virginia 1825-1841 Personal Property Tax Lists

Loudoun County, Virginia Birth Register 1853-1879
Loudoun County, Virginia Birth Register 1880-1896

Loudoun County, Virginia Clerks Probate Records
Book 1 (1904-1921) And Book 2 (1922-1938)

Loudoun County, Virginia Will Book Abstracts, Books 2a-3c, Jun. 1841-Dec. 1879
And Superior Court Books A And B, 1810-1888

Loudoun County, Virginia Will Book Abstracts, Books A-Z, Dec. 1757-Jun. 1841

Loudoun County, Virginia Will Book Index, 1757-1946

1850 Fauquier County, Virginia, Slave Schedule